The Correspondence of Catherine McAuley, 1818–1841

The Correspondence of Catherine McAuley, 1818–1841

Edited by
MARY C. SULLIVAN

FOUR COURTS PRESS
THE CATHOLIC UNIVERSITY OF AMERICA PRESS

Set in 10.5 on 12.5 Ehrhardt for
FOUR COURTS PRESS LTD
7 Malpas Street, Dublin 8, Ireland
e-mail: info@fourcourtspress.ie
http://www.fourcourtspress.ie
and in North and South America for
THE CATHOLIC UNIVERSITY OF AMERICA PRESS
c/o Hopkins Fulfillment Service, PO Box 50370, Baltimore, MD 21211–4370
http://cuapress.cua.edu

ISBN 978-1-85182-825-8 Four Courts Press
ISBN 978-0-8132-1395-8 Catholic University of America Press

Library of Congress Cataloging-in-Publication Data

The correspondence of Catherine McAuley, 1818-1841 / edited by
Mary C. Sullivan. – 1st ed.
p. cm.
Includes bibliographical references and index.
ISBN 0-8132-1395-9 (cloth : alk. paper)
1. McAuley, Catherine, 1778-1841 – Correspondence. 2.
Nuns – Ireland – Correspondence. 3. Sisters of
Mercy – Ireland – Correspondence. I. Sullivan, Mary C. II. Title.

BX4483.8.C67 2004
271'.9202--dc22

2004009164

Contents

Contents

Preface

The present volume is a new critical edition of the extant correspondence of Catherine McAuley (1778–1841), the founder of the Sisters of Mercy. The book attempts to collect all the surviving letters written by Catherine McAuley, to her, or about her during her lifetime. The research underlying the book included visits to the major archives in Ireland, England, Australia, and the United States, and requests for verified photocopies of letters in other archives in Australia and many regions of the United States. Presented in this edition are over 320 letters, each preserved in one authentic form or another. The letters that are relatively easy to find have now been found; what may still remain are hidden letters in places no one would suspect, letters that their owners may not even know they possess. Although one could continue the search for many more years, in the hope of turning up a few more letters, that approach seemed increasingly unwise, in view of the need to make the presently known letters available to readers.

It may be helpful here to define certain terms that are frequently used in this edition, to review the collecting and publishing history associated with Catherine McAuley's correspondence, to describe the primary sources on which the edition is based, and to explain the editorial methods that are followed in presenting the letters.

TERMS

An *autograph* is an original letter, on the original paper, in the handwriting of the author of the letter. Finding and verifying the exact current location of each extant autograph is a key aspect of the research supporting this edition. The autograph *cover* is the sheet of paper or, rarely, the envelope, on which the author wrote the name and address of the recipient. Unlike a hand-delivered letter, a posted letter has postmarks on its cover that help to date the letter (if the author did not). Sometimes the cover sheet is one side of a folded piece of stationery and is thus attached to the letter; however, over time a cover sheet may become detached from the letter itself, and may not even end up in the same archives as the letter. The term *photocopy* or *photostat* is used here to signify only a photographic reproduction of the original autograph, not of a later transcription. A *handcopy* or *transcript* is an early hand-written copy of an original autograph. Handcopies made by the original recipient or by an early collector (1840–1870) of the letters of Catherine McAuley are valuable if they can be verified by other handcopies or printed sources, especially in cases where the original autograph cannot now be found, or is not yet found. Of particular value is an *author's handcopy* or a *recipient's handcopy*, as in the case of the letters from Dr. Michael Blake, bishop of Dromore, and some of those to Mary Vincent Harnett for which there are no extant autographs. A *typescript* is a later type-written copy, and as such is somewhat unreliable because the typing often cannot be dated, the typist may not be identified, and the accuracy of the typescript cannot be known, unless the text can be verified or corrected by some other source. In this edition, the term *published transcription* refers to a letter for which there is no autograph, but which is published in one or other of the works of Catherine McAuley's first published biographers: Mary Vincent Harnett's *Life of Rev. Mother Catherine McAuley* (1864), Mary Austin Carroll's *Life of Catherine McAuley* (1866), or the same author's four-volume *Leaves from the Annals of the Sisters of Mercy* (1881–1894). Such letters are presented in this edition only when a substantial portion of a letter appears in one of these sources alone.

Included in this edition, wherever authentic texts have been discovered, are poems and poem-letters written by Catherine McAuley or her correspondents, including poems Catherine transcribed in altered form from published sources. The poems were usually written as letters to particular recipients or were enclosed in other letters. I have not included a few poems said to have been written by Catherine McAuley—when no autograph of a particular poem can be found and when there is the possibility that the poem was transcribed from a so far unidentified source. In addition, certain documents are presented in this edition which do not at first appear to be "letters" in the conventional sense, but are rather statements, notations, or records—communications in very special senses.

HISTORY

Systematic work on the letters of Catherine McAuley began in the middle of the twentieth century when Mary Dominick Foster, RSM (1877–1960), the bursar, and later secretary general, of the Dublin congregation of the Sisters of Mercy, began to collect documents in support of the canonization of Catherine McAuley. She was assisted by John MacErlean, SJ (1870–1950), who prepared extensive notes on the location and content of all the letters available to them. Foster secured photostatic copies of as many letters as she could locate, and five bound volumes of these photostats are now preserved in the Mercy Congregational Archives, Dublin. Every scholar working on the correspondence of Catherine McAuley is deeply indebted to the foresight and perseverance of Mary Dominick Foster and John MacErlean, especially, but not only, when the original autograph of a letter cannot be found, but a photostat is available.

Two published editions of Catherine McAuley's correspondence appeared in the later twentieth century: Mary Ignatia Neumann, RSM's *The Letters of Catherine McAuley, 1827–1841* (Baltimore: Helicon Press, 1969) and Mary Angela Bolster, RSM's *The Correspondence of Catherine McAuley, 1827–1841* (Cork: Congregation of the Sisters of Mercy, Diocese of Cork and Ross, 1989). Scholars of the life and teachings of Catherine McAuley and of the history of women and the church in Ireland in the nineteenth century have for almost four decades depended on Neumann's and Bolster's editions of the letters as indispensable records of Catherine McAuley's thought and activities.

In the editions of Neumann and Bolster, 249 letters were published; of these, 177 letters—all but one written by Catherine McAuley—were published in both editions. To this number Bolster added 71 letters not in Neumann, and Neumann included one letter not in Bolster. Of the 249 letters published in Neumann and/or Bolster, 214 were written by Catherine McAuley herself, and 35 were written to or about her by other correspondents. In addition, both editors included Catherine McAuley's essay on the "Spirit of the Institute" (also included in this edition) and her "Act of Consecration" (not included here). This impressive total represents an enormous amount of research on the part of Mary Ignatia Neumann and Angela Bolster, two women to whom those writing on Catherine McAuley owe lasting recognition and gratitude.

However, the 250 previously published letters and essay do not constitute the whole body of Catherine McAuley's extant correspondence. The total correspondence that is currently available includes 325 items, of which 269 are written by Catherine McAuley, and 56 by other correspondents: 26 letters written to her, and 30 written about her (or the Sisters of Mercy) in her lifetime, of which 15 involve correspondence between bishops and officials in Rome. Thus, a new edition will appreciably add to existing autobiographical and biographical data on the life of Catherine McAuley. But another factor contributes to the need for a new edition.

Mary Ignatia Neumann's *Letters of Catherine McAuley*, published in 1969, contains almost completely accurate transcriptions of the letters it publishes, but it presents only 178 letters, and the book itself has been long out of print. Mary Angela Bolster's *Correspondence of Catherine McAuley*, published in 1989, contains 71 more letters and many helpful footnotes. However, discrepancies, perhaps then unavoidable, appear in the transcriptions when one compares them with the autograph letters: for example, missing or incorrectly transcribed words. I say this with very great understanding and sympathy, and profoundly mindful of my own inevitable inaccuracies. Catherine McAuley's handwriting is very difficult to read, especially when she is tired or writing in a hurry, and in the past both finding and deciphering some of the autographs were often problematic.

PRIMARY SOURCES

The primary research underlying the present edition has been the search for the extant autograph letters themselves, or for authentic representations of now missing autographs. I have myself visited Mercy archives in Ireland (Dublin, Limerick, Charleville, Galway, Tullamore, Cork, Carlow, Birr and Bessbrook, Northern

Ireland); England (London, Birmingham, and Liverpool); Australia (Adelaide, Brisbane, and Melbourne); and Silver Spring, Maryland, as well as the Dublin Diocesan Archives, the Dromore Diocesan Archives, the Westminster (London) Diocesan Archives, and the Archives of Propaganda Fide in Rome. I have also corresponded with archivists of all the other Mercy archives in the United States, Australia, and New Zealand as well as several other diocesan and Mercy archives in Ireland and England, in each case requesting complete and verified photocopies of all the relevant autographs and early handcopies in their collections— sometimes with wonderfully positive results. The list of "Abbreviations of Archival Collections of Primary Sources," used to identify the present location of the letters presented in this volume, illustrates the global migration of Catherine McAuley's autograph letters in the decades after her death.

Of the 325 documents in this edition, I have located the autographs (or in the absence of the autographs, photostats or photocopies of the original autographs) of 293. Of the 32 "missing" autographs two are those of previously published letters, and 30 are of new letters, for which we have reliable paper sources: that is, two or more early handcopies or a complete text in Harnett or Carroll. A huge debt of gratitude and admiration is owed to those who preserved these letters over the past 160–170 years: the first recipients of the letters who saved and treasured them, and all the communities and archivists down through the decades who took steps to conserve them.

Most of the autographs are in excellent condition. Catherine and the other correspondents usually wrote with good ink on durable paper. However, some autographs have serious problems from an editor's point of view: some have missing covers so, if the author did not date the letter, there is no postmark to help date it; some have passages cut or torn out, evidently to remove an uncomplimentary or confidential comment on another person; a few have sizeable, relatively recent ink blotches that obscure the handwriting; a few are now very faded, having been once preserved in glass frames and exposed too long to light; some exist only as fragments of once complete letters, parts of the letters having been lost when the sides of the stationery became detached at the fold; and two have been inexpertly cleaned by conservators to the point where the wording is almost, if not completely, removed. Sometimes the text of the missing portions or illegible sections can be supplied by other reliable sources, but not always. Therefore, as one looks forward a hundred years, one realizes the necessity of creating now an accurate inventory and exact texts of all the presently known correspondence of Catherine McAuley.

EDITORIAL METHODS

The main operating principle in presenting the letters in this edition has been to transcribe completely and accurately the most authentic source of each letter, which in 90 per cent of the cases is the original autograph of the letter or an accurate and complete photostat or photocopy of the autograph. However, that high standard is more easily proposed than observed, for reasons related chiefly to Catherine McAuley's own writing habits (these comments and those that follow apply equally to the letters of the other correspondents).

The letters presented in this edition were all written in the period 1818–1841. The conventions of that age, as to vocabulary, spelling, punctuation, capitalization, and abbreviation, were all slightly different from present-day usage in some respects. Moreover, although Catherine McAuley wrote very well, certain idiosyncrasies appear in her written texts.

In terms of spelling, several things strike the reader of the autographs: for example, Catherine usually reversed the "i before e" convention, spelling "beleif," "releif," and "recieve" thus; she often used the suffix "-ance" where a present-day writer would use "-ence," and vice versa; she often did not "double the consonant" before adding an ending to certain verbs; and she was, one might respectfully say, hopeless about proper names, often spelling them simply phonetically, and sometimes differently in successive letters. An editor is torn between honoring the author's own spelling, staying alert to variant spellings common in her day, and not wanting to confuse the reader or use 'sic' either pedantically or too frequently. My compromise among these competing values has been to change the "ie/ei" and "ance/ence" words and the verbs without doubled consonants to present-day spellings; to leave Catherine's spelling of most other words (such as "salery," "novaship" for "noviceship," and "sysmatics" for "schismatics"), inserting bracketed alternative spellings or *sic* where this seemed necessary or helpful to the reader's understanding; and to use throughout the correct spelling of the proper names of those persons whose preferred spelling of their names can be verified—for example, Mary Cecilia Marmion, William Kinsella, Mary de Sales White, Mary de Pazzi Delany, Theobald Mathew (in all these cases Catherine McAuley often added, deleted, changed, or capitalized a letter in the spelling). My goal has been to alter Catherine's spelling as little as possible while at the same time removing unnecessary confusion in the texts.

Capitalization, abbreviation, and punctuation have been dealt with similarly. In general, I have preserved all Catherine McAuley's capitalization of the beginning letters of words (except in the case of proper names such as "de Sales"), even when she did not appear to be consistent in her own use of capitals. For example, she often did not capitalize the first letter of words beginning with "e," such as "English" or "Easter." I have left certain of her understandable abbreviations (such as "Revd.," "Dr.," and "rec'd") as well as her ampersands and frequent "etc.", but I have spelled out the months of the year, certain unfamiliar abbreviations (such as "yr" for "your") and her eccentric abbreviations with a squiggle at the end when she was in a hurry (such as "affect" for "affectionate").

Catherine's punctuation is not unlike that of most writers of her day. She generally uses commas and short and long dashes, rarely any mark that looks like a period, even more rarely a question mark, and never an exclamation point. She sometimes uses quotation marks, but not always where one might expect them. In this edition, periods have been often introduced as substitutes for some of Catherine's commas and dashes, but never where a full stop would over-determine the meaning of her wording. Her long dashes are clearly intended to be full stops. Often they also indicate the beginning of a new paragraph—although Catherine tended to paragraph very little. I have silently created additional paragraphing on my own, but conservatively, and only when the flow of the letter seemed to require a paragraph shift for clarity's sake.

Two additional points about Catherine McAuley's letter-writing habits bear noting. She very frequently added postscripts to her letters, sometimes several of them (evidently she always had more to communicate, especially to her sister-correspondents). Often these messages are written on the portions of the cover sheet that would be folded inside when the letter was folded for mailing. When, therefore, the autograph cover of a letter is missing, postscripts may be lost as well. Catherine generally signed her name in two ways only: "M. C. McAuley," for Mary Catherine McAuley, her name in religion, on letters to professed members of the community, women who were her longstanding friends; and "Mary C. McAuley" in more formal letters to bishops, priests, and lay friends, as well as in friendly letters to novices, postulants, and prospective members of the community. These two modes of signature are not universally observed, but appear frequently enough to be noted. In letters to her family, she usually signed her name "C. McAuley," and to Rome, "Mary Catherine McAuley." In presenting her letters in this edition, I have transcribed her signature as it appears on the autograph, and when she signed a letter or postscript simply "M. C. M.", I have replicated that as well. If an autograph (hers or that of another correspondent) has no signature, but the author's name is known with certainty, I have placed a signature in brackets.

Some comment on the use of handcopies in this edition is necessary. As noted earlier, a handcopy, as the term is used here, is an early handwritten transcription of an autograph letter, presumably made by someone who had access to the autograph. By "early" I mean roughly before 1870 or 1880, that is, while some recipients of Catherine's letters and some of her contemporaries were still alive. In some cases a handcopy is the only primary source for a letter, if the original autograph cannot now be found. However, since the copyist may have incorrectly or incompletely transcribed the letter, it seems prudent to include in this edition only those handcopied letters (having no autographs) for which more than one early handcopy exist. Fortunately, in nearly every case multiple handcopies are extant: for example, in the Liverpool or Limerick Annals, in one or other of the two Baggot Street manuscript books, in the Brisbane Book of Transcriptions, or in the Dundalk Manuscript Book. Moreover, four letters that Catherine McAuley sent to Mary Vincent Harnett were copied in 1856, if not by Mary Vincent herself then under her supervision. Sometimes the wording in handcopies of the same letter is different; discrepancies of this sort are discussed in the footnotes.

In addition, a few letters in this edition, for which there are evidently no other primary sources, are taken from the published transcriptions in the early biographies by Harnett and Carroll or in Carroll's *Leaves from the Annals of the Sisters of Mercy*.

A note of explanation on two particular sources of letters may be helpful. In the Dublin Diocesan Archives three different sets of correspondence were consulted: the papers of Daniel Murray; the papers of John Hamilton, Dr. Murray's priest-secretary; and a collection of letters written by or about Catherine McAuley. The latter letters were placed in a separate box years ago, in anticipation of the canonization of Catherine McAuley, and so were not cataloged. However, all the McAuley papers have been recently cataloged among the Murray papers. Therefore, in giving the source of letters from the Dublin Diocesan Archives, the full catalog numbers are provided. Readers should also note that none of the autograph letters Michael Blake, bishop of Dromore, sent to Catherine McAuley is extant, except the one she forwarded to Rome. However, Dr. Blake kept a Journal of all the letters he wrote, in which he transcribed each letter, either before or after he made the fair copy to post. In giving the source for these letters, I use the designation: "Author's transcript."

Finally, a word on interpolations in the text and on the footnotes. Bracketed interpolations in the text of a letter occur only for five reasons: to provide a present-day spelling where this seems needed; to expand an abbreviation that may not be clear in the context of the letter; to provide a word that was evidently inadvertently omitted by the author of the letter; to indicate a lacuna, an illegible word, or a damaged portion of the autograph; and to correct—this is done very rarely—a reference in a letter. In general, I have tried to avoid interpolations, but where they occur, they are always bracketed. Where parentheses appear, they are always part of the original letter and not editorial insertions.

Readers will find that many letters presented in this edition are heavily footnoted, though I trust not in a cumbersome way. The footnotes serve two purposes. Only rarely are they interpretive of a puzzling passage in the text of a letter. More frequently they are intended to be simply informative: to identify a person or place mentioned in the text, including, where necessary, the recipient or author of the letter; to explain an obscure reference; to cite related letters and footnotes in the edition; to provide background information not included in the letter; to identify the translator when the original letter was written in Latin or Italian; and to define obsolete words or expressions. In the latter instance, the Oxford English Dictionary (OED) is enormously helpful where Catherine McAuley or another correspondent uses words that may be somewhat unfamiliar to present-day readers. The goal of the footnotes is to support a full understanding of the meaning and significance of the letters without violating the integrity of the letters themselves. The footnotes can obviously be ignored by readers who prefer that approach, since each letter can be read and enjoyed without recourse to them.

References to *Catherine McAuley and the Tradition of Mercy* (1995), which I edited, appear frequently in the footnotes because the book contains the complete texts of many early biographical manuscripts written by Catherine McAuley's contemporaries, as well as Catherine's own manuscript of the original Rule of the Sisters of Mercy. Her first biographers—women who lived with her, sat beside her, and travelled with her—often give details that illumine passages in Catherine's letters, and her own text of the original Rule frequently clarifies points that might otherwise be obscure. Since *Catherine McAuley* is readily available, I cite it as a reliable source of the original manuscripts, noting also the original manuscripts themselves, which are housed in many different archives and are less easily consulted.

The footnotes also frequently refer to "Annals" and to the *Irish Catholic Directory*. Several of the early Mercy convents kept detailed Annals; these often provide background information for a particular passage in a letter. However, in some of the Annals the pages are not numbered; in these instances, the citation can usually be found by reference to the year, which is always indicated. In the footnotes I have also depended heavily on the *Irish Catholic Directory* for the years 1836 to 1842, for the full names, locations, and dates of priests and some bishops mentioned in Catherine McAuley's letters, as well as for other relevant information, and have generally indicated that dependence.

The letters in this edition are presented chronologically and numbered consecutively (one autograph letter, found as the edition was going to press, is inserted as 129a). Neumann's edition numbered the letters in groups, not consecutively. Bolster's edition numbered them consecutively, but since the present edition contains over seventy additional letters, frequently departs from Bolster's sequence and editorial presentation, and is in fact based entirely on a new and independent reading of the original autographs, or of authentic substitutes for missing autographs, it seemed wise to introduce a new numbering of the extant letters.

In the headings of the letters, I use the titles "Sister" (for members of the Sisters of Mercy), "Dr." (for archbishops, bishops, vicars apostolic, and priests who had that title), and "the Reverend" (for priests to whom Catherine McAuley, following the convention of the day, usually gave the title "Mr."—a practice dating from the penal era in Ireland). In speaking of sisters, priests, and bishops in the notes and narrative links, their titles are generally not needed for clarity, though Father (or Fr.) and Dr. are used when necessary. In giving the religious name of a Sister of Mercy, her baptismal name is often also given in parentheses—for example, Mary Clare (Georgiana) Moore. I have chosen to use "Catherine" rather than "McAuley" when referring to her without giving her full name, not only because that is common parlance among those associated with the Sisters of Mercy. Just as "Teresa" (Teresa of Avila) and "Catherine" (Catherine of Siena) appear to be common usage among Carmelite and Dominican scholars, so a similarly respectful freedom may prevail with respect to Catherine of Dublin. Using "Catherine" also reflects her own lack of pretension and distance, and the easy relations she invited.

The number of letters in Catherine McAuley's extant correspondence increases markedly from year to year, especially as the new foundations outside Dublin begin in 1836, and the second half of the decade unfolds. While there are 12 extant letters in the period 1818–1831, 13 in 1832–1834, and 16 in 1835–1836, starting with the 27 letters in 1837, the yearly number climbs steadily: 37 in 1838, 51 in 1839, 68 in 1840, and 101 in 1841, the year of Catherine's death. The gradual increase reflects the geographical expansion of the Sisters of Mercy beyond Dublin, developments in the ecclesiastical status of the congregation, and the increasing membership of the religious order—to the whole scope of which Catherine McAuley tried, to the end, to offer her guidance, wisdom, moral support and affection. In presenting the extant letters, especially of the later years, I have inserted periodic narrative links; these provide a brief overview of the letters that follow and situate them in the historical context of Catherine McAuley's life.

I hope this explanation of the terms, history, primary sources, and editorial methods underlying this new edition of the correspondence of Catherine McAuley will assist readers to appreciate the life that is revealed in the letters. To that end may the editorial methods fade into complete transparency so that the voice of "M. C. McAuley," the author and subject of these letters, may come through as clearly to her readers of today as it did to those to whom these letters were originally addressed.

Acknowledgments

To assemble a collection of letters such as this has involved widespread dependence on dozens of archivists, historians and others, who have contributed irreplaceable pieces, both material and spiritual, to the whole mosaic. Moreover, as the source notations at the foot of the letters imply, this edition of the correspondence of Catherine McAuley uses manuscript materials that are housed in the archives of many institutions worldwide, from whom permission to publish these materials has been graciously received.

The "List of Abbreviations of Archival Collections" names all the archives holding the original autographs and early handcopies of the letters by, to, or about Catherine McAuley that are presented in this edition. I wish to acknowledge publicly the generous help of all these archivists as well as others who assisted me in countless ways, even when their repositories held no primary McAuley materials relevant to this research project. Their names constitute a long, global litany of women and men from whom I have received help, on whom this edition has depended, and to whom I personally owe deep gratitude and admiration.

For help in Mercy archives in Ireland I wish to thank the following Sisters of Mercy: Angela Bugler, Kathleen Daly, Teresa Delaney, Helena Doherty, Mary Magdalena Frisby, Agnes Gleeson, Frances Lowe, Mary Lyons, Maureen McGarrigle, and Dolores Walsh, and especially the archivists of the two major Mercy collections of Catherine McAuley's letters in Ireland, Sister Scholastica Stokes (Limerick Archives), and Ms. Marianne Cosgrave (Mercy Congregational Archives) who have been extremely helpful. I also offer my gratitude to the Most Reverend Francis Gerard Brooks, former bishop of Dromore, and Canon Aidan Hamill, for help in the Dromore Diocesan Archives, and Aileen Havern, secretary at Newry Cathedral; Thomas May, Galway Diocesan Archives; John McEvoy, St. Patrick's College, Carlow; and especially David Sheehy, archivist of the Dublin Diocesan Archives, the holder of thirty autograph letters presented in this edition. I also wish to thank Peter Costello, Ken MacGowan and Teresa Whitington of the Central Catholic Library, Dublin; Nicholas Carolan and Maeve Gebruers at the Irish Traditional Music Archive, Dublin; and the librarians of the National Library of Ireland—for their expert help with many questions.

In England, I wish especially to thank the following Sisters of Mercy for their generous help in accessing archival material: Barbara Jeffery, Sheila Quinn, and Marion McCarthy, archivists of the major collections of the Sisters of Mercy, in Birmingham, Liverpool, and Bermondsey, London. While the Mercy archives in Scotland and elsewhere in England had no relevant archival material, I received ready encouragement from Mary Austin (Dundee), Mary Aelred Timmons (Edinburgh), Annette McCartan (Glasgow), and Dolores Magee (Sunderland), for which I am very grateful. In Fishguard, Wales, Johanna Moloney and Rose Berrie were extremely helpful in the discovery of a poem transcribed by Catherine McAuley. I also wish to thank the Reverend Ian Dickie, archivist of the Westminster (London) Diocesan Archives.

The archivists of the Mercy collections in Australia were generous and persistent in their contributions, and I especially wish to thank the following Sisters of Mercy who gave me access or sent me carefully identified photocopies of autograph letters and early handcopies: Deirdre O'Connor (Adelaide), Germaine Greathead (Brisbane), Mary Philip Sullivan (Grafton), Joan Doolan and Agnes Gleeson (Melbourne), and Moira Young (Singleton). I also thank the other Mercy archivists or congregational leaders in Australia who conducted careful searches, but could provide no material for this edition: Mrs. Lyn Snibson and Sisters Mary Ryan, Judith Carney, Eileen Casey, Margaret Barry, Veronica Earls, Anna Maria O'Shea, Joanne Molloy, Helen Mary Peters, and Norma Scheikowsky.

The archives of the Sisters of Mercy in Aotearoa New Zealand contained no relevant material for this edition, but I am grateful for the responsiveness of the congregational leaders or archivists: Marcienne D. Kirk (Auckland), Rita Bonisch (Dunedin), and Denise Fox (Wellington), and especially Eileen Burrell (Christchurch) who provided some useful photocopies. I also thank Mercy historian Kathrine Bellamy for information about the Newfoundland foundation and for her help in my eventually securing the Rice correspondence.

I am very grateful to the staff of the Archives of the Vatican Congregation for the Evangelization of Peoples (Rome)—formerly Propaganda Fide—for access to nineteen documents related to this research project; to Brother Peter E. Fogarty, secretary of the Congregation of Christian Brothers, Rome, for excellent photocopies of two letters in the archives of Propaganda Fide that I could not find myself: the letters of Catherine McAuley to John Rice, OSA, and of Saint Edmund Rice to his brother; and especially to Brother J. Bertrand Darcy for his having discovered these important letters.

Finally, to the Mercy archivists in the United States I owe a large debt, especially to those who provided materials presented in this edition: Helen Sigrist (Baltimore), Eleanor Nishio (Brooklyn), Marilyn Gouailhardou (Burlingame), Patricia Illing (Chicago), Joan Freney (Merion), Ellen Marie Robarge (New York), Rita Connell (Omaha), Patricia Hodge (Pittsburgh), Mary Shawn Sévigny (Portland), Dolores Liptak (West Hartford) and Christina Branswell (Windham). For their assistance, even when their archives held no documents for this edition, I wish also to thank Mary Berding, Katherine Doyle, Pauline Fox, Angelita Heinrich, Margaret Mary Hughes, Edith Langiotti, Michaeline Lewandowski, Gertrude Myrick, Susan Nowalis, Mary Andrew Ray, Jeanne Reichart, Rose Marie Rocha, Mary Agatha Smith, and Diane Szubrowski. In the United States the largest collection of autograph letters written by or to Catherine McAuley—over sixty—is preserved in the archives of the Institute of the Sisters of Mercy of the Americas, Silver Spring, Maryland. To Sisters Felicitas Powers and Paula

Diann Marlin, and Ms. Mollie McMahon, former archivists, I offer my sincere thanks for their care of this collection and for their help.

Several other Sisters of Mercy assisted me to prepare this edition, and I am very grateful to them: Agnes Gleeson, archivist at Mercy International Centre, Dublin, during most of the years of my research, who was constantly helpful; Dorothy Schlueter, who read the manuscript and offered suggestions; and especially, Mercy scholar and historian Mary Hermenia Muldrey, who reviewed the entire manuscript and provided much appreciated advice about needed corrections. I also offer my sincere thanks to Dr. Anne Coon, professor of literature at the Rochester Institute of Technology, who read early chapters and offered guidance; the Reverend Ernan McMullin, O'Hara professor emeritus of philosophy at the University of Notre Dame, who critiqued portions of the manuscript and supported the project throughout its development; and finally, Ms. Louise Novros, who typed the entire manuscript with great skill and cheerfulness.

The vast majority of the letters in this edition were written in English. However, most of the correspondence to and from church officials in Rome was written in Latin or Italian. English translations of these letters were made by John MacErlean, SJ, in the middle of the twentieth century when he was assisting Mary Dominick Foster, RSM, to gather Catherine McAuley's correspondence. Recently MacErlean's translations of the letters that were originally written in Latin were reviewed and slightly modified by Mary Eymard Hyland, RSM. His translations of the letters that were written in Italian were reviewed and slightly modified by Mary Borromeo Povero, RSM, and Dr. Pellegrino Nazzaro, professor of history at the Rochester Institute of Technology. To all these translators I express my deep gratitude.

Financial support for this project came from several sources. I am primarily grateful to the Sisters of Mercy of Rochester, New York, for their constant support; to the College of Liberal Arts, Rochester Institute of Technology, for research and travel grants; and to the Institute of Our Lady of Mercy (Great Britain), the Union of the Sisters of Mercy (Great Britain), and the Institute of Sisters of Mercy of Australia, for generous financial contributions to the project. To thank, by name and in the detail they deserve, all the many Mercy communities who gave me hospitality over the years of this research is not possible, for I might, regretfully, neglect to mention a community that welcomed and helped me. To them all I offer my gratitude and my hope that this volume will bring them joy and inspiration. My own Mercy community in Rochester—Gratia L'Esperance and Marilyn Williams—assisted me in every conceivable way, and I give them my special thanks.

Permission to publish the manuscripts presented in this edition has been received from the owner of each document. I wish to acknowledge this generous cooperation and to thank the following congregational leaders and bishops for their permission: Breege O'Neill, Congregation of the Sisters of Mercy (Ireland); Evelyn Gallagher, Union of the Sisters of Mercy (Great Britain); Noreen Cullen and Patricia Bell, Institute of Our Lady of Mercy (Great Britain); Marie Chin, Institute of the Sisters of Mercy of the Americas; the presidents of the respective regional communities of the Sisters of Mercy of the Americas—Barbara Wheeley (Baltimore), Mary Waters (Brooklyn), Mary Waskowiak (Burlingame), Joy Clough (Chicago), Eileen Dooling (Connecticut), Christine McCann (Merion), Ellen Kurtz (New Hampshire), Suzanne Elliot (New York), Patricia Forrett (Omaha), Georgine Scarpino (Pittsburgh), and Jean Little (Portland); in the Institute of Sisters of Mercy of Australia, Meredith Evans (Adelaide Congregation), Pauline Burke (Brisbane Congregation), Marleen Flaherty (Grafton Congregation), and Kathleen Tierney (Melbourne Congregation); His Eminence Desmond Cardinal Connell, retired archbishop of Dublin; and the Most Reverend John McAreavey, bishop of Dromore. Finally, permission to publish letters in the archives of the Vatican Congregation for the Evangelization of Peoples has been received from His Eminence Crescenzio Cardinal Sepe, Prefect, to whom I am very grateful. Through his publisher, Faber and Faber, Seamus Heaney has graciously allowed me to use lines from his poem "Sunlight" in the introduction.

With all the assistance I have received, one might hope that no errors or omissions will appear in this book. Regretfully, mistakes and oversights may well be discovered; for these I apologize to the readers and to the holders of the affected documents, trusting in their corrections and in their continuing regard for the correspondence of Catherine McAuley, founder of the Sisters of Mercy.

List of Abbreviations

of Archival Collections of Primary Sources

Adelaide	Archives, Sisters of Mercy, Congregation Office, 4 Victoria Street, Mile End 5031, South Australia, Australia
Baltimore	Archives, Sisters of Mercy, Mercy Center, 1322 E. Northern Parkway, Baltimore, Maryland 21239, United States
Bermondsey	Institute of Our Lady of Mercy, Bermondsey Archives, 1 Parker's Row, Bermondsey, London, SE1 2DQ, England
Bessbrook	Archives, Northern Province, Congregation of the Sisters of Mercy, 32 Convent Hill, Bessbrook, Newry, Co. Down BT35 7AW, Northern Ireland
Birmingham	Archives, Union of the Sisters of Mercy, 98 Hunters Road, Handsworth, Birmingham B19 1EB, England
Brisbane	Archives, Sisters of Mercy, Brisbane Congregational Offices, P.O. Box 299, Ashgrove, Queensland 4060, Australia
Brooklyn	Archives, Sisters of Mercy, 273 Willoughby Avenue, Brooklyn, New York 11205, United States
Burlingame	Archives, Sisters of Mercy, 2300 Adeline Drive, Burlingame, California 94010, United States
Carlow	Archives, St. Leo's Convent of Mercy, Carlow, Co. Carlow, Ireland
Charleville	Archives, Convent of Mercy, Charleville, Co. Cork, Ireland
Chicago	Archives, Sisters of Mercy, 10024 S. Central Park Avenue, Chicago, Illinois 60655, United States
Cork	Archives, Convent of Mercy, St. Maries of the Isle, Sharman Crawford Street, Cork, Co. Cork, Ireland
Dromore	Archives, Diocese of Dromore, Bishop's House, 44 Armagh Road, Newry, Co. Down BT35 6PN, Northern Ireland
Dublin Diocese	Diocesan Archives, Archdiocese of Dublin, Archbishop's House, Drumcondra Road, Dublin 9, Ireland
Dublin, Mercy	Mercy Congregational Archives, Congregation of the Sisters of Mercy, Catherine McAuley Centre, 23 Herbert Street, Dublin 2, Ireland
Galway	Archives, Western Province, Congregation of the Sisters of Mercy, 47 Forster Street, Galway, Co. Galway, Ireland
Grafton	Archives, Convent of Mercy, P.O. Box 278, Grafton 2460, New South Wales, Australia
Limerick	Archives, Convent of Mercy, Ashbourne Avenue, Limerick, Co. Limerick, Ireland

Liverpool	Archives, Convent of Mercy, Yew Tree Lane, Liverpool L12 9HH, England
Melbourne	Archives, Sisters of Mercy, Melbourne, Congregation Centre, 720–726 Heidelberg Road, Alphington 3078, Victoria, Australia
Merion	Archives, Sisters of Mercy, 515 Montgomery Avenue, Merion Station, Pennsylvania 19066, United States
New York	Archives, Sisters of Mercy, 150 Ridge Road, Hartsdale, New York 10530, United States
Omaha	Archives, Sisters of Mercy, 7262 Mercy Road, Omaha, Nebraska 68124, United States
Pittsburgh	Archives, Sisters of Mercy, 3333 Fifth Avenue, Pittsburgh, Pennsylvania 15213, United States
Portland	Archives, Sisters of Mercy, 605 Stevens Avenue, Portland, Maine 04103, United States
Propaganda Fide	Archives of the Vatican Congregation for the Evangelization of Peoples (formerly, the Congregation for the Propagation of the Faith), Piazza di Spagna 48, Rome 00187, Italy
Silver Spring	Archives, Institute of the Sisters of Mercy of the Americas, 8380 Colesville Road, Silver Spring, Maryland 20910, United States
Tullamore	Archives, Convent of Mercy, Tullamore, Co. Offaly, Ireland
West Hartford	Archives, Sisters of Mercy, 249 Steele Road, West Hartford, Connecticut 06117, United States
Wexford	Archives, Convent of Mercy, Clonard Road, Wexford, Co. Wexford, Ireland
Windham	Archives, Sisters of Mercy, 21 Searles Road, Windham, New Hampshire 03087, United States

Introduction

> And here is love
> like a tinsmith's scoop
> sunk past its gleam
> in the meal-bin.
>
> Seamus Heaney, "Sunlight"

What is most moving about the letters of Catherine McAuley (1778–1841), the founder of the Sisters of Mercy in Dublin in 1831, is not any gleam of overt or expected virtue, but everyday love immersed deep in the human grain of her friends' and co-workers' lives. Departing from the conventions of her day about how a well-bred woman should compose letters, Catherine wrote not from a script, but from her heart—to offer affection, to give encouragement, to cheer, to affirm the demands of justice, to console, to incite laughter, to express gratitude, to keep playfulness alive. Some of her letters were indeed written to launch or settle business matters: these she *had* to write. But most of them were unsolicited, penned late at night or in the last moments before a post, from no requirement, but the command to love.

In his introduction to a translation of selected writings of Catherine of Siena, the Dominican scholar Kenelm Foster, OP, wrote: "To study her letters is to be drawn deep into the history, both ecclesiastical and secular, of late fourteenth century Italy" (11). While their historical content is not the most important treasure in the letters of either the Sienese or the Dublin Catherine, any history of the church, in any century or place, which restricts itself, unconsciously or deliberately, to the writings of priests and bishops, reporting and indexing only their words and activities, is unrepresentative of ecclesial experience and incomplete in its analyses of effects and causes. As Patrick J. Corish wrote two decades ago: "religious history is coming to be seen as something much wider than succession-lists of parish priests or records of antiquities. Religious history is a history of flesh and blood, a highly important element in cultural and social history, perhaps the most important section" ("The Catholic Community" 32).

THE SIGNIFICANCE OF THE LETTERS

Today the larger church and society need the opportunity to hear not just pious, one-sentence summaries about the holiness of its past women leaders, but detailed presentations of their own voices, articulating in their own prophetic words and actions their own convictions and hopes. In this fusion of horizons, historians and theologians can pose questions to Catherine McAuley which perhaps she never addressed, and she can pose questions to them which perhaps they too rarely address.

After the Rule which she composed, the most authentic and authoritative documents by and about Catherine McAuley are her own letters, and, by implication, the extant contemporary letters written to her or about her. The autobiographical, biographical, and historical content of these letters is an irreplaceable voice, made available to present-day hearers in the oldest and arguably the most intimate of all literary forms: the personal letter written in one historical moment and place by one human being and then sent across time and space to another.

Whether a particular letter is written to inform or to console others or to relieve her own anxiety; whether it is written to an attorney, a dear friend, or a Roman official; whether it is hurriedly scribbled or painstakingly drafted, Catherine McAuley's letters in this edition, taken together, constitute a narrative utterance shaped by her words, emotions, thoughts, and actions. Even in her silences, her omissions, one can hear her speak. And in the antiphonal letters of those who wrote to her, one can hear further echoes and resonances of her own voice.

Catherine's letters are repositories of her affection, her religious standards, her faith, her weaknesses and annoyances as a human being, and her evolution as a woman and as a founder. They are the precious testimony of her wit and sense of humor, the recourse she found for her occasional complaints about certain church officials and medical practitioners, the record of her griefs and fears and of her anguish about her nieces and nephews. In this way they allow a fuller grasp of her own self-image and of her perception of the milieu in which she lived and in which the Sisters of Mercy were founded.

The range of purpose, with the corresponding differences of style and content in Catherine's letters, is refreshing. She writes to the archbishop to settle the date of a ceremony; to a former resident of the House of Mercy to assure her continuing support; to a priest in Carlow to tease him about departing from Baggot Street before breakfast; to the Limerick community to console them in the death of a young sister-poet; to the archbishop's secretary to represent the injustice of the chaplaincy crisis; to those at Baggot Street to describe a new foundation; to an old Dominican friend to announce the death of her niece; to a sister in London to assuage her homesickness; to superiors in all the foundations to encourage them; to her solicitor to clarify the history of the Kingstown debt controversy; to a child in Carlow to send her kisses; to the Pope to petition confirmation of the Rule and Constitutions of the Sisters of Mercy; to her brother to release money for her nephew Willie; to a bishop in England to arrange a new foundation; and gently, in the last months, to several sisters to alert them to her persistent cough. The style in these letters thus varies from the heavily elliptical to the carefully drafted; the tone, from the ironic to the tenderly sympathetic to the coolly logical; and the content, from the precisely focused and explicit to the tangential, allusive, and free-wheeling. Catherine McAuley wrote simply for the recipients of her letters, surely never dreaming of (or wanting) eavesdropping readers centuries later. This purity of purpose gives to her letters a fresh humanity and the kind of immediacy that is so attractive in a gifted letter writer. The justification for publishing her letters is the paradigmatic character of her life and the continuing historical, indeed prophetic, obligations that attach to such a life.

In the overall contours and trajectory of Catherine's collected letters, one can gain insight not only into her own relationships and preoccupations, but also into the personalities and preoccupations of the church in Ireland, and to some extent in England, especially in the years 1831 to 1841, though these insights may be unreliable to the extent that they rest on purely accidental factors: which of her correspondents chose to save her letters? who, if any, decided that it was better to destroy them? what external catastrophes befell some of the preserved letters, such as those possibly in Mary Austin Carroll's burned trunk? what sisters, priests, bishops, or family members, if any, decided there was no need to save her letters? Though many letters have survived, many have not. In probing and appreciating the extant correspondence, one needs constantly to remember the rich, but non-extant correspondence, the letters that are lost, the letters that were not saved, through carelessness or caution or scruple, including those to which the extant letters allude.

A listing of the major recipients of Catherine McAuley's extant letters may illustrate to some extent both her attitudes and theirs. Seventy-seven of the letters in this edition were written to Frances Warde, superior of the Carlow community and a future founder of the Sisters of Mercy in the United States; this number represents almost 30 per cent of all the extant letters Catherine wrote. Nineteen were written to Elizabeth Moore, superior of the Limerick community founded in September 1838; 13 to Mary Aloysius Scott, superior of the Birr community founded in late December 1840; 10 to Mary Cecilia Marmion, the mistress of novices at Baggot Street; and 10 to Teresa White, superior of the branch house in Kingstown in 1838 and then of the Galway community founded in 1840. One hundred seventy-seven, or 66 per cent of her total extant letters, were written to Sisters of Mercy, including novices and postulants. Among major correspondents beyond the Sisters of Mercy, 14 of the extant letters were written to John Hamilton, priest-secretary to Daniel Murray, archbishop of Dublin, during Catherine's life as a Sister of Mercy; 10 were written to Charles Cavanagh, Esq., the community's solicitor; and 25, to various other priests and bishops. Among the extant letters are also four written to church officials in Rome and a draft of one of them.

The major gaps among Catherine's surviving letters, at least according to present reckoning, are the apparent absence of any letters to Mary Clare Moore, superior of Cork in 1837 and then of Bermondsey, England, founded in November 1839; or to Michael Blake, her close friend and confidant, the bishop of Dromore; or to or from Redmond O'Hanlon, the self-effacing Carmelite priest appointed ecclesiastical superior and confessor of the Baggot Street community.

All three recipients can be presumed to have destroyed Catherine's letters to them, out of respect for their confidentiality, or merely out of undue caution. The O'Hanlon-McAuley correspondence may in fact have been slight since Catherine saw him on almost a daily basis. The letters sent to Clare Moore may have been destroyed in the 1944 bombing of the Bermondsey church and adjacent property, although a large quantity of early archival material in the Bermondsey convent was unharmed by the bombing. There are, finally, no extant letters of Catherine to Edward Armstrong, her close priest-friend who died in 1828. Moreover, Catherine apparently destroyed before her death every letter she ever received from a Sister of Mercy, except one from Mary Ann Doyle which she had sent on to Frances Warde. Thus, the presently extant letters, despite their large number, do not constitute the complete landscape of Catherine McAuley's correspondence, but only a sizeable sample that may be more or less representative.

The data in the letters, of course, complicate rather than simplify her portrait, making attempts to interpret her all the more intricate and tentative. The greater the quantity of supposedly accurate details about her, the more difficult become attempts to interpret and integrate them. Ought each extant letter be thought of as a frame in a film, related in relative continuity to the next frame, or ought each letter be regarded as a snapshot in an album, with significant psychological and spiritual, as well as temporal and physical, gaps and disjunctions between them, gaps that can never now be filled, and disjunctions that can never be bridged.

DISCOVERIES

Among the motives for this research was the belief that some new and previously unpublished letters would be found, letters that would add new evidence for the emerging portrait of Catherine McAuley. In this respect, and with the invaluable help of many archivists, the search has been quite successful. Among the important discoveries are the following letters and poems:

- An undated letter written to her brother James McAuley before Catherine moved into Baggot Street, perhaps before 1827. The letter was recently discovered among the papers of a deceased former Sister of Mercy.
- Catherine's letter to John Rice, a priest in Rome, dated December 8, 1833, accompanied by a letter from Edmund Rice to his brother, introducing Catherine McAuley and the Sisters of Mercy, and asking for his brother's help in furthering her request for initial church approbation of the young Mercy congregation. The letters were found by Brother J. Bertrand Darcy, a Christian Brother, among Canadian correspondence in the Archives of Propaganda Fide.

- A letter from Andrew Fitzgerald, OP, president of Carlow College, to Catherine McAuley, dated November 6, 1837. Fitzgerald's forthright letter, found in the Dublin Diocesan Archives, responds to the early and most painful phase of the chaplaincy crisis. Catherine evidently forwarded it to Daniel Murray in support of her position.
- The long, undated, private portion of a letter Catherine sent to Frances Warde immediately after the death of Dr. Patrick Coleman, dean of the Dublin chapter, in May 1838. The letter, now in the Portland archives, is a profoundly personal, confidential letter; it speaks of her weariness and worries, of Dr. Coleman's "great tenderness," and of his unsuccessful attempt to intervene in the chaplaincy crisis.
- A transcribed poem in Catherine McAuley's handwriting found in a framed collage in a nursing home of the Sisters of Mercy in Fishguard, Wales. The autograph is a much abbreviated version of a poem by the English writer Helen Maria Williams (1762–1827) and comments on the precept, "Do unto others as you would they should do unto you" (Matt. 7.12).
- Six autograph poems found in the Brisbane archives that go a long way toward upholding Catherine McAuley's reputation as a "hack" (her word)— a versifier who, as she said, wrote poems and poem-letters as a "prop."
- An undated letter presumably written from Limerick to Mary Magdalen Flynn in Baggot Street. The autograph, once in Sligo, then Athlone, is now in the Galway archives. In this letter, Catherine describes the first days in Limerick: "We are still crowded with visitors, but hope to be engaged next week and have done with them. The Priests refused to give us calls until we would rest, and indeed we are more fatigued talking and receiving strangers than we would be walking over the Town."
- A poem from Catherine McAuley to young Fanny Warde, enclosed in a letter to Frances Warde dated November 24, 1840. Fanny was Frances's niece. Enclosed was a brooch for Fanny that had once belonged to Catherine's beloved niece Mary Teresa Macauley, who died in 1833.
- Two important letters to Mary Teresa White, superior in Galway, written on February 16, 1841 and October 7, 1841, and now in the Galway archives. In the second, written just a month before her death, Catherine speaks about the recent profession ceremony in Galway which she could not attend and notes the disappointment of Mary de Sales White, Teresa's sister, who would have been her travelling companion.
- A draft letter from Catherine McAuley to Dr. Nicholas Foran, bishop of Waterford and Lismore, written in late September or early October 1841, and now in the Merion archives. She responds to Dr. Foran's request for a foundation in Waterford, advising him to send a few "educated persons with marked vocation—good constitution, young if possible" to the convent in Dublin where they will be well prepared for a foundation in Waterford.

TOWARDS A PORTRAIT OF CATHERINE McAULEY

No matter how large any edition of the extant correspondence of Catherine McAuley ever turns out to be, the portrait of her that the letters together afford can never be other than incomplete. Not only are there numerous gaps in the correspondence, even in the extensive series of letters to Frances Warde, and notable silences, but Catherine's self-representations in the letters differ from letter to letter.

The autobiographical "I" is represented differently each time Catherine writes: as a consequence of the historical and social context of the letter; the specific character, personality, and needs of the recipient; the present preoccupations, experiences, and mood of the author; and the circumstances—fatiguing or exhilarating, clarifying or perplexing, hurried or leisurely—in which the letter is written. The first-person protagonist of her letters is a living woman, exercising in a largely male-organized world what she perceives to be her God-given responsibilities, and doing so among differing communities of women who turn to her for guidance, encouragement, and affection.

Over the decade of her life as a Sister of Mercy, a mythical figure of "Catherine McAuley" developed in the minds of her colleagues and correspondents. Therefore, the persona she presents in each letter, the "I" she offers to each "Thou," especially to each sister-correspondent, often suggests an attempt to weaken or correct or redirect the myth while maintaining an authentic relationship. Increasingly visible is her desire to convey her dispensability, to recede to the background herself, to become the "grandmother" not the "mother," to become only a companion in love and hope, no longer needed for guidance or strength.

The self she projects in her letters never, of course, becomes completely invisible. This steady evolution gradually dwindles in the autumn of 1841 to her last, one-sentence plea that Charles Cavanagh secure for the Baggot Street community £20 bequeathed to her by the widowed Mrs. Ryan. This last extant letter, written in October 1841, is a remarkably symbolic conclusion to her career of letter writing: the now dying woman, whose own inner "self" surely felt great need, is now completely veiled, and only the poverty of the community is represented, and that indirectly.

THE READER'S RESPONSIBILITIES

Any editor of the correspondence of Catherine McAuley, as well as any reader of her letters, must inevitably become her biographer, with all the responsibilities and restraints that the proper exercise of biography entails. As Paula Backscheider cautions, while letters are "the closest approximation to a diary or journals that most biographers have," they may also be misleading. Because they are written to specific contemporaries, they do not offer "an unfiltered, clear window" to the personality of the author. "Letters, like diaries, can give a fleeting mood," but it "can be impossible to reconstruct their context, and what survives is always to some extent an accident" (Backscheider 74–75). While letters are an important, perhaps even an essential, category of evidence, by themselves they do not convey the whole life of their author. For "no matter how many, how varied, and how widely addressed" they are, they "give us the subject as nothing except letter writer, not a trustworthy picture of human beings in the fullness of their lives" (84). That is why "[l]etters *about* a person and descriptions of social actions and interactions must be sought as diligently and used as fully as [letters] by the subject" (85).

It is a difficult task to interpret a letter; it is an even more difficult task to interpret a life. The reader-biographer's role is not to create a life, but to interpret one. The values and perspectives of the subject have a reality independent of the values and perspectives of the reader-biographer, a reality that may to some extent be revealed, but not imposed from the outside. The constant temptation of students of so beloved a figure as Catherine is to make her over in their own image, to select those elements that appeal to their own preferences. But to commit oneself to accuracy in one's inquiry will in the end afford a portrait that will have the merit of being better-grounded historically.

The affection and admiration for Catherine McAuley that readers will experience as they read her letters and the letters to and about her are, I believe, fully justified. Though they bring to these letters their own distinct lives, something in her will assuredly reach out to them in ways as distinct, perhaps, as those lives themselves. These reactions, across time and space, are evidence that her work of inspiring and encouraging still goes on, and that her death over 160 years ago has not ended that merciful work.

The Correspondence

1818–1831

Catherine Elizabeth McAuley was born in Dublin in 1778, or possibly in 1781, of Catholic parents, James McGauley and Elinor Conway. Tradition assigns the earlier date. Her father died in 1783, leaving his wife and three children—Catherine, Mary, and James—relatively secure in the earnings of his real estate properties in Dublin. However, by 1798, the year of Elinor McAuley's death, the family's financial security had been severely reduced by the sale of properties and "pecuniary losses."[1]

Mary McAuley married William Macauley, a Protestant, in 1804, and the couple subsequently had five children: Mary (1811), James (1815), Robert (1818), Catherine (1819), and William (1821). Catherine McAuley's sister Mary died in August 1827, and her brother-in-law William, a physician, in January 1829, leaving Catherine the guardian of their five children. Her brother James, also a physician, and now a Protestant, married Frances Ridgeway in 1821.

Meanwhile Catherine herself lived first with her Catholic uncle Owen Conway, then with Protestant relatives, the William Armstrongs, and finally, from 1803 on, with Catherine and William Callaghan, a wealthy, elderly, Protestant couple, at their estate in Coolock, now a north Dublin suburb. Catherine Callaghan died in 1819, and when William Callaghan died in 1822, he left Catherine McAuley the sole residuary legatee of his estate. She continued to live at Coolock until she sold the property in September 1828, having used a sizeable portion of her inheritance to build a large House of Mercy on Baggot Street, in southeast Dublin. The House, opened on September 24, 1827, was intended to provide a school for poor girls, an overnight shelter for homeless servant girls and women, and a residence for lay women who wished to engage with Catherine in these works of mercy.

The atypical character of the resident community on Baggot Street, numbering twelve lay women by June 1830, had from 1827 on aroused intense lay and clerical criticism, in part because they were not a religious congregation with a recognizable religious status and rule, and in part because support of their works of mercy seemed, in the eyes of some benefactors, to compete with support of the Irish Sisters of Charity founded in Dublin in 1815. The criticism threatened to discourage young women from joining in Catherine's endeavors and thus to undermine the very stability of the works of mercy to which she was committed, including the visitation of the sick poor in their homes and in hospitals.

---

1 Bermondsey Annals, in Sullivan, *Catherine McAuley* 99. See also Burke Savage who favors 1781 as her birth year (418–19).

33

Consequently, and contrary to her earlier inclinations, Catherine and her colleagues at Baggot Street decided to found an unenclosed religious congregation of women devoted to "the service of the poor, the sick, and the ignorant"—a phrase that would eventually become part of the congregation's profession of vows. On September 8, 1830, she and two companions, Anna Maria Doyle and Elizabeth Harley, entered the convent of the Presentation Sisters on George's Hill in Dublin for the purpose of serving a novitiate prior to professing religious vows on December 12, 1831, as the first Sisters of Mercy.[2]

Catherine McAuley's extant correspondence for these early, but formative years of her life is extremely sparse, many letters no doubt having been destroyed or lost by herself or others. However, fittingly, the extant documentation begins with a Christmas poem-letter she wrote to her beloved niece Mary, then a child. The other extant letters in this period record her correspondence with her brother James about a family trip, her plans for the House on Baggot Street, her friend Father Edward Armstrong's dying wishes in her regard, her explanations of the community on Baggot Street, her efforts to seek the blessing of church officials on her undertaking, her decision to found the Institute of the Sisters of Mercy, and finally, her attempt to secure for the community some books on the spiritual life which she had given to her now deceased friend, Father Joseph Nugent.

The years 1818–1831 were a time of profound transformation in the mind and heart of Catherine McAuley: from the ease of managing the Callaghan household to the difficulties of founding a religious congregation; from the joys of relative wealth and comfort to those of freely chosen personal poverty; from the happiness of close involvement in a devoted extended family to quiet acceptance of the deaths of many whom she deeply loved; from the personal independence she enjoyed as a lay woman to the communal obligations of religious life; but also, from the uncertainties of living with hopes and desires about her life's work to the clarity and strength of her response to God's beckoning voice as the years and circumstances unfolded. Catherine McAuley was forty years old in 1818 and had received at least one marriage proposal. In late December 1831 she was the 53-year-old founder of the Sisters of Mercy, living in a large house on Baggot Street, not only with her religious community, but with dozens of homeless girls and women, and hundreds of poor girls who came in for school each day. As she was to write of her conviction and joy almost a decade later: "Hurra for foundations—makes the old young and the young merry" (Letter 226).

---

2 For a detailed summary of Catherine McAuley's early life, her Catholic practice and religious development, and her relations with her family and the Callaghans, see especially the Chronology and the Limerick Manuscript in Sullivan, *Catherine McAuley and the Tradition of Mercy*, 9–13 and 139–68. This volume is, in large part, a collection of biographical manuscripts about Catherine McAuley written by her contemporaries in the Sisters of Mercy.

1. To Mary Macauley [Christmas 1818–1821]

Dear Mary[3]
> One more revolving year has passed away
> > Since I address'd you, in a Christian lay
> For time rolls on, regardless, here below
> > Whether we dwell with happiness or woe;
> Then say, my child, have you fulfill'd your part
> > In serving God, with purity of heart
> To please Papa, Mamma, and all the tribe
> > Of little brethern, do you constant strive
> Who never ceasing, fondly look to you
> > For all the good, that they must learn to do.
> *I* answer, "yes," *I* know your gentle breast
> > Throbs with delight, in doing what is best
> But oh, my stars, can I believe my eyes
> > This child is grown to such a monstrous size
> Only I know we bipeds do not vary
> > I'd say, it cannot be my little Mary.
> Then my sweet Child, how thankful should you feel
> > What grateful offerings give, when ere you kneel
> To him who thus gives virtue days of length
> > To grow with your growth, and strengthen with your strength.
> Should you desire to know this World so wide
> > I send a little Traveller[4] for your guide
> Which will convey you without fear or dread
> > To any Port where you would rest your head
> But hark, 'tis twelve, I think I hear the clocks
> > Good night, my love, accept your Christmas Box.
> > > > [Catherine McAuley]

Autograph: Bermondsey

3 This poem-letter which was recently found among private papers in England was, I believe, written by Catherine McAuley to her young niece Mary Macauley, born in 1811. It is clearly a Christmas letter, and was probably written at Coolock. If one takes the reference to "brethern" in line 8 literally, then one can conclude that it was written after the birth of Mary's brothers James (1815) and Robert (1818), but before the birth of her sister Catherine (1819) and her brother William (1821); if "brethern" is not taken literally, then the letter may have been written as late as 1821 or 1822, when Mary was ten or eleven. While the handwriting is quite different from Catherine McAuley's writing in the 1830s, she may be attempting a kind of enlarged script in this poem, in deference to her young reader. 4 Catherine's gift to her niece is impossible to identify with confidence. In the early nineteenth century "traveller" was a name for a variety of things, including "a horse, or other beast of burden or draught, a vehicle, etc. that travels or goes along (fast, well)," including a bird, such as a duck, that made a long flight. The word could also designate "a suit

2. To James McAuley, Esq.[5]   [1825–1826]
Royal Hibernian Military School

My Dear James

   I would have seen you ere this, but I waited to hear Mr. Tigh's[6] answer
which he hesitated to give, probably through fear of exciting a little jelousy
between sisters, but he has settled that by promising to go with Rosina[7] next
year.

   I am now ready to join you and promise myself great pleasure in doing so.
We will give you as little trouble as possible and promise (for the time being) a
compleat surrender of our own will.

> So fully complying are we for the Trip
> That we'll go in a coach, in a car or a ship
> Not a word of complaint shall escape our sweet lips
> No head achs, no heart achs, no fainting, no Hips[8]
> No parcels forgot in a coach or a packet
> No calling on drivers and making a racket
> If a whimsical traveller perchance we should meet
> Who can't get a place for *his* head or his feet
> Who selfishly rude or determinedly cross
> Would not take a place with his back to a horse
> Who must have all the windows open all day
> or all shut – overcome by the smell of new Hay
> No matter – others may do as they please

---

case, trunk, or travelling bag" and "a metal ring or loop used to guide yarn in winding it on the
spindle" (OED). Of these options, the "Traveller" Catherine gave Mary *may* have been a toy animal
or bird—possibly as large as a child's rocking horse.   5 This letter, also found recently among private papers in England, is addressed, in Catherine McAuley's hand, to her brother James
"Macauley," although he generally spelled his name, as she did, "McAuley." James was a physician at the Royal Hibernian Military School in Phoenix Park, Dublin until February 1829 when he
transferred to the post of assistant surgeon at the Royal Hospital, Kilmainham, on the south side
of Dublin.   6 Mr. Tigh is undoubtedly the uncle of Frances (Fanny) Tighe, Catherine McAuley's
close young friend. Frances, originally from Galway, lived with her aunt and uncle in Dublin, but
spent a great deal of time at Coolock House. Catherine and Fanny had apparently been invited to
go on a trip with James and his wife Frances. Possibly this is the trip to France that, by tradition,
Catherine is said to have taken in 1825 (Burke Savage 57 and Degnan 45). The trip discussed here
could have occurred only in 1825 or 1826, several events precluding such a trip in the years before
or after these years.   7 It is difficult to read Catherine's spelling of Fanny Tighe's sister's name.
It may well be Rosina, but it may also be Korina or Rorina. So far it has not been possible to cor-
roborate her name through some other source. She died in January 1841 (see Letter 235).   8 In
Catherine McAuley's day, a "hip" signified a "morbid depression of spirits; the 'blues'" (OED).
She is here promising that James's traveling companions will not be annoyingly low-spirited or
hypochondriacal—which, so far as we know, Catherine never was in her whole life.

We'll always preserve an agreeable ease
and never unthinkingly, wickedly cruel
expose our kind guardian to fighting a duel
ah no—you may safely assure your D[ea]r wife[9]
That we will not ever endanger a Life
of such real value, at least in her mind
That sooner than lose it she'd leave us behind
But like unto clock work our journey shall be
or like music as set for a march in full glee
With the aid of three notes we'll go gaily along
"Bank of Ireland" our Travels & notes of a song

Farewell

a note from Miss T[10] accompanies this
give Ellen & Emily[11] each a sweet kiss
and believe me with
warm affection & truth
your sincerely attached
since the days of my youth

                                                                    C. McAuley

Autograph: Bermondsey

3. **To Bryan Bolger, Esq.[12]**   April 11, 1827
    L[ittle] Longford Street, Dublin

Dear Sir
    I send the specification and drawing of the building in Baggot Street for your
inspection, and from your very kind promise I feel great confidence the matter

---

9 James McAuley married Frances Ridgeway in Dublin in 1821. 10 Frances Tighe. 11 James
and Frances McAuley's two daughters: Ellen born in 1822, and Emily born in 1824. 12 Catherine
clearly addresses this letter to "Bryan Bulger, Esq.," but his name is Bolger. He is listed in the
Dublin Directory for 1824, 1825, and 1826 as a "Measurer," at the Little Longford Street address;
there is no listing for "Bryan Bolger" or "Bulger" among the "Merchants and Traders" in the
Directories for 1827 or 1828. In the *Dublin Directory* of 1830, the following listing appears: "Bryan
and Bolger, Architects, 42 G[rea]t Ship Street," which is probably a misprint. In the "Deed of
Appointment by the Trustees of the Will of Bryan Bolger, deceased"—which is preserved in the
Dublin Diocesan Archives (Murray Papers AB3/33/9)—he is listed as a Measurer. Mr. Bolger was
a Catholic; the Trustees of his Will included Daniel Murray, archbishop of Dublin, and Edmund
Rice, founder of the Irish Christian Brothers. Since the House on Baggot Street was largely completed by September 24, 1827, it is unclear exactly what inspection of the building Catherine sought
from him in April. The builder inserted a convent-style grate in one wall of the chapel, much to
her annoyance, and building delays are known to have occurred; perhaps she consulted Mr. Bolger
on one or other of these matters.

will be speedily brought to a conclusion. When you find it convenient to appoint a meeting, you will have the goodness to give notice of it to the Very Reverend Mr. Armstrong.[13]

I remain, dear Sir,
your very much obliged humble servant
C. McAuley

Autograph: Dublin, Mercy

4. Door-to-Door Petition[14]   [December 1827]

[Poor] Schools and House of Mercy, Baggot Street, [approved] by His Grace, The Most Reverend Doctor Murray, superintended by the Reverend Matthew Kelly[15] and kindly assisted by the Revd. Doctor Armstrong, under whose pastoral charge of this parish the intention was formed and building erected.

In these schools five hundred poor girls may daily experience the blessing of religious instruction, and being practised in various branches of industry, come forward, shielded from all the evils incident to ignorance and idleness—prepared as Christians to discharge the duties of the humble state in life to which it has pleased God to call them.

Young tradeswomen of good character who have employment yet not sufficient means to provide safe lodging are invited to this house at night as their home—practised in prayer and meditation, prepared for sacraments and guarded against the dangers that surround them.

You are most earnestly entreated to contribute to the support of this Institution.

D. Murray, D.D.

Autograph: Dublin, Mercy

---

13 Edward Armstrong had helped Catherine to select the building site on the corner of Baggot and Herbert Streets and is listed in the building agreement as one of her agents in the construction of the house. The Limerick Manuscript reports that he said of the site: "if you would have a public Institution be of service to the poor, place it in the neighbourhood of the rich" (Sullivan, *Catherine McAuley* 150).   14 This petition, in Catherine McAuley's handwriting, but signed by Daniel Murray, was evidently the master text of petitions that were copied and then handed out, from door to door, in the neighborhood of the House of Mercy—sometimes receiving positive responses, but often provoking complaints and insults from residents who regarded the House as an unbecoming intrusion into the social status of the neighborhood, and regarded "Miss McAuley" as an impertinent newcomer. The beginning of the autograph is damaged; the illegible words have been supplied from published copies; the words "of Mary" were inserted after "House" by a later hand.   15 Matthias Kelly was administrator of St. Andrew's chapel, then located on Townsend Street. The Baggot Street House was situated within the parish boundaries. In fact, he was relatively

5. **To Dr. Daniel Murray** Halston Street
March 16, 1828

My dearly beloved Doctor

I have executed a Will purporting to be my last, on the 27th of last month, by which I leave at your disposal any property I may die possessed of, or be in any manner entitled to.[16] I have appointed the Revd. Patrick Walsh and the Revd. Laurence Dunne of this Chapel the executors of it. I have requested in it, with your permission, to be interred in the vaults of the New Building Marlborough Street.[17]

Any property that I shall leave behind me, at least at the present period of my life, can consist only in the value of the effects which will be found about me, namely furniture, books, etc. It is my wish that these should be sold under your instructions and the monies applied principally for Masses for my poor soul; and for the advantage of Religion. I would wish to mark strongly my zeal and good will for our new Institute in Baggot Street, where I hope the Glory of Almighty God will be promoted, and the mental and corporal distresses of the poor in a great degree alleviated. But what can I do, not having, I fear, wherewith to accomplish other pressing good things. Could I hope to survive for the Easter dues of the current year, I should name a sum of £50 for the purpose.[18] I shall however name it and your good sense and prudence will determine for me.

To my servant maid Mrs. Elizabeth Farren I should wish a sum in money to be given her, not exceeding twenty pounds or less than ten pounds, over and above any wages that may be due to her at the time of my death, this of course provided she continues in my Service. She has been hitherto, indeed, a laborious tender and faithful servant to me. I would also wish not to pass in silence my two affectionate cousins, the Kennedys, to whom I would wish to mark my affection and gratitude by some small consideration for mourning.

---

unsupportive of Catherine McAuley and the Baggot Street community (see Sullivan, *Catherine McAuley* 51, 86, 167, 208–209). Catherine here gives his first name incorrectly.   16 Edward Armstrong was Catherine McAuley's close friend, at least as far back as his years as curate at St. Mary's, Liffey Street (1810–1823), but especially since the early 1820s when he visited Coolock House, while William Callaghan was still alive. At the time of this letter he was parish priest of St. Michan's church on North Anne Street, with its presbytery on Halston Street.   17 Father Armstrong died on Ascension Thursday (May 15), 1828. He was buried in the vaults of the new St. Mary's church on Marlborough Street, the parish where he had served as curate for so many years when the chapel was on Liffey Street.   18 The custom of giving to the parish priest the receipts of the collections taken up at the Masses on Easter Sunday was observed in Ireland at this time. Father Armstrong lived until well past Easter and the Limerick Manuscript, as well as the Derry Manuscript, records that "He had furnished the first dormitory in the House of Mercy on its opening [September 24, 1827], and at his death gave fifty pounds more to the charity" (Sullivan, *Catherine McAuley* 158).

I wish to give to my dear and valued Friend, Miss McAuley, for her use in the House in Baggot St., the large divisional maps and the mahogany case in which they are, together with my Ivory Crucifix and the Calvery in which it stands, with the Predieux belonging to it, and the pious pictures prints, to be had in my bed room and study.[19] The Madonna or Mater Amabilis which is placed over my fireplace in the drawing room I should wish to be given to my dear Friend Mrs. Stapleton as a token of my gratitude to her and my affection. I should likewise wish to give my work of the lives of saints together with the volume of moveable feasts to Mrs. Fagan of Capel Street. What is to be done with my Physician, and Executors in the way of retributions I know not. The produce of property only can regulate any of the aforementioned matters.

[My purpose][20] in transferring the produce of my property from the hands of the Executors to you, is that you may govern all according to your good prudence and in such a manner as you would wish I should act for you were I to survive you and be so entrusted by you. Whatever you shall do shall be according to my will of doing, and your conscience shall be perfectly free, not only in the things I have enumerated, but in every other disposition, which you may find it becoming to make.

The only great solicitude which presses on me is with respect to Miss McAuley. When I shall be taken from her, she will find herself in a great measure bereft of an Ecclesiastical Friend, which is a desideratum for her of the utmost importance. Surrounded on every side by protestant and prejudiced relatives and acquaintances, she will be much straightened to follow up her good purposes, unless protected and supported by some zealous and religious Friend. Could I pledge myself to her that you would be that good Friend, who would support and uphold her good purposes, there could not be any fear of her.[21]

---

19 The large ivory crucifix and the Calvary (a substantial, carved wooden base for the crucifix) are now in Catherine's Room, on the first floor (i.e., above the ground level) of Mercy International Centre, Baggot Street, Dublin. The two wooden priedieux, one currently in the room and one in the chapel, are Edward Armstrong's. The "large divisional maps and the mahogany case," as well as "the pious pictures prints," were undoubtedly given to Catherine McAuley in 1828, but they cannot now be identified and located with certainty.   20 The sentence begins "In transferring the produce ...," but it is clear from the syntax that Father Armstrong meant to say something like the words in brackets.   21 The intention and the outcome of this paragraph warrant an essay, not just a footnote. Certainly, Daniel Murray, archbishop of Dublin, appears to have had profound respect for Catherine McAuley, and the Sisters of Mercy were blessed to have been founded during his long episcopacy, rather than in that of his successor, Cardinal Paul Cullen, given that appropriate freedom of movement, local governance, flexibility, and a certain measure of self-regulation were essential to the congregation's early development. But, as her extant correspondence reveals, Catherine McAuley felt "bereft" of Daniel Murray's explicit support in the two controversies that most afflicted her: the chaplaincy issue and the Kingstown debt. In these and other trials, she finally clung most strongly to the stark injunction in Edward Armstrong's dying words to her: "Do not place your confidence in any human being, but place your confidence in God alone" (Sullivan, *Catherine McAuley* 158).

I would wish that my gold pabble snuff box[22] should be returned to Mrs. Sweetman, 4 Mountjoy Square N., from whom I got it, as a token of affection.

Now allow me, my beloved Friend, to say what shall be the portion which you will separate for yourself. I hereby give you full dominion over all, so cull and choose for yourself. If you could know the delight I would have in marking strongly my affection for you, you would not hesitate to possess out of any remnant of my effects whatever would be useful to you.

Here I must take my last farewell of you. As this letter is not to be opened until death shall stop all emotions of my heart, let me entreat of you to be mindful of me when you stand at the altar of God, offering the great sacrifice of the living and the dead. And may the Almighty who has hitherto supplied you with distinguished graces augment those graces in your soul until that day of death shall come for you, when I trust you will be entitled through the all saving blood of your Redeemer to a participation of glory in the church triumphant [*two illegible words*] to the high elevation to which his grace and mercy have raised you in his militant Church on Earth.

E[dward] Armstrong

Autograph: Dublin Diocese, Murray Papers AB3/33/9, no. 12

6. To the Reverend Francis L'Estrange, ODC[23]

Baggot Street
September 10, 1828

Very Reverend Sir

With full approbation of his Grace The Archbishop, the institution in Baggot Street is to go on according to the original intention. Ladies who prefer a Conventual life, and are prevented embracing it from the nature of property or connections, may retire to this House. It is expected a gratuity will be given,* and an annual pension paid sufficient to meet the expence a lady must incur.

The objects which the Charity at present embraces are daily education of hundreds of poor female Children, and instruction of young women who sleep in the House.

---

22 The word seems to be clearly "pabble", not "pebble" or "pobble." But the meaning of "pabble" seems not to fit, and there is no OED listing for "pobble", whereas the meanings of "pebble" relate well to "snuff box." A "gold pebble snuff box" could have been made of natural pebble, from the sea or from a quarry, having flecks of gold in the stone. The OED also connects "pebble" with "Egyptian jasper". 23 Francis L'Estrange, ODC, was then the prior of the Discalced Carmelites at St. Teresa's Church on Clarendon Street, Dublin. An ardent supporter and aide to Daniel O'Connell, the "Liberator," he was also a devoted friend to Catherine McAuley and her co-workers. In the early years the Carmelite friars on Clarendon Street regularly welcomed the Baggot Street community to St. Teresa's for Mass and the sacrament of Penance, and regularly provided the chapel on Baggot Street with vestments, incense, altar breads, charcoal, and other liturgical supplies. In this letter Catherine spells out her conception of the resident lay community in the House on Baggot Street.

Objects in view—superintendence of young women employed in the house, instructing and assisting the sick poor as may hereafter be approved.

I have the honor to remain, Very Reverend Sir,

with great respect, etc., etc.,

C. McAuley

*to create a fund for the school [*CMcA's own footnote*]

Autograph: Dublin, Mercy

7. **To Cardinal Mauro Cappellari, Prefect**   [Early 1830—
    Congregation for the Propagation of the Faith   before March 27]

Most Excellent and Reverend Lord[24]

Sister Mac-Auley of Dublin, most humble Petitioner of your Most Reverend Eminence, represents most respectfully that in the year 1828 she, with the previous approbation of the Most Reverend Monsignor Murray, Archbishop, and under his protection, founded at her own expense a Pious House after the manner

---

24 Though she would have desired that a similar request be forwarded to Rome, it is hard to imagine that Catherine McAuley herself actually drafted *this* petition. Had she done so, she would have written it in English, but no copy in English in her handwriting can be found. The Archives of Propaganda Fide in Rome contains the petition, written in Italian, but the handwriting has not been identified. The same is true of the Italian handcopy that was forwarded to Daniel Murray on March 27, 1830 (see Letter 8).

The petition—written in Italian—was probably not composed, even initially, by Catherine McAuley, but rather, on her behalf and in her name, by one of the Discalced Carmelites of Clarendon Street—either Francis L'Estrange (see Letter 6) or Redmond O'Hanlon, the confessor of the Baggot Street community since June 4, 1829. Both priests were in Rome on Carmelite business in early 1830, and both would have known that Catherine wished for some sign of ecclesial endorsement, especially in view of the lay and clerical censure the Baggot Street community was then experiencing, simply for being what it was: a group of lay women who, though not a religious congregation, dressed simply and lived and prayed together.

On July 26, 1938, in a letter to John MacErlean, SJ, who was then doing research on the life and letters of Catherine McAuley, Fintan O'Brien, ODC, archivist for the Carmelite community on Clarendon Street, wrote as follows:

> The rescript [see Letter 10] was got by the exertions of L'Estrange, and he sent it to Whelan, who was prior at Clarendon St., and Whelan brought it to the nuns. I can remember reading that among L'Estrange's letters to Whelan, which are still at Clarendon St.
>
> L'Estrange was a very active and business-like man, who loved taking on jobs for others. When he was in Rome he did a lot of business for our Fathers in Spain, our nuns in Ireland, etc. I have no doubt it was at O'Hanlon's instance he did this favour for the Sisters of Mercy. (Typescript transcription: Dublin, Mercy)

That the petition can be interpreted as over-reaching in its description of the nature of the House on Baggot Street and in its specification of the papal favors it seeks is clear from Daniel Murray's polite but firm clarifications in Letter 9.

of a Convent, in which she and others associated with her in the pursuit of the same end, occupy themselves in the following charitable works, namely:

1. They commit themselves and strive as much as they possibly can to give a Christian and truly Roman Catholic education to poor and wretched Girls who could not otherwise procure or obtain it.
2. They bring together and lodge poor Servant-girls who owing to the prejudice of heretical employers or other misfortunes find themselves deprived of employment, as well as others who, though they have some trade or profession, are unfortunately not able to find work and therefore stand in need of food and help.
3. They visit the Hospitals and there serve and assist the sick, performing for them the most necessary and useful services.

All such works of charity they exercise in the true spirit of Religion and obedience.

But, nevertheless, they do not remain fully satisfied and content, seeing that they have not got the principal Requisite, namely, the approbation and *Beneplacitum* of the Holy Apostolic See, in consequence of which many devout Persons who would be disposed to embrace such a laudable institute do not join it, and some who have already joined it live constantly in the greatest perturbation and doubt.

In this state of affairs your Petitioner, in the name also of her Companions, has recourse to the well-known piety and zeal of your Most Reverend Eminence, humbly praying you to deign to obtain from the Holiness of Our Lord, Pius VIII, now happily reigning, such faculties and graces as your exceptional ability and signal prudence will deem most opportune and beneficial for the establishment, confirmation and further encouragement of this devout Community, and thus to animate them to perseverance and to the accomplishment of their undertaking, which has been so well started and which tends wholly to the greater glory of God and the good of their neighbours. And they will not fail, united together, to pray to the Most High for the long conservation, greater prosperity and further advancement of Your Eminence.

[Catherine McAuley]

Autograph (Italian): Dublin Diocese and Propaganda Fide, Udienze, vol. 75, f. 645 rv[25]

8. To Dr. Daniel Murray

Rome
March 27, 1830

Most Illustrious and Reverend Lord

Annexed to this letter Your Grace will receive a copy of a suppliant petition forwarded to me in the name of Sister Mac-Auley, in which I am asked to get

25 The English translation of this Italian autograph was made by John MacErlean, SJ, in the middle of the twentieth century. The translation was recently reviewed and slightly modified by Mary Borromeo Povero, RSM, and Professor Pellegrino Nazzaro.

from our Most Holy Lord some faculties and graces for a Religious house established by the said Sister at Dublin in the year 1828 for the exercise of various works of charity.

I pray Your Grace to let me know plainly what you think of that petition, and also to be so good as to explain to me what in your opinion would be the most suitable favors and faculties for me to apply for.

In the meantime I pray that God may long preserve Your Grace in health and happiness.

> Ever at Your Grace's service
> D. M. Cardinal Cappellari, Prefect
> C. Castracane, Secretary

Rome, from the Office of the Sacred Congregation
for the Propagation of the Faith

Autograph (Latin): Dublin Diocese, Murray Papers AB3/34/15, no. 1[26]

9. To Cardinal Mauro Cappellari, Prefect   9 Mountjoy Square
Congregation for the Propagation of the Faith   Dublin
April 17, 1830

Most Eminent and Most Reverend Lord

I have received the letter of Your Eminence dated 27 March, with enclosed *Libellus Supplex* sent to Your Eminence in the name of Sister McAuley who desires certain faculties and favors for a religious house established by that Sister in Dublin in the year 1828 for the exercise of many acts of charity.

In order to comply with the demands of Your Eminence and signify to you my sentiments concerning the position of that house, I must say, by way of a beginning, that it is my opinion it cannot be called *religious*, since the women who live there, however pious, neither belong to a legitimately established congregation, nor do they live according to an approved rule, nor do they take vows, nor indeed can I rightly understand why Miss McAuley is designated *Sister*. Some years ago she began to build a house, which was said to be destined for certain works of charity; and although its opening was not signified to me, nor indeed was it as yet clearly stated by Miss McAuley what its function might be,

---

26 The English translation of this autograph was made by John MacErlean, SJ, in the middle of the twentieth century. It was recently reviewed and slightly modified by Mary Eymard Hyland, RSM. Mauro (Bartolomeo Alberto) Cappellari (1765–1846), the recipient of Letter 7 and the principal signatory of Letter 8, was a member of the Camaldolese religious order. He served as Prefect of Propaganda Fide from 1826 until February 2, 1831, when he was elected to the papacy, taking the name Gregory XVI. As Pope he gave formal approval to the religious congregation of the Sisters of Mercy (1835) and to their Rule and Constitutions (1841). In his signature "D. M." apparently stands for "Dom Mauro." Enclosed in Letter 8 was a handcopy, in Italian, of Letter 7.

I pronounced the pious project to be a favourable one because it appeared to be for the benefit of the poor.[27]

Miss McAuley spent part of this time among her friends and relatives. Meanwhile many of them died and she immediately felt herself freer to devote herself to pious works. Therefore, she took up residence in the above-mentioned already-established house,[28] and with other women who had joined her, began to perform the works of charity which are mentioned in the *Libellus Supplex*.

Shortly afterwards, as the work she had begun became permanent and stable, she requested of me that she and her companions be raised to the status of a Religious Congregation. I replied I could not do this, since no prior preparation had been done by them, nor had it been attempted according to the religious rules laid down for Novitiates.

In a matter of such great importance, I considered it wise to proceed carefully and slowly. Nor could I doubt but that these women needed to be trained in stricter discipline before they could be allowed to rejoice in the name of Religious Women, all the more so in view of the works which compel them to leave home daily and involve themselves among seculars. Finding themselves so circumstanced, they have recourse to the Holy See, without my offering any objection, in the hope of obtaining a satisfactory remedy.

As far as concerns me, these women, in spite of the good works to which they are dedicated, are not organised according to the norms of Religious Life, and I do not presume to ask favours for them which are seen to apply to a Religious Congregation.[29]

However, if it seems fit to Your Eminence to send any favors of this nature or any other grace or faculty to strengthen them in the path of virtue and to sustain them along that path, whatever Your Eminence will decide, I shall regard as most wise and I shall endeavour to fulfil it exactly.

Dublin
17 April 1830

Daniel [Murray], Archbishop of Dublin

Autograph (Latin): Propaganda Fide, Udienze, vol. 75, ff. 646 rv–647 rv[30]

---

27 The House of Mercy on Baggot Street, Dublin, was opened on September 24, 1827. Its purpose at that time was to provide an overnight shelter for homeless servant girls and women and a school for poor girls. The resident community of workers consisted only of Anna Maria Doyle and Catherine Byrn, Catherine McAuley's young adopted cousin.   28 Catherine McAuley probably moved permanently into the House of Mercy only after her sale of Coolock House on September 15, 1828, although there is some evidence that she was living there regularly after the death of Edward Armstrong on May 15, 1828. However, until the death of her widowed brother-in-law, William Macauley, on January 25, 1829—his wife Mary, Catherine's sister, having died in August 1827—she was also spending time at his home, caring for their five children.   29 On September 8, 1830, five months after Dr. Murray wrote this letter, Catherine McAuley entered the novitiate of the Presentation Sisters on George's Hill, Dublin, to begin preparation for founding the Sisters of Mercy.   30 The English translation

10. To Dr. Daniel Murray

Rome
May 23, 1830

From the Audience of His Holiness held on the 23rd May 1830

Our Most Holy Lord by Divine Providence Pope Pius VIII, having received a report from me, the undersigned Secretary of the Sacred Congregation for the Propagation of the Faith, and having maturely considered the whole state of affairs, kindly concedes and mercifully grants in the Lord, subject to the consent of the Ordinary, to all the ladies dwelling in the said House and engaging in the said Pious works, who, provided they be truly penitent, have confessed and received Holy Communion, shall devoutly visit any church, or oratory or chapel twice in a month on days they themselves select and shall piously pray to God for some time for the propagation of the holy Faith, a Plenary Indulgence applicable also by way of suffrage to the souls in Purgatory. Moreover, he also concedes and mercifully grants, subject also to the consent of the Ordinary, to these same ladies a Partial Indulgence of two hundred days once a day if they recite the Litany of the Blessed Virgin Mary, applicable also to the souls detained in Purgatory.

Given at Rome from the household of the Sacred Congregation on the day and in the year above mentioned. Free from payment under any title whatsoever.

Castruccio Castracane
Secretary

Autograph (Latin): Dublin, Mercy[31]

11. To Catherine McAuley

Saturday
August 28, 1830

Dear Miss McAuley

I am rejoiced at the arrangement which has been made, and I trust it will lead to most beneficial results.[32]

I fear from the occupations which I've before me, that it will not be in my power to call at Baggot Street within the time which you mention; but Dr. Blake will, on this occasion, be my substitute. Have the goodness to pray him to make

---

of this autograph was made by John MacErlean, SJ, in the middle of the twentieth century. It was recently reviewed and slightly modified by Mary Eymard Hyland, RSM, and Father Robert McNamara.   31 The English translation of this Rescript of Indulgences was made by John MacErlean, SJ, in the middle of the twentieth century and was recently reviewed and slightly modified by Mary Eymard Hyland, RSM. The text of Letter 7—i.e., the Petition (in Italian) to which this Rescript (in Latin) responds—is repeated at the beginning of the autograph of the Rescript, but since the text is given in Letter 7, it is not repeated here.   32 See note 29.

the necessary examination in my name.[33] With earnest wishes for the success of your pious project, I remain, Dear Miss McAuley,

Yours in Christ, very faithfully

D. Murray

Autograph: Dublin, Mercy

12. Act of Profession of Vows[34]   December 12, 1831

In the name of Our Lord and Saviour Jesus Christ and under the protection of His immaculate Mother Mary ever Virgin, I, Sister Catherine McAuley, called in religion Mary Catherine, do vow and promise to God perpetual Poverty, Chastity and Obedience, and to persevere untill the end of my life in the Congregation called of The Sisters of Mercy, established for the visitation of the sick poor, protection and instruction of poor females, according to the rule and constitutions of the Presentation order, subject to such alteration as shall be approved of by the Archbishop, under the authority and in presence of you, My Lord and Most Reverend Father in God Daniel Murray, Archbishop of this Diocese, and Reverend Mother Elizabeth Knowd, called in religion Mary Francis of Sales, Superioress of the Convent of the Presentation, Dublin, this twelfth day of December, in the year of our Lord one thousand eight hundred and thirty one.

Sister Catherine McAuley

In religion, Mary Catherine

Sister M. C. A. Doyle, Assistant

Sister Mary Francis de Sales Knowd, Superioress

+D. Murray, Archbishop, etc.

Autograph transcript: Propaganda Fide, SC America Settentrionale, vol. 3, f. 197

33 As part of the documentation required for Catherine McAuley's entrance into the Presentation Convent on September 8, 1830, a letter of recommendation from the archbishop was necessary. Dr. Murray is here deputing Catherine's good friend, Michael Blake, parish priest of St. Michael's and St. John's, to perform this function on his behalf.   34 Though not in itself an item of correspondence, the text of Catherine McAuley's Profession of Vows forms a fitting conclusion to the correspondence of this phase of her life. It represents the decision toward which she was led, by circumstances and sometimes unknowingly, ever since the death of her benefactor William Callaghan on November 10, 1822. The text of her vows incorporates language, approved by Daniel Murray, which allows for the future development of a Rule and Constitutions proper to the Sisters of Mercy. The text presented here is that contained, in her own handwriting, in the letter she wrote to John Rice on December 8, 1833 (see Letter 19 below). Catherine McAuley's Act of Profession and the Acts of Profession of Mary Ann (Anna Maria) Doyle and Mary Elizabeth Harley, also pronounced at the Presentation Convent on December 12, 1831, constitute the founding documents of the Sisters of Mercy.

1832–1834

The first three years of the new religious congregation of the Sisters of Mercy were not unlike the beginnings of any organization that hopes to endure beyond the lifetimes of its first members. Now, in addition to Catherine McAuley, Mary Ann Doyle, and Mary Elizabeth Harley—the three who had professed their vows at the Presentation convent on December 12, 1831—new members enlarged the congregation. Seven of the women who had waited for fifteen months at Baggot Street, while Catherine and the others made their novitiate at George's Hill, received the habit on January 23, 1832,[1] and four of them professed their vows a year later.[2] Meanwhile they were joined in these first years by others who chose to enter the community.

These quietly remarkable Irish women, most of them at least thirty years younger than Catherine McAuley, were not uniformly talented, but they were destined to become the vital nucleus of the future growth and spread of the Sisters of Mercy. Without their courage, zeal, good humor, and imaginative mercifulness, the young congregation would not have survived the difficulties of its first decade. Many of them became the founding superiors of the convents established outside of Dublin, in Ireland and England, prior to Catherine's death in 1841. Many of them also became, through the particular circumstances of their lives, major recipients of Catherine's letters, especially after the opening of the first branch house in Kingstown in 1835 and the series of new foundations that began in Tullamore and Charleville in 1836.

The names of these first Sisters of Mercy—who entered, received the habit, or professed vows before the end of 1834—will appear often as the addressees or subjects of the extant correspondence published in this volume: especially Mary Ann Doyle, Mary Frances Warde, Mary Angela Dunne, Mary de Pazzi Delany, Mary Clare Moore, Mary Elizabeth Moore, Mary Josephine Warde,

---

1 Mary Josephine (Catherine) Byrn, Mary Frances (Frances) Warde, Mary Angela (Margaret) Dunne, Mary Joseph Teresa (Mary) Macauley, Mary Clare (Georgiana) Moore, Mary Magdalen de Pazzi (Mary Anne) Delany, and Mary Agnes (Anna) Carroll. Shortly after the ceremony Anna Carroll left the Sisters of Mercy to join the Presentation Sisters on George's Hill. 2 Those professing their vows on January 24, 1833 were Mary Frances Warde, Mary Angela Dunne, Mary Clare Moore, and Mary de Pazzi Delany. Catherine Byrn (Catherine McAuley's adopted cousin) left the Sisters of Mercy on December 1, 1832 to join the Dominican Sisters in Cabra. Catherine's beloved adopted niece, Mary Teresa Macauley, had thoughts about becoming a Carmelite and so chose not to profess vows in January 1833. However, as the year unfolded her tendency to consumption worsened. On November 3, 1833, in a private ceremony she professed her vows as a Sister of Mercy, and nine days later, on November 12, 1833, just after midnight, she died, her aunt at her bedside.

Mary Teresa White, Mary Cecilia Marmion, Mary Ursula Frayne, and Teresa Carton. Others would join in the years that followed, but on the "first flock," as Catherine sometimes called them, depended greatly the "good beginning" for which she was always deeply grateful. As she later wrote of these first years:

> There has been a most marked Providential Guidance which the want of prudence, vigilance or judgment has not impeded—and it is here that we can most clearly see the designs of God ... in short, it evidently was to go on—and surmount all obstacles—many of which were great indeed—proceeding from causes within & without. (Letter 110)

The "obstacles" revealed in the correspondence of the years 1832–1834 were not always big ones, such as the cholera epidemic of 1832 which nearly exhausted the strength of the sisters who nursed for seven months in a temporary cholera hospital; or the deaths in 1832 of Anne O'Grady and Mary Elizabeth Harley, two young women of great zeal and promise, and in 1833 of Catherine's beloved niece Mary Teresa Macauley; or the decision of Walter Meyler, parish priest of St. Andrew's, to close the Baggot Street chapel to the public in 1834, thus depriving the community of income from the Sunday collection. The letters of these years also reveal the ordinary tasks Catherine had to learn to accomplish: how to judge the readiness of young women in the House of Mercy to be placed in private homes as servants; how to secure aids to spiritual growth for the community; how to provide continuing guidance for her three orphaned nephews; how to relate to Dr. Daniel Murray, archbishop of Dublin, and his secretary, the Reverend John Hamilton; how to select suitable postulants for the community; how to write a Rule for the congregation; and how to correspond with officials in Rome to secure ecclesiastical approval of the Sisters of Mercy. All of these duties taxed her own "prudence, vigilance or judgment."

But these were also years of laughter, instigated by Catherine's own marvelous sense of humor, as the poem-letter to Mary Ann Doyle demonstrates, as well as years of supportive friendships, as intimated in the letters to John Hamilton, and exhibited in those from Michael Blake, now bishop of Dromore. In addition, they were years of growth. By the end of 1834, there were twenty-four women living in the Baggot Street community, at various stages of membership. Indeed, "it evidently was to go on"—despite the deaths of those she dearly loved and despite the community's financial difficulties, the bulk of her inheritance now depleted.

Moreover, and this fact comforted her most intimately, the works of mercy to which she had dedicated her life were now in full swing on Baggot Street. As she wrote in December 1833 to Father John Rice, the brother of Edmund Rice: "In this Institute we lodge and support distressed unprotected women of good character ... and have extensive schools for poor girls ...Of the distressed women, seven hundred and seventy-two have been instructed and protected ... and several hundred children have partaken of the Holy Sacraments" (Letter 19). No wonder the community begged bedding and clothing from door to door, and no wonder the artist Mary Clare Augustine Moore later remarked, somewhat peevishly, about the period in 1832–1833 when the sisters also ran a soup kitchen: "There was soup to be made for a hundred, sometimes more, and they had to pass through the office down to the dining hall in squadrons, and this by a wooden staircase now replaced by stone, so there was work and dirt and discontent ... and inconvenience in the management of the House of Mercy" (Sullivan, *Catherine McAuley* 209).[3] Had she lived to read this passage of Clare Augustine's "Memoir," Catherine McAuley would simply have smiled, sweetly. It was the merciful care of the "squadrons" that worried her, not the "work and dirt."

13. To the Reverend John Spratt, OCC

Convent of Mercy
[1832]

Reverend Sir

We admitted to our Institution a young woman named Margaret Thompson who brought a note of recommendation from the Revd. Mr. Yore[4]—and having been twice in the house, the usual enquiries were not made. We sent her to Mrs. Murray in Sackville Street—a confectioner—where her foot was scalded, and she came again to us. Her conduct each time was approved.

A very suitable situation having now offered—"To attend young ladies at Mrs. Baker's boarding school"— we selected her and referred to her last mistress, Mrs. McDonogh, who presides over the orphan school. Mr. Baker saw Mr. McD., who said he would not recommend her.

I am now referred to you, Revd. Sir, who can judge of the evil consequences that must follow if we send from this Establishment a person of blemished character.[5]

> I remain very respectfully, etc., etc.,
> Mary Catherine McAuley

Autograph: Dublin, Mercy

3 Mary Clare Augustine Moore entered the Baggot Street community on August 8, 1837. Her long biographical "Memoir of the Foundress," written from notes and interviews in the twenty years after Catherine McAuley's death, is contained in Sullivan, *Catherine McAuley* 198–216.   4 William Yore was a vicar general of the Dublin Diocese and parish priest of St. Paul's on Arran Quay, 1828–1864 (Donnelly 10:25). John Spratt, OCC, the recipient of this letter, was at this time prior of the Calced Carmelites on Whitefriar Street, off Aungier Street.   5 It is not immediately clear why Catherine McAuley is writing to John Spratt about this problem. However, the *Dublin Directory* for 1833 notes that a Mrs. Baker operated a "Ladies Seminary" at 42 St. Stephen's Green, East, a fairly short distance from Whitefriar Street. This is probably the "boarding school" to which Catherine refers, and perhaps she hoped that John Spratt would intervene with the Bakers, or possibly with the McDonoghs, if either couple were parishioners of the Whitefriar Street Church. I have not been able to identify the McDonoghs. The letter suggests that Catherine McAuley trusted the earlier reports on the com-

14. **To Dr. Daniel Murray** Convent of Mercy
February 19, 1832

My Lord

I beg leave to engage your attention a few minutes in the cause of charity. My second nephew has expressed a strong wish to commence studies for a Priest—he is in his fifteenth year, of very healthy constitution, and is said to possess more than ordinary talent.[6] Doctor Fitzgerald speaks of him as follows: "Robert continues to excel in everything, and though always successful, has nothing of triumph about him. When raised above boys much older, he is quite embarrassed. I would trust anything to his head and heart—he is supported by a mind that will carry him through every difficulty—distinguished for candor and manly steadiness. In no instance has he ever been found to deviate from truth."[7]

My Lord, I considered this a little extravagant, and speaking of it to Dr. Kinsella[8] who called at George's Hill, I said: "Robert, in being diligent and successful at study, has secured Doctor Fitzgerald's good opinion in all things." He answered: "I do not think you have heard too much of him—from my observations whilst I was in the house and what I have since learned, I believe it to be fully merited." My Lord, he has not any property. It pleased God to take away Father, Mother, and six hundred a year in seventeen months.[9] He is an orphan child of your Lordship's diocese, and I most earnestly beg the Patronage and Bounty of your Grace to enable him to try his vocation to a state for which he has already received so many essential qualities.

I have the honor to remain, My Lord, with great respect,
your obedient humble servant
M. C. McAuley

Autograph: Dublin Diocese, Murray Papers AB3/34/15, no. 3

---

mendable "conduct" of Margaret Thompson, a resident of the House of Mercy, and would resent any unfounded blemishing of her character, or that of the House of Mercy, by the McDonoghs or Bakers.   6 Robert Macauley, the son of Catherine McAuley's deceased sister Mary and Mary's husband William, was fourteen years old at this time, a student in St. Patrick's College, Carlow (familiarly called Carlow College).   7 Dr. Andrew Fitzgerald, OP (1763–1843), was president of Carlow College, 1814–1843, and the devoted friend of Catherine McAuley, who had placed her three adopted nephews, James, Robert. and William, in Carlow College shortly after the death of their father on January 25, 1829.   8 Dr. William Kinsella (1796–1845) was appointed bishop of Ossory in 1829. He then resided in Kilkenny and was a good friend to Catherine McAuley, visiting her at George's Hill and always hoping she would found a community of Sisters of Mercy in Kilkenny or elsewhere in Ossory Diocese. He consecrated the Baggot Street cemetery on November 14, 1841 and attended Catherine McAuley's funeral liturgy on November 15, 1841. A professor in Carlow College until 1829, he continued his association with the Carlow faculty after his appointment as bishop.   9 Mary Macauley died in August 1827, and William Macauley died seventeen months later, on January 25, 1829. The "six hundred [pounds] a year" which Catherine notes may refer to the family's expenses since Mary's illness and death and especially since the death of William and the loss of his income as an apothecary at the Royal Military Hospital, Kilmainham, Dublin.

15. To Sister Mary Ann Doyle[10]   [1832]

Dear Sister Doyle, accept from me
for your poor suffering martyrs
a laurel wreath to crown each knee
in place of former garters.

Since fatal Cholera appeared
you've scarce been seen to stand,
nor danger for yourself e'er feared
when death o'erspread the land.

While on your knees from Bed to Bed
you quickly moved about
it did not enter in your head
that knees could e'er wear out.

You've hurt the marrow in the bone
imploring aid and pity
and every Cardinal in Rome
would say you saved the City.

Now that the story of your fame
in Annals may be seen
we'll give each wounded knee a name
Cholera—and—Cholerene.

Autograph: Dublin, Mercy

16. To the Reverend John Hamilton   [Baggot Street]
November 26, 1832

Reverend Sir

I think you were so kind to say you would see about the books which are amongst poor Mr. Nugent's.[11] It would [be] a charity indeed, as we find it diffi-

10 A severe epidemic of Asiatic cholera struck Dublin in Spring 1832. Sometime soon after April 25, at the request of the Board of Health, Catherine McAuley and other Sisters of Mercy began to work, in four-hour shifts, at a cholera hospital set up in a facility on Townsend Street. This work continued for seven months. Mary Ann Doyle was one of the nurses, and since the pallets of the cholera victims were low off the ground, she often moved from bed to bed on her knees. Several early manuscripts record this nursing experience which left the sisters bone-tired at the end of the day (see Sullivan, *Catherine McAuley* 64, 97, 112, 174, and 207). Catherine remained at the hospital all day. Sometime in the course of these months her sense of humor enlivened the community and Mary Ann Doyle with this witty eulogy—written on the inside of the front of an envelope addressed to "The Rev. Mother, Convent of Mercy." She often used scraps of paper for her poetic productions.   11 Joseph Nugent—Catherine McAuley's young friend from her days in Coolock,

cult to keep up a supply for school, sick, etc.—and would get a great stock for one fourth of the books I ask for. I should think they are not marked as Mr. Nugent's.

Reverend Sir, respectfully, etc.

M. C. McAuley

Autograph: Dublin Diocese, Murray Papers AB3/34/15, no. 4

17. To the Reverend John Hamilton

Baggot Street

23 Inst. [December 23, 1832][12]

Very Reverend Sir

I scarcely know how to apologise for troubling you about the books you were so kind to promise me. My dear friend Mr. Armstrong[13]—who knew the manner poor Mr. Nugent got them – very often said to me—"you ought to have those Books returned and I will speak to the Bishop of it"—so that I should not have any hesitation asking for all. Were it of any use—you mentioned, Revd. Sir, a few not marked as Mr. Nugent's—even these will be most acceptable, and I will send for them any time you appoint.[14]

I remain, very Reverend Sir, respectfully

Mary C. McAuley

Autograph: Dublin Diocese, Murray Papers AB3/34/15, no. 22

18. To Catherine McAuley

[Violet Hill, Newry]

[June 5, 1833]

Dear Madam

You should not have been so long without receiving an answer to your kind letter of the 27th of April had I not been ever since immersed in the duties

---

when she attended St. Mary's chapel, Liffey Street, Dublin—had died of typhoid fever on May 30, 1825, at the age of twenty-nine, while serving as curate in Saints Michael's and John's parish. Catherine often spoke of "his great friendship and readiness to serve in any way"; he died "after fifteen days of severe suffering, during which she attended him day and night" (Sullivan, *Catherine McAuley* 92, 46). Evidently, John Hamilton or others were now disposing of Joseph Nugent's remaining effects, among which were spiritual books, many of which Catherine had given him (see Letter 17), and which she now requested—for example, catechetical books and books of prayers for the sick and dying. **12** This is probably the second of Catherine McAuley's two letters about Joseph Nugent's books, so "Inst.," i.e. "of this month," may stand for December 1832, a month after her first letter to John Hamilton. **13** Edward Armstrong knew of Catherine's friendship with Joseph Nugent, having served with him at St. Mary's, Liffey Street. **14** The books were presumably received, but none of them appears to be still in the collection at Mercy International Centre, Baggot Street, or Mercy Congregational Archives, Herbert Street. Many books that were once in the Baggot Street library have, over the last 170 years, been lost or distributed to other convents.

belonging to the Jubilee time, and were I not anxious, before I would reply, to have my mind properly informed on the subject of your inquiry. As I have no personal acquaintance with the lady herself[15] and have not seen her but once for a moment, my information has been necessarily borrowed from others. But I have consulted several dispassionate persons, all have agreed in acknowledging the strict morality and religious habits of that lady. All are persuaded that she has means for doing extensive good, all finally regret that one little drawback from the excellence of her other qualities is found in a certain peculiar or a singular mode of thinking & judging by which [she] is distinguished.[16] I hope that you and your good community all continue to enjoy good health and that everything else is going on well—likewise I am. I shall always [*illegible words*]

[Michael Blake]

Author's transcript: Dromore

19. To the Reverend John Rice, OSA   Convent of The Sisters of Mercy
Rome   Baggot Street, Dublin
                                                  December 8, 1833

Reverend Father

Your good Brother called on me at your request—to read part of a letter which refers to our community—and I beg to return most grateful thanks for the kind interest you have taken. When you so charitably offered your services at Rome, perhaps I was too importunate to be rightly understood.[17]

15 The lady is Elizabeth Magenis. Various forms of her surname appear in letters of Catherine McAuley and in biographies and other works about Catherine McAuley—McGuinness, Magennis, for example—but in a legal document she signed on February 25, 1839, she spells her name "Magenis."
16 The story of Miss Magenis is not completely clear. It seems that, at first, she sought to be a member of the Sisters of Mercy and promised, by legal document, a very large dowry, totaling £1471 in stock, to be paid in installments over future years. She entered the Baggot Street convent on June 18, 1833 and received her habit as a novice on February 11, 1834, but when her behavior led to a negative judgment (on January 28, 1836) about her suitability to be a professed member of the community, she was evidently allowed to live in the branch house in Kingstown (Dun Laoghaire) as a boarding benefactress. When this arrangement also proved unsatisfactory, again due to her own conduct, she was released from any future financial obligations to the Sisters of Mercy and asked to leave the premises; the money she had already promised or given to the congregation minus what was needed to cover the expenses she had already incurred was returned to her through a formal deed of release dated February 25, 1839 (see Letter 115). Apparently, the "singular mode of thinking & judging" that Dr. Blake reports here eventually led to Miss Magenis's departure, although the deed of release cites only her "ill health and increasing delicacy of constitution" (Autograph: Mercy Congregational Archives, Herbert Street, Dublin).   17 John Rice, OSA, the brother of Brother Ignatius (Edmund) Rice, founder of the Christian Brothers, was an Augustinian priest stationed in Rome. Apparently he had visited Catherine McAuley at Baggot Street while he was on a visit to Dublin, and during their conversation Catherine had requested his help in Rome, perhaps to secure some form of

We do not seek to be engrafted with the good Sisters of Charity, who have only one noviciate, and one general superior—each branch of our Institute will have its own noviciate and be subject to the ordinary of the Diocese. This is the chief distinction. Our first Sisters were professed in a Convent of the Presentation order in George's Hill for the express purpose of establishing this House, with the full approbation of our venerable Archbishop, Most Revd. Doctor Murray. It is the first Convent that was erected in the midst of the Protestant nobility—when they were employing wealth and influence to allure Catholics from their faith.

We have an extensive poor Institution attached, called the House of Mercy— from which we have been entitled—Sisters of Mercy. In this Institute we lodge and support distressed unprotected young women of good character untill suitable situations are provided and have extensive schools for poor girls—entirely conducted by the Sisters who also visit the sick poor. Of the distressed women, seven hundred and seventy two have been instructed and protected, most of whom would have fallen victims to the Proselyting system—and several hundred children have partaken of the Holy Sacraments, who were all under Protestant influence in this neighbourhood. By the visitation of the sick, the poor are rescued from the dangerous interference of false teachers, at the awful period of death.

The benefit effected by this establishment is most remarkable and generally admitted. It has restrained the new lights in their attempts to pervert Catholic servants—who regard it[18] as a kind of tribunal, always ready to receive their complaints, and redress their wrongs—and from the liberal Protestant, tributes of approbation have been received. All public taxes are remitted, and contributions placed at the disposal of the Sisters. From what I know of Ireland—for twenty years—I am quite convinced, Revd. Father, that if Houses of such general relief were spread through the Country, all efforts to delude would—with the blessing of God—be entirely defeated.

initial ecclesiastical approval of the Sisters of Mercy. He had subsequently written to his brother about her request, not precisely understanding what sort of assistance she sought from him. Therefore, Edmund Rice himself came to Baggot Street to clarify the situation.

This letter from Catherine to John Rice, written as a consequence of her visit with his brother, and Edmund Rice's accompanying letter to John Rice (see Letter 20), written two days later on the *same* single large sheet of paper, have been only recently found by the Christian Brothers, in the Archives of Propaganda Fide in Rome where the document had been misfiled, apparently for years, among papers in the North American section of the Archives.

I am extremely grateful to Brother J. Bertrand Darcy, Canada, who originally found these two important letters, and to Brother Peter E. Fogarty, Congregation Secretary, Congregation of Christian Brothers, Rome, who—after my own unsuccessful search in Rome prior to my knowledge of Bro. Darcy's discovery—sent me a superb photocopy of the photocopy of the autograph in the Congregation's possession. I was assisted early on in my pursuit of these letters by Kathrine Bellamy, RSM, Newfoundland, and Noel Keller, RSM, Dallas, Pennsylvania, to whom I also express my gratitude. The story of the discovery of Letters 19 and 20 is also the story of the discovery of the face-to-face encounter between two great nineteenth-century Irish servants of the poor, Edmund Rice and Catherine McAuley.

18 That is, the House of Mercy.

I give you a copy of our vow, by which you will see we have professed according to the rule and constitutions of the Presentation order—already approved by The Holy See. What we humbly beg is to have our two Chapters—one on the visitation of the sick—the other, protection of poor women—added thereto, and that we may be regarded on religious equality with our Sisters of the Presentation order.[19] This indulgence would greatly animate our exertions—and with the assistance of God's Holy Grace, we would shew our gratitude to our Most Holy Father by unwearied efforts for the preservation of our sacred Faith amongst His poor beloved brethern. Our first Sisters were professed on the twelfth of December one thousand eight hundred and thirty one. Twenty three Sisters have united with us—and *were* we fully adopted by the Holy See many Houses would soon be established. We have been already invited[20]—and much encouraged—but our first and dearest wish is to obtain the entire concurrence of His Holiness.

I beg again to offer most sincere thanks for your kindness. We shall not neglect to pray most earnestly that God may be graciously pleased to bless your exertions for our spiritual advancement—and reward you for them.

I remain, Reverend Father, most respectfully,
your obliged servant in Christ
Mary Catherine McAuley[21]

Autograph: Propaganda Fide, SC America Settentrionale, vol. 3, f. 197rv

19 In December 1833 Catherine McAuley had not yet completed, or perhaps had not even begun, her revision of the Presentation Sisters' Rule and Constitutions for use by the Sisters of Mercy. However, she had written the two distinctive chapters which she intended to add to the Presentation Rule. Securing the Holy See's approval of these two chapters (which she transcribes at the end of this letter) is her first request of John Rice. In addition, Catherine entertained at this time the hope that, like the Presentation Sisters, the members of the Sisters of Mercy might profess solemn vows, rather than simple vows. For some reason, she felt that the profession of solemn vows (according to church practice in Catherine's day, professed only by cloistered congregations) would indicate a stronger degree of ecclesiastical approbation. John Rice must have forwarded this second request because when the Holy See responded on March 25, 1835, Cardinal Fransoni, then Prefect of the Congregation for the Propagation of the Faith, stated: "His Holiness, however, has decided that in the present state of affairs it would not be opportune to agree to the proposal that the ladies who are admitted into that Society make solemn vows" (Letter 26).   20 For example, Dr. William Kinsella, bishop of Ossory, had probably already invited the Sisters of Mercy to come to Kilkenny; Dr. Andrew Fitzgerald may have already invited them to Carlow; and the invitation to Tullamore may have been already on the table.   21 After her signature on this letter, Catherine McAuley then transcribes the complete text of her own "Act of Profession" on December 12, 1831 (see Letter 12 above), as well as an early version of the text of the proposed new chapter of the Rule: "Of the Visitation of the Sick," and an early version of the first three paragraphs of the proposed new chapter: "Of the Admission of Distressed Women." Her final versions of these two chapters, as she sent them to Rome in December 1839 or early January 1840, are contained in Sullivan, *Catherine McAuley* 297–300.

20. **To the Reverend John Rice, OSA**
Rome

Dublin, Richmond St.
December 10, 1833

My dear Father John[22]

You have at the other page of this a long letter of Mrs. McAuley about her Institute craving your exertions in its behalf which indeed it deserves, for already it has cost her a sea of trouble to bring it to what it is at present. I know not whether or not you have been acquainted with the history of her life. I shall give it to you as well as I know it. Her parents died whilst she & a brother & sister of hers were left young in care of a Gentleman of fortune in this City. They were all Protestants, & [when] Mrs. McAuley was grown up she was converted, and practised her religion a good many years without the knowledge of her Patron, but when he came to the knowledge of it, such was his regard for her that he, it seems, never opened his lips to her about [it] & gave directions to her brother & sister never to speak to her on the subject.[23]

Thus she lived for a good many years & when this old Gentleman was dying, instead of leaving his property to the other two who continued Protestants he left the whole of it to her, save a small share.[24] Thus was she left at the head of

[22] Previous versions of this autograph letter (for instance, that published in Bolster, *Correspondence* 16–17) are incomplete and the wording does not correspond with the autograph. Such versions were evidently transcribed from the Italian abstract (*estratto*) of the autograph that is filed in the Archives of Propaganda File: SOCG, vol. 950, f. 186. The extract, made in late 1833 or more likely in 1834, by John Rice or by someone in Propaganda Fide, attempts to capture the major points recorded at the beginning of Edmund Rice's letter, but does not include the details about Catherine McAuley (often inaccurate) offered in his letter, nor his suggestion about how his brother can secure for Catherine the sanction of the Holy See, nor his analysis of the political and economic situation in Ireland at the time, nor his more personal comments about his own health and the poverty of his community. The Christian Brothers regard this letter as one of Edmund Rice's "longest and most interesting letters, giving us an insight into his character, his desire to help all and his affection for his brother" (M. Austin Connolly, Typescript notes, November 10, 1996, a copy of which is now in the Mercy Congregational Archives, Dublin). **23** Edmund Rice's visit with Catherine McAuley may not have been the sole source of his knowledge of her life, but whatever his sources (possibly including rumor), the account given here is not fully accurate. For instance, Catherine was probably twenty (or at least seventeen) when her mother died in 1798, hardly "young" by the standard of her day; and if the "Gentleman of fortune" is William Callaghan, only Catherine (not her sister and brother) lived with him and his wife, and not until 1803, after living for some time with her uncle Owen Conway and then with the William Armstrong family where her sister Mary and her brother James also lived. Moreoever, Catherine McAuley was not a Protestant who "converted" to the Catholic church. She was born and raised a Catholic, but in the gradually increasing absence of any parental, familial, or social support for the Sunday obligations and sacramental dimensions of her faith, she had, after the early 1800s, begun to drift from observable Catholic practice; however, about 1810, through the perceptive counsel of Thomas Betagh, SJ, a revered priest in Dublin, and Daniel Murray, then a priest at St. Mary's, Liffey Street, she began to renew and deepen the external expressions of her Catholic faith. The best contemporary account of Catherine McAuley's religious development is in the Limerick Manuscript, influenced as it was by her close friend and confidant Mary Elizabeth Moore (see Sullivan, *Catherine McAuley* 139–44). **24** As a childless

a large property with carriage, horses, etc.; a great deal of it she gave amongst the poor & for other pious objects whilst she was deliberating on raising some pious foundation. She was at length advised to something like her present plan by a good man, Revd. Mr. Armstrong whom you know; & in all appearance they hit very right for to my knowledge they have done an immence deal of Good since their commencement. The Monastery, if it can be so called before it gets the sanction of the Holy See, has cost her several thousands of pounds & when I told her [on] Saturday last that you may be able to do something for her at Rome, her heart jumped for joy at the prospect of getting any thing from the H[oly] S[ee]. Now it seems to me that this document of hers is rather a loose thing[25] and should I be right in my conjecture perhaps you may be able to have the matter referred back to Doctor Murray which in my mind would be the best way of doing it;[26] however you must be the best judge, but at all events I hope you will do what you can for the poor Creatures who are sighing for it.

I wrote you about the 27th of last month & enclosed you a Bill of Sylvester Young on his brother in London for £11.0.0 for to say Masses @ 2/6 each, we are very low in cash, with 10 or 11 of us living together in this house. The repeal question every day getting new strength at a hint for a libel against the Pilot Newspaper. O'Connell made a speech for 4 hours in the Court of King's Bench, & flung back the speeches which were made by two of the judges before whom he was pleading, the Chief Justice & Judge Jebb, at the time of the Union, in themselves. Never were men so disappointed as the Gov't were for this prosecution in making the Court of King's Bench an arena for the question they thought to stifle. The Press in Ireland & in England also are teeming with eulogiums on O'Connell. Shiel is sticking close to him & a most powerful auxiliary he is. Is it likely you will be successful in Jn. Healy's business? I had a letter from him the day he rec'd yours. If it be contrary to our Vow to appropriate the penny a week for our rent, I hope you'l get us a dispensation for it, for we are rather in a distressed way. This country is growing worse and worse every day, people absolutely starving in the midst of plenty. Corn & Pigs [*illegible*] drug. Pork ab[ou]t. 21s [d?]

---

widower, William Callaghan's alternative, in designating Catherine McAuley as his sole residuary legatee, was not Catherine McAuley's brother and sister, but a relative of his wife—i.e., Catherine Callaghan's cousin, Mary Anne Powell (see Sullivan, *Catherine McAuley* 364 n. 43).   **25** Edmund Rice is referring to Letter 19, with its transcribed texts of Catherine McAuley's Act of Profession and the two chapters of the Rule. See note 21 above.   **26** Michael Blake, her devoted friend and the bishop of Dromore, also occasionally reminded Catherine McAuley that the best, indeed the only sure, route for securing approvals in Rome was through appeals to and from her own archbishop (see Letter 133). Catherine may have realized this intellectually, but her natural instinct— especially in matters relating to the Holy See with whom she felt personally ill equipped to communicate—was to turn for help to whoever offered assistance. Three or four times in the decade, 1830–1840, she attempted, or initially attempted, to contact Vatican authorities directly, having a kind of innocent, even somewhat admirable, ignorance of how church officials in Rome wished to relate to competent—but not hierarchically placed—women leaders of religious congregations.

per cwt. & wheat at ab[ou]t 21 or 23s [?] per barrell. I was glad to find that you had not abandoned the Idea of returning home. My health is, thank God, pretty good, with the exception of pains in my limbs.[27]

I remain, My Dear Fr. John
Yours most affectionately
E[dmund] Rice

Autograph: Propaganda Fide, SC America Settentrionale, vol. 3, f. 198

21. To Pope Gregory XVI [Late 1833–Early 1834]

Most Holy Father

Catherine McAuley, prostrate at the feet of Your Holiness, humbly begs that you may deign to confirm the congregation which she with several other pious women has founded. The principal aim of this congregation is to educate poor girls, to lodge and keep poor young women until they can provide for themselves in some suitable way, and to visit the sick poor. With the attentions which they find in this Institute, these poor girls escape those dangers which from every side threaten their habits and their faith.

Already, within a short space of time, 772 poor women have been provided for, more than a hundred young girls have been instructed and admitted to the Sacraments, and the poor come here with all their disputes and complaints, while the good that is done on all these occasions is unbelievable.

The Petitioner made her religious vows in the presence of Monsignor Murray, Archbishop of Dublin, and twenty three other sisters have joined her. They were professed according to the rules and constitutions of the Presentation Order, subject to those changes which will be approved by the Archbishop, so that the only thing which remains to be confirmed are two chapters, that by reason of their different aim, have been added to the rules of that Order, and for which confirmation they humbly beg Your Holiness, so that they can then be put on the same footing as the nuns of that Order ...

[Mary Catherine McAuley]

Autograph (Italian): Propaganda Fide, SOCG, vol. 950, f. 183 rv; Photostat, Dublin, Mercy[28]

27 The last part of this letter, while containing information not directly related to Catherine McAuley and the Sisters of Mercy, illustrates the ongoing efforts of Daniel O'Connell to secure Parliament's repeal of the Act of Union (1800) joining Ireland to England, and comments on the material poverty of the Irish people and the early Christian Brothers. Edmund Rice, born in 1762, was seventy-one when he wrote the letter. He will outlive Catherine McAuley by almost three years, dying in Waterford on August 29, 1844 (Normoyle 412–13). 28 This petition, written in Italian, was translated into English by John MacErlean, SJ, in the middle of the twentieth century. The translation

22. To Dr. Daniel Murray

Rome
May 6, 1834

The Sacred Congregation has received a suppliant petition in which a certain pious lady, Catherine Mac-Auley, prays our Most Holy Lord to deign to confirm a congregation of women set up by her which is called *of Mercy*, and which should be devoted entirely to the pious works of instructing poor girls, providing for women exposed to danger, visiting the sick, etc.

She mentions that she and twenty-three other ladies have made religious vows in this congregation in the presence of Your Grace, according to the Rules and Constitutions of the Order of the Presentation of the Blessed Virgin Mary. She asks that there should be added to those Rules two chapters having reference to the method to be followed in the Visitation of the Sick and the Admission of poor women. In this petition it is stated that this Institute has already been productive of great good and that greater good is expected in the future.

Since Your Grace knows all about this affair, I have judged it well, before presenting this petition to our Most Holy Lord, to write this letter to you that you may signify what your opinion is about the several points mentioned above, and may inform me at the same time, if you think that everything connected with this business is in such a state that a confirmation of the said Congregation may be asked of our Most Holy Lord.

In the meantime, I pray God may long preserve Your Grace in health and happiness.

Ever at your Grace's service
Rome, from the Office of the Sacred Congregation
for the Propagation of the Faith
6 May 1834
C. M. Cardinal Pedicini, Prefect

Autograph (Latin): Dublin Diocese, Murray Papers AB3/34/15, no. 6[29]

---

was recently reviewed and slightly modified by Mary Borromeo Povero, RSM. The petition was probably not composed by Catherine McAuley, but rather by John Rice in Rome, in her name and drawing on wording in her letter to him of December 8, 1833 (Letter 19). The postmarks on side four of the large folded sheet that contains Letters 19 and 20 indicate that the letters did not reach Rome until late December, so the petition was probably composed and forwarded then or in January 1834. The formulaic conclusion of the petition is abbreviated ("*Che etc. etc.*") and is noted here by an ellipsis. Gregory XVI had assumed the papacy in February 1831, following the death of Pius VIII. **29** Cardinal Carlo Maria Pedicini had succeeded Cardinal Mauro Cappellari (now Gregory XVI) as Prefect of the Sacred Congregation for the Propagation of the Faith. His letter to Daniel Murray is written in Latin. It was translated into English by John MacErlean, SJ, in the middle of the twentieth century. His translation was recently reviewed and slightly modified by Mary Eymard Hyland, RSM.

23. To Cardinal Carlo Maria Pedicini, Prefect   Dublin
Congregation for the Propagation of the Faith   June 21, 1834

Most Eminent and Reverend Father

On the 6th day of May of this year, Your Eminence kindly informed me that there had been presented to the Sacred Congregation a formal petition in which a certain pious lady, Catherine McAuley, requests the Holy Father that he would deign to confirm a Congregation of women founded by her, under the title of the Sisters of Mercy, which is to be entirely devoted to the pious works of instructing poor girls, of caring for women in danger, and of visiting the sick. She further states that she herself and twenty three other ladies have made, in my presence, in that Congregation their religious Vows according to the Rules and Constitutions of the Order of the Presentation of the B[lessed] V[irgin] M[ary]. She requests finally that to these Rules there be added two Chapters concerning those duties which are proper to this Congregation.

About all these things your Eminence orders me to state what I think, and whether I consider all things connected with this matter to be in such a state that the confirmation by His Holiness the Pope of the Congregation in question would seem to be called for. To these questions with due respect I reply as follows:

A few years ago, the above mentioned Catherine built a large house at her own expense,[30] so that she herself and other pious ladies, living a common life in it could devote themselves to the above mentioned pious works. When they were for some time living together in that way, they expressed the desire of binding themselves to this mode of life by being united into a Religious Congregation, and for that reason they petitioned me that they might be allowed to make perpetual Vows of Obedience, Chastity and Poverty. I said that this was not expedient until such time at least as some of them would have done some period of probation, so as to learn the discipline of religious life and to exercise themselves in it. And thus it came about that the above mentioned Catherine and two others were admitted into the Convent of the Presentation of the B.V.M.,[31] so that they would do their year's probationship and then return to their own house, to teach their own sisters the science of the Saints. Having completed that year of probation, the above men-

---

30 That is, the House of Mercy on Baggot Street, Dublin, the first, and as of the date of this letter the only, convent of the Sisters of Mercy. The House was first occupied on September 24, 1827.
31 Catherine McAuley, Anna Maria Doyle, and Elizabeth Harley entered the Presentation Convent on George's Hill, Dublin, on September 8, 1830. Mary Clare Moore, Catherine's contemporary, reports that Catherine "often said it was so hard a struggle for her to remain on account of meeting there many things repugnant to her feelings that had she not had the establishment of the Institute most deeply at heart she would (that very evening) have sent for a coach to take her back to Baggot St" (Sullivan, *Catherine McAuley* 93). Catherine was then fifty-two. She retained throughout her life a distaste for certain conventual practices, such as kneeling to superiors and the chapter of faults; she did not herself permit the former, and she implemented the latter only reluctantly, after much delay.

tioned three ladies made in my presence the perpetual Vows of Obedience, Chastity and Poverty on the 12th day of December in the year 1831. They also vowed that they would persevere until death in the new Congregation, which they asked to have called the Congregation (Sisters) of Mercy, under the Rule and Constitutions of the Presentation Order, but with such changes made in that Rule and Constitutions as His Grace, the Archbishop of Dublin, might deem suitable.

The seven other ladies, who while the above things were being done had remained in the aforesaid house of Catherine, living the common life together, then began their Noviceship. Having completed it, they in turn made their vows in the same form. Of these, two have already died.[32] There are at present in that House twenty three truly pious ladies. Of these, only eight have yet made their Vows, ten have been clothed with the holy habit and are trying to do their noviceship, and five (of whom two are lay sisters) are in their first period of probation and are asking for the religious habit. They devote themselves earnestly and with great fruit for souls to the pious works which are set down in the petition. And I consider that they fully deserve to receive from His Holiness all these signs of benevolence which may seem suitable for the firm establishing of the good work thus begun for the promoting of the glory of God.

I earnestly pray God to preserve your Eminence for very many years in health and happiness.

Dublin, the 21st day of June 1834
Your Eminence's most humble & obedient servant
Daniel, Archbishop of Dublin

Autograph (Latin): Propaganda Fide, SOCG, vol. 950, ff. 189r–190r[33]

24. To Catherine McAuley   [Violet Hill, Newry]
                                                        October 23, 1834

Dear Madam

Having been in spiritual Retreat for the last fortnight with my clergy, your kind letter of the 13th instant must have arrived in Newry, I should suppose, on the following [day], but as I was then just commencing a second week's spiritual Retreat with some of my clergy, it was not brought to me until that salutary business was entirely over. Otherwise you should have received a few lines from me before now.

---

32 Dr. Murray is inaccurate here. Of the first seven, only five professed vows. Two left the community as novices. Catherine's niece Mary Teresa Macauley, one of the first seven, professed her vows privately on November 3, 1833 and died on November 12, 1833.   33 Daniel Murray's response to Letter 22 is written in Latin. It was translated into English by John MacErlean, SJ, in the middle of the twentieth century. The translation was recently reviewed and slightly modified by Mary Eymard Hyland, RSM.

I most cordially sympathise with you and your edifying Community in the great trial which the closing of your chapel must have caused, although I am sure, from my knowledge of the natural kindness of your revered Archbishop and of his frequently declared sentiments respecting the merits of your Institution, that nothing short of an imperative sense of duty could have induced him to insist on such a sacrifice.[34] If he has not explained his reasons to you, be persuaded that they are strong and cogent.

I have not forgotten you in my poor prayers. Trusting in the efficacy of Divine grace, I hope that you and all the members of your Community will be superior to the workings of human weakness and will not utter a murmur of complaint. It would be right, however, that you should know clearly the will of his Grace, Dr. Murray, and beg as a favour that he would express it directly himself to you. You seek nothing from selfish motives: he will require nothing but what is right, and if his decision cause some pain, he will alleviate, he will reconcile you to it by his consoling & healing advice.[35]

I beg you to present my most respectful compliments to his Grace, and to remain assured that I shall always [cherish] the kindest sentiments towards you & your Community, being most sincerely, dear Madam ...

[Michael Blake]

Author's transcript: Dromore

25. To the Reverend John Hamilton [Baggot Street]
December 10, 1834

Reverend Sir
    I received your kind note. We are all very happy to hear of the recovery of

34 The convent on Baggot Street is located within the boundaries of St. Andrew's parish. The parish community had since 1814 worshipped in an old chapel on Townsend Street. However, when Dr. Michael Blake was parish priest of St. Andrew's (1831–1833), he initiated construction of a new parish church, prior to his consecration as bishop of Dromore on March 17, 1833. The new St. Andrew's Church was opened for divine worship on January 2, 1834, and some time afterwards, the new parish priest, Walter Meyler, closed the convent chapel on Baggot Street to the public, prohibiting celebration of the second Mass on Sundays which lay people had been attending. An immediate effect of his decision was the Mercy community's loss of the weekly income from the collection taken up at this Mass—income on which they had depended ever since the opening of the convent chapel on June 4, 1829. In this letter, probably on the basis of information in Catherine's letter to him, Dr. Blake seems to imply that Dr. Murray actively sanctioned Walter Meyler's decision. Although there is no other contemporary evidence to support Dr. Blake's view, the chapel did, in fact, remain closed to the public, perhaps to swell Sunday attendance and the collection at the new parish church, and there appears to be no extant documentation suggesting that Dr. Murray attempted to alter the situation.   35 Whether or not Catherine McAuley contacted Dr. Murray about this problem, as Dr. Blake recommended, is not known. Letter 25 (below) seems to suggest that Dr. Murray was ill at this time. Dr. Blake's copy of this letter is incomplete.

his Grace and will defer our ceremony until perfectly convenient to him.[36]

Reverend Sir, respectfully, etc.

M. C. McAuley

Autograph: Dublin Diocese, Murray Papers AB3/ 34/ 15, no. 5

---

36 A long delay occurred. The next public ceremony of reception and profession at Baggot Street took place on July 1, 1835. However, Mary Mechtildis Gaffney who was dying in early 1835 was allowed to profess her vows in a private ceremony on May 24, 1835.

1835–1836

The Sisters of Mercy entered a new phase of development in the years 1835–1836, guided throughout by Catherine McAuley's gentle, unself-conscious leadership. A branch house of the Dublin community was opened in Kingstown (present-day Dún Laoghaire) in late March 1835; in the same month Pope Gregory XVI confirmed the status of the Sisters of Mercy as an approved religious congregation; two new Convents of Mercy were founded: in Tullamore, Co. Offaly, on April 21, 1836, and in Charleville (Rath Luirc), Co. Cork, on October 29, 1836; and in the cracks of time left between other duties, Catherine completed and submitted to Daniel Murray her handwritten draft of the proposed Rule and Constitutions of the Religious Sisters of Mercy, a thoughtfully crafted revision of the already approved Rule and Constitutions of the Presentation Sisters.

But these notable public accomplishments were accompanied by, and indeed their integrity rested upon, many private sorrows and worries. What most grieved Catherine McAuley were the deaths of two young sisters: Mary Mechtildis (Bridget) Gaffney, on June 14, 1835, less than a month after her profession, and Mary Agnes (Frances) Marmion, on February 10, 1836, of erysipelas of the brain—and the ongoing illness of several other sisters with tendencies to consumption. New demands for taxes and other financial worries also dogged the Baggot Street community, to the point where a loan of £20 made a crucial difference. In addition, normal day-to-day activities required increasing attention in this period, as the community and their works of mercy grew: acquiring appropriate outside employment for the young women in the House of Mercy, arranging reception and profession ceremonies, explaining the "requisites" of prospective Sisters of Mercy to enquiring priests, and securing popular speakers for the annual Charity Sermons, a major source of income. Happily, the possibility that Redmond O'Hanlon, ODC, the solicitous and self-effacing guide and confessor to the Baggot Street community since June 1829, might resign in 1835, because of his heavy duties as Prior of the Discalced Carmelites on Clarendon Street, did not come to pass. Whether Catherine ever knew of this possibility is not clear from her extant letters.

Yet what is most striking about Catherine McAuley's letters in these years is her ardent, explicit, even winsome, affection for her sisters—manifest, for example, in her feast-day quatrain to the Baggot Street novices, in her long letter-poem about the first profession ceremony in Tullamore, and in her playful letter to a Tullamore postulant in which she plots a future "Nonsensical Club." In a poem-letter she wrote years later to a postulant at Baggot Street, she explained the relief and pleasure she found in composing verses. She says, in part:

When not far removed from life's earliest stage
at Rhyming I never could stop
and beginning to feel the pressure of age
I lean on it now as a prop

It affords some support and help on the way
recalling the days of my youth
in which 'twas my pastime, my folly, my play
and so it is still in good truth (Letter 174)

In this poem she admits she is a "hack." Nonetheless, her often anapestic dog-
gerels brought joy to their recipients, as well as a "prop" to their author. In this
and many other ways revealed in her letters, Catherine McAuley deflated her
role as Mother Superior, a title she had reluctantly accepted in December 1831
only at Daniel Murray's insistence, and which she never used of herself, except
in one official letter to Rome. As the Carlow novice-annalist would record in
1839: "The most amiable trait in her character which we believed we discerned
was a total absence of everything in her manner telling, I am the Foundress"
(Sullivan, *Catherine McAuley* 230). This is the woman whose hopes and concerns
are reflected in the following letters.

26. To Dr. Daniel Murray   Rome
                                                              March 24, 1835

Most Illustrious and Most Reverend Lord
    Your Grace will of yourself understand, without my having to express it in
words, how highly the Sacred Congregation and our Most Holy Lord approve the
resolution taken by the very pious lady, Catherine MacAuley, of establishing a society of ladies, called *of Mercy*, from the works in which it is to be dedicated. For I
need not tell you how deserving of praise that society must be which directs all its
efforts and aims to the special end of helping the poor and relieving the sick in
every way, and of safeguarding, by the exercise of charity, women who find themselves in circumstances dangerous to virtue. I shall merely say that from an Institute
of this kind the greatest benefit will result both in civil society and to religion.
    The Sacred Congregation has, therefore, praised in the very highest terms
the above-mentioned resolution of that very pious lady, and His Holiness, on his
part, has not only approved the establishment of that Society, but has declared
that it is truly worthy of his paternal benevolence and Apostolic Benediction.
    His Holiness, however, has decided that in the present state of affairs it would
not be opportune to agree to the proposal that the ladies who are admitted into
that Society make solemn vows.[1] But seeing that that Society has proposed to

1 The decision of the papacy in 1835 that the Sisters of Mercy should profess simple not solemn
vows was evidently based on the fact that the Sisters of Mercy were not intended to be cloistered,

follow the Rules and Constitutions of the Order of the Presentation of the Blessed Virgin Mary, approved by His Holiness Pope Pius VII, he has left it to the judgment of Your Grace to prescribe for the Society of Mercy, over and above those Rules and Constitutions, such observances as Your Grace will think ought to be decreed, considering the object of the Society and the pious works in which it is to be employed.

Meanwhile I pray that God may long preserve Your Grace in health and happiness.

Ever at Your Grace's service,

At Rome from the Office of the Sacred Congregation for the Propagation of the Faith

24 March 1835
Giacomo Filippo Cardinal Fransoni, Prefect
Angelo Mai, Secretary

Autograph (Latin): Dublin Diocese, Murray Papers AB3/34/15, no. 7²

27. To Sister M. de Chantal McCann [Baggot Street]
Kingstown [After March 1835]

My dear Sister de Chantal³

It comforts me exceedingly to hear you are happy. I would not make you otherwise for all this world could give, though it were to build convents all over

---

but rather to be free to minister outside the convent among people who were poor, sick, and uneducated. 2 This letter to Daniel Murray is the approval of Pope Gregory XVI—given in a papal audience in February 1835, and communicated through the Prefect of the Sacred Congregation for the Propagation of the Faith—of the petition submitted in Catherine McAuley's name in late 1833/early 1834 (Letter 21), and reflected in the subsequent correspondence between Rome and Dublin (Letters 22 and 23). The English translation of the letter was made by John MacErlean, SJ, in the middle of the twentieth century. It was recently reviewed and slightly modified by Mary Eymard Hyland, RSM. When this letter, approving the establishment of the Sisters of Mercy as a religious congregation, was received in Dublin on May 3, 1835, Dr. Murray either came himself or sent word immediately to Catherine McAuley at Baggot Street. As the Limerick Manuscript claims: "This approbation was notified in a letter to Dr. Murray of which he without delay informed her, knowing how anxious she was to have the approbation and benediction of the Holy See" (Sullivan, *Catherine McAuley* 178).

3 Mary Jane Frances de Chantal (Mary) McCann was the widow of Dr. John McCann, a Dublin physician in St. Andrew's parish who had attended the sick in the House of Mercy "from the beginning" (Degnan 159). She entered the Baggot Street community on October 18, 1832, received the habit on July 2, 1833, and professed her vows on July 1, 1835. On October 22, 1832, a few days after her entrance, she enrolled her 10-year-old daughter Kate in the boarding school of the Loreto Sisters in Rathfarnham where the child died shortly after of whooping cough (Degnan 367 n. 6).

Funds made available through Mary de Chantal's inheritance and subsequent profession of vows were used to purchase the house and property on Sussex Place in Kingstown (Dún Laoghaire),

Ireland. I will soon, please God, spend a day with you—I hope you will entertain me well. All here as you left—love to my dear Sisters.

Ever your affectionate in J.C.

M. C. McAuley

Autograph: Adelaide

28. To Catherine McAuley   [April 30, 1835][4]

Dear Reverend Mother, our cook & your namesake[5]
Wants to compose a most beautiful tea cake
For materials of which 'twill be needful to pay
And therefore for cash your petitioners pray

The Sisters of the Noviceship

Autograph: Dublin, Mercy

29. To the Novices at Baggot Street   [April 30, 1835]

Dear Sisters
Early this morning on leaving the choir[6]
I did anticipate this—your desire

---

and the convent was opened on March 24, 1835. This house was not intended as an autonomous (governmentally independent) foundation of the Sisters of Mercy, but rather as a branch house directly affiliated with the convent on Baggot Street, Dublin: it was to be a rest home where sick sisters from Baggot Street could convalesce, reaping the benefits of fresh sea air and lighter duties. The harbor town of Dunleary had been renamed Kingstown in 1821 in honor of the visit to Ireland of George IV; it was renamed Dún Laoghaire in 1921 (O'Donnell 138).

The exact date of this letter is unknown, but it may correlate with Mary de Chantal's profession on July 1, 1835, or with work she was doing in Kingstown. Although the house had been intended only as a rest home, the neglected state of the poor girls Catherine saw loitering about the streets of the town had almost immediately spurred her to arrange a poor school on the premises—a decision that eventually led to a disappointing controversy (see Letter 46).

4 The feast day of Catherine McAuley's patron saint, Saint Catherine of Siena, was celebrated on April 30 in the nineteenth century. The novices' desire to prepare a tea cake to celebrate Catherine McAuley's feast day—if only they can get "cash"—is typical of the easy relationships Catherine inspired. 5 Catherine McAuley's namesake was, of course, her niece Catherine Macauley who entered the community on January 28, 1834, received the habit on July 3, 1834, and professed her vows on October 22, 1836. Thus she was a novice on this date in both 1835 and 1836, but since Catherine McAuley was in Tullamore on her feast day in 1836, Letters 28 and 29 must have been written in 1835. 6 The "choir" is the convent chapel. Catherine McAuley accedes to the novices' wishes while saving them the trouble of baking a cake for a community of at least twenty-three sisters. Letter 29 is written on the same piece of paper (8″ x 5½″) as Letter 28; the paper is enclosed in a small envelope inscribed by a later hand, "A Petition from the Novitiate Sisters to dear Revd. Mother McAuley."

and sent out an order in time—to bespeak
what I hope you will find—a very nice cake

[Catherine McAuley]

Autograph: Dublin, Mercy

30. To Catherine McAuley

Violet Hill, Newry
[September 10, 1835]

Dear Madam

I regret very much that your letter dated the 27th of last month was not brought to me until this day, particularly as it regards a subject which has been and perhaps is still troublesome to you.

I do recollect that at your request I applied about 4 years ago with a petition in your handwriting to the head office near the Royal Exchange to have your Convent exempted from demands of taxes, and the impression seems clear on my mind that Alderman Darly[7] and another magistrate who sat with him, on account of the nature & purposes of your situation, received the petition favourably and promised that the demand should cease. An official answer to that effect was, I think, afterwards sent to me, and by me delivered to you, but your saying that you read it makes me quite sure that I received it. I should suppose that if the transaction book of the office were examined, all doubt or contention would be removed.

Hoping that you & the other ladies of your Community are all well and wishing to all every blessing which[8]

[Michael Blake]

Author's transcript: Dromore

31. To the Reverend John Hamilton

Rahan Lodge[9]
November 24, 1835

Dear Mr. Hamilton

I have compressed the Relatio Status[10] into twelve pages of this size; and as I am anxious to get it out of my sight as soon as possible, I pray you to pay the

---

7 The *Dublin Directory* for 1829 lists a Frederick Darley, Esq., on William Street as an Alderman among the "Magistrates of Dublin." 8 Like other letters in Dr. Blake's Journals of Letters, in which he drafted letters before or after he made their final copies, this letter is incomplete. 9 Perhaps because of his many duties, as his extensive correspondence and numerous pastoral visitations in and out of Dublin suggest, Dr. Murray was "often ill," and frequently went to Rahan Lodge, near Tullamore, to recuperate. The Lodge was the country estate of John and Anna Maria O'Brien, his neighbors on Mountjoy Square in Dublin (Enright 278–81). 10 The Relatio Status was the official

postage of it, together with that of the letter to Doctor Cullen. Let the letter to
Mr. Lalor be also thrown into the post.

The cough is, I may say, gone; and tho' the storm is at this moment somewhat menacing, I hope, by and by, to get my little walk. I did not expect to see
the correspondence with the London Tract Society, travelling back to us here;
but those gentry are, I suppose, fond of seeing themselves in print.

It appears that Revd. Mr. O'Hanlon is about to give up his charge of
Confessor at Baggot Street.[11] Doctor Meyler should take care that his Friend
Mrs. McAuley should suffer no inconvenience from this occurrence. This is not
a good season for long excursions in the North; so I suppose his return will be
rather speedy.[12] All here quite well, and join as usual in best regards.

Most truly yours

+D. Murray

Autograph: Dublin Diocese, Hamilton Papers P1/35/1–2, no. 38

32. To Charles Cavanagh, Esq.

Baggot Street

December 2, 1835

Dear Sir

We begin to feel the want of the interest due on the Bond—have we any
chance of getting it soon?[13] We have so often cautioned all those who supply us—
not to give any credit on our account—I doubt would they now, if we were to ask
them. Have your heard from Mr. Burke, do you know when he is to come home?[14]

Dear Sir, your much obliged

M. C. McAuley

Autograph: Dublin, Mercy

---

report on the state of his diocese that a bishop was required to send periodically to Propaganda Fide in
Rome. The Dublin Diocesan Archives contains the commendatory response from Propaganda Fide, written in Rome on January 9, 1836 (Murray Papers AB3/31/5, no. 29). Dr. Paul Cullen, rector of the Irish
College in Rome, served as agent of the Irish bishops at this time.   11 I have not been able to find any
other documentary evidence on this topic. Perhaps Dr. Murray's information was mistaken, or Father
O'Hanlon changed his mind. Redmond O'Hanlon, who had been appointed to the post on June 4, 1829,
remained confessor to the Baggot Street community until shortly before his death in 1864, at age seventy-five. For a detailed account of his many contributions to the Sisters of Mercy, see Sullivan, *Catherine
McAuley* 334–40. As events in 1837–1838 suggest, it would have been very difficult for Catherine McAuley
and the Baggot Street community had Walter Meyler, parish priest of St. Andrew's, become responsible for appointing their confessor, as well as the chaplain of their House of Mercy (see, for example,
Letter 66).   12 Walter Meyler evidently had relatives in the country north of Dublin whom he visited.
13 Charles Cavanagh notes: "about Robinson's bond—afterwards paid off to Mrs. McA." Much research
and analysis remains to be done on the extant financial records of Catherine McAuley and the Baggot
Street community during her lifetime. Charles Cavanagh served not only as her solicitor, but also as her
accountant.   14 Daniel Burke, OSF, was the chaplain to the women and girls in the House of Mercy
on Baggot Street. He was a good friend of Charles Cavanagh, sometimes staying with him and his family.

33. Notation

Mr. Cavanagh has lent me twenty pounds this day.[15]

2nd December 1835
Mary C. McAuley

Paid back to me
by Mrs. McAuley
in settling account.
   C. C.

Autograph: Dublin, Mercy

34. To Catherine McAuley

Violet Hill, Newry
January 17, 1836

Dear Madam

I am informed that in recommending young women to any situation, either of servitude or to assist schools, it is your practice previously to ascertain not only the merit of the person who desires a place, but also the character of the individual to whom she is to be sent.

The confidence which a recommendation coming from you inspires here, I am informed by Mrs. Brydon, principal of a most respectable Establishment for the education of young ladies in this town that, as she is in need of an assistant in her school, she has applied to you with hope of obtaining through your recommendation a young woman well qualified for such a situation, but that your practice is, in such cases, always to assure yourself beforehand ...[16]

Michael Blake

Author's transcript: Dromore

35. To Sister M. Ursula Frayne
    Baggot Street[17]

[Tullamore]
[c. May 27, 1836]

My own dearest child, your letter so kind

---

15 The immediate loan of £20, in response to Letter 32, is typical of the constant and generous solicitude of Charles Cavanagh towards the Sisters of Mercy, during Catherine McAuley's life and long afterwards.　16 Dr. Blake assures Catherine McAuley that Mrs. Brydon will be a trustworthy mistress of any young woman sent to her. In the first sentence "your practice" may be "imperative."
17 This poem—composed by Catherine McAuley after the profession ceremony of Mary Teresa (Bridget) Purcell in Tullamore on May 27, 1836—now exists only in handcopies made by sisters other than the author. Only the handcopy in the Liverpool Annals (followed here) identifies Mary

Was most gladly received by your Mother[18]
'Twas in every way quite to my mind
I pray you soon give me another.
I'm delighted that Sister Cecilia is well
And that dear Sister Frances is better
O'er Celia I wish you could cast your own spell
And make her write a fanciful letter.[19]
Poor Sister Joseph has something to do
Your partner in school is a treasure
I hope my Teresa is well employed too
And not wasting time out of measure.[20]
To dear little Ellen[21] pray give my best love
Tell her to tune well the harp
Let the notes be all soft, like those of a dove

Ursula (Clara) Frayne, then a novice, as the recipient. The handcopies in Brisbane and Grafton (Australia) do not identify the recipient.

Clara Frayne had entered the Baggot Street convent on July 2, 1834, and received the habit on January 20, 1835. She will profess her vows on January 25, 1837—eight months after the date of this poem. Since she wrote at least one poem to Catherine (Letter 120), and Catherine wrote several to her (Letters 93, 104, and 121), she is likely the recipient of this poem.

Catherine McAuley was in Tullamore, County Offaly, to establish the first foundation of Sisters of Mercy outside of Dublin. On April 21, 1836, she had left Dublin on the canal fly-boat, arriving at the new convent in the late afternoon. With her were her first co-worker and good friend Mary Ann Doyle, slated to be the superior in Tullamore; Mary Teresa Purcell, a novice, who was to remain in Tullamore; and Catherine's travelling companions: Mary Clare Moore, Mary Anne Agnes (Catherine) Macauley, Redmond O'Hanlon, and Daniel Burke. The convent provided on Store Street in Tullamore was a small house. The Tullamore Annals records that Mary Ann Doyle "whose ideas of spaciousness in convents nearly coincided with those of S[t]. Peter of Alcantara was well pleased with the straitness of the cells and parlor. Our V[enerated] Foundress notices this in a pleasant letter she wrote at this time to Baggot St., thus—'Mother M. Anne has met with her "beau ideal" of a conventual building at last, for our rooms are so small that two cats could scarcely dance in them. The rest of us, however, would have no objection to larger ones'" (Tullamore Annals 9). Unfortunately, Catherine's letter is no longer extant, but the image of two cats dancing survives as wonderful testimony to her wit.

18 That is, Catherine McAuley, the "Mother" of the community on Baggot Street.   19 Probably the sisters named are Mary Cecilia Marmion, then a novice, and Mary Frances Warde. "Sister Frances" cannot be Mary Agnes (Frances) Marmion who had died on February 10, 1836, or Mary Francis (Margaret) Marmion, the third of this family, who did not enter the Baggot Street convent until August 1, 1836.   20 Sister Joseph is Mary Joseph (Sarah) Warde, who later used the name Mary Josephine. She was the sister of Frances Warde; she had professed her vows on December 9, 1835. Mary Ursula's "partner in school" is unidentified: she is probably one of the sisters who came to Tullamore: Mary Teresa Purcell, Mary Clare Moore, or Mary Anne Agnes (Catherine) Macauley. And "my Teresa" is either Teresa (Mary) Carton, a lay sister on whom Catherine greatly depended, or Mary Teresa (Amelia) White—probably the former.   21 Ellen Potter had entered Baggot Street by this time. She subsequently left because of poor health, but later entered the Mercy community in Limerick after its founding on September 24, 1838. She and Catherine McAuley then developed an extensive correspondence in verse.

Like her own, sweet and lively, not sharp.
The Profession to-day went on very well[22]
We'd two voices of exquisite tone
Who as private singers are deemed to excel
One sang most sweetly alone.
About thirty priests, and ladies by dozens
Some of whom had got cards of admission
But their Nieces, their Aunts, and their Cousins
Came with them without our permission.
And while forcing their way in crowds thro' the hall
Feared much they did greatly intrude
And hoped that the chapel would not be too small
And that we would not think they were rude[23].
At the usual hour the preacher[24] began
And gave a most excellent view
Of God's various designs in relation to man
And His graces to carry them through.
He proved how both Martha and Mary were blest
By our Lord, while on earth He did stay
But did forcibly all our attention arrest
With "Mary has found the best way."
Then with a voice so subdued and so mild
Addressing our Sister, he said
"How consoling to you, my much favor'd child
Are the words of the Gospel just read.
For were our Redeemer on earth at this day
And saw you at the Altar appear
The very same words, I am sure would He say
For His words, my dear Sister, can ne'er pass away
He would lovingly bid you draw near.
The sick and the poor were His own constant care
You are trying His footsteps to trace
And He will invisibly oft meet you there
Till you see Him at length face to face.
Let us join in a prayer to this Saviour of love

22 Mary Teresa Purcell's profession of vows took place in the parish chapel in Tullamore on May 27, 1836. A remarkable woman, she became the superior of the Tullamore community in 1844 and continued in that office until her death on March 28, 1853. Letters 41, 242, and 251 are written to her. For a more detailed account of her life see D. Walsh 48–50. 23 The first ceremony of religious profession ever to be held in Tullamore drew a great crowd of townspeople, a fact that pleased Catherine McAuley as an opportunity to explain the nature and mission of the Sisters of Mercy. 24 The preacher was Walter Murtagh, curate in the Tullamore parish. The parish priest, Dr. James O'Rafferty, who could not do enough for the new community, presumably assisted the bishop.

That He may His best graces impart
That your Vows may this day enter Heaven above
And His blessing descend on your heart.
May He be your safeguard and guide in your way
May you to His counsels attend
And may you advance in perfection each day
And with joy persevere to the end.
And oh! may the Order to which you belong
Be increased by the power of the Lord
May the young and the virtuous round it still throng
And to Him greater glory afford."
Thus far, my dear child, I have been most exact
In telling you what the Priest said
But I have not, as yet, like you got the tact
To carry it long in my head.
The Profession now ended, the ladies proceed
To the rooms with refreshments provided
Though numerous, they all were nice persons indeed
In the first room the Bishop presided,
Who graciously hearkened to every call
To carve and to help condescended
Extending the kindest attention to all
With grace and with dignity blended.[25]
At length they are done, the guests gone away
And all is in peace as before
But oh! with what mingled sensations I say
That not far remote is that troublesome day
When they must assemble once more.[26]

Read this first alone, in an audible tone,
Till you gloss over every mistake.
What you can't read you'll spell
Till you know it quite well
Do this for your poor Mother's sake.

[M. C. McAuley]

Handcopies: Brisbane, Grafton, and Liverpool

---

25 Dr. John Cantwell had been consecrated bishop of Meath on September 21, 1830.   26 Catherine is here anticipating her return to Tullamore for the reception ceremony on August 1, 1836, when two young women who had entered the Tullamore community after its foundation would receive the habit: Mary Delamere and Eliza Locke.

36. **To Sister Mary Delamere**   [Baggot Street]
    Tullamore   [June–July 1836]

a preparatory meditation

My Dear Sister Mary[27]

It has given me great pleasure to find you are so happy, and I really long for the time we are to meet again—please God—but the good Mother Superior will not have equal reason to rejoice, for I am determined not to behave well, and you must join me.[28]

If I write to mention the day we propose going, you might contrive to put the clock out of order—though that would be almost a pity. By *some means* we must have till ten o'clock every night not a moment's silence—until we are asleep—not to be disturbed until we awake.[29] Take care to have the key of the cross door, and when those who are not so happily disposed go into Choir, we can lock them in until after breakfast. I fear Sister Mary Clare will join the "Divine Mother"—she is getting rather too good for my taste.[30] Sister Catherine is according to our own heart, and surely Sister Eliza will not desert us[31]—and if Mrs. Doyle should complain to the Bishop—remember, you and I are safe. We are not of his flock, most fortunately.[32]

I know very well Father Murtagh[33] will applaud our pious intention—for such it really is, when rightly considered. First, it will effectually remove all the painful remembrance of our former separation and animate us to go through a second parting. It will shew superiors and their *assistants* that it is necessary sometimes to yield to the inclinations of others, and convince them that authority, however good, cannot always last. It also affords them an opportunity—if they

---

27 Mary Delamere, a postulant in Tullamore, had entered the community there on May 10, 1836, and was now preparing, through prescribed daily meditations, for her reception of the habit. Thus, the humor of Catherine McAuley's title for this letter ought not to be overlooked.   **28** Catherine McAuley had departed from the new foundation in Tullamore on May 30, 1836, having spent five weeks there, and was looking forward to her return at the end of July for the reception ceremony of Elizabeth Locke and Mary Delamere. Here, and throughout this letter, she indirectly teases Mary Ann Doyle, the conscientious, and perhaps overly serious, new superior of the Tullamore community.   **29** Catherine is playfully planning to overturn two basic regulations of religious life as practiced by the Sisters of Mercy: night silence, which normally began at 9:00 p.m. and lasted until morning; and the standard rising time, which was 5:30 a.m. for all sisters unless they were ill.   **30** The "plan" includes locking Mary Ann Doyle (the "Divine Mother") and Mary Clare Moore (who will accompany Catherine from Dublin) in the chapel overnight—so they cannot bring a halt to the merriment.   **31** Catherine is anticipating an additional postulant: Catherine Barnewall, who was considering entrance into the Tullamore community and will do so on October 29, 1836. Eliza Locke was already a postulant, having entered on April 30 while Catherine McAuley was in Tullamore.   **32** Catherine McAuley lived in the diocese of Dublin, and Mary Delamere was from Geashill, a town southeast of Tullamore, in the diocese of Kildare and Leighlin. Hence, in Catherine's mischievous view, neither was under the jurisdiction of John Cantwell, bishop of the diocese of Meath where Tullamore was situated.   **33** Walter Murtagh, curate of the parish in Tullamore, had already proved himself a good friend of the community.

will take advantage of it—of seeing dispositions and manners, that might remain unknown to them, and consequently unchanged.

My dear Sister Mary Teresa[34] describes a melancholy night she passed while her mother was so ill. We must banish all these visionary matters with laughing notes ♫ ♫ ♫ hop-step for the ceremony, to be concluded with "The Lady of flesh and bone."[35] We will set up for a week what is called a nonsensical Club. I will be president, you vice-president, and Catherine can give lectures as professor of folly.

Of one thing, however, I am sure—and seriously so—that I seldom look forward to any change in this world with such happiness as I do to our meeting, and Sister M. Catherine,[36] who "was never to leave her dear Baggot Street again," is delighted to hear she is to go. I did hope to have brought one of our best singers, but am disappointed.

> Believe me, Dear Sister Mary,
> with sincere affection, etc., etc.
> M. C. McAuley

Remember me to your Mamma.

Autograph: Bessbrook

37. To Dr. Daniel Murray   **Convent of Saint Mary of Mercy**[37]
                                                    [July 26, 1836?]

My Lord

The Sisters will be happy to undergo the examination mentioned soon as you find it convenient.[38]

34 Mary Teresa Purcell, one of the founding members of the Tullamore community (see Letter 35).   35 Catherine had a large store of songs, including Dublin street ballads, in her repertoire, many of which she often sang at recreation. "The Lady of flesh and bone" was one of these: it was an ancient Irish version, sung to an Irish ballad melody, of an old English nursery rhyme. In the song an old lady comes slowly to a church, enters, sees a dead man on the ground, and asks whether she will look like that when she is dead; the parson assures her: "You will be so when you are dead" (Petrie, ed. 1:165–66). One line of the song—"The worms crawl'd out, the worms crawl'd in"— may be familiar to some readers. I am extremely grateful to the Irish Traditional Music Archive, 63 Merrion Square, Dublin, and to its director, Nicholas Carolon, for helping me locate this song and others, and for directing me to *The Petrie Collection of the Ancient Music of Ireland*.   36 Catherine is probably referring to her niece Mary Anne Agnes (Catherine) Macauley, who had accompanied her on the founding journey to Tullamore in April, and whom Catherine intended to bring with her in July. Young Catherine, now a novice, had received the name Mary Anne Agnes at her reception of the habit on July 3, 1834, but her aunt continued to call her Catherine. A number of early sources spell her name "Mary Ann Agnes" (which may be correct), but the Dublin Register spells "Anne" thus.   37 So far as the extant correspondence is concerned, this is the only time Catherine McAuley refers to the Baggot Street convent by this title. The correct date of the letter cannot be verified: Catherine dates it simply "26 Jul" or "26 Inst."   38 Novices preparing for their

I enclose the regulations you desired me to prepare and will make any alteration your Grace points out as well as I can.[39]

I remain, my Lord, with great respect,

your obedient servant
M. C. McAuley

Autograph: Dublin Diocese, Murray Papers AB3/34/15, no. 20

38. To the Reverend Gerald Doyle[40]   Convent of Mercy
Naas   September 5, 1836

Reverend Sir

I have been favored with a letter from you which I should have answered immediately, but expected the Lady to call, and am only just now informed by the Sister who presides in my absence, that Miss Wilson has returned to the Country.

In compliance with your desire, Revd. Sir, I shall submit what seems "generally" requisite for a "Sister of Mercy." Besides an ardent desire to be united to God and serve the poor, she must feel a particular interest for the sick and dying; otherwise the duty of visiting them would soon become exceedingly toilsome. She should be healthy—have a feeling, distinct, impressive manner of speaking and reading—a mild countenance expressive of sympathy and patience.[41] And there is so much to be acquired as to reserve and recollection passing through the public ways—caution and prudence in the visits—that it is desirable they should begin rather young, before habits and manners are so long formed as not to be likely to alter.

---

profession of vows were individually examined in private by the bishop or his delegate as to the sincerity and freedom of their decision—a safeguard against external coercion or personal unreadiness in taking such a serious step as perpetual vows. Here Catherine McAuley may be arranging for such an examination. The next profession ceremony at Baggot Street took place on October 22, 1836—after some considerable delay, as Catherine notes in Letter 39.   39 The "regulations" Catherine cites cannot be identified with certainty, but they may be her draft or a fair copy of the Rule and Constitutions of the Sisters of Mercy. We know that Dr. Murray inserted suggestions for revision of her draft and then dated his approval of a revised copy "23rd January 1837"—having kept the copy for some months. For a detailed history of the composition and approval of various extant copies of the Rule and Constitutions see Sullivan, *Catherine McAuley* 258–91.   40 Gerald Doyle was parish priest in Naas, about thirty-four miles southwest of Dublin, in the diocese of Kildare and Leighlin. In the early years a number of young women from Naas entered the Baggot Street community, and on September 24, 1839, a convent of Sisters of Mercy was founded in Naas, from Carlow.   41 In composing this list of qualities Catherine is thinking, in part, of the virtues and skills needed in the visitation of the sick, which always involved reading prayers for the sick and dying, and of the sisters' long walks to and through the slum areas of Dublin. See the chapter of the Rule, "Of the Visitation of the Sick," in Sullivan, *Catherine McAuley* 297–99.

I beg again to remark that this is what seems generally necessary. I am aware exceptions may be met, and that where there is a decided preference for the order, and other essential dispositions, conformity in practice might be accomplished at any period of life.[42] Recommending myself and community to your prayers

I remain, Reverend Sir, very respectfully, etc. etc.

Mary C. McAuley

Photocopy of autograph: Dublin, Mercy[43]

39. To the Reverend John Hamilton

Convent
October 14, 1836

Very Reverend Sir

May I beg your charitable assistance to relieve me from a very perplexing state. Two Sisters whose noviciate ended in June have been most anxiously waiting the return of his Grace—who has referred me to the Vicar General. Were it only a Reception, we would not make any remonstrance, though [it would be] a painful disappointment. But for Profession, it is extremely difficult to manage.[44] One of the Sisters, a sensible person, thirty three years old, "fears she will not feel happy, as she confided much in the efficacy of the prayers to be said by the Bishop—and cannot think they could be supplied by a representative."[45]

I was once before in a difficulty of this nature and you, Revd. Sir, forwarded an application to his Grace who was then in the King's County, which he most condescendingly and graciously answered. Quite sure that you will excuse this trespass on your time, I remain

Very Reverend Sir, most respectfully, your obedient servant

Mary C. McAuley

Autograph: Dublin Diocese, Murray Papers AB3/34/15, no. 8

42 Catherine McAuley was herself fifty-three when she professed her vows as a Sister of Mercy, and at least two widows had already entered the Baggot Street community—one, Mary Genevieve Jarmy, said to be "old," had professed her vows on July 1, 1835.   43 The original autograph of this letter, once available in Naas, is currently missing, but a photocopy and a photostat of the original are preserved in Mercy Congregational Archives.   44 Walter Meyler, parish priest of St. Andrew's, was vicar general of the diocese at this time. In an almost illegible letter to John Hamilton on July 19, 1836, Dr. Meyler, who had just made his annual retreat with the Dublin priests, wrote of his pastoral visits to other religious congregations in Dublin and then said of Catherine McAuley, and indirectly of the delayed profession ceremony on Baggot Street: "I am told that Mrs. McAuley is keeping 36 *in reserve* for his Grace—only I have just come from the retreat, I would say: May she be disappointed" (Dublin Diocesan Archives, Hamilton Papers P1/35/6, no. 68). The number is clearly "36" which can only be an exaggeration of the number at Baggot Street awaiting ceremonies of reception or profession. The tone of the comment is, however, helpful in clarifying, in part, the grounds of Catherine McAuley's strained relations with Walter Meyler.   45 Of the three sisters who professed their religious vows on October 22, 1836—the date subsequently arranged with Dr. Murray—only Mary Cecilia Marmion, whose birth year is not known, may fit this description. Mary Anne Agnes (Catherine) Macauley was seventeen, and Mary Martha (Susanna) Wallplate was twenty-five.

40. To Catherine McAuley

Newry
December 5, 1836

Dear Madam

I have been just now honoured by the receipt of your letter of the 3rd instant. To decline any request of yours is, I assure you, painful to me: but the duties I have here to perform and the circumstances of my condition oblige me to be here as much as possible, so much so that if the annual visit to meet the Prelates in Dublin were not considered a matter of serious obligation, I could scarcely be justified in making it.[46]

Being thus situated, I hasten to apprise you of my inability to preach your Charity Sermon on the 29th of January, and beg you not to mention that you had applied to me lest ...[47]

[Michael Blake]

Author's transcript: Dromore

41. To Sister M. Teresa Purcell
Tullamore

Convent
December 13, 1836

My Dear Sister Mary Teresa

I have just had the pleasure of seeing Revd. Mr. O'Rafferty and receiving your letter. Indeed, I am heartily sorry to hear of Mr. Murtagh's illness,[48] and earnestly hope God will soon restore him. We have been seriously alarmed about dear Sister Luby,[49] and thought we were going to pay our annual tribute to the tomb, but this day, thanks be to God, there is a more favorable opinion—though strong symptoms of rapid consumption appeared. Her Brother appointed Doctor Graves[50] to visit her, and his treatment has been quite different from what we

46 The bishops of Ireland met in Dublin each year, in January or February, to discuss and decide upon pastoral matters affecting the whole of Ireland. 47 Dr. Blake's autograph draft of this letter is incomplete. Presumably, given his characteristic courtesy, he wished that the speaker whom Catherine eventually engaged for the Charity Sermon might think that he was the first person approached. 48 Walter Murtagh, curate in Tullamore, had been attacked with a serious case of fever. Catherine McAuley was fond of him and deeply grateful for his generous solicitude toward the Tullamore community since its founding on April 21, 1836. 49 Mary Rose (Johanna) Lube was the sister of Andrew Lube, parish priest of St. James's and Catherine's steady friend until his death in 1831. She entered Baggot Street on August 30, 1835, and received the habit on February 29, 1836. Her illness continuing, she professed her vows on February 17, 1837, and died one month later, on March 11. 50 Dr. Robert Graves, MD (1796–1853), a distinguished Irish physician, soon gained an international reputation as a teacher and clinician. He "revolutionize[d] the management of fever patients by advocating that they should be encouraged to eat. Up to then these patients had been placed on a very sparse diet." In 1835 he described the disease of the thyroid gland now known as Graves's Disease (Coakley, *Irish Masters* 92–93).

have seen on similar melancholy occasions. So far it has been wonderfully successful, and we have great hope. I am sure you will pray for her recovery in choir—as we do. She is now so much affected by mercury[51] that a decided opinion cannot be given for some days.

Poor Sister Teresa Carton is very ill, but not dangerously. Your old Mother[52] coughing away, not up for two days, but in high spirits. Sister M. Clare's cough not gone.[53] All the rest well. Our last addition[54] is very pleasing and quite strong. She is equal to Sister M. Cecilia[55] in music—and just the size of Sister Margaret Marmion,[56] whose child she is.

I am delighted to hear Doctor Murray called to see you. It was a comfort to her Reverence, I am sure.[57] Mr. O'Rafferty gives a good account of you all and hopes you will multiply fast.

I shall be very anxious to hear of Mr. Murtagh and beg you to let me know soon how he is.

Remember me most affectionately to the Sisters all, including their good Mother—in which I am very numerously joined.

Believe me, Dear Sr. Mary Teresa,
most truly, etc., etc.
M. C. McAuley

Autograph: Tullamore

51 A preparation of one of the compounds of liquid mercury, such as calomel or corrosive sublimate, was until the mid nineteenth century used in medicine as a purgative. 52 It is not clear to whom Catherine is referring: Mary de Pazzi Delany, who served as mistress of novices for a time? Mary Frances Warde? Or probably young Catherine Macauley who had entered Baggot Street just before Teresa Purcell and so was regarded as her "mother." 53 Mary Clare Moore, then twenty-two, had a tendency to pleurisy. 54 Evidently this is a postulant who entered and then left sometime after this letter was written. The "last addition" listed in the Baggot Street Register is Margaret Marmion to whom Catherine likens this person in size. Mary Austin Carroll says the "last addition" is probably Mary Aloysius Scott, but this cannot be correct since Mary Aloysius had entered the convent on August 15, 1835 (*Leaves* 1:105). 55 Mary Cecilia Marmion had just professed her vows on October 22, 1836. 56 Margaret Marmion, a sister of Mary Cecilia, had entered the convent on August 1, 1836. 57 Mary Ann Doyle, superior of the Tullamore community, whom Catherine here teasingly calls "her Reverence."

January–August 1837

In January 1837, Catherine McAuley, at age fifty-eight, began an intense year of emotionally oscillating experiences that would have broken the grip of a woman less confident in the strength and providence of God. On January 23, Daniel Murray, having made earlier minor suggestions for revision, approved her text of the Rule and Constitutions of the Sisters of Mercy; on January 25, four young women professed their religious vows, including Ursula Frayne who would one day take the congregation to Newfoundland and Australia; on February 9, Mary Veronica (Ellen) Corrigan, an orphan who had lived with Catherine since she was a child, died of virulent typhus, just two weeks after her profession; on February 17, Mary Rose Lube professed her vows on her deathbed and died of consumption three weeks later (March 11); on April 10 Catherine led a party to found a Convent of Mercy in Carlow, choosing as the new superior one of her most helpful companions at Baggot Street, Mary Frances Warde; sometime before June 7, the controversy over payment of the building costs for the poor school in Kingstown escalated; on June 30, the epidemic still raging, Mary Aloysius Thorpe, a novice, died of typhus at Baggot Street; the next day, at a ceremony that could not be postponed, four women professed their vows and two received the habit; and on July 5, Catherine McAuley, Mary Clare Moore, and the rest of the founding party embarked by steamer for Cork where they established a new Mercy convent. This series of events alone would justify the apparent fatigue that led Catherine to write from Dublin on July 27: "I am weary of all my travelling, and this morning I fell down the second flight of stairs" (Letter 49).

Catherine returned early from Cork, not staying her usual full month, because she was "sent for." Two weeks later, on August 8, she wrote from Baggot Street to her good friend, Dr. Andrew Fitzgerald, OP, president of Carlow College: "We feel just now as if all the House was dead" (Letter 50). On the previous night, just before midnight, her beloved niece and godchild, Catherine Macauley, age eighteen, died of consumption, her aunt at her bedside. The full pain of this human loss Catherine McAuley never directly expressed.

All in all, 1837 was not an easy year. The journeys to and from Carlow and Cork were demanding enough, the mail coach to Carlow taking six hours each way, and the trip to Cork a full night by boat, or two days if one travelled by land. Gone now, as well, was the daily assistance of the talented Frances Warde and Clare Moore, even as the "unjust transaction" in Kingstown was heating up. Moreover, in the first eight months of the year eight young women had entered the Dublin community as postulants, all needing Catherine's special instructions and guidance. But the heaviest toll on Catherine's mind and heart during these months was the deaths of the four young sisters, and her persistent concern that the ailing Maria Sausse receive "great tenderness." Years later Mary Clare Augustine Moore wrote in her "Memoir": "I believe the greatest trial of all to her were the frequent deaths of the Sisters. While she preserved her health she had a great awe or even fear of death, and she never saw the approach of a Sister's death or spoke of one who had died without great emotion. She had a really tender affection for us" (Sullivan, *Catherine McAuley* 209).

Yet during these months Daniel Murray's approval of the Rule and Constitutions remained a continuing source of comfort and gratitude, as did the prospects for extending the works of mercy to the poor in Carlow and Cork. And, regarding cheerfulness as her special obligation to the community, Catherine continued to write poems when she could—to bring amusement or consolation to others. Charles Cavanagh, the community's solicitor, Andrew Fitzgerald, John Hamilton, Elizabeth Moore, and Frances Warde became her most trusted correspondents. Typically, she closed the last extant letter of this period sending "My love to the children" in Kingstown (Letter 52).

42. Statement of Approval

We approve of these Rules and Constitutions compiled for the Religious Congregation of the Sisters of Mercy, and we declare that it is not our intention that they shall oblige under pain of mortal or venial sin, only in as much as the transgression of any article may be a violation of the vows or in itself a sin independently of the Rule.[1]

+D. Murray, Abp., etc.

Dublin
23 January 1837

Autograph: Dublin, Mercy

1 This statement, which Daniel Murray, archbishop of Dublin, wrote directly on Catherine McAuley's final text of her proposed Rule and Constitutions of the Sisters of Mercy, appears stark on a first reading. It was, however, standard language, intended to highlight the spiritual freedom and zeal with which the Sisters of Mercy were to pursue the rich possibilities of ever deeper fidelity to the Gospel inherent in the provisions of their Rule and Constitutions. The document supports the fulfillment of the vows, but is not, in itself, an expansion of the commandments incumbent upon all Christians. In reviewing an earlier draft, Dr. Murray had penciled in a number of recommendations for revision. These revisions are indicated in detail in Sullivan, *Catherine McAuley*, where the full text of the original Rule and Constitutions is presented (295–328).

43. **To Sister Anna Maria Harnett** [Carlow]
   Baggot Street [After April 14, 1837]

My Dearest darling youngest Daughter²

> I know you would like to hear all in Rhyme
> of our journey³—and how we have passed away time
> We were not two miles and a half on our way
> when Sr. M. Teresa got sick & remained so all Day
> She was moaning & looking as white as a sheet
> almost ready to drop—and lie down at our feet
> About half past 2 we got into the Town
> and passed by our own House—where we should be set down
> at least half a mile taken out of our way
> through the midst of a crowd—on the chief market day
> We drove up to the Inn—but would not get out
> nor the coach had not room for to turn about
> So there we remained set up for a shew
> until a nice person whom we did not know
> had the two first horses unlincked from the coach
> so that nothing impeded our speedy approach
> to a very neat convent— prepared very nice
> The Priest and the Bishop⁴ were there in a trice⁵
> and conducted us on to our Sisters in Love⁶
> who gave 78 kisses⁷—their fondness to Prove
> and a very nice dinner—set out in good form
> all exceedingly nice—and pleasantly warm
> We had plenty of laughing—and cheering & fun
> and music & singing when dinner was done
> The Bishop and good Father Andrew⁸ at Tea

2 At age twenty-six Anna Maria Harnett had entered the Baggot Street Community on February 5, 1837. As the most recent postulant she was the "youngest daughter" in the community. On July 1, 1837 she will receive the habit, taking the name Mary Vincent. 3 The Carlow community of the Sisters of Mercy was founded on April 10, 1837, with Mary Frances Warde as superior, and Mary Josephine (Grace) Trennor, a novice. According to the Carlow Annals, Mary Teresa White, Mary Cecilia Marmion, and Mary Ursula Frayne accompanied Catherine McAuley, to assist the new community in its first weeks. 4 Dr. Edward Nolan, bishop of the diocese of Kildare and Leighlin, and James Maher, administrator of the bishop's parish in Carlow. Before the year was out Dr. Nolan died of typhus. James Maher, uncle of the future Cardinal Paul Cullen, remained a devoted and lifelong friend of Catherine McAuley and the Carlow sisters. 5 That is, immediately, at once, forthwith (OED). 6 The Presentation Sisters who had founded a community and a school in Carlow in 1811 (T. J. Walsh 202–203). 7 Apparently, a kiss from each of the Presentation Sisters to each Sister of Mercy. 8 Dr. Andrew Fitzgerald, OP, president of Carlow College and a long-time friend of Catherine McAuley. Upon the death of her brother-in-law William Macauley in

soon after nine we all went away
Ever since we are settling & running about
some staying at home & some going out
The new Sister Green[9] is a very nice creature
unlike to the old one in manner or feature
Your Mother[10] has said now the 4th or 5th time
"Don't forget my best love in the midst of your Rhyme"
Sister Frances—Mary Teresa & Grace[11]
Beg also to get for their love a good place.

Write to me soon a poetical letter
no matter how long—the more nonsense the Better
I hope e'er long to write you another
and remain your fond and affectionate Mother.

Don't let this be seen—by any but your little party at home at the fire side.[12]

[Catherine McAuley]

Autograph: Brisbane

44. To Catherine McAuley

Cork
April 29, 1837[13]

Rev. Mother,
    Down to this period I have not had it in my power to announce to you that we have at length procured a house here in which your spiritual daughters can commence the work of mercy. Altho' it will take a month to fit it out, I deem it

January 1829—her sister Mary having died in August 1827—Catherine had placed their three sons, James, Robert, and William, in boarding school at Carlow College under Dr. Fitzgerald's fatherly eye. In April 1837, he loaned the Sisters of Mercy a building on the property of Carlow College to use as a temporary convent.   9 Rebecca Greene entered the Carlow community as its first postulant on April 14, 1837. Her sister Jane had earlier entered the Dublin community and received the habit, but poor health forced her to leave. Jane subsequently entered the Tullamore community where she professed her vows on October 18, 1839, and died on September 11, 1843. Rebecca, taking the name Mary Agnes at her reception, became a member of the Naas community founded from Carlow in 1839. In 1851 she was sent to Little Rock, Arkansas, as part of the founding party from Naas. She died in New Orleans in 1903 (Muldrey 253, 408 n. 26).   10 Probably Mary Cecilia Marmion, who had accompanied Catherine McAuley to Carlow.   11 Mary Frances Warde, Mary Teresa White, and Mary Josephine (Grace) Trennor. Throughout her letters Catherine McAuley spells Frances Warde's name thus, which is, I believe, the correct spelling, not "Francis" (see Sullivan, *Catherine McAuley* 218–19, 354 n. 25, 380 nn. 6–7, 383 n. 2).   12 That is, the Baggot Street community.   13 This letter from John Murphy, bishop of Cork, arrived at Baggot Street while Catherine McAuley was still in Carlow. She returned to Dublin with Mary Cecilia Marmion in early May, having learned that fever continued to afflict the community on Baggot Street.

necessary to give you this information that you may make the necessary arrangement to supply [us] with at least four efficient subjects.

Last week I saw Mr. Deasy of Clonakilty, who informed me that it was not his intention to carry into effect his intention of making a foundation in Clonakilty & that he wished to have his daughter Margaret in our Community in Cork & requested of me to make this intimation to you. I am now informed that [she] is sick & that Mr. & Mrs. Deasy are [to] go to Dublin. If God spare her life & this arrangement take place, it will tend very much to the propagation of your Institute in this country.[14]

In the latter end of next week I intend, God willing, [to go] to Limerick with Presentation Nuns, to make a new Establishment in that City. We afford subjects & assign to their support the dividends of the sums which they brought into our Convent.[15]

I understand that there is to be a Ceremony in your Charleville House in the beginning of May, at which your presence is expected. I hope to visit your Ladies there on Tuesday the 9th of May on my return from Limerick: it would afford me much pleasure to meet you there.[16]

The following is the state of our Finances: we have £80 per An[num] from one good tenant & £2400 in the 3½ per cents, independent of an expenditure of £400, in fine [i.e. in short], for the house & fitting it up. We shall be under £40 a year rent.

I request the favor of a line at your earliest convenience & remain, with hearty prayers for the recovery of Miss Deasy and the propagation of your valuable Institute,

Rev. Mother
Your faithful Servant in Christ
+John Murphy

Autograph: Dublin, Mercy

45. To the Reverend John Hamilton   Convent, Baggot St.

June 7 [1837]

Very Reverend Dear Sir

As you have been always kindly disposed towards us—may I beg you will

---

14 On December 17, 1835, Margaret Deasy entered the Baggot Street community, before plans for a foundation in the south of Ireland materialized. She received the habit on April 20, 1836, and was a novice when Dr. Murphy wrote this letter. In July 1837 she became a founding member of the new Convent of Mercy in Cork; in 1843 she founded the convent in Sunderland, England.   15 That is, the South Presentation Convent, Douglass Street, Cork. Honora (Nano) Nagle (1718–1784) had founded the first Presentation community in her own home in 1775 (T. J. Walsh 98–113).   16 The profession ceremony of Mary Joseph (Alicia) Delaney occurred in Charleville in May 1837, according to Charleville records, but I have not been able to discover any evidence that Catherine McAuley attended this ceremony. The *Irish Catholic Directory* for 1838 says that the profession ceremony took place on June 30, 1837 (430), but the *Directory* may be incorrect.

call here, any time convenient. I think you could settle a matter relative to the Sisters in Kingstown which has become too serious for me without assistance.[17]

I remain, Very Revd. Sir
with much respect and gratitude, etc.
M. C. McAuley

Autograph: Dublin Diocese, Murray Papers AB3/34/15, no. 23

46. To Charles Cavanagh, Esq.   [Baggot Street]
June 20, 1837

Dear Sir

When we went to the convent in Kingstown, I expressed to Revd. Mr. Sheridan a particular desire to have a school for the poor girls whom we every day saw loitering about the roads in a most neglected state, and I proposed giving the coach house, stable, and part of our garden, with some gates, doors, and other materials for that purpose.[18]

Mr. Sheridan seemed quite disposed to promote it, and brought Mr. Nugent of Kingstown to speak about the plan.[19] When that was fixed on, I most distinctly said in the presence of Mr. Sheridan that we had no means to give towards the expence, but to encourage a beginning I promised to give all the little valuable things we had for a Bazaar that year and to hand over whatever it produced.[20] We got fifty pounds, which I gave immediately to Mr. Nugent though we were six pounds in debt for things got at Nowlans on the Batchelor's Walk.

While the Building was going on Mr. Nugent repeatedly said he had not any doubt of Mr. Sheridan getting from the Board of education a grant nearly sufficient to pay for it, and always added, "I will only charge what it costs me." Mr. Sheridan also said this with full confidence, and whenever I spoke to him of making application to the board, he answered: "I am waiting for the account."[21]

The letter[22] which I enclose to you, Sir, says the account was furnished to me. It never was, nor could Mr. Nugent have ever—in sincerity—regarded me

---

17 The controversy—between Catherine McAuley and James Nugent, the builder, and between Catherine and Bartholomew Sheridan, the parish priest in Kingstown—over financial responsibility for the cost of building the poor school in Kingstown was already heating up in June 1837, as Catherine makes clear in Letter 46.   18 For background information see the notes on Letter 27. Bartholomew Sheridan was parish priest in Kingstown.   19 The *Dublin Directory* for 1836 lists "James Nugent, builder, Kingstown"; the *Dublin Directory* for 1839 lists "Nugent, James, grocer and builder, George's Street, Kingstown" (187).   20 A bazaar of handmade goods prepared by the sisters and friends of the community was an annual source of needed income for the Baggot Street community.   21 A board of education to supervise the national education system had been set up following the institution of the national system of education in Ireland in 1831. Grants were made to localities for schools agreeing to operate under the rules of the national system.   22 The letter Catherine enclosed has not been found.

as answerable to him. The charge seems to be a most extraordinary one for the coarse plain work that is done.[23]

With great confidence in your kindness, I remain,

Dear Sir, respectfully, etc., etc.,
Mary C. McAuley[24]

Autograph: Dublin, Mercy

47. To Sister M. Frances Warde Carlow

[Baggot Street]
[1837]

Though absent, dear Sister
I love thee the same
That title so tender
Remembrance doth claim

Your name oft is spoken
When kneeling alone
I sue for high graces
At God's Mercy throne

Then say not Religion
To friendship is foe
When the root is made healthy
The plant best doth blow

O grieve not we're parted
Since life soon is flown
Let us think of securing
The next for our own.

This day of our mourning
Will quickly be passed
While the day of rejoicing
For ever shall last[25]

M. C. McAuley

Handcopies: Brisbane and Dublin, Mercy

23 In her "Memoir" Clare Augustine Moore reports that a woman in Kingstown estimated the cost of renovating the coach house and stable which Catherine McAuley had to pay at £400 (Sullivan, *Catherine McAuley* 210). When the lawsuit was settled against her in 1838, Catherine had to pay £375, including "taxed costs," in addition to the £50 which she had earlier and voluntarily given toward this expense (see Letter 87). 24 Apparently Catherine started to sign her name "Mrs. Mary C. McAuley," but then smudged out "Mrs." She often wetted a corner of her handkerchief to erase errors in her writing. 25 The original autograph of this poem, in Catherine

48. To Dr. Andrew Fitzgerald, OP   Convent of the Sisters of Mercy
Carlow   July 1, 1837

My Dear Reverend Father

I received your kind letter, which was very consoling to me. Robert[26] seemed delighted with your invitation, and had every hope of getting leave to go.

It has pleased Almighty God to visit us with another affliction. We have just sent a fine young Sister to the tomb.[27] She died on the tenth day of violent fever. She was exactly like a person in cholera—cold and purple coloured. Some kind of circulation was kept up by wine, musk cordials, and warm applications, but no hope of recovery from the first 3 days.

As the Archbishop had appointed this day we were obliged to go through our ceremony and had four Professed and two received this morning.[28] My poor little Catherine is cheerful as ever, but no symptoms of recovering strength.[29] A new Sister entered yesterday,[30] and another is to come on Sunday.[31] This is five in a few weeks. I believe we are to go to Cork on Wednesday.[32] Doctor Murphy has waited for us as long as he could.

McAuley's handwriting, has not been located and may be no longer extant. However, two identical handcopies dating from the early decades of the Sisters of Mercy and addressed to "Sister Mary Frances" are available: on page 121 of the small Baggot Street Manuscript Book preserved in Mercy Congregational Archives, Dublin; and on page 203 of the Brisbane Book of Transcriptions assembled for Mary Vincent (Ellen) Whitty. Ellen Whitty (1819–1892) entered the Baggot Street community on January 15, 1839, and founded the Sisters of Mercy in Brisbane, Australia, in May 1861, having sailed, with the founding party, from Liverpool on December 8, 1860. In letters written in 1863 and in 1887, Mary Vincent refers to handcopies of Catherine McAuley's letters in Brisbane (Whitty 66, 120). It is possible that this poem is not an original composition of Catherine McAuley's, but rather a transcription she made of a published poem by another author. She is known to have made, for herself or others, transcriptions of poems she especially liked (see Letters 153, 322, and 323). I have been unsuccessful in finding the published poem she may have copied; the use of "thee" in this poem is not typical of Catherine's writing, but that does not automatically prove the poem is not her composition. Her reason for sending the poem sometime in 1837 was undoubtedly the early pain of separation she and Frances Warde both felt after the founding of the Carlow community, with Frances Warde as superior, on April 10, 1837. See Letter 55 for Catherine's later comment on Frances's feeling at parting from her.   26 Robert Macauley, Catherine's nephew.   27 Mary Aloysius (Margaret) Thorpe, a novice, died of typhus on June 30, 1837, the day before this letter. She had entered the convent on July 23, 1836, and received the habit on January 25, 1837. Hers was the third death at Baggot Street in less than five months.   28 The four sisters who professed their religious vows on July 1, 1837, were Teresa (Mary) Carton, a lay sister; Agatha (Mary) Brennan, a lay sister; Mary Monica (Anna) Murphy, and Mary Vincent (Margaret) Deasy (see Letter 44). The two who received the habit were Mary Francis Xavier (Jane) O'Connell and Mary Vincent (Anna Maria) Harnett.   29 Young Catherine Macauley, Catherine McAuley's niece, was suffering the final stages of consumption.   30 Elizabeth Blake entered on June 30, 1837. She will later take the name Mary Gertrude at her reception of the habit on February 21, 1838.   31 The Baggot Street Register does not list any woman who entered on Sunday, July 2, 1837. The woman who entered that day may have left before profession of vows and thus would not be in the Register.   32 The new convent of Sisters of Mercy in Cork was

Begging you to give my most affectionate love to my dear Sisters,[33] and assured that you will not forget to pray for me, I remain, my dear Revd. Father with great respect and gratitude, your attached

Mary C. McAuley

Autograph: Silver Spring

49. To Sister M. Elizabeth Moore Kingstown[34]

Convent, Baggot Street
July 27, 1837

My Dear Sister Mary Elizabeth

My poor dying child[35] requested I would be sent for—and as she was quite anxious that I should remain to the end of the month with Sister M. Clare, etc., I concluded she was drawing near to the end, and hastened back immediately.[36] She is so much changed that if I had not seen similar cases greatly protracted, I would say she was going very rapidly out of this miserable world.

I am weary of all my travelling, and this morning I fell down the second flight of stairs. My side is quite sore, but if ever so well able, I could not leave my poor child.

Sister Sausse (for whom we are all particularly interested) is recommended sea air.[37] I would be delighted to be any way instrumental in enabling her to go on in the state she prefers—which cannot be except some favorable change takes place in the state of her health. Will you, my dear, get the room our darling Catherine was in prepared for her and Sister Teresa Mary,[38] and give her all the

---

founded on July 6, 1837. The founding party travelled by steam boat from Dublin to Cork. In the group were Mary Clare (Georgiana) Moore, the new superior, Mary Josephine (Sarah) Warde, Mary Vincent (Margaret) Deasy, and Mary Anastasia (Caroline) McGauley, a novice (Dr. John Murphy had asked for "four"), as well as Catherine McAuley and Mary Teresa (Amelia) White, her travelling companion. If the party departed from Dublin on Wednesday, as Catherine indicates, they would have left by boat on the night of July 5. **33** The Sisters of Mercy in Carlow. **34** Mary Elizabeth (Anne) Moore was the local superior of the branch house in Kingstown from October 1836 until sometime in 1838, when she returned to Dublin to prepare for the foundation in Limerick later that year. **35** Catherine Macauley. **36** Catherine McAuley had been at the new foundation on Rutland Street in Cork since July 6, assisting the new superior, Mary Clare Moore, who was then twenty-three years old. It was Catherine's practice, beginning in Tullamore, to stay at each new foundation for at least one month, during which she helped to select postulants who presented themselves as prospective Sisters of Mercy. During this time she always led the new community in praying the "Thirty Days' Prayer to the Blessed Virgin Mary, in Honour of the Sacred Passion of our Lord Jesus Christ" to implore God's blessing on the new foundation and its works of mercy (see Sullivan, *Catherine McAuley* 66–67, 211). The text of this prayer is contained in *Praying in the Spirit of Catherine McAuley* (70–73). **37** Maria Sausse had entered the Baggot Street community sometime before this date. Sadly, her poor health eventually forced her to leave the community, probably in early 1838. **38** Mary Teresa (Catherine) White, who entered on May 9, 1834, was the second sister in the Baggot Street community with the name "Mary Teresa White," and she can be easily confused with—though

care you can for a little time—she is so gentle, it will be no difficult matter to please her—a little broiled meat, or whatever she tells you she can take, not to get up till Breakfast time except you have Mass, and that she feels able—not to go out except she likes to try a short walk. Great tenderness of all things.

You & Sister Chantal[39] might come in the steam [train] tomorrow to see me & and the two Sisters can return with you. Sister Mary Angela[40] will have the room ready. Come in early. Give my most affectionate love to all.

Your ever attached
M. C. McAuley

Autograph: Wexford

50. To Dr. Andrew Fitzgerald, OP   **Convent, Baggot Street**
Carlow   **August 8, 1837**

My Dear Reverend Father

Our innocent little Catherine[41] is out of this miserable world. She died a little before twelve o'clock last night. She suffered very little, thanks be to God. Not more than one hour of distressed breathing, and her playfulness continued to the end— mingled with an occasional awful feeling, but nothing like melancholy. She represented Mrs. Deasy,[42] on her arrival from Cork, yesterday morning most perfectly. She received the last Sacraments on Saturday, with delight and great fervor. We feel just now as if all the House was dead. All are sorry to part our animated, sweet little companion.

---

their personalities were very different—Mary Teresa (Amelia) White who had entered the community on May 2, 1833. Catherine McAuley had allowed them to choose the same name and patron saint (Teresa of Avila) at their reception of the habit, but she sometimes tried to distinguish them by calling Catherine White "Teresa Mary" or "Teresa the Less." Catherine White departed from the Sisters of Mercy in 1848. **39** Mary de Chantal McCann. **40** Mary Angela (Mary) Maher, then a novice, had entered the Baggot Street community on July 10, 1836, and received the habit on January 25, 1837. She was now in Kingstown, but in 1846 she became part of the community founded in New York City on April 13. She died there on May 28, 1873. **41** Catherine Macauley was the fourth of Mary and William Macauley's five children. They had been adopted by their aunt after their father's death in January 1829. Young Catherine entered the Baggot Street community on January 28, 1834, at age fifteen; she received the habit on July 3, 1834, taking the name Mary Anne Agnes, but her aunt continued to call her Catherine. She professed her religious vows on October 22, 1836, and died ten months later of tuberculosis, the disease that had taken her sister Mary Teresa, also a Sister of Mercy, in November 1833, and would take her brother Robert in 1840 and her brother James in 1841. **42** Marianne Deasy of County Cork was the mother of Mary Vincent (Margaret) Deasy who professed her vows at Baggot Street on July 1, 1837. Surely Mrs. Deasy came to Dublin for the ceremony as well as earlier. Dr. John Murphy of Cork indicates that the Deasys—from Clonakilty, southwest of Cork—were going to Baggot Street in late April or early May when Margaret was ill (Letter 44). Young Catherine, always the playful mimic, had evidently developed a wonderfully humorous imitation of Mrs. Deasy's Cork accent.

I hope you have been pretty well since I had the pleasure of seeing you.[43] I suppose the Sisters are in retreat,[44] as they are here, except those who were engaged in the scene of sorrow with me. Thank God it is over. I know you will pray for me. As to her, I believe she was fit to unite with the angels—so pure and sincerely devoted to God.I shall be obliged to return to Cork[45] after the retreat. May I beg you to give my affectionate love to my Dearest Sister Frances [Warde] and little community, and to believe me, Dear Revd. Father, with great respect

your attached & faithful
M. C. McAuley

Autograph: New York

51. **Sister M. Frances Warde**   [August 15–30, 1837][46]
    Carlow

My Dearest Sister Mary Frances

I am glad to have an opportunity of forwarding a few lines to you. Thanks be to God you are all so well and happy, and doing so much for the afflicted poor. Blessed and happy life which makes death so sweet. Our dear Catherine might indeed have sung in the last hours of her innocent life, "oh death, where is thy sting," for she did not seem to feel any.

I have suffered more than usual with my old pain of sorrow and anxiety. My stomach has been very ill.

Poor Sister de Pazzi was twice very bad, with a short interval.[47] I am almost sure Maria Sausse cannot remain, her delicacy increases daily. I pity her very

---

43 Catherine McAuley visited Carlow on May 20, 1837, when the first stone was laid for the new Carlow convent made possible by John Nowlan's gift of £2000. On this occasion she brought young Catherine with her as her travelling companion.　44 According to the Rule and Constitutions of the Sisters of Mercy, an annual retreat of eight days was made in each convent, preceding the feast of the Assumption of the Blessed Virgin Mary (August 15).　45 Although it was Catherine McAuley's custom to remain with each new community for at least a month, in late July when her dying niece requested that she be sent for (see Letter 49), she returned in haste to Dublin, leaving Cork, as she later said, in an "unfinished state" (see Letter 51).　46 This letter is undated. It was definitely written after the close of the annual retreat at Baggot Street (August 15), and must have been written before August 31 when Catherine was again in Cork (see Letter 52). Carroll dates the letter September 8, but that date cannot be correct (*Leaves* 1:226–27).　47 Mary de Pazzi Delany, one of the first Sisters of Mercy, suffered from spells "identified with epilepsy" (Degnan 229). Mary Clare Augustine Moore says that she "was afflicted with severe disease which injured her mental much more than her bodily powers, so that she became inconceivably melancholy and captious" ("Memoir," in Sullivan, *Catherine McAuley* 214). Although Clare Augustine does not identify the sister she is speaking of, she describes her as one whom Catherine McAuley "loved and trusted more than others." Of those remaining at Baggot Street when she entered, Clare Augustine's comments seem to fit only Mary de Pazzi Delany.

much. She is so desirous and so gentle & complying. Teresa Byrne took the Postulant's dress on the Assumption, to fill my dearest child's vacancy.[48] She is delighted, and promises great things. May God give her grace. Sister Mary Clare's eldest sister has joined us—she is Mary Clare by Baptism.[49] A Miss Fanning from the Co. Meath comes in tomorrow, which will make 10 Postulants—including Bessy Hughes & Eliza Smith, Lay Sisters.[50] This is all the news I have for you, my own dearly beloved child.

The Rule is ready for you, but we wait, hoping to get His Grace to affix his approbation. I expected to be in Cork before this. I am waiting for a packet.[51] One got off without my hearing of it, and my poor Sister Mary C.[52] will be sadly disappointed—indeed I have left her in an unfinished state. She writes, full of fears and doubts. Indeed I know she has too much to encounter untill the way was made more easy for her. Please God I will soon go there.

God preserve and bless you, my ever dear child. Give my most affectionate love to all the dear Sisters.

Your very fondly attached
M. C. McAuley

You are truly fortunate in all the circumstances of your little foundation[53]—*nothing* that I know of like it.

Photocopy and photostat: Dublin, Mercy

52. To Sister M. Elizabeth Moore   [Cork]
Kingstown   Friday, August 31, 1837

My Dear Sister Mary E.

I trust in God you all continue well and happy. I suppose you are preparing your poor children for Confirmation.[54] You will not forget to make them

---

48 Teresa Byrn was Catherine McAuley's adopted sixteen-year-old cousin, the child of her cousin Anne Conway Byrn who died in 1822. Teresa had lived at Baggot Street from the beginning of Catherine's residence there. On August 15, 1837, the feast of the Assumption of the Blessed Virgin Mary, she formally entered the religious community. Catherine started to write that Teresa took young Catherine's "place," then crossed out "place" and wrote "vacancy"—a subtle revision signifying her special affection for her dead niece.   49 Mary Clare Augustine (Mary Clare) Moore was the elder sister of Mary Clare (Georgiana) Moore, now the superior in Cork. She entered the Baggot Street community on August 8, 1837, and at her reception on February 21, 1838, took the name Mary Clare Augustine. Catherine McAuley sometimes called her simply Mary Clare which adds to the confusion with her younger sister.   50 Unfortunately, the entrance dates of Miss Fanning, Bessy Hughes, and Eliza Smith are not recorded in the Baggot Street Register. This fact further prevents the precise dating of this letter.   51 An overnight passenger boat carrying mail and cargo from Dublin to Cork.   52 Mary Clare Moore, the superior of the new foundation in Cork.   53 The Sisters of Mercy in Carlow, founded in April 1837. Frances Warde was superior of this community.   54 The children are those in the poor school in Kingstown, where Mary Elizabeth Moore

repeat the Hymn often and the ejaculatory prayers—we used make them understand well the nature of the Sacrament, the gifts and graces it imparts, which depends so much on the preparation: to impress particularly—the great necessity of a pious good preparation, as the Sacrament can be received but once, and that if the benefit is lost now, they never can receive it again. I always found this produce good effect. Do all you can to get them to understand the nature of retreat for 10 days before. Tell them how far they can practice it, but above all things, constant fervent prayer. I am sure you know all this—and would not fail to put it in practice—but I like to help you. What a comfort it would be to me to see them all.

Give my most affectionate love to my dear Sister Chantal, Sr. Genevieve, Sr. Ursula, Sr. Ann Clare & Sr. Maher.[55] I hope Sr. Lucy is getting better. May God preserve and bless you all.

Your ever affectionate Mother in Christ
M. C. McAuley

Sister Mary Clare desires her affectionate love to all—also Sr. Mary Joseph, Sr. Mary Cecilia & Sr. Mary Anastasia.[56]

My love to the children.

I suppose your Garden looks beautiful as every thing does at this season.

Autograph: Limerick

---

was local superior. It is notable that in writing this letter about the Kingstown school children, for whom she had such great and tested affection, Catherine does not mention the ongoing controversy over paying the cost of building the school. Typically, she does not burden others with her own sufferings.   **55** The sisters mentioned are Mary de Chantal McCann, Mary Genevieve Jarmy, Mary Ursula Frayne, and Mary Angela Maher; Lucy is probably Teresa (Maria) Breen, a lay sister in Kingstown whom Catherine sometimes called "Lucy Teresa." In writing "Sr. Ann Clare," who cannot be identified, Catherine may have meant to write "Sisters Ann, Clare," in which case she may be referring to Annie O'Brien and Mary Clare Moore (later Clare Augustine) who entered the Baggot Street community on August 19 and August 8, respectively, though it is unlikely they would be sent to Kingstown so soon after their entrance. Given the kind of summer Catherine had experienced, her lapses about names and locations are understandable.   **56** Mary Clare Moore, Mary Josephine Warde, and Mary Anastasia McGauley were now members of the Cork community; Mary Cecilia Marmion was Catherine's travelling companion on this return visit to Cork.

September–December 1837

In the six years since its founding in Dublin on December 12, 1831, the Institute of the Sisters of Mercy had merited episcopal approval and support, and had been invited to open houses in four other parts of Ireland: Tullamore (1836), Charleville (1836), Carlow (1837), and Cork (1837). But the last months of 1837 were a very painful period in Catherine's life for one specific reason: in September a deep conflict arose between her and Dr. Walter Meyler, parish priest of St. Andrew's Church, over his unwillingness to assign a regular chaplain to serve the sacramental needs of the homeless women and girls sheltered in the House of Mercy on Baggot Street. This "unwarranted abuse of Church authority"—to quote Dr. Andrew Fitzgerald—caused her more anguish than the saintly death in October of Mary de Chantal McCann, the fifth to die in 1837, or the pain she suffered in November when she broke her left wrist, severely injuring the sinews, in a fall down stairs while visiting the sisters in Kingstown. Catherine made light of her broken arm, and though the death of any sister affected her profoundly, she was consoled by the memory of Mary de Chantal's holiness (see Letter 67). But the "bitterness" she felt at the injustice of the chaplaincy controversy was a new kind of suffering for her; it was assuaged only with prayer, effort on her part, and the support and counsel of friends. The year ended in worry about the stability of the Charleville community and especially about "the poor of Charleville" for whose sake the community had, in fact, been established. Catherine McAuley was now fifty-nine.

53. To Sister Mary de Pazzi Delany Convent of the Sisters of Mercy
Dublin [Cork]
October 3, 1837

My Dear Sister Mary de Pazzi

Your packet of notes and letters afforded me great comfort, and I am most grateful to you and all my Dear Sisters for them. They were real recreation to me. Please God, I will soon have the happiness of thanking each personally. The time though long is drawing to a close—it would have been useless for me to take such a long journey if I did not remain until my poor Sister Mary Clare got fixed in her new office, and I know you feel very anxious about her and would not wish me to leave her too soon.[1] She continues extremely timid and will not appear

1 By August 31, 1837, Catherine McAuley had returned to the new foundation in Cork (see Letter 52). Mary de Pazzi Delany now served as Catherine's assistant superior at Baggot Street, but she

without me on the most trifling occasion—to visitors, etc., etc. She promises to overcome this, is in excellent health, thank God, and looks remarkably well. I am quite surprised to find no remark made as to her youth, in any quarter.[2]

We were all quite at home for two mornings with our poor Mr. Burke who celebrated Mass for us. Doctor Griffith called and is quite animated with the success they have had so far.[3] He left this [city] for Kilkenny where he was to preach. Mr. Burke went before to prepare the way. Mr. Burke told me he had an introduction to your good Papa.[4] We have a Father William Delaney, as well as you. I have just been writing to him and found out his Christian name, and indeed he does not disgrace the Delaneys in any way. He has a true Irish countenance, abounding in 'gras' and good humour. An exemplary priest.[5]

The expected ceremony[6] is exciting the greatest curiosity, they fancy it is to be something wonderful. There has been so much anxiety to have ceremonys [*sic*] for the sick poor order in Cork. The Bishop says that at least sixty persons must be invited. It will not be very easy to enter here, the terms are high—and *no abatement.*[7] This is a drawback—perhaps for the better. All that I could say on the matter—quite fruitless. Sister Mary Clare will not be teased with importunitys [*sic*] from Priests or people. Every applicant is to be referred to the Bishop, provided she approves of them, and all settled by him. This will save her from many painful concerns, and to this part of the regulations I could feel no objection. I only wish the terms were not so high—for a beginning.

---

was not comfortable during Catherine's necessary absences from Dublin.   2 Mary Clare Moore was then twenty-three years old, a young and "timid" superior. However, two years later she would become the founding superior of the Sisters of Mercy in Bermondsey, London, where she would serve with courage and creativity until her death in 1874, including almost two years of nursing under Florence Nightingale in the Crimean War. Dr. Thomas Griffiths, vicar apostolic of the London District, told Catherine McAuley, while she was in Bermondsey from November 1839 to mid January 1840, that "he never saw such maturity in so young a person—that she had judgment in her countenance" (Letter 158).   3 Daniel Burke, OSF, had been the much-appreciated chaplain at the House of Mercy, Baggot Street, from June 1829 until September 1837 when he was assigned to accompany Dr. Patrick Griffith, the newly appointed vicar apostolic of the Cape of Good Hope, Africa. Dr. Griffith and Father Burke solicited volunteer clergy and financial support throughout Ireland before sailing for southern Africa.   4 Mary de Pazzi Delany was from Castle Durrow, Co. Kilkenny. Her father was William Delany. Catherine, who often spelled personal names in a variety of ways, sometimes spelled their surname "Delaney," as on the cover of this letter.   5 William Delany, no relative of Mary de Pazzi, was then a priest in Cork. On the death of Dr. John Murphy in 1847, he became bishop of Cork. Catherine's 'gras' is her attempt at "grace" in a Cork accent.   6 The first profession and reception ceremonies of the Sisters of Mercy in Cork were held on Thursday, October 25, 1837. Mary Anastasia McGauley, who had come from Dublin as a novice, professed her vows that day, and Margaret O'Connell, the first postulant to enter the Cork community, received the habit, taking the name Mary Aloysius.   7 Catherine McAuley was always willing to lessen the dowry expected of women who entered the congregation, to meet their particular financial circumstances, and often asked for no dowry or only a nominal sum. But John Murphy, bishop of Cork, and other bishops, fearing the financial collapse of new convents, were often adamant about the designated sum. Six hundred pounds, to be paid at the time of profession, was the figure set in Cork.

Private[8]

My dearest Sister Mary, will you relieve me from the distressing business about the chaplain. It is constantly before me, and makes me dread going home. I know it is not possible for me to have any more argument with Dr. Meyler without extreme agitation. I am so strongly opposed to the measure,[9] and when I explained the nature of the Institution—that a confessor might be necessary for some days in succession to prepare a person or persons for going into situations, and that we might want him at night in case of sudden illness, where there was such a crowd of persons—he immediately admitted it was just, and said had he seen it in that view, he never would have proposed it. Putting this all aside, Mr. Armstrong[10] has engraved on my mind an objection not to be overruled. Will you, my Dear, speak to Mr. Lynch[11] and say in the most decided manner that we require a chaplain to the House, *and cannot nor will not* call on any of the Parish clergymen to attend to the Institution. This will imply that no salery [*sic*] will be given. You may add that Mr. Armstrong told me it would be injurious—indeed he said if we were a religious community it could not be attempted, and he was deeply afflicted on his death bed that we were not *so* established. You may say that the Revd. Mr. Kelly who was P.P. of Townsend St.[12] knows he never would consent to it, and that Mr. Kelly kept us a year and half walking to Clarendon St.[13] every day—poor women and children—after Mr. A's death, and say that I would rather do so again than consent to it. We will all find room enough in Westland Row.

Do get me through this—don't be afraid. I know the Bishop will be rather pleased than otherwise. Dr. Griffith said we ought to have a Chaplain *and more*— but we won't speak of that.

Take Mr. Lynch into the parlour and speak with decision. Should Dr. Meyler call, assure him that I never will depart from the advice Mr. Armstrong gave me, that I would sooner leave the parish entirely, and that I am sure the Bishop would not ask me to do what Mr. Armstrong so long and so determinedly objected to.

---

8 Since her letters, no matter to whom addressed, were usually read aloud to the community of the recipient, Catherine occasionally labeled parts of letters "Private" when she discussed topics intended only for the recipient.   9 Dr. Walter Meyler, parish priest of St. Andrew's, wished the curates of the parish to rotate the chaplaincy duties at the House of Mercy, and for this service he asked an annual salary of £50 to be paid to the parish. Catherine McAuley wished to have a single consistent chaplain, as Daniel Burke had been, and she claimed, correctly, that the community could not afford to pay more than £40.   10 Edward Armstrong, administrator of St. Andrew's until 1826 and then parish priest of St. Michan's until 1828, had been Catherine's most supportive clerical friend during the years in which she was planning and building the House on Baggot Street (see Letter 5). When he died in May 1828, Catherine herself still did not envision founding a religious congregation, although this had been Armstrong's hope for the community she had begun to assemble at Baggot Street.   11 Gregory Lynch, one of the eight curates at St. Andrew's in 1837.   12 Matthias Kelly had been parish priest of St. Andrew's when the parish chapel was still on Townsend Street. By 1837 the parish had built and occupied a new church on Westland Row.   13 St. Teresa's Church on Clarendon Street was served by the Discalced Carmelites. The priests at St. Teresa's had long been supportive of the Sisters of Mercy, especially Redmond O'Hanlon who served, in Dr. Murray's capacity, as ecclesiastical superior of the Baggot Street community.

Perhaps one third of what I have said will be more than sufficient—and this is the reason I dread the subject because I find myself impelled to say too much.

[*Here a sizeable portion of the autograph letter has been cut out.*] sad consequences were to follow. However, the poor shall not be deprived of the comfort that God sent them while we can avoid it, and I want you to send me a one hundred pound note you will get in the next drawer of the Book stand—to lodge here.[14] I wish to stop the lamentations, and surely we will spend Miss Clanchy's £500[15] before we break up. Perhaps she might recall that now, but I will prevent that. Perhaps you would hear of some person coming. I would fear sending it [the money] in a parcel. You will not speak of it. If you had a frank [a post-paid envelope] you could send half. I am sorry I did not think of it before Mr. O'Hanlon left.

As to Sister O'Callaghan,[16] I do not know what she wants with Mr. Cavanagh.[17] Remain present at the conversation, and ask Mr. Cavanagh in an *earnest* manner, has he got any money for us. Think of the name Clarendon,[18] ask has he not paid any—appear quite acquainted with the matter.

There will be great *woe* if the Rule gone to Carlow has *half* as many mistakes as the one for Charleville. Poor Sister Mary Clare was worn out at the work when she wrote it.[19]

Nothing can be more as we would wish than the conduct of the Sisters here. The new one is quite edified.[20] Sister Deasy unceasing in her delightful description of the noviciate in Baggot Street when she does not think I am paying any attention—it seems to be her favorite subject with the stranger. She really would excite veneration for the whole system. Sister Joseph[21] is a Rock—as to propriety and composure, and poor Anastasia[22] amiable in the highest degree.

14 Catherine is here speaking of the Mercy community in Charleville. Mary Angela Dunne, the superior, had become frightened at their dwindling financial resources and relatively few new members. 15 Mary Clanchy had promised £500 to the Charleville community, to be paid in installments, but her marriage to Arthur French raised doubts about the continuation of this donation. 16 Evidently Miss O'Callaghan entered the Baggot Street community, but did not persevere. She does not appear in the Register of professed sisters. 17 Charles Cavanagh, Esq., a solicitor with offices at 18 Fitzwilliam Street, was Catherine McAuley's and the Sisters of Mercy's attorney. He continued to provide legal services for the community long after Catherine's death (1841)—in fact, until his own death in 1862. 18 Apparently a donor or creditor by the name of Clarendon. 19 After Dr. Murray approved Catherine McAuley's text of the Rule and Constitutions of the Institute of the Sisters of Mercy on January 23, 1837, fair copies were made for each of the new foundations. Mary Clare Moore was given the laborious work of making the handcopies. She evidently worked to finish the Carlow copy before she left for Cork on July 5, 1837. The Rule was not printed until after it was returned from Rome in 1841. See Sullivan, *Catherine McAuley*, 270–72. 20 Margaret O'Connell entered the Cork community on July 23, 1837 and was scheduled to receive the habit on October 25. The postulancy of the first seven sisters to enter a new foundation lasted only three months; normally it lasted six months. 21 Mary Josephine (Sarah) Warde, the sister of Mary Frances Warde, had entered Baggot Street on April 9, 1833. She was a professed member of Cork founding group. In Baggot Street she was known as Sister Mary Joseph, but the Cork Register lists her as Mary Josephine. She remained in Cork for the rest of her life, serving as superior of the community from late August 1839 until her death in 1879, except for one six-month interval in 1841. 22 Mary Anastasia McGauley, a native of London and now a novice in the Cork

I would like to tell you all the little cheering things that God permits to fall in our way, though it does not do so well for reading out—as it might sound like boasting—but it has so happened that all our little ways are particularly liked here, and our dress within & without meets general admiration. The Priests say we have the nicest convent in Cork—that is, our settling [setting?] & laying out— and the poor say they never heard such prayers. We have had the cross too— but of that when we meet—no disedification, thank God. [*The words on the reverse side of the cut-out portion of this letter are here missing.*]

May God bless you, my Dearest Sister, and preserve you in grace and health.[23]

Your ever affectionate
Mary C. McAuley

Autograph: Bermondsey

54. To Sister M. Frances Warde   Convent—Cork
Carlow   October 12, 1837

My dear Sister Mary Frances

I have just heard with deep concern that Doctor Nolan has got fever.[24] The manner it is reported gives me some hope it may be [a] mistake. It is said that he took it from his curate who died—and the Priest who told me did not know how long Mr. Kelly was dead.[25] Write me a particular account soon as you can.

Sister Locke at Tullamore has had fever,[26] and one of the Sisters who came last to Baggot St. has been very ill and is still, I believe.

Mr. O'Hanlon gave them a gratifying description of your healthful appearance and happiness, also of the new Convent which is admired by all who see

---

community, went on the foundation to Pittsburgh, Pennsylvania in 1843 and died there the following year.   **23** In 1868 Mary Clare Moore cut off this sentence and the closing of the letter to form a memento of Catherine McAuley's handwriting which was then photographed and distributed to all the early Mercy foundations (Bermondsey Annals 2:124–30). The text of this sentence has been copied from the memento.   **24** Dr. Edward Nolan, bishop of Kildare and Leighlin, had been consecrated on October 28, 1834. He lived in Braganza House, Carlow, almost across the road from the Sisters of Mercy. Early in October he contracted typhus fever in the course of his pastoral work. He died a few minutes before 7 o'clock on the evening of October 14, 1837, "surrounded by several of his priests, and by the Sisters of Mercy, who had attended on him throughout his illness" (Comerford 1:136). He was forty-four. See also the Carlow Annals (Sullivan, *Catherine McAuley* 226) for an account of the sisters' nursing Dr. Nolan during his last days.   **25** In the *Catholic Directory* for 1837, the Revd. Kelly's first name is omitted (231). He was a curate in the bishop's parish in Carlow, and presumably lived with Dr. Nolan at Braganza House.   **26** Mary Catherine (Eliza) Locke, a novice, had received the habit in Tullamore on August 1, 1836. She recovered from this illness, professed her vows on February 2, 1838, and subsequently became the founding superior of the Sisters of Mercy in Derry (1848) and in Dundee, Scotland (1859).

it.[27] We go on pretty well here, a second Sister is to enter on Wednesday,[28] and the ceremony on the Wednesday following.[29]

I was very glad to hear you got the Rule with the Approbation, but if this melancholy report is true, your ceremony will be delayed a little.[30] I trust that is all.

The Sisters unite in affectionate love to you and the Sisters. Write me a few lines soon as you can, and believe me your ever attached

M. C. McAuley

Give my respectful remembrance to Dr. Fitzgerald.

Autograph: Pittsburgh

55. To Sister M. Teresa White   Convent, Cork
Carlow   October 17, 1837

My Dear Sister Mary Teresa

I was in part prepared to receive the melancholy news conveyed in your letter by the account which reached Mr. Lynch of this Town—a few days previous.[31] The dear saintly Bishop has got an early crown—and we have now a valuable friend in Heaven whose advocacy will be soon experienced by those who humbly bend to the adorable will of God.

My ever dear affectionate Sister Mary Frances will soon, I trust, give great edification to you all by her perfect composure and entire resignation. Submit we must, but we should do much more. We should praise and bless the hand that wounds us—and exhibit to all around us a calm quiet appearance and manner. I trust in God this will be manifest amongst you, afflicted as you are.

When I promised to go to my dear Sister Frances in time of trial, you may be sure, my Dear child, I did not mean the trial which death occasions, with which I am so familiarised that the tomb seems never closed in my regard. I alluded to those difficulties which her new state[32] exposed her to—such as incurring the displeasure of her spiritual superiors, without intention, or experienc-

---

27 Shortly after the Sisters of Mercy arrived in Carlow, living in temporary quarters, the construction of a new convent began, supported by the £2000 donation of John Nowlan. The building was not yet ready for occupancy.   28 Catherine Mahony entered the Cork community on October 18, 1837.   29 Mary Anastasia McGauley's profession of vows took place in Cork on October 25, 1837.   30 Dr. Nolan's illness would, of course, delay any planned profession and reception ceremony in Carlow. As events turned out, the next ceremony there occurred on November 14.   31 Mary Teresa (Amelia) White of the Baggot Street community was temporarily in Carlow to assist the community there. She must have written to Catherine McAuley in Cork immediately after the death of Dr. Edward Nolan on the evening of October 14. Evidently, she also described to Catherine the profound effect on Frances Warde of this sudden loss of the support and friendship of Dr. Nolan.   32 Frances was, at age twenty-seven, the founding superior of a new community, with all the personal difficulties her new duties might entail.

ing marks of disapprobation, and not knowing why. These are some of the bitter-sweets incident to our state—and most of all requiring support and council.

The sorrow in which she now so deeply shares is extensively divided and equally the affliction of many. The poor Presentation Nuns who were so long his spiritual children had not, I suppose, the happiness of seeing him, and the Priests and people, what must they feel. To regard it as an individual sorrow would not be right. Our portion of it may well be lost in the lamentations of his poor and destitute people.[33] Yet I can account for my dear Sister Mary Frances feeling so much on this distressing occasion. The good Bishop afforded her the first and chief comfort she experienced on parting me, etc., etc.,[34] but I know she will not continue unmindful of the exalted obligations of our holy state, and I will confide in the generous bounty and never ceasing kindness of our Blessed Saviour—to which we must put no impediment—that He will pour down on you all, my dear Sisters, His sweet abundant consolation, and that I will find you in a few days perfectly tranquil—and reasonably cheerful.

You do not mention Dr. Fitzgerald—if at home, I am sure he is kind.

With the most fervent prayers and fondest affection for my tender, ardent, beloved Sister Mary Frances and for you all, I remain,

My Dear Sister Mary Teresa, most sincerely
your attached Mother in Christ
Mary C. McAuley

Autograph: West Hartford

56. To Sister M. Frances Warde   [Cork]
Carlow   Tuesday 23rd [October 1837][35]

My Dear Sister Mary Frances

I have now an afflicting account from Dublin—Sister Chantal in bad typhus fever—Dr. Marsh attending her in Kingstown.[36] The worst symptoms appeared

<hr>

33 Always more conscious of the sufferings of others than of her own, Catherine encouraged others to adopt this perspective. Here she is especially aware of the grief of the Presentation Sisters in Carlow: Dr. Nolan had served as their chaplain and then confessor for many years, from his ordination in 1819 to his consecration as bishop in 1834 (Comerford 1:137).   34 A close friend of Catherine McAuley's niece Mary Macauley in the mid 1820s, Frances had come to know Catherine at Coolock. She then lived with her at Baggot Street from June 1829 until her departure for Carlow in April 1837. Over their years of working together a deep friendship had developed, strengthened no doubt by Frances's many talents and Catherine's reliance on them.   35 The reference to Mary de Chantal McCann's illness and anticipated death (she died on October 27) indicates that this letter was written in October 1837, but "Tuesday 23rd" is an error on Catherine McAuley's part. In 1837, October 23 was a Monday, and October 24, a Tuesday. In either case, Catherine is writing from Cork just before the profession ceremony there on October 25. She plans to stay in Cork on Wednesday the 25th, and then go to Carlow on Thursday the 26th. Mary de Chantal will die on October 27 before Catherine can reach Kingstown.   36 Sir Henry Marsh (1790–1860) was, like

on Friday—till then Sister M. E.[37] did not write to me. Of course I expect to hear of her death by tomorrow's post. Whatever the case is, I will return by Carlow to see you, if only for a few hours.[38] I hope to be there by half past 12 o'c on Thursday night. You will have Mary Ann sitting up—but I entreat you may all go to rest as usual. I will not be able to speak till morning. If you can, let me into a room alone to sleep a few hours, and not where I was with my child.[39]

May God bless and animate you with his own divine Spirit, that you may prove it is Jesus Christ you love & serve with your whole heart.

Your ever affectionate
M. C. McAuley

Autograph: Silver Spring

57. **To Sister M. Josephine Warde**   **[Late October–**
    Cork   **Early November 1837][40]**

My Dearest Sister Mary Josephine

Accept these few lines which proceed from my heart, earnestly hoping you are as well and happy as I wish you to be. We found dear Sr. M. Frances much more reconciled to her great affliction than I expected. Revd. Francis Haly, who is expected to succeed the beloved Dr. Nolan, was the most particular friend of your uncle, William Maher, and has been quite affectionate to our Sisters in Carlow.[41]

---

many of the physicians who attended the early Sisters of Mercy, a distinguished Dublin surgeon. A member of the Church of Ireland, he had an extensive private practice that in 1832 forced him to resign as professor of medicine at the Dublin College of Surgeons. In 1837 he was appointed "physician in ordinary to the queen in Ireland," and beginning in 1841 served four separate terms as president of the Irish College of Physicians (*Dictionary of National Biography* [DNB] 36:211). 37 Mary Elizabeth Moore, the local superior in Kingstown. 38 Given Frances Warde's grief at the death of Dr. Edward Nolan, Catherine will stop in Carlow en route to Dublin and Kingstown. 39 Catherine's niece, young Catherine Macauley, had accompanied her to Carlow for the laying of the first stone of the new Carlow convent on May 20, 1837 (Carlow Annals, in Sullivan, *Catherine McAuley* 226). 40 This letter is undated. Since its primary purpose is to reassure Mary Josephine Warde that Catherine found her sister Frances Warde in better spirits when she saw her in Carlow, the letter was probably written soon after Catherine McAuley's return to Dublin (prior to or just after Mary de Chantal McCann's burial on October 29) and before Catherine broke her left arm during a visit to Kingstown (see Letters 61, 62, and 64 below). 41 According to the *Irish Catholic Directory* for 1838, the clergy of Kildare and Leighlin assembled on November 15, 1837 to decide the *terna*: the three names recommended to Rome for appointment of a successor to Dr. Edward Nolan (435). Among Daniel Murray's Papers in the Dublin Diocesan Archives is a copy of the letter Dr. Murray sent to Propaganda Fide on November 16, 1837, notifying officials there of the names selected by the Kildare and Leighlin clergy; Francis Haly's name is the first (AB3/31/5, no. 116). However, Catherine McAuley's awareness that Francis Haly was "expected to succeed" may have come from information available before the *terna* vote was taken. Dr. Haly was consecrated bishop on March 25, 1838 (Comerford 1:144).

Mary Maher who entered in Maraborough is likely to join Sr. Frances, which was her first vocation.[42]

Remember me most affectionately to my Dear Sister Mary Anastasia and Sister Aloysius and Catherine, each of whom I trust are [*sic*] happy.[43]

Pray fervently for me and believe me most affectionately
M. C. McAuley

Autograph: Cork; photocopy: Dublin, Mercy

58. To Catherine McAuley

Monday Evening
November 6, 1837[44]

My dear Friend

Though reluctantly, I shall accede to your wish. My reluctance arises from a desire of having the office filled by a higher Church authority, which I see we

---

42 Mary Maher of Killeany, Queen's County, entered the Carlow community on November 30, 1837. The present letter was written well before that date. "Maraborough" should probably be Maryborough, also known as present-day Portlaoise. Here in 1824, the Presentation Sisters from Carlow had established a convent and school (T. J. Walsh 203–204). Evidently, Mary Maher had earlier entered the Presentation Sisters in Maryborough.   43 Catherine Mahony was the most recent addition to the Cork community, having entered on October 18, 1837, while Catherine McAuley was in Cork.

44 Sometime in early November 1837—the exact date is not known—Catherine McAuley broke her left arm at the wrist, while she was in Kingstown to console the community there on Mary de Chantal's death. Mary Vincent Harnett—who was in Baggot Street at the time and would have heard, then or later, the story of Catherine's accident directly from Mary Elizabeth Moore—gives this detailed account:

> On her return from Cork, dear Reverend Mother met with a severe accident. She went to console the sisters out to Kingstown, where Mary de Chantal breathed her last. By some accident there was no light on the stairs, and when dear Reverend Mother was going to the choir to say the Angelus, she missed the first step, fell forward, and, in endeavouring to save her head, broke her arm against the architrave of the window. She also seriously injured the sinews of her hand; in fact, her whole frame was much shaken by the fall.
>
> The noise brought some of the sisters, who helped her to rise; and, after some time, the poor arm was set. So great was her patience, that she scarcely moaned or gave any manifestation of suffering; and, after she recovered the first shock, she did not fail to rise in the mornings, as before, among the first, and attend all the community exercise as usual. Indeed, she managed even to dress herself without aid, except for a few mornings at first, when the arm was very painful. (*Life*, 135–36)

Andrew Fitzgerald's letter from Dublin to Catherine on Monday, November 6, implies that she was not then in Dublin. One may assume that she was in Kingstown at this time, "to console the sisters," and that her accident occurred near this date. (Although Dr. Fitzgerald asks her, at the end of his letter, to present his "kindest wishes to Sister Mary Frances and her dear little community," this reference does not necessarily imply that Catherine was then in Carlow.)

cannot obtain. I know the Vicar Capitular from a nervousness would scarcely be adequate to the business.⁴⁵ I hope I have quieted Sister Delany to wait your arrival.⁴⁶ I saw her on Saturday greatly agitated by the afflicting circumstances in which Dr. Meilor [Meyler] has placed her and the community, exposed as they [have] been to the inclemency of the weather and the inquisitive gaze of the publick on going to the Parish Chappel [sic].

I sought an interview this morning with Dr. Meilor [Meyler]. I did not succeed. I met Mr. Carroll⁴⁷ and asked him why it was necessary I should have asked leave to say Mass on Sunday at Baggot Street. He told me Dr. Murray sanctioned the proceeding to oblige you to take one of the Curates as Chaplin [sic]. I solely remarked it was rather an extraordinary proceeding, seeing all the other Convents had Chaplains, not Curates, to which observation I received no reply. I know not what advise [sic] to give you, but, this I know, if some arrangement is not made much scandal and injury will arise. What would you think of applying to your old Friend the Bishop of Kilmore⁴⁸ and beg his intercession with Dr. Murray to extricate you out of what I consider a wanton unwarranted abuse of Church authority. Call up all your firmness, and I have no doubt, having such just ground for supplication against the unprecedented intrusion, you will succeed. I hope to return on Friday or Saturday. In the mean time I beg to present you with assurances of my most tender regard. Fondest wishes to Sister Mary Frances and her dear little community.

I am most faithfully yours,
Andrew Fitzgerald

Autograph: Dublin Diocese, Hamilton Papers P1/35/7, no. 59⁴⁹

In the period, November 1837—January 1838, Catherine evidently wrote about her broken arm in one or two (or three?) letters to Frances Warde, but the original autograph or autographs are apparently lost. The missing autographs may have been separate letters or simply postscripts to extant autographs. Numerous transcripts of fragments of this correspondence are available, however, and are presented below (Letters 61, 62, and 64).
45 Catherine McAuley had apparently asked Dr. Andrew Fitzgerald to intervene on her behalf in the chaplaincy controversy with Dr. Walter Meyler, parish priest of St. Andrew's. Dr. Meyler was also vicar general of the diocese at this time, and Dr. Patrick Coleman, parish priest of St. Michan's, was dean of the diocesan chapter (i.e., vicar capitular). Evidently Dr. Fitzgerald felt that Dr. Coleman would not be able to handle the necessary dialogue with Dr. Meyler; however, Catherine herself subsequently expressed gratitude for the efforts of Dr. Coleman (see Letter 89). 46 Mary de Pazzi Delany, Catherine McAuley's assistant and acting superior in her absence. 47 Thomas Carroll, a curate at St. Andrew's Church, Westland Row. 48 Dr. Fitzgerald writes "Kilmere" or "Kilmore." The bishop of Kilmore at this time was Dr. James Browne, who is not known to have been one of Catherine McAuley's "old" friends. Probably Dr. Fitzgerald is thinking of Dr. Michael Blake, bishop of Dromore, who was indeed Catherine's "old Friend." 49 Catherine McAuley must have given this letter, so strongly in support of her position, to John Hamilton, Dr. Murray's secretary. She may even have enclosed it with Letter 59 (below).

59. To the Reverend John Hamilton   Baggot Street
                                                          November 22, 1837

Dear Reverend Sir

I beg you to accept my most grateful thanks for your kind letter to Carlow, and if it is not too much to ask—perhaps you would call here any time convenient—for a few minutes. I think you could assist us in our present state without much difficulty. I remain

Very Revd. Sir, most respectfully
M. C. McAuley

Autograph: Dublin Diocese, Murray Papers AB3/34/15, no. 9

60. To Sister M. Frances Warde   Baggot Street
Carlow   November 22, 1837

My ever dear Sister Mary Frances

I was greatly comforted by your letter. Please God Sister M. Ursula[50] will be soon quite restored.

I am delighted you all got the venerable Archbishop's blessing.

I have had a melancholy account from Tullamore. Sister Delamere's death hourly expected in Typhus fever.[51]

When I went to Kingstown, Sister Elizabeth was heavy and far from well. I remained three days and made her stay in Bed. She is recovered, thank God.

All here are well. We go to Westland Row every morning, which gives us a very good appetite for our breakfast. I was greatly surprised to see a Church very little larger—if any—than the Cathedral in Carlow.

I have not heard from Cork.

I am sure dear Sister Mary Josephine Gabriel is happy in her state and the new novices quite at home in the coife, etc., etc.[52]

Remember me with respect and affection to my dear friend Dr. Fitzgerald who has taken such a kind feeling part in my troubles. Tell him all will end well. Remember me also most gratefully to the other good clergymen from whom we

---

50 Mary Ursula Frayne, who was evidently ill in Carlow. 51 Mary Clare (Mary) Delamere recovered, and in 1844 she went on the foundation to Kells, where she served as assistant to Mary Ann Doyle, superior of the convent in Kells. In 1847, Mary Clare became the superior of the Kells community, following Mary Ann Doyle's return to Tullamore, and died there in 1870. It was Mary Clare Delamere, and not Mary Clare Cantwell, who went to Kells in 1844 (D. Walsh 47, 69). 52 Mary Josephine Trennor professed her vows in Carlow on November 14, 1837, and on the same day Mary Agnes (Rebecca) Greene and Mary Catherine (Kate) Meagher received the habit. Mary Josephine Trennor had taken the Archangel Gabriel as a patron and sometimes added "Gabriel" to her name. Her surname is occasionally spelled "Trenor"; however, the Carlow Annals and the current Carlow Register use "Trennor."

experienced such attention—Mr. Rafter, Mr. Taylor, Mr. McCarthy, etc., etc., and Father Dan.[53]

To Mr. Maher you could not omit to offer my grateful remembrance.[54] God has given you in him a good Father. All here unite in most affectionate love—with

your ever fondly attached Mother in Christ

M. C. McAuley

It will give you pleasure to here [hear] that James and Robert[55] have been to see me—*both* respectable and going on remarkably well, living together and studying for the Bar every day—with real attention. Robert's pay increased.

Autograph: Silver Spring

61. To Sister M. Frances Warde   [Late November–
Carlow   Early December 1837][56]

... I went to Kingstown to condole with the Sisters on the death of their dear holy companion, Sister M. de Chantal. Going down to Matins, I missed the first step of the stairs, fell forward, and, in endeavouring to save my head from the window, broke my left arm across the wrist, and injured the sinews in the back of my hand so much, that I am not likely to have the use of it for some months to come, if ever.[57]

... I remained in care of an apothecary without taking off my clothes for two days, and as the inflammation was so great nothing could be done but apply

---

53 The priests mentioned are Michael Rafter, parish priest of Killeshin (Carlow-Graigue); James Taylor, vice president of Carlow College; Daniel McCarthy, curate in Carlow; and Daniel Nolan, curate in Killeshin and brother of the deceased Dr. Nolan. The young "Father Dan" was especially dear to Catherine McAuley as later references indicate (see, for example, Letter 68). He once gave Catherine a copy of *Vespers; or The Evening Office of the Church in Latin and English* (Liverpool: Rockliff and Duckworth, 1829) which is now in Mercy Congregational Archives, Dublin. He signed the book: "To Revd. Mother Catherine McAuley of the order of SS. of Mercy from her affectionate and dutiful son D. Nolan."   54 James Maher, administrator of the bishop's parish in Carlow, proved to be, over many years, the good friend not only of Catherine McAuley herself, but of the Sisters of Mercy in Carlow.   55 Catherine McAuley's nephews, James and Robert Macauley, now twenty-two and nineteen years old, respectively.   56 I have pieced this letter together from three transcripts (as indicated in notes 57, 59, and 60). The date given in brackets is simply an estimate of when Catherine McAuley may have told Frances Warde about her broken arm. Letter 60 to Frances Warde (preceding this letter) is a complete autograph with cover and postmarks, and no earlier autograph in which Catherine could have told Frances of her accident is extant. That Catherine did not wait too long to describe her fall to Frances is certain from the nature of their friendship.   57This paragraph is quoted in Carroll, *Life* 332, where it is dated December 6, and in Carroll, *Leaves* 1:79, where it is also dated December 6 and where Mary Austin Carroll indicates that the letter was sent "to Carlow." The paragraph is similar, but not identical, to the second paragraph of the autograph letter to Mary Angela Dunne on December 20 (Letter 67), but there is no indication that Carroll is quoting that letter.

leeches. I returned here and Surgeon White bound me up in boards.[58] This is the twenty-first day. I have great hopes of soon getting my old companion on duty again and am happy to tell you from experience that a broken arm is by no means so distressing a matter as I always supposed. The want of its use is the chief inconvenience. However, take great care of your bones and, if you go through your convent before stairs are put up, be extremely cautious, for though not proportioned to all the lamentations we hear on such occasions, yet it gives a general shock to the frame that is not easily recovered.[59]

No arrangement has been made for us yet as to chaplain ... We go to Westland Row every day ... Twelve couples start as gay as when traveling to Clarendon Street in our first happy days. Father McDonogh waits for us and we have three Masses and are home at nine o'clock.[60]

[M. C. McAuley]

Published excerpts: Carroll, Life *332–33 and* Leaves *1:79–80; Degnan 208*

62. To Sister M. Frances Warde   [December 8, 1837, or
Carlow   later in December][61]

We go to Westland Row every morning. I carry my child in its cradle.[62]
Twelve couples start as gaily as we did when traveling to Clarendon-street in our

58 Surgeon White may be Matthew Esmonde White, MD, the brother of Mary Teresa (Amelia) White and Mary de Sales (Jane) White, whose mother's maiden name was Esmonde. Dr. White is listed in the *Dublin Directory* for 1836 under the heading, "Royal College of Surgeons in Ireland": "White, Mat. Esm., MD Wexford" (128); and listed in the *Dublin Directory* for 1839, under the same heading: "White, Matthew E., MD Lunatic Asylum, Carlow" (152). His location in 1837 has not yet been discovered. However, "White, Francis, 41 Dawson Street [Dublin]" is listed in the *Dublin Directory* for 1837, under the Members of the Royal College of Surgeons in Ireland (147–49); whether this Surgeon White is related to Mary Teresa and Mary de Sales is not known, but he may be the surgeon who attended Catherine McAuley.   59 This paragraph is partially paraphrased and partially quoted in Carroll, *Life* (332–33) and in Carroll, *Leaves* (1:79–80); the entire paragraph is quoted in Degnan (208), where it is undated, but said to be addressed to Frances Warde, although no source is given. Catherine's claim that "This is the twenty-first day" since the accident suggests that, if the accident occurred in the early days of November, as seems likely, this letter was written in late November. Roland Burke Savage also quotes some sentences of this paragraph, but gives no date or source (225).   60 This paragraph, with its two ellipses, appears as the second paragraph of Degnan's excerpt (208).   61 There are three sources for this fragment: Carroll, *Life* 334; Carroll, *Leaves* 1:195–96; and Burke Savage 225–26. The fragment may be a continuation of Letter 61 (Degnan, page 208, adds a much abbreviated version of this paragraph to that letter) or it may be part of a separate letter. No autograph of the fragment has been found. As Michael Blake indicates in Letter 63, Catherine McAuley wrote to him on December 8, 1837. Thus Catherine's claim in *this* letter that she "wrote to Dr. Blake" suggests that the present letter was written on or after that date. Burke Savage says it was written on December 8; Carroll does not date her citations of this fragment. One suspects that Burke Savage's source is Carroll, and that possibly Degnan is quoting a different source.   62 Her broken arm, in boards or a sling.

first happy days. We remain for three Masses, and are home at nine.[63] I wrote to Dr. Blake, stating our grievances, and will act according to his advice. You know how difficult it is to get the poor women and children out and home again on days of obligation, and their confessions are, of course, neglected. The Archbishop does not interfere. He permitted Dr. Blake, when Vicar,[64] to give us a Chaplain and two Masses; now he allows another in the same authority to act as he pleases. All is fair and right, and will end well if God is not offended.

[M. C. McAuley]

Published excerpts: Carroll, Life *334 and* Leaves *1:195–96; Burke Savage 225–26*

63. **To Catherine McAuley** [Newry]
December 12, 1837

Dear Madam

Some very urgent duties have prevented me from answering immediately your letter of the 8th instant[65] as I would have wished, but the subject of it has frequently engaged my attention since that day, & I avail myself of the first moment of leisure to communicate my sentiments candidly upon it.

I must in the first place commend your prudence in avoiding, whatever your trials may be, every appearance of resisting just authority. This will secure to yourself and to your excellent Community great interior peace, and as far as your case is known, will enable you to give very edifying example. It will also, I am persuaded, tend most forcibly to interest your kind-hearted Prelate in your favour: and what might be refused or declined on the ground of justice may be obtained through the recommendation of love and paternal feeling.

It appears to me from your letter that our worthy friend Dr. Meyler is not absolutely opposed to your having a distinct chaplain, but that his objection rests on a persuasion that the salary you could offer for the support of a chaplain would be insufficient, and that therefore it would be for the advantage of your Community to have the duty of chaplain performed by a curate of the parish. If he requires that for this benefit the old salary be given to him,[66] I conceive that

---

63 Degnan's quotation of this sentence within this paragraph is more detailed: "Father McDonogh waits for us and we have three Masses and are home at nine o'clock" (208), but she gives no source for this fragment.   64 Michael Blake, now bishop of Dromore, was vicar general of the Dublin diocese in June 1829 when Daniel Burke, OSF, was appointed chaplain of the House of Mercy, and the chapel was dedicated and opened to the public for the second Mass on Sundays (see Sullivan, *Catherine McAuley* 53–54).   65 Dr. Blake refers to the letter that Catherine McAuley mentions in Letter 62, and he notes that it was dated December 8. Unfortunately, Catherine's letter is not extant. 66 The adjective "old" is confusing here, but the word is clearly in Dr. Blake's draft. Probably an annual salary was paid to the former chaplain, Daniel Burke, OSF, but I have not discovered evidence of that.

he certainly does not intend it for himself, but to make it, by a discreet arrangement amongst his clergy, a conditional bond for an exact fulfilment of the duties
for which it is given.

A little explanation on both sides might perhaps have prevented so many
uneasy feelings. I am confident, however, that when nothing is sought on either
side but what is perfectly consistent with justice and charity, it will not be difficult for your wise and benevolent Archbishop to settle the point at issue in a
reasonable and satisfactory manner—to give you a distinct chaplain, if you can
afford a salary sufficient for his support, or if otherwise, to have such an arrangement made in the parish Chapel, that *one individual* clergyman belonging to it
shall have it as his peculiar duty to be an *efficient and regular* chaplain to your
Community.

I would request of you again to submit your case to his Grace. Your own
prudent mind will easily suggest the time and the manner most agreeable to him.
Your good friend, the Rev. Mr. Hamilton, whose kindness you have experienced,
will not refuse his valuable cooperation in so good a work. Whilst using these
exertions, put your trust in God, pray to him fervently, but with perfect resignation to the ways of his providence, and rest assured that all things shall work
together for good to those who love & obey him.

Please to present my kindest compliments to your very interesting
Community, and my humble petition that they will pray for me, and believe me
always with perfect sincerity, Dear Madam ...

[Michael Blake]

Author's transcript: Dromore

64. To Sister M. Frances Warde   [November–December 1837][67]
Carlow

[My dear Sr. M. Frances]
   Though I find it difficult to write without the assistance of my second hand,
yet I am going to depart from my rigid rule of not writing more than six lines,

---

67 This letter, for which no autograph is extant, is published only in Carroll, *Life* 467. Carroll's
version of the letter, which she dates "St. Patrick's, Kingstown, January 1838," is entirely presented
here. Readers will notice that paragraph one of the postscript contains sentences that are almost
identical to paragraph two of Letter 61 (above), and that paragraph two begins with the first sentence of paragraph three of Letter 61. The most confounding part of this letter is the reference to
"Kingstown" in Carroll's heading and the word "here" in Catherine's sentence: "The day after I
arrived here I broke my arm." There is no evidence to support the view that Catherine McAuley
broke her arm in January 1838, or that this letter was written in its entirety in January 1838, or
even that it was written from Kingstown. I strongly suspect that the "letter," as Carroll received
it, perhaps in transcribed form, from her correspondent, is a pastiche of two or more letters. The
reasons for including this letter, with all its problems, in this edition are twofold: Carroll must have

or what is barely necessary. I will tell you all I can collect, but first, must heartily congratulate you on the arrival of Miss Maher, to whom I beg you to offer my affectionate regards. If Miss Coffey has come, remember me to her, and tell her we all pray that she may get good health and the grace of perseverance.[68] The account of Sister M. Ursula is consoling indeed. She will not feel the winter passing in Carlow, the air is so mild and clear. I am sure she will be a grateful child for all your affectionate care and solicitude, and make herself, like Missie Rice, "generally useful."[69] Then she will be quite prepared for Booterstown.[70] I am comforted to hear of all the fatherly affection you meet. The beauty of your convent has become a town talk. Father Carroll is proclaiming it as the handsomest in Ireland.

Remember me, with great respect and esteem, to all our good pastors and friends. I hope to have a strong party of exquisite singers for the blessing of the chapel. Tell Father Dan his teacher will expect to find him well prepared after diligent practice.[71]

P.S. *All private*.

As if you and I, like old Darby and Joan,[72] were sitting together at the community-table. The day after I arrived here I broke my arm. The inflammation

---

been working from transcriptions of authentic autographs, however flawed the transcriptions; and the letter contains, in those parts that are not repetitious of Letter 61, important commentary by Catherine McAuley that is not available in any other letter and that must have been once expressed in one or more authentic letters, now no longer extant. I have estimated the correct date of the parts of the letter to be November–December 1837.   68 Mary Maher entered the Carlow community on November 30, 1837. Kate Coffey entered on December 8, 1837. These dates help one to estimate the date of this letter.   69 Mary Ursula Frayne of the Baggot Street community had been asked to remain with the Carlow community for some time after its founding in April 1837. Whether her presence in Carlow in late 1837 is a continuation of that earlier assignment, or whether she had returned to Baggot Street and then returned again to Carlow, for reasons of health, is not known. Mary Austin Carroll provides this footnote: "Missie Rice was a delicate orphan child Mother McAuley took in some time before [perhaps as early as the 1820s]. This little lady used sometimes grow tired of Baggot-Street, and ask for 'change of air.' 'If I could go to Cork or Carlow,' said she, 'I'd make myself generally useful'" (*Life* 467). Catherine is confident Ursula Frayne will do the same.   70 A branch house Catherine McAuley intended to open in mid 1838.   71 Daniel Nolan, curate in Killeshin, Co. Carlow, was a favorite "son" of Catherine McAuley. Catherine's reference to "the blessing of the chapel" in Carlow is a puzzle. The chapel of the new convent in Carlow was blessed "pro tem" sometime before April 2, 1839, but probably not as early as the first months of 1838 (Carlow Annals). This fact raises further question about the original dating of parts of this letter, or at least of this paragraph.   72 Catherine compares the easy confidence and trust of her friendship with Frances Warde to the mutual attachment of the legendary old husband and wife, Darby and Joan. While the first portrait of Darby and Joan may have been in a poem by John Pomfret and published in his collected poems in 1724 (D.F. Foxon, *English Verse, 1701–1750*, 2:C157), several references to and descriptions of the devoted couple exist in other English poems and songs. The *Gentleman's Magazine* (March 1735) contains a poem entitled "The joys of love never forgot: a song" which begins "Dear Chloe, while thus beyond measure..." In the third stanza are the lines: "Old Darby, with Joan by his side, / you've often regarded with wonder: / He's dropsical, she is sore-eyed, / Yet they're never happy asunder" ("Darby" in OED). A later version has

was so great that nothing could be done but apply leeches. After two days, Surgeon White bound me up in boards. A broken arm is by no means so distressing a matter as I always supposed—the want of its use is the chief inconvenience. However, take great care of your bones, and, if you go through the new convent before stairs are put up, be extremely cautious.

No arrangement has yet been made as to chaplain. Poor Sister M. de Pazzi is after getting one of your old mother's best and strongest lectures and reasoning. She is perfectly happy. I know you will be particularly kind to Miss Doyle's aunt, who goes as housekeeper to the College. You have a high name in that quarter.

Sister M. Magdalen[73] gave a few lectures, while I was absent, on the duty of a Superioress, and on being away from the Convent. She has reason to think I heard it, and is as meek as a lamb.

May God bless and preserve you all, is the constant prayer of

your ever fond Mother
M. C. McAuley

Published transcription: Carroll, Life *467*

65. To Sister M. Frances Warde   [December 1837][74]
Carlow

My dear Sr. M. F.

I cannot express the gratitude I feel to all the truly kind good priests who shew such feeling & attention to you, etc. Sr. M. T.[75] has given me great comfort.

I rejoice to find Sisters Mary & Kate[76] feel so happy—may God bless them and grant them health and the grace of perseverance.

My dear Sister Mary Agnes and Mary Cath.—I hear are so happy, thank God—and my old child Mary Josephine G. whose *9 lines* I received.[77]

---

the refrain: "Always the same, Darby, my own / Always the same to your old wife Joan." I am very grateful to the staff of the Irish Traditional Music Archive, Dublin, for their help in gaining even a minimal understanding of the complicated history of this reference and of the humble man and woman who are immortalized in it.   **73** Mary Magdalen (Marcella) Flynn, one of the earliest associates of Catherine McAuley, had joined the resident community at the House of Mercy, Baggot Street, on July 15, 1829, and professed her vows on February 11, 1834.   **74** Previous editors have dated this letter "September 1837," but that date is not possible, given the entrance dates of Mary Maher and Kate Coffey.   **75** Mary Teresa (Amelia) White, still in Carlow.   **76** Mary Maher and Kate Coffey entered the Carlow community on November 30, 1837, and December 8, 1837, respectively.   **77** Mary Agnes (Rebecca) Greene and Mary Catherine (Kate) Meagher had received the habit in Carlow on November 14, 1837, the same day Mary Josephine Gabriel Trennor professed her vows. Apparently Catherine McAuley was looking for a longer letter from Mary Josephine than nine lines!

I enclose a note from Sister Josephine Warde[78]—which will gratify you—as it did me. I hear great accounts of her prudence & nice regular example. I saw in Cork all that was amiable in her character.

God bless you my Dear Child —

your ever affectionate
M. C. M.

Autograph: Silver Spring

66. To the Reverend John Hamilton

Convent, Baggot Street
December 19, 1837

Dear V. Reverend Sir

I ought to have acknowledged the receit of your letters and enclosure—two pounds ten for the servant and one pound subscription—for which we are very much obliged to you and Madam O'Connor.

I am sure, Revd. Sir, you are disappointed to find our unpleasant business not settled.[79] I wrote to Doctor Meyler the day you were here; he called—we acceded to his will—promised forty pounds a year. He appeared perfectly satisfied at first, then complained of the salery [*sic*], but in the end said he would send Mr. Farrily.[80] Three of who were present considered all settled. In the evening I received a note to say the salery could not be accepted, and that even if Mr. F. were satisfied, Doctor Meyler would think it his duty to prevent him, in answer to which I wrote as follows.

Very Revd. Sir—I am sorry to find the salery proposed is not deemed sufficient—as we could not promise anymore. We received a gratuity towards the alter [*sic*] which is now withdrawn (the particulars can be made known if required). We are ready to submit an account of our funds, and the expenses of our Institution, where it will appear that we have not near forty pounds left for the purpose. Perhaps Revd. Sir, you would think proper to add five pounds which you give and we might make up the remainder.[81] I remain, etc.

78 Mary Josephine Warde, Frances Warde's sister, was in the Cork community.   79 That is, the chaplaincy dispute. This letter to John Hamilton contains within it two letters of Catherine McAuley to Walter Meyler. These two letters were published as distinct letters in Bolster, *Correspondence* (41–43), but since no autographs or other sources for these letters are extant, beyond Catherine's own transcription of them within this letter, I have decided not to present them as separate letters. 80 No Revd. "Farrily" or "Farrilly" is listed among the eight curates at St. Andrew's at this time. However, the *Irish Catholic Directory* for 1838 notes that "In addition to the Clergymen attached to the Parish Churches, Friaries, and Nunneries, there are others who officiate in Monasteries, or public establishments in this Archdiocese" and then lists "Rev. Mr. Farrelly, Westland-row" (287). Perhaps Dr. Meyler had arranged for him to serve as chaplain on a partial or temporary basis. A Revd. Paul "Ferrally" was then a member of the Jesuit community at St. Francis Xavier Church, Upper Gardiner Street.   81 The particular gratuity Catherine McAuley mentions has not been

After this I had another note from Doctor Meyler—rejecting the proposal—to which he added: "I think I feel your friend Mr. Armstrong[82] urging me in this decision."

Sunday was let to pass in the same disorder, our poor persons did not return home till it was late.[83] When I missed them from their Sunday School, my heart became sore and bitter, and I wrote a letter which is proclaimed a threatening one. I will write you every word of it:

> Very Reverend Sir—When I read in your last note that you felt as if my dear respected Mr. Armstrong was urging you to your decision, I thought that in gratitude for the affectionate friendship with which he so long honored me, I ought to mention how he acted towards a religious community. The Revd. Mr. Wall, his predecessor in Ann Street, had been contending with the Sisters in Georges Hill about some temporal matters.[84] When Mr. A. was appointed he immediately visited the convent, gave his most cordial sanction to their two public Masses and a Charity Sermon if they required it—not all this world could give would induce him to harrass or annoy a society of women devoted to the service of God and the poor.
>
> We were happily at home today in time for all our different duties, hence for ourselves we ask for nothing—but our poor young women are still about the streets, taking advantage, to be sure, of the irregularity which has been introduced among them. I will make one effort more in their regard. I will endeavour to prevail on the Sisters to accompany me to their Bishop—representing that the Chapel and Institute which he blessed in all the ceremonial form, carrying his Benediction to its outer walls,[85] is now under some kind of condemnation, that even a friendly priest is not permitted to celebrate Mass, that the Blessed Eucharist has not been renewed for near three months, that the poor inmates are deprived of the Holy Sacraments. We will shew what is lost by the change that has been made, and that far from withholding the necessary compensation, we are promising more than we possess. This sad alteration in

---

identified. Dr. Meyler had asked for an annual salary of £50. Catherine had proposed that the community could afford only £40. However, she is here offering a compromise of £45.   82 Father Edward Armstrong died in 1828. Catherine McAuley had attended her good friend constantly in his last illness.   83 By depriving the House of Mercy of a chaplain, Walter Meyler had, in effect, removed the possibility of daily, and even Sunday, Mass at Baggot Street. This meant that the forty or more servant women and girls living there had to go out to a parish church on Sundays, with the consequent freedom to dally in the city and delay their return to the House—the very shelter created to protect them from the sexual and other dangers lying in wait for them on the city streets.   84 Catherine refers to the Presentation convent on George's Hill where she had made her novitiate and professed her vows as the first Sister of Mercy. Christopher Wall was parish priest of the neighboring parish of St. Michan's on North Anne Street from 1804 until his death in 1826. Edward Armstrong succeeded him (Donnelly 11: 60).   85 On June 4, 1829, Dr. Daniel Murray had dedicated the chapel of the House of Mercy on Baggot Street and blessed the building and gardens. On the same day he had appointed Daniel Burke, OSF, as chaplain of the House of Mercy and Redmond O'Hanlon, ODC, as confessor.

our once orderly Establishment cannot fail to excite pity in a mind like his. If we have incurred displeasure and drawn this heavy malediction on our House, we will on our knees beg his pardon and implore a renewal of his Paternal protection. I remain, etc., etc.

At eight o'clock on Sunday evening, a letter was handed me from Doctor Meyler. It began thus: "When is your procession to take place? I should like to see the Theatrical exhibition—the Bishop must be apprised—perhaps you may not admire the reception you will meet, for he is too strait forward [*sic*] a person to be caught by your Juggle."

I read no more and put it out of my power ever to do so by burning the letter. I must now be done with the matter entirely. I will attempt nothing more. The means that contributed to pay a Chaplain is taken from us, and we are to be forced to promise what we cannot be sure of having. We will shew you our accounts, and you will find there is no prevarication in the statement made. I have no one to appeal to.

Begging you to forgive all this trouble, I remain, Very Reverend Sir, with lively gratitude for the kind interest you have manifested,

Very respectfully, etc., etc.
Mary C. McAuley

Mr. Lynch[86] was sent on Monday to say Mass, but not since. You told me, Revd. Sir, we were to have Mr. Farrelly entirely, except his last Masses. Dr. Meyler said we were to have two.[87] Of course, we could not know who to call on as a friend—but even to this we assented, distressing as it is.

It is said that we all dislike the Parish Clergy—God forbid—and that we give freely elsewhere. Indeed, Reverend Sir, I should fear that God would be displeased at my ingratitude, did I not declare that Mr. O'Hanlon has been the most generous friend—and that all he ever received for his nine years constant attendance—often every day for a week preparing for Profession—was thirty two pounds in different sums from the Sisters—to get Mass for them etc., etc.—in all, the entire sum—£32—in nine years.

The only apology I can offer for all this writing is that it comforts and relieves my mind to declare the truth where I trust I am not suspected of insincerity.

Autograph: Dublin Diocese, Murray Papers AB3/34/15, no. 10

67. To Sister M. Angela Dunne   [Baggot Street]
Charleville   December 20, 1837

My dear Sister Angela

I confided, that Sister Mary Clare had written to inform you of the death of our innocent dear Sister de Chantal, as the letter announcing it to me arrived in

---

86 Gregory Lynch, a curate at St. Andrew's.   87 That is, two curates from St. Andrew's alternating as chaplain.

Cork when I had left it—exactly the same fever which was sent by God to take the pious valued Bishop—Dr. Nolan—came, I trust, from the Divine hand for her. She had quite a saintly death—continually repeating aloud—"My God, I love you—forgive me and take me to yourself." The Physicians were astonished.

I have not been able to write or do much since I returned. On the second day I went to Kingstown—to condole with them on the loss of their lively dear companion. When the Angelus Bell rang, I was hastening to the choir from the Community room, missed the first step of the stairs, fell forward and in endeavouring to save my head from the window, broke my left arm across the wrist—and injured the sinews in the back of the hand so much that I am not likely to have the use of it for months—if ever.[88]

My Dear Sister M. Angela, the Charleville foundation has been a source of great anxiety to me. One of the Curates called on me in Cork, asking in a kind of disguised way—but like as if called on to do so—would any of the Sisters be sent to Limerick—would Sister Delaney. I felt quite distressed, as if we were like persons in the world, changing our House or lodgings on trifling occasions. Since I left Cork, Mr. Reardon, the Monk, made some such enquiry.[89]

What could excuse us before God—for casting off any charge which we had freely undertaken, except compelled by necessity to do so. Are not the poor of Charleville as dear to him as elsewhere—and while one pound of Miss Clanchy's five hundred lasts, ought we not to persevere and confide in his Providence. The Sisters of Charity in Cork have been but 5 in number & a Lay Sister for 10 years. It is wonderful all they do—and they are not all in good health, and live in most confined bad air. I am grieved to find such feint-hearted symptoms amongst us.

I had a letter from Mrs. French.[90] She says that £50 per an[num] will be paid. Your 30 & the interest will make 97. Surely that will do.

I cannot hope to see you till May. Perhaps it would be well to get the 2 Sisters received as Mr. Croke has power from the Bishop.[91] Let us not forget that you and Community are subject to Dr. Crotty, who surely would not approve of any such change—and I really feel that God would not grant his blessing—while we can avoid it.

I am sorry to hear such an account of Jane Taaffe.[92] The sooner she leaves, the better. I write with difficulty, not having the second hand to hold my paper.

---

88 This is Catherine McAuley's only extensive reference to her broken arm in an extant autograph letter, although, as noted earlier, some references to it appear in fragments of transcriptions of other letters (see Letters 61, 62, and 64).   89 Brother Michael Paul Riordan was a member of the Christian Brothers living in the North Monastery, Cork. Edmund Rice was at the time still superior general of the Christian Brothers, and Riordan was part of "the anti-Rice faction" (Rushe 130–31).   90 The former Miss Mary Clanchy, a benefactor of the Charleville community.   91 Dr. Bartholomew Crotty was bishop of Cloyne and Ross, and former president of the Royal College of St. Patrick, Maynooth. Thomas Croke was parish priest of Charleville (*Irish Catholic Directory* [1837] 278).   92 Jane Taaffe was received as a novice in the Charleville community on June 30, 1837. However, she did not persevere.

I will venture the 2 half notes. Write when you receive this. Remember me most affectionately to my dear Sr. M. Joseph, Sister Ann & Sister Lawless,[93] whom I hope you continue to like. Remember me to Mary and the children.

Present my respectful remembrance to Mr. Croke. Remember me to the Mrs. Clanchys, etc., etc. Tell me all the news you have about your school & sick poor—your little collection, etc., etc.

Put your whole confidence in God. He never will let you want necessaries for yourself or children. It would afflict me and it would be a disgrace to our order to have a break up.

Believe me, my Dear Sister Mary Angela, your ever affectionate
Mary C. McAuley

All unite in fondest love.

Remember you are to charge Jane Taaffe £20 per year from the time she went to you—and anything expended for her. I request you will do this exactly.

[*illegible words*][94]

Autograph: Charleville

68. **To Sister M. Frances Warde**   **Convent, Baggot Street**
    Carlow   **December 23, 1837**[95]

My Dear Sister Mary Frances

It is no wonder I should take a fancy to my adopted son[96]—for he is a real rogue, according to my own taste. I must let you into the plot. We had sent to buy franks[97]—and of course your name was on the list. They came when Father

93 Mary Joseph (Alicia) Delaney came to Charleville from Baggot Street as a novice; she professed her vows in Charleville in May 1837, but returned to Baggot Street in 1839. "Sister Ann" is presumably Anne Kent who entered the Charleville community in 1837, received the habit on March 2, 1838, but apparently left before professing vows. Miss Lawless is evidently Margaret Lawless who entered the Charleville community in 1837 and professed her vows there on August 5, 1840; in 1845 she transferred to a Ursuline community in Ennis. Evidently, Mary Agnes Hynes, the second novice who had come from Baggot Street on the Charleville foundation in October 1836, had by now left the community. Thus, in 1837, and particularly in 1839, Mary Angela Dunne, the superior, had some reason to anticipate that the Charleville community would not take hold, although the rumors of its closing that reached Catherine McAuley in 1837 may have been clerical speculations that did not originate with Angela Dunne. Actually, in the ensuing decades the community developed and by 1866 was able to send a new foundation to Bathurst (New South Wales), Australia. 94 Catherine's second closing is tantalizingly illegible; it may be an abbreviated "Affectionately yours." 95 Previous editors have dated this letter December 29, 1837. However, the number in the autograph is clearly 23 or possibly 27, not 29. Moreover, December 23 or December 27 makes more sense, given the content of the letter. Each Mercy convent, including Baggot Street, observed a year-end spiritual retreat of three days, December 29, 30, and 31, and the retreat would seem to rule out Catherine's taking the time on the 29th to write an interesting, even playful, but not really necessary letter. 96 Daniel Nolan, curate in Killeshin, Co. Carlow. 97 Envelopes or cover sheets

Dan was here. I said I had nothing to put in yours. He then proposed, and I agreed to write hinting—or in part saying—that he was likely to become our chaplain, etc., etc., and to endeavour by degrees to reconcile you to this. Though I had all ready—artfully done so as not to tell an untruth, etc.—I found I could not send it lest it would give you even passing uneasiness. *Play your part well. My son will.* Appear quite embarrassed—be surprised that I would wish to take any more comfort from you, etc., etc., and when you have him well cheated, then discover the plot.

I was heartily delighted to see him. I think he is remarkably like my Mary Teresa[98]—and certainly as innocent.

A very pleasing young person of plain education called here yesterday to say she wished to join the Carlow Sisters of Mercy, and the Revd. Mr. McSweeney advise[d] her to call on me to know would 300 pounds be accepted—her name is Kelly. She has a brother at the College—they live 5 miles from Carlow.[99] I like her very much—very nice looking & sweet countenance, and when I say plain education, I do not mean any thing objectionable. I referred her to Dr. Fitzgerald—and recommended *Mrs. Warde* in the highest possible terms. I hope she will not disgrace my judgment. Miss Kelly said she would like to enter in Lent.

Write to me soon. Sister Mary Teresa has delighted me telling of the instructions you give—shew them in your actions as much as you can, my Dearest Child, and your Institution will outdo us all.

May God preserve and bless you—and grant you all the graces and precious gifts reserved for this holy season.

Your always fond Mother in Christ
M. C. McAuley

Autograph: Silver Spring

---

marked to signify that the postage was prepaid. In Ireland in 1837 postal rates correlated with the distance travelled and the number of enclosures. See also Letter 88, note 19.   **98** Catherine McAuley's beloved niece Mary Teresa Macauley, who had died on November 12, 1833.   **99** Maria Kelly entered the Carlow community on February 23, 1838. In 1840 she became the founding superior in Wexford.

January–March 1838

The first three months of 1838 saw no resolution of the chaplaincy controversy with Dr. Walter Meyler, but Catherine McAuley's energies were also focused in other directions: consoling the Carlow community after the sudden death of Kate Coffey, arranging a speaker for the Charity Sermon scheduled for February 18, preparing a profession and reception ceremony for eight women at Baggot Street on February 21, selecting employment situations for numerous women and girls in the House of Mercy, and planning for a new branch house soon to be opened in Booterstown. In the midst of her business activities, Catherine's lightheartedness overflowed in a wonderfully humorous letter "chastising" her good friend James Maher, now parish priest of Carlow-Graigue, and in a poetic exchange with Mary Francis Marmion, one of Baggot Street's indefatigable workers among the Dublin poor.

In this period Catherine McAuley continued to defend the sacramental needs of the women and girls in the House of Mercy, but she was at peace, even with the law proceedings now in process to force her to pay the debt incurred in building the poor school in Kingstown. She saw in these two controversies "the Cross of Christ which we so often pray to 'be about us,'" yet she still needed support. She found she could speak with James Maher "with all the confidence of one addressing a long, well proved friend, and such comfort does not often fall to my lot" (Letter 71).

69. To the Reverend James Maher
Carlow-Graigue

Convent, Baggot Street
January 10, 1838

My Dear Father Maher

I am very sorry you did not complete the full week's attendance, which according to the regulations of this diocese, would have entitled you to one pound or guinea, whichever you liked best.[1] The statutes are now most rigorously observed

---

1 This letter to Catherine McAuley's friend James Maher has sometimes been misinterpreted as a serious complaint. Father Maher, whom she had met at the founding of the Carlow community in April 1837, had evidently spent a few days in Dublin, and celebrated Mass each morning at Baggot Street. When he returned to Carlow-Graigue where he was now parish priest, Catherine wrote him this teasing letter, insisting on "the regulations of this diocese." This straight-faced letter is no doubt a sustained parody, set in another context, of the serious conversations they must have had about the chaplaincy issue and the chaplain's salary she was expected, but could not afford, to pay. Catherine's claim to be writing "in real sincerity" is an ironic tip-off to the tongue-in-cheek

and I really cannot say, without making enquiry, whether a broken week is payable. You will excuse me, I am sure, for taking this little advantage, for you know, although I should be simple as a Dove, I must also be prudent as a serpent—and since there is very little good can be accomplished, or evil avoided, without the aid of money, we must look after it in small as well as in great matters.

I have now to deplore the loss of a superfine veal cutlet, specially provided for this morning, also a dear nice little kettle to supply boiling water for the second or third cup as might be required—and then my poor infirm hand, employed far beyond its power making the fire burn brilliantly, giving a sharp edge to a knife to set off the cutlet, roasting a plate, etc., etc.

Most sincerely thanking you for past services, and earnestly wishing for a renewal and continuance of the same, I remain

My Dear Father Maher in real sincerity,
your ever grateful
Mary C. McAuley

Don't forfeit all chance of the pound—perhaps we can make up the week—without violating the Law.

Autograph: Silver Spring

70. To Catherine McAuley   Friday [January 1838]

Dear Mrs. McAuley

I have finally determined on the arrangement I made yesterday.

I hope you will consider me the sincere and zealous friend to the interests of your institute. I have not the least doubt of the advantages of this arrangement, both to the House of Mercy & to the Parish.

If it should appear otherwise—after the sermon and a sufficient trial—new regulations can be made.[2]

When the time of the Charity Sermon will draw near, I shall afford you every assistance in my power and beg that you will enroll me as an annual subscriber of £5—which I shall remit in a few days.

Believe me most sincerely and faithfully, etc., etc.
W[alter] Meyler

Autograph: Dublin, Mercy

---

character of the letter. Would that James Maher's reply were extant!   2 Dr. Meyler is referring to the upcoming Charity Sermon on behalf of the House of Mercy which was scheduled to be given in St. Andrew's church on February 18, 1838. His letter is undated, but was probably written some time in early January, perhaps even before Letter 69. The Fridays in January 1838 were January 5, 12, 19, and 26. The specific details of the chaplaincy "arrangement" Dr. Meyler has decided are not known, but presumably they involved the curates of St. Andrew's serving on a rotating, as-needed basis at the £50 annual salary he had earlier stipulated (see Letter 71).

71. To Sister M. Frances Warde
Carlow
January 17, 1838

Convent, Baggot Street

Private

My Dearest Sister Mary Frances

If I have inspired you with the melancholy view you take of our situation I assure you I did not intend to do so. We have just now indeed more than an ordinary portion of the Cross in this one particular[3]—but may it not be the Cross of Christ which we so often pray to "be about us." It has not the marks of an angry cross—there is no disunion, no gloomy depression of spirits, no departure from charity proceeding from it. The difficulties lessen every day. We get our poor inmates to Confession by six at each time, with Eliza Liston[4] to bring them safe home—and please God we will have all prepared for Holy Communion first Friday.

We get an occasional charitable Mass—and never go out on very wet mornings. I am sure Doctor Meyler would wish the matter were settled according to his own plan—we would have at least three Priests, and never know who to call on as friend or chaplain—and for this must pay or promise to pay £50 per annum, which we really have not, independent of casual events. Mr. Delaney, Sister de Pazzi's father, would contribute to pay a chaplain, as we had before, but not under the present circumstances. Miss McGuinness [Magenis] would also. I offered £40 to Dr. Meyler, and I now believe it is well it was rejected, for if we had not twenty to give at the end of the half year, we would be suspected of withholding it, and all the dispute would be renewed—and whenever I have the happiness of seeing Mr. Maher again, I will tell him—and him only—another strong reason why the proposed connection should be avoided if possible.

I am not unhappy, thanks be to God—nor do I see any disedification likely to arise from the matter. Some think that after having Mr. Burke[5] eight years, we are not now easily pleased—and most of those who know the cause that we go out [to Mass] seem to think we ought to have a distinct chaplain, and only say, Dr. Meyler is a little positive. This is the extent of it at present. It is humiliating no doubt, a smart attack on self importance, and if this part of it is well managed, it must turn to good account. I humbly trust it will end very well.

Sister Mary Teresa is in Kingstown— "greatly tempted" she says "to wish she were back with the Fathers in Carlow."[6] There also we find a nice little cross. Law proceedings for building the school—though we expressly said we could not contribute more than the ground, coach house, & fifty pounds from

---

3 The chaplaincy situation.   4 Eliza Liston was a young woman from Limerick who initially lived in the House of Mercy on Baggot Street. She later entered the Baggot Street community on September 8, 1838, and professed her vows as a lay sister on May 4, 1841.   5 Daniel Burke, the former chaplain, now gone to southern Africa.   6 Mary Teresa (Amelia) White, who had spent several months assisting the Carlow community, was now the local superior of the convent in Kingstown.

the Bazaar. By giving that £50 Mr. Sheridan says I am, what he terms, committed, and he has left me in the hands of Mr. Nugent.[7] I am hiding from some law person who wants to serve a paper on me personally & sent in to say he came from Doctor Murray. I am afraid to remain five minutes in the small parlour. This has caused more laughing than crying, you may be sure, for every man is suspected of being the process man, and kept at an awful distance by my dear Teresa Carton.[8] They make a demand of 4 hundred and fifty pounds.[9] I suppose we must sell Kingstown when Booterstown is nearly ready. Now you have the double cross[10]—the cross of the Diocess—out of it, all is consoling and animating, thanks be to God.

The contributions go on well—great relief afforded. The extern Dinner encreased and the House crowded.[11] Twenty went to situations in one week—and twenty more came in. We have got three times more than the Chapel would have produced with the 2 Masses. Since it was closed entirely, it is now our choir—and the dear choir a parlour, the grate boarded up. Pray fervently for me, and you will see me young and handsome at the grand consecration.[12]

The kind interest Mr. Maher manifested was most consoling because it is genuine. Indeed I could speak to him with all the confidence of one addressing a long, well proved friend, and such comfort does not often fall to my lot. He promised to do something about the charity sermon—we have only one month.[13] Will you coax him with all the earnestness you can. You know the contributions won't last very long in a flourishing way. This is the season of particular pity, and if these means stop, we must stop. Oh how you should bless God who has made provision for the poor about you, not depending on daily exertions.

---

7 James Nugent, the builder of the poor school in Kingstown, where Bartholomew Sheridan was parish priest. 8 Teresa (Mary) Carton was, at this point, a lay sister, having professed her vows on July 1, 1837 (in August 1844 she became a choir sister, by a decision of the Baggot Street Chapter). She was deeply devoted to Catherine McAuley and assisted her in all sorts of household tasks, including, as here, preventing a subpoena from being served. 9 Three months later the law proceeding was decided in favor of the builder, James Nugent, and against Catherine McAuley (see Letter 87). 10 The chaplaincy and the Kingstown "crosses." 11 The House of Mercy was originally intended simply as an overnight shelter, the residents going out to work, or to find work, each day. However, by 1837 Catherine had concluded that merely providing a night shelter was not sufficient assistance to these poor women and girls whose skills were often, if not usually, inadequate to secure them suitable employment. She therefore began a training program for them at Baggot Street. At this time fifty or sixty women and girls were regularly living in the dormitories of the House of Mercy and receiving all their meals at Baggot Street. The "extern dinner" Catherine mentions may refer to their noonday meal, or to the annual Christmas dinner that was, from the beginning, provided to poor children. 12 Catherine McAuley anticipated attending the episcopal consecration of Francis Haly, the new bishop of Kildare and Leighlin, in Carlow cathedral on March 25, 1838. However, as the event drew near. she realized that she could not leave Dublin. 13 The Charity Sermon for the House of Mercy was scheduled for February 18, 1838, according to an archdiocesan plan—published in the *Irish Catholic Directory*—that distributed dozens of Charity Sermons for various charitable institutions in Dublin across the Sundays of the calendar year. Catherine McAuley had asked James Maher of Carlow to give the Charity Sermon in 1838 (see Letter 72).

Give my affectionate love to all my dear Sisters—Fathers and Son.[14] All unite with me in fondest remembrance—who am your most truly attached Mother in Christ—

M. C. McAuley

You have written twice without mentioning your coajutor [*sic*], Sr. M. Teresa.[15] I will not shew her the letter. Always remember her distinctly.

Autograph: Silver Spring

72. To the Reverend James Maher   Convent of the Sisters of Mercy
Carlow-Graigue   Baggot St., January 23, 1838

My Dear Mr. Maher

You created some little hope in my mind relative to the Charity Sermon— which is appointed for the 18th of next month. Will you have pity on us now, and we will feel particularly grateful—and pray most fervently for you. I will look out anxiously for a favorable answer, perhaps I may not be disappointed.[16]

I remain Dear Mr. Maher with much respect—

your faithful and obliged etc., etc.
Mary C. McAuley

Autograph: Omaha

73. Poetic Exchange: Catherine McAuley   [January 25, 1838]
and Sister Mary Francis Marmion[17]

[To Mary Francis Marmion]
To my great surprise you demanded last night
The enclosed as your own—your particular right
I am sorry to find such a matter distract you

---

14 The priests of Carlow, including Daniel Nolan.   15 Mary Teresa (Amelia) White had been Frances Warde's temporary assistant in Carlow for several months, and always spoke fondly of her experience there. Catherine McAuley is anxious that Frances's letters, which she will share with Teresa, indicate some remembrance of her and her contributions in Carlow.   16 Whether Father Maher actually preached the Charity Sermon on February 18 is not known. Writing on March 13, Catherine says, "Charity Sermon very bad" (Letter 80). It is difficult to imagine that James Maher didn't agree to give the sermon, for Catherine's sake, but it is nearly impossible to imagine that he was not a profoundly stirring public preacher. Rather, Catherine must be referring to a low atten- dance and collection.   17 Evidently the occasion of this exchange of verses was Mary Francis Marmion's having begged half a crown (a British coin worth two shillings and sixpence) from a vis- itor to Baggot Street, so she could buy food for the sick poor whom she visited. She gave the money to Catherine McAuley, with the request that she might have it back for the poor. Catherine's teas- ing response and Mary Francis's further request that, in commemoration of the anniversary of her

I did not suppose such a crown could attract you
But since with reluctance from it you would part
Take it—there is no such tie on my heart.

[M. C. McAuley]

[To Catherine McAuley]
Dear Mother, in spite of your jesting I own
That I ever ambitiously sigh for a crown
Which the one you surrender may aid me to gain
And therefore the right of my poor I maintain
This very day twelvemonth it was that you bound
With a black leather cincture my waist & will round
And to tell of my happiness humbly I pray
That the Sisters may have recreation today.

[Mary Francis Marmion][18]

[To Mary Francis Marmion]
I rejoice in your motive for liking this day
But not in your wishing to spend it in play
I must freely confess it were more to my mind
If to reflection your heart were inclined
But since you're not weaned, nor alone cannot walk
I suppose you must do what you can do—then *talk*!

[M. C. McAuley]

Handcopies: Liverpool Annals (123–24) and Brisbane Book of Transcriptions (190–91)

---

receiving the Mercy habit (January 25, 1837), the community might have "recreation," that is, conversation rather than silence, at the day's meals culminate in Catherine's final mock-serious poem. The whole exchange illustrates the ease with which novices interacted with Catherine McAuley, as well as her own ever ready playfulness and flexibility. No autographs of the three poems have been found, but handcopies are extant in the Liverpool Annals (123–24) and in the Brisbane Book of Transcriptions (190–91). The two handcopies are identical except in two places: the Liverpool copy inserts "your" before "wishing" in the third poem, and the prefatory wording is slightly different. The Liverpool Annals says: "To Sister M. Frances who had begged 2 [shillings] 6 [pence] from a visitor, and wanted it for the sick poor of whom she had the charge" (123); the Brisbane handcopy reads: "From Revd. Mother to Sr. M. Francis who had charge of the Sick Poor and who begged half a crown from a visitor to get food for the Poor" (190).   18 Mary Francis (Margaret) Marmion was the third of three Marmion sisters to enter the Baggot Street community: Mary Agnes (Frances) Marmion entered on July 1, 1832, professed her vows on October 8, 1834, and died on February 10, 1836; Mary Cecilia (Mary) Marmion entered on January 5, 1834, professed her vows on October 22, 1836, and having been elected superior of the Baggot Street community in 1844, and subsequently re-elected, she will die in office on September 15, 1849; Mary Francis (Margaret) Marmion, the correspondent in this poetic exchange, entered the convent on August 1, 1836. She will profess her vows on January 21, 1839, and die of consumption fourteen months later, on March 10, 1840. 19 Mary Frances Warde, Mary Josephine's sister in Carlow.

74. To Sister M. Josephine Warde   Saturday, January 27, 1838
Cork

My Dear Sister Mary Josephine
    In a flying hurry, I am going to say a few words to you. Sister Mary Frances[19] tells me she had a most consoling letter from you. Thanks be to God you are so happy, indeed it affords me real comfort. The contrary would afflict me very much. The union which exists amongst you will draw the favor and blessing of Heaven, and you will soon be an edifying Community, please God.
    Do not neglect praying for me particularly, and believe me always
                                            your affectionate Mother in Christ
                                                            M. C. McAuley

Autograph: Cork; photocopy: Dublin, Mercy

75. To Sister Mary Vincent Deasy   [February 1838]
Cork

My very Dear Sister
    When you heard the facts contained in this little Controversy related in conversation, you expressed such an ardent desire to have it in the form of a Tract, that immediately on my return I had it prepared for you. I earnestly hope it may be useful for your poor patients, who require something amusing as well as instructive; you may assure them, that it is a true story, and that the distinguished personage, and the humble Margaret were living not long since.[20]
                                            Dear Sister Mary Vincent,
                                            your very affectionate, etc. etc.
                                                            M. C. McAuley

Published letter: Carroll, ed. Cottage Controversy, *unnumbered prefatory page*

20 I have chosen to include this letter, as presented in the front of Carroll's reprint of *Cottage Controversy*—despite the fact that no autograph or handcopies of it have been found—because its contents pertain to an ongoing discussion among scholars of Catherine McAuley's life and writings. The letter is said to relate to a document titled "Cottage Controversy" which is said to be composed, not simply "prepared," by Catherine McAuley, and is said to have been "published" by Catherine McAuley, or if not by her, probably by Mary Vincent Deasy, if not in 1838, then some time after Catherine's death. Copies of the original publication were sent to Mary Austin Carroll in 1882, and she reprinted the work in 1883 (New York: O'Shea). No manuscript in Catherine McAuley's handwriting has been found (Carroll did not see one), and copies of the first edition which Carroll received cannot now be located (Muldrey 204–205, 393 n. 279, and 395 nn. 42, 45). Letter 131 in this volume contains a passage that has been cited to support the view that Catherine's "work" was written for Mary Vincent Deasy.
    I remain convinced that *Cottage Controversy* (Carroll's reprint was recently reprinted) is not an original composition of Catherine McAuley's, but at most a transcription, probably an abbreviated

76. To the Reverend John Hamilton

Convent, Baggot Street
February 6, 1838

Very Reverend Sir

Though I am aware I ought not intrude on your time which must be fully occupied, yet I feel as if indifference was taking place in my mind when I give up every effort to raise the Institution from its fallen state. Since the first of this year, thirty seven young women went to situations from the House, most of whom merely approached the Sacrament of Penance to obtain a note for admission. We are quite full again of persons under similar circumstances. On such occasions, Mr. Burke attended to the confessional for four or five days together, very often till after four o'clock, to afford them the means of reconciliation, before employment was obtained.

They leave us now, as they came, and there is noise and quarrelling amongst them, which the participation of the Holy Sacraments with due instruction used to cure. The alteration in the school is quite evident. [21] They went to Confession every week in turn, and I assure you, Revd. Sir, Mr. Burke has frequently said he was very tired. Mr. Cavanagh of Fitzwilliam Street, with whom he resided for some time, mentioned here a few days since that Mr. Burke used to say, "That House gives work enough for any man."

I think it was providential that Doctor Meyler refused the salery, [22] for I still hope that God will grant the spiritual assistance required, to meet the expense

---

transcription, of a previously published treatise by an as yet unidentified author. A great deal of research remains to be done on this topic, guided by an understanding of Catherine McAuley's penchant for transcribing parts of published works that appealed to her (or asking others to "prepare" them), and by a developed knowledge of her writing style and habits. So far, hours spent in the British Library, the National Library of Ireland, and the Central Catholic Library in Dublin have not yielded discovery of the original source of *Cottage Controversy*.

However, the title "Cottage Controversy" or "Cottage Conversation" or "Cottage Dialogues" is used by many authors of religious tracts that present debates between Protestant and Catholic proponents. In fact, "cottage controversy" appears to be a genre of apologetic writing that was popular in Ireland and England in the early nineteenth century, the authors of the debates or dialogues favoring either the Protestant or the Catholic doctrinal positions by the way in which they represented the arguments of the characters in the controversy. In the six conversations contained in the document said to have been composed by Catherine McAuley, the Catholic cottager Margaret Martyn, married to Thomas Lewis, a Protestant tenant, argues more convincingly than her landlord's wife, the Protestant Lady P[embroke]. However, in the second edition of J. S. Monsell's *Cottage Controversy; or, Dialogues between Thomas and Andrew, on The Errors of the Church of Rome* (Limerick: Goggin, 1839), first published in 1838, the opposite outcome is presented. In this volume Thomas is a Protestant and Andrew, a Catholic; at the end of their nine dialogues, the dying Andrew is gratefully converted to Protestantism.

21 As well as the young women in the House of Mercy, the children in the Baggot Street school for poor girls also used to receive the sacrament of Penance from Daniel Burke, the former chaplain.   22 Walter Meyler asked for an annual salary of £50; Catherine McAuley offered £40, and then £45, which he did not accept.

of which, we would make every exertion and be very kindly assisted. Relying on the charitable allowance you will make for this intrusion, I remain

Very Reverend Sir, with much respect, etc., etc.
Mary C. McAuley

Autograph: Dublin Diocese, Murray Papers AB3/34/15, no. 11

77. To the Reverend James Maher

Convent, Baggot Street
February 15, 1838

Dear Reverend Father

I have just received your kind letter and feel exceedingly concerned at the melancholy communication.[23] Thanks be to God the event has been atten[d]ed with such consoling circumstances. It must be a severe trial to her attached relatives from whom she so recently parted.[24] To my dear Sister Mary Frances it is I know a real portion of the Cross, and as such I trust she will embrace it—with humble resignation to the holy will of God. I have great happiness in knowing that she will receive all the solid council [counsel] and animating comfort which affectionate fatherly feelings can dictate. The usual suffrages for a deceased Sister will be offered here. The most sensible participation of the trial has already spread through the House,[25] and all unite in most earnest prayers for our poor Sister Frances and Community.

I remain, Dear Reverend Sir, with great respect, etc., etc.
Mary C. McAuley

Autograph: Brooklyn

78. To Sister M. Frances Warde
Carlow

Convent, Baggot Street
February 17, 1838

My ever Dear Sister Mary Frances

How deeply, how sincerely, I feel this second trial[26] which it has pleased Almighty God to visit you with, not in His anger—we will humbly hope—but to purify and render the foundation solid and according to His own heart—established on the Cross. The innocent amiable young person you have parted was,

---

23 On February 12, 1838, Kate Coffey, a postulant in the Carlow community, while "on the Visitation of the Sick, slipped in the snow, and fell; she only seemed a little stunned for the moment, but after retiring to bed that night, she got a severe attack of hemorrhage of the lungs" and died on February 14 (Carlow Annals). 24 Kate had entered the Carlow community only two months before, on December 8, 1837. Her family lived in Carlow. 25 The community on Baggot Street. 26 The death of Kate Coffey, a Carlow postulant, occurred on February 14 (see Letter 77). The first "trial" Frances experienced was the death of Dr. Edward Nolan on October 14, 1837.

it would seem, particularly designed for what has come to pass—for we did every thing that was calculated to alter her intention, at least I did.[27] Knowing how much these afflictions press on your mind, I will be most anxious to hear that you are yourself again.

You have given all to God without any reserve. Nothing can happen to you which He does not appoint. You desire nothing but the accomplishment of His Holy Will. Every thing, how trivial soever, regarding you will come from this adorable source. You must be cheerful and happy, animating all around you. This [advice] is quite unnecessary, for I know you do not want[28] counsel—or comfort—yet I cannot entirely give up my poor old Child. You may be sure we all pray fervently for you, which is the best we can do. If you could have seen the general feeling that prevailed at recreation yesterday evening, you might almost have thought we were strangers to such sorrows.

You will soon now have an increase—the comfort comes soon after a well received trial. May God preserve and bless you, my own dearly loved child. Remember me most affectionately to all. Sister Ursula forgets me.[29]

> Your ever faithful and fondly attached
> M. C. McAuley

I have been 3 hours out in the snow—walking—so I am growing young. 8 Sisters in retreat and so much to be done, I was obliged to assist. 7 to be received & Sister Scott professed on Wednesday next.[30]

Autograph: Silver Spring

79. To Sister M. Frances Warde   [Late February–March 1838]
Carlow

My dear Sister Mary Frances

The Register[31] ordered by Revd. Mr. Maher has been here two months, waiting for Sister Moore who prints beautifully in every type to write the title

27 Kate Coffey was apparently sickly before she entered, perhaps with some weakness of the lungs, and Catherine McAuley had evidently tried to discourage her entering the Carlow community on the grounds that convent life might be too hard for her. 28 That is, lack. 29 Mary Ursula Frayne was still temporarily in Carlow, and had apparently not written recently to Catherine McAuley. 30 The extensive work of visiting the sick poor while so many of the sisters at Baggot Street were in retreat before their reception or profession meant that Catherine herself, who usually worked full-time in the House of Mercy, had to go out to visit the sick in their homes or in hospitals. Mary Aloysius Scott will profess her vows on February 21, and those who will receive the habit that day are Mary Catherine (Ellen) Leahy, Mary Gertrude (Elizabeth) Blake, Mary Clare Augustine (Clare) Moore, Mary Anne Teresa (Annie) O'Brien, Veronica (Mary Anne) Duggan, a lay sister, Mary Frances (Frances) Boylan, and Mary Camillus (Teresa) Byrn, Catherine McAuley's cousin and adopted child. All seven had been approved to receive the habit by a vote of the Baggot Street Chapter (the professed members of the community) on January 20, 1838. 31 The Register is the

page.[32] She has been constantly employed, and now Bazaar work engages all their time.[33] I constantly spoke of your book—for a long time, indeed, a cut finger prevented her.

What pleasure it would afford me to be at your approaching ceremony, but it is quite impossible—two new Sisters and other circumstances must deprive me of that great indulgence.[34] I shall be anxious to hear from you as you say you are not quite well.

Your ever affectionate
M. C. McAuley

Miss Grace waits while I write.[35]

Handcopy: Silver Spring

80. **To Sister M. Frances Warde**   [March 13, 1838]
    Carlow[36]

... immediately after Easter—I have been there, it is quite finished, and will have a good garden for the weak ones.[37] I will find it difficult to add this charge

---

record kept in each convent of the important dates and appointments of each professed sister: her birth date (if known), her parents' names and location, and the dates of her entrance, reception of the habit, and profession of vows, as well as of her election or appointment to leadership roles (if applicable). In Catherine McAuley's day, the Register of each convent was a large, often artistically illuminated, volume with a page devoted to each professed sister. Often, as in Baggot Street, the relevant facts were recorded in a notebook before being transcribed by a calligrapher into the permanent Register.   **32** Mary Clare Augustine Moore, the sister of Mary Clare (Georgiana) Moore, now superior in Cork, had entered the Baggot Street convent on August 8, 1837, and received the habit on February 21, 1838. The present letter was probably written after that date. Mary Clare Augustine was a superb artist and calligrapher, as her many surviving art works testify. Catherine McAuley naturally sought to have her do the calligraphy and illumination of the Baggot Street Register, and at least begin the Register for Carlow, but Clare Augustine's timing and Catherine's did not always jibe, as will be apparent in future letters. James Maher visited Baggot Street in early January 1838 and may have ordered the Carlow Register then—hence my dating of this undated letter.   **33** As a fundraising activity, the Baggot Street community held a bazaar of handcrafted goods each year after Easter. In 1838 the bazaar was scheduled to occur sometime after April 15, so preparations would have been well underway at the time of this letter.   **34** Catherine McAuley had earlier planned to go to Carlow for the episcopal consecration of Francis Haly (March 25) and the reception ceremony of Mary de Sales (Mary) Maher (March 26), but circumstances now prevented her. Anna Markey had entered the Baggot Street community on February 16, 1838; the other "new Sister" cannot be identified, unless Catherine is anticipating the entrance of Clare Butler and Mary O'Connor, which did not occur until April 15 and April 27, respectively. All new sisters needed Catherine's guidance in their early days in the convent. Moreover, the Kingstown lawsuit and the unsettled chaplaincy situation still hung over her head.   **35** The messenger who will hand-deliver this letter.   **36** This letter is composed of two autograph fragments which appear to belong to the same letter. Paragraphs one and two are on the front and back of one fragment, which was apparently cut off the bottom of the letter, probably off pages 1 and 2 of a folded (four-sided) sheet of stationery. Paragraph three with the closing was probably on page 3 because the reverse side of this second fragment

to the present. When quite overwhelmed, I reanimate myself with the words of the Dear saintly Dr. Nolan—"It is my lot."

She[38] would have printed your Register long since—but knowing there was one could do it more fancifully, she was quite anxious to get it done so. *That one*[39] has more of her own ways yet than of ours—and it is not very easy to fix her to a point. She finds the duties sufficient to fill up her time, and as her constitution is strong, she is much employed in out door work.[40]

Sister Cecilia will bring our Register and print for you Friday, Saturday & Sunday.[41] God grant she may not get fresh cold. Please God, all will go on well and your ceremony will be very nice. Tell Sister Ursula[42] to be ready to return. I trust we will go to the consecration or dedication of the Chapel.[43] Charity Sermon very bad—Chapel closed—Bazaar unpromising.[44]

All unite in most affectionate love with

your ever fondly attached Mother in Christ

M. C. McAuley

Autograph fragments: Silver Spring; and photostats: Dublin, Mercy

contains the address: "Mrs. Warde, Convent of Sisters of Mercy, Carlow," and the postmarks: Dublin "MR 13, 1838" and "Carlow, MR 14, 1838." Catherine usually used side 4 of a folded piece of stationery for the cover—that is, the place for the address after the whole sheet was folded down to letter size. These two fragments have been a conundrum for previous editors as well. Neumann inserts paragraph two in a letter dated March 29, 1841 (321), although the autograph passage does not appear to be a cut-out part of that autograph letter. Bolster treats paragraph two as a separate fragment (214), and presents paragraphs one and three, in reverse order, as fragmentary parts of the same letter, dated "c. 13 March 1838" (54). The key point of my arrangement is that paragraphs one and two are on the front and back of the same autograph fragment, and the address and postmarks are on the back of paragraph three and the closing. **37** Catherine is undoubtedly speaking about the new branch house in Booterstown scheduled to be opened some time in the spring or early summer of 1838. **38** Mary Cecilia Marmion. **39** Mary Clare Augustine Moore, the artist. **40** That is, the visitation of the sick poor in various slum areas of Dublin such as Townsend Street and Bull Alley. **41** In a few days Catherine will send Mary Cecilia Marmion and Mary Elizabeth Moore (see Letter 83) to Carlow to attend, in her place, the episcopal consecration on Sunday, March 25, and the reception ceremony on Monday, March 26, and to assist the Carlow community beforehand. **42** Mary Ursula Frayne returned to Dublin with Mary Cecilia Marmion and Mary Elizabeth Moore after the ceremonies in Carlow. She was then chosen to be a member of the branch house in Booterstown. **43** The chapel of the new convent in Carlow was not consecrated until April 2, 1839. Perhaps Catherine McAuley assumed that the building and its occupancy would move along more quickly, and that the consecration would be her nearest opportunity to visit Carlow. As it turned out, her next visit was nine months away, when, en route home to Dublin from Limerick, she stopped in Carlow for a reception ceremony there on December 10, 1838. **44** No wonder she was "overwhelmed" (see paragraph one). What was "very bad" about the Charity Sermon on February 18, especially if James Maher preached it, was probably not the sermon itself, but rather the attendance and hence the collection of money on which the community depended so heavily for its work in the House of Mercy. The bazaar would not take place until after Easter (April 15), but Catherine may have been assessing the "unpromising" quality and quantity of the goods that would be for sale, and the small number of raffle tickets already sold.

81. To Sister M. Frances Warde
Carlow

Convent, Baggot Street
March 24, 1838

My Dear Sister Mary Frances

I am sure you and the Sisters are very anxious to hear of our dear Sr. Aloysius.[45] Thanks be to God the feverish symptoms have passed away, though she continued heavy and ill all Thursday. She was up a little yesterday and now only complains of weakness. She did not sleep till after four this morning, and seems still to be apprehensive—but please God, there is no fear. I trust my poor Sr. M. C.[46] has been pretty well, and taking great care to avoid cold & hunger, as desired. The weather here has been fine though frosty. I suppose it is milder in Carlow. I trust the ceremony will go on very nicely. We all pray for dear Sister Maher.[47] I have charged the travellers to bring me a full account—and hope to hear all on Tuesday.[48]

Mr. Bacon was here yesterday about our going to Booterstown. [49] There is a good room in which the caretaker's family have lived all the winter. I intend to put Sister Mary C. and Sr. Ursula in that.[50] Indeed every part is perfectly dry—it has been so long building.

I saw Sister Mary Teresa on Sunday last.[51] She desired a thousand loves to you. She is doing great good for the poor, thank God. I expect to find Sister Ursula very much improved from what I see of the effects of Carlow. Sister Mary Teresa would never tire speaking of the instruction and advantages she received there. She is uneasy about her young brother who writes—very dissatisfied, etc., etc. She hopes you will advise him. His family are in Dublin. It would be better for him to write to his eldest sister. Poor Sr. M. Teresa can do nothing now that she cannot see him.[52]

---

45 Mary Aloysius Scott, who had professed her vows on February 21, 1838, suffered from weakness of the lungs, an ailment that would claim her life six years later. Perhaps the illness Catherine here reports was related to this condition.   46 Mary Cecilia Marmion had arrived in Carlow for the ceremonies on March 25 and 26.   47 Mary Maher was scheduled to receive the Mercy habit at the reception ceremony in Carlow on March 26, taking the name Mary Francis de Sales, though she was usually called simply Mary de Sales.   48 Catherine McAuley expects that Cecilia Marmion, Elizabeth Moore, and Ursula Frayne will return to Dublin on Tuesday, March 27.   49 Mr. Bacon was the agent of Mrs. Barbara Verschoyle, now deceased, who had been the widow of Richard Verschoyle, an agent of Lord Fitzwilliam. At her death she bequeathed funds for the building and endowment, at twenty guineas a year, of a convent in Booterstown in the hope that the religious community who would live there would continue her husband's and her own charitable work among the poor Catholic tenants on Lord Fitzwilliam's property.   50 At this point Catherine intends that Mary Cecilia Marmion and Mary Ursula Frayne will both live in Booterstown, with Cecilia serving as superior of the branch house. However, in time, Ursula Frayne was appointed superior in Booterstown, and Cecilia Marmion returned to Baggot Street.   51 Mary Teresa White was now superior of the branch house in Kingstown.   52 Mary Teresa White's brother in Carlow was probably Matthew Esmonde White, MD, who in the 1836 *Dublin Directory* is listed as practicing in Wexford (128), the Whites' original home city, but the 1839 *Dublin Directory* lists him as serving at the Lunatic Asylum, Carlow (152). Since Teresa was in Kingstown now, no longer in Carlow as

I trust I shall hear you are quite well. Remember me affectionately to all, particularly Sister Mary Joseph.[53] I heard you are likely to get another Sister soon. Mrs. Carpenter told me. The passengers on the stage coaches are bringing a description of the new Convent in all directions. I hear of it constantly.

God bless and preserve you and all with you, my very Dear old child.

M. C. McAuley

The character of your Bishop is most amiable.[54]

Autograph: Silver Spring

---

she had been for some months, she was not in a position to help him.   53 Mary Josephine Trennor. 54 Catherine McAuley speaks encouragingly about Francis Haly, the new bishop of Kildare and Leighlin, residing in Carlow. While the Carlow Annals is discreet in its comments about the working relations of Frances Warde and Dr. Haly, Mary Austin Carroll suggests that some tension may have existed between them. In speaking of the departure of the new foundation from Carlow to Pittsburgh, Pennsylvania in 1843, she notes that Dr. Haly requested Frances Warde to return to Carlow in two years, even though "it was well known that personally she was no favorite with him" (*Leaves* 4: 281). See also Catherine McAuley's encouragement of Frances's confidence in his opinion in Letter 108. Perhaps to Frances Warde, who had known the kindness of Dr. Edward Nolan, no one could seem fit to replace him.

April–August 1838

The spring and summer of 1838 brought new concerns to Catherine McAuley: the illness of Frances Warde in Carlow; an unsuccessful bazaar at Baggot Street, "very unlike past days"; the Kingstown lawsuit settled against her in the amount of £375; the decision to use an unexpected legacy to build a commercial laundry at Baggot Street, as a means of training and employing the large number of young women in the House of Mercy; the death on May 25 of Dr. Patrick Coleman, a vicar general of the Dublin archdiocese, who had tried, even in his waning health, to resolve the chaplaincy issue on her behalf; the opening of the branch house in Booterstown, "an additional weight on my mind"; the minimally satisfactory settlement of the chaplaincy controversy; the recurrence of her gum disease; and the decision to establish a new foundation of Sisters of Mercy in Limerick in September, the first new foundation in a year.

In the letters of this period, Catherine remembers the road the Sisters of Mercy have travelled since 1831 and the unfailing providence of God that has accompanied their journey, as well as the human instruments of that providential help. As she writes to Andrew Fitzgerald in Carlow on July 3: "I never can forget all the animating lively hope that you created in my mind when we were rising out of nothing" (Letter 92). In her mind the community is still an inadequate resource before the severe and beckoning needs of the poor: "We are very near a Stop—I should say, a full Stop—feet and hands are numerous enough, but the heads are nearly gone." Yet she will go forward to Limerick, asking only of Frances Warde, her "very dear old child": "Get all the prayers you can for me—that I may get through this new business as well as I can" (Letter 94).

Catherine McAuley was now almost sixty years old. There were seven postulants to be guided at Baggot Street; her always dependable aide, Teresa Carton, was ill and needed to be temporarily relieved of her duties; and the community was receiving "endless" invitations to establish new foundations elsewhere in Ireland. All of Catherine's executive management skills were called into play, but what claims attention in the letters of these months is not primarily her organizational ability, but her gratitude for the help she received and her tender affection for her sisters and the poor women in the House of Mercy.

82. To Sister M. Frances Warde   Convent, Baggot Street
Carlow   April 9, 1838

My Dear Sister Mary Frances

I feel very grateful indeed for Mr. Maher's kindness in writing to me—but afflicted to find such powerful remedies necessary for you. Thank God, Mr. M. says you are better, and I confidently hope that the approaching season and your delightful situation will soon quite restore you.

Our dear Teresa Carton is much better, Sister Cecilia[1] very delicate, but we must live and die between Baggot St., Booterstown and Kingstown. No Sister can go to Carlow who is not to remain there—they get too fond of all that is there. My poor Sister M. T. White will never like any place so much.[2]

We are likely to have the long desired public laundry built this season. Through the Providence of God and the kindness of Mr. O'Hanlon we have got a legacy nearly equal to the expense. What a comfort if I am permitted to see some secure means of supporting our poor women & children established, not to be entirely depending on daily collections which are so difficult to keep up. We would soon have a valuable laundry as the neighbourhood is so good.[3]

I look forward with joy & happiness to the time when I hope to see you.

Remember me respectfully to the Clergymen I have the pleasure to know— and most affectionately to all the Sisters.

Believe me always your fondly attached
M. C. McAuley

Let me soon have a letter from your own dear self. Mr. Carroll was surprised to hear you were ill—he thought you looked so well.[4] Sr. Elizabeth was delighted with the Convent.[5] She says it will be a real trap—that it is quite irresistible. You would wonder how much it is spoken of—it is said to be beautiful.

It is very gratifying to hear you are to have the comfort of it so soon. Mr. Maher says the end of June. You will be all making a holy preparation for that happy day, to draw down the blessing of Heaven—by the regular observance of all regulations—and a salutary cautious fear of every departure from rule & observances. Then God will make it His own and love to dwell amongst you.

May every blessing be with you. How I should rejoice to find your Institute excel in every way the poor old Mother House.

Autograph: Chicago

1 Mary Cecilia Marmion.   2 Catherine only half means this claim about Carlow, for she will later send Mary Aloysius Scott there for her health. Mary Teresa (Amelia) White had indeed grown fond of Carlow during her months there in 1837; however, in 1840 she became the founding superior of Galway, and in 1855 moved on to found a new community in Clifden, on the western coast of Connemara.   3 Mary Clare Augustine Moore claims that in 1838 "a legacy of £1000 was bequeathed to the Institute, and Foundress resolved to build the laundry, hoping that the labour of the inmates might be able to render the House of Mercy self-supporting, as the closing of the chapel had so greatly curtailed our resources" ("Memoir," in Sullivan, *Catherine McAuley* 212).   4 Mr. Carroll is probably Thomas Carroll, then a curate at St. Andrew's, Westland Row.   5 Mary Elizabeth Moore had been in Carlow for the reception ceremony of Mary de Sales Maher on March 26, 1838.

83. **To the Reverend John Hamilton**   [Convent, Baggot Street]
                                                                  April 11, 1838

Dear Reverend Sir

I have received a most satisfactory letter from Catherine.

She begs me to send the enclosed to you[6] and to assure you of her gratitude & prayers.

Dear Reverend Sir, respectfully, etc., etc.

M. C. McAuley

Autograph: Dublin Diocese, Murray Papers AB3/34/15, no. 12

84. **To the Reverend John Hamilton**   Cheltenham
                                                                  April 6, 1838
                                                              8 St. James's Square

Dear Revd. Sir

Pardon the liberty I take in troubling you with this note, but as Madam O'Connor requested of me to leave word with you when I would get a situation, and as I am in the situation I was speaking to you about in Dublin, I will feel now obliged to you if you let her know that I like my situation very well and am very comfortable in it. I know she will be very glad to hear of it, for she was always anxious for my welfare, and also if you [would] be kind enough to let the Revd. Mr. Murphy of Denmark Street know the same.[7] By doing so you will ever oblige

your most humble and most obedient servant

Catherine Divine

Autograph: Dublin Diocese, Hamilton Papers P1/36/1, no. 150

85. **To Sister M. Frances Warde**   [c. April 25, 1838][8]
     Carlow

My Dearest Sister Mary Frances

Mr. Maher and Dr. Fitzgerald give me every hope that you will soon be quite well, please God. I look forward with joy to the time of your chapel being blessed, as I trust we shall then meet.

---

6 The letter from Catherine Divine to John Hamilton is Letter 84. Presumably she was a former resident in the House of Mercy.   7 Madam O'Connor—apparently an acquaintance of John Hamilton—has not been identified. A Miss O'Connor operated a "seminary for young ladies" on Usher's Quay (*Dublin Directory* [1836], 210). "Revd. Mr. Murphy" is evidently James Murphy, OP, a member of the Dominican community in charge of the Church of Saint Dominick, Denmark Street (*Irish Catholic Directory* [1837] 154). Presumably Catherine Divine is writing from London.   8 There is no date or postmark on this letter, but since Catherine discusses the Bazaar, which always took place shortly after Easter, and since Easter was April 15 in 1838, the letter was probably written in late April.

The Bazaar, all summed up—after expenses—we will have about forty five pounds, very unlike past days. Mrs. Sullivan[9] has given us up, and almost all the Protestants. I am told there were not ten Protestants in the room.[10] Mr. Maher[11] the best purchaser—every one tormenting him. Poor Sister Gertrude[12] made a carpet 5 yards square –which cost us £10—cloth cut in various colours & patterns. One ticket only was sold. I suppose we are done with Bazaars.

Remember me affectionately to dear Sister Trennor[13] and all the good children. Dr. Fitzgerald gives a description of your little Cath[erine] that exceeds all we ever had. I hope Mary goes on as you wish.[14]

Dr. Murphy[15] will not let them have a Lay Sister in Cork, though Sr. M. Clare has one long in view—a convert and, she says, most desirable.

Sister Mary J. Warde[16] is very anxious to hear of her brother & family. I think you got a letter.

God bless you, my Dear Sr. M. F., and send you every comfort and restore you to health.

Your ever attached
M. C. M.

Autograph: Silver Spring

86. To Sister M. Frances Warde [Baggot Street]
Carlow [April 1838]

My Dear Sr. M. F.[17]

I this moment received a letter directed "Mrs. Warde, Convent of the Sisters of Mercy, Rutland Street, Dublin." I can forward it tomorrow, by a person

9 Mrs. Sullivan is likely the wife of Cornelius Sullivan of Mount Street, the estate agent for the Earl of Pembroke from whom Catherine McAuley had leased the property on Baggot Street. 10 Roland Burke Savage notes that beginning in April 1832, the annual bazaars in aid of the House of Mercy on Baggot Street excited considerable support among women of the Protestant nobility and upper class residing in Dublin. He cites contemporary newspaper articles that list dozens of patronesses of these charity events which were generally held in Morrison's Hotel, Dawson Street, or in the Rotunda at the northern end of Sackville Street, present day O'Connell Street (157–61). However, by 1838 fashionable interest in these occasions had apparently waned—just when the financial needs of the House of Mercy were most severe, owing to the loss of income from the chapel collections and to the great increase in the number of women moving in and out of the House, now regularly about sixty at any given time. 11 James Maher, of Carlow. 12 Mary Gertrude (Mary) Jones of Worcester, England, had professed her vows on February 11, 1834. She will die about a year after this letter, on May 9, 1839. 13 Mary Josephine Trennor, one of the first members of the Carlow community. 14 The reference to "little Cath[erine]" cannot be firmly identified. It may be Catherine Meagher, a widow, who entered the Carlow community in May 1837 and received the habit on November 14, 1837, taking the name Mary Catherine. "Mary" is probably Mary Maher who had received the habit on March 26, 1838, taking the name Mary de Sales. 15 Dr. John Murphy, bishop of Cork. 16 Mary Josephine Warde, Frances's sister in Cork. 17 This brief note to Frances Warde is simply a message written on the inside flap of a sheet of

returning to Cork. I am not surprised you should make some mistakes, writing so much just after your ceremony, before your mind rested itself.

[M. C. McAuley]

Autograph: Silver Spring

87. To Charles Cavanagh, Esq.

Mrs. C. McAuley's Account with [James] Nugent[18]
9 May 1838

Judgment debt	£360. 1. 10½
Taxed costs	15. 13. 4½
	£375. 15. 5

46 L[owe]r Gardiner St.
May 9, 1838

Dear Sir
    Above you have the particulars in Mrs. McAuley's case.

Yours,
J[ohn] Martin

Typescript of autograph: Dublin, Mercy

---

paper used as a cover. Presumably Catherine McAuley forwarded to Cork the mis-addressed letter which Frances had intended to send to her sister Mary Josephine Warde at the convent on Rutland Street, Cork. The cover addressed to "Mrs. Warde, Sisters of Mercy, Carlow" contains no post-marks; it and whatever contents it contained were hand-delivered. Thus the date of the note is uncertain. The reference to Frances Warde's recent "ceremony" may be to the reception ceremony in Carlow on March 26, 1838. Bolster dates this letter "c. 5 April 1841," but the evidence for an 1841 date is no greater than for an 1838 date. 18 This account furnished to Charles Cavanagh, solicitor for the Baggot Street community, by John Martin, solicitor for James Nugent, the builder of the poor school in Kingstown, records the outcome of the lawsuit brought against Catherine McAuley by James Nugent. The court found Catherine liable for the full cost of remodelling the coach house and stable on the Kingstown property into school rooms for the poor girls in the neigh-borhood—even though Bartholomew Sheridan, the parish priest, had assured her that the expense would be covered by a special parish collection or by a grant application to the Board of National Education. In addition to the £375 noted here, Catherine had already voluntarily contributed £50 at the beginning of the building project, a goodwill gesture on her part that was interpreted as acknowledging her accountability for the project.

88. To Sister M. Frances Warde   Convent of Mercy

Carlow   May 15, 1838

My own Dearest Child and Sister

We have been every day looking for franks[19]—but I cannot wait any longer to write to you. We had some days of real summer which had the most beneficial effect on our Sisters Cecilia and Teresa.[20] Sharp cold returned yesterday, and they have felt the change already. We had sleet this morning. I trust it continues mild in Carlow, and I have no doubt of your perfect recovery. I expect, please God, to hear that you have improved very much—you may be sure I am very anxious to get a letter from you.

I did hope to have our weak ones in Booterstown this week, but am now afraid to venture, though it is very sheltered and quite dry—and Father Doyle very pressing.[21] We are too full here for hot weather and expect two more. Thus we go on, my Dear Sister Frances, flourishing in the very midst of the Cross—more than a common share of which has latterly fallen to my lot, thanks be to God. I humbly trust it is the Cross of Christ. I endeavour to make it in some way like to His—by silence.

Dr. Fitzgerald was exceedingly kind and affectionate to me when in Town, and really felt like a sincere friend, for he did not care to whom he spoke, or what remarks were made. He exclaimed privately and publickly against what he conceived unjust and unkind. Indeed he gave me great comfort, for while he condemned the proceeding—he reasoned with me so as to produce quiet of mind and heart. Believe me, there is not the smallest dimunition [diminution] yet in his rational powers or discernment—though they may not be always equally exercised.[22]

I hope you hear from our dear Sister M. J.[23] sometimes. She writes to me when she can do so by a private source—and each note or letter is more expressive of affection and gratitude than the former, which is consoling indeed as it shews her happiness increases—thanks be to God.

---

19 Franks were prepaid envelopes or covers that permitted the contents to be posted free of further charge. When the reforms proposed by Sir Rowland Hill in 1837–1838 were instituted some time in the late 1830s, inland postal rates in Ireland were determined by weight at the rate of a penny for each half ounce (no longer also by distance and the number of enclosures) and were paid in advance by the sender rather than by the recipient (Hemmeon 60). Postage to Carlow cost sixpence in 1839 (*Dublin Directory* [1839] 58). **20** Both Mary Cecilia Marmion and Teresa Carton were ill in the spring of 1838. **21** A new branch house of the Dublin community was scheduled to be opened in Booterstown in May or June. The house and an annual grant of 20 guineas had been given for a religious community by Mrs. Barbara Verschoyle, widow of Richard Verschoyle, before her own death in 1837. Patrick Doyle, parish priest in Booterstown, was anxious to see the convent occupied, but cold weather made Catherine McAuley hesitate to place infirm sisters so close to the Irish Sea. She anticipated that Booterstown would replace Kingstown as a place for convalescing sisters, should she be forced to close the Kingstown convent. **22** Dr. Andrew Fitzgerald, OP, Catherine's faithful friend at Carlow College, was now seventy-five years old. **23** Mary Josephine Warde, in Cork.

I scarcely ever felt more surprised than on reading a letter from Sister Mary Teresa to Sister Mary Clare on Geraldine entering the Cork Convent—indeed, if you saw it you would say she improved in Carlow.[24] Every Sr. here who heard it was astonished—Sister de Pazzi[25] should have it in her hand to believe it was written as I read it. I regretted very much that the packet was going before I could shew it to her Mamma. I have been so often severe to her on that subject—that I lost no time thanking her for this *first* creditable production. She frequently has said since her return that she felt considerably enlightened and improved in mind—by her stay in Carlow. She is proving it—is never troublesome, complaining of anything or pressing me to go to Kingstown—and all with her are most happy, even my perverse Teresa Byrn.[26]

The noviciate duties are regularly carried on. I fear poor Jane Sausse will not be able to remain. She often looks like poor Maria—quite blue. Her mother made a small settlement on her this time—or as we term it now—*"settled for the Bread & Butter."*[27]

For Booterstown we have marked out M. Cecilia, Superior, Ursula, J. Sausse, Lucy, Teresa. Sr. Scott will manage the Collection business & the ser-

---

24 Elizabeth Constantia Agnew, an English convert from London and the author of the novel *Geraldine*, entered the Mercy convent in Cork on April 4, 1838, at the age of forty. Two volumes of her novel were published before she entered; the third and final volume was written while she was in the convent and published in 1839. Her entrance into the Sisters of Mercy, together with Maria Taylor, also from Bermondsey, London, created a stir of publicity which amused Catherine McAuley. Catherine is here referring to Elizabeth by the name of the title character in her novel. **25** Mary de Pazzi Delany, one of the senior members of the Baggot Street community. **26** This paragraph does not lend itself to easy interpretation. Evidently, Mary Teresa White in Kingstown had heard about the entrance of Elizabeth Agnew and had written about it either to Mary Clare Augustine Moore in Dublin (whom Catherine often called simply "Mary Clare") with the intention that her letter or comments be forwarded to Cork, or directly to Mary Clare Moore in Cork. She may even have encouraged Catherine to read the letter before it was delivered or posted. If in these sentences Catherine is speaking about Mary Teresa (Amelia) White (who I assume is the author of the letter about Elizabeth Agnew), her criticism of Mary Teresa—whether of her letter-writing skills or of her behavior—is most unusual. Mary Clare Augustine Moore claims that Catherine once said to her: "'Of all the sisters Sr. M. Teresa has most of my spirit and I trust more to her guiding the Institute as I wish than to any other Sister'" ("Memoir," in Sullivan, *Catherine McAuley* 212). Perhaps Catherine was speaking only of sisters then in the Baggot Street community. Apparently, Catherine read the letter, or the portion about Elizabeth Agnew, to the Baggot Street community after she received it for posting and before it was posted in the mail packet to Mary Clare Moore in Cork, but too late to show it to Mary Teresa's mother, who lived in Dublin. These sentences are clearly not about Mary Teresa (Catherine) White, whose indecisiveness gave Catherine reason to be uneasy, but about Mary Teresa (Amelia) White, then the local superior in Kingstown. Perhaps what is at stake in Catherine's sentences is nothing more than Teresa's improved writing skills, enhanced by her months in the Carlow community which included several competent writers. **27** Because of very poor health, neither Maria nor Jane Sausse was able to remain in the convent. Catherine McAuley often expresses her own sorrow at their disappointment. The "small settlement" Mrs. Sausse made was a contribution toward the cost of her daughter Jane's living expenses. Maria Sausse had evidently left the community by this date.

vants.[28] Teresa must go off duty except walking a little in good air. Little Sr. Teresa Mary is quite changed. She is, I may say, strong and most useful— has the whole House on her shoulders—Infirmarian—and cell-regulator—quite a dear valuable little Sister. She has also Mrs. Duffy—who is like a part of herself, is every where she is.[29]

All goes on well in Tullamore. Miss C., now Mrs. French, has not fulfilled her engagement for Charleville, perhaps she may—but they will not give up while her five hundred pounds lasts, which has not been touched yet.[30] I have seen a lady from Charleville who says Sister[s] Angela and Delaney[31] were very ill after Lent. I suppose there was imprudent fasting to which Sister Dunne is much inclined, you know.

I did hope our Laundry would have been commenced by this, but no— delays innumerable. We are leaving it to Mr. Mullins—by Dr. Fitzgerald's particular advice —though higher than others.[32] What would I not go through to see it at full work. We have got all information on the matter. You would be surprised to know all that can be earned by this means. New persons coming into the neighbourhood every day. We are asked to take washing. Since the Townsend St. Asylum was removed to Donny Brooke,[33] we have constant application. Yesterday it went to my heart to send away a large parcel which would have paid well. In one Institution they earned 7 hundred pounds in 14 months, clear of all expenses. We must give up all the garden for drying ground & grass plot—but there can be a walk round it. God grant it may be soon done.[34]

---

28 Catherine anticipated that Mary Cecilia Marmion would be the local superior in Booterstown. Eventually Mary Ursula Frayne was given that responsibility. Jane Sausse, Mary "Lucy" Teresa Breen, and Teresa Carton, who was ill at the time, were also slated for Booterstown. Teresa Carton's work of managing the material needs of the House of Mercy and the daily door-to-door collection of money and goods to support the women in the House was to be temporarily handled by Mary Aloysius Scott. The "servants" were simply the residents of the House of Mercy who answered the door and performed other household chores.   29 Mary Teresa (Catherine) White—often called Teresa Mary, or "Teresa the Less" to distinguish her from Mary Teresa (Amelia) White—was evidently a favorite of Mrs. Duffy, a long-term and somewhat frail resident of the House of Mercy whom Catherine McAuley had befriended.   30 Mary Clanchy, the benefactress of the Charleville community, had recently married a Mr. Arthur French. Her marriage raised doubts that the annual portions of the £500 which she had promised the Charleville community would actually be granted to them.   31 Mary Angela Dunne was the superior of the Charleville community, and Mary Joseph (Alicia) Delaney, part of the founding community in Charleville in October 1836. In 1839 she returned to the Baggot Street community.   32 Bernard Mullins, Esq., lived at 1 Fitzwilliam Square South and was a partner in the architectural firm of Henry, Mullins, and MacMahon (*Dublin Directory* [1839] 670). On the advice of Andrew Fitzgerald, he was chosen to design the public laundry and other additions to the House of Mercy, which were to be joined to the Baggot Street convent and front on Herbert Street.   33 The Townsend Street Asylum for Penitent Women, managed by the Irish Sisters of Charity since 1833, had moved to its new location in a country mansion known as Donnybrook Castle in 1837 (Rushe 52–53).   34 Catherine McAuley's hopes for the financial success of the commercial laundry, as a means of supporting the women and girls in the House of Mercy, never really materialized. As Clare Augustine Moore notes in her "Memoir": "the expense of the building greatly exceeded her calculations, and the building itself was a continual worry.

Remember me most affectionately to all the dear Sisters—and respectfully to Dr. F., Fr. Maher, etc., etc., etc.—all you wish I should remember. Believe me at all times and under all circumstances, the very same fondly attached

M. C. McAuley

We had heard of poor Mr. Burke—he arrived safe.[35]

I must stop now—Sr. Elizabeth is taking a memorandum of my writing across.[36]

Autograph: Silver Spring

89. **To Sister M. Frances Warde**   [Late May 1838][37]
    Carlow

Not fit to appear

Perplexed and weary—out of conceit with everything—I sit down to talk to my own dear old companion and affectionate child. Your packet was most joyfully received, and your letter read again and again—as a solace and comfort which God sent me. To hear you are recovering was the best and happiest communication I could receive, though I did not for a moment let myself think otherwise.

Dear Teresa Carton continues most delicate, the least breeze brings a return of the cough. She is taken from every occupation—and is to try Booterstown

---

Neither were the returns when it was built at all equal to her expectations; in fact, for long enough after her death they were miserably insignificant" (Sullivan, *Catherine McAuley* 212). **35** Daniel Burke, OSF, the former and much loved chaplain of the House of Mercy, had gone to southern Africa, accompanying Patrick Griffith, OP, vicar apostolic of the Cape of Good Hope. According to the *Irish Catholic Directory* for 1839, they arrived in Cape Town on April 14, 1838 (291). **36** Mary Elizabeth Moore was now living at Baggot Street, after serving for a time as local superior in Kingstown. The nearest postal receiving station to the Baggot Street convent was at 39 Lower Baggot Street (*Dublin Directory* [1839] 55). **37** This undated letter, which also has no salutation or return address, is a long, private postscript to a letter to Frances Warde that is probably no longer extant. The Sisters of Mercy of Portland, Maine, who possess the autograph, tentatively dated it "February 1840," but that estimate cannot be correct, given several datable references within the postscript itself: plans for opening the Booterstown convent in late May or June 1838 (see earlier letters); the death of Dr. Patrick Coleman on May 25, 1838; Frances Delaney's joining the Charleville community in May 1838; Elinor Cowley's entrance into the Baggot Street community on May 6, 1838; and preliminary plans for the new foundation in Limerick (which took place in September 1838). In resolving the conflict between Elinor Cowley's entrance "yesterday" (May 6, according to the Dublin Register) and Catherine's having heard "this moment" of the death of Dr. Coleman (May 25, 1838, according to the *Catholic Directory* for 1839), I have chosen to date the postscript "[Late May 1838]," on the grounds that the death day of Dr. Coleman is certain, whereas Catherine McAuley may be imprecise about the day of Elinor Cowley's entrance, and the Register may also be inaccurate (as is occasionally the case in the early years). Dr. Coleman's death day, May 25, is also confirmed by the memorial plaque in St. Michan's church. Thus the letter was written in May 1838, not in February 1840.

early next week, provided there is no blast. You would be surprised to see how uneasy Mr. O'Hanlon is about her. He has just lost his favorite sister of decline—and he perceives the alteration from week to week in my poor Teresa. Sister Mary Cecilia not worse, very little better—all the rest well.

I have not seen them in Kingstown for a long time, cannot go—or at least I think so. The thought of Booterstown is an additional weight on my mind[38]—I have no happiness in it—& endless difficulty in who will go, etc.—and, animating circumstance except the earnest hope that God may receive some small portion of glory in the help that will be given to His poor.

I have this moment heard of the death of Doctor Coleman—and indeed I have reason to be heartily sorry.[39] Doctor Blake mentioned to him how much I was afflicted at the arrangement making as to Chaplain. Though he was then exceedingly weak and the weather most severe, he came here several times—went from me to Doctor Meyler—and used all the means in his power to have it according to our wishes—and when he could not succeed wrote me a feeling, fatherly letter. I can never forget his great tenderness and most Christian manner of acting. He desired me to regard him as a particular friend—and immediately he is called away. May God receive him into the Glory of Heaven. His death was quite sudden at his sister's, where he intended to remain for some time.

Our Mass is celebrated very regularly every day, and the Confessions pretty well attended to—but I never will feel reconciled to it—however we are perfectly silent.[40]

I have just got a letter from Cork by a Clergyman. Sister M. Clare says—"we go on Piano—Pianio".[41] They have commenced visiting the Jail. She says

---

38 Catherine McAuley actually appears to have written "The thoughts of Booterstown is ...," but this verb agreement problem is no doubt a slip of the pen.   39 Dr. Patrick Coleman was at the time of his death vicar general and dean of the chapter of the Dublin diocese. He was also parish priest of St. Michan's. The *Irish Catholic Directory* for 1839 lists his death day as May 25, 1838 (284). Catherine McAuley's gratitude for his solicitude in the chaplaincy controversy with Dr. Walter Meyler is fully evident in this postscript. Following Dr. Coleman's death, Dr. Meyler, who was already a vicar general of the diocese, became the dean of the Dublin chapter, a fact which illustrates Dr. Daniel Murray's regard for him and highlights the sensitivities involved in the chaplaincy dispute.   40 Evidently, by the date of this letter, a curate from St. Andrew's—though not the same curate each day—celebrated daily Mass at Baggot Street and heard the confessions of the residents of the House of Mercy and the school children, in an arrangement which still did not satisfy Catherine McAuley. The *Irish Catholic Directory* for 1838 lists no chaplain for the House of Mercy (291–92); the *Directory* for 1839 lists "Rev. G[regory] Lynch," a curate at St. Andrew's, as chaplain (181–82). Although no precise and uniform contemporary evidence of when and how the chaplaincy controversy was settled appears to be available, it is reasonable to assume that an unsatisfactory arrangement, with the tension surrounding it, continued into 1839, the *Directory* listing notwithstanding, and possibly into 1840. Apparently Catherine McAuley had to agree to a higher salary for the chaplain (the precise figure is not known), but the regularity of a distinct chaplain, not the salary, was always her primary concern. Carroll (*Life* 338), Burke Savage (222–32), and Degnan (264) all comment, sometimes in conflicting ways, on the chaplaincy situation, but they do not cite any sources for their claims, beyond the references in Catherine McAuley's own letters. In Letter 90, Catherine uses an unusually strong word for her feelings about the situation: "bitterness."   41 Catherine clearly writes "Piano—Pianio," though this may not have

Mr. Croke of Charleville called to them in great spirits—said Lord Cork had given a fine piece of ground for a Convent. We hear Miss *Fanny* Delaney has joined them. Sr. Angela did not consult me you may be sure. I should fear very much, it will not turn out well. Sister de Pazzi cannot conceive how she could ever bend to Sister Angela as a Superior—it is quite a puzzle to her. I trust in God we are not going to have any disedification introduced amongst the Sisters of our order—but I certainly feel uneasy on this subject.[42]

We got a merry little Sister yesterday—one of the Cowleys—very musical.[43] We have not one who appears doubtful, of Novices or Postulants—7 Postulants now.

I wrote so much to you lately that I suppose I will say the same things again. All unite in affectionate love to you. Tell the dear Sisters I felt most grateful for their kind notes and will answer them soon. They were great amusement and comfort to me.

Mr. Scott promised to take this, we expect him soon. I am in a kind of fear lest the summons to Limerick should come in the way of that to Carlow. I trust it will not.

Your ever fondly attached
M. C. McAuley

I have just heard that Mr. Scott will not go to Carlow till Wednesday so this will be an old letter—he waits for Doctor Kinsella.[44]

A small parcel came here for Sister Mary Catherine. The Books are not fit for her present state. Some very objectionable—poetry. You could not venture to read it over, so when I take all that out I will send the rest which is amusing. The sugar sticks are for her.[45]

Autograph: Portland

---

been Clare Moore's spelling. As a borrowed musical term, used in the context of the progress in Cork, the expression may mean "softly—and more softly." As is seen in other letters about the Cork community, John Murphy, bishop of Cork, exercised considerable control over what was permissible, and Clare Moore, always patient and cautious at this stage in her development (she was now twenty-four), had to learn even greater patience and diplomacy.   42 Frances Delaney is not listed in the Charleville Register of professed sisters, although Carroll says that she "persevered at St. Joseph's [Charleville] with great edification to all" (*Life* 302). The 1838 "Annals" in the *Irish Catholic Directory* for 1839 notes that on "[October] 30. Miss Delany, formerly a Protestant, took the white veil at the Convent of the Sisters of Mercy, Charleville" (299). In Letter 98, Catherine McAuley writes: "Miss Delaney, I believe, is much changed. She was quite satisfactory when I saw her [in September 1838] and is to be received on the 29th [of October 1838]."   43 According to the Dublin Register, Elinor Cowley entered the Baggot Street community on May 6, 1838. She received the habit on January 21, 1839, taking the name Mary Veronica.   44 William Kinsella was bishop of Ossory and resided in Kilkenny, the home of Mary Aloysius (Elizabeth) Scott, whose parents were Barnaby and Elizabeth Scott. The Mr. Scott referred to here may be her father.   45 The parcel was for Mary Catherine (Kate) Meagher who had received the habit in Carlow on November 14, 1837. Apparently Catherine McAuley, herself a lover of poetry, found some of the poems in the books unsuitable for a novice to read, and relieved Frances Warde of the task of expurgating the

90. To Sister M. Frances Warde   Convent, Booterstown
    Carlow   June 16, 1838

My Dearest Sister Mary Frances

    Yesterday I received your letter, which is dated the 3rd. The music was ready. Sister Mary Cecilia had it finished and is now quite annoyed, but as usual I was left to guess all about it. We have a sad practice of not mentioning in time what is to be forwarded, etc. I felt so mortified that you should be disappointed.

    I hurried out here to get poor Teresa into change of air. She is already evidently better, but is fretting so much for being taken from her employment that I fear the good effect will be lost. She has given me much uneasiness by the gloomy peevish manner she behaves every day since she came. The collection goes on just the same with Sister Aloysius—though I was alarmed enough—seeing how constantly she attended to it. She distressed me very much yesterday— I almost thought she was sorry to hear the collection children went on as usual—perhaps I was mistaken. Please God she will triumph over this human weakness—and I rejoice at the good which must result from her seeing that those things do not depend on any one in particular, but on the continuance of God's blessing.[46]

    This House is better than I expected. The cells are all uncomfortable—doors so exceedingly large and in the center of the wall—so that the head of [the] Bed would not fit at either side, and the window as large opposite the door.[47] The only way with room—is across—which scarcely leaves a pass at the foot—just like this

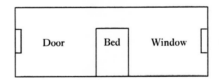

There is good ground for a garden, quite unmade. Mr. Ennis called[48] —to ask would the Sisters sing in the P[arish] Church. I left Sister M. Cecilia to do as

objectionable ones. This is the only recorded instance of Catherine's exercising any censorship over convent reading material. At least she spared the "sugar sticks"! **46** Apparently Teresa Carton, whom Catherine brought to Booterstown to improve her health, feared that others at Baggot Street might do her work there as well as she had done it. Sufficient evidence exists in Catherine's letters to suggest that Teresa was dependent on Catherine's affection and that she associated this affection with her own successful handling of various household tasks. **47** The Booterstown convent, which is still a Mercy convent, is situated on a slight hill just off a road heading due east to the town and the sea. The convent was opened in late May or early June 1838, and dedicated to Saint Anne on July 26, 1838. By mid 1838 Catherine McAuley had had enough experience of small convent bedrooms ("cells") to know where the bedroom door should be positioned for maximum convenience. The drawings in this letter attempt to replicate her own ink drawings in the autograph. **48** Dr. John Ennis, who had been a curate at St. Andrew's, Westland Row, Dublin, was appointed parish priest of Booterstown,

she pleases.[49] At present she is not well enough—the same complaint. My poor Teresa is coughing now. I am sure she has this cough more [than] 7 months—but not expectoration—her appetite is better, thank God.

I had a note from Sister Mary Joseph.[50] She says— "I have a packet ready for Carlow, but our english Sisters [*sic*] hearing of the long delay in the delivery of letters sent by Friends advises me to send it to London, and promises that it will reach Carlow sooner than by any other way that she hears of." Sr. M. J. always writes me most satisfactory notes. Dr. Murphy likes her very much—he has been in town.

Miss Fanny Delaney is gone to Charleville. Mr. Croke wrote to me to say Lord Cork had given some ground for a Convent, and that he will begin immediately. He mentioned M. D.'s[51] arrival.

They have commenced a Convent in Tullamore. Mr. Molloy, a very wealthy pious Catholic, has taken the House they are in for an Hospital. Their convent is to be joining the new school—and they are to have a passage to the Hospital through their present garden.[52] Such is the account Sister M. A.[53] gives me—to which she adds— "notwithstanding this prosperity, I am grey with care."

There is too much *caution* in Cork—to build in a hurry—but they have a very good residence for their number.

I trust your cells will not have too much door—and will have a good place for a Bed—which might have been here—had the doors been put to one end, thus

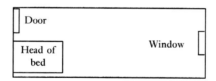

Blackrock, Stillorgan, Kilmacud, and Dundrum in 1838. He succeeded Patrick J. Doyle who "had commenced, and nearly completed, the Convent of the Sisters of Mercy in Booterstown, when in 1838, he was transferred to the Parish of St. Michan" in Dublin (Donnelly 3:112). Nicholas Donnelly further notes that "Two characteristic features stand out in all the work undertaken by Dr. Ennis; first his desire to establish efficient schools, and secondly the promotion of temperance" (3:113). In Letter 92, Catherine McAuley remarks: "Mr. Ennis is remarkably kind and anxious to do all in his power to promote our comfort. He seems to regret the past [when he was curate at St. Andrew's] and says if he lives seven years more it will be atoned for." **49** This sentence might seem to suggest that initially Mary Cecilia Marmion, who was an accomplished musician, was appointed superior in Booterstown, as Catherine McAuley had originally planned. However, Mary Ursula Frayne was, if not initially, subsequently appointed to that role. **50** The verb agreement problem in the next sentence is no doubt a slip of the pen as Catherine McAuley copies Mary Josephine Warde's note from Cork. **51** Miss Delaney's. **52** In addition to their first benefactor, Miss Elizabeth Pentony, Michael Molloy, a distiller, was a major benefactor of the Convent of Mercy in Tullamore. He "re-established the Tullamore distillery (Flanagan's) in 1829. In 1838 he laid the foundation of the [new] Mercy Convent in Tullamore" (Byrne 36). **53** Mary Ann Doyle, the superior of the Tullamore community.

in place of which we have great wide doors in the center exactly opposite a large window.

Mrs. Duffy is very bold. She has the hooping cough. This is a queer mixture—but she is just making a great noise. We brought her for change of air.

We are in the very midst of the Sandymount Patronesses—and feel it. Dr. Murphy is cast off—he came here and to Kingstown.[54] We have a majority of Bishops at all events. Take care you do not let this nonsense be subject to any eye but your own.

Pray fervently to God to take all bitterness from me. I can scarcely think of what has been done to me without resentment. May God forgive me and make me humble before he calls me into His presence.[55]

May He bless and protect you—and make you the Instrument of His glory—and may he prepare you to enter the new House with a Heart entirely devoted to Himself.[56]

[M. C. McAuley]

I went in to town—& forgot this letter.[57] I am so confused—and *never* dressed so neat and nice as *my Dear Darling Fanny* used to dress her *old* Mother. I am this moment in a fuss—at being obliged to appear in Disorder.

Autograph: West Hartford

---

54 The "Sandymount Patronesses," as Catherine McAuley identifies them, were Catholic lay women, many of them living in Sandymount or other areas south of Dublin, who supported the charitable endeavors of the Irish Sisters of Charity and Mary Aikenhead, their founder. No personal rivalry whatsoever appears to have existed between Mary Aikenhead and Catherine McAuley, but their lay and clerical supporters sometimes yielded to a certain party spirit especially where publicity or financial support was involved. The Sisters of Charity opened a new convent in Sandymount in 1831, in a house built for them by Mrs. Barbara Verschoyle, the same woman who, before her death in 1837, funded what was to become the Mercy convent in Booterstown. Already an invalid when she lived in Sandymount from 1831 to 1833, Mary Aikenhead inspired not only her sisters who worked in the poor school built by Mrs. Verschoyle and visited the sick poor tenants on the Fitzwilliam estate, but also numerous lay women who remained faithful supporters of the Sandymount works of mercy (Flanagan 114–17). A disagreement between Mary Aikenhead and John Murphy, bishop of Cork, over his desired measure of control over the Sisters of Charity in Cork, created tension between him and the Sisters of Charity, who were centrally governed from Dublin as a single religious congregation. This tension evidently spilled over to their supporters. Because each new foundation of the Sisters of Mercy was autonomous—i.e., not governed from Baggot Street—and had as its ecclesiastical superior the diocesan bishop, the potential for violation of the proper authority of the religious congregation was quite different, though not without its pitfalls.   55 The provocations to resentment which Catherine McAuley sought to resist were—as noted in previous letters—two-fold: the chaplaincy dispute with Dr. Walter Meyler and the Kingstown financial judgment against her, to which Bartholomew Sheridan, the parish priest, had abandoned her, reneging on his earlier assurances of financial assistance.   56 The new convent under construction in Carlow will not be occupied until July 2, 1839.   57 This letter is dated June 16, 1838, but the postmarks on the attached cover are Dublin "Ju[ne] 25, 1838" and Carlow "Ju[ne] 26, 1838."

91. To Catherine McAuley[58]   [Tullamore]
                                                       [Early July 1838]

My dear Reverend Mother

Knowing how anxious you will be to hear that our ceremony went on happily, I am anxious to give you an early account, lest the papers should get the start of me. At 2 o'clock, the procession entered the church which was awfully crowded, yet wonderful order and quiet prevailed. We had nothing to regret but your absence, which I felt the more, as I know how delighted you would be to hear the Objects of our Order so beautifully described in a sublime sermon preached by Very Rev. Dr. Curtis, Rector of Tullabeg College.[59] [I wish I could give you some idea of it.] His text was: "This is true religion: to visit the widow and the fatherless in their affliction, and to keep oneself unspotted from the world." Reviewing nearly every Order in the Church, he introduced [the Trappists, who were driven out of France, and to whom some Protestant gentlemen have given tracts of land so barren, that neither the avarice of the rich nor the misery of the poor could induce them to break the soil. He described the fertile appearance now presented where for ages no sound had been heard but the whistling of the wind, or the scream of the bird of prey. In that once desolate spot, a hundred voices now sing the praises of God. He described] at last the Order of Mercy for the Redemption of Captives, telling how its mem-

58 No autograph of this letter has been discovered. However, the letter is transcribed in the Tullamore Annals (26–28) and published in Carroll's *Life* (288–90). The text in the *Life* is longer than, but generally matches, the text of the Annals. Since this letter is one of the very few extant letters addressed *to* Catherine McAuley by a Sister of Mercy, it seems wise to include it in this edition. The additional phrases, sentences, and paragraphs that are presented in Carroll's text are included here in square brackets. Although the Tullamore text is in some sense the primary text because it was transcribed in the convent of the author of the letter, Mary Ann Doyle, it is entirely possible that the letter was copied into the Annals, in abbreviated form, after it was first seen in Carroll's *Life* which was published in 1866. The Annals themselves were recopied in 1875, according to the preface in the volume.   59 Tullabeg Seminary, located near Tullamore, was a boarding school operated by the Society of Jesus for boys ages seven to eleven. John Curtis, SJ, the rector of the seminary, proved to be a devoted friend of the Sisters of Mercy in Tullamore. The Tullamore Annals notes at length the many contributions of the Society of Jesus: "The Jesuits of Tullabeg shewed the most lively interest in this establishment from its very beginning and should be regarded as our first spiritual benefactors ... The Fathers often came to instruct the sisters both privately and publicly in the Retreats which they offered to give, sent them books of instructions which at that time were very rare, and even left written lectures which were most useful to the community, and served for its guidance for many a year ... It was usual for the Jesuit Fathers to leave the notes of their meditations, considerations and examens after them, which the sisters did not fail to copy out carefully, and thus leave a store for future generations. Thus we have in our library Retreats from the early Fathers of the Society of Jesus in Ireland, viz. Fathers Kenny, S. Leger, Curtis, Esmonde, Bracken, etc. The convent was scarcely a year founded when Rev. J. Curtis, Rector of Tullabeg, was appointed Extraordinary Confessor" (16–17). The reception ceremony described in this letter occurred on July 1, 1838: Mary Aloysius (Arabella) Deverell and Mary Agnes (Mary Anne) Murtagh received the habit that day.

bers bound themselves by vow, should gold fail, to lay their consecrated hands on the chains of the captives, and become slaves in their stead. [He pictured the Alps covered with unthawing snow, where the wild beast could not dwell, and the Brother of St. Bernard, accompanied by his faithful dog, seeking the perishing traveller. In the most appropriate language he introduced whatever is most attractive in each Institute, ending with the Order of Mercy], introducing our little Congregation for the redemption, not of captive bodies, but of captive souls, and leaving nothing unsaid that was calculated to fix a preference in the hearts & judgments of all present for it [the Order of Mercy as established in our own country].

He complimented the Bishop & Dr. O'Rafferty[60] in the strongest terms [though he said he was restrained by their presence]. He could not avoid, he said, picturing to himself a future day, when many a parent would point out to his children the edifice now in course of erection, and say: "At such a period a prelate ruled this diocese whose virtue added lustre to his mitre & who restored religion in this part [of Ireland] to a splendor to which for ages it had been a stranger. Under him an illustrious pastor governed this parish whose whole life long was spent in deeds of benevolence. It was such a Bishop, it was such a Pastor, introduced the Sisters of Mercy to this town and built that beautiful convent." He exhorted the immense multitude never to prove ungrateful for such a blessing, spoke of Abraham supplicating God to spare the sinful city if ten just souls could be found therein, reminded the people of the cholera, which had so lately desolated their town, and said that if God in his justice should ever again visit his people for their sins, this new convent would be like a tower before Him to remind Him of his Mercy which its title proclaims, and upon which He would look with more complacency than on the Rainbow of old which He himself had formed.

[Dear Rev. Mother, I hope you will recommend the whole Society, and particularly Dr. Curtis, to the prayers of the community. He deserves to be enrolled among the warmest friends and most zealous advocates of our Order.

The new convent is getting up rapidly. Dr. O'Rafferty is constantly on the spot, even at six in the morning.

Ever, with deep affection,
and love to all at St. Mary's,
Your devoted child in Christ,
Sister M. Ann Doyle]

Handcopy: Tullamore Annals (26–28); published transcription: Carroll, Life *(288–90)*

---

60 Dr. James O'Rafferty, vicar general of the diocese of Meath, "was perhaps Tullamore's most distinguished parish priest and presided over the parish for thirty-seven years from his appointment in 1820 until his death in 1857" (Byrne 39).

92. To Dr. Andrew Fitzgerald, OP
Carlow

Convent of Mercy
Booterstown
July 3, 1838

My Dear Reverend Sir

I had the pleasure to receive your kind letter, and have admitted the poor girl for whom you are so interested. When I return to Baggot Street, I will give every attention to your wishes respecting her.

Every thing here is much more satisfactory than we expected. I know you will be pleased to hear that Mr. Ennis is remarkably kind—and anxious to do all in his power to promote our comfort—he seems to regret the past and says if he lives seven years more it will be atoned for.[61]

When you were in town last I mentioned to you a young widow who had returned from Madrass [*sic*]—that seemed disposed to unite with us. Her Director recommended Rathfarnham Convent. She entered there, and has now left—saying she feels a strong preference for the order of Mercy. I hope I will have her to introduce to you when I have the happiness to see you again.[62]

Mr. Mullins has undertaken to build the Laundry, etc., etc., in Baggot Street—and I was greatly surprised indeed to find his estimate five hundred pounds less than one we got—and two hundred less than any.[63] He is quite interested, and thinks it will give much value to the Institution. The sincere affectionate concern which you, dear Sir, have always manifested makes me feel desirous to communicate every thing to you. I never can forget all the animating lively hope that you created in my mind when we were rising out of nothing.

61 John Ennis had been a curate at St. Andrew's, Westland Row, Dublin, from well before the founding of the Sisters of Mercy in 1831 until his appointment as parish priest of Booterstown in 1838 (Donnelly 3:112).   62 The Loreto Sisters were founded by Teresa Ball (1794–1861) in 1821, after she and two others had served a seven-year preparatory period in the Bar Convent of the Institute of the Blessed Virgin Mary in York, England. In 1822 they moved into Rathfarnham House; Daniel Murray, who had been Teresa Ball's spiritual director for many years, "paid £2,300, on Teresa Ball's behalf, for the house and forty acres in 1821" (Enright 284–85). The widow who had returned from Madras in southeast India has not been identified, unless she is Mary Rose (Catherine) Lynch who entered the Baggot Street community on July 3, 1838. Since Catherine McAuley was in Booterstown on that day, the day of this letter, she may have been unaware of Catherine Lynch's actual entrance.   63 The final cost of building the addition to the House of Mercy, including the commercial laundry, was £1924.7.11, minus one shilling credit for "Error in Totting up deductions," according to signed account sheets preserved in Mercy Congregational Archives, Dublin. This figure was said to be considerably higher than the original estimate which did not include the necessary equipment for the laundry. The cost was also much greater than the £1000 legacy which Catherine McAuley directed to the building project. Letters 141 and 161, among others, record her difficulties with the laundry construction. Considerable research remains to be done on all the extant financial records, especially from the period 1822 (the year of William Callaghan's last will and death) to 1841 (the year of Catherine McAuley's death). Such analysis is, unfortunately, beyond the scope of this edition of her correspondence.

The delightful description I get of the Carlow Convent makes me very anxious to see it. My innocent Sister M. Frances—says she has the poplars in full bloom, with evergreens between, and Roses blowing on the mount.

I am almost afraid to hear of the Limerick foundation lest it should come in the way of my visit to Carlow. I have reason to expect a conclusive arrangement but must put it off a little.

Mr. Croke, the P.P. of Charleville, has been here. He commences a Convent immediately.[64] I advised him to see the Carlow plan. They have begun in Tullamore. Mr. Croke comforted me very much with the account he gave of the Sisters. I asked him would Miss Clancy's marriage be any draw back. He said if he were obliged to go to England to beg for them, they should not feel any loss. This was very strong language—from rather a cold character.

We have a striking example before us here every day of the power we possess of exercising unwearied efforts of Body and mind—in the perpetual movements of the steam train carriages—which do not cease from morning till night—and seem to be just passing our windows.[65]

I know you will not forget me—and remain

My Dear Reverend Sir, your ever grateful and affectionate
Mary C. McAuley

My Brother came here to see me—and I find that the apprehension I expressed to you about religious influence with James and Robert was without foundation—thank God.[66]

Autograph: Silver Spring

93. To Sister M. Ursula Frayne   [Mid 1838][67]
Booterstown

Dear Sr. Ursula, we parted you know Monday last
hear what from that to Wednesday past

---

64 Thomas Croke, parish priest in Charleville, having received a parcel of land from Lord Cork (see Letter 90), intended to replace the small, damp convent in Charleville by a new building. The foundation stone would be laid on September 24, 1838, when Catherine McAuley was in Charleville en route to found a new convent in Limerick.   65 Steam railway service from Westland Row, Dublin to the New Wharf in Kingstown (Dún Laoghaire), passing through Booterstown, was inaugurated in December 1834. Trains were "dispatched from each end of the Railway every half hour from Six o'clock, A.M. in summer, and Seven A.M. in winter, until half past Ten P.M." (*Dublin Directory* [1839] 186).   66 Catherine McAuley's brother James W. McAuley was raised a Protestant after his mother's death in 1798, when he was fifteen. Catherine had raised her adopted nephews, James, Robert, and William Macauley, the sons of her sister Mary and William Macauley, as Catholics, after their father's death in January 1829. The young men had attended Carlow College and were well known to Andrew Fitzgerald. James was now twenty-three, and Robert twenty.   67 It is not possible to date this poem-letter precisely, although some facts about its timing are evident: it followed a visit of Catherine McAuley to Booterstown—if not her first visit in June 1838,

After walking and waiting and looking in vain
to try could we see any sign of a Train
We went to the stop house to try were we late
and found we had yet half an hour to wait
I said Come, my Dear Sister, we'll step on towards town
It is better to do so, than here to sit down
We got to Merrion exceedingly tired
No sign of a train—no car to be hired
went slowly and feebly to next stand house gate
and were told we yet had a long time to wait
—that from some mischance the Packet did fail
and the train would not come without bringing the mail
Just as they spoke—one came in to view
going to Kingstown, so in we got too[68]
by this we had finished our own meditation
I now turned my thoughts upon—predestination
and fancied that some good spirit directed
to bring us to Kingstown—so much unexpected
Well—so it turned out—for a matter was pending
about which to B Street[69] they were just sending
and it was one—to few things inferior
which could not be answered without the Superior
And what above all—should ne'er be forgot
It was well I that day appeared on the spot
and although my old bones were weary and sore

then a subsequent visit; her knowledge of the frequency of train times on the Dublin-Kingstown railway is not well formed, as it might have become after several such trips, thus suggesting a mid 1838 date; Mary Aloysius Scott is on the trip described in the poem; and the serious Kingstown "matter" noted in the poem could have arisen only before the sisters were removed from the Kingstown convent in November 1838. The Booterstown convent was dedicated to St. Anne on July 26, 1838. Perhaps this letter followed Catherine McAuley's presence in Booterstown on that occasion. Bolster dates the poem "December 1838" (*Documentary Study* 441), which is not possible, given the presence of sisters in Kingstown. Moreover, cold weather does not appear to be a factor in the poem. The autograph in the archives of the Sisters of Mercy, Brisbane, has no date or cover. A typescript of the poem, done some time in the twentieth century, dates it "1839," but that date does not seem correct. The autograph postscript of the poem which was for many years in the archives of the Sisters of Mercy in Singleton, Australia, has been recently given to Brisbane. There is no signature on the poem; however, a detached autograph signature—simply "M. C. McAuley"—is now in the archives of the Sisters of Mercy, Bathurst, Australia, and may have been cut off the autograph of the poem. The fragmentation of this poem-letter illustrates well how treasured autographs of Catherine McAuley were spread throughout the world. **68** Having walked northwest, in the direction of the city of Dublin—probably to Merrion Road, and to what would be the present-day DART station at Sydney Parade—Catherine now got on a train headed southeast to Kingstown, past Booterstown and in the opposite direction from Dublin. **69** Baggot Street.

yet to be there then, I'd have gone through much more
You may think after all we made pretty good speed
since we reached—just in time the Lecture to read
Next morning we left about half past ten
but—how shall I say it—missed the steamer—again
My Dear Aloysius—so smart and so airy
proposed that we should walk on to Dunleary[70]
and the day that she brought me that round about race
will hold in her memory—a long lasting place
By hills and by hollows—through great rocks and stones
expecting each moment to break my poor bones
untill quite exhausted of temper and strength
I gave up to despair and lay down at full length
on a deep slooping [sloping] Rock—from which the least tip
would—or I thought so—have caused me to slip
At length I got up and did fervently pray
that the good guiding spirit would bring me through that Day
Again we arrived at a steam train House gate
and had not now more than 10 minutes to wait
by our long walk—the rest of the way seemed much shorter
and—we reached our dear Convent in time for the quarter[71]

P.S.　　All things that you've asked for I'm trying to get
　　　　But pray ask no more—my own dearest Pet
　　　　I'll now take my leave—Be a good child
　　　　Humble—and merry—diligent & mild
　　　　Work hard for the poor, love one another
　　　　and believe me your ever affectionate Mother

[M. C. McAuley]

Autograph: Brisbane

94. To Sister M. Frances Warde　　　　　　[Baggot Street]
Carlow　　　　　　　　　　　　　　　　August 23, 1838

My ever Dear Sister Mary Frances

I have felt quite uneasy at not writing to you. I received your letter announcing your new child—the Sister Whites are delighted. They say you will like Miss

---

70 Since Catherine was now in Kingstown (called Dunleary before 1821), she must be referring to the old Dunleary Road, just to the west, and to the next train station on the route to Dublin.　71 That is, in time for noonday community prayers at a quarter to twelve.

Johnson very much.[72] Revd. Mr. Hughes[73] is also most happy, he was greatly interested for her.

As to my delay in writing, I have been tortured with my unfortunate mouth—only just getting a little better[74]—and in the midst of other matters, the Limerick foundation was prepared—and concluded—for the first week in September.[75] You may be sure this is sorrowful news to me if I am to forfeit the happiness of going to Carlow—but it is impossible to put it off. Indeed the season does not admit of delay, we are too late as it is. We have not yet fully determined who will go besides Sr. M. E. and Sister Harnett[76]—we would give no more if possible. The account that is given of all our dear Sisters who have gone forth is so satisfactory that our invitations are endless.

Mr. O'Hanlon is just returned from Cork, Charleville & Tullamore and is pleased beyond every expectation.[77] When we said—Oh, not in Carlow—he answered, that was his *first* visit last year. He never was such an advocate for founding as he is now, so that I do not mention to him where we are asked—for fear he would be pressing what cannot be done. We are very near a Stop—I should say, a full Stop—feet and hands are numerous enough, but the heads are nearly gone.

I send you the copy of a letter from Sister Mary Ann[78]—it is very interesting.

Get all the prayers you can for me—that I may get through this new business as well as I can—and I need not bid you pity me and yourself for our mutual disappointment, but please God I will avail myself of the permission I got on my

72 Mary Teresa White and her sister Mary de Sales White apparently knew Charlotte Johnson who entered the Carlow community on August 2, 1838, received the habit on December 10, 1838, taking the name Mary Angela, and professed her vows on January 8, 1840 (Carlow Annals).   73 The *Irish Catholic Directory* for 1838 lists no priest with the name Hughes in the diocese of Kildare and Leighlin, and only one in the diocese of Dublin: Very Rev. Henry Hughes, provincial of the Franciscan community, Merchants' Quay, Dublin. Charlotte Johnson's native town is not known; she is not listed in the Carlow Register of professed sisters.   74 Catherine McAuley suffered from gum disease. Clare Augustine Moore notes that early on (1832) some members of the Baggot Street community, perhaps including Catherine, had "virulent scurvy," a disease of the gums caused by lack of ascorbic acid (Vitamin C) as found in fruits and leafy vegetables ("Memoir," in Sullivan, *Catherine McAuley* 206).   75 Catherine McAuley and the founding party for Limerick left Dublin by boat in early September, intending to stop in Cork and Charleville before proceeding to Limerick. 76 Mary Elizabeth Moore, as superior, and Mary Vincent Harnett, a novice.   77 Redmond J. O'Hanlon, ODC (1789–1864), then prior of the Discalced Carmelite community at St. Teresa's on Clarendon Street, had been appointed confessor of the Baggot Street community in June 1829 and was later Dr. Murray's deputy as ecclesiastical superior of the religious community. In his low-keyed solicitude for the welfare of the Sisters of Mercy he regularly visited the Mercy foundations outside of Dublin. His evident respect for and deference to Catherine McAuley's judgment, and his own self-effacing manner may obscure the steady, thoughtful assistance he gave to the Sisters of Mercy until his death.   78 Perhaps the letter from Mary Ann Doyle, superior of the Tullamore community, that Catherine encloses here is Letter 91, which would explain why it survived when, according to Mary Elizabeth Moore, Catherine "arranged," and disposed of, papers before her death (see Sullivan, *Catherine McAuley* 255). It would also explain Mary Austin Carroll's access to the letter as she composed her *Life* of Catherine McAuley.

return—and if I cannot see the Convent blessing, I can hope to see it blessed—which is as good.[79]

Remember me affectionately to all the Dear Sisters—now a fine flock, thank God—to Dr. Fitzgerald, Father Maher, Frs. Nolan, Rafter, etc., etc.[80]

May God bless and preserve you, my very Dear old Child.

> Your fondly attached
> M. C. McAuley

Sister Teresa still delicate. Sister M. Cecilia as usual—Sr. Ursula pretty well. Your faithful and indeed fond Sister Mary Teresa—who still sighs after Carlow—is well & doing a great deal for the Poor of Kingstown.[81]

The letters you send by hand do not reach me until long out of date. I have just heard of your 2nd addition.[82] I believe you will soon have enough to divide.

Autograph: Silver Spring

95. To James McAuley, Esq.   **Baggot Street**
                                                     August 31, 1838

My Dear James

I received your two kind notes and trust you will be able to do something for our affectionate Mary's poor spoiled child[83]—and I hereby empower you to

---

79 As it turned out, the blessing of the new convent in Carlow did not occur until July 2, 1839, although its chapel was blessed pro tem on April 2, 1839. Catherine McAuley was away from Baggot Street for about three months in 1838, but returned from Limerick to Dublin through Carlow, where she attended a reception ceremony on December 10, 1838. **80** Andrew Fitzgerald, James Maher, Daniel Nolan (brother of the late Dr. Edward Nolan), and Michael Rafter are the priests mentioned. **81** Teresa Carton, Mary Cecilia Marmion, Mary Ursula Frayne, and Mary Teresa White, the local superior in Kingstown, are the sisters mentioned. **82** Eliza Maher entered the Carlow community on August 10, 1838. She received the habit on December 10, 1838, taking the name Mary Clare. In 1841 she left because of ill health, but returned on July 22, 1845 (Carlow Register). **83** William Armstrong Macauley (1821–1904), the youngest of the five children of Catherine McAuley's sister Mary and her husband William Macauley, was seven years old when, after his mother's and father's deaths (in August 1827 and January 1829), he chose his Aunt Catherine as his legal guardian. He attended Carlow College, and was then apprenticed to a physician whom he did not respect and subsequently to a wholesale merchant on Usher's Quay. But his profound grief at his sister Catherine's death in August 1837, coupled with his feeling that his Aunt Catherine did not fully forgive him his faults, or did so reluctantly, led him to pursue a seafaring life. He visited his aunt at the time of his sister's death as well as one further time, went to sea, returned some months later, and then in late 1838, after the time of this letter, left Ireland for good. In London, with his Uncle James's help he got a post on an East India Freetrader, and sailed from St. Katharine's Dock on the *Mary Catherine* on December 26, 1838, never to see Ireland or England again (Keena, ed. 1–4, 16–17). Catherine McAuley died in 1841 assuming that Willie had died at sea or of consumption. However, he eventually settled in Australia where he and his wife Jessie Tompkins had thirteen children. Australia is now home to numerous great and great great grandchildren of William and Jessie, the great great and great great great grandnieces and nephews of

apply the Share in the Hall in whatever way you think most useful for him.[84] Should any legal assistance be necessary, Mr. Cavanagh, Solicitor, 18 Lower Fitzwilliam Street, will afford it. Love to all.

Your ever affectionate
C. McAuley

Autograph: Bermondsey

Catherine McAuley. William's is a touching story that can be presented only superficially in a footnote. It is best told in his own *Letters of William Armstrong McAuley*, edited by Mary Imelda Keena. These letters are preserved in the archives of the Institute of Our Lady of Mercy, Bermondsey, London. I am very grateful to Mary Dennett, RSM (Melbourne) for her unpublished chart of William's descendants.   84 At his birth on December 9, 1821, William Macauley received from William Callaghan, Catherine McAuley's employer and future benefactor, a share of stock in the Apothecaries Hall, Dublin, where Mr. Callaghan was a member. With this letter, Catherine, as William's guardian, released the stock for his future expenses. He was now almost seventeen years old.

September–December 1838

Catherine McAuley spent most of the last four months of 1838 away from Dublin: establishing a new foundation of Sisters of Mercy in Limerick, the fifth foundation outside of Dublin since April 1836, and visiting the communities in Cork and Charleville at the beginning of this trip, and Carlow at the end. But her happiness in seeing the works of mercy extended to some of the most impoverished children and adults in Ireland overlay the deep pain of a seemingly sudden, and unfortunate, development in the Kingstown controversy: the departure of the Sisters of Mercy from Kingstown in early November. Her grief for the poor girls and sick poor who would be left behind revealed her profoundly personal identification with them: "God knows I would rather be cold and hungry than the poor in Kingstown or elsewhere should be deprived of any consolation in our power to afford" (Letter 100). On December 19, Catherine McAuley returned to the Kingstown parish the £26 remaining in the Poor Fund of the parish which the sisters had been asked to distribute to those in need.

Two other worries nagged at Catherine's heart. Her seventeen-year-old nephew William ("Willie") Macauley was going to sea, sailing from London on December 26, apparently without having come to see her again, before she left Dublin in early September or after her return. They were never to see one another again, a fact she could not have known. In writing to her brother James in late August, she had called Willie a "spoiled child." He left Ireland resolved not to seek any greater evidence of her forgiveness of his youthful flounderings than he had received in the past. Yet a deep bond of memories and longstanding affection united them. Willie's extant letters from Australia over the next six decades speak lovingly of her, whereas her extant letters over the final three years of her life are silent about him—with the silence not of unconcern, one assumes, but of unspeakable sorrow and regret.

While she was away from Dublin, Catherine also worried about Baggot Street—in particular, about Mary de Pazzi Delany's reluctance to have her away from home. Lacking, at least at this point, Catherine's understanding of the need to support new foundations in their early months, Mary de Pazzi exercised, perhaps indeliberately, a kind of subtle constraint on Catherine's travelling that put her in the position of justifying and apologizing for her necessary absences. In the letters of these months, covering her longest period away from Baggot Street, one sees Catherine defer raising alarms about the intended length of her absence.

In Cork, Charleville, Limerick, and Carlow, Catherine saw encouraging signs of God's blessing: two English women had entered the Cork community to prepare for a new foundation in London; the foundation stone for a new convent was laid in Charleville, and fears about the future of that community were eased; in less than three months from its founding on September 24, four young women entered the new Convent of Mercy in Limerick; and in Carlow three women received the habit of the Sisters of Mercy on December 10. As Catherine will write a month later, the Institute of Mercy "evidently was to go on" (Letter 110)—welcoming its "real portion of the Cross," and giving thanks for God's "Providential Guidance."

96. To Sister M. Teresa White Kingstown

Convent of the Sisters of Mercy, Limerick October 1, 1838[1]

My Dear Sister Mary Teresa

Your letter which I this day received was truly acceptable, indeed it was great comfort to me. I am rejoiced to find you all so well and have no doubt you will get through the little difficulty about the Children. Revd. Mr. Carroll[2] wrote to me a few days before I left, asking admission for a poor child. I remember he added: "She would be just fit for a collector." You might write to him if you are not provided. I do not think it would be well to have a child who could not remain always—but I leave you free to do what you think best—as I am satisfied you will not act imprudently, and this conviction makes my mind very happy far as you are concerned.[3]

We have found much more here than we expected. A very nice old Convent, enclosed by the walls of an abbey—a beautiful ruin. There is a most simple inviting tomb just opposite the cell I occupy. A holy Abbess and a Lay Sister are deposited there—a very large weeping ash hanging over the Grave[4]. It looks delightful and excites meditation of the most consoling kind. A very nice chapel and choir—good garden—and extensive school rooms. The approach is very bad—yet enough of visitors have found the way passable—to us it is of but little consequence, as we should often have to visit in the immediate neighbourhood— it is exactly as if our Dublin Convent was in the center of the lanes & courts about Townsend Street instead of returning to Baggot St—but the House is surrounded by trees & walking ground, and all enclosed with fine old walls entirely lined with ivy, and it is capable of being made a valuable Institution—if God will

1 The date on the autograph of this letter is "1st October"; Catherine McAuley crossed out "Novr" and inserted "October." However, the postmark on the cover (probably the Dublin mark) is "OC 12/38," indicating that some delay in posting the letter occurred, as well as in the route to Dublin and Kingstown. The letter was written shortly after the new Convent of Mercy was founded in Limerick on September 24, 1838.   2 This is probably Thomas Carroll, a curate at St. Andrew's, Westland Row, Dublin.   3 Capable young girls were often chosen to participate in door-to-door begging to support the various works of mercy, such as the House of Mercy on Baggot Street and the school for poor girls in Kingstown.   4 Catherine wrote "Grace" here, but she must have meant "Grave"—that is, the graves of the two Poor Clares.

grant His blessing to our exertions. We are the third order who have made a trial—first Poor Clares, then Presentations, & now Sisters of Mercy. God grant them the grace of perseverance, there are difficulties every where.[5]

We found dear Sister Mary Clare & Community in excellent health and spirits. The english converts are very pleasing, Sister Agnew particularly so.[6] We left Cork on the 12th—intending to stay a day in Charleville and go into Limerick on the Exaltation of the Holy Cross—but I found I could be more useful there than perhaps I have ever been. There was danger of all breaking up—and my heart felt sorrowful when I thought of the poor being deprived of the comfort which God seemed to intend for them. I made every effort & praised be God, all came round. The first stone of a nice convent was laid on our dear festival, the 24th—and leaving all in joy and happiness we proceeded to our present abode on the same favoured Day.[7]

We are saying the two Thirty Days prayer—one in the morning and one after Vespers.[8] I am sure you will unite with us in obtaining all the intercession you can. Get the Sisters to invite their patron saints and implore Saint Teresa who loved foundations to intercede for poor Limerick where no seed has yet taken root.[9] Visitors pray us not to be discouraged by the past failures and

5 The founding community in Limerick consisted of Mary Elizabeth Moore, the new superior, and Mary Vincent Harnett, a novice who would profess her vows on October 24, 1838. Assisting them during the first months were Catherine McAuley and her traveling companions Mary Aloysius Scott and Mary Francis Xavier O'Connell, a novice. Some sources say Eliza Liston, a postulant, had also come to assist, but she did not enter Baggot Street until September 8, 1838; she later went to Limerick for a period of time. The community moved into the old convent building formerly occupied by the Poor Clares who had disbanded in 1831 because of financial difficulties, but left behind three lay sisters who continued the poor school they had begun. Two of these Poor Clares were still living in September 1838: Mary Shanahan and Anne Hewitt, age forty-eight and forty-two, respectively. Catherine McAuley immediately invited them to live in the Mercy community, gave them the place their seniority deserved, and "did not require them to discharge the duties of Lay Sisters" (Limerick Annals 1:16). 6 In early September, having come by steamer from Dublin, the party visited Mary Clare Moore and the Cork community, where the English converts, Mary Clare (Elizabeth) Agnew and Mary Augustin (Maria) Taylor, were preparing to profess their vows in August 1839, prior to founding a new Convent of Mercy in Bermondsey, London. Catherine McAuley frequently used a lower case "e" where a capital "E" would now be expected, as in "easter" or here in "english." 7 Catherine McAuley had hoped to move on from Charleville to Limerick on September 14, the feast of the Exaltation of the Cross, but found she was still needed in Charleville. Financial worries and the slow progress of the Charleville community tempted the superior, Mary Angela Dunne, to think that the community should disband. In the end, the foundation stone of a new convent in Charleville was laid on September 24, the feast of Our Lady of Mercy, the patronal liturgical feast of the Sisters of Mercy, and with Catherine's encouragement, fears about the future were calmed. (See Letter 67, note 93.) 8 "The Thirty Days' Prayer to our Blessed Redeemer, in Honour of his Bitter Passion" and "The Thirty Days' Prayer to the Blessed Virgin Mary, in Honour of the Sacred Passion of our Lord Jesus Christ": these prayers, among Catherine McAuley's favorites, are found in the standard prayerbooks available in Ireland in her day, including William A. Gahan, ed. *The Christian's Guide to Heaven, or, A Complete Manual of Catholic Piety;* and *The Poor Man's Manual of Devotions.* For the texts and further explanation of Catherine's use of these prayers see Sullivan, "Prayers" 48–51 and 68–73. See also Letter 49, note 36. 9 Mary Teresa White probably received

promise us it will not be so in our regard. We were called upon to visit a respectable person who is in a disponding [desponding] state of mind, and to encourage us, he gave six pounds for the poor sick on our first visit. Sister Ellen Potter has joined and is in very good spirits.[10]

It was not Mr. Hogan[11] who brought your letter, but a Parish Priest near Limerick—he said Mass for you twice. The Bishop[12] has been here—he was absent when we came. I think he will be very kind. The furniture is exactly what we asked for. All in Cork, Charleville and Limerick send their most affectionate love to all with you. Sister M. Joseph sent 10,000 loves to Sister Genevieve.[13] I trust in God she is well, and that I shall see all my old flock once more. A Wexford Priest told a Cork Priest that our Sisters are going to Wexford immediately. Indeed I believe he said they were to be there in a week positively. I think they will wait for me. I am so experienced now in such affairs that it would not be well to go without me.[14]

I am not uneasy about the school business—you will do all you can.[15] God bless and preserve you, my Dear child. Pray fervently for

your sincerely attached Mother in Christ
Mary C. McAuley

Write to me whenever you can.

Give my most fond remembrance to each of my very dear Sisters. Present my best thanks to Mrs. Kelly, and any person you please. I am delighted to hear you go on so well with Father S.—keep it up if possible.[16]

Autograph: Galway

97. To Sister M. Magdalen Flynn[17]   [Limerick]
Baggot Street   [October 1838]

My Dear Sister Mary Magdeline

I felt very much obliged for the very affectionate letter you sent me—and

---

this letter before October 15, the feast of St. Teresa of Avila. **10** Ellen Potter, a native of Adare, Co. Limerick, had earlier entered the Dublin community, but left because of poor health. The first young woman to enter the Limerick community, she became—until her sudden death in March 1840—a much loved correspondent of Catherine McAuley, often exchanging poems with her. **11** Patrick Hogan was vicar general of the diocese of Limerick and parish priest of St. Michael's, Limerick (*Irish Catholic Directory* [1838] 369). Apparently he made the final arrangements for the Mercy foundation in Limerick. In Letter 102 Catherine McAuley claims that he was "the favorite Priest of Limerick." **12** Dr. John Ryan, the bishop of Limerick, was consecrated December 11, 1825. He proved to be a very helpful support to the Sisters of Mercy, imposing only one restriction on Elizabeth Moore, the new superior: "'not to incur debt' of which his Lordship had a just horror!" (Limerick Annals 1:16). **13** Mary Josephine Warde in Cork, and Mary Genevieve Jarmy in Kingstown. **14** The foundation in Wexford was made by the Carlow community on December 8, 1840. **15** The ongoing welfare of the poor girls in the school in Kingstown was on Teresa White's mind—and Catherine's. By November 15, 1838 the school and convent in Kingstown will be closed (see Letter 101). **16** Bartholomew Sheridan, the parish priest in Kingstown. **17** The recipient of this autograph, which was for many years in the Mercy

the pleasing account you gave of the Building which I suppose is raising its head high.[18]

We like every thing here very much, and although the immediate approach is very bad, yet we pass it all in about ten minutes. There is a Lodge at the entrance gate, and a very orderly man & his wife living in it who have charge of the ground and two gardens, for which they are paid by disposing of fruit and vegetables not required in the Convent.[19]

Poor Mr. Burke was Chaplain here for many years—we see several little things that remind us of him.[20]

We are still crowded with visitors, but hope to be engaged next week and have done with them. The Priests refused to give us calls—until we would rest—and indeed we are more fatigued talking and receiving strangers than we would [be] walking over the Town.[21]

God bless you, Dear Sister Mary Magdeline—pray for your ever affectionate

M. C. McAuley

Autograph: Galway

---

convent in Sligo, and then in the Mercy archives in Athlone, has been difficult to identify, since it has no date or place of origin, and no extant cover with an address. However, internal evidence suggests that it was written from Limerick to Mary Magdalen Flynn at Baggot Street, even though Catherine McAuley spells Magdalen's name in a way that does not correspond with the Dublin Register. The description of the convent setting could fit Limerick or Galway, but the "Building" on which the recipient has reported is probably the addition to the House of Mercy on Baggot Street begun in 1838; and the Franciscan, Daniel Burke, the former chaplain of the House of Mercy and now in southern Africa, had earlier ministered in Limerick, not in Galway.

Mary Laurentia Flaherty, the former archivist in Athlone, once thought the letter might have been written from Galway in May or June 1840, to Mary Magdalen (Ellen) O'Brien in Carlow, who professed her vows in Westport in 1842 and subsequently went to Sligo. In this case, the "Building" to which Catherine refers might be the new convent in Carlow. However, Ellen O'Brien did not enter the Carlow community until July 9, 1840, when the Carlow convent was already completed and occupied, and did not receive the name Mary Magdalen until her reception of the habit on November 16, 1940 (Carlow Annals).

Catherine McAuley was in Galway in early October 1840, but the contents of the letter suggest that it was written at the beginning of a new foundation, not when the foundation was some months in operation. The contents also imply that the letter was not written from Baggot Street. All in all, Mary Magdalen Flynn seems to be the most likely recipient, there being no other Mary Magdalen in the Sisters of Mercy at the time who would fit the circumstances of the letter—and despite the historical locations of the autograph. In Letter 96 also, Catherine speaks about the "very bad" approach to the Limerick convent.

18 See note 17 above.   19 See note 17 above.   20 See note 17 above. If the letter was written from Galway in 1840, word of Father Burke's death in Grahamstown, southern Africa on April 11, 1839 had already reached Catherine McAuley.   21 As already indicated, I interpret this entire letter as a description of the early days in the Limerick foundation.

98. To Sister M. Frances Warde   **Convent of the Sisters of Mercy**
      Carlow   **Limerick**
                                                              October 25 [1838]

My ever Dear Sister Mary Frances

My mind has been uneasy at not writing to you—and even yet I cannot say when I shall be able to leave this foundation—which with much to excite hope and expectation, has still much, very much, to contend with. It is quite novel to see those who have the smallest means most afraid to join—in which they are encouraged by the Priests—who say: If this breaks up—as three other communities have done—they would be nuns—but what House would take them in without support, as they never could be regarded like full subjects. The friends of such as have property excite their fears that they would be obliged to go where they might not like. Such a perplexing conflict as we have almost daily. Notwithstanding, I hope two will soon come. Sister Potter and a Miss O'Farrell are come.[22]

I cannot go for a full month. No person of less experience could manage at present—and I am very insufficient for the task. As to Sister Elizabeth, with all her readiness to undertake it—we never sent forward such a feint-hearted [*sic*] soldier, now that she is in the field. She will do all interior & exterior work, but to meet on business—confer with the Bishop—conclude with a Sister—you might as well send the child that opens the door. I am sure this will surprise you. She gets white as death—and her eyes like fever. She is greatly liked—and when the alarms are a little over and a few in the House, I expect all will go on well.[23]

Sister Vincent was professed yesterday, thank God[24]—we were obliged to admit many persons.

They do not know in Baggot Street that I am to be so long away. It seems providential that the charge there is very much lessened—on account of the

22 Ellen Potter entered the Limerick community on the evening the foundation party arrived, September 24, 1838. Miss O'Farrell received the habit on December 4, 1838, and may have been one of "the three" who professed their vows on December 9, 1839, but she is not listed at this point in the Limerick Register of professed sisters. However, she is mentioned—as "Sister O'Farrell"— in two letters of Catherine McAuley in February 1841. In the present letter Catherine may have written "O'Farrell" and then wetted out the O. For more discussion of Miss O'Farrell (or Farrell), see Letter 238, note 82. The two postulants Catherine anticipates are presumably Joanna Bridgeman and Mary Anne Bridgeman who entered the Limerick community on November 1, 1838 and December 8, 1838, respectively.   23 Mary Elizabeth Moore, the superior of the Limerick community, was thirty-two years old at the time. She subsequently became one of the most courageous early Mercy founders—opening new foundations in numerous places in Ireland and Scotland, ministering during the Famine, and serving those in jail who were condemned to death. See Courtney, "Fearless Mother Elizabeth Moore," and Sullivan, *Catherine McAuley* 247–57.   24 Mary Vincent (Anna Maria) Harnett, now twenty-seven years old, had come from Baggot Street as a novice, having received the habit on July 1, 1837. She professed her vows on October 24, 1838, one month after their arrival in Limerick. For a discussion of the correct spelling of her surname, and for biographical details, see Sullivan, *Catherine McAuley* 130–38.

Building—only 10 young women are kept and no school. Still I must announce
it by degrees—as my poor Sister de Pazzi is now subject to *dreadful* attacks.[25]

Sister Mary Teresa expressed such disappointment at not going to the consecration of your Convent that she must come & Sr. Cecilia—with three from
this. Can you pack five of us—and will we be time enough in about a month? I
had a letter from Sister White—but did not yet tell her she should go—as it
would not be well the others knew it till the time comes.[26]

Write to me and say particularly how you are. Mr. McCormick was here.
He said you looked very well, but had some return of your distressing feelings.[27]
I look forward with delight to the day I shall see you once more.

This House is fully in the old conventual style—very bad all around as to
neighbourhood—but when within the gates, quite a nice place—enclosed by

25 Mary de Pazzi Delany did not become Catherine McAuley's formally appointed assistant at
Baggot Street until March 1840 (see Letter 166). However, as one of the earliest members of the
Dublin community, having joined on July 12, 1830, she was—after Mary Ann Doyle, Frances Warde,
and Clare Moore went to their respective foundations in 1836 and 1837—regularly left in charge
when Catherine went out of town. Her noted reluctance to have Catherine away from Baggot Street
and the effect of this reluctance on her propensity to "attacks" similar to epilepsy made Catherine's
necessary travel to new foundations very difficult. Messages were often sent to her, urging her to
return before her work at a new foundation was completed. The trip to Cork, Charleville, and
Limerick, with the stop in Carlow on her return to Dublin, was the longest she ever took—just
over three months. Her apprehension about the situation in Dublin is revealed in her letters from
Limerick, especially in Letter 101 to Mary de Pazzi herself.   26 Catherine was planning to attend
a reception ceremony in Carlow on her way home from Limerick. Mary Aloysius Scott, Mary Xavier
O'Connell, and she would be coming from Limerick, and Mary Teresa White and Mary Cecilia
Marmion from Dublin. Catherine's reference to the "consecration" of the Carlow convent is confusing, unless she means the episcopal consecration of Francis Haly (March 25, 1838), which she
missed, and not the consecration of the new Carlow convent which did not occur until July 2, 1839,
though the new chapel was blessed on April 2, 1839. It is entirely possible that Catherine has simply
lost track of what events have occurred in Carlow in the last seventeen months—not having been
there herself since the first stone of the new convent was laid on May 20, 1837 (Carlow Annals).
In this paragraph, one sees her unwillingness to let Mary de Pazzi know too soon that she will stop
in Carlow on her way home and thus add two days to her time away.   27 As mentioned in earlier
letters, Frances Warde was ill in April and May 1838. The exact nature of her ailment is not known.
Although a Reverend M. McCormick served in the diocese of Limerick in 1838, Catherine is probably referring to a visit from her longtime friend, John McCormick, a curate in the Booterstown,
Blackrock, and Dundrum parish (*Irish Catholic Directory* [1838] 285, 269). Father McCormick died
on September 17, 1841, at the age of sixty-eight (*Irish Catholic Directory* [1842], 437. In his will,
signed on August 6, 1835 or 1831, he bequeathed "My three Houses Value one Thousand pounds
for Miss McGauley & the Sisters of Mercy in Baggot Street"; in the will he notes that "My niece
is in Baggot St. Convent on the income of the Houses" (Dublin Diocesan Archives, Murray Papers,
AB3/33/9, no. 20). His niece Anne O'Grady entered the Baggot Street community on January 21,
1829, but died of consumption on February 8, 1832, just after the founding of the Sisters of Mercy
on December 12, 1831. Since I am unaware of any other niece of Father McCormick who entered
the Baggot Street community, I am inclined to read the not altogether legible year in his will as
1831, even though the Diocesan Archives reads it as 1835 (*Archivium Hibernicum* 42:52). John
McCormick had visited Catherine McAuley's sister Mary in 1827, when she was dying in Dundrum,
and had received her back into the Catholic Church (Sullivan, *Catherine McAuley* 41, 47).

the Ruins of an abbey—and green in every view. It has been put into the best repair and furnished in our own style. We have never seen the foundress—this is Gospel perfection. She would not even ask for a Ticket to the Ceremony.[28] We had a very good sermon—good private singers—and my most *angelic* Sister Aloysius at the piano—I never knew her perfectly till now. Sister Elizabeth often says she believes there is no mixture of human feelings remaining in her[29]—so unalterably sweet and placid and unceasing day and night in her efforts to promote this object. She is everything at all times—how did I live so long with such a person and not know her? The sweetest we ever had could be a little disturbed, particularly on occasions like this—but she is never moved—in looks or manner.

We finished the two 30 days' Prayers[30]—on the 23rd—one in the morning and one in the evening—and are now going to say the whole Psalter for 15 days—this is our best hope.[31]

Miss Delaney, I believe, is much changed. She was quite satisfactory when I saw her—and is to be received on the 29th. A niece of Sister Angela's—Miss Lawler—I believe from Kilkenny—is coming to them. She has 38 pounds per year. They have commenced building a convent.[32]

Do not say a word of any fears about Limerick that could reach a Limerick person. Revd. Mr. Rouley [Raleigh] knows your Sr. Kelly.[33] Every word takes wing—and I have not given this account to any one but you—not to Sr. de Pazzi. If they thought I was speaking unfavorably, I would get nothing done these three months. All my language must be encouraging. Some Carlow Priests write to Priests here.

---

28 The principal benefactor of the Limerick community was Miss Helena Heffernan who in 1836, if the Sisters of Mercy could be persuaded to come to Limerick, "assigned for that purpose [a major portion of] the estate bequeathed to her by her brother, Patrick McMahon Heffernan, of the County of Limerick" (Limerick Annals). She established a Trust which allotted "one hundred pounds annually to [the] Institution of Mercy [in Limerick] during her life; two hundred annually after [her] death," as well as several annuities to other charitable projects (qtd. in M. L. O'Connor 25). Miss Heffernan died on August 4, 1860. For a full account of this remarkable woman, see M. L. O'Connor, "Helena Heffernan, a true Limerick Woman." 29 That is, in Mary Aloysius Scott. 30 Catherine McAuley wrote "2 30 days Prayer," but for clarity I have changed this to "two 30 days' Prayers." (See Letter 96, note 8.) 31 The Psalter of Jesus was one of Catherine McAuley's most frequent personal prayers. For the text and further explanation, see Sullivan, "Prayers" 48–51, 57–67. The Psalter of Jesus consists of fifteen petitions; Catherine is planning to pray one petition each day. 32 Frances Delaney, who entered the Charleville community in May, will receive the habit on October 29. She is not listed in the Charleville Register of professed sisters. Margaret Lawless entered the Charleville community on July 4, 1838; in August 1845 she will leave to join an Ursuline community in Ennis. The Register gives England as her native place. Margaret Lalor will enter the Charleville convent on October 29, 1838. The Register lists her native place as Tully, Co. Kildare. Catherine McAuley may have confused these two women. 33 Catherine wrote "Rouley," but she evidently means James Raleigh, a curate in St. Michael's parish, Limerick, since no other priest's name in the Limerick diocese at this time comes close to her spelling. She often spelled names phonetically—especially ones she had not seen in print. James Raleigh served in the parish where Patrick Hogan was parish priest.

Give my most affectionate love to all. Sisters M. E. & Aloysius, M. Xavier and Mrs. Harnett desire their best love to you—the latter is in good spirits—read her vows very well.

May God bless and preserve you, my ever dearest child, is the constant prayer of your ever fond

M. C. McAuley

As yours is the first convent erected for our order, except our first—B. St.[34]—we ought to pay it every tribute of regard—& bring our best music.

Remember me to Doctor Fitzgerald and all the good Priests.

If I left this before a month, I should leave Sister Aloysius—and that I think better not to do.[35]

Autograph: Silver Spring

99. To Sister M. Elizabeth Moore   Newry
     Limerick   October 25, 1838

Dear Rev. Mother,

I have felt great joy in learning from your own esteemed letter and subsequently from one which I have had the happiness of receiving from the venerated Foundress of your Order that you have been placed at the head of a Religious Community where with the solicitude and cares of a tender mother you are likely to have the comfort of doing immense good, not only to the immediate objects of your care and thousands of poor children and young women, but also by your example and the influence of your exertions to a large and populous city.[36]

That you never sought so responsible a charge I am fully persuaded. You know too well the difficulties and anxieties which even in a well regulated establishment are inseparable from the office of Superior: you are too well assured that without the grace of God you can accomplish no real good in such a situation, and that his grace has been promised only to the humble and unassuming; your mind in short is too well instructed by Religion, you have meditated too much and practised too fruitfully that lesson of our Redeemer—choose the lowest place—to suffer a temptation of vanity to spread its dazzling mirrors and delu-

---

34 Baggot Street, Dublin.   35 The three postscript sentences are written in the top or bottom margins of pages 2 and 3 of the letter.   36 Catherine McAuley may have written to Michael Blake in Newry about what she perceived to be Elizabeth Moore's "faint-heartedness" as a new superior. He was one of Elizabeth's longtime friends, having been her confessor before she entered the Sisters of Mercy on June 10, 1832. It was to her that he sent his letter of grief and sympathy on November 13, 1841, two days after Catherine McAuley's death (Sullivan, *Catherine McAuley* 190–91). The present letter is typical of Dr. Blake's generous encouragement of others and his constant upholding of the basic virtues of religious life.

sive fallacies over your mind. Yes, I am persuaded that not only you never thought, but, moreover, that you never would seek to be placed over others, and therefore I feel joy in hearing that you have been called up to a higher place, and regarding that movement as the work of divine Providence, I feel no doubt that God has blessed [your community] and will continue to bless and make it a source of blessing to many.

I most cordially congratulate with you on the auspicious circumstances which have cheered the commencement of your charitable labours in Limerick. The paternal kindness and manifest encouragement of the Venerable Bishop of that Diocese[37] did not surprise, though it gladdened me. It was in perfect accordance with the character he has always maintained. But the extraordinary benevolence and welcome you have experienced from the people was indeed rather more than [was] anticipated from the failure of other convents in that city. The eagerness also with which postulants already present themselves, and the spacious schools which are already provided for the reception of poor children – so many advantages must afford you comfort, they must exhilarate your hearts. They are at present a reward for the purity and sanctity of your motives, and I hope they will facilitate your progress to still happier results.

I will only add that I shall continue to feel a lively interest in the success of all your undertakings and concerns, being most truly, Dear Rev. Mother,

Your sincere friend & faithful servant in Christ
[Michael Blake]

Author's transcript: Dromore

100. To Sister M. Teresa White
Kingstown

Convent of the Sisters of Mercy,
Limerick
November 1, 1838

My Dearest Sister Mary Teresa

How can I sufficiently thank you for the kind cautious manner in which you communicate the painful news—and above all, I bless & praise your recollection of the ever adorable Sacrament. We have done all that justice and prudence demands—to avert this affliction. If it must come, let us receive it as the Holy Will of God in our regard. It will mortify us and that will be salutary, please God. As to removing the Blessed Sacrament—God will direct you. Be a good soldier in the hour of the trial—do not be afflicted for your poor—their Heavenly Father will provide comfort for them, and you will have the same opportunity of fulfilling your obligations during your life.

---

37 Dr. Michael Blake had been bishop of Dromore for over five years, and would have known Dr. John Ryan, bishop of Limerick, at least during that time.

I charge you, my very dear child, not to be sorrowful—but rather to rejoice if we are to suffer this humiliating trial. God will not be angry—be assured of that—and is not that enough. I feel that it would give you no consolation were I to say—"God would not be displeased with you—though He may with me." He will not be displeased with me—for He knows I would rather be cold and hungry than the poor in Kingstown or elsewhere should be deprived of any consolation in our power to afford—but in the present case, we have done all that belonged to us to do—and even more than the circumstances justified.

May God in His mercy bless and protect you all. Perhaps the next letter will inform me of your removal to Baggot Street.[38]

The Sisters here unite in love—with your ever affectionate

Mary C. McAuley

Autograph: Galway

101. To Sister Mary de Pazzi Delany   Convent, Limerick
Baggot Street   November 15, 1838

My dear Sister M. de Pazzi[39]

Your letter was the greatest comfort to me, as from your communications I had reason to think you were ill—but your long letter, written as well as usual, has quite removed my fears.

The Kingstown business is a real portion of the Cross. From what you say, I should think you do not know all the circumstances. They were submitted to the Bishop[40] already and I cannot see any use in teasing him with another statement. Indeed, when I think of what my poor Sisters suffered, I do not wish they should return, though I feel very much for the poor souls they have left.

---

38 This sentence reveals the specific nature of the "painful news" mentioned in the first sentence: the Sisters of Mercy had to move out of the Kingstown convent and return to Baggot Street. Whether their removal in November 1838 was instigated by the parish priest (Bartholomew Sheridan), the builder of the poor school to whom Catherine McAuley was said to owe £375 (James Nugent), or by Catherine McAuley or Mary de Pazzi Delany in consultation with Charles Cavanagh, their solicitor, is not known. In earlier letters Catherine had been aware that they might have to move from Kingstown and sell the house to pay the building debt, but her extant correspondence prior to this letter does not indicate that she thought all other efforts would fail or fail so soon. There is no extant correspondence with Charles Cavanagh at this time, though he tended to save many of her letters, if not all of them. However, Letter 101 to Mary de Pazzi gives further background on the problem, and Catherine reports that she wrote to Daniel Murray sometime in the preceding year. As she notes, that letter was forwarded to Bartholomew Sheridan; it has not so far been found.   39 The autograph of this letter is damaged by stains. I have been assisted in reading the text by a photostat in the Mercy Congregational Archives (*Letters of Mother McAuley: 1827–1839*) and by two typescripts made independently: one at the Archives, and one in Adelaide.   40 Daniel Murray, archbishop of Dublin.

In my letter to his Grace I mentioned that Father Sheridan said I made myself accountable for the whole debt—by giving fifty pounds—and added, "perhaps, my Lord, I cannot be said to have given it since the builder took it from the table—a heavy parcel of silver." This letter was forwarded to Mr. Sheridan. Mr. Nugent got it to read and conceived it charged him with taking away the bag of silver forcibly. He went to Sister Elizabeth in a violent rage, called me cheat & liar.[41] He did just the same in Mr. Cavanagh's public office in Fitzwilliam Street, and from that time, no proposal Mr. Cavanagh could make would be attended to—and a bitter feeling has existed towards the poor Sisters ever since.

Even Father Sheridan was greatly excited, and said that while I appeared to be a quiet simple person—I was cunning & clever. These things were never told to me until I pressed Sr. Elizabeth for her reason for disliking Kingstown so much, and for appearing quite in terror lest Mr. Nugent should come whenever I was there. It has been said that not giving the profits of the second Bazaar occasioned the law proceedings—but we never promised it—and one hundred children were then preparing for Confirmation, for whom 100 dresses were bought.[42]

Two watches were given to that Bazaar for the children, but not for building. Mr. Nugent got £12 each time for putting up the tent—though we had all the trouble of getting permission from Col. Burgoyne[43]—and borrowing sail cloth. In all, Mr. Nugent has got from us eighty four pounds—and ten which Mr. Sheridan sent me for him. I suppose he did not keep a regular account of the expense incurred, for he sent a measurer which he seemed to think we would not allow, for he sent some message the Sisters did not understand—about wanting to know the dimensions, etc.—the plainest work that ever was executed is charged at a high rate—and the promise that was made in the beginning of applying to the board of education—never fulfilled.

They give £40 per year to this school[44]—which is as much under the direction of the superintending Priest and the Sisters as could be desired. I think the inspector would not make a remark which could be objected to. Religious instructions are given every day from 3 till half past 3, and any hour in the day we may say what we please to them—hence I could have no objection to be subject to the regulations anywhere. In Charleville and Tullamore the Inspectors are equally unobtrusive—the Priests and our Sisters are in full authority, sometimes three Priests teaching in the school at once.[45]

---

41 The reference to Elizabeth Moore indicates that the event Catherine describes occurred sometime in 1837 or 1838, before Elizabeth was replaced as superior in Kingstown by Mary Teresa White.   42 The "second Bazaar" probably occurred in 1837 and may have taken place in Kingstown, as the next paragraph suggests. Letter 52, written to Elizabeth Moore in Kingstown on August 31, 1837, speaks of preparing the girls in Kingstown for the sacrament of Confirmation. 43 Colonel Burgoyne, Easton Lodge, Monkstown Road (*Dublin Directory* [1839]).   44 The poor school in Limerick, begun by the Poor Clares, was affiliated with the Board of National Education in 1833. The school received an annual grant of £40 from the Board to cover some of its expenses (Courtney, "Careful Instruction" 14).   45 Like Dr. Daniel Murray and many, though not all, of

Now as to my return, I assure you I will not stay one day for recreation. You must be aware that great caution is necessary selecting persons to commence an Institution, where there is so much to fear and to hope. If a prudent, cautious beginning is made, there is every prospect of success. More judgment that I possess might be useful, but less would not distinguish between the characters that present themselves—as to steadiness of purpose, capacity for the Institute. A House of Mercy is opened, and I, please God, will leave this about the 4th or 5th of December.[46]

I cannot express the consolation Sister M. Teresa has afforded me by her manner of concluding the Kingstown business—and the few quiet lines she sent to Father Sheridan. Thanks be [to] God, I find the Sisters can act as well as could be desired when I am not at home—though they cannot write a note then—but I hope to keep them in practice and to rest myself in future.

Doctor Ryan[47] has just been here for nearly an hour. You would like him very much—he is very feeling and kind to all.

If it is necessary to give an immediate answer to the young person you mention, give her my affectionate regards and say that if she can now be admitted in Stanhope Street,[48] I advise her not to delay—and as her sister is there, it must be an attraction.

Sisters Elizabeth, Aloysius & Xavier unite in affectionate [love] to all. We have three very nice new Sisters and a fourth coming. Tell dear Sr. Genevieve her poetry was most acceptable. Sister Ursuline[49] might have chosen a happier subject for hers than the runaway from Kingstown. However, it was made the most or rather the best of.

How anxiously I long to be with [you] in the community room—alone—telling you all the queer things I met since we parted.

---

the Irish bishops, Catherine McAuley supported the national system of education established in 1831. She saw its educational benefits for poor children, and believed that under the right conditions—proper textbooks, strict observance of the end-of-day regulations about religious instruction (both Protestant and Catholic), good relations between teachers and inspectors, and attentive oversight by the commissioners of national education, of whom Dr. Murray was a member—the potential danger of proselytism, by textbooks or teachers, could be averted. By 1841, Mercy schools in Carlow, Charleville, Cork, Dublin, and Tullamore, as well as Limerick, were affiliated with the national board. The commissioners were charged with "administering the funds placed at the disposal of his Excellency the Lord Lieutenant, for the education of the poor in Ireland" (*Irish Catholic Directory* [1838] 339).   46 According to Catherine McAuley (see Letter 102), the temporary House of Mercy for poor women and girls in Limerick was opened on November 19, 1838. Catherine left Limerick on December 9, 1838, the day after Mary Anne Bridgeman entered the community.   47 Dr. John Ryan, bishop of Limerick.   48 The motherhouse of the Sisters of Charity founded by Mary Aikenhead was located on Stanhope Street, in the western area of Dublin, below the River Liffey. The young woman has not been identified.   49 Catherine obviously meant to write "Ursula"—Mary Ursula Frayne in Booterstown. Evidently Ursula had sent Catherine a poem, possibly about the departure of the sisters from Kingstown. No individual "runaway" as such has been identified.

God bless and preserve you, my very Dear Sister. Pray for your fondly attached

M. C. McAuley

I expect to get a pointer from Miss Roach.
I find this is written on the wrong side.[50]

Autograph: Adelaide

102. To Sister M. Frances Warde   Convent, Limerick
Carlow   November 17, 1838

My Dearest Sister Mary Frances

I would have written to you sooner but waited to tell you when we expect to leave this—which was not decided till yesterday. The Bishop has granted a remission of time, on account of the necessity, and three Sisters are to be clothed in the Holy Habit on the 4th of December. We propose going on the 6th—and hope to be with you on the 8th,[51] but as it is a fast day,[52] I suppose you would not have a ceremony.

I have said I hope to be with you, but am not yet sure that circumstances will admit of it. Sister de Pazzi has been so frequently ill since I left Dublin that I dread every account. She continues to write to me and is not aware that I have been told. I did not stay one day for rest or recreation—but extreme caution was necessary in selecting sisters who were likely to make a steady good beginning where there was so much to fear—and I trust we have succeeded—a Miss Bridgman and Miss O'Farrell, about 24 years old, of as much mind and formed

50 Catherine wrote on side 3 of the folded sheet of paper, before concluding the letter on side 2. Miss Roach has not been identified. She was probably a woman with opinions about correspondence style or etiquette.

51 In the end Catherine did not leave Limerick until December 9, and the reception ceremony in Carlow was held on December 10. In Limerick, Mary Teresa Vincent (Ellen) Potter, Mary Francis (Joanna) Bridgeman, and Miss O'Farrell received the habit on December 4 , and Mary Anne Bridgeman from Quin, Co. Clare, entered the community on December 8. Joanna Bridgeman was from Tulla, Co. Clare, and may have been a cousin of Mary Anne.

The Limerick Register lists Ellen Potter's name in religion as "Mary Vincent," but in a poem to her Catherine McAuley writes, "Mary Teresa Vincent de Paul / your names are so pretty—I give you them all" (Letter 107). Moreover, the Limerick Annals, in recording her final illness in 1840, calls her "Sister M. Teresa Vincent Potter" (1:69). Since Mary Vincent Harnett was also in the Limerick community, it was undoubtedly helpful to give Ellen Potter a longer name, if she too wished to have St. Vincent de Paul as her patron.

52 In Ireland at the time the Fridays and Saturdays in Advent were "Fasting Days on One Meal." In 1838, December 8 was a Saturday in Advent. Although it was the feast of the "Conception of the Blessed Virgin Mary," it would have been listed in the *Irish Catholic Directory* among the "Retrenched Holidays, or Days of Devotion," as it was in 1837 when the feast fell on a Friday (*Irish Catholic Directory* [1837] vii).

character as our darling Mary Teresa[53]—and Sister Potter was certainly designed for the Institute. Her ardent zeal for Limerick made her uneasy & restless elsewhere, and her being on the spot, with good connections and interest, promoted the object very much. But we had some difficulties which required experience to manage. They are over, thank God, and I have great reason to think & hope that a lasting foundation is made. The House of Mercy opens on Monday.[54] The collection children are very well received. Priests and people very much pleased.

What would I do or say to have a Carlow Priest at the ceremony on the 4th. Try all the influence you possess—it would comfort and delight me to see them. I have a bad account of Sr. M. Cecilia's health—& fear she cannot come. She & Sr. M. Teresa were to be at the ceremony here and then to go with us to Carlow.[55] If one or more of our dear Carlow Priests were here, we could not avoid going with them—though Mr. O'Hanlon has been prevailed on to order me home. I wrote to him and think he will approve my reason for remaining so long—it was as strong as it could be.[56]

Carlow is keeping pace with Baggot Street as to progress. I suppose it will be spreading through the Country in less time.

The poor here are in the most miserable state—the whole surrounding neighbourhood one scene of wretchedness and sorrow. By staying for the reception I can bring Sr. Aloysius [Scott] away—otherwise I could not.

We find they[57] would not do well until attired in the Religious dress. The people are very sharp and say queer things—even the poor don't like the nett [*sic*] caps so well to speak to them, but turn to the others. Every place has its own particular ideas & feelings which must be yielded to when possible.[58]

3 of the Presentation order came here—about a year and half before us—to a House built by the favorite Priest of Limerick—*Father Pat* Hogan.[59] Every one that wishes to shew their true love turns away from the S[isters] of Mercy—at least, just call to tell them that they are engaged—as to patronage, etc., etc. A great war is going on now about a Lady who has changed her vocation from them

---

53 Catherine is recalling her beloved niece Mary Teresa Macauley, who died on November 12, 1833.   54 November 19, 1838.   55 Mary Cecilia Marmion and Mary Teresa White were scheduled to come from Dublin to Limerick, to swell the musical expertise at the reception ceremony on December 4, and then, if possible, to go on to Carlow with Catherine McAuley.   56 Mary de Pazzi Delany had succeeded in getting Redmond O'Hanlon, the acting ecclesiastical superior of the Baggot Street community, to instruct Catherine to come directly back to Dublin. His letter and Catherine's to him have not survived.   57 The three postulants in the Limerick community.   58 Typically, Catherine McAuley accommodated to the preferences of the locale, whose citizens, in this case, did not regard the postulants—attired in black dresses and black net caps, their hair visible—as "real nuns."   59 According to Courtney, the first group of Presentation Sisters had come to Limerick from Galway in 1833, but "withdrew in 1836 for lack of subjects" ("The 'Nuns'" 6). T. J. Walsh, the biographer of *Nano Nagle*, records the first Presentation foundation in Limerick as that made in 1837 from the South Presentation Convent, Cork (*Nano Nagle* [Chart of Foundations] 404–405). In a letter to Catherine McAuley on April 29, 1837, John Murphy, bishop of Cork, notes the journey "next week" of these Presentation Sisters to Limerick. He says: "We afford subjects & assign to their support the dividends of the sums which they brought into our convent" (Letter 44).

to us. We have received a friendly caution to take no part, but let it work its own way. They are in the best part of the city, but not well supported except by words—and a party. The gentlemen are all with us—Fathers, brothers & uncles will give no assent to any other.[60]

It is getting dark. I may, I trust, say I will see you at the time I mention. I do not yet know how we should travel, but if dear Father Dan would come, we would find the way.[61]

Remember me affectionately to all—and believe me your ever fond

M. C. McAuley

Be sure to give my affectionate regards to Dr. Fitzgerald, etc., etc.

My Dearest Sister M. F.

I have only this moment got a satisfactory letter from Baggot St. Sisters M. C. and M. Teresa will be here on the 4th of December, and we will leave this for Carlow on the 6th, please God—but cannot remain beyond the 10th—quite impossible, from many circumstances which I will tell you.[62]

Autograph: Silver Spring

103. **To Sister M. Elizabeth Moore** [Limerick]
    Limerick [December 9, 1838]

My Dearest Sister M. E.[63]
    Don't let crosses vex or tease
    Try to meet *all* with peace & ease
    notice the faults of every Day
    but often in a playful way

60 A zealous rivalry evidently erupted initially in Limerick, between supporters of the Presentation Sisters and of the Sisters of Mercy. In time, both religious congregations flourished, for the sake of the poor people they served, the Presentation Sisters eventually sending a foundation to Castleisland, County Kerry in 1846 and one to Windsor, Victoria, Australia in 1873. From the Castleisland foundation evolved, directly or indirectly, fourteen additional foundations, twelve of them in Western Australia (T. J. Walsh [Chart] 404–405). 61 Daniel Nolan, curate in Killeshin, Co. Carlow, was, by now, a good friend of Catherine McAuley. Whether he or any other priest from Carlow accompanied Catherine from Limerick to Carlow is not known. 62 As indicated earlier, the timing of the plans in this postscript was subsequently changed. See notes 51 and 55 above. Although this letter was written on November 17, the postmarks on the attached cover are "Limerick NO 26, 1838" and "Carlow NO 27, 1837." Catherine McAuley either delayed mailing the letter, awaiting word from Dublin, or neglected to mail it when the postscript was completed. 63 Mary Elizabeth Moore was the superior of the Limerick community founded on September 24, 1838. In October, Catherine McAuley had commented on Elizabeth's faint-heartedness, but expressed confidence that, in time, she would get over it (Letter 98). The Limerick Annals records that on hearing these lines of poetry, John Ryan, bishop of Limerick, "admired them so much that he observed 'They ought to be written in letters of gold'" (1:22).

And when you seriously complain
let it be known— to give you pain
Attend to one thing— at a time
you've 15 hours from 6 to 9
be mild and sweet in all your ways
now & again—bestow some praise
avoid all solemn declaration
all serious, close investigation
Turn what you can into a jest
and with few words dismiss the rest
keep patience ever at your side
you'll want it for a constant guide
Shew fond affection every Day
and above all—Devoutly pray
That God may bless the charge He's given
and make of you—their guide to Heaven.

The parting advice[64] of your ever affectionate
M. C. M.

Autograph: Limerick

104. To Miss Joanna Reddan   [December 1838][65]
Limerick

My dear Miss Reddan

I had great pleasure in receiving your kind letter; the friendship and regard you express are very acceptable to me. I have not known many whose esteem

64 Catherine McAuley stayed with the new Limerick community for two-and-a-half months, departing for Carlow and Dublin on December 9, 1838.   65 No autograph of this letter exists, but the complete text, as presented here, is published in Carroll, *Leaves* 4:13; with some abbreviation, in Burke Savage (249–50); and in Carroll's article, "Joanna Reddan," in the *Irish Monthly* 20, no. 227 (May 1892): 225–36, where it is also somewhat abbreviated. Burke Savage acknowledges Carroll's *Leaves* as his source, noting that in her text (as well as in her article) "it is dated November 1838, but the month is clearly wrong, as Catherine remained in Limerick until 9th December" (250). I agree. The content of the letter, especially paragraph three, suggests that it was written from Dublin, shortly after Catherine returned from Limerick and Carlow on December 11—probably in December, but possibly in January 1839.

66 Joanna Reddan (1799–1857) was a woman after Catherine McAuley's own heart. On November 1, 1838, she had brought her niece Joanna Bridgeman to the convent in Limerick, rejoicing in her entrance and regretting her own inability to follow her example. The adoptive mother of six children (of her deceased sisters), including Joanna Bridgeman, Joanna Reddan was deeply engaged in ministry in Limerick, a garrison town, where occasions of soldiers taking sexual advantage of young women were prevalent. She "opened a house of refuge in Newgate Lane, but soon removed to Clare

and friendship I should be more desirous to possess.[66] I should have written to you sooner, but have been kept quite a busybody. When absent, I find all goes on very well without me. But, within call, it is nearly impossible not to be forthcoming on almost every occasion, and thus I am doomed to pass many an unprofitable hour. The Sisters at home seem to regard all my excursions as pastime, and expect me to make restitution for the additional charge they had to sustain.

I have great reason to rejoice in our visit to Limerick. Every report is animating and delightful. The institution in that quarter will be very valuable to the afflicted poor, and very edifying to all. I trust you will soon be added to their number—more than in spirit. And I shall never be surprised to hear that you are an obedient, humble Sister. For, being so capable of fully understanding the nature of the state, its obligations and recompense, you could not feel satisfied to lessen its value in your regard. And as God inclines you to desire ardently a more perfect separation from the world, He will not permit any unfavorable results to follow, but will render you more instrumental in perpetuating the establishment over which you have so meritoriously and efficiently presided, and for which you feel so deeply interested.

I have not any communication to make to my dear Sisters, as some parcels were sent lately. I could not put my letter to you among them, thinking it would better atone for my delay to write express. I shall not omit to pray as you desire, with all the sincerity and fervor I am capable of, that God may guide you safely to the fulfilment of His adorable will.

Earnestly begging you to remember me, I remain, my dear Miss Reddan,

Your faithful and affectionate
M. C. McAuley

Published transcription: Carroll, Leaves *4:13*

Street, an historic district where she owned property … She afterwards purchased a factory belonging to a Scotch firm, which she transformed into a chapel and dormitory." To support the young women, "she took in needle-work and washing, and had some of them taught to make the delicate material known as Limerick lace" (Carroll, *Leaves* 4:9–11). In 1832, when cholera raged in Limerick, as in Dublin, she and her protégées attended the sick and dying.

When Catherine McAuley met her in late 1838, Joanna was fully responsible for the Magdalen Asylum she had established, and Dr. John Ryan would not hear of her leaving it in other hands, so she could enter the Sisters of Mercy. In 1847 she brought a group of Sisters of the Good Shepherd from France, planning that they would manage the Asylum on Clare Street, and she could then enter the Sisters of Mercy. But according to Carroll, Dr. Ryan required her—if she wished to enter a convent—to enter the Good Shepherd Sisters. She did so for a year. In 1848, she finally secured Dr. Ryan's acquiescence to her entering the Sisters of Mercy in Kinsale, where her niece Mary Francis (Joanna) Bridgeman was superior (Carroll, *Leaves* 4:14–15). In 1854 she was part of the founding community sent from Kinsale to San Francisco, where she died in 1857, as beloved by the poor people of that city as she had been by the poor women of Limerick.

105. To Catherine McAuley   December 19, 1838

Mrs. McAuley has this day handed me the sum of Twenty Six Pounds Thirteen Shillings and two pence halfpenny being the balance of the Poor Fund in the hands of the Ss. of Mercy at the time of their leaving Kingstown.[67]

William Walsh

Typescript: Dublin, Mercy

---

[67] This brief memorandum (no autograph has been found) represents the final gesture of Catherine McAuley in the departure of the Sisters of Mercy from Kingstown: her return to the parish of every halfpenny remaining in the Poor Fund which the sisters in Kingstown had dispensed on behalf of the parish. Catherine presumably asked William Walsh, a curate in the parish who had tried to avert the departure of the sisters, to provide this memorandum. On May 1, 1842, William Walsh was "consecrated by Dr. Murray co-adjutor bishop of Halifax, Nova Scotia, and some years later succeeded as archbishop" (Donnelly 4:159).

January–April 1839

On November 13, 1841, two days after Catherine McAuley's death, Dr. Michael Blake, bishop of Dromore, wrote to Mary Elizabeth Moore about "the dear departed friend whom I ever esteemed and reverenced." He said of Catherine: "A more zealous, a more prudent, a more useful, a more disinterested, a more successful benefactress of human nature, I believe never existed in Ireland since the days of St. Bridget" (Mercy Congregational Archives; qtd. in Sullivan, *Catherine McAuley* 190–91).

Such thoughts never entered the mind of Catherine McAuley—certainly not in the early months of 1839. In January, in a brief and now much-treasured history of the early years of the Sisters of Mercy, she wrote: "we have been deficient enough—and far, very far, from cooperating generously with God in our regard, but we will try to do better ... will try to repair the past" (Letter 110).

A destructive hurricane swept through Ireland on the night of January 6–7—later popularly known as "the night of the big wind"—leaving hundreds of Dublin houses blown down and the windows of the Baggot Street community room in shambles. But the events that most shook Catherine's spirit in early 1839 were of a different sort: the need, in late February, to dismiss Elizabeth Magenis, a novice, from the Baggot Street community, and the ongoing issue of the Kingstown property and debt. In these two matters she was compelled to act in ways that seemed to run counter to her natural compassion for the weak and her profound reverence for priests. Miss Magenis was "acting in the most rude and unchristian manner," and Bartholomew Sheridan, the parish priest in Kingstown, was asking for £470. There were no solutions short of formally releasing Elizabeth Magenis from her financial donation in return for her immediate departure, and leasing the Kingstown convent. To Charles Cavanagh, the community's solicitor, Catherine wrote: "I regret exceedingly being obliged to engage your time and attention so much" (Letter 115).

Yet, somehow, the "prop" of poetry did not fail Catherine during this period. In January she penned a long poem about the opportunities of the new year to Mary Teresa Vincent Potter in Limerick, and on April 30, her feast day, she sent a playful response in verse to the sisters in Booterstown, promising them "a party will make your heart glad / a nice pick nick dinner" (Letter 120). No, in writing to Frances Warde in April, she did not think of herself as a successor to St. Bridget, but only as "your fond and most affectionate mother" (Letter 118).

106. To Catherine McAuley

Violet Hill, Newry
[c. January 2, 1839][1]

Dear Revd. Mother

I had the honour & pleasure this day of receiving your letter requesting that I would officiate at the profession of three of the Sisters of your House while I shall be in town to attend the next annual meeting of the Irish Prelates.

I am very sorry to learn from your communication that your dear & venerable Archbishop is in such delicate health as to prevent him going out in the morning, and if any services in my power could afford him comfort, I should be delighted in testifying by them my gratitude for the innumerable acts of kindness I have received from him, among which I consider the encouragement he has always shewn to me in my little endeavours to promote the welfare of your establishment.

As to the matter of your request, I cannot give you a refusal. You consider the mitre as an ornament that would add to the solemnity of your Religious Profession. I think so, too, if it have other accompaniments in which I am deficient. However, I will at least shew my good will and readiness to do what you desire. By a letter which I received this day from the Rev. M. Flanagan[2] I am informed the meeting of the prelates will be held on Tuesday, the 22nd instant. I will therefore go up to Dublin on the preceding Saturday, and then on the Monday following[3] I can be at your service without neglecting any other duty.

I must request, however, that you will again see Dr. Murray as soon as you conveniently [can], that you will present to his Grace my most respectful and affectionate compliments and ardent wishes for the perfect re-establishment of his health, and that besides the general leave which he has again & again been pleased to give me of administering sacraments or preaching to his flock, you will receive from him the expression of his special approbation.[4]

[Michael Blake]

Author's transcript: Dromore

107. To Sister M. Teresa Vincent Potter
Limerick

[Early 1839][5]

Dear Mary Teresa—Vincent De Paul
Your names are so pretty—I give you them all

1 This letter is undated, but in his Journal of Letters Dr. Blake transcribes it between letters dated December 28, 1838 and January 4, 1839; the reference to "the 22nd instant" (paragraph three) indicates that it was written in January, not December. 2 Matthew Flanagan, parish priest of St. Nicholas Without on Francis Street, Dublin, and chancellor of the archdiocese of Dublin. 3 That is, January 21, 1839, the day on which Catherine McAuley could schedule the proposed profession ceremony. 4 Ever the courteous bishop, conscious of ecclesiastical protocol, Dr. Blake here requests that Catherine secure Dr. Murray's permission for him to officiate in Dublin. 5 Lines 19 and

I hope you don't think I've been very remiss
In not answering all your nice Rhyme
I should have done so indeed long e'er this
Could I snatch but one hour from time
that monarch who bears us away
In his chariot of measureless flight
to whom we can never, oh never, say Nay
but go with him from morning till night
Stern foe to our beauty and youth
which he steals as he passes along
while he makes us acknowledge as truth
that Life is no more than a song
Oh what shall we do to defeat him
while he is smiting us so
let us try by what art we can cheat him
and make him—a deep "fallen foe"
Let us now with the new year begin
to wrest from this tyrant his power
not only avoiding all sin
but piously passing each hour
our humours and pride we'll subdue
and be mild and be meek as we can
we will try to become quite—a new
and entirely cast off the "old man"
The 38th year is now past
Its cares and its pleasures are gone
the 39th may be our last
since the last is so surely to come
Let us beg for renewed animation
in discharge of our duties each Day
let us smile under every privation
that religion has strewed in our way
All coldness and cholar we'll smother
and watchfully shun all dejection
we will cordially love one another
since that is the mark of election

[M. C. McAuley]

Autograph: Limerick

27–29 of this poem-letter indicate that it was written at the turn of the year, about a month after Mary Teresa Vincent Potter's reception of the habit in Limerick on December 4, 1838. The poem, in response to an earlier poem (or poems) no longer extant, continues a correspondence in verse that will end only with the death of Catherine McAuley's "sweet little poet" on March 20, 1840.

108. To Sister M. Frances Warde   [January 6, 1839][6]
Carlow

My Dearest Sister Mary Frances

Mr. Lynch called late this day and said he would leave town for Carlow at one tomorrow, but finding from his sister[7] that he may go at eight, I am come back to my corner after all are gone to Bed—to write a few lines to my poor old child.

I have not seen Mr. Maher. Mr. Fitzpatrick called—he said you were pretty well, thank God.[8]

We are exactly as you left us, except that a new Sister was concluded for this day from the Co. Wexford. She comes in a week. I thought we should be without a postulant after the ceremony, not knowing anything of the expected one. She will not be 20 till next month. Very pleasing and musical.[9]

It is striking 10, the fire is out and the windows making an awful noise, so I must be done.[10] Praying God to bless and guide and protect you—and all your charge.

6 This undated letter was hand-delivered, so its cover has no postmarks. However, two references in the letter help to date it: the entrance of Ellen Whitty, from Wexford, on January 15, 1839; and especially, the hurricane that struck Ireland on the night of January 6–7, 1839.   7 Catherine Lynch of St. Paul's Parish, Dublin, entered the Baggot Street community on July 3, 1838. She will receive the habit on January 21, 1839, taking the name Mary Rose. No priest by the name of Lynch is listed as serving in a Carlow parish or at Carlow College at this time, but the architect of the new Carlow convent was Joseph Lynch (Carlow Annals for 1837). Moreover, there were two curates with that surname at St. Andrew's, Westland Row, Dublin: Gregory Lynch and Joseph Lynch (*Irish Catholic Directory* [1839] 177). Perhaps one of these was Catherine Lynch's brother.   8 James Maher was now professor of Theology and Sacred Scripture at Carlow College (Moran, ed. xliii), and Bartholomew Fitzpatrick was dean of the College (Carlow Annals for 1838 and 1839). The *Irish Catholic Directory* for 1840, perhaps erroneously, lists two Fitzpatricks at the College: P. Fitzpatrick, as dean, and B. Fitzpatrick, as professor of Logic and Mathematics (363).   9 Ellen Whitty (1819–1892) entered the Sisters of Mercy, Baggot Street, on January 15, 1839, six weeks before her twentieth birthday. She received the habit on July 24, 1839, taking the name Mary Vincent; professed her vows on August 19, 1841; and attended Catherine McAuley in her final illness, writing five detailed letters about her last days. Although she was not the recipient of any of the extant letters of Catherine McAuley, Mary Vincent Whitty was an important early leader of the Sisters of Mercy, initiating construction of the Mater Misericordiae Hospital in Dublin, recruiting Mercy sisters to nurse in the Crimean War (1854–56), serving as novice mistress, mother assistant, or mother superior of the Dublin community from 1844 to 1858, and leading a new foundation to Brisbane, Australia in 1860. From her arrival in Brisbane in 1861 to her death there in 1892, she was an imaginative, courageous servant of the needs and interests of poor Irish immigrants and aboriginal peoples. For fuller knowledge of her life, see Whitty, *Mercy Women* (a collection of her letters, 1860–1891); O'Donoghue, *Mother Vincent Whitty;* and Sullivan, *Catherine McAuley* 235–46.   10 The storm brewing at 10 p.m. on January 6 proved to be a major catastrophe, as later recorded: "Jan. 7 [1839]. Between the hours of 12 [midnight] and 5 o'clock this morning, there was an awful hurricane in Dublin, and in most parts of Ireland, by which several lives were lost, many churches, chapels, and other sacred places were damaged, and an immense number of houses and trees were destroyed." Within the Dublin police district alone, 157 houses were partly or completely blown down, 5089 houses were partly or completely unroofed, and 1527 chimneys were blown down, to say nothing of shattered walls and windows (*Irish Catholic Directory* [1840] 342).

I could not describe the extreme kindness of Doctor Healy [Haly][11] when he called last. He was afraid I would be uneasy lest the little arrangement he made should occasion any unhappiness to you—and he gave the most full—and unquestionably—faithful assurance of the deepest interest and regard. You have a true Father in him.

Good night, my Dearest Child—affectionate love to all.

Pray fervently for your ever fond
M. C. McAuley

Photostat and photocopy: Dublin, Mercy

109. **To Sister M. Frances Warde**   Monday, January 7, 1839
    Carlow

My ever Dear Sister Mary Frances

I have been very uneasy about you since I heard how you have been affected, though I am aware there may not be any serious cause, for Sister Mary Teresa White had the same kind of attack—yet I know you are not sufficiently cautious, and this is what I fear most. Now let me entreat you not to be going through the new Convent, or out in the garden even the mildest day during this month—without careful caping up. Have your shawl crossed on your chest and your feet very warm. I am sorry I did not look at the flannel you are wearing—is it very good? I could send some if you have it not. Again I entreat you to be prudently cautious.[12]

Last night's storm has done great injury in Dublin—I hope you had it not in Carlow. 16 panes of glass broken in the Community room—the pictures all blown down and even the heavy book stand quite upset—the cabinet moved from the wall to near the middle of the room. You may suppose what an appearance on opening the door this morning. Poor Sister Teresa[13] was afraid to enter and came running for me to the choir. The school room as bad. No more here, but many houses blown down and a dreadful fire in Dorset Street from the breaking of chimneys. I have not heard from Booterstown, but suppose they felt it very much. We are obliged to remain in our broken state, as they say new glass would come out immediately.

We were very glad to see Mr. Maher, I mean my child.[14] I suppose he is at home with you. He told me you are still on the increase, quite outdoing the old Mother House—as to rapid progress.

---

11 Francis Haly, bishop of the diocese of Kildare and Leighlin, where Carlow was situated.   12 Word that Frances Warde was again showing signs of illness prompted this second letter to her in two days, as did worry over the possible effects of the hurricane (see note 10) in Carlow.   13 Teresa Carton.   14 The sentence is confusing: Catherine may have intended to refer to James Maher, who was fifteen years younger than she, but she has not previously called this robust and politically powerful priest "my child"; or she may have meant to write "Mr. Nolan," and corrected herself by writing, "I mean my child." She often called Daniel Nolan "my son."

I am glad you are to have the balcony since you like it—but I charge you, if you have any affection for me, not to be looking after it at present. Let this month pass over.

I had letters from Limerick yesterday—everything going on well, thank God— from Sister Mary Clare[15] also—whose account is not cheering. She feels very much their progress being kept back—says that none like to propose now, there is so much scrutiny into family concerns and so much about means—though she adds, "we find that very limited means will suffice" and have plenty of money to spare. The House next to them has been purchased to enlarge their Convent, and this seems to perplex her more. No wonder it should.[16]

I fear the Kingstown business is going to be settled. I cannot wish the poor Sisters to go there—they never shall, except a private choir is made for them in the P[arish] Chapel, but I fear this will be done. *Do not say anything of it yet.*[17]

Remember me to Doctor Fitzgerald—and give my most affectionate love to all the dear Sisters. Tell them to take care of my child—yourself.

Praying God to bless and guide you with His own Divine Spirit,

I remain, my Dearest old Child,
your ever fond
M. C. McAuley

Autograph: Silver Spring

110. **Sister M. Elizabeth Moore**   **Baggot Street**
     Limerick   **January 13, 1839**

My Dear Sister Mary Elizabeth

I received your letter yesterday and thank God that you are all safe after the storm. The accounts from Limerick were as usual exagerated [*sic*], but we heard the Convent was safe—from some person who called. We remained in Bed all night—some in terror, others sleeping, etc. The morning presented an altered scene from what we had left at 9 o'clock. The Community Room a compleat ruin in appearance, though not much real injury—the Prints and pictures all on the ground—only two broken. The maps and blinds flying like the sales [*sic*] of a ship—the Book stand down—the cabinet removed from its place, and the chairs all upset—16 panes broken—and such a body of air in the room that we could scarcely stand. The windows are still boarded up—it is almost impossible to get a glazier—a fine harvest for them.

15 Mary Clare Moore in Cork.   16 Dr. John Murphy, bishop of Cork, was apparently exercising determined control over the size of the dowries young women brought to the Cork community, as well as planning for a larger (and therefore, in his view, more financially sound) community.   17 Some conversation was occurring to get the Sisters of Mercy to come back to their house in Kingstown. However, see Letters 112, 113, 114, 116, and 117. Sisters did not return to Kingstown until April 1840, and then only at Daniel Murray's direct request.

The Hospital at the green[18] greatly broken—a chimney fell. Several Houses blown down—and many lives lost. Your friends and Sister Vincent's safe. The Sisters in Carlow passed the night in the choir—part of their very old roof blown down. The Beautiful Cathedral much injured. The chimneys of the new Convent in Tullamore blown down—the old one & Sisters safe. We have not heard from Cork or Charleville.

My dear Sister E., I would find it most difficult to write what you say Mr. Clarke[19] wishes for, the circumstances which would make it interesting could never be introduced in a public discourse. It commenced with 2, Sister Doyle & I. The plan from the beginning was such as is now in practise—& in '27 the House was opened. In a year & half we were joined—so fast that it became a matter of general wonder. Doctor Murray gave his most cordial approbation and visited frequently—all was done under his direction from the time we entered the House—which was erected for the purposes of charity.

Doctor Blake & Revd. Mr. Armstrong were chiefly concerned—received all the Ideas I had formed—and consulted for 2 years at least before the House was built. I am sure Doctor Blake had it constantly before him in all his communications with Heaven—for I never can forget his fervent prayers—when it was in progress.

Seeing us increase so rapidly, and all going on in the greatest order almost of itself—great anxiety was expressed to give it stability. We who began were prepared to do whatever was recommended—and in September 1830 we went with Dear Sister Harley[20] to Georges Hill—to serve a noviciate for the purpose of firmly establishing it. In December '31 we returned—and the progress has gone on as you know. We now have gone beyond 100 in number—and the desire to join seems rather to encrease. Though it was thought the foundations would retard it—it seems to be quite otherwise.

There has been a most marked Providential Guidance which the want of prudence—vigilance—or judgment has not impeded—and it is here that we can most clearly see the designs of God. I could mark circumstances calculated to defeat it at once—but nothing however injurious in itself has done any injury.

18 The new St. Vincent's Hospital on the eastside of St. Stephen's Green had been founded by Mary Aikenhead and the Sisters of Charity in 1834 in the former mansion of the Earl of Meath. It opened for women patients in 1835, for men patients in 1836 (Blake 55–57). 19 During the spring of 1839, John Clarke, a curate in St. John's parish—the bishop's parish in Limerick—was scheduled to preach a Charity Sermon on behalf of the poor schools there (Limerick Annals 1:31). He had apparently asked Elizabeth Moore for some information about the origin of the Sisters of Mercy. His request led Catherine McAuley to pen the brief, but moving account of the first years of the congregation that is the centerpiece of this letter, all the while claiming that she could not write such a history. 20 Mary Elizabeth (Elizabeth) Harley, a friend of Frances Warde, had joined the Baggot Street community on November 30, 1829. She went to George's Hill with Catherine McAuley and Anna Maria Doyle, and on December 12, 1831 professed her vows as one of the first three Sisters of Mercy. Four and a half months later (April 25, 1832), she was dead, victim of a consumptive condition that had worsened while she was at George's Hill. All the contemporary biographical manuscripts about Catherine McAuley speak fondly of Elizabeth Harley, and of Catherine's confidence in what she contributed, and might in the future have contributed, to the young congregation. See, for example, Sullivan, *Catherine McAuley*, 63–64, 105, 109–110, and 171–72.

This is all I could say. The loss of property has been supplied. The Death of the most valuable Sisters passed away as of no consequence. The alarm that was spread by such repeated deaths—did not prevent others crowding in. In short, it evidently was to go on—and surmount all obstacles—many of which were great indeed—proceeding from causes within & without. One thing is remarkable—that no breach of charity ever occurred amongst us. The sun never, I believe, went down on our anger. This is our only boast—otherwise we have been deficient enough— and far, very far, from cooperating generously with God in our regard, but we will try to do better—all of us—*the black heads*[21]—will try to repair the past.

This is a repetition of what you already know. To prepare a detail fit to give Mr. Clarke would be to me now a difficult task—I should write it 10 times at least before it would be fit for his purpose—and as my sight is getting worse and my fingers stiff, I would consider it a hopeless attempt. This is the worst scribble I ever wrote—in this way I cannot hope to improve.

Write soon—it is a great comfort to me to hear from you often. Do not get tired—half your paper not written on—a little nonsense even will be acceptable.

Two Sisters to enter next week.[22] We are too full at present and going to divide the old school room to get more accom[m]odation.

Doctor Blake is to perform the ceremonies here on the 21[st]—as our Bishop does not go out early since his last severe illness. Mr. Lynch[23] is to Preach. I had a most kind affectionate letter from Doctor Blake—he tells me of your having written to him.

Tell me, could you read all this? God preserve and bless you, my Dear Sister—pray fervently for your

> ever affectionate
> M. C. McAuley

On reading this over—I find it quite in a random style. It must stay so. I charge you not to let *this* out of your hand.

The next frank I will write to all my Dear Sisters.

Autograph: Limerick

111. **To Sister M. Frances Warde**   **Sunday—commenced on Friday**
     Carlow   **[January 25, 27, 1839]**

My Dearest Sister Mary Frances

We got through our ceremony under most painful circumstances.[24] Poor Mrs. Marmion got her last illness just when the retreat commenced. We concealed it

---

21 That is, the professed sisters, who wore black veils, in contrast to the white-veiled novices. 22 Ellen Whitty entered the convent on January 15, 1839, but Annie Fleming, whom Catherine is evidently anticipating, did not enter until February 5, 1839. 23 Either Gregory Lynch or Joseph Lynch, both of whom were curates at St. Andrew's, Westland Row. See Letter 108, note 7. 24 Dr. Michael Blake presided at the ceremony at Baggot Street on Monday, January 21, 1839, during which three

from Sister Francis—but on the third day she heard a message given as she passed in the hall, yet remained perfectly quiet till the day of her Profession. She could merely read her vows—and went immediately after to her dear Mamma, who was in great joy to see her a nun—and have her constant attendance in her last moments. She lived four days, her two children about her bed.[25] She said, "I wonder is there a woman in the world dying so happily as I am." All is now peace & joy. They are delighted—indeed she was greatly favored by God—thought of nothing but her sins.

I have only a few moments more—expecting the Bishop[26]—he most kindly celebrated Mass for us & promised to call again. This is, I believe, the last day he proposed remaining.

Will you tell dear Sister Mary Josephine that her Sister is not so ill as she fears—I expect she will call here in a few days. Mrs. Lynch of Dorset Street came as Sr. M. J. requested—but agreed with me that I could not go to Mrs. Barrett's house under the present circumstances. Mrs. Lynch said she would prevail on her to come to Baggot St. I will not part her till she promises to do all that is necessary.[27]

I had a letter from Sister Mary Ann Doyle. She expresses great fears about Sister G. and asks what is thought of her sister—says she cannot hear if she has been professed—prays God to direct herself in this matter & says she thinks Sr. G. would die of grief if obliged to go—says the means are reduced to half, and adds "at this the Bishop will be very angry." I read such sentences with great satisfaction. When not carried quite so far as Cork—they prove a fatherly guidance & shield from censure.[28]

---

sisters received the habit: Mary Veronica (Elinor) Cowley, Mary Rose (Catherine) Lynch, and Mary (Eliza) Liston; and three professed their vows: Mary de Sales (Jane) White, Mary Angela (Mary) Maher, and Mary Francis (Margaret) Marmion. These women had made a week-long spiritual retreat prior to the ceremony. In 1841 Mary Veronica Cowley changed her name to Mary Aloysius. 25 Mary Francis Marmion was the third of the Marmion sisters to profess her vows at Baggot Street. Her sister Mary Agnes (Frances) Marmion had died there on February 10, 1836. With her sister Mary Cecilia, Mary Francis attended the deathbed of Mary Marmion, their mother. By all accounts the Marmions were a remarkable Catholic family in St. Andrew's parish; a son, Francis Marmion, Esq., often did legal work for Catherine McAuley. Catherine's reference to "four days" (since the profession ceremony) helps one to read correctly her dating of this letter: "Sunday—commenced on Friday," *not* "Tuesday—continued on Friday" as in Neumann and Bolster. 26 Dr. Francis Haly, bishop of Kildare and Leighlin. 27 Mary Josephine Trennor was a professed sister in the Carlow community. The particular circumstances to which Catherine alludes have not been identified. 28 Evidently Mary Ann Doyle, the superior of the Tullamore community, was concerned that Mary Josephine (Jane) Greene could not provide the dowry on which Dr. John Cantwell, bishop of Meath, normally insisted. Earlier Jane Greene had been a novice in the Baggot Street community, but delicate health had forced her to leave. She then entered the Tullamore community on March 30, 1837. Her term of postulancy "shortened on account of being in Religion before" (Tullamore Annals 23), she received the habit on May 21, 1837. Still a novice in January 1839, there was now some question, related to the bishop's known views, about whether she could profess vows, having an insufficient dowry. The issue was

I am rejoiced at your wonderful increase—in two years more Baggot St. will be outdone. When I want to have some real amusement I talk to Sr. Mary Teresa of your going to London. She becomes impatient and expresses surprise in various terms: "do I want to break up the Carlow Convent"—"do I think it is past all danger"—"has a miracle been worked for it." Certainly she must have some attachment by right of birth— for we have only to touch the subject to have her all concerned.[29] She is now *labouring* at the Charity Sermon letters. She cannot do them in the best style, but is so anxious that I am silent. We have not Sister M. C. yet able, but I trust she will [be] next week.[30]

Are you taking great care of cold? The weather is now very severe.

The invitation is very nicely done. I think the printing remarkably good. The *Judge* thinks the etching would be exceedingly good if not so heavy, which she says gives it the appearance of a print—but I do not mind half what she says on these scientific points, which she delights in unfolding to the fools that will hearken to her. She will do anything in the Register you wish, but what is mentioned. She calls three weeks work—and she could not give that time until the Bazaar is over. She is very slow.[31]

Give my most affectionate love to all the dear Sisters—best regards to the Priests—respects to Dr. F.[32] Earnestly praying God to bless you—I am always

your attached

M. C. McAuley

I am rejoiced you pray so often for me.

Will you send the enclosed to wherever Miss Fitzgerald is—you may read it and then seal it.

---

apparently resolved, after some further delay (allegedly because of Dr. Cantwell's absence in Rome), for she professed her vows in Tullamore on October 15, 1839 (Tullamore Annals 30–31). Jane's sister Rebecca Greene had entered the Carlow community on April 14, 1837, received the habit on November 14, 1837, taking the name Mary Agnes, and was slated to profess her vows on June 11, 1839. Apparently Mary Ann Doyle wished to know whether Mary Agnes would be professed, and how Frances Warde, the superior in Carlow, was handling the issue of the dowry. Mary Josephine Greene died in Tullamore on September 11, 1843.   **29** Having been born in Carlow and having spent considerable time assisting the Carlow community, Mary Teresa White was partial to its well-being; she regarded the leadership of Frances Warde as essential to its welfare.   **30** Mary Clare Augustine Moore, the best artist and calligrapher in the Dublin community, was likely occupied in other work, probably for the Spring Bazaar.   **31** The "Judge" of calligraphy is surely Mary Clare Augustine Moore. The invitation in question may be the invitation to the Charity Sermon on behalf of the House of Mercy in Dublin, scheduled for February 3, on which Teresa White was working, or to an event in Carlow. One sees in this paragraph a confidential expression of Catherine's impatience with Clare Augustine's expertise, particularly with the amount of time required to produce her art work. The irony of Catherine's complaints is reflected in the admiration for Catherine's virtues that Clare Augustine expresses throughout her "Memoir of the Foundress" (see Sullivan, *Catherine McAuley* 198–216). To Catherine's credit, the Bermondsey Annals records an occasion when she publicly apologized to a sister, presumably Clare Augustine, for having "spoken, as she thought, rather sharply to her" (Sullivan, *Catherine McAuley* 119).   **32** Dr. Andrew Fitzgerald, in Carlow.

We were anxiously looking out for Doctor Healy [Haly] this morning, but he did not come.

Autograph: Silver Spring

112. To Charles Cavanagh, Esq.   [Baggot Street]
Saturday [January 26, 1839][33]

Dear Sir

The Sisters are just returned from Kingstown. Mr. Sheridan met them according to his appointment, but said he thought there was a misunderstanding—that we would have to pay four hundred and seventy pounds—before he would make the Choir.[34] This is very different from what he said to you.

Dear Sir, respectfully, etc., etc.

M. C. McAuley

Autograph: Dublin, Mercy

113. To Sister M. Frances Warde   [February 1839]
Carlow

My Dearest Sister Mary Frances

I am delighted to hear you are to have your ceremony at Easter—it is a most animating season, after the dreary winter. I hope Sister M. de Sales [Maher] is in great spirits for her most happy engagement in which she will every day find something more endearing. Neither her own unworthiness or the crosses inseparable from every earthly state can deprive her of the sweet peace she will enjoy, because I am sure she will be faithful. I am so happy to find Sister Strange is sufficiently strong to give hope that she will be stronger, and Sister Kenny, I suppose, is in rapture and in full health. I would dearly like to be one amongst them on the occasion.[35]

---

33 Charles Cavanagh dated this letter, on the back of Catherine McAuley's stationery.   34 Normally the Sisters of Mercy worshipped in their own convent chapel—if their house had a chapel, which some early convents did not—or in the parish chapel or church. Given the coldness of the dark, empty parish chapel during their times of daily prayer, Catherine McAuley had asked for a "private choir" as a condition for considering a return of the sisters to Kingstown (see Letter 109). Exactly what she meant by a "private choir" (space in a transcept? in a room adjoining the sanctuary?) is not known. Letter 113 indicates that Mary Teresa White and Mary Aloysius Scott were the sisters who met with Bartholomew Sheridan, the parish priest.   35 A profession and reception ceremony, as well as the blessing pro tem of the new convent chapel, was scheduled in Carlow for April 2, 1839, two days after Easter (Carlow Annals). Mary de Sales (Mary) Maher had already received, two months in advance of the April date, the positive vote of the Carlow chapter (pro-

All as usual. I am afraid to let myself hope that Dear Teresa Carton is better. She does not cough near so much—and is more cheerful. She calls herself quite well.

We have two new Sisters since the ceremony—neither quite twenty. The last we call the Queen, she is exactly her age—an exceedingly nice young person—a cousin of Father Hume of Naas.[36] Her family live in this street. The other Co. Wexford. I believe another is on the way—quite unexpected. When I think we are done, we seem to be beginning again. Only yesterday I found your note to Sister M. C. It must have dropt in among my papers. I sent it to her this day.[37]

Mrs. & Miss White called this morning. The rest of the family are on the way. When Sister de Pazzi heard you were preparing for a ceremony she said you would want some of the meditations, if Mr. Kenny can take them.[38]

I wrote to you so lately, I cannot think of one sentence more.

Saturday—a new account about Kingstown. Mr. Sheridan told Mr. Cavanagh that if the School House were assigned to trustees—for the children—the debt should be paid & a choir made in the P[arish] Church for the Sisters if they would return. Mr. Cavanagh agreed to this. Mr. Sheridan then wrote to me requesting two Sisters would go out to select such portion of the church as was deemed necessary. Sister Mary Teresa and Aloysius went on the day he appointed. After taking all their plan, he recalled what he had agreed with Mr. Cavanagh—and said in presence of Mr. Walsh that he never invited them to Kingstown and therefore could not be called upon to do what he heard was done for us in other places. I could not describe Mr. Cavanagh's surprise. He said Mr. Sheridan could not speak plainer. He wrote to him expressing his surprise and shewed me a copy of the letter. If it was to me he said it—he would think it was my imagination.[39]

---

fessed sisters) for admission to profession (Rule 20.3, in Sullivan, *Catherine McAuley* 315). Rosina Strange, who entered the Carlow community on October 15, 1838, and Margaret Kenny, who entered on November 28, 1838, will receive the habit on April 2, taking the names Mary Rose and Mary Vincent, respectively. The Carlow Annals for 1839 records that "Our Foundress always seeking to gratify her children came down for the ceremony—it was the last [ceremony] in St. Leo's [the Carlow convent] which she favoured with her presence."   **36** Ellen Whitty, of Wexford, and Annie Fleming had entered (see Letter 108, note 9, and Letter 110, note 22). Annie, the cousin of George Hume, curate in Naas, was one of two sisters whom Catherine McAuley called the "Queen." Queen Victoria was born in 1819.   **37** Sister M. C. is probably Mary Cecilia Marmion, then in Booterstown, or possibly Mary Clare Moore in Cork.   **38** Numerous handwritten copybooks of "Meditations for Retreat before Reception [or Profession]" can still be found in the archives of the earliest Mercy convents. These Meditations were usually selective transcriptions from published books on spirituality and religious life. Considerable research is needed to identify the sources of the content in these meditation books which were widely used by the early Sisters of Mercy. Mr. Kenny has not been identified—unless he is John Kenny, the father of Margaret Kenny of Newgarden, Co. Carlow. Peter Kenny, SJ, was then superior of the Jesuit community at the Church of St. Francis Xavier on Upper Gardiner Street, Dublin, but he seems an unlikely messenger since Catherine McAuley appears to have had no direct contact with this celebrated Jesuit leader.   **39** About this meeting with Bartholomew Sheridan, parish priest in Kingstown, see Letter 109, note

I think it would seem like defiance—if we were to go now, after the Parish Priest saying to two Sisters, in the presence of his curate, that he never invited them. Sister Mary Teresa could not avoid saying in reply—that none of them liked to come. It is a perplexing business.

Pray for me. God preserve you and bless you, my Dearest Child. Love to all.

Your ever affectionate
M. C. McAuley

Autograph: Baltimore

114. To the Reverend John Hamilton

Convent, Baggot Street
February 7, 1839

Very Reverend Sir

I beg leave to send you some papers just received. If I were to draw from our fund what would pay the demand,[40] the concerns[41] must be sold to return it, as we have not two pounds a year more than is required for our support, etc.

Mr. Sheridan has the rooms locked—and the furniture may get damp. I never could come to any conclusion as to retaking the charge, without seeing his Grace—if you, Revd. Sir, would be so kind to prevail on him to appoint any time, I would keep the Sisters all at home that they might get his blessing—as we have not seen him for thirteen months.[42]

With a grateful sense of your kindness on all occasions, I remain

Very Reverend Sir, with much respect, etc., etc.
Mary C. McAuley

I suppose, Revd. Sir, something must be done to prevent more law proceedings.

Autograph: Dublin Diocese, Murray Papers AB3/34/15, no. 13

---

17 and Letter 112, note 34, as well as Letters 114, 116, and 117 below. William Walsh was a curate in Kingstown.   40 The demand of Bartholomew Sheridan, Kingstown.   41 That is, the house on Sussex Place in Kingstown and the poor school on the property.   42 As Donal Kerr points out, Daniel Murray was from 1838 to 1841 the leading proponent in one of the most serious controversies facing the Irish hierarchy during his episcopacy: the attempt of John MacHale, archbishop of Tuam, to persuade Rome to condemn Catholic participation in the National School system "as dangerous to Catholic children" (255). Dr. Murray and a majority of Irish bishops favored participation. The author of a biographical sketch of Dr. Murray in the *Irish Catholic Directory* for 1839 also notes that following his return from Rome in October 1836, "his Grace has had two or three severe attacks of illness; yet, although in the 71st year of his life, [he] is still enabled to discharge the duties of his high and weighty office" (151). These duties are amply documented in Dr. Murray's (and John Hamilton's) extensive correspondence in 1837 and 1838, now preserved in the Dublin Diocesan Archives. Although Catherine McAuley was surely sympathetic towards the reasons for Dr. Murray's inaccessibility—at least the reasons of which she seems to have been aware—her lack

115. To Charles Cavanagh, Esq.　　　　Convent, Baggot Street
February 14, 1839

Dear Sir

I regret exceedingly being obliged to engage your time and attention so much, but I cannot arrange this matter myself—were it merely personal, I would soon put an end to it, by giving Miss McGuinness [Magenis][43] what she now violently demands. She is acting in the most rude and unchristian manner—she called me a wretch twice before two or three and says I prepared a drink for her with something to stupify her and sent it by Sister White, that you and I got her to sign the deed after she had taken this draught. This has spread through the House— and may be productive of very injurious consequences. Sister White's father has been appointed a Stipendiary Magistrate and is at present in Town.[44] I was thinking of consulting him—of course he would take up very seriously such a charge brought against his child.

Miss McG. seems to forget entirely that she is to observe any regulations— she interrupts our religious exercises—always saying that she acts by the direction of her Lawyer who, she says, tells her she may go into every room in the Convent—what no religious Sister could do.[45]

I will copy here what our Rule prescribes—in reference to this case. It is signed and sealed by the Archbishop:

> Chapter 8—4th Section: "...as many shall be received on the Establishment as the funds will admit of and no more—unless the subject bring with her a sufficient dower for her support in every necessary. Lodgers shall not be admitted—with an exception in favor of a foundress or very particular Benefactress."[46]

---

of direct contact with him could not have come at a worse time, given the chaplaincy and the Kingstown disputes. Whether she had an opportunity to meet with him after this letter is not known. Walter Meyler and Bartholomew Sheridan were both close friends of Daniel Murray, as one can infer from regular invitations to dinner preserved in the Murray and Hamilton Papers in the Dublin Diocesan Archives.　**43** Elizabeth Magenis had entered the convent in 1833 and was received as a novice. She attempted to live a religious life, but was eventually found unsuitable for admission to religious profession, confirming the impression of her reported to Catherine McAuley by Dr. Blake in 1833 (see Letter 18). She evidently remained in the convent, either as a novice or as a boarder until her behavior led to the crisis described in this letter to Charles Cavanagh.　**44** Mary Teresa (Amelia) White's father was Laurence White. Although she was born in Carlow in 1809, the family had moved to Fairy Lawn, Co. Wexford before the birth of her sister Mary de Sales (Jane) White in 1810 (according to the Liverpool Register) or 1813 (according to Carroll, *Leaves* 2:387). Whether the family was still living in Wexford in 1839 is not known. I have not so far identified a source citing Laurence White's appointment as a stipendiary magistrate, beyond Catherine's claim which is presumably accurate.　**45** For example, a sister did not enter the bedroom (i.e., cell or dormitory) of another sister without permission.　**46** In Catherine McAuley's original text of the Rule and Constitutions as approved, after some suggested revision, by Dr. Murray on January 23, 1837, the chapter "Of the Reception of Postulants," of which this paragraph is the 4th section, was Chapter

Miss McG. wants to be a Lodger without being either foundress or Benefactress, but that cannot be—except we were permitted to violate our Rule.

If Miss McG. will give a release, I will propose (with permission) returning her one thousand pounds—though we never could consider a person giving four hundred—and paying her expenses—eligible to be admitted as Benefactress.

It has been said here that Miss M. has incurred damages by the manner she has spoken of the Establishment before strangers—her language indeed is dreadful—I am sure her poor head must be in a distracted state.

Will you in charity to all—make the above proposal—and I will get it concluded soon as possible.[47]

With many thanks for your great kindness, and begging you to excuse all this trouble, I remain,

Dear Sir, your very grateful etc., etc.

Mary C. McAuley

Autograph: Dublin, Mercy

116. To the Reverend John Hamilton

Adelaide Place
Kingstown
February 19, 1839

My dear Mr. Hamilton,

Someone lately told Mr. Sheridan that a Priest commissioned by the S.S. [Sisters] of Charity had been making enquiries at Baggot St. concerning the deserted Convent in Sussex Place[48]. Mr. Sheridan expressed a wish that I should write to ascertain from you whether they have any real intention of settling in

---

20. In Clare Moore's fair copy of the document the chapter became Chapter 8. Catherine is here following the placement in the fair copy, now signed and sealed by Dr. Murray, which is the version she will send to Rome in late 1839. See Sullivan, *Catherine McAuley* 270–72, 292, 315–16.   47 The Indenture of Release, dated February 25, 1839, was signed by Elizabeth Magenis, Catherine McAuley, and J. M. Cantwell of 19 Bolton Street, Dublin. It acknowledged the original Indenture of Agreement, dated January 28, 1836, by which Miss Magenis transferred to Catherine McAuley, Anna Maria Doyle, and Frances Warde "One thousand four hundred and seventy one pounds four shillings new three and a half per cent Government stock", to be held in Trust for the use and benefit of the Sisters of Mercy. The Indenture of Release provided that in view of the lodging, board, and other services provided to Elizabeth Magenis by the Sisters of Mercy for "five years eight months," a sum of "nine hundred and eighty five pounds fourteen shillings and six pence of Government new three and a half per cent stock equivalent at the price of the day to the sum of one thousand pounds sterling" should be transferred to Miss Magenis upon her departure. Thus, about £485 in Government stock was retained by the Sisters of Mercy to cover Elizabeth Magenis's past expenses in the convent. The autograph Indentures are preserved in Mercy Congregational Archives, Herbert Street, Dublin.   48 The deserted convent on Sussex Place, Kingstown, was the convent of the Sisters of Mercy. Further evidence that enquiries were made at Baggot Street on behalf of the Sisters of Charity has not been located, nor has "someone" been identified.

Kingstown. He seems very favorably disposed towards them and says they can have the place at a dead Bargain—say 500£. There would be an ample field here for their charitable zeal. I believe he would be disposed to render them every attention & says they might reckon on a Charity Sermon for the Poor besides Subscriptions [*illegible word*]⁴⁹ the Convent is now the property of Mr. Sheridan himself & he can sell it for what he likes. Though I have made one hundred ineffectual attempts in behalf of this most unfortunate place I cheerfully discharge this commission in the hope that it may lead to some good.

I wish I could fully impress your mind with the state of the children in this town. As many as 40 or 50 are attending the Church School within 3 or 4 doors of me. Several of them actually go to Church⁵⁰ on Sundays! and three or four Adults unblushingly frequent it, who are said too to have gone through a form of recantation. I have been for a long time an agonized though silent witness of these proceedings. I was unwilling even to allude publickly to the matter for many reasons—the chief of which was that a word from the Pulpit on the frightful state of the children might do more harm than good in the excited state of feeling here consequent on the melancholy departure of the Nuns.⁵¹ Besides, I hoped to the last, that they might return. Last Sunday, however, I felt that I could be no longer. During the Sermon I read the Parents a Lecture which I trust they will never forget. But alas! of what avail is all this, if we are to have no Female School or no means to counteract the insidious, persevering efforts of the wealthy Bigots who swarm in this place, whom no child can escape, and whom no labor nor expense will deter from their proselyting career.

I am no alarmist & I have been now for three months silent. But, would to God, our dear Archbishop could see the state of this place as I do, and I am convinced he would soon apply a remedy.⁵²

I again called today on George Roche⁵³ after the Station at Bray. As usual he received me most kindly. I am certain I have gained his confidence. May we

49 At this critical point in the narrative, the handwriting is unfortunately illegible. There appears to be no period after "Subscriptions"; the next word is a capitalized, two-letter word that appears to be followed by a period. It is possible that the word is "If," in which case the following clauses are conditional, or a strangely abbreviated "Etc.," in which case the following sentence is declarative, although it is not clear to me that the opening word, "the," is capitalized. What is at stake in a correct reading of the word is whether William Walsh, a curate in Kingstown, is reporting that Bartholomew Sheridan is now the owner of the property, or whether he is conveying uncertainty about that. The sentence above, stating that the Sisters of Charity "can have the place at a dead Bargain—say 500£," implies that Father Sheridan did indeed regard himself as the current owner. 50 Presumably, given his concern, William Walsh means that the children are attending the school and services of the Established Church—or those of another Protestant denomination. 51 That is, the departure of the Sisters of Mercy in early November 1838. In cataloguing this letter for the Dublin Diocesan Archives, Mary Purcell mistakenly said that the deserted convent belonged to "the Discalced nuns" (*Archivium Hibernicum* 49 [1995]: 54). 52 In transcribing the two preceding paragraphs of this letter, Burke Savage frequently interpolates words that do not appear in the autograph of the letter (179–80). However, these interpolations do not alter the meaning of the letter. He does not transcribe the paragraph containing the problem discussed in note 49. 53 "George Roche" may have been a priest of

humbly hope that I shall be the means of bringing him to a sense of his duty at this important crisis in his life. He is much better and if we could induce him to come to Kingstown for a short time, I would endeavor to see him every day & follow up the good work.

Believe me, my dear Rev. friend

yours very sincerely
William Walsh

Autograph: Dublin Diocese, Hamilton Papers P1/36/2, no. 33

117. To Charles Cavanagh, Esq. [Baggot Street]
Wednesday Morning [April 17, 1839][54]

Dear Sir

I forgot to acknowledge the receit of your note enclosing £1.16.4.

May I beg to trouble you again about Kingstown. I hear of places letting all about & fear the season may pass with us. We want knives and many other things in the household way which must be quite spoiled there.[55] Will you in charity conclude the matter for us?

Dear Sir, respectfully, etc.
M. C. McAuley

Autograph: Dublin, Mercy

118. To Sister M. Frances Warde [Late April 1839][56]
Carlow

My Dearest Sister Mary Frances

Our poor Sisters M. Teresa and de Sales are in great affliction. An account

---

the Dublin archdiocese whom William Walsh was trying to help. The content of this paragraph is unrelated to that of the rest of the letter. The *Irish Catholic Directory* for 1839 lists Alexander Roache as parish priest of Bray (178).   54 Catherine McAuley did not date this letter, but Charles Cavanagh wrote "17 Apl 1839" on the reverse side of Catherine's stationery. The date of the letter is important because in it Catherine urges the community's solicitor to conclude the Kingstown matter and implies that she wishes to "let" (i.e. lease) the property while the season for letting seaside houses is active. Two months separate this letter and Letter 116. If in that letter Bartholomew Sheridan was understood to be the owner of the Kingstown convent, in this letter Catherine McAuley clearly regards the Sisters of Mercy as the owner.   55 In her "Memoir," Mary Clare Augustine Moore—who entered the Baggot Street community on August 8, 1837—reports that in November 1838 the Sisters in Kingstown "had to come into Baggot St. with all haste to avoid being in the [Kingstown] house when an execution [presumably a judicially approved seizure of the house] should be laid upon it" (Sullivan, *Catherine McAuley* 210).   56 Previous editors and archivists have dated this undated letter January 10, 1839, but that date cannot be correct, in view of the references to the Bazaar, now passed, and to the upcoming profession of Mary Agnes Greene in Carlow (see notes below).

of Brother William's death came on Monday—without Priest or friend.[57] We have just returned from a visit to his poor little widow. I never witnessed such a scene. She seems quite deranged, and her Mother nearly as bad. They all say he was so good and amiable. The poor Sisters here are as sorrowful as they could be, but a quiet silent sorrow of course.

Your last letter was the greatest comfort to me, and Dr. F's description of the ceremony is romantic.[58]

Miss Fitzgerald of Geraldine called about servants. She praised the arrangements in your Convent in the strongest terms—said it was most attractive in every way, and admired Mrs. Warde beyond expression.[59]

Dr. Fitzgerald is uneasy about your health. I entreat you not to give public instructions or make any exertion you can avoid. I was very ill for about 10 days, but am getting on again.

The Bazaar like last year—about 40 or 50 [pounds] after all expenses—dearly earned.[60]

Sister Teresa [Carton] much better—all the rest well. Take care of yourself, my Dear Child. Remember me affectionately to all. I am delighted to hear Sister Mary Agnes is to be professed.[61] Please God she will be very good & happy.

Dr. F[itzgerald] goes off in the morning. I must send this now. God bless and preserve you, my Dearest Child. Pray often for your fond & most affectionate mother

M. C. McAuley

My poor little Teresa Byrn not going on well. She cannot remain, I think, much longer.[62] My poor James & Robert gone from me. I have not seen them—though in Dublin—for 17 months.[63]

Autograph: West Hartford

---

57 The exact day of death of William White, brother of Mary Teresa (Amelia) White and Mary de Sales (Jane) White, has not been identified. The *Dublin Directory* for 1839 lists a William White, "apothecary, 49 Thomas St." 58 The ceremony Dr. Fitzgerald has described is presumably the profession and reception ceremony held in Carlow on April 2, 1839—which Catherine McAuley herself attended, *if* the Carlow Annals for 1839 is correct. Later in this letter, Catherine indicates that Dr. Fitzgerald is now in Dublin. 59 Miss Fitzgerald has not been identified. 60 Easter Sunday fell on March 31, 1839, and the annual bazaar of hand-crafted goods always occurred in the early weeks following Easter. 61 According to the then-proposed Rule of the Sisters of Mercy, "two months before the expiration of the period of their probation, [novices] shall ... present their request in Chapter to be admitted to Profession" (Sullivan, *Catherine McAuley* 315). Since Mary Agnes (Rebecca) Greene professed her vows in Carlow on June 11, 1839, she must have presented her request and received a positive vote of the Carlow Chapter in early April 1839. This sentence—which is not about the profession of Mary Agnes O'Connor (as in Neumann and Bolster)—helps to date this letter. 62 Teresa Byrn, Catherine McAuley's adopted godchild and cousin, was now about eighteen years old. She had lived at Baggot Street as long as Catherine McAuley had lived there. On August 15, 1837, she entered the religious community, and on February 21, 1838, she received the habit, taking the name Mary Camillus. Catherine occasionally expresses reservations about her suitability for religious life in terms of her health and behavior. However, Mary Camillus eventually professed her vows on May 4, 1841,

119. To Catherine McAuley [Booterstown]
[April 30, 1839][64]

My dear Reverend Mother, on this festive day
Some words in your honor I gladly would say
But vain the endeavor, in vain do I try
My muse is too humble for subject so high
Yet, tho' *louder* expressions of joy you may hear
I'll answer for it, they are not more sincere
Than that felt by your children who with me unite
In begging the favor, about which I write
That you'll send Sister Celia, your 'presentative here
And M. Aloysius,[65] to the Sisters so dear
Before dinner to day, as it would not be fair
To leave us *here* orphans and keep both Mothers there
A pity it were that a day of such joy
Should bring with it even a shade of alloy
Which must be the case unless you will please
To grant us this favor, as you can with great ease
If they come in the Train[66] they'll be here in less time
By far than I spend in writing this rhyme
I know you will grant us this favor to day
As on reading those lines I expect you will say
"I cannot refuse them so just a request
Then go back my dear Sisters, I think it is best
Be merry and joyous in B town tonight—
St. Catherine's Day should to all bring delight."

[Mary Ursula Frayne]

Autograph: Brisbane

and in 1846 became one of the founding members of the new St. Catherine's Convent in New York City. See Sullivan, *Catherine McAuley* 12, 345 n. 7, and passim.   63 If Catherine McAuley's calculation is correct, and if this letter is written in April 1839, she had not seen her nephews James and Robert Macauley since November 1837, although both were living in or near Dublin. In Letter 60, written on November 22, 1837, she tells Frances Warde that "James and Robert have been to see me."   64 This undated poem-letter and its response (Letter 120) were written on the liturgical feast of St. Catherine of Siena (April 30), which was the feast day of Catherine McAuley. They were probably written in 1839 because on that day in 1838 the Booterstown convent was not yet opened; in 1840 Catherine was preparing to go to Galway on May 2; and in 1841 her nephew James had just died on April 29. An early transcript of this poem in the Liverpool Annals (112–13) says that it was written by Mary Ursula Frayne, then in Booterstown. The autograph in Brisbane, Australia, does not bear a signature.   65 The community in Booterstown is requesting that Mary Cecilia Marmion and Mary Aloysius Scott come to Booterstown later that day and stay overnight. Mary Cecilia was at this point serving as mistress of novices, at least informally, and Mary Aloysius, as bursar—hence the title "Mothers," which Catherine McAuley did not use, except rarely, and never of herself.   66 The steam railway from Westland Row, Dublin, to Booterstown.

120. To Sister M. Ursula Frayne   [Baggot Street]
Booterstown   [April 30, 1839][67]

My own dearest Child you must eat, laugh & pray
without Aloysius or Celia to day
and though you're not with us at this little feat
we are planning to give you a very nice treat
"To this *our* great feast—an octave *we'll* add"
and give you a party will make your heart glad
a nice pick nick dinner—just fit for the sod
the white veils—in high joy will be off at a nod
So merry a party I'm sure was ne'er seen
In parlour or drawing-room—garden or green
Kirwan[68] will take them, for about half a crown
If you can contrive to let them lie down
on the same day they could never come back
It would spoil all the fun & break down the hack
You can make up some pallets & place them all so
that we'd lie down together like pins in a row
In the steamer to Cork[69] we lay down altogether
and slept mighty well with blanket or feather
for the sake of our innocent pastime and play
we'll call Booterstown Convent a steamer that day
and wonder there's half so much room on the sea

[M. C. McAuley]

Autograph: Brisbane

---

67 For the date of this response to Letter 119 see note 64 above. Although it is not consistent, Catherine McAuley's use of capital letters at the beginning of lines has been followed.   68 Kirwan was a "car" (carriage or cart) owner who had sometimes transported the sisters, at least as early as the cholera epidemic of 1832 (see Sullivan, *Catherine McAuley* 97).   69 In September 1838, Catherine McAuley and the founding community for Limerick had traveled at night by mail steam packet to Cork, since the day mail coach to Cork from Dublin, whether through Cashel or Clonmel, took twenty hours (*Dublin Directory* [1839] 69).

May–October 1839

Catherine McAuley always remembered the serene words of Edward Nolan, late bishop of Kildare and Leighlin: "It is my lot." She saw the events of her own life as the "lot" which God's providence offered for her embrace. In the middle of 1839, these events included the death of Mary Gertrude Jones in Booterstown; the near completion of the addition to the House of Mercy, with the need to re-open the poor school in the building, and the hope that the commercial laundry would soon be in operation; the trip to Cork in August for the profession of the English novices destined for the Bermondsey foundation; the long journey home to Baggot Street—through Charleville, Limerick, Tullamore, and Carlow, so the English sisters could see other Mercy communities and their variety of ministries; plans for submitting the Rule and Constitutions, with accompanying documents, to Rome for final confirmation; and preparation for the journey to London on November 18, to found the first Convent of Mercy in England.

Catherine was now in her sixty-first year, full of zeal and still relatively healthy. She rejoiced that the Carlow community established a new foundation in Naas in September, even though she could not attend, and that Mary Xavier O'Connell and Mary de Chantal Markey professed their vows at Baggot Street on October 3. In the midst of business she found time to send a teasing poem to Ursula Frayne in Booterstown, humorously complaining that Ursula's sense of "sweet holy poverty" had "flitted away" (Letter 130). October ended with generous endorsements of the Sisters of Mercy by John Ryan, bishop of Limerick, and Michael Blake, bishop of Dromore—encouraging letters that Catherine would soon forward to Rome.

121. Notation   May 2, 1839

Mr. Thomas Butler has handed me twelve pounds ten shillings, in payment of his sister's pension up to the 15th of April 1839.[1]

M. C. McAuley

Autograph: Dublin, Mercy

1 Mary Elizabeth (Clare) Butler had entered the Baggot Street community on April 15, 1838 and received the habit on September 4, 1838. She professed her vows on November 26, 1840, and joined the Liverpool community in June 1845. During the Crimean War (1854–1856) she volunteered, with other Irish and English Sisters of Mercy, to serve the sick and wounded soldiers. On February 23, 1856, she died of fever in a military hospital in Balaclava, on the Crimean peninsula.

122. To Sister M. Frances Warde   Booterstown
    Carlow   May 11, 1839

My Dearest Sister M. Frances
    Our poor Sister M. Gertrude is no longer an inhabitant of this passing world.
She died on Ascension Day.² For the last year she has been chiefly confined to
Bed—fourteen weeks since she was removed here, for change of air and chiefly
in the hope that she could have the comfort of being present at Mass, without
many stairs to go up. No evident symptoms of death appeared until Monday last.
She had every spiritual consolation—Mr. O'Hanlon came to her three times. Her
dear remains were this morning deposited with her eleven Sisters in religion. We
hope to have them all home before another year.³
    Reviewing all the past, I regard poor Sister Gertrude as a martyr to the faith.
The violent efforts she made to embrace and practice it, and the entire seperation
[*sic*] from all to whom she was ever known, gave a shock to the whole nervous system
which could not be recovered. Delighted as she felt with the Catholic faith, she fancied all who faithfully observed it must be divine—hence she was disappointed. Yet
for one moment she would not entertain a thought of returning lest there might be
danger of losing it. Soon after her death—before I made any remark—Sister Mary
Cecilia said—"Well, Revd. Mother, though poor Sr. G. was sometimes very tiresome, I often thought she was like a martyr." She seemed every day to be offering
great violence to feelings which were not in any degree overcome. All her mind
turned to england & english manners. We could not converse so agreeably, cut out
a cap, make a pudding, or spread a plaister as they could in Bridgnorth, which she
often said had every attraction under Heaven but the true faith.
    When describing the amiable and—as she used to say—exalted principles &
dispositions of her Brother & his daughters, she seemed to think they were all
lost—for want of a knowledge of the faith.⁴ This feeling was engraved on her
heart by some supernatural means. Her case was an extraordinary one. God only
can appreciate its value. I believe she may be truly said to have taken up her

2 Mary Gertrude (Mary) Jones, a convert and a native of Bridgenorth in North Wales, had joined
the Baggot Street community before Catherine McAuley went to George's Hill in 1830. Her early
story is told in the Limerick Manuscript (Sullivan, *Catherine McAuley* 170). She entered the religious
community preparing at Baggot Street on May 26, 1831, received the habit on October 8, 1832, and
professed her vows on February 11, 1834. She died on Ascension Thursday, May 9, 1839 at
Booterstown. Though this letter is dated May 11, the postmark is May 18, 1839.   3 Like all the
Sisters of Mercy in Dublin who died before November 15, 1841—including Caroline Murphy who
died at Baggot Street before the congregation was founded—Mary Gertrude Jones was buried on May
11 in the Discalced Carmelite vaults in the basement of St. Teresa's Church, Clarendon Street, Dublin.
Contrary to Catherine McAuley's expressed hope, and to the claims of some writers, the remains of
these sisters were not removed to the garden cemetery at Baggot Street after it was opened. A plaque
in St. Teresa's Church now commemorates their burial there.   4 Catherine McAuley, like most of
the Catholics of her day, as well as converts like Gertrude Jones, had not the benefit of present-day
ecumenical and ecclesiological understandings of the workings of God's salvific love.

Cross—while, in general, we only carry it when it comes—and keep it away as long as we can. I am certain her reward will be great. She suffered in mind and Body for nine years from no visible cause, but a rending of the heart—from violent sacrifice of all the predelictions [*sic*] of 37 years. A vocation to religious life has its joys—but her whole concern was the preservation of faith, and guarding against whatever would put it in danger—and she would not trust to her own perseverance—if not shielded as she was.

Her countenance was sweetly composed in death, her teeth perfectly white—and not the slightest swelling in [her] feet—which are strong signs of not being in an unhealthy state of Body. She expressed a strong desire to die on Ascension day. Sister Monica[5] and I were watching her. We had read all the last prayers—three or four times—and after eleven o'clock—on Wednesday night—concluded she would live a day or two longer as no change appeared. The instant the clock struck 12—which was just at her door—she stretched out her arms, and as if it were an immediate call on her to go, she settled her head & before we could read the departing prayer, she was gone.

Sister Teresa Carton is better—except in looks—which are bad—teeth discoloured and the whole countenance expressive of some vital part being affected. Sister de Pazzi not well—and Sister Lynch of Everton very ill[6]. Her Brother from Naas has been to see her and placed her under Surgeon White's care. I fear very much she cannot remain, which will afflict her greatly.

A Priest from Cork said Mass for us yesterday. He said he was in company with some clergymen who were speaking of our Institutions—and that it was said the progress of a House in Carlow was like a miracle. I suppose they are adding to the real number in imagination—hearing so much said about it.

Great expectations in Limerick [*several words obliterated by ink scribbling*].

My dear Sister Mary Clare has a trying station.[7]

Remember me most affectionately to all. I trust your health is pretty good and all with you well. Mr. Rafter[8] was so kind to call though he had only a few hours. God bless you, my Dearest Sister M. Frances.

Pray for your ever attached
M. C. McAuley

5 Mary Monica (Anna) Murphy, who had professed her vows on July 1, 1837.   6 This is probably Maria Lynch, who received the habit on January 21, 1839, but is not listed in the Dublin Register of professed sisters—and not Mary Rose (Catherine) Lynch who lived until August 6, 1891, serving in Birr; St. John's, Newfoundland; and Geelong, Victoria, Australia.   7 Mary Clare Moore, the superior in Cork, may have experienced "trying" relations with Dr. John Murphy, although except for Catherine McAuley's occasional allusions to the situation, often quoting Clare Moore, I have found no further contemporary evidence to this effect. However, Bolster notes that "the various congregations in his diocese found him less than easy to deal with" (*Mercy* 4).   8 Michael Rafter, parish priest of Killeshin, Carlow, was a devoted friend to the Sisters of Mercy from the beginning of the Carlow foundation. He will die in less than a year, on January 16, 1840 (*Irish Catholic Directory* [1841] 357).

Give my respectful and affectionate remembrance to [*several words obliterated by ink scribbling*] and all our good friends.

Autograph: Silver Spring

123. **To Sister Mary Vincent Harnett**   [Baggot Street]
     Limerick   [May–July 1839][9]

My dear Sister M. Vincent

Will you get all the instructions for me as to the school, and send the person you have designed soon as you please—I will rely on your giving every direction possible. You know we are quite unprepared here—we shall be quite perplexed on the New School opening if not ready to receive them in good order. We hope to get in connection with the Board. Our room is a very fine one—with space for 400. To begin well is a great point.[10]

Sister Mary will write any observations you would think it well to make.[11] This you may consider a real charity, it will so relieve my mind. I dread the

9 No autograph of this letter can be found. However, Mary Vincent Harnett herself had handcopies made of letters she had received from Catherine McAuley and sent them to Mary Josephine Warde in Cork. In her cover letter, written from Roscommon on "2nd August," probably in 1856—since she refers to opening a branch house in Athlone "next month," which in fact did not occur until March 25, 1857—she says: "when I received your note I gave dearest Rev. Mother's letters to be copied for you & I send the copies of the four, the only ones that were kept." Mary Vincent's cover letter and the four handcopies are preserved in the archives of the Convent of Mercy, St. Maries of the Isle, Cork, and I am very grateful to Mary Angela Bolster who gave me photocopies of them in 1990. Mary Vincent Harnett labeled the undated handcopy of this letter "1st," implying that, chronologically, it precedes the letter dated April 20, 1840. Catherine McAuley's reference to "August 1" (in her request for information) offers two options for dating this letter: May–July 1839 or May–July 1840. (Mid 1841 is out of the question, given the large number of letters in that period, none of which refers to the opening of the school.) In light of Mary Vincent's own labeling of this letter as the first she received, I have proposed the 1839 date. In Letter 124 (below), which according to internal evidence was written in 1839, Catherine McAuley also speaks of having the school on Baggot Street "connected with the Board of education."   10 Construction of the addition to the House of Mercy, including the new commercial laundry and new schoolroom, began in 1838, and during the construction the poor school conducted at Baggot Street was temporarily suspended. As soon as possible, perhaps by August 1, 1839, Catherine McAuley hoped to re-open the school, to serve hundreds of poor girls who had no other means of education.   11 Sister Mary may be Mary Liston, a native of Limerick, who had entered the Baggot Street community on September 8, 1838, received the habit on January 21, 1839, and was loaned to the Limerick community sometime in the following year. She did not profess her vows at Baggot Street until May 4, 1841. More likely she is Mary Shanahan, one of the Poor Clares in the Limerick community, an experienced educator who had taught in the national school in Limerick before the Sisters of Mercy arrived. Mary Vincent Harnett was herself an excellent teacher, having taught in the Baggot Street poor school. She was certified by the National Board shortly after coming to Limerick. In time she authored a *Catechism of Scripture History* used by the Sisters of Mercy in their schools. For further biographical details about her, see Sullivan, *Catherine McAuley* 130–38.

crowd rushing in as formerly—without a good arrangement—and such rules as you think may bring about a regular attendance as to hour.[12] Say something of the Infant School. We hope to open on the 1st of August.

Give me all the help you can collect.

Your ever affectionate
M. C. McAuley

Harnett handcopy: Cork; photocopy of handcopy: Dublin, Mercy

124. **To Sister M. Frances Warde**   [May–August 1839][13]
     Carlow

My Dearest Sister Mary Frances

I cannot attempt to describe the joy your letter afforded me. I fear I am in danger of getting a little jealous—poor Baggot Street is outdone if you make a foundation already. I may retire from business—and certainly without making a fortune. Doctor Fitzgerald is delighted. The school exceeds all he hoped for. "I knew when I first cast my eye on her she was the girl that would do all." He is really gratified—which is a great comfort to me.[14]

Doctor Murphy celebrated Mass. Dr. Fitzgerald attended him. You could not think of any thing more venerable than the two white heads. Dr. Murphy says he must go to look at the wonderful Institution.[15] I hope he may see all together. They say the english Sisters must be brought to visit you. We are getting the old school room fitted up as Community room—before they come. Mr. Boylan came to look at it—& said he would have his papers looked over for some old church pattern to cover the walls. "This," he said, "I will do for Geraldine."[16]

---

12 The *Irish Catholic Directory* for 1841, giving 1840 attendance figures, notes that 300 poor female children were educated in the poor school at the House of Mercy on Baggot Street, as well as "72 young women supported" (286)—these were the "rushing" crowd whom Catherine McAuley both "dreaded" and loved.   13 Dating this undated autograph involves harmonizing a number of datable references that appear incompatible. I have tried to address the problem in the notes that accompany the text. In Bolster's edition, this letter is dated "Early 1839" (78–80); in Carroll's *Life*, where it appears in a somewhat altered and abbreviated form, it is dated "February 1839" (474). However, internal evidence suggests that it could not have been written before May 1839 (after the Carlow pension school opened on May 1), nor later than mid August 1839 (before the profession of the English sisters in Cork on August 19). Note 26 identifies a portion of the letter that may not, in fact, belong to this letter, but if it does, the references there further complicate the dating of the letter.   14 The Carlow community was already contemplating a new foundation in Naas, which took place on September 24, 1839. The pension school in Carlow, for tuition-paying students—for which Andrew Fitzgerald credits Frances Warde—opened on May 1, 1839, according to the Carlow Annals.   15 The new convent in Carlow was now completed and would be formally blessed on July 2, 1839. As Catherine notes later in this paragraph, the paint ("colour") was, fortunately, not put on the walls of the chapel before the plaster had dried.   16 The English sisters—Mary Clare Agnew, author of the three-volume novel *Geraldine*, and Mary Augustin Taylor—were preparing for their profession of vows in Cork on August

He told me he never saw anything prettier than the choir in Carlow and rejoiced he was just in time to prevent the same mistake that was made here—putting on colour too soon.

We hear the Convent in Naas is beautiful—the garden laid out in the neatest style—and Father Doyle will have none but Sisters of Mercy. I long to hear if it is determined, and who are to go. This is a trial you have to pass through. Remember your venerated dear Doctor Nolan's words, "It is my lot." To reflect that it is the lot or portion which God has marked out will be sufficient—and in the cheerful performance of every part our sanctification rests. There is every reason to think that you have been an obedient child—to your Superior[17]—since to the obedient victory is given. May God continue his blessings to you, and render you every day still more deserving of them.

In all Mother M. A.'s letters, she is what I call "doing the humble"—greatly afraid of that cunning thief, vain glory. I heard a very nice description of the new Convent from a Dr. O'Brien who was in Tullamore lately preaching.[18] He says the cematery [*sic*] would invite anyone to become an inmate, and he heard of a rich widow who intends to join them—but all are slow when compared to Carlow.

Sister M. Clare has a similar tendency. She never mentioned a Sister who entered last week, nor a Lay Sister they have 3 months.[19] I do not yet know how the London House is to commence. The english sisters beg to have Sister M. Clare. Dr. Murphy has not given a conclusive answer. It is said that the increase in London will be immediate—they hope to open the Institution on the 24th September[20]—they are to be professed on the 19th of August. I fear I must go

---

19, 1839. After the ceremony, which Catherine McAuley plans to attend, they will journey to Dublin by land, stopping in the Mercy convents in Charleville, Limerick, Tullamore, and Carlow. They will then stay in Baggot Street for over two months prior to their departure for the new foundation in Bermondsey, London in mid November. Mr. Boylan has not been identified. Like Catherine, he referred to Clare Agnew by the title of her novel.   **17** That is, Dr. Francis Haly, bishop of Kildare and Leighlin.   **18** Mary Ann Doyle, the superior of the Tullamore community, where a new convent was under construction, was both happy about the situation in Tullamore and worried about expressing the reasons for her happiness, lest it seem like boasting. Dr. O'Brien is Richard Baptist O'Brien, the newly appointed president of St. Mary's College, Halifax, Nova Scotia, who was delayed in Ireland prior to his departure for Halifax. He reports that he was "engaged to deliver a few discourses to the nuns in Tullamore" and that on a visit to Baggot Street in 1839 Catherine McAuley offered to devote herself, "if permitted, for her remaining years to Nova Scotia. To every representation of the loss which would accrue to her native country she calmly replied: 'The Institute requires me not at home; it has young, intelligent, and devoted children. We ought to provide for the instruction of the poor and the relief of the sick in the colonies'" (Harnett, *Life* 204–205).   **19** This sentence, to the extent that it is accurate, would seem to date this letter in August 1939. However, *two* women entered the Cork community on August 6, 1839: Margaret Lyster and Ellen Lane, according to the Cork Register. Since Catherine McAuley's information did not come directly from Mary Clare Moore, the superior in Cork, but probably from Dr. John Murphy, her information may be incorrect. I am grateful to the archivist, Mary Lyons, RSM, for verifying the names and dates of women who entered that community in 1839.   **20** The September date proved impracticable since the newly built convent in Bermondsey was not even partially ready for occupancy until November.

to the ceremony. Doctor Murphy says it would be necessary—that every aid should be given to england—we all feel—and every mark of interest shewn—but I got [get?] a surfeit of travelling in my old days.

However, I would have some comfort returning by Carlow and seeing my old child and her flock. If I go—I think Sister de Sales White will be my companion. She has not been looking well latterly—thin as a Ghost. Sister M. Cecilia is such a very *troublesome* traveller that I would not think of her, and Sister M. Teresa is in the midst of business—preparing for Wexford.[21]

Our Laundry will soon open, please God—how I rejoice to have a resource within doors—for the support of our poor people. The Poor Law Tax is breaking up all contributions.[22]

We intend to have the new school connected with the Board of education. The children improve so much more expecting the examination. I suppose you have seen Geraldine's 3 volumes—all about Sisters of Mercy. She is getting the 3 volumes fancifully bound for her Grandmother. I wish my dear respected eldest son[23] would come to her profession. That would make me feel quite a charming young woman. Give my most affectionate love to all my dear grandchildren,[24] and believe me

your ever fond

M. C. McAuley

I am expecting Dr. F. every moment. He said he was going in the morning. Mr. O'Hanlon was delighted with your letter—there scarcely ever was so disinterested a friend—I wish you would remember him always.

Sister Teresa[25] is just in the same state—old looking—and occasionally fretful—but most ardent in all her employments. Mr. Hume sent us our last Sister— a relation of his in the immediate neighbourhood—a sweet young creature—puts me in mind of our first flock.[26]

21 Mary Cecilia Marmion was frequently ill on long trips. At this point Catherine McAuley envisioned that a future foundation in Wexford would be made from Baggot Street, but it was eventually made from Carlow, on December 8, 1840. 22 "The Act 'for the more effectual Relief of the Destitute Poor in Ireland' passed into law on 31 July 1838" (J. O'Connor 68). Unfortunately, this Act of the British Parliament—which aimed to provide relief primarily to the aged, the infirm, the developmentally disabled, and children through workhouses financed by a "poor rate" tax levied on property owners—misled many prospective donors to non-governmental charitable agencies into thinking that, since they were already taxed to help "the poor," their donations were no longer necessary. O'Connor's detailed description of the workhouses, which by 1840 Catherine McAuley had come to abhor, offers a telling contrast to the early Houses of Mercy established by the Sisters of Mercy (68–110). 23 Daniel Nolan, curate in Killeshin, a parish of Carlow. 24 Early on, Catherine McAuley began to refer to the young women who entered the various foundations of Sisters of Mercy outside of Dublin as her "grandchildren." 25 Teresa Carton. 26 This paragraph is the first paragraph of what is now a separate autograph sheet that may or may not belong to this letter. If this sheet—which is preserved in the Windham archives where the autograph of the rest of the letter is preserved—does not belong to this letter, then I have so far not found any other letter to which it could belong. The folds of the sheet do not appear to match those of Letter 113 which is preserved in the Baltimore archives. However, the last sentence of the paragraph complicates the

Sunday— I expected Dr. F. would have gone yesterday. He celebrated Mass for us this morning—and indeed you would have felt—if you heard how deject-edly he said that you did not invite him to the ceremony.[27] I am sorry—very sorry—you did not write to him in Dublin—he could not go as he was waiting on the Dentist—and that you could pardon—but not asking him seems remarkable.

Pray often for your affectionate

M. C. M.

No Mrs. Bridgman entered in Limerick. 2 Miss Bridgmans. They have not the honor of a widow yet.

Autograph: Windham

125. To Sister Mary de Sales[28]   [June–July 1839]

My dear Sister M. de S.

Accept my thanks for your kind note, which was quite cheering. You are timely in thinking of your profession, and I feel satisfied you will make due prepa-

---

dating of this letter. As Catherine McAuley identifies her, the "last sister" is Mary Justina (Annie) Fleming, the cousin of George Hume, curate in Naas. She entered the Baggot Street community on February 5, 1839 and received the habit on July 23, 1839. However, Mary Ann Creedon of Colowen, Co. Cork, had entered the community on July 4, 1839, "for the purpose of establishing a convent in [St. John's, Newfoundland]." (She became the founder of that community in 1842.) Given Mary Ann's intention, perhaps Catherine McAuley did not think of her as the "last sister" entering specifically for the Baggot Street community. If that is not the case, and if this paragraph in fact belongs to this letter and was written before Mary Ann Creedon entered (i.e., before July 4), then this assumption conflicts with the August date suggested by the entrances in Cork dis-cussed in note 19.   **27** The ceremony in Carlow to which Catherine McAuley may be referring is the profession and reception ceremony held there on June 11, 1839 at which Mary Agnes Greene and Mary Teresa Kelly professed their vows, and Mary Paul or Paula (Anne) Cullen, a first cousin of the future cardinal, and Mary Bridget (Margaret) Hackett received the habit; *or* the formal Blessing of the new St. Leo's Convent in Carlow by Dr. Francis Haly on July 2, 1839. However, the Carlow Annals records that Dr. Andrew Fitzgerald attended both of these ceremonies. Letter 118 implies that Dr. Fitzgerald also attended the profession and reception ceremony in Carlow on April 2, 1839, at which Mary de Sales (Mary) Maher professed her vows and Mary Rose (Rosina) Strange and Mary Vincent (Margaret) Kenny received the habit. However, if that is not correct, that is, if Catherine McAuley is referring to the April 2nd ceremony, and if these postscript paragraphs do indeed belong to this letter, then the date of this letter could be simply "[May 1839]," and the infor-mation Catherine received about women who entered in Cork, as discussed in note 19, should be regarded as incorrect. What is certain, I believe, is that the letter and the postscript were written in 1839, sometime after the opening of the Carlow pension school on May 1, not in February. **28** No autograph of this letter has been found; however, the letter appears in four sources: Harnett, *Life* (191–92); Carroll, *Leaves* (1:426); Burke Savage (316); and Moore's *Practical Sayings* (25–26). Harnett, who was familiar with the Limerick community and its archives, says the letter was sent to "Sister M. de S." and identifies her as "a novice who, on the day of her reception, wrote to [Catherine McAuley] expressing anxiety for profession" (191). Carroll does not name the recipient.

ration for it, and that you will never be unworthy of so great a favour. I expect to see a sweet and holy reserve in all my dear sister novices, which will be as a shield around them. This word 'reserve' is most extensively useful for meditation; if we acquire religious reserve, we shall never speak too much, write too much, grieve too much, laugh too much: and when we do all things in due order, and do not exceed in any, then a good foundation will be laid for advancement in religious perfection. May God grant to us all this beautiful reserve, that restrains words, looks, and actions, and that continually whispers 'go back—stop—say no more.' It is much to be desired, and of immense value.[29]

I am anxious to hear of the last postulant. I must select a nice one for you, and endeavour to induce her to help the poor sisters. Some person has said that a great barn must be opened in B—— to admit all that are talking of going there. Perhaps their pious intentions will all evaporate in talk, for want of that Heavenly reserve we were speaking of. Now, like a dear child, pray for me, and believe me most affectionately yours in Jesus Christ.[30]

[M. C. McAuley]

Published transcription: Harnett, Life *(191–92)*

126. To Sister M. Elizabeth Moore — Limerick

Baggot Street
July 24, 1839

My Dearest Sister Mary Elizabeth

We have this moment received your sweet fruit & flowers—I seldom see any so fragrant—to me. The offering of genuine affection has every thing to enhance its value. I am looking at them now, and think the Roses have some unusual

Burke Savage says the letter was written "(in June 1839) to Sr. de Sales Bridgeman, then a novice in Limerick" (316). He may be using Harnett as his source, but he is also known to have consulted the research notes of John MacErlean, SJ, who did extensive work on the letters of Catherine McAuley. Many Sisters of Mercy had the name "de Sales" in Catherine's lifetime—at least four in 1839, in Baggot Street, Carlow, Limerick, and London (after December 12). In the absence of a stronger possibility, as to both recipient and date, it may be reasonable to think of this letter as addressed to Mary de Sales (Mary Anne) Bridgeman in Limerick, shortly after her reception of the habit on June 7, 1839. The text presented here is Harnett's.   29 Burke Savage's text of the letter stops here.   30 Only Harnett and Carroll include this paragraph. Carroll fills in "B——" with "Birr," which would place the paragraph in 1841, after the founding in Birr on December 27, 1840. Since "B——" (surely not abbreviated in the original autograph) could stand in 1839 for Baggot Street or after 1839, for several places where many young women were ready to enter, I have chosen to leave the abbreviation as in Harnett. If the letter was not written in 1839, the other possibilities emerge: Birr, Bermondsey where Mary de Sales Eyre received the habit on December 12, 1839, and possibly Baggot Street or Birmingham. Moreover, it is entirely possible that this paragraph does not belong to this letter. If this letter was written to Limerick in June–July 1839, the "last postulant" to have entered the Limerick community was Ellen Bowles, on May 16. The "nice one" Catherine will select "for you" is unclear, unless she means that she will send a young woman from Dublin.

shade—and such bright purple—and rich yellow flowers. The gooseberrys—liquer—jams and jellys all safe—apples, etc.

Ann—[31] gone to take some tea—and then go to Bed.

I wrote a long letter to Sister Harnett which Mr. Malone promised to forward—immediately. [It is] 10 days since he took it. Now what could possess you to think I could feel the slightest displeasure—I exerted myself to write some nonsense in return, being deeply in debt to my Dear Sister M. Teresa[32]—but I could not even say that I felt any regret—at what was written to me or had one serious thought about it. Never suppose you can make me feel displeased by giving every opinion that occurs to you. I am sure you ought to know me well—and I wonder you could mistake.[33]

I have seen many who do not admire the 3 books of *Geraldine*—though nothing ever exceeded the sale—not a copy to be had in Dublin.

Sisters Fleming and Whitty—two very nice young persons—not 21—& Jane Starling were received yesterday by—*Dean* Meyler[34]—gracious as possible. Mrs. McA[35] a very good child—smiling and praying alternatively—attended at table—and paid great attention to.

The votes have passed for the Profession of Sisters O'Connell— and Markey, in whose favor the Bishop remitted a year.[36] She is truly edifying in every respect.

Mr. Maher of Carlow preached a delightful sermon—shewing the vows of Religion to be the perfection of the Baptismal engagement—pronouncing woe to the Parent or Guardian that will stop the child whom God calls to that state.[37]

I fear not getting this forward in time for the post. I expect to have the real heartfelt joy of seeing you in five or six weeks—I rather think in 5. I hope to remain two days—the english Sisters say only one. They speak of being in London on the 24th Sept.—which I suppose cannot be accomplished—but they are most eisily [easily] guided—nothing positive in their character.[38]

---

31 The word "Ann" is not capitalized in the autograph, but it seems to begin a new sentence. The word is not "I'm" or "am"—though either might be a somewhat easier word to interpret. Rather it seems to be a person's name, possibly that of the messenger who brought the fruit and flowers from Limerick.   32 This sister may be Mary Teresa Vincent Potter in Limerick, to whom Catherine often wrote verses, but the "nonsense" Catherine wrote has not been identified. The sense of the paragraph does not suggest that she is speaking of Mary Teresa White in Dublin.   33 The nature of Elizabeth Moore's misunderstanding and its cause are not clear from the wording of this paragraph. What is needed is the other side of the dialogue, but no such letter is extant.   34 After the death in May 1838 of Dr. Patrick Coleman, dean of the chapter of the archdiocese of Dublin, Daniel Murray sought the approval of authorities in Rome to appoint Dr. Walter Meyler to that position. Word of Rome's approval reached Dublin on April 20, 1839 (*Irish Catholic Directory* [1840] 347). Catherine McAuley is speaking of the reception ceremony on July 23, 1839.   35 Mrs. McA is Catherine McAuley herself.   36 By a positive vote, the Dublin Chapter of professed sisters had admitted Mary Xavier O'Connell and Mary Jane Frances de Chantal Markey to profession of vows. They will profess their vows at Baggot Street on October 3, 1839. Perhaps because Mary de Chantal was a widow, Dr. Murray required her to serve a novitiate of only one year.   37 James Maher preached this sermon at the reception ceremony on July 23.   38 See Letter 124, note 16. Catherine McAuley intends to stop in Limerick and elsewhere on the way back to Dublin from Cork.

Our Building is nearly finished—a fine school room & Dormitory—the Laundry not yet opened but every prospect of its doing well. Our memorial to the board[39] was signed by the most respectable protestants—the Surgeon General,[40] Sir Henry Marsh, Mr. Hume & several others—it was presented by Doctor Murray and well received. We have great hope of a favorable answer.

God bless and preserve you, my Dearest Sister M. Elizabeth.

Pray for your ever fondly attached
M. C. McAuley

Sister de Pazzi has not read your letter yet. I would not stand up till this was finished. I opened the letter & find it is from Sr. Vincent[41]—to whom, and all, give our fondest love.

I ought to say all that could animate and comfort you—for you are a credit and a comfort to me. Every week I hear all that is edifying and respectable of your Institution. [*illegible name*][42] is doing all he can to get his niece with you— he says you will soon have plenty.

Every one who came in since I began—said, oh, the sweet smell, where did you get all the lovely flowers—and when answered, "from Limerick"—I think they fancied them somewhat out of the common way.

Autograph: Limerick

127. To Sister M. Frances Warde[43] **Convent, Baggot Street
September 23, 1839**

My dear Sister Mary Frances

I suppose you have heard of the death of poor Mr. Carroll[44]—since it was the holy will of God to call him away, there is reason to rejoice in the pity & mercy which was manifested. Though there was every symptom of sudden death, he was rescued from it—and also from protracted decline, which Mr. Crampton said would continue till the end of November. His death is considered a happy one, & if so, that his journey should be shortened is a blessing indeed.

---

39 The Board of National Education.　40 Sir Philip Crampton, MD, a distinguished physician, had long been a supporter of Catherine McAuley's endeavors.　41 Mary Vincent Harnett's letter may be her response to Letter 123.　42 Neumann (167) and Bolster (94) read this illegible name as "Mr. Maher."　43 The autograph of this letter—once thought to be in Cresson, Pennsylvania (according to an old list of letters in Mercy Congregational Archives, Dublin)—cannot now be found. However, a handcopy is preserved in the Mercy archives in Silver Spring, Maryland. Whether Catherine McAuley sent this letter to Carlow or Naas is not known. Frances Warde and members of the Carlow community established a new foundation of Sisters of Mercy in Naas on September 24, 1839. The founding party traveled from Carlow on the morning of September 23; it included Mary Josephine Trennor, the new superior, Mary Catherine Meagher, and Mary Agnes Greene, as well as Frances Warde and Mary Angela Johnson who "was lent for a month" (Carlow Annals).　44 Thomas Carroll, a curate at St. Andrew's Church, Dublin, died on September 20,

I rejoice with you, my dearest child, in the little branch you are forming this day, and humbly beseech God to grant it a blessing. Many circumstances unite to keep me from you—it would have been a very particular gratification to me. A young Priest is to celebrate his first Mass—Mr. O'Hanlon bring home a new Sister—and if I were to desert them it would not do well at present for the poor old House.[45] May God preserve & bless you and all with you.

Your ever affectionate,
M. C. McAuley

Handcopy: Silver Spring

128. To Sister M. Frances Warde   Convent, Baggot St.
Naas   September 27, 1839

My Dear Sister M. Frances

Another disappointment to me—I cannot have the happiness of being with you and dear Sister Josephine at the joyful blessing of the Convent which of all things I delight in.[46] When the Bishop called to visit the English missioners, I mentioned the Profession of Sisters Markey & O'Connell—his Grace appointed the 3rd of September [October].[47] If any good chance would bring you to me the evening before, after all your ceremony ended, what a comfort it would be to have you—once more—one of the number—and if we had a hope of your good Bishop, that indeed would be cheering—perhaps Dr. Fitzgerald & Mr. Maher, but I suppose this is all too much to think of.

The new Bishop Doctor Hughes[48] called here, and seemed to expect to meet Sister Angela Johnston [Johnson]—he said her Mamma informed him she was to be here. I believe he had some business to settle, etc.[49]

1839, at the age of thirty-six (*Irish Catholic Directory* [1840] 338). He had been very supportive of the Sisters of Mercy on Baggot Street. **45** Catherine McAuley had recently returned from a long trip: to Cork for the profession ceremony of Mary Clare Agnew and Mary Augustin Taylor on August 19, and then—with these two English sisters, as well as Mary Clare Moore, who was destined to be the founding superior in London, and Mary de Sales White, Catherine's traveling companion—to Charleville, Limerick, Tullamore, and Carlow. Catherine wished the English sisters to see other Mercy convents in operation. It was on this trip that the novices in Carlow made an acute observation about Catherine McAuley: "The most amiable trait in her character which we believed we discerned was a total absence of everything in her manner telling, I am the Foundress" (Carlow Annals, in Sullivan, *Catherine McAuley* 230). **46** The blessing of the Naas convent occurred sometime after September 27. The former national school building in Naas "had been just converted into a Convent" (Carlow Annals, in Sullivan, *Catherine McAuley* 230). **47** Catherine wrote "September," but certainly meant "October." The profession ceremony took place on October 3, 1839. **48** Henry Hughes, provincial of the Franciscans in Ireland, was consecrated vicar apostolic of Gibralter on April 21, 1839 (*Irish Catholic Directory* [1840] 374). **49** Mary Angela Johnson, a member of the Carlow community, was now temporarily in Naas.

While the stage horses were changing at Naas we looked in at the sweet little Convent from the window—it is a nice spot—the walks and shrubs so neatly arranged.

On our ceremony day[50] we expect to have 45 Sisters at dinner—you & child would make 47—at Tea.

Sister Agnew is a delightful addition—every day more pleasing & amiable. She is evidently selected for a great work—always recollected, but never too solemn—no shew of any kind—yet all that is valuable shews itself continually. She yields to the opinion of others like a little child, and you find yourself irresistably drawn to hers—by the very manner in which she submits. Had I met her as she now is—10 or 12 years since—I might have been greatly benefitted indeed, and even now, she teaches me by her example what genuine meekness and humility are. The adage—"never too old to learn"—is a great comfort to me.[51]

Our dear Father Carroll is exceedingly regretted by every class—who are most anxious to raise a monument as a tribute of their respect & affection.

I hope Sister M. Josephine will soon—by the grace of God—enter cheerfully on the various duties of her new state. Poor Mrs. Cassin[52] is delighted to get her favorite child so much nearer and intends going to see her soon. She looks extremely well. Fanny is growing quite a nice little girl and pretty.

I found my poor Teresa[53] in the same state of health—how little I thought she would see Mr. Carroll gone—he was most anxious about her latterly.

Give my most affectionate love to my dear Sister M. Josephine for whom we will all fervently pray—& to Sister M. Catherine.

I have been so much interrupted all day with enquiries about "Geraldine." This will not be in time for the post.

[M. C. McAuley][54]

Autograph: Silver Spring

50 October 3.   51 Catherine McAuley's generous first impression of Mary Clare (Elizabeth) Agnew did not, and probably could not, penetrate to the latent characteristics and opinions that were revealed in 1841 when Clare became superior of the Bermondsey (London) community. For Catherine's view at that time, see, for example, Letter 284.   52 Neumann (171) and Bolster (95) have "Cassin" here, but the word looks as if it might be Cogsin or Cagsin. However, according to the Carlow Register, Mary Cassin was the mother of Mary Catherine Meagher, now in Naas.   53 Teresa Carton.   54 This letter is unsigned. However, the autograph appears to be complete: it is a single large sheet of paper, folded once, with text on pages 1, 2, and the top of 3, and the address on page 4. The Dublin postmark is "SE 28, 1839." Conceivably, Catherine McAuley could have inserted another sheet of paper with further text and her signature, but the large amount of available space on page 3 would seem to argue against that hypothesis. All available letter-fragments have been examined—including part of Letter 124 which has two signatures, one abbreviated—and none appears to belong to this autograph.

129. To the Reverend John Hamilton   Convent, Baggot Street
September 30, 1839

Very Reverend Sir
    May we hope for the favor of your presence at the ceremony of Profession
on Thursday next⁵⁵—at eight o'clock.

                                Very Reverend Sir, respectfully, etc,
                                            M. C. McAuley

Autograph: Dublin Diocese, Murray Papers AB3/34/15, no. 14

129a.   To Mrs. Dunn   Tuesday, October 1 [1839]
          Tighe Street

Dear Mrs. Dunn
    On Thursday morning at eight o'clock our dear Sister Markey is to make
her vows. We hope to have the pleasure of seeing you on that happy occasion—
and any Priest you wish to ask. Doctor Yore has kindly promised to be present.

                                Dear Mrs. Dunn, faithfully etc.
                                            M. C. McAuley

Autograph: Dublin, Mercy

130. To Sister M. Ursula Frayne   [October 1839]⁵⁶
      Booterstown

        My dear Sister Muse, I am sorry to find
        That sweet holy poverty's not to your mind.

---

55 The profession ceremony of Mary Xavier O'Connell and Mary de Chantal Markey (from Co.
Louth) on October 3, 1839. Letter 129a, also about Mary de Chantal Markey's profession, was
found as this edition of Catherine McAuley's correspondence was going to press.   56 No autograph of this teasing poem on poverty has been found. However, at least three early handcopies
survive—in the small copybook labeled Baggot Street Manuscript Copies, in the Liverpool Annals,
and in the Brisbane Book of Transcriptions. Each identifies Mary Ursula Frayne, in Booterstown,
as the recipient of the poem, as does the conclusion of the poem. The text followed here is the
Baggot Street handcopy. Lines 9 and 20 seem to suggest, though not unequivocally, that the poem
was written in the late summer or early fall, when fruit was plentiful ("fruit" is also a metaphor
here), but just before "the frost." The reference to John Ennis, parish priest of Booterstown, in
line 30 limits the dating of the poem because "Father John" and William Meagher were sent to
Rome as delegates of the Irish bishops in favor of the national system of education, from at least
October 29, 1839—when William Meagher wrote to John Hamilton from Paris, while en route to
Rome—until September 1840 when the two made plans to return from Rome to Ireland (Dublin

What in your case would a poor girl do
But look[57] for a cobbler to mend her old shoe
Is soling and heeling a language obscure
To those who have freely made vows to be poor
How many bleak winters were safely passed through
With nothing to keep out the wet but a shoe
And now, when we should be abounding in fruit
We are wishing to dress up our foot in a boot
The advocates here did wisely discover
That a break in the stocking the boot would quite cover
Oh shame for a Sister of Mercy to own
That she'd cover up what she ought to have sewn
May we not fear 'tis the enemy lurking
Our fears & our fancies so artfully working
Who at the word Cobbler would teach us to blush
And whisper—get boots made of leather & plush
But where reason is not, all reasoning is lost
Then, pray get the boots to keep out the frost.

Now as to the China, your taste must be bad
If you don't like what we send, more than those that you had
They were once, I assure you, nice breakfast cups[58]
And no mouth but your own could make them 3 sups
They hold full as much as the modern grand shapes
And each cup & saucer have different landscapes
Here again holy poverty's flitted away
'Tis plain you want nothing in this but display
I pray you, dear child, cast these feelings away
Should good Father John your breakfast e'er favor
Let his Tea be well made and of exquisite flavor
I'll answer for him, he'll chat all the time
And know no more of these cups than he does of this rhyme
You say that they are safe there as here
But 'tis far more convenient to keep them all near
For when we have much things in haste to prepare
It makes a great difference to be here or there

Diocesan Archives, Hamilton Papers P1/31/7, no. 72 and P1/31/8, no. 75). I have placed the poem-letter in 1839, rather than 1838 (another possibility), simply because Catherine McAuley was occupied in Limerick from September to December 1838. However, the poem may have been written in the summer of 1838 or earlier in 1839. Finally, the content of the poem is more significant than its date.   **57** The handcopy in the Liverpool Annals (124–26) has "send" here.   **58** The Liverpool handcopy reverses the order of this line and the next, but that switch cannot be correct.

They might without damage make 2 or 3 trips
Yet 'tis very likely they'd meet a few chips
And although they went safely day after day
They'd at length get a fall & break on the way
You remember the story when learning to spell
Of the pitcher that often was sent to the well
Though many times it in safety had passed
Yet on the way it was broken at last.

As I have not got a poetical name
Borrowing yours—I beg to remain
The affectionate Mother of Ursula Frayne

[M. C. McAuley]

Handcopy: Baggot Street Manuscript Copies (43–45), Dublin, Mercy

131. **To Sister M. Josephine Warde**   **Baggot Street**
    Cork   **October 18, 1839**

My Dearest Sister Mary Josephine[59]

I cannot tell [you] how very anxious I feel to hear that all with you goes on happily, with good prospect of increase. I pray most earnestly and indeed constantly for you—and I have a confident hope that the Institute over which you now preside will not be excelled by any. I could even wish it to excel poor Baggot Street.

Tell my dear Sister Mary Vincent I am quite disappointed that she never writes me one little note. I fear she will not patronise my next work—I dare not venture to dedicate it to her—if she does not give me more encouragement.[60] Is Sister Anastasia[61] very useful—I know she is very good. In dear Sister Mary Aloysius and Mary Francis you have all that could be desired—and the last additions I trust are all desirable.[62]

How is your venerated Bishop, Mr. Delany and Mr. Mathew,[63] whose fame has reached the most remote cornor [*sic*] of the land—the walls of Dublin covered with placards proclaiming the good he has accomplished. It is no longer a

59 When Clare Moore left Cork in August 1839, to become the temporary superior of the forthcoming foundation in Bermondsey, London, Josephine Warde was appointed superior of the Cork community.   60 This sentence has been frequently cited to support the view that Catherine McAuley composed *Cottage Controversy* for Mary Vincent Deasy. See Letter 75.   61 Mary Anastasia McGauley had come to Cork as a novice in July 1837. She professed her vows there on October 25, 1837.   62 On July 23, 1837, Mary Aloysius (Margaret) O'Connell entered the Cork community as its first postulant. On October 18, 1837, Mary Francis (Catherine) Mahony joined her. Within five months of this letter, Mary Francis will die in the Cork convent—the first of three Sisters of Mercy to die in March 1840.   63 Dr. John Murphy, William Delany, a Cork priest, and Theobald Mathew, OFM Cap., who came to be known as the "Apostle of Temperance."

laughing matter. All description of persons speak most seriously of his extraordinary success—and all wish he could extend his influence to every place.[64]

How is Miss Goold— give my love to her.[65] How does your collection go on—are the dear children as attentive, as is reasonable to expect? I feel confident you will never seek any thing unreasonable. I trust that on my return from London, I shall be able to make some excuse to go see you.

The pension school in Carlow is making great progress. You must get their regulations—it is quite simple and does not seem to add to their toil—some sweet young persons amongst them who bid fair to become Sisters. They are all interested and some prefer it to any other duty. Sister Vincent I am sure would enter into the spirit of it and give one hour every day. It thus becomes easy to all. The girls are obliged to acquire a perfect knowledge of the lessons at home—so that to hear the classes is all—one the french class, another Grammer & Geography, [and] so on. They have already commenced at Naas and have 18 pupils—also a poor school.

Write to me every particular. Give my most affectionate love to all, and believe me, my very Dear Sister

your fondly attached
M. C. McAuley

We all love the english Sisters more every day—you know by this time that we leave for London on the 18th November—as appointed by Dr. Griffiths.[66]

Autograph: Cork; photocopy of autograph, Dublin, Mercy

---

64 Catherine McAuley had enormous respect for the character and mission of the Capuchin priest Theobald Mathew. The *Irish Catholic Directory* for 1840 reports that in March 1839 he "commenced in a marked manner the formation of a Temperance Society. In nine or ten months he has enrolled about 100,000 persons who have kept their pledge of not drinking any intoxicating liquors; and under his patronage, branch Societies have been formed in Cork, Limerick, Cove, Dungarvan, Charleville, Nenagh, Tipperary, and lately in the City of Dublin ... with the most incredible benefits" (345–46). Fitzgerald, quoting an unnamed source, claims of the pre-Famine period: "'the sudden conversion of a drinking into a temperance country by the eloquence and enthusiasm of a single man is one of the most remarkable facts in the history of morals'" (2:6). 65 "The foundress of the Cork Convent of Mercy was Miss Barbara Ann Goold, a gentlewoman of great wealth and greater charity, who allowed herself none of the luxuries of life, and stinted herself even in the necessaries, that she might have the more to devote to works of beneficence ... a spacious, well adapted mansion [on Rutland Street], fully furnished in conventual style, and a gift of two thousand pounds were presented to Mother McAuley in 1837 by this most charitable, mortified, and unostentatious woman" (Carroll, *Leaves* 1:221–23). Like Elizabeth Pentony in Tullamore, Mary Clanchy in Charleville, Michael and John Nowlan in Carlow, Barbara Verschoyle in Booterstown, Helena Heffernan in Limerick, and later, John and Barbara Hardman in Birmingham, Barbara Goold provided not only the initial financial help, but the inspiring example of lay holiness, compassion for the poor, and far-reaching vision on which the original foundations of the Sisters of Mercy depended. Catherine McAuley never forgot their collaborative role in whatever good the Sisters of Mercy might accomplish in the future. 66 With Peter Butler, the parish priest in Bermondsey, Dr. Thomas Griffiths, vicar apostolic of the London District, arranged the forthcoming foundation: the first convent of Sisters of Mercy in England. Until the restoration of the English hierarchy in 1850,

132. To Mrs. Turnbull[67]   Convent
                                                                October 25, 1839

My Dear Mrs. Turnbull

Mrs. Kinsela called on me to ask—could I give you an introduction to the Very Revd. Mr. Hamilton. I would most willingly write, or say, everything in my power for you—but I am quite certain that your own personal application will have more effect—which with the reference you can give as to the character of your nephew—will be sufficient to interest Mr. Hamilton in his regard.

I am very truly, etc.,
M. C. McAuley

Autograph: Dublin Diocese, Murray Papers AB3/34/15, no. 15

133. To Catherine McAuley[68]   Newry
                                                                October 30, 1839

Dear Revd. Mother

Instead of hesitating a moment I would wish to comply at once with every request that comes from you, and particularly when the request is that I would commend your petition for the approbation of the Holy See. In complying with such a request, I am sure I could not say too much in praise of your Institute, or of the intrinsic excellence of its rules and constitutions, or of the perfect adaptation of these to the great and peculiar duties of your community, or of the strict observance by which they are carried into effect. But as the sincere friend of your Institute, I think it my duty to suggest rather the regular and most approved mode usually adopted on such occasions, of having your petition sanctioned and corroborated by the joint request and signature of your venerable Archbishop. Whatever is asked in that way, if it be at all reasonable, is usually and almost as a matter of course, granted. I give this advice because, from my experience in such matters, I believe it to be the best I can offer.

---

the title of bishop was not used for episcopal appointments in England, as was the case in other countries that the Vatican viewed as missionary territories.   **67** The *Dublin Directory* for 1839 lists a Mrs. Turnbull as matron of the City of Dublin Hospital, Upper Baggot Street, across the canal from the Mercy convent (314). Perhaps she is the Mrs. Turnbull to whom Catherine McAuley writes this letter. The hospital was established in 1832 "for the purpose of affording additional relief to the sick poor of the metropolis" (314), and Catherine would surely have known its matron. Since the letter is now preserved in the Dublin Diocesan Archives, it must have been forwarded to John Hamilton as a letter of recommendation.   **68** This letter and Letter 134 are the first of many letters Catherine McAuley will receive in response to her request for episcopal letters of recommendation to forward to the Sacred Congregation for the Propagation of the Faith in Rome with the proposed Rule and Constitutions of the Religious Sisters of Mercy for which she will seek final

I was much gratified in hearing from the Revd. Prioress of St. Clare's, that you and your venerated companions in your late visit to Newry are all well after the journey.[69] That you and they may always be well and daily receive an encrease of every good and perfect gift of God is the sincere wish, dear Revd. Mother, of

Your faithful servant in Christ
+ M. Blake

Autograph: Propaganda Fide, SOCG, vol. 957, ff. 317r–318v

134. To Catherine McAuley

Limerick
October 30, 1839

Dear & Revd. Madam

I feel much pleasure in testifying my approbation of the edifying conduct and valuable exertions of the Branch of the Institute of the Sisters of Mercy in this city and am happy to be informed, that their zeal & efficiency entitle them to similar praise, wherever they have been established in this country. I therefore consider, their claim to every favorable consideration from the Holy See to be well founded & trust they will experience that attention so justly due to so meritorious a society.

I remain, dear & Revd. Madam
Your faithful Servant in J.C.
+John Ryan
Bishop of Limerick

Autograph: Propaganda Fide, SOCG, vol. 957, f. 319rv

---

confirmation by Pope Gregory XVI. She will take these letters with her to London on November 18, and when all are assembled, including those of Dr. Thomas Griffiths, forward them from London in December or January, under his guidance. The letters from Michael Blake and John Ryan are written in English; some of the other episcopal letters are written in Latin; some are addressed to Catherine McAuley, others to Gregory XVI; all are now preserved in the Archives of Propaganda Fide in Rome. In this letter, Dr. Blake advises Catherine to seek the sanction and corroboration of Dr. Murray, which of course she has done, as evidenced by Letters 138 and 142. Letters 139 and 140 are apparently the only surviving examples of the letters of request she sent to bishops in whose dioceses the Sisters of Mercy were then located.   69 Carroll says that early in October 1839, Catherine McAuley, Clare Moore, Mary Clare Agnew, and Mary Augustin Taylor visited Newry, staying in the convent of the Poor Clares. However, she also says that Catherine asked for accommodation for "three Sisters of Mercy for a few days" (*Leaves* 2:45–46). She clearly indicates that Catherine was part of the group, as does Degnan who quotes records in the Poor Clare convent and says that the visit of the four took place on October 5–9, 1839 (247–48).

November–December 1839

Catherine McAuley spent most of the last two months of 1839 in Bermondsey, London, where on November 19 she and the founding party, including the temporary superior Mary Clare Moore, established the first Mercy convent in England. During this period Catherine also prepared the large packet she sent to the Congregation for the Propagation of the Faith in Rome, seeking Gregory XVI's final confirmation of the Rule and Constitutions of the Religious Sisters of Mercy.

The weather in London was often rainy, and the Bermondsey convent, cold, damp, and unfinished, yet warmth and gaiety characterize Catherine's letters in this period. She was exhilarated by the trip, by the reception ceremony for six English women on December 12, and by the example and friendship of Thomas Griffiths, vicar apostolic of the London District, and Peter Butler, the severely ill pastor of the mission in Bermondsey. She called herself "Kitty" among intimates; teased Peter Butler about the English stereotype of the "wild Irish"; wrote long, detailed letters to Limerick, Cork, and Charleville; and gave free rein to her verse-making. Though problems had arisen in early November about the contract for the commercial laundry on Baggot Street, and she had confided to Frances Warde on the eve of her departure: "I need not tell you all the difficulties I have to meet in getting away from this poor old charge" (Letter 142), once she was in London, she gave herself completely to the demands of the new setting, making clothes for 200 girls in the parish poor school, visiting with English nobility related to one of the Bermondsey sisters, and helping the new foundation in every way she could.

Catherine carried with her to London, or received there, for forwarding to Rome, the most extensive written expression of episcopal support she had ever received: letters of recommendation from Daniel Murray and William Crolly, the archbishops of Dublin and Armagh, and from six bishops familiar with the Sisters of Mercy: John Ryan (Limerick), Michael Blake (Dromore), William Kinsella (Ossory), John Murphy (Cork), Francis Haly (Kildare and Leighlin), and Thomas Griffiths (London). All praised the work of the Sisters of Mercy and recommended confirmation of their Rule and Constitutions.[1] Catherine probably did

---

1 No such letter from Dr. John Cantwell, bishop of Meath, or Dr. Bartholomew Crotty, bishop of Cloyne and Ross, appears to be extant, though in Letter 231 Catherine lists one from Dr. Cantwell. Perhaps both bishops wrote letters that were subsequently lost, before or after reaching Propaganda Fide in Rome, where the other episcopal letters are preserved. In materials prepared for meetings of the Congregation for the Propagation of the Faith no reference is made to

not advert to the fact—or if she did, she was silent—that these generous letters were a far cry from the complaints made by some in Dublin nine or ten years earlier: claims that she was a parvenue, one of the "unlearned sex," doing "mischief by trying to assist the clergy" (Moore, "Memoir," in Sullivan, *Catherine McAuley* 208). Rather, she was deeply grateful. For her, these letters were, quite simply, a gift of God, a sign, she humbly accepted, that the journey begun so long ago, at the death of William Callaghan in November 1822, had indeed been guided by a mysteriously benevolent Providence in whose presence her own deficiencies were not decisive.

Perhaps it was now that Catherine turned to Helen Maria Williams's poetic paraphrase of Matthew 7:12—"do to others as you would have them do to you"—and transcribed for the Bermondsey community an abbreviated version of Williams's "Precept divine, to Earth in Mercy given" (Letter 152). Catherine had never had a limited understanding of Jesus' precept. Repeatedly, as Clare Moore knew, she had taught novices at Baggot Street "the advantages of Mercy above Charity. 'The Charity of God would not avail us, if His Mercy did not come to our assistance. Mercy is more than Charity—for it not only bestows benefits, but it receives and pardons again and again—even the ungrateful'" (Bermondsey Annals, in Sullivan, *Catherine McAuley* 117). In Bermondsey, at the end of 1839, Catherine McAuley evidently felt the pardon and assistance of God; in the strength of such mercy she gave herself wholeheartedly to the foundation that—as it turned out—she would never see again.

135. To Pope Gregory XVI

Kilkenny
November 5, 1839

Most Holy Father

Most humbly prostrate at the feet of Your Holiness, I ask, unworthy though I am, that I may be allowed to proffer briefly testimony concerning the Institution of the Sisters of Mercy, formed a few years ago in Ireland.

Although I was unable as yet to introduce any of these holy virgins into this Diocese, nevertheless, from an abundant experience of their labours in other places, I can faithfully assert that the members of this Institution in visiting the sick, in protecting young girls who would be otherwise exposed to grave danger, and in educating the children of the poor, have produced the most fertile fruits of charity and piety.

And if Your Holiness deign to approve of the rules of this Institution and to confirm them, there is no doubt that it shall advance honor in the Church and most of all the salvation of souls.

---

letters from these bishops in whose respective dioceses the convents of Tullamore and Charleville were located.

Imploring on bended knee the Apostolic Benediction, I earnestly beseech God that He may long preserve Your Holiness safe and most happy.

Your most humble, obedient and devoted servant
+ William Kinsella
Bishop of Ossory

Autograph (Latin): Propaganda Fide, SOCG, vol. 957, ff. 279r-280v[2]

136. To Miss Emily Molloy[3]   Baggot Street
November 6, 1839

My Dear Emily
    Having known you so intimately for six years, I could have no hesitation in saying all that would tend to your welfare—and I am satisfied I should not have any reason to regret doing so. I feel exceedingly interested for you—and most earnestly wish you may be happily settled according to your inclination—which has continued so long unchanged. Believe me

Dear Emily, your affectionate friend
Mary C. McAuley

Autograph: Dublin Diocese, Murray Papers AB3/34/15, no. 16

137. To Catherine McAuley   Armagh
November 8, 1839

My dear Mrs. McAuley
    In compliance with your request, I feel much pleasure in stating that I have lately visited Convents of the Sisters of Mercy in Limerick and Carlow, where their charitable attention to the poor merited the unqualified approbation of the Prelates in whose Dioceses they have been established. I am convinced that the Order of the Sisters of Mercy is calculated to render important services to the poor of Ireland. With the highest esteem and respect I have the honour to remain, my dear Mrs. McAuley,

Your faithful and obt. [obedient] Servant
+ W[illiam] Crolly
[Archbishop of Armagh]

Autograph: Propaganda Fide, SOCG, vol. 957, f. 320rv[4]

2 The episcopal letters sent to Rome that were originally written in Latin have been recently translated by Mary Eymard Hyland, RSM, with help from earlier translations made by John MacErlean, SJ. Dr. William Kinsella (1796–1845), Catherine McAuley's longstanding friend, wrote this letter in Latin. 3 Emily Molloy has not been identified. She may have been a resident of the House of Mercy, Baggot Street. Since this letter of recommendation is preserved in the Dublin Diocesan Archives, she may have applied for a servant's position through John Hamilton or an acquaintance of his.   4 Dr. William Crolly,

138. To Pope Gregory XVI

Dublin
November 12, 1839

Most Blessed Father

Prostrate at the feet of Your Holiness, I humbly beseech that you may kindly deign to confirm by your Apostolic authority the Rules already approved by me for the government of the Pious Congregation which is called by the name Sisters of Mercy, and which is spreading more and more every day, far and wide throughout Ireland, to the great benefit of souls and the great consolation of Pastors.

Humbly begging your Apostolic Benediction, I sign myself
Your Holiness's
Most Obedient, Most Respectful, Most Loving Son
+ Daniel, Archbishop of Dublin

Autograph (Latin): Propaganda Fide, SOCG, vol. 957, ff. 275r–276v[5]

139. To Dr. Francis Haly
   Carlow

Baggot Street
November 13, 1839

Dear and respected Lord

I took the liberty of sending you a little circular which I was directed to forward to the Bishops in whose Diocess [sic] a branch of our Institute was formed.

Perhaps, my Lord, I should have explained the nature of the application more fully. In the year 1830 our venerated Archbishop obtained permission from the Holy See for three of us to serve a noviciate in a Presentation Convent with intention to add the visitation of the sick and charge of distressed women.

In 1835, our progress was represented, and the Pope then imparted to us his approbation and Benediction. The Bishop prepared our Rule—and finding it after due trial well suited to our purpose—we now seek its final confirmation—in form of a petition from ourselves, a memorial or request from His Grace, and all the recommendation we can obtain from other Prelates.

The Primate has given his in very gratifying terms—and Doctor Kinsella has enclosed me a letter to His Holiness—though we are not in either Diocess.[6] We take all our documents to London on Monday next, and trust you will be so kind to add the tribute of your approbation.

I have the honor to remain, My Lord
Most respectfully, etc., etc.
Mary C. McAuley

Autograph: Carlow

---

the primate of All Ireland, wrote this letter in English.   5 Dr. Murray's letter is written in Latin. See note 2 regarding translation.   6 Dr. William Crolly was, since 1835, the archbishop of Armagh and the primate of All Ireland; Dr. William Kinsella was the bishop of Ossory since July 26, 1829.

140. To Dr. John Murphy   **Baggot Street**
    Cork   **November 13, 1839**

Dear and much respected Lord
    His Grace called here yesterday to affix his approbation and seal to the copy
of our Rule going to Rome—and left with me his memorial to the Holy Father.
Your own Mary Clare,[7] the best Latin reader amongst us, finds that your name
is not introduced. My Lord, the Primate has sent us a strong recommendation,
and Doctor Kinsella a letter addressed to the Pope—and I am sure that you who
have so long honored us with your patronage and valued friendship will not withhold what would certainly give great weight to our application.
    My Lord—in the year 1830—His Holiness gave permission for our novici-
ate to be served in a Presentation Convent. In 1835 our venerated Archbishop
represented the successful progress—when[8] the Holy See imparted to us full
approbation. Doctor Murray then prepared our Rule, and finding it after due
trial well suited to our different duties, we now seek for its final confirmation.
We take all our documents with us to London on Monday next, and indeed, my
Lord, I would feel the parcel very light without a small tribute from you.
    I have the honor to remain, Dear and much respected Lord,
                                    with great respect and gratitude, etc., etc.
                                                            Mary C. McAuley

Autograph: Cork; photocopy: Dublin, Mercy

141. To Charles Cavanagh, Esq.   **Baggot Street**
                                    [November 15, 1839][9]

Dear Sir
    Will you be so kind to send me the contract to look at the words relative to
the Laundry, as it seems now as if we only expected a Room capable of being
made into a Laundry. I most distinctly repeated—that a *perfect* Laundry[10] was
the chief object in view. Certainly Mr. Brophy[11] is bound to that.
                                    Dear Sir, your respectful, etc.
                                                            M. C. McAuley
Autograph: Dublin, Mercy

---

7 Mary Clare Moore, the former superior in Cork, was now temporarily loaned to the forthcoming Bermondsey (London) foundation as its first superior.   8 Catherine McAuley often used
"when" in the sense of "then."   9 Charles Cavanagh dates this letter on the back of the stationery.
10 Catherine McAuley expected a laundry properly fitted with equipment for washing, drying,
and mangling, as well as heating and water connections. The original contract apparently did not
imply these features. In a bill for "Extra Work done by Mr. Brophy, in the Erection of New
Addition to the House of Mercy, Baggot Street—Materials & Workmanship" (which was reviewed

142. To Sister M. Frances Warde   [Baggot Street]
     Carlow   [November 17, 1839]

My Dear Sister Mary Frances

I need not tell you all the difficulties I have to meet in getting away from this poor old charge—which would—and will do as well without me.[12]

The six travellers leave dear Ireland tomorrow, all in tolerable good health—and more than tolerable spirits. Sister Agnew rejoiced, Sister Taylor in rapture, and their Mother all animation. Sister M. Cecilia greatly improved and Mary Teresa smart as a lark.[13] I have my list of songs prepared for the journey.

We visited our old Georges Hill—they were delighted and so was I, said I would kiss the chairs & tables—but by some mistake I kissed a grand new chair in the Parlour.[14] However, I managed, as ducky Mary Quin used—(your mother)—I took it back and brought it up to the old rush chair I used to sit on in the novaship.

---

by the architect Bernard Mullins and is now preserved in Mercy Congregational Archives, Dublin) many additional expenses, beyond the original estimate, are itemized: for example, "Framing of Cistern to Supply Wash Troughs in Laundry—£0.16.7½," "Yorkshire flagging to Hot Closet—£3.18.9," "Additional Clothes Horses to [Hot] Closet—£2.0.0," "Framed & Moulded Wainscott (reduced) in door between Mangling & drying Room—£1.12.8," and "14 Days, Carpenters time, making Tables, Cloths presses, etc. for Mangle Room, out of Old Materials supplied by the Establishment, Nails & Glue included—£2.16.0." The extra construction amounted to £128.8.7, from which was deducted credit for works in the original estimate that were not executed, leaving a final additional construction bill of £41.19.4, exclusive of the plumber's work. In reviewing this bill on January 20, 1840, Bernard Mullins wrote: "I consider the sewer leading from the Wash House along the area of that building & across the court yard of the front Building & thro' it into the Main Sewer in Baggot Street too small & insufficient for the purpose & that the part constructed by Mr. Brophy is in this respect as defective as the old House Sewer previously built into which the new part discharges—B.M." 11 Thomas Brophy was the contractor hired for the project by Bernard Mullins, the architect. A detailed architectural analysis of the original House of Mercy on Baggot Street (the original convent) and of the addition to the House constructed in 1838–1840 is badly needed. Such an analysis, for which many primary source materials are available, would explain the evolution of the community's living quarters and its ministries and would elucidate the courageous balance achieved between the growth and poverty of the religious community and its expanding works of mercy within the house. To say that the first Sisters of Mercy were uncloistered is an understatement. 12 Catherine McAuley and the founding party for Bermondsey, London, departed by steamer from Kingstown (Dún Laoghaire) at six o'clock in the evening on Monday, November 18, 1839. "They arrived the next morning in Liverpool, travelled thence to London by Railway, and reached Bermondsey at eleven o'clock on Tuesday night the 19th of November, from which time is dated the establishment of this Convent" (Bermondsey Annals 1:7). 13 The six travellers were Mary Clare Agnew, Mary Augustin (or Austin) Taylor, Mary Clare Moore (who was to be superior in Bermondsey for one year), Catherine McAuley, and her travelling companions Mary Cecilia Marmion and Mary Teresa White. 14 This was evidently Catherine McAuley's first visit to the Presentation Convent on George's Hill, Dublin, since December 12, 1831—the day she, Mary Ann Doyle, and Mary Elizabeth Harley professed their vows there and then departed immediately for Baggot Street. The visit was obviously an affectionate reminder of her novitiate days among the Presentation Sisters.

My poor Sister Teresa[15] is much better, thanks be to God. She has passed through all the great damp—without much cough—yet I dread frost for her more. She takes nourishment enough now—except for a day or two. The little excitement of my going will last a few days—I trust only a few.

We have had *long* and most kind visits from our poor Bishop, a cordial leave taking—and fervent prayers for safe return. Nine masses are to be offered for us tomorrow, thank God. I am sure Mr. O'Hanlon is a little alarmed at the angry things which are said in the English papers—he gave me 10,000 cautions yesterday.[16]

I hope you find my intended child a very good one.

Begging to be most affectionately remembered to all and to Naas when you write, believe me always

your affectionate
M. C. McAuley

Get all the prayers you can for poor me.

Written in the greatest haste on the eve of departure.

Sister Teresa will give this a respectable appearance and forward it to you when I am gone.

Autograph: Brooklyn

143. To Pope Gregory XVI

Cork
November 18, 1839

Most Holy Father

Prostrate at the feet of Your Holiness, I humbly beg that you would deign to grant full confirmation to the Rule and Constitutions prescribed for the Sisters of Mercy by the Most Reverend Daniel Murray, Archbishop of Dublin. By confirming this Institute which is so completely suitable to the present state of things amongst us, Your Holiness will be conferring a most precious benefit on the Prelates, Clergy and Ro[man] Catholic people of Ireland.

Within the space of six years, eight convents[17] are already flourishing; and the Sisters in these convents, glowing with charity, bring both temporal and spir-

---

15 Teresa Carton.   **16** Protestant-Catholic controversy, not always unmixed with bigotry, characterized this period in England, frequently inflamed in the press by the conversion of notable Protestants to Catholicism, the erection of new Catholic churches, the immigration of Irish Catholic laborers, public debates between Protestant and Catholic theologians, and the publication of intemperate tracts and letters.   **17** This letter is written in Latin (see note 2 regarding translation). The autograph clearly says "*Intra sex annorum spatium jam florent octo Monasteria*," as does the printed text prepared in Rome and distributed to the members of the Sacred Congregation for the Propagation of the Faith prior to their July 1840 meeting. It is not clear how Dr. Murphy calculates "six years" (it was eight, from the founding in 1831; or four, from the approval of the congregation in 1835). The "flourishing" convents at the time—Dublin, Tullamore, Charleville, Carlow, Cork, Booterstown, Limerick, and Naas—do in fact number eight if the branch house in

itual help to the sick poor, whether they be in their homes or in public hospitals. They give alms to the faithful, to the convalescents, and they educate young girls. They take in poor servant maids after serious illness, feed them and instruct them, and finally find for them masters and mistresses with whom they can earn honestly for themselves food and clothing and be free from all the danger of falling, through poverty, into the hands of impious and wicked men, and of endangering their chastity and their faith.

May God long preserve Your Holiness in health for the greater glory of His Name and for the exaltation of His Church is my fervent prayer.

Of Your Holiness,
the most humble and obedient servant
+ John Murphy
Bishop of Cork

Autograph (Latin): Propaganda Fide, SOCG, vol. 957, ff. 281r–282v

144. To Cardinal Giacomo Filippo Fransoni

Carlow
November 22, 1839

Most Eminent and Reverend Lord

Since the Congregation of pious women not unknown to Your Eminence, which under the protection of the Blessed Virgin Mary of Mercy has flourished for about four years in this kingdom, now humbly petitions that His Holiness may deign to approve and confirm their Rules; and since there are two Convents of this Congregation in our diocese,[18] it seems just for us to declare our opinion of this very useful and holy Institution.

How fortunate for religion this Institution is in other parts of this region we have often heard, and we have seen with joy this Congregation bringing much fruit of its piety into our diocese. For the Sisters of this Institution, who are called "Sisters of Mercy," instruct the ignorant in the principles of faith and morals, encourage and uplift the needy and the miserable, visit and console the infirm, assist the dying, and therefore, this Congregation increases good works, augments piety, adorns religion and seems especially suited for promoting the greater glory of God.

Therefore, desiring earnestly that this Institution may be strengthened and rendered perpetual, we humbly and fervently beseech His Holiness to yield to the prayers of the Sisters and to confirm their Rule.

That God may long preserve Your Eminence is the prayer, Your Eminence, of

Your most obedient and most dutiful servant
+ Francis Haly
Bishop of Kildare and Leighlin

Autograph (Latin): Propaganda Fide, SOCG, vol. 957, ff. 285r–286v[19]

Booterstown, which Dr. Murphy had visited, is counted. **18** In Carlow and Naas. **19** This letter

145. To Pope Gregory XVI   [November or December 1839][20]

Most Holy and beloved Father, we your devoted children—called Religious Sisters of Mercy, with profound reverence and dutiful respect, approach your sacred person to implore the confirmation of our Rule and to represent the blessings and favors which God has bestowed on our humble efforts since we had the happiness to receive the Approbation and Benediction of Your Holiness— imparted to us by our ever venerated Archbishop in one thousand eight hundred and thirty five. From that period to the present—Branches of our Institute have been established in the Diocesses of Meath, Cloyne, Kildare [and] Leighlin, Cork, Limerick, and in the City of London where the venerable Vicar Apostolic cherishes strong hope it will increase and multiply as it has done in the Capital of Ireland. His Lordship regards it as a circumstance of great promise, that the Religious who form the foundation are distinguished converts to the Catholic Faith—and now join with us as the devoted children of Your Holiness praying the grant of this our humble petition which will give new fervor and animation to our united exertions—[and] fill our hearts with lively gratitude to God and dutiful attachment to you, our Most Holy Father.

Convent, Baggot Street, Dublin
    Diocess of Dublin. . . . . Mother Superior, Mary Catherine McAuley
Convent, Tullamore,
    Diocess of Meath . . . . Mother Superior, Mary A. Teresa Doyle
Convent, Charleville,
    Diocess of Cloyne . . . . Mother Superior, Mary Angela Dunne
Convent, Carlow,
    Diocess of Kildare & Leighlin. . . . . Mother Superior, Mary Frances Warde
Convent, Cork, Diocess of Cork . . . . . Mother Superior, Mary Joseph Warde
Convent, Limerick,
    Diocess of Limerick . . . . Mother Superior, Mary Elizabeth Moore
Convent, Naas,
    Diocess of Kildare & Leighlin . . . . Mother Superior, Mary Joseph Trennor

---

was written in Latin (see note 2 regarding translation) to Cardinal Fransoni, the Prefect of the Sacred Congregation for the Propagation of the Faith, but it was posted on November 24 to "Mrs. McAuley, Convent of SS. of Mercy, Bermondersey [*sic*], London," for her to include in the packet to be sent to Rome. It is Dr. Haly's response to Letter 139. **20** This autograph petition, in Catherine McAuley's handwriting, was probably written either before she left Dublin on November 18, or—and this is more likely, given the references to Dr. Thomas Griffiths, vicar apostolic of the London District—sometime later in Bermondsey. The whole packet, including the petition, the Rule and Constitutions signed and sealed by Dr. Daniel Murray, and the episcopal letters, was probably ready to be sent to Rome by the end of December, though by what means—post or messenger—is not known. Side four of Catherine McAuley's large folded sheet is addressed by an unknown hand: "To His Eminence Cardinal Franzoni [*sic*], Prefect of the S. Congregation de Propaganda Fide," but there are no postmarks.

Convent, London,
London District. . . . . Mother Superior, Mary Clare Moore[21]
[Catherine McAuley]

Autograph: Propaganda Fide, SOCG, vol. 957, ff. 321r–322v

146. To Cardinal Giacomo Filippo Fransoni **London**
December 3, 1839

Most Illustrious and Most Reverend Lord
    The pious Congregation called the Sisters of Mercy has already for six [*sic*] years been of the greatest help to the poor of Ireland, as is apparent from the letters of its superiors.[22]
    Wishing that the poor of my jurisdiction might enjoy the same benefits, I caused some pious virgins to proceed to Ireland to take the accustomed vows in this Congregation,[23] so that they might return to this District in order to educate the young and visit the sick.
    I therefore most humbly seek from Your Eminence, that His Holiness, to whom I address this petition, may deign to grant confirmation of this Congregation.

Your Eminence's most humble and most dutiful servant,
+ Thomas [Griffiths]
Bishop of Olena[24]
Vicar Apostolic, London

Autograph (Latin): Propaganda Fide, SOCG, vol. 957, ff. 283r–284v

---

21 The names of the various superiors, except Catherine's own, are not in Catherine McAuley's handwriting, but in another hand or other hands. They are not personal signatures. Mary Ann Doyle's full name in religion is given: Mary A[nn] Teresa Doyle, as it appears on her Act of Profession. A photocopy of the autograph of a very rough draft of this petition is preserved in Mercy Congregational Archives, Dublin; the original autograph of the draft has not been located. The autograph of the final petition (written in English) differs from the draft only in the sequencing of the convents and dioceses; here in the final petition they are listed in the order of their founding. 22 This letter to the Prefect of the Sacred Congregation for the Propagation of the Faith is written in Latin (see note 2 regarding translation). Dr. Griffiths had evidently read the letters Catherine McAuley received from the Irish bishops before writing his own. 23 With Peter Butler, pastor of Bermondsey, Dr. Griffiths had encouraged Elizabeth Agnew and Maria Taylor to serve a novitiate and profess their vows at the Mercy convent in Cork. 24 Dr. Griffiths was titular bishop of Olena. He was consecrated coadjutor vicar apostolic of the London District on October 28, 1833 (*Irish Catholic Directory* [1836] 25) and became vicar apostolic at the death of Dr. James Yorke Bramston on July 11, 1836 (*Irish Catholic Directory* [1837] 272).

147. To Pope Gregory XVI **London**
December 3, 1839

Most Holy Father

Prostrate at the feet of Your Holiness, most humbly do I join my prayers to the prayers of the Most Illustrious and Most Reverend Lord, Daniel, Archbishop of Dublin, that you may deign to confirm and to enrich with the Apostolic Blessing the Sisters of Mercy who already in many places in Ireland educate poor girls, visit sick women, and support and instruct those in danger.

A home for housing these Sisters has been established in London and very recently occupied by them, so that shortly their manifold work will be a help to the Clergy and people of this District.

I pray that you will impart of Your Beatitude the Apostolic Blessing to me and to my flock.

Your most humble and obedient son
+ Thomas [Griffiths]
Bishop of Olena
Vicar Apostolic, London

Autograph: Propaganda Fide, SOCG, vol. 957, ff. 277r–278v[25]

148. To Sister M. Elizabeth Moore **Convent of the Sisters of Mercy**
Limerick **Bermondsey, London**
December 17, 1839

My ever dear Sister Mary Elizabeth

I know you are anxious to hear from me, but not more than I am to write you a full account of our journey and the progress we have made in our new undertaking.

We sailed from Kingstown on Monday evening, the 18th of November, at 6 o'clock in the *Queen Victoria*, arrived in Liverpool at half past six next morning—were conducted to the Mersey Hotel where breakfast was ready—laughed and talked over the adventures of the night—particularly my travelling title— changed from your Kitty[26] to 'friend Catherine'—an improvement, you will say.

---

25 Dr. Griffiths's petition to Gregory XVI is written in Latin (see note 2 regarding translation).
26 Catherine McAuley's brother James called her Kitty. She shared this fact with her friend Mary Elizabeth Moore, as well as with the traveling party on the boat to England. The Limerick Annals notes that in this letter: "The name of 'Kitty' was in playful allusion to a little circumstance which occurred when they were coming on the foundation here in Sept. '38. They travelled by steamer from Dublin round to Cork, and Mother McAuley desiring that no seculars present should know her asked the Sisters not to address her as 'Rev. Mother.' All were sick from the motion of the vessel & to dispel their seriousness, Mother M. Elizabeth said jestingly, 'O Kitty, what shall I do?'

Proceeded in the train most comfortably—and reached London in very good time. Just think a moment what [an] extraordinary expedition—we dined in Baggot Street on Monday—and arrived in London time enough to take refreshment, say our prayers, and go to bed early on Tuesday night. Very different from our travels in Ireland—we were 16 hours going from Limerick to Tullamore.

The Convent is built in the old heavy monastic style. It will not be finished for another year, nor dry in three years, but our unceasing engagements have contributed to preserve us from the bad effects of a damp House—indeed we have been 'Busy Bodys.'

The Bishop[27] called the day after we arrived—he was exceedingly kind—said the Irish Sisters must be entertained by him and insisted on giving me a fifty pound note. In vain he was assured that all was provided which we were accustomed to—he would not be refused. He is remarkably gentle—his appearance—between Doctor Blake and Doctor Murray[28]—wears a gold chain and large cross outside his dress and purple stockings.

His Lordship celebrated Mass and blessed the Convent on the feast of the Presentation[29]—he also appointed Thursday last, 12th of December, for the reception of six who have been waiting with pious anxiety more than a year. The Bishop left everything to me—and as the test of their sincerity was not to be questioned, we concluded that it would be well to get all into religious order—first. On the morning of the ceremony, the Church[30] which accomodates [sic] four thousand was crowded to excess. Tickets had been circulated by the Bishop's direction—and none, that we could call poor, was amongst them. The seats next the sanctuary were filled with nobility—The Countess of Newburgh, Countess Constantia Clifford—Lady Bedington Dowager Countess Newburgh—Lady Petre—the Miss Cannings, Mrs. Weld, Mrs. Maxwell. You will be surprised that I remember all these titles, but they are the particular friends of Sister Agnew,[31] and familiar visitors—some the immediate family of one of our new novices—of whom you shall hear a description.

At eleven o'clock a grand High Mass commenced—the organ and choir are considered very fine. After Mass the hymn "O Gloriosa"[32] was performed—and we advanced from the entrance leading to our convent. The Bishop wished the ceremony to be last, lest any of those high persons should be late. Procession: Sister Mary Teresa—carrying an immense Cross; Sisters M. Cecilia, M. Clare Agnew, M. Augustin Taylor[33]—one by one, to make the most of a few—Mother

---

This had the desired effect and amused Mother McAuley much—it was the favorite name by which her brother called her" (1:60–61). **27** Thomas Griffiths, vicar apostolic of the London District. **28** Michael Blake, bishop of Dromore, and Daniel Murray, archbishop of Dublin. **29** November 21, 1839—feast of the Presentation of the Virgin Mary. **30** The newly built Church of the Most Holy Trinity, Dockhead, Bermondsey, London. **31** Mary Clare (Elizabeth) Agnew, age forty-one, had made her novitiate at the convent of the Sisters of Mercy in Cork and professed her vows there on August 19, 1839, intending to be part of the Bermondsey founding community. **32** The hymn "O Gloriosa Virginum" was the processional hymn at reception ceremonies of the Sisters of Mercy from the beginning of the congregation until at least the mid to late twentieth century. **33** Mary Teresa

Mary Clare[34] and her valuable assistant, "Friend Catherine" or your "Kitty," with their 6 postulants—following. All were admitted to the Sanctuary. The altar is the highest I ever saw—9 steps—2 platforms—the Bishop at the top—in very rich episcopal dress. Kitty had to go up and down eighteen times—3 times with each—indeed I might have said, poor Kitty. First, the Lady Barbara Ayre [Eyre], daughter of the late and sister to the present Earl of Newburgh—about Sister Agnew's age—has been a beauty—very dignified appearance—humble and pleasing—wore a full court dress worth 100 guineas—besides valuable diamonds—her train went below the last step when [she was] at the top. Next, a Lancashire Lady,[35] not young—very nice and amiable. Next, one from Gravlin [Gravelines][36]—young. A fourth [from] London[37]—about 30—and two lay Sisters[38]—all desirable. 36 priests—sermon preached by Doctor McGuire[39]— explaining the nature of the order and the spiritual and corporal works of Mercy. You would think the Bishop performed the ceremony every month, he did not make one mistake and pronounced every word most audibly. Nothing could exceed the joy manifested by all at living to see the Institute established.

The situation of the Convent is exactly what Kilmainham is to Dublin, only this a better neighbourhood. Amongst the visitors after the ceremony we had our *friend* Miss Lizy O'Rielly and Miss Granger, sister to Mrs. Thomas Farrell, who claimed Irish acquaintance with Kitty—in the most gracious manner. There is great work here for the poor Sisters—2 large hospitals—Guy's and St. Thomas's—4 work houses—endless converts—the people delighted.

Miss Birch[40] of Manchester Square enters next week—young & very nice. Miss Best[41] of Bath soon after—every application is referred by the Bishop to Kitty—who is major domo.

White and Mary Cecilia Marmion had come to Bermondsey as Catherine McAuley's travelling companions, to assist the new community. Mary Augustin (Maria) Taylor, age thirty-three, had made her novitiate in Cork and professed her vows there on August 19, 1839, intending to be part of the Bermondsey founding community.   34 Mary Clare Moore, the temporary superior of the Bermondsey community.   35 The six women who received the habit at the first reception ceremony in Bermondsey had all been ministering to the poor of the parish for some time, while they awaited the coming of the Sisters of Mercy. Mary Xaveria (Jane) Latham, "who had been a Professed Nun in France for twenty five years," entered the convent on November 26, 1839 (Bermondsey Annals 1:9). In 1840 she was dismissed from the community.   36 Mary Vincent (Susan) Weller, a friend of Jane Latham, also left the community in 1840.   37 Mary Ursula (Mary) O'Connor had assumed responsibility in 1837 for the poor school operated by the parish in the basement of its old chapel. On November 1, 1840 she died of typhus contracted while visiting a sick family in the parish.   38 The lay sisters were Mary Teresa (Elizabeth) Boyce and Mary Joseph (Sarah) Hawkins—two remarkable young women who contributed enormously to the life and ministry of the Bermondsey community. Mary Teresa Boyce became a founding member of the Brighton community in 1852 and remained, even at a distance, a lifelong friend and support of Clare Moore. Mary Joseph Hawkins served as a nurse in the Crimean War, earning the highest praise from Florence Nightingale (see Sullivan, *Friendship*, passim).   39 Dr. John Maguire.   40 Louisa Birch entered the Bermondsey community on January 17, 1840, subsequently taking the name Mary Agnes. She professed her vows on April 22, 1841, and in time became a member of the Chelsea community.   41 Cecilia Best entered the community in April 1840. Taking

The following note will amuse you, it is from her Majesty's hair dresser: "By desire of the Countess Constantia Clifford—Mr. Trufitt will wait on the Sisters of Mercy at 9 o'c on Thursday morning to adjust a court head dress." Lady Barbara was my charge on that morning. I went to her cell and said in a disguised voice: "Please, your Ladyship, Mr. Trufitt is come." She was at the other side of her Bed—did not see me—and answered—"Take down that box with my feathers & diamonds." When she discovered her mistake, she was sincerely distressed and said: "oh what shall I do—is it to Revd. Mother I have spoken." Indeed, they have all, thank God, a nice sense of religious respect—yet we cannot avoid preferring our sweet Irish Sisters every where—and Sister Augustin, though such an attached english woman, says she loves the Irish Sisters more.

Mrs. Agnew, Sister's Mamma, is a most delightful woman. Though 68 years old—you could never think of age when conversing with her. Her residence is Brighton. She came to remain in London for a few weeks—on her daughter's arrival—is most affectionate and delighted to see her child so happy. A younger daughter & one married is all her family—they are also very kind—and evidently astonished to find such wild Irish—nuns. Mrs. Agnew particularly pleased with "The young Lady Superior"[42]—acknowledges she did not expect her daughter would meet such a companion in the South of Ireland. The Marchioness Wellesley wrote a most kind note—regretting she was prevented by severe cold from visiting the Convent—but would take the first opportunity to do so. The poor Sisters of Mercy—are great persons. Lady Barbara—is Sister Mary de Sales.

I do not admire Mr. Pugin's taste[43]—he has put the windows up to the ceiling—we could not touch the glass without standing on a chair. Sister M. Cecilia has not been quite well since we came. I suppose we shall return in about a month or five weeks. When Sister Agnew's cards come out, she will send you a set. You heard of them—"The Spiritual and Corporal Works of Mercy illustrated with etchings by A Sister of Mercy."

How I long to hear of you and dear community—your ceremony—any new additions. You will write a long account to me—a letter that I may shew to all. Will you remember that.

Give my love a thousand times to my dear Sister Vincent, and M. Teresa and all my very Dear Sisters—particularly Sisters Mary and Ann.[44] I could wish this moment with all my heart that I were with you and them—even for a little time. I had a letter from Baggot Street lately—all are as I left them—but I believe they would not tell me if it were otherwise. I am often weary of myself. [*A small portion of the autograph letter is here cut out, by some later hand.*]

---

the name Mary Catherine at her reception of the habit, she professed her vows on August 21, 1841. She was at that time the eighth professed member of the Bermondsey community.   42 Mary Clare Moore.   43 Augustus Welby Pugin (1812–1852), the celebrated English convert and architect whose neo-Gothic designs of church buildings drew praise from many, was the architect of the Bermondsey convent. Catherine McAuley found his design of that convent wasteful and unconducive to community living.   44 Mary Vincent Harnett, Mary Teresa Vincent Potter, Mary Shanahan, and Anne Hewitt.

Farewell, my ever Dear Child. May God preserve and bless you.

Pray for your fondly attached

Kitty

M. C. McAuley

Remember me to Revd. Mr. Fitzgibbon & Mr. Nash.[45]

We have High Mass every Sunday. I like the irish piety better—it seems more genuine—though not near so much exteriorly.

You may judge how unceasingly we have been employed—besides the spiritual and temporal preparation for the Sisters, we had to prepare dresses for 200 poor girls of the school—who were to attend the ceremony.

Will you remember to return my most grateful and respectful thanks to your Bishop[46]—for the very kind and valuable letter his Lordship sent me.

Autograph: Limerick

149. To Sister M. Josephine Warde
Cork

Convent of the Sisters of Mercy
Bermondsey, London
December 24 [1839]

My Dearest Sister Mary Joseph

I have felt quite anxious to give you a full account of our grand ceremony. I fear it is now too late to be the first—but I will tell you up to the present day. We sailed from Kingstown on Monday at 6 o'c in the evening in the *Queen Victoria*—a beautiful Packet. We arrived in Liverpool at half past 6 next morning—not one of us sick. We were met by a carriage and brought to the Mersey Hotel—where breakfast was ready. We proceeded in the train – a most comfortable conveyance—it was just like 6 very cosy arm chairs. We reached London in full time to get a very good night's rest. Just think what extraordinary travelling. We dined in Baggot Street on Monday and slept in London on Tuesday.[47]

The Bishop called on us next day—he was exceedingly kind. His Lordship celebrated Mass and blessed the Convent on the Feast of the Presentation—also appointed the 12th of December—our first profession day—for the reception of six sisters who had been waiting in pious anxiety for the establishment of the order, and as they were led to expect us on the 24th of September—it would not have been fair to keep them longer in expectation. You may be sure the poor Habit makers, etc. had a busy time. Worldly dress was also to be prepared[48]— and nett [*sic*] caps—bibs and tippets[49] for all the children of the poor school.

45 Curates in Limerick.   46 Dr. John Ryan, bishop of Limerick.   47 This letter to Cork repeats much of the information contained in Letter 148 to Limerick.   48 At the beginning of a reception ceremony, in these early years, simple white dresses, remotely akin to bridal attire, were worn by the women about to receive the religious habit of the Sisters of Mercy. After the ceremony the dresses were converted to other purposes, such as liturgical vestments or altar cloths.   49 A tippet

On the 12th the fine church was crowded at an early hour. The High Mass commenced at eleven o'clock, after which the "O Gloriosa" was performed by the choir—and we then approached to the sanctuary—Sister Mary Teresa bearing a *very heavy* Cross—Sisters M. Cecilia, Agnew, and Taylor—one by one, to make the most of a few—Revd. Mother Clare—and her valuable assistant, with their 6 Postulants, advanced to the sanctuary.[50] The altar is very high – two platforms – the Bishop at the top—we had to ascend & descend—in the full view of thousands—and many of the ancient English nobility.

Our first postulant—The Lady Barbara Ayre [Eyre]—daughter of the late and sister to the present Earl of Newburgh—was in full court dress—a white satin petticoat covered with white crape richly embroidered in gold down the middle and at the bottom—a satin body and train of violet hue—embroidered all round—full half yard deep—the train from the waist 3 yards long. I never saw such a splendid thing. Hair dressed with long lace lappets—feathers and most valuable diamonds. [51] She is said to be about Sister Agnew's age, very pleasing, and has commenced her noviciate in the most edifying manner, quite a model of humility and obedience. All her noble relations were at the ceremony and came in after to congratulate her.

The next a Yorkshire lady—one from Gravlin [Gravelines]—one from London—and two lay sisters—all very desirable and—so far extremely promising. A sermon was preached by Dr. McGuire—I could not hear it well—I am told it will be published.[52]

The Convent is not more than half built—I do not admire Mr. Pugin's taste, though so celebrated—it is quite the old heavy monastic style. He was determined we should not look out at the windows—they are up to the ceiling—we could not touch the glass without standing on a chair. We have got one good room finished, with brown walls and a long table.

The schools are not commenced yet—they intend to put cells over them, which are much required—for the part that is compleated is not well laid out— too much room in some places and too little in others. We are obliged to go to the church to say our Office—but it is perfectly free to our use and nearer to the Community than the choir in Baggot St. is to the reception parlour—we have a private door—however it is certainly cold & bleak for a few. Mother Mary Clare often says she likes Rutland Street Convent[53] much better, and so do I.

---

was either "A long narrow slip of cloth or hanging part of dress, ... either attached to and forming part of the hood, head-dress, or sleeve, or loose, as a scarf or the like" or "A garment, usually of fur or wool, covering the shoulders; a cape or short cloak, often with hanging ends" (OED). In this case, the tippets were probably scarves or, more likely, capes; however, in Letter 148, Catherine McAuley reports that they prepared "dresses" for the 200 poor girls. Carroll says they made "a uniform of brown cashmere and white capes" for the children, at the expense of the Newburghs (*Leaves* 2:61–62). **50** See Letter 148, notes 31–33. **51** A lappet is an "appendage or pendant to head-gear of any kind; esp., one of streamers attached to a lady's head-dress" (OED). **52** See Letter 148, notes 34–38. **53** The convent in Cork.

There is every prospect of two more joining very soon—one from Manchester Square and one from Bath.[54] There are many others spoken of—some think that the young Countess of Newburgh—Lady Barbara's eldest Brother's widow—will join. It is most consoling and animating to read the pious letters of congratulation written by these very high persons—and one of which I will get a copy— from a Protestant Minister—to Sister Mary de Sales—with beautiful lines on the striking of the Clock.

Sister M. Clare Agnew's Mamma and Sister have visited most affectionately. Their home is Brighton, but they came to stay in London—in order to see Sr. A frequently. They took leave of us on Monday. Mrs. Agnew is a most amiable benevolent woman—much more animated than her daughter, of dignified manners and appearance and although 68 years old you never would think of age when conversing with her. She believes much of Catholic doctrine—the Real Presence, prayers for the Dead, etc., etc., but cannot receive the faith entire—looks to concessions— which, she says, the Catholic church will grant e'er long. I fear very much she will go on to the end—in this uncertain way. I have never [met] a person who appears more sincere—or less disposed to censure any party. Sister Taylor's Mamma, Sister and Brother all are affectionate and offering their assistance in every way.

You will judge what high prices are here. Mrs. Agnew paid thirteen shillings for a turkey to send us on our ceremony day. She always came in her own carriage—though it was thought at first that she would not come so publickly. She was most evidently surprised and greatly pleased with the "young Lady Superior"—she certainly did not expect her child would meet such a companion in the South of Ireland.[55] When speaking to me of Sister Agnew's whole proceedings she said—"Elizabeth's character from infancy has been marked with such noble disinterested feelings, and such love of candor—that I never could continue to oppose her." Five of the Sisters are converts.

The Refectory is very neat—with tables like Cork—novaship very small. Kitchen fit for a castle—ovens, boilers, etc.—I am sure Mr. Pugin likes to have dinner well dressed. It is boarded—and nearly the best room in the House. The enclosed ground will be very nice when settled—at present it is not formed or even levelled.

Poor Mr. Butler—if recovering—is very slow—he looks so badly that though going about, I doubt very much his getting through the Spring—you heard he broke a blood vessel—before we arrived.[56]

54 See Letter 148, notes 39 and 40. **55** The "young Lady Superior" was, of course, Mary Clare Moore, born in Dublin in 1814, and now twenty-five years old. Here, and even more in the comparable paragraph of Letter 148, one hears allusion to the ethnic prejudice that afflicted some English persons at the time, causing them to imagine that anyone born in Ireland was unlikely to possess intelligence and cultivated manners. The well educated, courteous Clare Moore was the ideal foil to such views. However, as some of Catherine McAuley's letters in 1841 make clear, prejudice against the Irish afflicted even the Bermondsey community for a time. **56** Receiving a gift of £1000 from Lady Barbara Eyre, Peter Butler (1799–1848), the pastor in Bermondsey since 1831, had arranged to have the convent built by A. W. Pugin adjoining the new Church of the Most Holy

My poor Sister M. Cecilia has been extremely delicate ever since we came—obliged to be taken great care of—confined 3 & 4 days at a time to her Bed. Sister M. Teresa coughing—all the rest travelling on. My poor Mother Clare looking thin and anxious—but keeping up. We propose returning on the 20th January. All were well when I heard. I had a long letter from Sister M. Frances[57] written in good spirits. I think I have told you all.

Give my most respectful remembrance to the Bishop[58] when you see him—best regards to Miss Goold—my affectionate love to dear Sisters Mary Vincent, M. Anastasia, M. Aloysius, M. Francis—and the last received—the lay Sister and dear children, particularly Hanera [Hanna?].[59] I will expect a long letter on my return to Baggot St.—telling me every particular—how the collection goes on, etc. We are eating Cork butter here—at 1/6 per pd. [lb.].[60] Everything very high.

Mother and Sisters desire love to you. Believe me, my very Dear Sister M. J.

your sincerely attached
M. C. McAuley

Autograph: Cork; photocopy: Dublin, Mercy

---

150. To Sister M. Angela Dunne Convent, Bermondsey, London
  Charleville December 26, 1839

My Dear Sr. M. Angela

I have felt most anxious to give you an account of our very interesting ceremony—but was so often prevented that I am now too late. However, you will

---

Trinity in Dockhead, on the south side of the Thames River, east of what is now Tower Bridge (see also note 43 above). The son of an Irish carpenter, Butler had himself built some of the furniture in the convent. But according to the Bermondsey Annals, he suffered since his youth from asthma, over-exerted himself in attempting to prepare the convent, and in mid November 1839 burst a blood vessel after a preaching engagement (1:148). On arriving in Bermondsey, the sisters "found their good Reverend Father in a very dangerous state of health which prevented him giving the assistance they so much required" (1:7–8). Always in poor health, he lived for nine more years, but by October 1848, "Dropsy, the usual termination of asthma, had been slowly making its way for several months." He died in the early morning on November 18, 1848, having been attended in his last days by Mary Clare Moore (1:159–60). The Bermondsey Annals provides a long biography of Peter Butler (1:141–62), a priest whose life can serve as an emblem of the kind of generous priestly assistance the first Sisters of Mercy received in so many places in Ireland and England.   57 Mary Frances Warde, in Carlow. 58 Dr. John Murphy, bishop of Cork, who had lent Mary Clare Moore to the Bermondsey community for one year.   59 Mary Vincent Deasy, Mary Anastasia McGauley, Mary Aloysius O'Connell, and Mary Francis Mahony are the Cork sisters mentioned. Margaret Lyster, Ellen Lane, and Jessie McCarthy had received the habit on December 9, 1839, taking the names Mary Clare, Mary de Sales, and Mary Joseph, respectively. Hanera or Hanna or Honora has not been identified, though she may be Honoria Barry who entered the Cork community on April 27, 1840, according to the Cork Register. See also Carroll, *Leaves* 1:232–33.   60 Catherine McAuley writes "pd.," apparently creating her own abbreviation for "pound"—a form not found in the OED.

like to hear all that concerns us. We sailed on Monday the 18th of November from Kingstown at 6 o'c in the evening—in the *Queen Victoria*—arrived in Liverpool about 6 next morning, proceeded in the Train—and reached London— in full time to get a good night's rest. Just think what extraordinary expedition— dined in Baggot Street on Monday—and slept in London on Tuesday night.[61]

The convent is not more than half built—it is quite in the old monastic style—very heavy. Mr. Pugin, the architect, was determined we would not look out of the windows—they are up to the ceiling—I could not touch the glass with- out standing on a chair. I do not admire his taste, though so celebrated.

The Bishop called on us next day—was exceedingly kind—celebrated Mass and blessed the Convent on the feast of the Presentation—also appointed the 12th of December, my profession day, for the reception of six postulants who were waiting with pious anxiety for the establishment of the order.

The ceremony was public. Many of the old english Catholic nobility were present. We first presented Lady Barbara Ayre [Eyre], daughter of the late and sister to the present Earl of Newburgh. She is about Sister Agnew's age—very pleasing manner & appearance. She appeared in full court dress—very valuable diamonds which soon will belong to the poor. Then a Yorkshire lady—one from Gravlin [Gravelines]—one from London—two Lay Sisters—all desirable. Lady Barbara's example will be extremely useful—she has commenced in the most edi- fying manner—a model of humility—and conformity.[62]

Sister Agnew's Mamma and Sister have visited most affectionately—they were greatly pleased with the "young Lady Superior"—as they termed our dear Sr. M. Clare—and were evidently surprised to see so little of the wild Irish—

---

61 In some passages this letter is nearly identical to Letters 148 and 149. Please see the notes to those letters. 62 The Bermondsey Annals provides a long biography of Mary Francis de Sales (Barbara) Eyre (1:164–78), and speaks of her as "the first Religious received and professed in this Convent, and in some degree its Foundress and great Benefactress" (1:164). Her father Francis, her sister Charlotte, her brother James (all Catholics) and her mother Dorothy (a determined Protestant) had all died before she entered the convent, her mother having struck Barbara from her will for deciding to work in the poor school in Bermondsey and enter the Sisters of Mercy when they arrived in the parish. However, when the document was judged invalid, the inheritance was ""divided equally among the younger children"; Barbara "became entitled to a fortune of about £10,000, and the first use she made of it was to give £1000 towards the erection of the new Convent at Bermondsey" (1:170).

Lady Barbara had an understandably difficult time adjusting to religious life. She struggled to curb her independence of movement, her desire to dispose freely of gifts and money, and, on the very day of her reception, her taste in clothes. Her fashionable court-dress being low-cut or sleeve- less, Catherine McAuley thought it unsuitable for the reception ceremony and indirectly suggested Lady Barbara wear a lace shawl; when she declined, Clare Moore simply took the shawl to her, and said: "'Sister, you will wear this,' and she did so" (Bermondsey Annals 1:172). However, Mary de Sales persevered in her desire to be a Sister of Mercy, professing her vows on April 22, 1841, at the age of forty-three. She died on April 13, 1849, after a long illness that included a tumor in her arm, having "by degrees and when life must have been much more burdensome ... brought herself to an entire submission to whatever Almighty God might please to appoint." Often in life she had, with a feeling of comfort, contrasted "the poverty of the Religious funeral with the state and grandeur which accompanied the Funerals of her near relatives" (1:177–78).

coming from the South. Mrs. Agnew is quite an accomplished person of very dignified appearance and benevolent mind—is half Catholic—yet I fear she will let the time pass without doing what is essential. Though 68 years old, you never would think of years when conversing with her. She is fondly attached to our religious Sister—and says she had from infancy such a noble candid disposition—so perfectly disinterested—and so unquestionably sincere, that she never could continue to oppose her. Yet she regrets very much that she would not wait for this *fancied* change in the Catholic church. Her fixed home is Brighton, but she came to stay in London a few weeks—in order to see her daughter frequently. First she came privately, but seeing we were more respectably formed than she expected, came ever after in her own carriage to the public entrance.

The Marchioness Wellesley[63] sent a most kind note regretting that she was prevented visiting the Convent by a severe cold, but would take the earliest opportunity of doing so. The Countess of Newburgh—Countess Constantia Clifford—Lady Bedingfield,[64] etc., called and made every offer of patronage.

My poor Sister Mary Clare, though thin and delicate as usual, goes—or rather flyes—through her various duties. Sister M. Cecilia very poorly ever since we came—four & five days at a time confined to Bed. Sister Mary Teresa gives much assistance and all the newly received are getting into the spirit of their state.

I trust all goes on well with you, dear Sister Angela—I expect we shall yet have a useful and flourishing Institution in Charleville. I often lay out plans for it—please God they will succeed. It [has] hitherto been a sick branch—but it will be a strong one yet.

Two more are about to join here immediately.

I have just been interrupted by a visit from the Countess of Newburgh—the widow of Sister de Sales's eldest brother—a beautiful young woman who has lived quite retired since the death of her Husband. It is said she has some thought of joining them here.[65]

---

63 Richard Colley Wellesley, Marquess Wellesley (1760–1842) was born in Ireland and served as lord lieutenant of Ireland from 1821 to 1828 and briefly in 1833 to 1834. The Marchioness Wellesley was, therefore, familiar with the House of Mercy founded in Dublin in 1827. In fact, Burke Savage, citing Dublin newspapers, notes that after 1832 the Easter Bazaar on behalf of the House of Mercy "became even more fashionable, attended in different years by two successive Vicereines, the Marchioness Wellesley and the Countess Mulgrave" (161). In early December 1853, when the widowed Marchioness, herself a Catholic, was dying at Hampton Court, Dr. Thomas Grant, bishop of Southwark, asked Clare Moore to allow two Sisters of Mercy from Bermondsey to care for her during her last days. Mary Helen Ellis and Mary Anne, a lay sister, "remained at Hampton Court until after her death and she derived much comfort from their care both for soul & body" (Bermondsey Annals 1:202).   64 In Letter 148, Catherine McAuley named this woman Lady Bedington. The woman has not so far been identified with certainty.   65 The Countess of Newburgh did not enter the Bermondsey community. When Mary de Sales Eyre was dying in 1849, she refused to see any visitors, including her sister-in-law. The Countess angrily assumed that this decision was Mary Clare Moore's, but Dr. Nicholas Wiseman, then vicar apostolic of the London District, convinced her otherwise, after he visited Mary de Sales and learned firsthand her preference for solitude (Bermondsey Annals 1:175).

I expect to return about the 20th of next month and will hope to find a long letter from you on my arrival. All were well when I heard last.

Remember me respectfully to Mr. Croke[66]—and most kindly to Mrs. Clanchy and family, if you see them. Give my love to the Sisters, and believe me, Dear Sister M. Angela,

with sincere affection, etc.

M. C. McAuley

Sisters M. Clare, M. Cecilia, M. Teresa, Agnew & Taylor particularly desire their affectionate remembrance.

Autograph: Charleville

151. **To Sister M. Teresa Vincent Potter**   [November 1839–
       Limerick   January 1840?]

My dear Sister Poet, we may give up all claim
To the palm or the laurel as emblems of fame;
The lines I transcribe will afford you delight,
Tho' they cast o'er your own a dull shade of the night.
But perchance you might catch a small spark of the fire
That warmed the young heart which has here touch'd the lyre.

Lines on a Profession

With downcast eyes and pallid cheeks,
The virgin band kneel one by one,
To ask the lonely garb which speaks
The pomps and joys of Earth foregone.

Let no contemptuous glance be given,
But reverent list the holy vow,
Which plights their purity to Heaven,
And breathes their charity below.

How glorious is the life they plan,
How sacred is their chaste abode!
Ne'er quitted but to solace man,
Ne'er entered but to worship God.

Fearless their step where sorrow calls,
Though death and danger mark the scene;
No terror from without appals;
Watchful against each foe within.

66 Thomas Croke, parish priest of Charleville.

And is it woman can retire
And choose this stern, determined part,
Stifle every fond desire,
Repress each impulse of the heart?

Gentle, and fond, and sweet, and young,
The willing sacrifice is given,
Triumphant midst the maiden throng,
Behold the chosen bride of Heaven.[67]

[M. C. McAuley]

Published transcription: Harnett, Life *150–51*

152. **Poem-transcription**[68]   [November 1839–January 1840?]

"Do unto others as you would they should do unto you"[69]

Precept divine, to Earth in Mercy given
oh sacred rule of action worthy Heaven

---

67 The only source for this undated poem-letter is Harnett's *Life*, 150–51. Mary Teresa Vincent
Potter professed her vows in Limerick on December 9, 1839, while Catherine McAuley was in
Bermondsey. This poem-letter may have been written in early November, in anticipation of the
event, and then inadvertently not posted, or it may have been written sometime after the event. It
was probably not written immediately after Catherine departed for London on November 18 because
in Letter 155 Mary Teresa Vincent implies that Letter 148, written on December 17, was the first
news from London they received in Limerick. She also says that enclosed in Letter 148 she found
"no letter in poetry which you know I expected / … you may have it written / In the corner of
your desk perchance it lies hidden." It is thus probable that this poem-letter, whenever it was written, was not posted to Limerick until some time after Mary Teresa Vincent's profession on
December 9. The letter, as it appears in Harnett's *Life*, consists of six lines of verse composed by
Catherine McAuley, followed by a six-stanza poem, "Lines on a Profession," which Catherine probably transcribed from another source. Despite considerable effort, her source, whether published or
unpublished, has not so far been discovered. The value of this poem-letter is its illustration of
Catherine's ongoing verse-correspondence with Mary Teresa Vincent Potter, and perhaps of her
habit of transcribing the poems of other authors, as will be seen again in Letter 152 below.   68
Catherine McAuley transcribed this poem from a longer poem by Helen Maria Williams (1762–1827).
Catherine's autograph was recently discovered in a framed collage on a wall of Saint Teresa Convent
of Mercy in Fishguard, West Wales. It is now in the Mercy archives in Handsworth, Birmingham,
England. Before the autograph was taken to Fishguard, it was for many years, possibly 140 or 150
years, in the Hospital of St. John and St. Elizabeth in St. John's Wood, London. This hospital was
founded as the Hospital of St. Elizabeth on Great Ormond Street by the Sisters of Mercy of
Bermondsey in November 1856, after eight of them returned from nursing service in the Crimean
War. Mary Clare Moore was the superior of the Bermondsey community at the time, and Mary
Gonzaga Barrie—who later nursed Cardinal Nicholas Wiseman when he was dying in 1865, and
whom Florence Nightingale deeply loved—was named the first superior of the hospital community.

wert thou the guide of life, we all should know
a sweet exemption from the worst of woe
No more the powerful would the weak oppress
but all would learn, the luxury to bless
and av'rice[70] from its hoarded treasures give
unasked the liberal boon that want might live
Thou righteous law – whose dear and useful light
sheds o'er the mind a ray divinely bright
condensing in one line whate'er the sage
has vainly taught in many a laboured page
May every heart, thy hallowed voice revere
to justice sacred and to nature dear

[M. C. McAuley]

Autograph: Birmingham

The history of this autograph transcription, with its long presence at the Hospital of St. John and St. Elizabeth, strongly suggests that Catherine McAuley made the transcription while she was in Bermondsey, London, from November 1839 to mid January 1840, and that she gave the transcription—with its clear message about the need for mercifulness—to the Bermondsey community, who later gave it to the hospital community. There it remained until it was given to a sister moving to the convent in Fishguard (when the Sisters of Mercy closed their community at the hospital). In 1868, when Clare Moore published the *Practical Sayings* of Catherine McAuley, she included this transcription, as it appears here (except for punctuation and capitalization), among the "Favourite Verses of our Foundress" (37)—further evidence that the transcription was once in her possession.

Helen Maria Williams, whose life and writings are summarized in the *Dictionary of National Biography* (61:404–405), was apparently a Protestant. Born in England, she lived many years in France and produced poems and essays (some in political support of the French Revolution), as well as plays, translations, short stories, and at least one novel, *Julia*. It is doubtful that her life and other writings were well known to Catherine McAuley, who was nevertheless sufficiently moved by her paraphrase of Matt. 7.12 to transcribe it for her own and others' guidance.

69 The title of Williams's poem is "Paraphrase"; immediately following the title is the epigraph: "'Whatever ye would that men should do to you, do ye even so to them.' Matt. vii. 12". The poem appears in her two-volume *Poems* published in 1791 (1:187–90), and in her *Poems on Various Subjects* published in 1823 (288–90), where the verse from Matthew is incorrectly printed as "22". In the 1791 edition the poem is forty-four lines in length; in the 1823 edition, thirty-six lines. The wording of Williams's two versions is also slightly different.

In making her transcription, Catherine McAuley used either the 1791 or the 1823 version—although where and how she acquired access to it is not known—and greatly abbreviated the poem, using only the epigraph and lines 1, 2, 7–10, 15,16, and 39–44 of the 1791 version (lines 1, 2, 7–10, 13, 14, and 31–36 of the 1823 version) to form her fourteen-line poem. She changed Williams's wording in the epigraph and in several other places: "mankind might" to "we all should" (l. 3); "calm" or "soft" to "sweet" (l. 4); "tyrants" to "all would" (l. 6); "his" to "its" (l. 7); "clear" to "dear" (l. 9); "on" to "o'er" (l. 10); "rule" to "line" (l. 11); "proudly" to "vainly" (l. 12); and "Bid" to "May" (l. 13). In addition to altering the masculine wording, she slightly tilted the poem to first-person and removed the punctuation.

70 avarice

153. To the Reverend Peter Butler   [December 1839—January 1840]

F = For wild Irish did you take us
A = As some English folk would make us
T = Thinking we just ran away – from
H = *Hirish* houses made of clay
E = Ever glad to change our station
R = Rushing to another nation

B = Bermondsey – we'll not forget
U = Under cold and damp & wet
T = Tis true we must all seasons meet
L = Leaving our calm—our loved retreat
E = Engaged in sorrows not our own
R = Refreshed—by all that's neat at home[71]

[Mary C. McAuley]

Photocopy of autograph: Bermondsey

154. To the Reverend Peter Butler   [December 1839—January 1840]

F = For pity's sake, Sir, will you cover the Porch
A = As now the wet season draws nigh
T = Too often we've passed by the light of a Torch
H = Heavy rain drip[p]ing down from the Sky
E = Every Sister caught cold in the dreary damp Way
R = Repeatedly they'd to pass over

B = Beyond eighteen times in the course of a Day
U = Under rain—without foot path or cover
T = To the young & the old it alike was severe
L = Lungs—teeth—eyes or head felt the smart
E = Each one could say—oh, tho' tis so near
R = Run fast—the cold pierces my heart[72]

[Mary C. McAuley]

Photocopy of autograph: Bermondsey

71 Catherine McAuley wrote this acrostic poem to Peter Butler, the pastor, while she was in Bermondsey—teasing him about the stereotype of the "wild Irish" she had encountered in England, though not from him, and humorously complaining about the damp convent and the London weather. "Hirish" is a concession to the spelling demands of the acrostic as well a mimicking of English pronunciation of "Irish." The autograph of this acrostic poem, once said to be in Liverpool, cannot now be located.   72 This second acrostic poem to Peter Butler, also written while Catherine McAuley was in Bermondsey, half-humorously continues the theme about the weather and the uncovered passage between the convent and the parish church. In calculating the "eighteen times" a day the sisters need to pass "under rain" she is evidently thinking of the separate times in the

155. To Catherine McAuley [December 1839]

My dear Revd. Mother, your letter of news[73]
Was to our drooping spirits like those morning dews
Which refresh the parched earth and nourish the flowers
Such was its effect on those fond hearts of ours.
We were beginning to wonder, to think and suspect
That your poor Irish Sisters you'd nearly forget.
But we quickly repressed this ungenerous feeling
Which week after week to our bosom was stealing—
At length came your packet—dispelled all our fears,
Restored all our smiles, removed all our tears.
But again comes a gloom o'er my heart and my mind—
In four well-written pages no promise I find
Of a letter in poetry[74] which you know I expected
These are your words "lest I should be dejected"
Having set off for London instead of for Limerick
Which Sisters all say was a runaway trick.
But perhaps I am judging, you may have it written
In the corner of your desk perchance it lies hidden.
With this supposition I'll try to amuse you
And not of forgetfulness longer accuse you.
Of my failings & faults I'll make no confession
But give you an account of our Holy Profession.[75]
The Sisters had cramps from printing & writing
The letters & tickets which they were indicting
Agreed on all sides that it was but in vain
To hope that the chapel could the crowd contain.
The architect Deighan was consulted thereon
And he most ingeniously settled upon

---

horarium when they gathered in the church for the liturgy, the Office of the Blessed Virgin Mary, or other prayers: morning prayers, Mass, a visit before the work of the day, noon prayers, Vespers, Matins and Lauds, and night prayers, as well as individual visits to the Blessed Sacrament. For two slightly different versions of the horarium see Letters 203 and 204. In addition to the coldness and dampness of the "unfinished and unsettled" convent itself—which had no chapel set up until December 17, 1840 (Bermondsey Annals 1:22)—the path to the church, though short, was unleveled, muddy, and often puddled. Carroll correctly notes that Catherine McAuley "grieved, knowing how little [the sisters] could do if health failed them" (*Leaves* 2:56). The autograph of this poem, once said to be in Liverpool, cannot now be located.   73 Letter 148, which Catherine McAuley wrote from London on December 17, 1839.   74 Perhaps Letter 151 was the "letter in poetry" that Mary Teresa Vincent hoped for. If so, it arrived in Limerick after she wrote this poem-letter.   75 Mary Teresa Vincent Potter and Mary Francis Bridgeman professed their vows in Limerick on December 9, 1839. Whether Sister O'Farrell, who was still in the Limerick community, professed vows at this time is not known.

An arrangement in form of a hanging saloon
Which he said with confidence would give sufficient room.
This surprising invention was the wonder of all
And strange to relate—not one got a fall!
The Bishop[76] appointed the hour to be nine
His Lordship, as usual, most punctual to time—
Attended by priests in sacerdotal array
Presenting indeed an imposing display.
The company assembled before it was light,
Indeed I may say it was all but dark night.
The excitement it caused was so very great
Before the Bishop arrived there was no vacant seat—
10–20–30 mile some of these came
The Sisters of Mercy have acquired such a name
They would not be absent for aught consideration
And every thing surpassed their high expectation.
A beautiful sermon preached by Mr. Murrane[77]
From weeping the auditors could not refrain.
If you were but here you'd be pleased beyond measure
And store it in your mind as a most precious treasure.
A slight sketch I'll try to give you in rhyme
And attempt something serious now for the first time
But remember the grave does not lie in my way
So excuse all defects dear Mother I pray.

Blessed are the Merciful, such was the text
With the end of the verse which to it he annext.
In language most touching there was depicted
The love of our Saviour for all the afflicted
Those lessons of Mercy which He came to teach
On the banks of the Jordan He commenced to preach.
O'er the hearts of His hearers there rose a new morn
Of sweetness & calm after a long night of storm
As He opened his mouth in blessings & meekness
And promised a Kingdom after this life of fleetness.
From a heart that was mild & humble & meek
He instructed those who in pleasures did seek
For contentment & joy which would not be found
By those who in the wealth of this world abound.
And tho' he drew on Him the frown of the great

---

76 Dr. John Ryan, bishop of Limerick.   77 "Mort. Murrane,"—his first name thus abbreviated—
was a curate at St. Michael's in Limerick, according to the *Irish Catholic Directory* for 1840 (297).

Yet many attracted to that holy state
Which He chose for Himself, recommended to all
And to it daily so many doth call:
To think on nought but Him He many invites
Assists with His grace, inspires with His lights.
Man flies to this desert to make life a thought
And that thought was that God Who so dearly had bought
His poor creatures soul with His own precious life
Still supporting His followers in this world of strife
And others again raised up walls of stone
And knelt in the presence of that Being alone;
Lifted their hands & their hearts to His throne of grace
Not a thought of this world or its vain joys you'd trace:
And saints have prayed within these aisles,
Whose faces beamed with Heavenly smiles.
And heads that diadems too had worn
Whose hearts by sadness oft were torn
And countenances where beauty oft did play
Are now lit up with holiest ray.
And hearts for this world far too pure
Its joys and pains could not endure
The glory of Christ & Heaven's child
May its fair inmate oft be styled.
A life of holy contemplation
Spent in sweetest meditation
Some to this devote their days
Singing forever their Maker's praise.
Others with this blend tender care
The child of the poor to fondly rear
Teaches to know her God her all
And on Him for Mercy daily call.
But blest above these orders all
Is that of our patron, St. Vincent of Paul[78]
Which teaches the daughter of the rich & the great
To forego the convenience of wealth and of state
Devote her life to the service of Christ & His poor
And for His holy sake many labors to endure.
Mark her by the bed of that poor dying man
Whose days are now wasted to life's shortest span—
Forgotten by all save his Creator and one

78 In the Rule of the Sisters of Mercy, which Catherine McAuley had just sent to Rome for final confirmation, Saint Vincent de Paul is listed as one of the patron saints of the congregation (see Rule 16.3, in Sullivan, *Catherine McAuley* 311–12).

Who kneels by his side on the cold rugged stone
With tenderest care she helps at first
To slake his fevered burning thirst.
He raises to Heaven his languid eyes
As she speaks of his home beyond the skies
Tells him his father waits him there
And lights up hope where dwelt despair.
Blessings on her are his last sigh
And angels waft them both on high.
She dries the mourning widow's cheek
And bids the orphan cease to weep
Oft shields her from distress and shame
For she on Mercy has a claim.
She challenges with heroism holy & high
Each change of disease, each last dying sigh
With new ingenuity devises means of relief
To soften the pains of a life tho' but brief.
The eloquence of Mercy how oft do they borrow
From the deep and the heartfelt outpouring of sorrow
Oh this is charity, not that showy thing
Puffed up in the world by applause of men:
But that being unobtrusive & Oh how much fairer
The less known by the world to her Saviour the dearer
"Who seeketh not her own," who is patient & kind
Who to everyone's failing but her own she is blind—
It's thus gentle Mercy teaches her child
Who for the bed of the poor leaves her fond parents' side,
Claims their woes for her portion, to soothe their sorrows her lot:
In the hearts of Christ's favorites she shall ne'er be forgot.
And if yet there should hover round the ruins of our nature
One pure holy feeling, one undarkened feature
Tis that spirit of humanity which thus calls away
The kind mother's child thus to tend and to pray
For the forsaken and the destitute, the despised and unknown,
Oh these are pure offerings for Heaven's great throne.
With gentle steps day after day
These holy Sisters cross our way
Pursuing their mission of holy love
With hearts & thoughts fixed on above.
Wherever grief and pain abound
There are these seraphs to be found
And when at eve returned home
They kneel before their Father's throne

Pouring forth prayers for those they left
Of earthly comforts quite bereft,
Laying their labors at His feet
Whose yoke to them is light and sweet.
If e'er a prayer was pure and holy
It sure is hers thus bending lowly,
Before the throne of her great King
Imploring blessings thus from Him.
And when her day of life is o'er
And toil and labor are no more
That Father, gentle, sweet and mild
Will welcome home His faithful child—
Place her in joys that ne'er shall cease
In mansions of unending Peace.

I feel, my dear Mother, I have done my best:
And for fear I'd do worse, I'll curtail the rest.
Of our three holy vows[79] he spoke in detail
That they were perpetual he did not fail
Full well to impress it—oh if you were but here
How we read these said Vows—your spirit would cheer.
Of Poverty he spoke in language sublime

79 The Sisters of Mercy have traditionally proclaimed the following words at their religious profession: "I vow and promise to God poverty, chastity, and obedience and the service of the poor, sick, and ignorant," and have interpreted the "service" phrase as their fourth vow. It is not clear that Catherine McAuley herself regarded the commitment to service as a distinct vow as such, or that the earliest Mercy communities did so. The words, "and the service of the poor, sick, and ignorant" were explicitly introduced into the vow formula in 1837 at the recommendation of Dr. John Murphy, bishop of Cork, though Mary Clare Moore and Mary Austin Carroll differ as to the precise occasion. In the Bermondsey Annals, Clare Moore says:

> On the 25th of October [1837] ... a novice [Mary Anastasia McGauley] made her holy Profession [in Cork]. It was on this occasion that Bishop Murphy wished an alteration to be made in the formula of the Act of Profession; before that, only the three Vows of Poverty, Chastity, and Obedience, common to every Religious society, were expressed in it; but he proved to our Foundress the necessity of declaring the special object of the Institute distinct from others, and therefore the following words were introduced "and the service of the poor, sick, and ignorant." But this was not generally adopted until after the Confirmation of our Holy Rule in 1841 (Sullivan, *Catherine McAuley* 122).

Carroll says the event was the profession of Mary Vincent Deasy, which occurred on July 1, 1837 (*Leaves* 1:229–30). However, since Clare Moore was present for the event, her date (October 25, 1837) is no doubt correct. Catherine McAuley was also present, yet writing to Angela Dunne in Charleville on January 20, 1841, she says: "I do not understand what you mean by the other question—the vow is that of all religious orders—'poverty, chastity and obedience—to the end of life'—the fourth of enclosure has been added to suit other communities" (Letter 231). For an analysis of the evolution of the "fourth vow" see Lappetito, "Our Life Together in Mercy."

To put it in verse is really a crime.
Blessed are the Poor said our divine Lord
In the heart of the holy this touches a cord
Which makes them rejoice in the resemblance they bear
To Bethlehem's nakedness in that abode drear.
The Lord of all things despised this world's dross
And to it preferred the bitterness of the Cross.
Poverty is holy—it's the birthright of the Saints
Linked with every death-less passage which our sacred Gospel paints.
Tis the rugged teacher which forms children of grace
To the hardiest virtues which no trial can efface.
We find stars the brightest the farthest from earth
So is it with souls freed from this world's wealth—
They shine before God with a still purer ray
And their life shall pass on as a bright summer's day
While wealth without pity in the Heaven-lit page
Is described as the cause of the rich glutton's rage.
In Heaven's blest hopes the hard rich have no share
For the poor of this world they ne'er had a care,
And these holy Sisters have chosen this state
Ennobled by Him who was great of the great.
The handmaids of the poor they become for His sake,
And with joy & delight this holy vow make.
Thus 'twill be [to] the wretched a sweet consolation
In their dark haunts of misery & sad desolation
To see taken for choice by the rich and the great
The privations & toils of their own distressed state.
From their visits they learn to be patient & meek
Wipe the fast falling tear from their care worn cheek.
Painful indeed are the scenes that they view—
To bend o'er the body where contagion's dark hue
Has colored the lip, and tho' late for relief
She can sigh [her] support, for his sorrows can weep:
Be he clothed in rags, no matter how wretched—
Enough—he is one of Christ's own afflicted—
Your mission is mercy, how truly it's styled,
You truly are Heaven's best beloved child.
You realize the ideas of holy St. Paul
Mercy & charity ascend above all.
Persevere then, my Sisters, in your office of love
You'll meet your reward in the realms above.

All were delighted, the Bishop contented,

The old married ladies only lamented
That Sisters of Mercy were not in their time
Or they would have joined them—alas my poor rhyme.
Were there Brothers of Mercy the Bishop did say
He would join them himself the very first day.
Our organ was beautiful, our singers enchanting,
To make us all happy, you were but wanting.
From priests & from laymen, in papers and all
In the town and the country, in parlor and hall
The Sisters of Mercy are everywhere known—
Their fame will soon reach to the Torrid Zone.
We're getting new Sisters, they're coming in plenty,
Before you come next we at least shall have twenty,
But when will that be—can you give us a light
And that to our hearts will be one so bright
That we would not exchange it for aught other so fair
In the earth, in the sky, in the deep or the air:
With heartful affection we wish you a happy new year
Years of peace in this world, for the next no sad fear
But endless felicity in the Realms above
Give all our dear Sisters our affectionate love.

    P.S. I ne'er again shall write so fine
        I can scarcely believe this letter's mine:
        No wonder, for over it I have given many a moan
        I'm fairly worn to skin and bone.
        My eyes are sunk into my head
        My cheeks that were so nice and red
        Are nearly pale as were I dead.
        My fingers as slight as any taper
        My desk is filled with scraps of paper.[80]

---

80 The text of this poem-letter as given here is a manuscript (which I believe is the author's) inserted in an early notebook of manuscripts preserved in the archives of the Sisters of Mercy in Limerick. The autograph sent to Catherine McAuley has not been found. This text is probably Mary Teresa Vincent's final draft, before she made the copy to post and before a later hand, modifying it somewhat or using a different draft, inserted a version of the poem into the Limerick Annals (1:41–55). Slight differences in wording appear in almost every line when the two versions (this manuscript and the text in the Annals) are compared, though none of these alters the sense of the respective lines. I regard the text presented here as Mary Teresa Vincent's own. Because the rhythm and meter of the lines (evidently intended to be a mixture of anapestic tetrameter and iambic and/or trochaic tetrameter) are frequently "off," one is tempted to leave out or put in a syllable, to rearrange a line, or to use the wording in the Limerick Annals. But I can well appreciate Mary Teresa Vincent's struggles with wording, as symbolized in her "scraps of paper," and I have refrained from tampering with the poetic "defects" she acknowledges early on (l. 52) or with the integrity of her manu-

My sight is every day more dim
Each one remarks I am grown quite thin
It's true—no one could do it better
I hope you'll own—you are my debtor.

[Mary Teresa Vincent Potter][81]

Autograph: Limerick

script. I have, however, inserted some additional periods to assist in reading the poem. 81 At the end of this manuscript, the following sentence is written in a different hand: "The enclosed lines were composed by Sister Mary Vincent Potter on a sermon preached at her Profession by Revd. M. Murrane December 9th 1839."

January–April 1840

The chill and dampness of the London foundation took a toll on Catherine McAuley's health. Although her own letters from London are silent about this, Mary Teresa White notes that while they were in Bermondsey:

> Our dear mother had a miserable time of it ... being almost constantly ailing. I always thought the Bermondsey foundation was the beginning of her death-sickness, for she was never perfectly well after ... While she was very ill and confined to bed in London, one morning I prepared her breakfast and brought it to her; but because I brought the best I could get—white sugar, china tea-pot, and cream-ewer—she said: "My heart, why did you not bring me a little tea in a mug, as you would to a poor person?" Scarcely had she spoken when the tray upset and everything was spilled on her bed. Then she said pleasantly: "Now you are punished for not remembering that your old mother is only a poor nun." (Qtd. in Carroll, *Leaves* 2:58)

Catherine left London on Monday, January 13, 1840, arriving in Dublin the next day. For much of January she was confined to bed—with an inflammation in her stomach and her "old mouth complaint."

Yet the first months of 1840 were filled with personal heartaches and business obligations that far overshadowed Catherine's recuperation. Her nephew Robert Macauley, toward whose lifestyle she had shown some displeasure before leaving for London, died of suddenly increasing illness—probably consumption, like his two sisters—on January 4, while she was still in Bermondsey, and without receiving her letter of forgiveness in response to his request.[1] Then severe illness, including typhus, began to afflict sisters in Baggot Street, Carlow, Tullamore, Cork, Charleville, and Limerick—resulting in three deaths, including that of Mary Teresa Vincent Potter in Limerick on March 20. It was a season of sorrows, and Catherine wrote plainly: "My heart is sore."

Simultaneously, business matters needed attention: construction of the commercial laundry proved to be a near disaster, the architect calling Catherine's letters about the contract "graciously offensive" (Letter 161); plans for a new

---

1 Neumann gives the date of his death, as cited in Dublin newspapers (194). Extensive discussion of Catherine McAuley's grief over Robert Macauley's death appears in the Bermondsey Annals, the Limerick Manuscript, and Clare Augustine Moore's "Memoir" (Sullivan, *Catherine McAuley* 122–23, 185–86, and 211) and in Carroll's *Life* (349–51).

foundation in 1841 in Birmingham, England, got underway, through correspondence with Dr. Thomas Walsh, vicar apostolic of the Midland District; income became an issue when the Charity Sermon failed, the preacher falling ill on the spot; sisters had to be chosen for formal appointment as assistant, bursar, and mistress of novices at Baggot Street; Dr. Daniel Murray asked her to re-open the convent in Kingstown after Easter; and preparations were needed for the promised foundation in Galway, the party scheduled to depart in late April.

On February 27, 1840, five women professed their vows at Baggot Street, and two received the habit. But by the end of April there were seven additional postulants in the community, including four from Birmingham. Any thoughts Catherine McAuley had had about "retiring from business" in Dublin were now groundless. She would leave for Galway, hoping to return by way of Limerick where "I will greatly feel the loss that will be visible on entering the convent": the absence of her "sweet little poet," Mary Teresa Vincent Potter, to whom she had written in January.

156. To Sister M. Teresa Vincent Potter [January 1840][2] Limerick

My Sweet Sister Poet—I think it much better
not to be waiting to write a very long letter
But acknowledge at once I'm deeply your debtor[3]

For your lengthened description so full & so plain
Of Reception and Sermon by Mr. Marane [Murrane][4]
Who is really now quite a Preacher of fame

Your refreshments so nice and your Bishop so kind
How seldom we have all things so much to our mind
Very often when reading my heart was inclined

2 Several internal references (discussed in the notes below) strongly suggest that this poem-letter was written in response to Mary Teresa Vincent Potter's long poem about her profession on December 9, 1839 (Letter 155), and not earlier, after a "Reception" ceremony in Limerick—for example, that on June 7, 1839. Although Catherine McAuley refers to Mary Teresa Vincent's description of a "Reception" (which she, in fact, did not describe, and no Reception ceremony took place on December 9), she may be referring to the luncheon-reception after the ceremony, which could have been described to her in a letter from Elizabeth Moore. Catherine was undoubtedly ill when she wrote this poem-letter; Mary Teresa Vincent's poem was long to re-read, and she was anxious to get a response in the post.   3 In calling herself Mary Teresa Vincent's "debtor," Catherine McAuley is agreeing with the last line in Letter 155.   4 Father Mort. Murrane preached the sermon at the profession ceremony in Limerick on December 9, 1839—as reported in Letter 155 and in the Limerick Annals (1:41).

To wish I were with you even now, if not then
To rejoice with my Sisters—again and again
and express with my voice what I can't with my pen

Now—as I think—I'll no more be a rover[5]
You shall soon have a full sheet written all over
With—Mrs. Potter[6]—in real good style on the cover.

[M. C. McAuley]

Autograph: Brisbane

157. To Sister M. Elizabeth Moore   Baggot Street
          Limerick   January 18, 1840

My ever Dear Sister Mary Elizabeth

How can I sufficiently express my gratitude for your tender charitable remembrance of my poor Robert. Accept my most affectionate thanks.

Tuesday—12 o'clock—after I had written the above—on Saturday—Mr. O'Hanlon ordered me to Bed—and a Doctor to be sent for. I suffered much in the passage from Liverpool—my stomach continued very sore—and he thought—from my looks and feel—that there was some inflammatory symptom. I am now quite well but weak, of course, after passing through the hands of a Doctor.[7] My first work—on being restored to my old post—is to finish my letter.

We left the Sisters in London well and happy. Sister Mary Clare's leave will expire on the 22nd of August—on that day Sister Clare Agnew becomes Superioress. The Bishop authorised me to announce this before we parted. I had a letter on Friday—a new Sister was to enter on Sunday.

---

5 Catherine McAuley's saying she will "no more be a rover" indicates that the poem was written after she returned from London on January 14. She was ill at the time and had no plans for future travel; the trip to Galway in early May was not yet settled.   6 Catherine used the title "Mrs." on the cover of letters mailed to professed sisters, and sometimes the title "Miss" for letters posted to novices and postulants. As a newly professed sister, a letter to Mary Teresa Vincent would be addressed to "Mrs. Potter."   7 Catherine McAuley discreetly does not say what medical procedure or procedures caused her weakness. But it is reasonable to suppose that blood-letting and/or purgative medicines were employed; both were more or less common medical treatments until the middle of the nineteenth century when humoral interpretations of illness were replaced by bacterial theories and more sophisticated understandings of disease and of human blood. See "Bloodletting" in McGrew, *Encyclopedia* 33–34. Crawford notes that some Irish doctors "valued purging of the bowel as a treatment above all others," but that by mid-century "purging … like bleeding was falling out of favour" (133). Catherine's physician on this occasion is not known, though generally those who visited the sick at Baggot Street were among the most respected physicians and surgeons in Dublin—men whom Catherine had come to know through her brother James and her now deceased brother-in-law William Macauley. Redmond O'Hanlon also had a good knowledge of the Dublin medical community; in late September 1841 he recommended the very distinguished Dr. William Stokes to diagnose and treat Catherine in what turned out to be her last illness.

Your letter to London afforded me great happiness. God is evidently pleased with the Limerick House—five ceremonies in 14 months—this far outsteps all. May our Blessed Redeemer dwell with you in such manner as will shield you from everything could be any draw back—above all from particular attachments, or ought that could produce jealousy—coldness—or party spirit. I have no fears for you on the subject—but I have a conviction on my mind of its fatal consequences.[8]

I suppose poor Baggot Street may retire "on a pension"—no proposals for us—and I suppose also that the foundations will soon be made from you & others.

A prevailing influenza amongst the poor of Dublin and great poverty. The Sisters are constantly engaged.

I will write soon again. All unite in love with your ever affectionate

M. C. McAuley

Tell my dear newly professed Sisters that I heartily rejoice in their happy fate—and tell my Dear Sister M. Vincent[9] she must write to me or I will be out with her.

Autograph: Limerick

158. **To Sister M. Frances Warde**   **Convent, Baggot Street**
     Carlow   **January 30, 1840**

My Dear Sister Mary Frances

I have been chiefly confined to Bed since my return—not down until yesterday. First, an affection[10] of my stomach, etc., for which I was obliged to have a Physician—and then my old mouth complaint[11] to a great degree which has kept me on Infants diet for more than 10 days.

I received your letter in London. As to what you said of the application to Rome, I did exactly what was marked out for me—a Petition from the "Mother House"—a Memorial from the A[rch]bishop of Dublin praying a confirmation of the Rule to which his approbation is attached—and letters of recommendation from the Bishops in whose Diocess Branches of the order were established.

8 The fifth article of the chapter "Of Union and Charity" in the proposed Rule and Constitutions which Catherine had sent to Rome speaks of "particular friendships, attachments and affections" in a community as "the source of discord and divisions, and as hostile to purity of heart, to charity, and to the spirit of religion" (Sullivan, *Catherine McAuley* 304).   9 Mary Vincent Harnett.   10 An "affection," as Catherine McAuley used the term here, is "an abnormal state of body; malady, disease" (OED).   11 In the absence of specific evidence for a diagnosis, one may speculate that Catherine's chronic "mouth complaint," some times worse than at others, may have been related to scurvy, a deficiency of vitamin C, due to a lack of fresh fruits and vegetables. "One of the classical signs of scurvy, the swollen, purple, and soft gums, does not appear until about 30 weeks of a diet free of vitamin C" (French 1001). Or she may have been suffering from pyorrhea, "an outflowing of pus from the gingival (gum) tissues of the oral cavity"—what today would be called periodontal disease—in which the gums may be "tender, swollen, and red" (Levin 924–925).

This has been most fully executed—the letters were as favorable as they could be. I am sure Mr. Maher feels sufficiently interested in our regard to do all in his power—a private letter to his nephew would even have more effect than one obtained through influence or entreaty, and I am certain he has done whatever he thought would promote success.[12]

Poor Father Rafter—I only heard of his death yesterday—and that Mr. Maher was his successor.[13] Mr. Butler, the Priest so deeply interested in the London Convent, was attacked in the same way—and I fear we left him on his death Bed. I expect the next letter will tell me so. They have got a new Sister with prospect of two more.

I had a long letter yesterday from poor Sister Mary Joseph.[14] She is in affliction. Sister M. Francis Mahony—one of the first who joined—is in deep decline. She says: "only for this we should be too happy. Our House of Mercy is opened[15]—and all our debts paid—though the addition cost five hundred pounds. On the morning we commenced, our dear Bishop gave us £50. He is delighted to see the young women protected. I almost think it[16] is the best branch of our Institute."

Her letter was quite a comfort to me. She expects two new Sisters and has nearly got leave to take a lay sister she was most anxious about.

I do not know how my poor Sister Mary Clare will be disposed of. She is superior in London until the 22 of August. On that day Sister Agnew takes her place. I am sure they will all be anxious to keep her[17]—if Doctor Murphy consents. The Bishop of London said he never saw such maturity in so young a person—that she had judgment in her countenance. She is, thank God, perfectly indifferent where or how she shall be.

All here pretty well, going on as usual. They unite in love to all with your ever affectionate

M. C. McAuley

Autograph: Silver Spring

12 James Maher was the uncle of Paul Cullen, then rector of the Irish College in Rome and later archbishop of Dublin (1852–1878). While in Rome, Cullen served as an agent of the Irish bishops in relations with the Vatican.   13 According to the *Irish Catholic Directory* for 1841 (357), Michael Rafter, parish priest of Killeshin (Carlow-Graigue), died on January 16, 1840. He had been a devoted friend of the Sisters of Mercy since their arrival in Carlow in 1837. Comerford says his day of death was "the 18th of January, 1840" (1:197). James Maher was appointed in January to succeed him as a parish priest in Carlow-Graigue.   14 Mary Josephine Warde, now the superior of the Cork community.   15 "The original House of Mercy in Cork was an annexe to the Rutland Street Convent and was opened in 1838/1839 on a budget of £8.00 sterling" (Bolster, *Mercy in Cork* 11).   16 That is, the Cork foundation.   17 Mary Clare Moore did not return to Ireland until June 1841, and then only for six months. She was recalled to London in December 1841 by Dr. Thomas Griffiths, with the consent of Dr. Murphy.

159. **To Catherine McAuley**   Benedictine Convent
                                                          The Mount
                                          [Wolverhampton, England]
                                                  February 1, 1840

Dear Madam

I had the honor of being introduced to you at Bermondsey Convent, & of having some interesting conversation with you on the holy order of the Sisters of Mercy. I intimated on the occasion that it was in contemplation to establish ere long Sisters of Mercy in the important town of Birmingham. This most desirable object I am desirous of accomplishing without loss of time, at least on a small scale at first.

The Earl of Shrewsbury[18] has already offered for the purpose two thousand pounds, the interest of which – £100 per annum – it is proposed to devote to the support of the Sisters, which will no doubt be increased by contributions etc. Mr. Hardman,[19] a respectable Catholic, who for some time past has in great measure supported an orphan school of from twelve to twenty poor children, is desirous of placing the dear little ones of Jesus under the Sisters of Mercy, and offers at his own expense to build and to furnish a small convent for the Sisters of Mercy. He wishes to know what would be required for the building to render them comfortable. The convent would be adjoining St. Peter's Catholic Chapel & to spacious schoolrooms. Any particulars, dear Madam, you will have the kindness to mention, will be most gratefully received & attended to.[20]

May I expect that, when every thing is ready for their reception, you will kindly allow two or three members of your community to devote themselves to the works of Mercy in Birmingham & to commence the establishment of a branch of the Order in that town? Were two respectable females from this country sent to the novitiate in Baggot Street, would they be received, and on what terms? Would they be allowed to prepare themselves for the convent in Birmingham, as Miss Agnew & Miss Tailor [Taylor] were permitted to do so for Bermondsey?

An answer, at your earliest convenience, dear Madam, to these lines will be esteemed a great favor, the more so, as Mr. Hardman is advanced in years and wishes to make a provision for the grand object as soon as possible and to settle his temporal affairs. He has a most excellent son[21] who cordially enters into all his charitable views.

18 John Talbot, the sixteenth Earl of Shrewsbury, was a major benefactor of the Birmingham convent. Although the expense of actually building the convent was undertaken by John Hardman, Sr., John Talbot contributed an endowment of £2000 toward the future expenses of the convent (Degnan 327–28).   19 John Hardman, Sr.—the father of Mary Juliana Hardman, the future superior of Birmingham—and Barbara Ellison Hardman, his third wife, were the primary benefactors of the proposed Birmingham Convent of Mercy. They gave the land, arranged and paid for the construction of the building, and provided all the furnishings (Degnan 327).   20 This invitation will give Catherine McAuley the opportunity to propose correction of the defects she found in Pugin's construction of the Bermondsey convent. See Letter 148, note 43, and Letter 160.   21 John Hardman, Jr.

You will have the kindness to address your letter to me at *Wolverhampton, Staffordshire*.

Praying that every blessing may descend on you, Dear Madam, and on the holy community under your care, I have the honor to remain,

Respectfully,
Your faithful, humble servant
+ Thomas Walsh[22]

Autograph: Dublin, Mercy

160. To Dr. Thomas Walsh	Convent of the Sisters of Mercy
Wolverhampton	Baggot Street
	February 4, 1840

My Lord

I have had the honor of receiving your esteemed letter—and would feel great happiness in co-operating to the full extent of my power in the accomplishment of your desire. If two persons who manifested a vocation for the religious state were sent here—one year and three months would finish the time of probation for a new Institute. They could then return, accompanied by one or two well acquainted with our regulations. The pension for each during the noviciate is twenty five pounds per annum—if circumstances required a reduction, it would be made.

Perhaps, my Lord, the persons in view would rather not come to Ireland—but join our Sisters on their arrival in Birmingham, which would save expense—and having the ceremony of reception at home might produce a pious excitement that would animate others to follow. Whatever you think best suited to the views and inclinations of those who are disposed to promote the object shall be met in every possible way.

My Lord—as to building—I beg leave to suggest the advantage of not doing so on a very limited scale. We should hope that an Establishment in Birmingham would be productive of others. Your Convent should have at least twenty cells—10 feet by 7—a small window—and small door made so close to the partition wall as to leave a sufficient space for the Bed's head—a novaship [noviceship]—about 18 feet by 14—a Community room—Refectory—and Choir—each to be 25 feet by 19—a good room for Infirmary—and a small reception parlour. It is very desirable there should be only two floors above the basement story. The refectory should be close to the Kitchen—all executed in the plainest style, without any cornice—cheap grates and stone chimneypieces.

---

22 Dr. Thomas Walsh, vicar apostolic of the Midland District of England in which Birmingham was located, resided for a time in the Benedictine Convent in Wolverhampton.

This could be compleated in ten months—and would not cost more than a smaller building—where ornamental work would be introduced. Or, my Lord, if you would think it better—merely to commence preparations for building—and to hire a small House for a beginning—perhaps the people would be induced to contribute more freely to its completion—but it should be commenced, my Lord, as the Sisters would not feel happy—except they had a convent in prospect.

The Convent in Bermondsey is not well suited to the purpose—the sleeping rooms are too large—the other rooms too small—the corridors confined and not well lighted—all the gothic work outside has made it expensive. A plain simple durable building is much more desirable.

Earnestly begging that you will give me and Community a place in your charitable remembrance—I have the honor and happiness to remain

My Lord—with great respect—your obedient Servant in Christ

Mary C. McAuley

The sum your Lordship mentions for support would do very well.

Autograph: Birmingham

161. To Charles Cavanagh, Esq.   [Convent, Baggot Street]
                                              February 26, 1840

Dear Sir

I enclose you a copy of the two notes I wrote to Mr. Mullins,[23] which he terms "graciously offensive." In as much as he has made himself a very principle [*sic*] party, complaints must necessarily be addressed or referred to him. The man called the contracter [*sic*][24] could not alter the most glaring defect without his permission—and repeatedly said "he got enough to starve" on—by the engagement.

My first note was occasioned by receiving three messages from Mr. Mullins—requesting I would give directions for the water pipes—not clearly saying that it was not part of the contract work— but that "I wrote so well." This inclined me suspect & when I decidedly refused to give the order—Brophy told me it would be an extra charge.

I then wrote to Mr. M[ullins]—& next day the work was begun. Immediately after my second note, the man[25] was taken away, bed & all in 2 hours. The keys have been given us. All the time I was[26] away—this man was constantly amongst our poor people—and even more troublesome when the Sisters were there—saying he was not to go away till all accounts were settled.

---

23 Catherine McAuley's two notes to Bernard Mullins, the architect of the addition to the House of Mercy on Baggot Street, including the commercial laundry, are apparently no longer extant. 24 Thomas Brophy, the contractor for the building project, was selected and supervised by Bernard Mullins. 25 This man is probably a laborer hired by Thomas Brophy. 26 Catherine wrote "way," not "was," but this must have been an inadvertent slip of the pen.

It is an unkind unjust transaction. I have good reason to say so.

Dear Sir, your grateful, etc.
M. C. McAuley

I send the copy with the remarks I made at the time.

Autograph: Dublin, Mercy

162. To Sister M. Elizabeth Moore   **Convent, Baggot Street**
Limerick   **February 29, 1840**

My dearest Sr. M. Elizabeth[27]

How heartily, how fervently, I rejoice in every circumstance that contributes to your spiritual and temporal happiness. All that I hear of our Dear Limerick Sisters brings comfort and joy to my mind. They are pronounced "good seed"—thanks be to God they are placed in good soil. Miss Reddin[28] came in just as I received your letter. She had not heard of Dr. Hanrahan's death,[29] but on hearing of the successor[30] you mention, she said it delighted her so that she scarcely felt the disappointment she had just met relative to her nephew. She says you have indeed got a Prize. May God preserve him & grant you lively gratitude & profound humility. Then indeed you will be a child of Benediction. Our poor Sr. M. F[rancis][31] lingers on—one day a little cheerful—another all debility.

A great trial in Carlow—a postulant[32] who had entered retreat for reception was suddenly visited with Typhus fever which has proved so fatal in Carlow for three or four years past. She is an only child of wealthy respectable parents—about 20 years old.

The last account from Tullamore was favorable.

---

27 No autograph of this letter has been found. However, three early handcopies of the letter are extant; all agree on the recipient and date of the letter. Two of the handcopies agree almost exactly in wording: the copy in the "Small Baggot Street Manuscript Book: Copies of Poems and Letters" (Mercy Congregational Archives) and the copy in the Brisbane Book of Transcriptions (Brisbane Congregational Archives). The text given here follows these two handcopies. The third handcopy, in the large book of Baggot Street manuscript copies which is called "Annals" (Mercy Congregational Archives), has slightly different wording in some places; only one passage is somewhat significant (see note 35 below). The first paragraph of the letter is also published in abbreviated form in Harnett's *Life* (163).   28 Miss Joanna Reddan, of Limerick. See Letter 104.   29 Charles Hanrahan, dean and vicar general of the diocese of Limerick, was parish priest of St. Mary's where the Mercy convent was located. The *Irish Catholic Directory* for 1841 says that he died on February 22, 1840 (357); the Limerick Annals says his death occurred on February 23 (1:69), and that he bequeathed £300 to the Sisters of Mercy in Limerick.   30 John Brahan, administrator and curate of Kilmallock parish in the diocese of Limerick, was appointed parish priest of St. Mary's upon the death of Charles Hanrahan.   31 Mary Francis Marmion was dying of consumption at Baggot Street.   32 Julia Redmond, a postulant in Carlow, became severely ill with "bad typhus fever" just before February 25, 1840, the day she was scheduled to receive her habit (Carlow Annals).

I must now tell you of our poor Sermon. Dr. Cahill commenced so as to attract great attention, and in less than 10 minutes became so ill as to give up.[33] £25 collected—of which he got 3 and the printer 4. Better (after) donations than usual are coming in. We are advised to publish it, which will be done next week.

I am sure your collection will be very good. I am told Mr. C. is greatly improved & produces remarkable effect on the feelings, which extends to the end of the purse where if anything can be found, it will come forth.[34] I am told we never had such an assemblage of persons at any charity. The few old friends gave as usual—all the rest went away disappointed—not a word had been said of the charity.[35] The opening was the Prodigal Son. I suppose you will have the same sermon. I will be quite curious to hear how the connection is joined—between us and the Prodigal Son. The remarks made on his style, etc. has induced Dr. Meyler to engage him for Lent.

After writing the above I recollected your Sermon will be over before you get this.

We have good accounts from London—2 or 3 about to join[36]—one in all in good health.

Do you ever write to Sr. Angela? I wish you could meet a well qualified person, who had very small means—that had a good vocation. Their pension day school will soon be ready, & I have not one to give.

We go to Galway after Easter and have made arrangements with Dr. Walsh, Bishop of the midland district, England to admit 2 or 3 ladies to serve a noviciate for Birmingham—we must lend one to return with them.[37]

About three weeks before the ceremony, I spoke to the junior postulant for not having a successor to her cap & charged her with lukewarm, bad ineffectual

---

33 The Dr. Cahill who preached the Charity Sermon on behalf of the House of Mercy on February 23, 1840 was probably Dr. Daniel W. Cahill. According to McEvoy, Dr. Cahill "taught in Carlow [College] from 1825 to 1834. Having left the College, he based himself in Dublin with the address: Ballyroan Cottage, Rathfarnham. He gained quite a reputation for himself as a speaker and pamphleteer" (13). The same Dr. D. W. Cahill may also have been the principal of the Catholic Seminary, Prospect, Blackrock. "In this seminary [was] taught the usual course to a very large number of scholars and boarders." Dr. Cahill "opened a new establishment for the special education of young gentlemen preparatory to their entrance into Trinity College" (*Irish Catholic Directory* [1841] 395–96). 34 The same Dr. Cahill was scheduled to give the Charity Sermon in Limerick. 35 This sentence ("The few … charity.") is not transcribed in the Brisbane handcopy, but is transcribed in the handcopies in the Baggot Street manuscript books. See note 27. 36 In April 1840, two postulants joined the Bermondsey community: Cecilia Best and Frances Burroughs; and in May, two more joined: Louisa Murray and Anne Brown. 37 Easter Sunday in 1840 fell on April 19. On April 29, five young women from England were scheduled to enter the Baggot Street community to begin preparation for a new foundation in Birmingham in 1841: Juliana Hardman, Ann Wood, Lucy Bond, Elizabeth Edwards, and Marianne Beckett. As soon as they were settled, probably by May 1, Catherine McAuley, Mary Teresa White, and the rest of the founding party would depart for Galway. In the end, Elizabeth Edwards entered on May 17, 1840 (Dublin Register) or May 12, 1840 (Birmingham Register)—not at the end of April.

style of praying—she took this quite seriously and was observed praying in every direction. In 10 days after, a very fine young person of whom we had never heard before came with a Priest from Drogheda with all satisfactory arrangements made for her to remain if agreeable to us—so that we have still one fools cap—quite the fruit of prayer.[38]

The new Laundry is all loss so far, but we must work on—a year, please God, will bring it forward.

I shall be anxiously looking for a letter—don't forget to remember Mr. O'Hanlon for he must have your letter to read whenever he hears of one—"don't forget to remember" brings to my mind how the English Sisters, to whom we were strangers, were watching to catch us making an Irish blunder—& I was equally so looking out, & was first to catch an English one. The Countess C. Clifford came to visit the Lady B[arbara] Eyre who had a cough. To the inquiries about her health she said "Oh you know a cold breaks one up so"—and in a minute after, "a cold breaks you down so." I told her at recreation that we must suppose up and down was all the same in her country. She was greatly amused to hear us talking of "going astray"—in England it is only applied to departure from rectitude—our fears for the Sisters going out was a source of much amusement—this was all we said that surprised them.

I have long stories to tell you if it please God we meet again. Pray for me—I will write very soon to my Dear Sr. M. Vincent. Give my most affectionate love to each—all unite in same to you, with

your ever fondly attached
M. C. McAuley

Newly Professed Mrs. Blake, Mrs. Leahy, Mrs. Moore, Mrs. O'Brien—Sister Boylen [Boylan] not well enough, etc.

Received Sister Credon [Creedon], Newfoundland—Sister Horan, Dublin— M. Francis and Mary Augustine.[39]

Handcopies: Dublin, Mercy; and Brisbane

---

38 At a ceremony in Baggot Street on February 27, two days before this letter, five sisters professed their vows: Mary Gertrude Blake, Mary Clare Augustine Moore, Mary Anne Teresa O'Brien, Mary Veronica Duggan, and Mary Catherine Leahy (who was destined for Galway); and two received the habit: Mary Francis (Mary Ann) Creedon (who was destined for the foundation in Newfoundland in 1842) and Mary Augustine (Frances) Horan (who will go in the foundation party to New York City in 1846). The "junior postulant" whom Catherine teased about not having a successor to wear her black net postulant's cap was Frances Horan who had entered the community on September 24, 1839. The postulant who came unexpectedly, Anne Gogarty, from the parish of Beamore, Co. Meath, entered the convent on February 3, 1840. 39 See note 38. Mary Frances (Frances) Boylan was scheduled to profess her vows on February 27, 1840, but illness forced her to delay until September 24, 1840.

163. **To Sister M. Frances Warde**   Convent, Baggot Street
     Carlow   March 2, 1840

My Dear Sister M. Frances

I feel exceedingly anxious about you in your present state of trial and fear for the health of your community, but please God the contagion will not spread.[40] They have had three in fever in Tullamore— Sister Purcell & two Lay Sisters, all recovering, thank God.[41] I am sure no place or convent could be better situated for recovery than yours—it has everything desirable. Poor Sister M. Francis goes on in the same hopeless way.[42] Most melancholy are those protracted maladies— six fevers would be preferable in my opinion. They have a similar case in Cork.[43]

I did hope that God would have spared you all these severe trials for longer time—but His Holy will be done in all things. May He never leave the choice to us. We never can be unhappy while we love and serve Him faithfully. I trust you use every prudent precaution. I am sure you do for others, but remember, well regulated charity begins at home.

May God preserve and bless you. Let me hear often until you have a favorable change.

Your ever affectionate
Mary C. McAuley

Autograph: Silver Spring

40 Irish historians of medicine do not usually cite 1840 as a year in which typhus fever was particularly prevalent in Ireland, yet Catherine McAuley's letters in February and March 1840 report cases of "typhus" or "fever" in the Carlow, Tullamore, Charleville, and Limerick communities— with a total of six sisters affected. In Carlow, the postulant Julia Redmond was still seriously ill, though recovering. Crawford notes that in Ireland in the nineteenth century "four major epidemics [involving "typhus symptoms"] occurred in 1816–19, 1826–7, 1836–7 and 1846–9." Like other medical historians she points out that in the first half of the century "typhus was generally referred to in Ireland simply as 'fever' ... 'Fever', in fact, was an omnibus term that embraced several febrile conditions, such as relapsing fever and typhoid fever, as well as typhus ... it was not until William Jenner published his work in 1849 that typhus, typhoid and relapsing fever were accepted as distinct diseases" (121–22). Frederick Cartwright's *Disease and History* provides a helpful historical account of these diseases and of the evolution in recognizing their bacteriological causes.   41 In Tullamore, Mary Teresa Purcell, Mary Martha Gilligan, a novice, and Elizabeth Molloy, a postulant, all had "fever" which "still continued to rage in the town and of course the poor were the victims. As the sisters were unceasing in their visits to the poor sufferers, they naturally caught the infection." Eventually, Dr. Cantwell "formally forbade the sisters to attend infectious cases, and although often called upon to revoke the prohibition, he could not be prevailed on to do so" (Tullamore Annals 32).   42 Mary Francis (Margaret) Marmion was dying at Baggot Street of consumption. The sister of Mary Cecilia Marmion, she had professed her vows only fourteen months before. She will die on March 10, 1840 (see Letters 164 and 165).   43 Mary Francis (Catherine) Mahony was dying in Cork, evidently of consumption. She was one of the first postulants to enter the Cork community and had just professed her vows on February 11, 1840 (Cork Register).

164. To Sister M. Frances Warde   [Baggot Street]
     Carlow   Tuesday, March 10, 1840

My Dear Sister M. Frances

At half past five o'clock this morning we were reading the last prayers for our dear Sister Francis Marmion—it is now past twelve and she is yet alive, but has not spoken since 6. She is in the novaship[44]—we had the Community Mass celebrated there at quarter past 7—from that to this she has not been more uneasy than she often was in unquiet sleep. I think she will speak again. Do you remember our sweet Sister Agnes spoke long after we thought she never would.[45] It is melancholy consolation to look for, yet I think we would all like to hear her gentle voice again. In your Sister Julia's case recovery may be hoped[46]—but none in this. May God grant us all humble resignation to His Divine Will.

My poor Sr. Teresa Carton is much weaker—nearly fainted last night.

This is a shameful letter. I am nervous. We will be anxious to hear from you.

                                              Your affectionate
                                              M. C. McAuley

Autograph: Silver Spring

165. To Sister M. Frances Warde   [Baggot Street]
     Carlow   Thursday, March 12, 1840

My Dear Sister M. Frances

I have just taken of[f] my white cloak after walking to the door with the dear remains of our beloved very edifying Sister Francis Marmion.[47] This seems to be a season of sorrows with us. Sister M. Francis Mahony died in Cork this week[48]—and I expect to hear of my poor Sister Angela's death in Charleville—a very bad typhus fever—wandering & constant hycup [hiccup].[49] May God support her. She received the last Sacraments before her reason was impaired. Our poor Sister here[50]

44 Catherine McAuley occasionally used the word "novaship" for "noviceship."   45 Mary Agnes Marmion—the first of three Marmion sisters to enter the convent—had died at Baggot Street on February 10, 1836.   46 In Carlow, Julia Redmond recovered slowly. "The Doctors considered change of air necessary to the re-establishment of [her] health, so as soon as she was equal to the fatigues of the journey, she returned for a time to her father's house" in Wexford. She later returned to Carlow and received the habit on September 24, 1840 (Carlow Annals).   47 Part of the original religious habit of the Sisters of Mercy was a white cloak, modeled on that of the Carmelites, which was worn at liturgical celebrations on major feasts and at ceremonies, including the funeral liturgies for deceased sisters. Mary Francis Marmion was, like the Mercy Sisters in Dublin who preceded her in death, buried in the vault of the Discalced Carmelite community on Clarendon Street.   48 Mary Francis Mahony died in Cork on March 8, 1840.   49 Mary Angela Dunne, one of the earliest Sisters of Mercy (she had received the habit on January 23, 1832) and now the superior in Charleville, recovered from her typhus infection and lived to her seventy-fifth year, dying in Charleville on November 12, 1863 (Charleville Register). (Carroll's date for her death—in *Leaves* 1:155—is incorrect.)   50 That is, Mary Francis Marmion.   51 "About the second week in March it pleased the Almighty to send

received them on Saturday & died a quarter before 2 on Tuesday, the day I wrote to you. She did not speak as I expected—expired without any struggle.

I now expect a good account from you.

God bless you, etc., etc.

M. C. McAuley

Autograph: Silver Spring

166. To Sister M. Elizabeth Moore
Limerick

Convent

March 14, 1840

My Dearest Sister Mary Elizabeth

Your letters are always most acceptable to me. I rejoice to see one. Please God, our sweet little poet will soon be well.[51] All will pray for her.

We have sent our dear edifying Sr. Mary Francis Marmion to the Tomb. On Tuesday at half past five in the morning her agony commenced—we expected she would expire before Mass. Her distress increased—we got permission to have the Community Mass—quarter past 7—celebrated in the Infirmary (novaship). Although she appeared to us insensible, all her uneasiness ceased immediately after the elevation. She turned on her side, got into a quiet sleep—and remained so till a quarter before 2, when she departed. The last Sacraments were administered on Saturday [*a portion of the autograph is torn off here*] her pure genuine piety was strongly manifested during her illness[52] [*one third or more of pages 1 and 2 of the autograph is here torn off*].

Nothing more was done for us. We have all our offices now filled up. His Grace came here on the 6th to make the appointments: Mother de Pazzi, Assistant—Sister Aloysius, Burser—Sr. M. Cecilia, Mother of Novices.[53]

I have just been speaking to Father O'Hanlon of your request—he says he will go himself, but that is very doubtful. It would add fifty miles to my travelling—who am journeying fast enough out of this world.[54] Every day I am weak at some time. My stomach has never recovered its last attack—frequent swelling & soreness.

What writing this is. Did I tell you we expect at easter some ladies from Birmingham to serve a noviciate for that great town. Doctor Walsh, Vicar-

---

our little Community the first portion of His Cross in the illness of Sister M. Teresa Vincent Potter ... This loved Sister had never been strong; yet it was often a subject of wonder, how she accomplished such an amount of laborious work as her zeal engaged her in ... Our sister sank rapidly under the low fever with which she was attacked" (Limerick Annals 1:69, 72). **52** The words "strongly manifested during her illness," which are missing from the damaged autograph, have been supplied from the handcopy on pages 34–35 in the Baggot Street Manuscript Book called "Annals." **53** The appointees were Mary de Pazzi Delany, Mary Aloysius Scott, and Mary Cecilia Marmion. It is noteworthy that Dr. Daniel Murray visited the Baggot Street convent on March 6, 1840. **54** The nature of Elizabeth Moore's request is not fully clear. Probably she had asked Catherine to visit Limerick on her way to Galway in early May, or on her way home to Dublin.

Apostolic of the Midland District, has arranged for them. I do not much like a pet in a bag—not a pig. I like greatly to see and speak first but this cannot be[55] [*a portion of the autograph is torn off*].

May God bless you and all with you. Tell Miss Reddin I got her letter, and set [got?] a Sister to copy the enclosed lines for her.[56] She admired them greatly.

Your ever affectionate

M. C. McAuley

Sister M. Teresa—for Galway 6 months—Sister Leahy to remain—3 postulants.

We return to Kingstown in 3 weeks by Dr. Murray's desire on the spot.

Ashamed of my writing I got Sister Mary Teresa to write the other letters—but I know you would rather have this—such as it is, and I owe you all in my power— and I take pleasure in giving you my poor tribute of affection and esteem.

Autograph: Limerick

167. To Sister M. Elizabeth Moore   [Baggot Street]
Limerick   Thursday [March 19, 1840]

My Dearest Sister M. Elizabeth

No words could describe what I felt—on reading the first line of your letter. Though the accounts from Carlow were as hopeless—yet I fear much in this case.[57] The dear sweet innocent creature—you will indeed have a child in heaven.

---

55 The words "a pet ... first" have been supplied from the handcopy in the Baggot Street book labeled "Annals" (see note 52). What Catherine McAuley means is that she does "not much like" accepting the Birmingham postulants sight unseen, without an opportunity to interview them before admitting them, but since Dr. Walsh has selected them, her preference "cannot be." One of the proverbial uses of "pig" is the expression "To buy (or sell) a pig in a poke (or bag)" which means "to buy anything without seeing it or knowing its value" (OED)—an expression that fits Catherine's concern, though she is trying to avoid using the word "pig" for the "ladies from Birmingham"! Probably the large portion of this autograph letter that has been torn off contained more wording than the handcopy has supplied.   56 Neumann (203) and Bolster (125) both read the words "set a Sister" as "got a Sister," but the middle letter of the word is clearly "e". However, the word may be "set" or "get." Catherine McAuley is saying that (or asking that) some lines, presumably of poetry, which she encloses in this letter were (or may be) copied for Joanna Reddan. It seems doubtful, though possible, that she would ask to have the copying done in Limerick when she could as easily have it done at Baggot Street. The intriguing question is, which lines of poetry? Although this is pure speculation, the poem in question is possibly the extant autograph transcription, in Catherine McAuley's handwriting, of selected lines from a long poem by Hannah More (1745–1833), titled "Sensibility: An Epistle to the Honourable Mrs. Boscawen." Catherine's untitled transcription begins with the line, "Since trifles make the sum of human things," and has sometimes been given the title "Trifles." The transcription is included at the end of the present volume (Letter 323), among undated manuscripts in Catherine McAuley's handwriting, with notes describing the use she made of Hannah More's much longer poem.   57 The illness—presumably typhus—of Mary Teresa Vincent Potter in Limerick.

God will support you in this great affliction—His Holy Will be done. If He calls her away it will be to shield her from some impending evil—or to exercise your patience—and to try do you love Him as much when he takes—as when He gives. Some grand motive must actuate all His visitations.

I will be in great anxiety to hear—though I will be agitated at the sight of the next letter.

May God bless and preserve you—and grant you all—humble, cheerful submission to the Divine Will.

Your ever affectionate
M. C. McAuley

Autograph: Limerick

168. To Sister M. Elizabeth Moore [Baggot Street]
Limerick Saturday morning [March 21, 1840]

My Darling Sister M. Elizabeth

I did not think any event in this world could make me feel so much.[58] I have cried heartily—and implored God to comfort you—I know He will. This has not been done in anger. Some joyful circumstance will soon prove that God is watching over your concerns which are all his own—but without the cross the real crown cannot come. Some great thing which He designs to accomplish—would have been too much—without a little bitter in the cup. Bless and love the Fatherly hand which has hurt you. He will soon come with both hands filled with favors and blessings.

My heart is sore—not on my account—nor for the sweet innocent spirit that has returned to her Heavenly Father's Bosom—but for you.

You may be sure I will go see you—if it were much more out of the way[59]— and indeed I will greatly feel the loss that will be visible on entering the convent.

Earnestly & humbly praying God to grant you His Divine consolation—and to comfort and bless all the dear Sisters—I remain

your ever most affectionate
M. C. McAuley

Autograph: Limerick

169. To Sister M. Elizabeth Moore [Baggot Street]
Limerick Tuesday, March 24, 1840

My ever Dear Sister M. Elizabeth

Your last letter was a great comfort to me. When I read it in the Community

---

58 The death in Limerick on Friday, March 20, 1840, of Mary Teresa Vincent Potter, in her twenty-eighth year. 59 In Letter 166, Catherine McAuley had indicated that she could not stop in Limerick on her way to or from Galway (see note 54). Now she says she will come to Limerick no matter what the added distance (over 100 extra miles).

room all exclaimed, "I don't know who would not like to die under such circumstances. Oh, that's not death"—they were astonished & delighted. It was indeed a Heavenly ceremony,[60] more so than any reception or Profession. It was like a grand entrance into Paradise—thanks be to God you had such solid consolation—it will be a powerful attraction to many to put themselves in the way of such a Blessed departure from this passing world. I have never heard of anything like it.

Mr. Mulhall, a very spiritual Priest removed from Ann St. to Westland Row,[61] came to see us on the death of our dear Sister M. F[rancis Marmion] and said—"I congratulate you—you have—or will soon have—another friend in Heaven. How delightful to be forming a community there." I asked him, would it be wrong to hope that it was now formed. He answered, "What are they here for but to prepare for Heaven. They ought to go as soon as they are ready—to make room for poor souls that are in the midst of danger—there is no other way of carrying on this holy traffic so as to meet the designs of God. It is His own divine plan." This good Priest is quite a comfort to us.

You can't think how the Limerick House is spoken of in Dublin. This day a high fashionable gave a grand description of the attendance at the Charity Sermon[62]—and the veneration in which the Sisters are held.

Sorrow clings close to poor Baggot Street. Since I commenced this letter Sister Aloysius has broke a blood vessel. Doctor Corrigan just gone—says it will not be serious.[63] She was preparing children in the school for Confirmation—and made too much exertion.

I will write in a few days.

Preparing to return to ill fated Kingstown and three new Sisters expected.[64] Ah, if my weary head was beside my darling little Poet— under the sweet invit-

60 The funeral of Mary Teresa Vincent Potter in Limerick—probably on Saturday, March 21.   61 William Mulhall, formerly a curate at St. Michan's on North Anne Street, was appointed curate at St. Andrew's, Westland Row, in late 1839 or early 1840 (*Irish Catholic Directory* [1840] 250).   62 The Charity Sermon preached in Limerick by Dr. D. W. Cahill was apparently a great success, in contrast to the one he attempted to preach in Dublin (see Letter 162).   63 Dr. Dominic John Corrigan, MD (1802–1880) was, unlike many physicians who came to Baggot Street, a Catholic. He "gained an international reputation in medicine ... all the more remarkable when one considers that [he] did not have the type of patronage often thought essential for professional advancement in Victorian Ireland." He made two significant contributions to cardiology. "Although not the first to describe the pathology of aortic incompetence, his paper [in 1832 in the *Edinburgh Medical and Surgical Journal*] was the most lucid on the subject up to that time." His second major contribution was his discussion in 1838 of aortitis, "as one of the causes of angina pectoris" (Coakley, *Irish Masters* 107, 109). Catherine McAuley had some reservation about his medical skill in treating consumption when he attended Mary Aloysius Scott in 1840 and Mary Justina Fleming in August 1841 (see Letter 290). For further biographical details see Talbott's *Biographical History of Medicine*, 1058–60.   64 The Sisters of Mercy returned to the convent on Sussex Place in Kingstown in April 1840. Mary Clare Augustine Moore, who notes in her "Memoir" that "in 1840 I had charge of the House in Kingstown for a couple of months," explains the return: "In the beginning of 1840, at the close of some troublesome litigation, the debt was paid by the Institute and Foundress was persuaded to open the House again. Other inconveniences occurred, however, and within a few months after her death it was sold" (Sullivan, *Catherine McAuley* 210). At this point Catherine expected "three" new sisters in the month of April. Actually, at least five women

ing willow. When I think rest is coming—business only seems to commence. The prospect of my visit to Limerick will animate me. I need scarcely tell you that it will be a source of great happiness—for which I thank God—a pure heartfelt friendship which renews the powers of mind and Body.

I have not a moment to spare. May God bless you and all with you. Mother de Pazzi, Sisters M. C[ecilia] and Teresa beg their best love.

Your most sincerely attached
M. C. McAuley

Autograph: Limerick

170. To Dr. Thomas Walsh
Wolverhampton

Convent of the Sisters of Mercy
Baggot Street
April 9, 1840

My Lord

I have been favored with your kind letter. It is very agreeable to our wishes that the english Ladies should come about Easter, being well suited to other arrangements. The number your Lordship expects is quite animating. The opening in Birmingham will give good promise of future establishments. I humbly and confidently trust that not one of them will look back, but return with delight to enter on their engagement.[65]

As to the payments, my Lord, they can be made as you please. The ordinary time of probation is two years and half—our Rule gives power to the Bishop, on extraordinary occasions, to reduce it to one year and quarter. You will be so kind to inform Doctor Murray if you wish this to be done, and we will endeavour to make months into years with the Grace of God.

Our branch convent in Kingstown, which has been repairing, will be open about the time your spiritual children arrive. Any person on the beach will conduct them—it is not more than five minutes walk.[66] They can take a little rest and refreshment there and then proceed to the Mother House. I long to receive them all. May God bless them.

I have the honor to remain, my Lord, most respectfully, etc., etc.
Mary C. McAuley

Autograph: Birmingham

---

entered Baggot Street that month: Isabella Corbett on April 7, and four from Birmingham on April 29 (see Letter 162, note 37).   **65** Evidently Dr. Walsh had informed Catherine McAuley that five women would be coming from Birmingham: Juliana Hardman, Ann Wood, Lucy Bond, Elizabeth Edwards, and Marianne Beckett.   **66** The women from Birmingham will travel to Ireland at night, by boat from Liverpool to Kingstown (Dún Laoghaire), arriving in the morning.

171. **To Sister Mary Vincent Harnett**   **Easter Monday**
     Limerick   **April 20, 1840**

My dear Sister Mary Vincent[67]

I never for one moment forgot you or ceased to feel the most sincere interest and affection—so forgive all my past neglect, and I will atone in due season.[68]

A thousand thanks for the really nice articles for the Bazaar. Tell my dear
Sisters I did not expect any thing this time. The Rotundo was engaged for all Easter
week. We are obliged to wait till the 29th & 30th. A letter from Birmingham informs
us we are to have five postulants this week or next, accompanied by a Clergyman
who is to bring Plans of a Convent to shew me—this unavoidably puts me under
arrest—though Low Sunday was fixed by Mr. Daly for Galway. Immediately after
the Bazaar and the arrival of our new Sisters, we shall go by Tullamore—where
Revd. Mr. O'Hanlon joins us—and we proceed to Limerick with our whole heart.[69]

Mother de Pazzi sends her love—and is delighted you like the things she bought.
She is greatly amused at the Bishop's intention to bring her—she says she would be
rather a heavy parcel in every respect, except to go in his Lordship's luggage.[70]

A new child enters here on Thursday. That will make our third since the
last ceremony[71]—and if five come from England, we shall have a nice lot again—
just when I thought we were retiring from business.

God bless you, my dear Sister and own child. Give my fondest love to all
and pray for

> your affectionately attached
> M. C. McAuley

Harnett handcopy: Cork; handcopies: Brisbane and Dublin, Merc

67 This is the "3rd" of the handcopied transcriptions of Catherine McAuley's letters to her that
Mary Vincent Harnett had prepared for Mary Josephine Warde in Cork. In addition to this copy,
which was presumably checked by the recipient, there are handcopies of the same letter in the Book
of Transcriptions in the Brisbane archives and in the large Baggot Street Manuscript Book called
"Annals" preserved in Mercy Congregational Archives, Dublin. The text presented here is that of
the handcopy Mary Vincent Harnett sent to Josephine Warde, unless otherwise noted. The text of
the letter was also published in slightly abbreviated form in Harnett's *Life* of Catherine McAuley
(168–69). 68 The words, "so forgive ... season," are not in Harnett's handcopy, but are in the
other two handcopies and in the published version in Harnett's *Life* (168). 69 The timing of events
must have been very difficult: four postulants from England entered on April 29, the Annual Bazaar
was held at the Rotundo on Sackville Street on April 29 and 30, and the founding party for Galway,
including Catherine McAuley, had to be ready to depart from Dublin on May 2 or 3. Low Sunday
in 1840 was April 26. 70 This reference to Dr. John Ryan, bishop of Limerick, is obscure. Harnett
did not include the sentence in the *Life*, but it appears in all the handcopies. Harnett's handcopy
has "luggage," I think; the other two handcopies have "baggage." 71 Among the "three" who were
still postulants at Baggot Street, since the ceremony on February 27, 1840, were Anne Gogarty who
entered on February 3 and Isabella Corbett who entered on April 7. The third postulant Catherine
McAuley has in mind may have left before profession of vows and so is not listed in the Baggot
Street Register.

May–July 1840

Catherine McAuley spent May and June 1840 in Galway founding a new community of Sisters of Mercy. The joyful beginning of this foundation, reflected in her poem to Marianne Beckett (about creating "a little foolish party") and in the earlier, often humorous poem she sent back to Baggot Street, was soon clouded by the sudden illness and death from typhus fever of Mary Bourke, one of the first women to enter the Galway community. With Teresa White, the new superior in Galway, Catherine sat beside Mary when she died at 3:15 a.m. on June 11, the very day she would have received the habit of the Sisters of Mercy.

Catherine remained in Galway for three more weeks, meeting prospective postulants and negotiating with Peter Daly, the priest who had arranged their coming to Galway. But her thoughts were often with Baggot Street, where five postulants for Birmingham had arrived, four of them before she left Dublin; where Mary Aloysius Scott was severely ill, of what Dr. Corrigan called "rapid decline"; and where Mary de Pazzi Delany was doing her best to manage, but also sending alarming reports to Galway. Finally, at the end of June, Redmond O'Hanlon sent word that Catherine was to return to Dublin "immediately"— thus foreclosing any possibility of her visiting Mary Elizabeth Moore and the sisters in Limerick on her way home. Catherine deeply felt the loss of this longed for reunion: "I could not recollect any circumstance that inflicted such painful disappointment on me as not going to Limerick on my return ... I desired it too ardently" (Letter 180).

Back in Baggot Street on July 6, she found that Mary Aloysius Scott, now in Booterstown, was not so ill as had been reported, though very thin and pale. But the English sisters filled the Dublin house with joy and youthful generosity. After a sixth young woman from England joined them in late July, Catherine marveled at their willingness "to consecrate themselves to the service of the poor for Christ's sake. This is some of the fire he cast on the earth—kindling" (Letter 180).

By the end of July she was arranging a reception ceremony for the English postulants on August 10, treating with homemade remedies the cough that she had developed in Galway, and trying to be optimistic that the commercial laundry, now in operation, would soon pay for itself. She assured Frances Warde: "These things take time. The expense of coal is very great—sometimes a ton a week ... the fire will not cost more when the work is much encreased ... We have not lost anything of consequence, and only a few borders of fashionable night caps torn" (Letter 182).

On July 20 in Rome, far from the practical realities of soap and coal at Baggot Street, the Sacred Congregation for the Propagation of the Faith unanimously approved a resolution to forward its Italian translation of the Rule and Constitutions of the Sisters of Mercy to Gregory XVI for final confirmation. Catherine will hear unofficial reports of this positive outcome in August, but in late July her mind focused on good news that construction of the Birmingham convent was progressing rapidly. She was overwhelmed with gratitude: "May God bless the poor Sisters of Mercy and make them very humble that they may not be unworthy of the distinguished blessings God has bestowed upon them" (Letter 180).

172. To the Sisters at Baggot Street

Galway
[c. May 12, 1840][1]

> My dearest Sisters, kind and sweet
> Though 'tis not long till we shall meet
>   I'll tell you all
> That may perhaps amusement give
> But nothing that could pain or grieve
>   Oh, not at all.
>
> In truth we have been greatly spared
> And very well so far have fared,
>   Not one cold frown.
> Were this to last, we'd suffer loss
> Since independent of the Cross
>   There is no crown.
>
> Stopped on Mount Carmel[2] on our way
> And passed a most delightful day

1 The foundation party for Galway departed from Baggot Street in early May perhaps on May 2 or 3. The group consisted of Mary Teresa (Amelia) White, the new superior, and Mary Catherine Leahy who were to form the community; Catherine McAuley and her travelling companion Mary de Sales White (Teresa's sister), and Redmond O'Hanlon. They travelled to Tullamore, then to the Carmelite convent in Loughrea, thence to the Presentation convent in Galway, and finally to the house on Lombard Street that would serve initially as the Mercy convent. Staying at least one night at each of the stops along the way, they arrived at their destination in Galway around May 8, 1840 (Carroll *Leaves* 1:380). The autograph of this poem—the only contemporary description of their journey—has not been located. However, at least three early handcopies are extant: in the Liverpool Annals, in the Brisbane Book of Transcriptions, and in the small copybook of Baggot Street Manuscript Copies. The text given here is that in the Baggot Street and Brisbane handcopies which match exactly; the Liverpool handcopy has slightly different wording in about nine places. All the handcopies say the poem was written "from the Galway Foundation, established May 2nd 1840"— giving the date the group probably departed from Dublin, although Burke Savage says they departed on May 4 (305). 2 Loughrea, the site of an ancient Carmelite Monastery founded in 1300, was in 1840 the site of both a convent of Carmelite Sisters and a priory of Carmelite Friars (Burke Savage 306). Loughrea is about twenty-eight miles from the city of Galway.

Sweet simple nuns.
Got lamb and salad for my dinner
Far too good for any sinner
    At tea, hot buns.

Got use of a Superior's cell,
And slept all night extremely well
    On a soft pillow.
When lieing down in my nice bed
I thought how very soon this head
    Must wear the willow.

Next morning we had Mass in choir
To the very heart's desire
    Our own dear Father.
Then we had breakfast nice and neat
Tea and coffee, eggs & meat
    Which we'd rather.

At eight o'clock we started fair
One car and horse, one chaise and pair[3]
    The car went first.
Not long we travelled ere a wheel
Mounted by illtempered steel
    Completely burst.

A youthful driver naught dismayed
A real Irish fearless blade
    Said: "Sorra fear
The forge is just below the river
We'll get it minded, smart and cliver[4]
    the place is near."

When to the expected forge he came
And no assistance could obtain
    Aloud he said
"Oh such a forge, no nails, no sledge

---

3 Since five were travelling, and bringing a quantity of essential luggage to establish the new convent, a driver, possibly one passenger, and some baggage probably rode in the uncovered, two-wheeled Irish car, and the other passengers (or perhaps all of them), a driver, and some baggage rode in the four-wheeled, covered carriage drawn by two horses—at least on this final leg of the journey. From Dublin to Tullamore the group had probably taken the fly-boat on the Grand Canal, and from there to Loughrea a post-chaise or stage coach. However they travelled the more than 130 miles from Dublin to Galway, it was a difficult journey—even without the broken wheel (see below).
4 In "minded" (for "mended") and "cliver" (for "clever") Catherine McAuley is attempting to reproduce the pronunciation of the young driver.

Pat Lurgan wouldn't take the pledge
   He drank his bed.

"Many a time I said, oh Pat,
I'm but a gossoon—for all that
   The pledge I took.
But not an inch would Paddy go
Though the fine man was just below
   That brought such luck.[5]

"I'll mend the wheel now, I'll be bail
I've got a stone and fine long nail
   Yees needn't fear.
I'll give the horses male[6] & water
That mare, I'm sorry sure I brought her
   She's down lame near."[7]

The wheel well mended, horses fed
First-rate for Galway now we sped
   All blithe and gay
Dashing in true John Gilpin style[8]
The post-boy calling every mile—
   "Clear the way."

Peeped at our fix'd habitation[9]
Then drove up to the Presentation
   Where all was love.
My dear old friend, sweet Sister Tyghe[10]

---

5 The "pledge" is the pledge of the Total Temperance Society—the promise "to abstain from all intoxicating drinks, except for medicinal and sacramental purposes"—administered to thousands by the "fine man," Theobald Mathew. Father Mathew had been preaching total abstinence in Galway and Loughrea in early March 1840 (*Irish Catholic Directory* [1841] 251–52, 256).   6 "Male" is, again, the author's attempt to re-create the young fellow's pronunciation of "meal."   7 That is, the mare's "nearly lame."   8 Catherine McAuley evidently enjoyed the amusing English legend of John Gilpin flying away on his uncontrollable runaway horse—a tale she may have known from William Cowper's poem "The Diverting History of John Gilpin; showing how he went farther than he intended, and came safe home again" (*Poetical Works* 353–61). She refers to John Gilpin again in Letter 228.   9 The house on Lombard Street had evidently been donated earlier to Peter Daly, parish priest of St. Nicholas parish in the town, by a Mrs. Martyn whose daughter Elizabeth subsequently entered the Sisters of Mercy (Degnan 268). Father Daly had originally intended the house for a community of two Sisters of Charity who were trained in Paris by the French Sisters of Charity and returned to Galway in 1835. But by January 1840, this community, "being local and little known, did not hold out a realistic hope of growth and development," so Peter Daly, "desirous of extending and increasing the efficacy of said institution," turned to Catherine McAuley in Dublin (Mitchell 40–43).   10 Fanny Tighe (or Tyghe) (1798–1876) was Catherine McAuley's dear friend from Coolock days. A native of Galway and about twenty years younger than Catherine, Fanny had lived in Dublin with relatives for some years and shared Catherine's charitable aspirations. Although

By every tender means did try
    Her joy to prove.

Next morning our new cares began
Each proposing their own plan –
    All different tastes.
What some approved, some deemed bad
But all agreed that we had
    No time to waste.

The work is now progressing fast
Not one waste hour we yet have passed
    And Sisters many.
We hear of Crissy, Jane, and Bess
All ready to put on the dress.
    We have got Nanny

Bridget, Margaret, and Mary[11]
Who were of this poor world weary
    Tho' free from care.
And now with all their mind and heart
Of all its joys give up their part
    The Cross to bear.

Farewell, loved Sisters, old and new
With joy shall I return to you
    And count you o'er
And if my number full I find
United in one heart and mind
    I'll bless my store.

                           [M. C. McAuley]

Handcopies: Dublin, Mercy; Brisbane; and Liverpool

Catherine had hoped that she would be part of the Baggot Street project, Fanny chose to enter the Presentation Convent in Galway on May 3, 1827. She received the habit in Galway on November 6, 1827, taking the name Mary Louis (or Lewis), and Catherine McAuley attended her reception ceremony (Degnan 44–45, 62, 356 n. 10). Their meeting in Galway in early May 1840 was their first reunion since November 1827. 11 The names Crissy, Jane, Bess, Nanny, Bridget, Margaret, and Mary can be only partly identified. Crissy is probably Christina Joyce, and Mary is certainly Mary Bourke—both of whom are discussed in subsequent letters. Nanny, Bridget, and Margaret, whom "we have got," may be the three women who received the habit in Galway on June 25, 1840 (see Letter 176). Their names do not obviously match, but Catherine may be using familiar names, or she may be simply incorrect. "Nanny" is probably the familiar name of Anne O'Beirne who received the habit on June 25, and "Margaret" may be Miss Curran. "Bess" may be Elizabeth Martyn (see note 9). These names may also include women who entered the Galway community and then left before profession of vows, and therefore are not listed in the Galway Register. The early Galway records are incomplete in terms of names and dates.

173. To Sister M. Frances Warde   **Galway**
     Carlow   **June [6, 1840]**[12]

My Dear Sister Mary Frances

    I received your letter and am delighted to find you so well recovered. Be cautious now for a little time, until your usual strength is restored.

    I am very sorry to hear of your dear little Sister's disappointment—and regret that it would not be possible to take her to Baggot Street.[13] I have been obliged to guard against any increase of expense since Miss McGuinness [Magenis] withdrew her aid. No chance here—this is quite a pious Catholic place, I am sure there would be fifteen in the Convent before six months, if two or three hundred pounds could be taken, but the poor funds will not admit of it.[14]

    We have four postulants who were to be received on Thursday next, as they have been kept waiting our arrival for some months, and are so much approved that the Bishop would have received them the day after we came[15]—three have merely enough—one—Miss Burke [Bourke]—who is fully arrived at the eleventh hour—has forty seven pounds per an[num] during life and five hundred pounds to bequeath. She became suddenly ill on Thursday evening, the second day of her retreat,[16] and this morning there is much appearance of fever—a Doctor attending. Of course, no prospect of her reception. Our order is greatly liked, but there is really no money amongst the people—all high consequence and poverty. A very nice young person—Miss MacDonnell, quite accomplished, daughter to what is termed an estated gentleman in the Co. Galway— is coming, and with all the influence—Bishops & Priests [*a top corner portion of the letter is here cut out*] more than five hundred pounds cannot be [*words missing*] six. The

---

12 This autograph is damaged: a piece of the letter (2 inches x 3 inches) is cut out of the upper right hand corner of sides 1 and 3 of the folded sheet, and out of the upper left hand corner of sides 2 and 4. The letter was written in early June 1840 from Galway before Mary Bourke was anointed late Sunday night, June 7. It may have been written, as both Neumann (214) and Bolster (132) claim, on Saturday, June 6, even though the Galway postmark on the cover is "Ju 8, 1840." Given its description of the progress of Mary Bourke's typhus infection, the letter was probably not written later than June 7, Pentecost Sunday. 13 Kathleen Healy has, I believe, correctly researched the ironic story of Anna Maria Maher whom Dr. Francis Haly would not permit to enter the Carlow convent because of insufficient dowry, but who entered the Kinsale community in 1845, taking the name Mary Teresa, and became the founding superior of the congregation in Cincinnati, Ohio in 1858. From early 1840 to well into 1841, Frances and Catherine both tried to find Anna Maria a place, but to no avail (Healy 120–21). See also Molitor, "Mary Teresa Maher." 14 Peter Daly, the priest who invited the Sisters of Mercy to Galway, required that each postulant who entered the convent in Galway present before her profession of vows a dowry of £600—a sum that was out of reach of many aspirants. 15 The reception ceremony for the first four postulants to enter the Galway community was scheduled for Thursday, June 11—the time of probation having been shortened to one month by the bishop of Galway, Dr. George J. Browne. However, the ceremony was deferred to June 25, as Letter 175 explains. 16 Mary Bourke became more seriously ill on Thursday, June 4, the second day of her eight-day spiritual retreat before her projected reception of the Mercy habit on June 11.

generality of respectable inhabitants could [*words missing*].[17] Walter Joyce, Esq. of Merview, one mile from town, who commonly drives four horses in his carriage, will, the Priests say, make as hard a bargain for his Daughter who is expected to enter Corpus Christi. She is a nice young person, the first Christina we ever had, and quite as pretty as Christina White.[18] The Bishop is all sweetness to all. Revd. Mr. Daly is Guardian and says he does not see any more who could bring what is absolutely required. The Bishop asked me would it be possible to take a person most anxious to come, with whom he would give two hundred pounds—it could not be done.[19] Sister Burke, who is ill, is a most pleasing person, quite of modern fashionable style.

The Revd. Mr. Mathew made me promise that immediately after Galway was done—I would endeavour to make up a branch for Birr where the unfortunate Crottys have done so much injury to religion.[20] He said they must be truly spiritual souls—confiding entirely in Divine Providence as there was no foundation fund. The Revd. Mr. Spain, P.P.,[21] proposed giving up his House and garden, he is so very anxious. Mr. M., the Apostle of Temperance, says he will preach often for them. If I can get two, perhaps your little pious soul might join them. At present I cannot fix my mind on any as head—but little Sister White— a perfect *mistress*—very faithful to her vocation and well versed in all our ways. Tell me what you think of her for such a purpose—I fear a little tendency to party spirit—which yet remains—would be a great impediment.[22] I shall be pressed very much until it is done. I should like to remain in Birr as one stationary. I would not fear begging my bread.[23]

I feel very much for your poor Sister in Law, but I would fear very much your taking her child.[24] These engagements never were designed for our state,

---

17 The damage to this autograph greatly confuses its discussion of the financial arrangements in Galway.   18 Christina Joyce entered the Galway community on Thursday, June 18, 1840, the feast of Corpus Christi.   19 Dr. George Joseph Plunket Browne had been consecrated bishop of Galway on October 23, 1831. Upon their arrival in Galway, he had designated Peter Daly as ecclesiastical superior, or "guardian," of the Mercy community. Yet when the bishop himself wished to allow a young woman to enter the community with only £200 in dowry, Peter Daly would not permit it. Catherine McAuley valued financial prudence, but she did not share Father Daly's intransigence about money in relation to religious vocations, though she was initially powerless to contradict it. Later, Mary Teresa White evidently found ways to manage the finances of the community less rigorously. 20 The Crottyite schism, instigated by two priests, Michael Crotty and William Crotty, had by 1840 caused considerable religious turmoil in Birr. Theobald Mathew believed that the presence of Sisters of Mercy in Birr might help to heal the situation.   21 Dr. John Spain, parish priest in Birr.   22 Mary Teresa (Catherine) White—not to be confused with Mary Teresa (Amelia) White, the superior of the Galway community—did not in the end become the superior of the Birr community, founded on December 27, 1840.   23 The words "should like to remain in Birr" and "bread" are supplied from an early, but also flawed, photostat of the autograph in Mercy Congregational Archives, Dublin. Catherine McAuley here expresses her own willingness to be a permanent member of the Birr community, a foundation that would begin in great poverty.   24 The words "would fear very much" are supplied from the photostat in Mercy Congregational Archives, Dublin; they are missing from the autograph. The child in question was Frances Warde's niece, either Mary or

and whatever is contrary, or not actually belonging to it, will ever create agitation of mind. If you had a school like the Ursulines, then it would be different—and the circumstances need not be known. God will assist such a good mother, not one of her children will want. The english Catholics are wealthy and truly zealous—they are every day providing for converts—not one is suffered to go to Protestant religion for want of means. It is in this Country that danger exists.

I suppose you have heard of Dear Sister M. Josephine's[25] great progress. She has got 4 Postulants since Sr. M. Clare left. Some Priest said there was a charm in the name of Warde.

Our english Sisters are greatly liked. They are all nice. Sister Beckett, a convert of high connections,[26] is quite equal to Sister Moore[27] in all arts and sciences—languages—painting, etc., etc. She brought her finery to Ireland, her under dresses trimmed with lace. It is very animating to see five [fine?] persons most happily circumstanced, leave their friends and country, to enter on a mission so contrary to our natural inclinations, but the fire that Christ cast upon the [earth][28] is kindling very fast. Several others have proposed following them, but the spiritual guides think it better they should wait their return and enter the new foundation. Sisters M. T., M. de S. & M. C.[29] unite in best love to all.

Pray for me and believe me always your affectionate

M. C. McAuley

Autograph: New York; photostat: Dublin, Mercy

174. To Sister Marianne Beckett[30]   [Galway]
      Novitiate, Baggot Street   [c. June 7, 1840]

Dear Sister
        Tho' so long I've delayed to reply to your note
        I never unmindful could be

Fanny Warde, the daughter of her brother John [William?] Warde who had died in Wakefield, England. Frances wished to help his widow by bringing the child to live in the Carlow convent. Had the Carlow pension school been a boarding school, Catherine McAuley would have sanctioned the plan. Carroll names Frances Warde's deceased brother John and says that he left four children (*Leaves* 1:255); Healy calls him William, and names only two children, Mary and James (84).   **25** Mary Josephine Warde, the superior in Cork.   **26** Marianne Beckett, to whom Letter 174 is addressed, had entered the Baggot Street community on April 29, 1840, to prepare for the Birmingham foundation in 1841. An English woman, she was a convert of the Honorable and Reverend George C. Spencer, himself a recent and celebrated convert to the Roman Catholic church.   **27** The artist, Mary Clare Augustine Moore.   **28** Catherine McAuley wrote "upon the is kindling." She probably meant to write, not "them," but "the earth"—a more exact paraphrase of Jesus' words in Luke 12:49: "I came to bring fire to the earth, and how I wish it were already kindled" (NRSV).   **29** Mary Teresa White, Mary de Sales White, and Mary Catherine Leahy—all of whom were known to Frances Warde and the Carlow community.   **30** There are two almost identical autographs of

of the metre so varied—so sweet that you wrote
and so kindly to gratify me

When not far removed from life's earliest stage
at Rhyming I never could stop
and beginning to feel the pressure of age
I lean on it now as a prop

It affords some support and help on the way
recalling the days of my youth
In which 'twas my pastime,[31] my folly, my play
and so it is still in good truth

Of this one poor talent I've made such a hack
That—unimproved it must remain
and ah, when obliged to deliver it back
I'll have losses much rather than gain[32]

This strain would make me very sad
I'll therefore cast it off for ever
Since gloomy thoughts are very bad[33]
The heart from God they often sever

I sometimes wish that we could form
A little foolish party
who common sense would loudly scorn
and aim at laughing heart'y.

Even now, I can select a few
Would suit our purpose well
V——a—J——a—too[34]
M.——A—— and I——ll[35]

---

this poem-letter, both addressed to Marianne Beckett, one of the English postulants who had entered the Baggot Street community on April 29, 1840, to prepare for the foundation in Birmingham the following year. The autograph followed here is in the Mercy Congregational Archives, Dublin. The second autograph is in the archives of the Sisters of Mercy, Melbourne, Australia; the Melbourne autograph differs from the Dublin text in a few places, as indicated in the notes, and its poetry seems less polished. The poem-letter was probably written on or just before Pentecost Sunday (June 7)—certainly before Mary Bourke's illness became acute on Sunday night. **31** The Melbourne autograph has "my whole pastime." **32** This line in the Melbourne autograph is "I'll have not one portion of gain." **33** The Melbourne text has "are always bad" for "are very bad." **34** "Veronica—Juliana too": this line names, without naming, Mary Veronica Cowley, a novice, and Juliana Hardman, one of the English postulants. Before she was approved in March 1841 for profession of vows, Mary Veronica changed her name to Mary Aloysius, once Mary Aloysius Scott had gone to Birr (see Letters 232 and 238). **35** "Mary Ann and Isabell": this line names, without naming, Mary Francis (Mary Ann) Creedon, a recent novice, and Isabella Corbett, a postulant who had entered the Baggot Street community on April 7.

A President we next should seek
of folly a Professor
Try Sister V——t for a week[36]
we'll soon get a successor

Dear Sister Marianne adieu
Since last I wrote—there's nothing new[37]
save—Habits, guimpes and veils
which they have wrought like any Bee[38]
plaited as nice as you could see
not creeping on like snails

I'll conclude with a prayer which I promise to say
from this till we meet—at least twice a day[39]
"May the Spirit of fervor, of light and of Love
which descended from high in the form of a Dove
our dear Postulants visit at this Holy time[40]
and prepare them to enter a life so Divine
May the fruits of this Spirit each evil efface
and infuse in their hearts an abundance of grace.—Amen."

[Mary C. McAuley]

Autographs: Dublin, Mercy; and Melbourne

---

175. To Sister M. Elizabeth Moore   Galway
     Limerick   June 10, 1840

My Dearest Sister Mary Elizabeth

It has pleased Almighty God to visit us with a large portion of the cross. Miss Bourke— a very amiable person whom I believe I mentioned, having joined us—is now in typhus fever. She was a little heavy on Monday week— like a slight cold—on Thursday was prevailed on with difficulty not to get up. On Sunday night at eleven o'clock the last sacraments were administered—and yesterday, Tuesday—the 9th day—her death expected, sinking all day. A favorable change has taken place, but not such as to give hope of recovery—4 physicians are attending. They visit four times a day. She is greatly esteemed and

---

36 "Try Sister Vincent for a week" refers to Mary Vincent Whitty, a novice. The Melbourne autograph has "Say" for "Try" and "the first week" for "for a week." **37** The Melbourne text has "I wrote last" for "last I wrote." In the next line Catherine spells guimpes "gaumps." **38** For this line the Melbourne text has "Oh if you could two Sisters see," and for the next line, "working diligent—as the Bee." **39** The Melbourne text has "which I purpose to say" for "which I promise to say," and "three times a day" for "twice a day." **40** The feast of Pentecost and its Octave: June 7–14, in 1840.

respected and so closely connected with many around us that it is quite a public matter.

My Dearest Sr. Elizabeth—a sudden bad change took place—I stopped writing. This morning at quarter past 3 o'clock she expired. She died most happily— in fervent sentiments of gratitude to God—and bequeathed five hundred pounds to the Sisters.[41]

We are founding on the cross now indeed—only eight days since she was forced to stay in bed, not thinking herself seriously ill. They reckon it the 11th day of the fever, supposing she was keeping it off a day or two. I never saw a person who seemed to have a more amiable disposition, never thought of religious life till she heard of the Sisters of Mercy coming to Galway—and embraced the inspiration the moment it came. She was most pleasing, and quite a lady— in manners and appearance—enjoying the gay world in all its fashion to the week of our arrival. God has certainly accepted her offering, and she is—I have no doubt, gone before him—received & professed by Himself.

I travelled 100 miles to meet this cross—and another has travelled after me. Sister Aloysius is very seriously ill—her case pronounced a bad one—appearance of rapid decline, after throwing up blood.[42] God preserve her.

God bless you, my Dearest Sr. M. E. If you have time, write me a few words of comfort—and say you are all well & happy.

Your ever affectionate
M. C. McAuley

Autograph: Limerick

176. To Sister M. Frances Warde Galway
    Carlow June 30, 1840

My Dear Sister Mary Frances

I would have written to you sooner but expected each day to know when we were to return. The calls now are very pressing, some proposing to enter who are impatient for an arrangement. Fearing I would not be let to go, Mr. O'Hanlon wrote to the Revd. Mr. Daly, requesting our immediate return. I will, please God, be in Baggot Street on Monday next.[43]

I enclosed your letter to Sr. M. T.—relative to Sr. Aloysius—to Sr. de Pazzi, requesting she would be sent to you without delay. In her answer she

---

41 The first paragraph of this letter was written on Wednesday, June 10. The second paragraph and the rest of the letter were written after Mary Bourke died of typhus at 3:15 a.m. on June 11, 1840. Her sudden illness and her death on the very day when she was to have received the habit of the Sisters of Mercy were a shock to the new community in Galway. Her final bequest of £500 was an extraordinary gift in the midst of her suffering and theirs.   42 Mary Aloysius Scott, at Baggot Street.   43 Catherine expects to be back in Dublin on July 6.

says—"Dr. Corrigan thinks Booterstown as good air for her [as] any other. She is gone there."[44]

We have got a sweet postulant,[45] a second Mary Teresa McAuley in look and manner—all ardor—sighing for the bleak winter to be cold and wet. Just when it was concluded that we were to come to Galway, her family were going to travel, and although she would have seen the Pope and all the religious splendor of the Holy City, she entreated to be left at home, having determined to join us as soon as possible. In writing, she communicated her ardent desire. Her Mamma is very pious, and on their return they visited the Sisters in London—were much pleased—and soon gave consent. Perhaps I told you this before. It is very probable Dr. Fitzgerald knows something of her Father— Walter Joyce of Merview— said to be the Richest man in the Co. Galway.

We had our reception of three on Thursday last.[46] The Bishop said a few nice words and wore grand ornaments just arrived to him from France—which he said he would not wear until our ceremony. He could not be kinder—and as to Mr. Daly, we all love him. Since the death of our first Sr.[47] he has been making it his study to comfort and oblige us. He is delighted at being constantly called on—and so proud of the new Sr.[48]—he says, "the Root has struck." He feels all will now flourish.

We said our two sweet Thirty Days Prayer—the one to our Saviour in the morning—to the B[lessed] V[irgin] in the evening. We did this also in London— my faith in it has encreased very much.

Poor Sister Angela[49] has had unceasing trial—scarcely recovered from her severe fever when Sr. Lawless caught it and was fifteen days very bad. I have not heard for a week.

44 Perhaps because they grew too fond of Carlow, Mary de Pazzi Delany was reluctant to send sisters there, even for health reasons. Claiming it was Dr. Dominic Corrigan's preference, and acting in Catherine McAuley's absence, she sent Mary Aloysius Scott (who had just burst a blood vessel in her lungs) to Booterstown—probably before receiving Catherine's request that she be sent to Carlow.   45 Christina Joyce, who entered the Galway community on June 18, 1840, the feast of Corpus Christi.   46 At the reception in Galway on Thursday, June 25, three postulants received the habit: Anne O'Beirne, who took the name Mary de Chantal; another woman whose baptismal name and name in religion are not known with certainty; and probably Miss Curran, who was in the community of Sisters of Charity that Peter Daly had earlier tried to form in the house on Lombard Street. Possibly the early Galway records misname as "Frances" a woman named Mary de Sales (Ismena) McDonnell who entered in July 1840, received the habit on October 1, and professed her vows in October 1841. Since Miss Curran apparently did not remain in the Mercy community, no further information about her is available in the Galway Register. However, Mitchell refers to the "obituary of Miss M. M. Curran, *Galway Vindicator*, 16 November 1878" (43); this suggests that her name may have been Mary Margaret (or Margaret Mary) as listed in Letter 172.   47 Mary Bourke, who died on June 11, 1840.   48 Christina Joyce.   49 Mary Angela Dunne, the superior in Charleville.   50 Mary Ann Doyle had invited Theobald Mathew—widely celebrated, especially at this time, as the "great" apostle of temperance who administered the pledge of total abstinence to thousands— to preach at the upcoming reception ceremony in Tullamore on September 8, 1840. Not only were there several major distilleries in or near Tullamore, but leaders of these businesses, such as Michael Molloy, were major contributors to building projects in

I had a letter yesterday from Sister Mary Ann—who says they have the mortification of *declining* the most kind offer or consent of Mr. Mathew to preach at a reception for them. The great supporters of all public matters in and about the Town are Distillers, and the Bishop, I believe, thinks it would be imprudent to excite their feelings—and—I suppose—hopes that the good work may go on quietly.[50]

Sr. M. A. wrote to Mr. Mathew with Revd. Mr. O'Rafferty's[51] consent— you may judge what she feels at being obliged to write again to say he is not to come. This is a good lesson—to teach us to be extremely cautious in asking extraordinary favors. If it was a little presuming—a great penance has followed—and we are certain the intention was pure. However, the kind complying answer by return of post might have created a spark of self complacency, and God in his Mercy sent the cure. She feels it—and writes—"It was too much for me to seek."

Our postulants have names new to us—Miss Joyce, Christina—Miss McDonnell (who comes tomorrow), Ismena—Miss Curran, one of those Mr. D. sent to France to be made a Sr. of Charity—plays & sings remarkably well, all sacred music. She is a novice now. Miss O'Beirne also—very, very nice person. Miss McDonnell plays the Harp & sings—we expect she will bring one—is only 19 years old.

The novaship is very nice—the table fifteen feet long with 12 drawers—grey carpet & community table 7 feet, 6 drawers—grey carpet, rush chairs, piano, etc., etc. Choir—beautiful crimson cloth carpet—seats like Baggot St., which Sr. M. C. and M. T.[52] wished. Refectory tables full as long as Baggot St.—very convenient to the choir & Community room—close to the Kitchen. Thank God they are very comfortable before I leave them.

All unite in affectionate love to you—& Sisters. Remember me affectionately to Dr. Fitzgerald—& Mr. M. & Fr. D.[53]

> Pray for me and believe me always your fondly attached
> M. C. McAuley

I had a letter from Sr. M. Clare—she says Dr. Murphy has written to say he will go for her in August—tho' he adds, "your place is well supplied." She says the Bishop of London wishes her to stay another year—and she adds, "Let their Lordships settle it between them. I feel no anxiety."[54]

---

the diocese of Meath and to the new convent and schoolrooms under construction for the Sisters of Mercy. **51** James O'Rafferty, parish priest in Tullamore. **52** Mary Catherine Leahy and Mary Teresa White, the founding community in Galway. **53** Father James Maher and Father Dan Nolan. **54** In August 1839, Mary Clare Moore, then the superior in Cork, was loaned for one year to be the superior in London. Dr. John Murphy, bishop of Cork, wished her to return to Cork in August 1840; Dr. Thomas Griffiths, vicar apostolic of the London District, wished her to remain a second year. She did not return to Cork until June 1841. However, in December 1841, at the urgent request of Dr. Griffiths, and with Dr. Murphy's concurrence, Clare returned to London where the eccentric leadership of Mary Clare Agnew, as superior in the intervening months, had severely threatened the stability of the Bermondsey community. Except for a period of fifteen

Your next letter will be to Baggot St.—where it will find me, please God, on Monday next. We shall be immediately preparing for our reception[55] there. The english Postulants are quite impatient for the votes.

God bless you and all.

Autograph: Silver Spring

177. To Sister M. Elizabeth Moore   Convent, Galway
      Limerick   July 1, 1840

My own ever Dear Sister Mary Elizabeth

I have waited to the latest moment to know what I would be obliged to do. To leave this sooner would certainly have been injurious, it was thought. We were quite alarmed at the fever—and if we moved—it would have been said— all was broken up—this was quite evident.

The difficulties are over, thank God. Three are received. A very nice postulant entered and another expected this week.

Endless letters from Baggot Street—with bad accounts of Dear Sr. Aloysius— though I believe I have not heard all. Revd. Mr. Daly had a letter from Mr. O'Hanlon—which he would not shew me—but informed me I was to return immediately.[56] Our places are engaged for Sunday. In Mr. O'Hanlon's letter he promises Mr. Daly that if I am not detained longer (for Mr. Daly would not suffer me to go)—I should return in a few weeks. You may be certain Galway will never see me again but from Limerick. I do think it would be very well for me to come to Miss Joyce's reception, which will be in September, my own favorite month. Our ceremonies in Baggot St.—reception of English Srs. & Profession of three will be about the 5th or 6. I would then set off—for Limerick direct—and most certainly keep them waiting in Galway—as long as Mr. Daly would have patience.

You would like him very much, though he is the greatest master we ever met. I really could not leave this without his full concurrence, except I were to become angry or stiff. All reasoning and entreaty was fruitless. He said—"You shall not go—not a vehicle in Galway should carry you. I will not suffer the foun-

---

months in 1851–1852, Clare was thereafter the beloved and remarkably successful superior of the community until her death on December 14, 1874—having been elected or re-elected every three years. **55** The reception ceremony at Baggot Street was eventually scheduled for August 10, 1840. **56** Either Mary de Pazzi Delany had urged Redmond O'Hanlon to write to Galway requesting Catherine McAuley's immediate return to Dublin, or he had sized up the situation at Baggot Street himself and concluded that she should return. Since he had met Peter Daly at the beginning of the Galway foundation, he undoubtedly saw or suspected Daly's tendency to dominate. By writing to him, rather than directly to Catherine, Father O'Hanlon spared her one more "fruitless" argument. See note 57.

dation to be injured."[57] This makes me fear he has a melancholy account—as he so quickly assented. I shall be truly glad of the excuse to return—in order to get to you and my Dear Sister Vincent.

I thank God for your wonderful progress—and I comfort myself thinking I shall so soon see them all—and everything about you will look so beautiful. The only disappointment I fear—is that the Bishop may be at the sea. I would be very sorry not to see him. You remember he was there when we arrived first in September '38.[58]

All unite with me in love to you and Sr. M. Vincent. I will write from Dublin on Tuesday or Wednesday next. May God forever bless you, my Dear Sister M. Elizabeth. Absence has much increased my affection for you—even the new Sisters here are sorry for our mutual disappointment this time, I have talked so much of it.

Pray for your fondly attached
M. C. McAuley

Autograph: Limerick

---

57 James Mitchell's long, thoroughly researched article on "Father Peter Daly (c. 1788–1868)" is a necessary amplification of the thin sketch of this complex Galway priest that emerges from references to him in Catherine McAuley's letters. Mitchell documents Daly's many admirable goals and accomplishments, but also his serious weaknesses: his excessive interest in civic leadership roles and commercial enterprises, his insubordination towards two successive bishops, and his proprietary attitude toward church property and revenue and towards the Sisters of Mercy in Galway and their assets. One can perhaps see in his behavior in 1840 intimations of attitudes and actions that in 1858 led Dr. John MacEvilly, bishop of Galway, to complain of him to Rome on three grounds:

> a very large amount of ecclesiastical property was registered in Peter Daly's name, in respect of which he refused to execute a deed of trust or to furnish an inventory. Secondly, during the previous few years he had been treating the Sisters of Mercy "most barbarously"; in particular, they claimed he had used their money to purchase an estate in Salthill, but that he refused to admit this. Thirdly, he had expended a very considerable amount of their financial resources in building the chapel adjoining their convent at Newtownsmith [to which the community had moved from Lombard Street]; not only was it too large and, consequently, very cold in winter, but he now claimed that he had been authorized to declare it a public chapel, by a papal rescript—which, however, he declined to submit to the bishop (Mitchell 70).

In 1844, Dr. George Browne, bishop of Galway—apparently at Peter Daly's implicit request, but supported by five members of the Mercy community in Galway—petitioned the Holy See "that, in the event of his [Dr. Browne's] being translated to Elphin, Peter Daly should be constituted the local [ecclesiastical] 'Superior and Father-for-life,' under the bishop, of the Sisters of Mercy," on the grounds that their "'permanence and value vitally depend on his connexion with them'" (Mitchell 45). Dr. Browne evidently executed this arrangement in writing, perhaps innocently ignorant of the negative potential of such a designation. Before her death in November 1841, Catherine McAuley too may not have foreseen any future serious difficulties arising from "the greatest master we ever met."
58 Dr. John Ryan, bishop of Limerick, tended to take his holiday in September each year.

178. To the Cardinals of the Congregation [Rome]
for the Propagation of the Faith[59]   [July 20, 1840]

Most Eminent and Most Reverend Lords

In the General Congregation of the 26th January 1835 amongst the matters pertaining to the churches in Ireland, of which reference is made in Article 3, there was submitted to Your Eminences the appeal of the *Sisters of Mercy* (as they are called) for the approval of their most edifying religious association established in Dublin. To that petition, which was accompanied by the earnest commendation of the Archbishop, your Eminences, resolving the third Doubt [Question] on the list, replied *affirmative in omnibus* [approved in all aspects]. That resolution was reported to His Holiness, who in His wise counsel directed that Propaganda should write to Monsignor Archbishop of Dublin in accordance with the terms expressed in the letter reported in Summary No. I.

Meanwhile, in the course of the years, the very great usefulness of this pious Institute has been more and more demonstrated, and for that very reason it has spread not only in Ireland where it originated, but also in England, and has given long proof of the suitability of the Rules adopted from the beginning by this Institute. And now the Archbishop, united with other Prelates and the Vicar Apostolic of London (Summary Nos. II to VII)[60] comes again to petition His Holiness for the confirmation of this praiseworthy Institute, and for the Pontifical recognition of the above-mentioned Rule, which for that purpose is submitted to Your Excellencies for examination, accompanied by the proper Vote [opinion] made by one of the distinguished Consultors of Propaganda, the Reverend Father Gavino Secchi Murro, Procurator General of the Order of the Servants of Mary (Summary Nos. VIII, IX, X).[61]

---

59 This document consists of two parts: the printed document (in Italian) sent in "July 1840" to the members of the Sacred Congregation for the Propagation of the Faith as part of the agenda for their General Congregation on July 20, 1840 (APF: SOCG, Vol. 957, f. 271r and repeated in APF: ACTA, Vol. 203, ff. 206r–208r); and the decision reached on July 20, 1840 and recorded (in Latin) by Cardinal Paolo Polidori, the *Ponens* (Petitioner) assigned to this particular Doubt (or Question to be decided) presented to the Sacred Congregation.   **60** See Letters 135, 138, 143, 144, 146, and 147. The letters from Dr. John Ryan of Limerick (Letter 133), Dr. Michael Blake of Dromore (Letter 134), and Dr. William Crolly of Armagh (Letter 137)—all originally written in English— were not included in the printed ACTA prepared *after* the meeting on July 20, 1840, but were included in their original autograph form in the agenda (SOCG) prepared *before* the July 20, 1840 meeting.   **61** On March 3, 1840, Paul Gavino Secchi Murro submitted his long Votum, written in Italian, to Ignatio Cadolini, secretary of the Congregation for the Propagation of the Faith (APF: SOCG, Vol. 957, ff. 307r–313r). In his report, he praises the content of the "Rule" proper, i.e. the First Part (see Sullivan, *Catherine McAuley* 295–317), but finds fault with the "Constitutions" proper, i.e. the Second Part (317–28). He notes that "there is not much detail given, nor does one find that methodical and positive prescription of actions and things which serves to regulate at all times and in every place the conduct of the individuals united in a Religious community" (f. 310r). Five pages follow, citing instances where the document should be more specific with respect to horarium, assigned occupations, curriculum in the school, admission of externs, the penitential system, and

The said Vote needs no comment, and the distinguished Consultor agrees fully that the required approval should be implored, except for some minor changes, which are to be sent, together with related instructions, to Monsignor Archbishop of Dublin—and, so, the Most Eminent and Most Reverend Lords are asked to resolve according to their wisdom the following

Doubt [Question]

Should His Holiness of Our Lord be implored for the approval, with only those modifications proposed by the Reverend Consultor?

In the General Congregation held on the 20th of July 1840, to the proposed Doubt [Question]—"Should His Holiness be petitioned for the approbation, with only those modifications recommended by the Reverend Consultor?"—their Eminences responded *Affirmative*, and left it to the Cardinal Prefect with the Cardinal Petitioner to have certain things in the Constitutions, to which attention has been drawn, appropriately emended or more accurately expressed.

P[aolo] Cardinal Polidori, Ponens

Autograph (Italian and Latin): Propaganda Fide, ACTA, Anno 1840, vol. 203, ff. 206r–208r[62]

179. To Sister M. Teresa White	**Baggot St.**
Galway	**July 27, 1840**

My Dearest Sister M. Teresa

I know you are anxious to have a more circumstantial account of all that relates to your own old habitation and its inmates. First then, I have a real old man's cough night and morning—old woman is entirely exploded from the new fashionable vocabulary—no such character is to [be] recognised in future. I sleep well, have good appetite, and feel improving in strength every day, so that I hope my "old man's cough" will not impede my journey in September,[63] to which I look forward with joyful impatience.

Sister Aloysius is exceedingly thin, pale, and weak. She has no cough nor any other alarming symptoms—she is in Booterstown. Sister Austin quite deli-

---

the process of dismissal, etc. Some of these recommendations were alien to Catherine McAuley's spirit and intentions, although it seems clear that she never saw Secchi Murro's document. Whether Dr. Daniel Murray ever received a detailed summary is not known. Some changes were made in the text of the Rule and Constitutions before it was confirmed in June 1841 and posted to Dublin on July 31, 1841 (see Letters 288 and 314). See also Sullivan, *Catherine McAuley*, 274–75, 278–82. **62** The translation of this two-part document was made in the mid twentieth century by John MacErlean, SJ, and was recently reviewed by Professor Pellegrino Nazzaro. **63** Catherine McAuley plans to return to Galway in September, for the reception ceremony of Christina Joyce and Ismena McDonnell, who entered the Galway community on June 18 and in early July, respectively.

cate—with prospect of recovery. Sister Teresa—exactly as we left her.[64] Mother pretty well recovered. The little Infirmarian as busy in her office as ever, and all going on in the old way.[65] Five new candidates, with one of whom I believe we shall soon close.[66] The sixth English Sister has arrived—Miss Polding.[67] It seems so extraordinary not to find one vacant seat in the Refectory after all the dear Sisters we have parted in life and death.

Miss Edwards—who came while I was in Galway—is a sweet creature, quite refined, simple and interesting. Sister Marianne Beckett—a prime pet with Mother Cecilia—tho' not to be seen by every eye. She is very gentle and all that is desirable. Sister Juliann [Juliana] Hardman very satisfactory—all her doubts and fears have passed away. Sister Ann Wood very amiable tho' not so pleasing as others, from a natural disposition to silence and too much reserve. Sister Lucy Bond greatly improved, not near so much of the wild English girl. All have every sign of solid genuine piety and strong vocations to their state. Their Mother M. Cecilia is in better spirits than I ever saw her before, and looks very well. Her laughing at recreation is fully equal to dear little Mary Ann Agnes.[68] The Postulants for this house are all she could wish. Our venerated Arch-Bishop has promised to receive them, but cannot yet appoint the day. The Irish Sisters are going to treat the English to a great christening cake, to impress them with a sense of "Irish hospitality", and even now when some fruit is dividing, the English Srs. get the best share.

All well in Kingstown—just as we left them. The invalids are in Booterstown, all the rest well. Sister Mary, Lay Sister, is rather seriously ill since last night— some remote symptoms of fever—it may not be so.[69]

I have been able to go through the preparation for reception with the postulants every day for the past week—and with the novices for profession—for three days—and to go on with both parties to the last day.

The Revd. Mr. Parker from Liverpool—who brought the last postulant— says the convent in Birmingham is getting on very fast.[70] The basement story

---

64 Mary Augustine (Frances) Horan, who received the habit on February 27, 1840, evidently also used the name Mary Austin. Teresa Carton was still ailing.   65 The infirmarian is probably Teresa White's sister, Mary de Sales White.   66 The five new candidates are not new postulants, but rather those that on July 10, 1840 were approved by the Dublin Chapter for reception of the habit: "Anne Gogarty, Ann Wood, Juliana Hardman, Lucy Bond, and Eliza Edwards." Eliza Edwards had entered in May 1840—as the fifth English sister. Marianne Beckett, who entered on April 29, 1840, as one of the first four English sisters, is not listed as one of those who on July 10 requested to receive the habit, nor is she listed in the Baggot Street Register. Perhaps she is the sister with whom, as Catherine says, "I believe we shall soon close." Since Catherine continues to speak of the "five English sisters" who will receive the habit on August 10, it is probable that Marianne Beckett was one of them. She subsequently left the Baggot Street community, but then returned to the Sisters of Mercy in 1842, entering the Birr community on February 9.   67 Margaret Polding entered the Baggot Street community, for the Birmingham foundation, on July 23, 1840.   68 Catherine McAuley's beloved, deceased niece Mary Anne Agnes (Catherine) Macauley.   69 Mary (Eliza) Liston, who had entered on September 8, 1838.   70 William Parker, one of the curates in Liverpool, had accompanied Margaret Polding to Dublin.

is finished. He says Mr. Hardman, the generous father of our Sister, is every day on the spot—taking the deepest interest, and appears quite delighted. His very nice child will be a source of great comfort to him. She is all animation, at the account she hears of her good Father, and the general kind feeling that is manifested.

You have now a faithful statement of all our concerns. Tell Mr. Daly a particular friend of his, Mrs. Kennedy, called to enquire for the Galway branch, hoping most anxiously it would do well. I have not seen any of Sister M. C.'s[71] friends yet.

We got an immense wedding cake from Francis Marmion[72] ornamented with Doves, etc., etc. I told the little Cowleys I would give them all leave to get married if they would remember us so well. They seem to think Kate is looking another way. She is here very much and likes to be with Mother Cecilia. Mrs. Cowley begged me to tell you she was so sorry for not seeing you, but thought we were not to go till next day.

Doctor Fleming (my Bishop) is quite pleased with his child.[73]

I very much fear Doctor Browne[74] would not inflict many mortifications on me. He would let me pass off too quietly. Write soon—tell me how all goes on. I cannot make up any excuse to write to Father Daly as you say he is kind as ever—if you would complain, I could then alarm him by saying I would go to Galway immediately to look after my poor fatherless Children. Give my affectionate love to each [*illegible words*] & the children.[75] I often think of them.

All desire love to you and dear Mother Mary Catherine. Pray for me frequently and fervently and believe me always

your fondly attached
M. C. McAuley

My respects to the Bishop and affectionate regards to Father Daly, in which Sister de Sales unites.

Autograph: Galway

---

71 Mary Catherine Leahy's friends.   72 Francis Marmion, an attorney, was the brother of Mary Cecilia Marmion.   73 Dr. Michael Fleming, vicar apostolic of Newfoundland, visited Rome, England, and Ireland at this time. His "child" was presumably Mary Francis Creedon, a novice, who was preparing to found a community of Sisters of Mercy in Newfoundland. In calling Dr. Fleming "my bishop" Catherine may be confusing Newfoundland with Nova Scotia, where she had offered to go. She had never met William Frazer, vicar apostolic of Nova Scotia—only Dr. Richard Baptist O'Brien, president of St. Mary's College in Halifax. However, given her generosity of spirit, she may also have been thinking of going to Newfoundland—in which case, Dr. Fleming would indeed have been her bishop.   74 Dr. George J. Browne, bishop of Galway.   75 This autograph is severely damaged by ink blotches in several places. Sometimes the words under the blotches can be deciphered, but not in this sentence. In the following sentence the obscure words may be "pray for" rather than "think of."

180. To Sister M. Elizabeth Moore Limerick

Convent, Baggot Street
July 28, 1840

My Dearest Sister M. Elizabeth

I know you are anxious to hear of us all. I had a very fatiguing journey, travelled all night. Indeed from the letters sent me—I expected to find Sister Aloysius near death and three others very bad. She looks exceedingly thin and pale—has no cough—is now in Booterstown, which Dr. Corrigan prefers for her to any other air.

Poor Mother de Pazzi had a most severe attack a few days before my return. This was also written to me.

I had not been well for a month before I left Galway—and have still a cough and bad appetite.

Mrs. O'Reilly called here with Mrs. Baggott. She said she had promised you to do so. She spoke with the warmest regard of you and the Institution, said it was highly valued. I could not recollect any circumstance that inflicted such painful disappointment on me as not going to Limerick before my return, and I suppose it is for this very reason I was not permitted to go—because I desired it too ardently—and I rejoice now at my mortification, for it was a real one.

They talk seriously of the *absolute* necessity of my going to the reception of Srs. Joyce and McDonnell[76]—two as desirable nice sweet postulants as we ever had here or elsewhere. Their ceremony will be towards the end of Sept. If my cough continues, I could not prudently go—but if I am to travel—Limerick must be the road that will lead to Galway, and there I will remain until Father Daly comes for me. Travelling charges are to be remitted before we move. Indeed the Galway founders have been very generous in this and every other way.

You know the english postulants were quite strangers to me. They were only three days here before I left. They are all that is promising—every mark of real solid vocation—most edifying at all times, and at recreation the gayest of the gay. They seem so far to have corresponded very faithfully with the graces received— as each day there appears increased fervor and animation. A sixth has arrived since I came back. They renew my poor spirit greatly—fine creatures fit to adorn society, coming forward joyfully to consecrate themselves to the service of the poor for Christ's sake. This is some of the fire He cast on the earth—kindling.

Mr. Hardman, the father of one of them, is the chief contributer to the Convent now erecting.[77] It is getting on rapidly, and we hear he is on the spot every day rejoicing at its progress. His child—about 21—is as nice and pleasing as you can imagine. A few days after he proposed building the Convent—his daughter got the vocation as the reward of his generosity.

May God bless the poor Sisters of Mercy and make them very humble that they may not be unworthy of the distinguished blessings God has bestowed upon

---

76 The reception of Christina Joyce and Ismena McDonnell in Galway.   77 The convent now under construction in Birmingham, England.

them. If one spark of generous gratitude exists in the first born children[78]—they will labour to impress humility and meekness by example more than precept—the virtues recommended most by our Dear Saviour—and chiefly by example.[79]

The Bishop[80] has promised to receive the english Srs.—but has not yet appointed the day.

It looks quite extraordinary to see the Refectory without a vacant seat—after all we have parted in life and death, and four proposals since I returned. I do not know how many you have now.

Dr. Murphy has been with the Sisters in London. He says he will bring Sister M. Clare back to Cork. We hear the Bishop of London intends to press for another year. God will direct them.

I have told you all I can recollect. Write soon—not such a short letter as lately. Mother de P. is writing to Sr. Vincent. Give her my most affectionate love—and to all the dear Sisters, never forgetting Sisters Mary & Ann.[81]

Remember me to Mr. Nash, and present my best respects to your Bishop. Pray for me often and believe me always

your fondly attached
M. C. McAuley

Autograph: Limerick

181. To the Reverend John Hamilton

Convent, Baggot Street
July 30, 1840

Very Reverend Dear Sir

We have some english postulants, designed for an establishment in Birmingham. The Archbishop promised to receive them on the eighth or tenth of August, his Grace could not at the time say which. We have had letters from Doctor Wareing and Revd. Mr. Moore, requesting to be informed of the day appointed for the ceremony.[82]

---

78 Catherine McAuley frequently referred to the earliest Sisters of Mercy—those who then became the founders of other convents outside of Dublin—as the "first born."   79 Catherine often repeated her conviction that people learn more by example than by precept, and that Jesus taught chiefly by example.   80 Dr. Daniel Murray.   81 The sisters mentioned here are the Poor Clares—Mary Shanahan and Anne Hewitt. By this date, three new postulants were also in the Limerick community: Mary McNamara had entered on April 21, 1840; Anne McNamara, on June 17, 1840; and Mary Purcell, on June 24, 1840. Mary Teresa (Ellen) Bowles, now a novice, had entered on May 16, 1839, and received the habit on November 25, 1839. Having not been in Limerick since December 9, 1838, Catherine McAuley had not met these four women.   82 Dr. William Wareing had been vice president of St. Mary's College, Oscott, Birmingham. However, in May 1840 he was appointed vicar apostolic of the newly formed Eastern District in England (comprising the counties of Bedford, Buckingham, Cambridge, Huntingdon, Lincoln, Norfolk, Northampton, Rutland, and Suffolk). His episcopal consecration was scheduled for September 21, 1840. John Moore was a

Recollecting that you, V. Revd. Sir, assisted me a few years since when his Grace was out of town—in a matter somewhat similar—I feel induced to beg this favor of you. It is probable his Grace could now say, which of the days mentioned will be convenient to him, if you will be so very kind to ask him, that I may answer Doctor Wareing's letter.

I remain, Very Reverend Sir, with much respect, etc., etc.

Mary C. McAuley

Autograph: Dublin Diocese, Murray Papers AB3/34/15, no. 17

182. **To Sister M. Frances Warde**   **Convent, Baggot Street**
     Carlow   **July 30, 1840**

My Dearest Sister M. Frances

I know you will be gratified to hear that I am in your own old habitation once more, engaged in my usual occupations, etc. I left the Sisters in Galway with every prospect of doing well, and expect a new Convent will be erected for them very soon.

The english Sisters were strangers to me. I had only seen four, two or three days before I left. We have now six. They have so far manifested every sign of a true vocation. They are most interesting, two so playful that they afford amusement to all at recreation. One about 20—not looking so much—thinks she will be best suited for superioress at Birmingham, makes up most amusing reasons.[83] Revd. Mr. Colgan[84] came to the community room at recreation yesterday evening—he called her Mother Eliza, and she affects to think that all is now confirmed.

---

priest assigned to St. Chad's Cathedral, Birmingham (*Irish Catholic Directory* [1841] 110, 330, 378). In Bolster's text of this autograph letter, "Wareing" is incorrectly read as "Manning" (*Correspondence* 142). Dr. Wareing and Father Moore were supporters of the Birmingham postulants and were evidently planning to come to their reception ceremony as representatives of Dr. Thomas Walsh, vicar apostolic of the Central (formerly, Midland) District. John Moore was asked to preach at the ceremony which was eventually scheduled for August 10, 1840 (*Irish Catholic Directory* [1841] 388). Dr. Wareing was presumably the uncle of Juliana Hardman, the brother of her deceased mother Lydia Wareing Hardman, John Hardman, Sr.'s second wife. I am extremely grateful to Barbara Jeffery, RSM, archivist in Birmingham, for information about Juliana Hardman's family.   83 Eliza Edwards, a native of St. Bride's parish, London, had entered on May 12, 1840, according to the Birmingham Register—while Catherine McAuley was in Galway.   84 Richard Colgan, OCC, a member of the Calced Carmelites in Dublin, had been in Rome on business in 1840. By the end of 1840, he became prior of the Calced Carmelite community on Whitefriar Street. He is said to have offered, when in Rome, to translate the Rule and Constitutions of the Sisters of Mercy into Italian (not Latin), prior to the deliberations of the Congregation for the Propagation of the Faith and its consultor (Degnan 248). The document was, in fact, dealt with and approved in Italian translation. Richard Colgan may also be the unnamed priest "coming to Ireland" to whom Catherine McAuley refers in Letter 186.

We get a delightful description of the Convent. Dr. Murphy & Dr. Mayley [Meyley?] have seen it.[85] Indeed it could not be too nice—for the first inhabitants that God has destined for it. May He continue his blessings to them.

I found all here rather better than I expected. Sister Aloysius—though very thin and looking exceedingly delicate—has no cough or other dangerous symptoms. Little Sr. Mary Teresa had one of her low tedious fevers—she is recovering. Our poor indefatigable Teresa[86]—in the same state, thin as possible, bad rest and scarcely any appetite—doing more for the Institution than ever. Every action seems to be followed by a blessing. She is most patient—and amiable in every way.

All the other Lay sisters very good. Sr. Agatha,[87] head laundress—very diligent—getting on pretty well. These things take time. The expense of coal is very great—sometimes a ton a week. You may suppose the work must be very great that would leave much surplus after this—soap, etc., etc.—but the fire will not cost more when the work is much encreased—as the hot closet must be prepared in the same manner for a small or large quantity. We have not lost anything of consequence and only a few borders of fashionable night caps torn, etc., etc.

They are going on well in Kingstown. Such a number of persons to be instructed on Sunday, that they cannot sit down.

All the delicate flock in Booterstown—except my poor Teresa who clings to her charitable employment. I am expected to return to Galway for the reception of the last two postulants, but fear I shall not be able. I have a cough for six weeks—and they say I am very thin. I may be well enough by September if God pleases.

I am very glad to hear Dr. Fitzgerald is so much better. Give my affectionate regards to him. I know I shall be interrupted presently, so will not go farther lest I miss this post. Give my best love to all the dear Sisters, and believe me

your fondly attached
M. C. McAuley

Remember me to Father Maher, Father Dan, etc., etc.

Autograph: Silver Spring

85 Dr. Murphy may be Dr. John Murphy, the bishop of Cork, but "Dr. Mayley" or "Meyley," as in the autograph, is confusing. Neumann (228) and Bolster (143) both read this name as "Meyler," but it seems strange that Catherine McAuley would misspell the name of Dr. Walter Meyler, now Dean Meyler, about whom she had so frequently written. She may be referring to Dr. John Miley, a curate at St. Mary's, Dublin—and spelling his name as she pronounced it—or to another priest travelling with Dr. Murphy. The spelling and handwriting in this letter are occasionally awry. 86 Teresa Carton.   87 Mary Agatha (Marianne) Brennan had entered the Baggot Street community as a lay sister on September 24, 1834, and professed her vows on July 1, 1837. She will die on December 27, 1841, six weeks after the death of Catherine McAuley.

August–October 1840

In August 1840 Catherine McAuley focused her energies on matters at Baggot Street: planning the August 10 reception ceremony for six postulants, most of them preparing for the foundation in Birmingham to be launched a year later; assessing the health of Mary Aloysius Scott and arranging for her to go to Carlow at the end of the annual retreat; teaching the young women in the House of Mercy how to do commercial laundry without losing or ruining their customers' clothing; responding, hopefully but indefinitely, to Dr. Thomas Walsh's request for a future foundation in Nottingham, England; welcoming a seventh young woman who wished to be part of the foundation in Birmingham; and engaging in a competitive "concert" of sighing and moaning with Mary de Pazzi Delany to jostle her assistant out of a slump.

But Catherine was tired, and privately nursing the persistent cough she had brought back from Galway. The 77-year-old Andrew Fitzgerald knew this. In one of the most tender of the extant letters she received, he pleaded with her to come to Carlow for a visit, or for the August retreat: "come to the quiet and calm residence of your dear children here. A few days with us would renovate both body and mind, and send you home fresh for new toils and labors ... have compassion on yourself and on so many interested in you." He closed his letter begging her to come for "good air" and acknowledging that "With all the affections of my heart, I remain, my dearest, your ever attached in Christ." The reception on August 10 prevented her going to Carlow for the needed "repairs" that he, though "almost blind," had so well divined (Letter 185).

September and October brought Catherine additional concerns: her nephew James, now living in Blackrock, appeared to be in the final stages of consumption; Anna Maria Maher, the young Carlow woman, still wanted to find a Mercy convent where her small dowry would be acceptable to the local bishop or his deputy; plans had to be made for a profession and reception ceremony at Baggot Street on September 24, and then for her own immediate departure for the reception ceremony in Galway on October 1. By mid October she had travelled well over one hundred miles across the country four times in five months—from Dublin to Galway and the reverse.

The need to return "immediately" from Galway to Dublin on July 6 had meant that she could not visit Limerick on her way home, nor have the comfort of seeing again her good friend and confidante Elizabeth Moore. Throughout August she entertained the hope that she could go to Limerick on the way to the reception ceremony in Galway. But this plan too was dashed by the date set for the Baggot Street ceremony (September 24) and the consequent need to go straight to Galway. Finally, in early October she was able to visit Limerick on her way back from Galway; it would be her last visit with that Mercy community, and her first since the death of Mary Teresa Vincent Potter in March 1840.

Catherine also hoped to visit Carlow on her return to Dublin, but unexpected demands intervened. Dr. Griffiths of London requested (wisely, as it turned out) that the Baggot Street community loan two professed sisters to Bermondsey; one of these was to be Mary de Sales White, Catherine's travelling companion to Galway and Limerick; but while they were in Limerick, Father Peter Butler, still ailing, arrived in Dublin to escort the two to England. So, once again, Catherine had to rush back to Dublin on October 10 or 11 to put Mary de Sales and Mary Xavier O'Connell on the boat on October 12. On October 13, she wrote: "Thank God, I am at rest again, and now I think the name of another foundation would make me sick—but they say I would get up again" (Letter 193).

Meanwhile unofficial word had been circulating in Ireland since early August that the Congregation for the Propagation of the Faith in Rome had forwarded the Rule and Constitutions of the Sisters of Mercy to Gregory XVI for papal confirmation, but Catherine McAuley had heard nothing directly. So on October 14, she wrote, probably with clerical guidance, to Cardinal Fransoni, Prefect of Propaganda Fide, soliciting "the valuable aid which your Eminence can afford" (Letter 194).

183. To the Reverend John Hamilton

Sheepwalk
August 1, 1840

Dear Hamilton

I am just thinking how gratified you must have been this morning, when the Post-Man passed by, without handing you a letter to check your Mathewistical ardour. Well then, I suppose your arrangement must go on; and my excuse for having refused that which is now granted will be that the present affair was settled during my absence. The blame will then fall on the proper head ...[1]

I mentioned the 8th Inst. as the earliest day that I could promise to attend Mrs. McAuley. But if she will prefer the 10th I will hold myself in readiness, on receiving due notice, to accommodate her.[2]

1 John Hamilton may have been trying to arrange the sermon on behalf of the Widows Asylum, Clarendon Street, which Theobald Mathew gave in St. Mary's Pro-Cathedral, Marlborough Street, Dublin on September 27, 1840, and the event the next day at which Father Mathew administered the pledge of total abstinence to 65,000 persons (*Irish Catholic Directory* [1842] 394). Since Theobald Mathew's sheer presence would draw thousands, the gentle-tempered Dr. Murray was evidently trying to distance himself from the spectacle. However, Kerr notes that "Murray, unlike some of the bishops, was a friend of the temperance leader, and had welcomed him warmly to his diocese" (262). 2 Heeding Catherine McAuley's request (Letter 181), John Hamilton had asked Dr. Murray to choose the date for the reception of the English postulants. Catherine subsequently settled on August 10.

Our four days of Confirmation have been little more than days of amusement; and I am now enjoying the most delightful repose, and renovating this old shatter'd frame by large draughts of the balmy air which first set the springs of life agoing and put it into motion ...3

Regards, etc. as usual.

Most truly yours
+ D. Murray

Excerpts from Autograph: Dublin Diocese, Hamilton Papers P1/35/1–2, no. 105

184. **To Sister M. Frances Warde**   **Convent**
    Carlow   **August 1, 1840**

My Dearest Sister Mary Frances

I would with delight—and without any hesitation—do exactly as you have recommended, but for the following circumstance.4 The time for receiving the english postulants is come. I felt exceedingly anxious that Doctor Murray should perform the ceremony in order to make the most pious impression on their minds. He is greatly engaged just now administering Confirmation in the Co. Wicklow & there about. The only days he could name for us are the 8th or 10th of this month. We must come out of retreat for the purpose, and will joyfully do so. His Grace is looking so heavenly and venerable now, the english Sisters never will forget him. The effect will be most valuable to them, and we esteem it so great a favor to get him that we would not make any difficulty.

I am writing this in a great hurry—before Mr. O'Hanlon comes. I wish very much Sister Aloysius was in Carlow for a little time. She is not improving much. Her loss would be felt indeed, she is so much beloved by all. After the retreat I will urge her going. She is afraid of giving trouble—though indeed she never gives any that could be avoided. Still in her present state she requires assistance.

God bless you. Pray for your own old affectionate Mother

M. C. McAuley

I should tell [you] that the Bishop is aware that we are to come out of retreat for the ceremony day—which he assents to.5

My cough is better.

Autograph: Silver Spring

3 Daniel Murray was born on a farm at Sheepwalk, Arklow, Co. Wicklow on April 18, 1768, and had family still living there (Kerr 251).   4 Frances Warde had, it seems, invited Catherine McAuley to come to Carlow for a visit, perhaps even for the annual retreat on August 7–14, prior to the feast of the Assumption of the Blessed Virgin Mary (August 15).   5 Since this letter was written on the same day as Letter 183, Catherine is not yet aware that the reception ceremony can take place on August 10.

185. **To Catherine McAuley**   Carlow
                                        August 4, 1840

My dear Friend

I do not think that my holy Patron, St. Dominick,[6] ever received more sincere devotional feelings from me, his unworthy son, than I offered him this day. You are not aware that you contributed to excite this warmth of devotion. Yet so it is. The dear Sisters of Mercy attended my Mass in the College—and partook with me of the Bread of Life. Could my heart be cold is such company—was it not you, who assisted by the Holy Spirit formed that company, and gave them to us, to dispense and obtain Mercy. Truly I may say that God took you out of darkness to spread his light, and are you not still under his vocation spreading it, in humility of heart, knowing that of yourself you are *nothing*, but everything in him who strengthens you.

It is delightful to reflect on the success of your late mission. England, as in former times, sends her virgins amongst us to be taught how Ireland has learned from long suffering to be compassionate towards human misery; and God has made you an agent for these purposes. See now the big house, the purpose of which could not be devised by the wise ones of this world, and the special purpose of which, there was a time, you could not distinctly see. Now what a teeming mother, her children reared under one roof, proclaiming in distant quarters the mercies of God to his people. How you should be humbled, to think that God had selected you with all the infirmities that encompass you, to diffuse His bounty there [thus?] to his suffering children. Now, dear friend, glory in these infirmities that the power of Christ may still be perfected in you.

But I must beg of you to think sometimes that you carry the treasure of God in a fragile vessel, liable to break and chink, and requiring frequent repairs. To effect those,[7] you cannot have leisure amidst the various intrusions of all immediately about you. Break from them, and come to the quiet and calm residence of your dear children here. A few days with us would renovate both body and mind, and send you home fresh for new toils and labors. Now, dearest Friend, may I in union with all here earnestly beg of you to have compassion on yourself and on so many interested in you to come down here as soon as possible. Remember God has given you in charge your health, which you employ in his service. Come to us, and we shall send you back loaded with that blessing. Remember, I hate that cough which annoys you, but here we have a cure for it, and tell Eliza if she comes, she shall have a visit from her father.[8] I am sure she has too much filial piety to refuse that favour to the best of Parents.

---

6 St. Dominic (1170–1221) was the founder of the Order of Preachers, of which Dr. Andrew Fitzgerald, the president of Carlow College, was a distinguished member.   7 That is, those bodily "repairs."   8 Mary Aloysius (Elizabeth) Scott was born in the town of Kilkenny. Andrew Fitzgerald, also a native of Kilkenny, evidently knew her father, Barnaby Scott, and knew her well enough to continue to call her Eliza.

Though almost blind, I can scarcely give up scribbling to you, as long as the sheet permits. I will conclude with earnestly repeating to you your obligation of coming down to our good air and obliging Eliza to accompany you.

With all the affections of my heart, I remain, my dearest,

your ever attached in Christ
Andrew Fitzgerald[9]

Autograph: Silver Spring

186. To Sister M. Frances Warde   [Baggot Street]
    Carlow   Wednesday, August 5, 1840

My Dear Sister Mary Frances

I have it only just in my power to tell you that our ceremony is appointed for Monday the 10th. I hope we may be so fortunate as to see dear Father Maher. You say Doctor Cullen[10] might call during the retreat. I would of course see him. We are expecting Dean Gaffney[11] will give us some instructions, but you know he disappoints sometimes.

Two english young Ladies and a Priest have arrived at the Shelbourne this morning for the ceremony. It is said one has a vocation.[12] As we could not answer their enquiries about the day fixed, they came lest they should be late.

Sister Aloysius is very grateful for your affectionate letter, and desires me to answer it as I wish, which is that she should go[13]—indeed, any trouble she gives will be found a pleasure. Immediately after the retreat, please God, I will get Mr. Farrelly to accompany her.[14] I cannot move while these english persons are coming—it is said we shall have more postulants.

9 Catherine McAuley was beloved by many, but this letter from Andrew Fitzgerald, who was now seventy-seven years old, is surely one of the most tender of the extant letters she received.   10 Dr. Paul Cullen, a nephew of James Maher in Carlow and rector of the Irish College in Rome, had numerous family members in Counties Carlow and Kildare and was currently home in Ireland for his summer holiday.   11 Myles Gaffney, a priest of the Dublin archdiocese and dean of St. Patrick's College, Maynooth, directed the annual retreat at Baggot Street in 1832 and perhaps in other years, as well as in 1840. He also assisted Catherine McAuley to compose two original chapters of the Mercy Rule and Constitutions, though precisely how is not known. A close friend and supporter of the Baggot Street community, he will accompany the founding party to Birmingham in August 1841. After Catherine McAuley's death he wrote a long, appreciative letter that is appended to several of the early biographical manuscripts about her (see Sullivan, *Catherine McAuley* 126–27, 191–92), and he is assumed to be the author of the anonymous article on Catherine McAuley and the Sisters of Mercy that was published in the *Dublin Review* in March 1847 (Muldrey 56–7, 348–49, 356–57).   12 John Moore will preach at the reception ceremony on August 10, 1840. Caroline Borini will enter the Sisters of Mercy at Baggot Street on August 15, 1840. A year later she will become part of the Birmingham foundation.   13 On August 14 or 15, Catherine McAuley will send Mary Aloysius Scott to Carlow, in an effort to restore her health. James Maher will accompany her (Carlow Annals).   14 This may be Father Paul Ferrally (or Farrelly) of the Jesuit community on Upper

I am not surprised at what you say as to the confirmation of our Rule—though we have been led to expect it all the past month—but these matters seldom go on so rapidly at the Holy See. It is however certain that the process of examination has been gone through—and most strong promises made for the conclusion, so much that a Priest coming to Ireland was asked could he wait a few weeks to carry it with him. Yet I suppose all possible interest and attention may be necessary to prevent its being delayed.[15]

Poor Sister de Pazzi had a severe attack a few days before my return, and she is now—(as you may well know)—in great agitation at the retreat being interrupted and parting Sister M. Aloysius. May God preserve her from any return.

Pray for our poor retreats—five english and one Irish girl.[16] God bless you and all with you.

Your ever affectionate
M. C. McAuley

Autograph: Silver Spring

187. To John Hardman, Esq. [Mid 1840]

Instructions for Works at the Birmingham Convent[17]

I herewith send the drawings for the convent in which you will perceive I have studied the greatest economy, but if you observe anything in which a still further saving may be effected, pray mention it.

Gardiner Street, Dublin. However, see note 13. 15 Catherine McAuley had no doubt heard indirectly of the positive decision on July 20, 1840 of the Sacred Congregation for the Propagation of the Faith (Letter 178), recommending to Gregory XVI confirmation of the Rule and Constitutions of the Sisters of Mercy. Probably James Maher and others in Carlow were urging Dr. Paul Cullen to see what he could do to hasten the process of confirmation, when he returned to Rome after his visit to Ireland. 16 Those making their retreat prior to reception of the habit on August 10 were the English sisters, Juliana Hardman, Lucy Bond, Ann Wood, Eliza Edwards, and possibly Marianne Beckett, as well as Anne Gogarty. However, the Acts of the Dublin Chapter of professed sisters, held on July 10, does not include Marianne Beckett among those admitted to reception of the habit. The Chapter book may be in error, and Marianne may in fact have received the habit; or the Chapter book may be correct, and Marianne may not have requested the habit. She left the Baggot Street community sometime before January 1841, though exactly when is not known. The "Annals" in the *Irish Catholic Directory* for 1841 lists all the clergy who attended the reception, but not the sisters who received the habit. The Dublin Register does not list Marianne because she did not profess vows in Dublin; she is listed in the Birr Register, but with only those dates relevant to her membership in that community, which she entered on February 9, 1842. The English woman Margaret Polding, who entered on July 22 or 23, had not yet served the three months probation normally required before reception of the habit when the sister is destined for a new foundation. 17 The autograph of these instructions written by Augustus Welby Pugin, the architect of the Birmingham convent under construction in 1840–1841, is addressed to "John Hardman, Esq." On side four of the folded sheet, in the handwriting of John Hardman, Sr., or of his son, John Hardman, Jr., is

I intend 2 paints for all the walls with blue headors occasionally, work in pattern.

I wish the roof tiled with blue tile over the front part of building & chapel, but over cells may be slated as well as cloisters.

As regards joist flooring boards & roof over kitchen & offices, I leave the dimentions to you, as you must estimate for them, as light as can be consistent with the required strength.

The partitions between cells of nuns may be exceedingly light & plastered, but the partitions which run up & down must be well framed as they will help to carry the joist[18]—for the whole bearing is too long without. The upper partitions over them must help the roof as the walls are so much lower than the ceiling of the upper storey, I cannot get a tie beam to the principals—these partitions above and below must be well framed and well braced and then plastered on both sides. The whole of the rooms, alleys, etc. are quite plain plastering without any moulding whatever, a plain chamfered skirting 4¾ round the rooms[19]—cloister and cell windows to be framed in deal—the rafters of cloisters dressed & stained, plastered between.

The rooms marked paving are blue & red tile like Derby. The paving of chapel not to be estimated for except the altar steps which will be of inlaid[?] stone. You will observe which are stone: entrance doorway, inner door, door into chapel. All the others are wooden door frames—doors according to drawing, staircase according to drawing.

Lead lights and quarries with casements to windows

Fire places according to drawing

You must arrange a stove [stone?] chamber under the chapel—which must be arced over—with an entrance door.

A cess pool must be provided for privies and a flue for hot air to be carried from stove [stone?] chamber under chapel & brought up by the side of kitchen fire place—as shown in dotted lines.

Front wall according to plan.

Items not in the contract:

---

written this notation: "Mr. Pugin's Instructions for the Building the Convent to Mr. Myers for him to make out the particulars and to Estimate for the same." Mr. Myers was presumably the builder. Since these almost illegible instructions seem to take into account Catherine McAuley's preference –for "a plain simple durable building," as stated in Letter 160, it is conceivable that when John Moore came to Dublin on August 5 (see Letter 186), he brought them with him to share with her, to reassure her about Pugin's design of the Birmingham convent, in contrast to that in Bermondsey. In Letter 190 to Dr. Thomas Walsh she says she has had "a delightful description of the Convent ... I am not so much afraid of Mr. Pugin as I was." However, it is possible that these instructions were written much earlier, when construction was just beginning (see Letters 148 and 182).   18 The joists of the hallway were the parallel timbers that would hold up the laths of the ceiling and the floor of the next storey, as well as the roof of the convent.   19 Probably Pugin is describing the beveled baseboards he wished to be placed around the walls of the rooms.

Chapel floor excepting the altar part
Grates
Bell
Fittings of chapel

[Augustus Welby Pugin][20]

Autograph: Birmingham

188. **To Dr. Thomas Walsh**   **Convent, Baggot Street**
Nottingham   **August 5, 1840**

My Lord

I had it not in my power until this day to inform you that our ceremony of religious clothing is appointed for Monday the 10th Inst. His Grace, the Archbishop, has most kindly promised to perform it, though engaged very much just now administering the Sacrament of Confirmation in the towns and villages surrounding Dublin, and it is indeed in some degree inconsiderate to ask him to do anything that might be spared him. But on this occasion we are so anxious to make a deep impression, which his venerable appearance and most pious manner is particularly calculated to produce.

They are going through their retreat with great attention and fervor. The Revd. Mr. Moore and two ladies arrived this day.[21] Miss Polding came on Saint Magdelin's day[22]—we like her—and find her very promising so far.

We have had a delightful description of the Convent in Birmingham. Every person who has seen it admires it. I am not so much afraid of Mr. Pugin as I was. He is so fond of high walls and few windows.

At present, my Lord, I cannot say what might be done for the new congregation you mention, but in some time hence we might make an arrangement. You will find, please God, that the Institution in Birmingham will soon begin to spread. From all I can learn, the prospect of progress is very good.[23]

---

20 Catherine McAuley and Augustus Welby Pugin may have met in late August or early September 1841 when she went to England to found the Convent of Mercy in Handsworth, Birmingham, the second foundation of the Sisters of Mercy in England. To Pugin's credit as an architect, the beautiful convent he designed, whose construction he supervised, is still functioning today as a convent and heritage center of the Sisters of Mercy.   21 John Moore, Caroline Borini, and another unidentified young woman arrived at the Shelbourne Hotel in Dublin on August 5, in order to be present in time for the upcoming reception ceremony.   22 Margaret Polding may have entered the Baggot Street community on July 22, the feast day of St. Mary Magdalen. The Birmingham Register says she entered on July 23.   23 Evidently Dr. Walsh had written to ask Catherine McAuley whether a foundation of Sisters of Mercy could also be made in Nottingham. Mary Austin Carroll notes: "After the appointment of Bishop [Nicholas] Wiseman as coadjutor to the Midland district [on May 11, 1840], Bishop Walsh resided chiefly at Nottingham, and his lordship was desirous that a Convent of Mercy should be established in that town as soon as Sisters could be spared from St. Mary's." As Catherine McAuley predicted, on February 6, 1844, a foundation was established in Nottingham, from Birmingham, with Mary Angela (Caroline) Borini as superior (*Leaves* 2:327).

Your children in religion are praying most fervently for you, particularly your dear Juliana, who was quite delighted when she heard her uncle was a Bishop.[24] They are to pray most earnestly when prostrate at the altar—and I am sure, my Lord, such pure innocent supplicants will not be unfruitful.

Begging you to remember us, I have the honor to remain
My Lord, most respectfully, etc., etc.
Mary C. McAuley

Autograph: Birmingham

189. To Sister M. Frances Warde   [Baggot Street]
   Carlow   [August 17, 1840]

My Dearest Sister M. Frances

I am quite uneasy at not getting a few lines this day, to say how our dear Sr. Aloysius feels after her journey. Mother de Pazzi says she is confined to bed, and that you wait till she is better. I trust in God it is not so. Will you tell me how she seems, and if her appetite is improving—it had not time yet.[25]

All are well here—making great resolutions to benefit by the excellent instructions we got during retreat.[26] Letters from Galway this morning—all going on well. We have a delightful new postulant here who came to the ceremony and would not go back.[27] She has put on the dress and looks so nice. Sister Aloy[sius] will tell you all the news of ceremony, etc.

Give my affectionate love to each and believe me ever your attached
M. C. McAuley

Autograph: Pittsburgh

24 Dr. William Wareing, vice president of St. Mary's College, Oscott, Birmingham, was named vicar apostolic of the Eastern District of England on May 11, 1840, and was scheduled to be consecrated on September 21, 1840 (*Irish Catholic Directory* [1841] 110, 378). It seems likely that he was Juliana Hardman's uncle. In Letter 181, Catherine McAuley reports that he planned to attend the reception ceremony of the sisters destined for Birmingham. In late April 1840 he had apparently escorted the first four of them to Dublin (Carroll, *Leaves* 2:309). 25 The ailing Mary Aloysius Scott had left Baggot Street for Carlow probably on August 14 or 15, accompanied by Father James Maher. There was, of course, "not time yet"—for a good appetite or for a considered report from Carlow—but Catherine McAuley is anxious about her sick sister, and apparently expected Frances Warde to write immediately. Although this autograph letter is undated, the Dublin postmark is "AU 17, 1840"; the Carlow mark is "AU 18, 1840." 26 Myles Gaffney, dean of St. Patrick's College, Maynooth, had preached the annual retreat at Baggot Street. 27 Caroline Borini entered the Baggot Street community, for the Birmingham foundation, on August 15, 1840, according to the Birmingham Register.

190. **To Sister Mary Ann Doyle**   Convent, Baggot Street
     Tullamore   August 20, 1840

My Dear Sister M. Ann

I had a letter this day from Limerick. Sr. E[28] says you are about to send two Srs. to learn the education system—indeed she speaks as if you were to be one. Surely not. I suppose you will never be one of the appointed teachers, though you might oversee. Would it not be better to try to get a well qualified Monitress from the Model School—until your Sisters would know the method. They sent us such a one from Limerick, quite a poor girl. I should think they could send you one. She should be paid a small salery [*sic*] out of what the board allows. I do not think they permit any one to attend the Model School in Dublin except those who are settled with them for the purpose and remain all day—paying a certain fee.[29]

There could not be a more delightful school than they have in Limerick—if one of your Sisters went there Sister Harnett, who is exceedingly clever, would teach her in a very short time—if a Priest could be met to accompany her. I need not add that you have this house at your command if you think of Dublin.

Sr. M. Cecilia hurries me lest Sr. M. Teresa should not have her note in time to answer it.[30]

I am much better—the cough almost gone. Write to me soon—and tell me how all goes on. Sr. M. Cecilia was delighted to get a note from her old favorite.

God bless you. Give my affectionate love to each and believe me always

                                                                  your attached
                                                                  M. C. McAuley

Sister Angela has moved into her new Convent.[31]

Autograph: Bermondsey

---

28 Mary Elizabeth Moore, superior in Limerick.   29 As part of the construction of the new convent in Tullamore, new schoolrooms were provided. Evidently Mary Ann Doyle, the superior in Tullamore, now planned to have the school affiliated with the national school system, once the teachers were prepared to meet its standards. The mode of instruction Catherine McAuley recommends is the Lancastrian method wherein a team of monitresses is employed to hear the students' lessons after they have received instruction from a head teacher or have studied the material on their own. Catherine advocates drawing on the expertise of Mary Vincent Harnett in Limerick, urging Mary Ann Doyle not to burden herself with a teaching role in addition to her other duties as superior. Model Schools were established in some of the major cities of Ireland to prepare teachers and monitresses for the national system, the one in Dublin apparently requiring a prior commitment to the Dublin schools. In the next paragraph Catherine seems to suggest that a sister could also study in the school at Baggot Street for service in Tullamore.   30 Mary Cecilia Marmion, and Mary Teresa Purcell in Tullamore.   31 Mary Angela Dunne in Charleville.

191. To Sister M. Elizabeth Moore
Limerick

Convent, Baggot Street
September 7, 1840

My Dearest Sister Mary Elizabeth

I believe I will resolve never to fix any little plan for my own gratification, that has not some particular duty, or appointed work connected with it. It is now determined that Sisters O'Connor and Boylan are to be professed on the 24th, from which I dare not be absent.[32]

Sister Aloysius in Carlow, little Sr. M. Teresa[33] in Booterstown recovering, Mother de Pazzi very nervous. It is decreed that I am to be in Galway on the first of October for what Mr. Daly terms the grand reception. Father Mathew to preach. I will not venture even to hope that I shall return by Limerick, but my Dear Sr. M. E., do not speak of my going. It has been talked of in Dublin without my asking leave—and in consequence of the report, I have had a most pressing letter from Mr. Croke to go see the Sisters in their new Convent. He will be quite offended if he hears I am in Limerick—and indeed I am not able to add forty miles to my long journey—by going & returning to Charleville. Could I not steal in and away—would Father Fitzgibbon publish me.[34]

My cough is gone—and I am getting quite strong.

I have just had a visit from Miss Roach—she says Mrs. Moore is one of the greatest favorites in Limerick. Dear Sr. Potter's cousin called.[35] She gives a romantic description of the little organ—chapel, etc., etc. How I long to see and hear it. I will not promise myself that comfort.

I began this immediately after the 12 o'c prayers—it is now near two. I have been so much interrupted. I must write to Mother Mary Clare who is to remain in England till Easter—her Bishop, tho' determined to bring her back, has been prevailed on.[36] Our english postulants go on very well.

I hope you will soon begin to spread.[37] Never give more than two Sisters and—let your agreement be that when four enter one of yours is to return. If I

---

32 Mary Agnes O'Connor, the future founder of the Sisters of Mercy in New York City (1846), and Mary Frances Boylan, a future member of the community in Liverpool, were scheduled to profess their vows on September 24, 1840. Catherine had hoped the profession would be earlier, so she could go to Limerick *before* she had to be in Galway for the reception ceremony on October 1. 33 Mary Teresa (Catherine) White. 34 Catherine now hopes to stop in Limerick *after* her trip to Galway, but she cannot also visit the sisters in Charleville, even though the parish priest, Thomas Croke, is pressing her to come. The full journey to Galway, then Limerick, and back to Dublin from Limerick, without going to Charleville, will be about 315 miles by stage coach, at the rate of about six miles an hour. Yet she is concerned that word of her coming to Limerick may be spread by Henry Fitzgibbon, a curate in St. Mary's parish where the Limerick convent is located (*Irish Catholic Directory* [1840] 296). 35 This woman is Ellen Griffin who entered the Limerick community on November 14, 1840, subsequently taking the name Mary Aloysius. 36 At the entreaty of Dr. Thomas Griffiths, Dr. John Murphy, bishop of Cork, agreed that Mary Clare Moore could remain as superior in Bermondsey until after Easter 1841. 37 Numerous foundations were made from Limerick, beginning in 1844 with foundations in Kinsale and Killarney, followed by Mallow

was as wise when we began as I am now in this particular, I would have Sisters returning, who would keep up the Mother House,[38] and though it should be painful to them, yet in justice the contract must be kept—and the opportunity of embracing mortification would also be afforded. As for example, if Sister Vincent had to return at the expiration of 2 years—Sister Purcell— Sr. M. J. Warde—Sr. Trenor, what renewed animation & strength it would give to the poor old concern—and the new ones not suffer.[39]

I have just had a letter from Galway. They are in great want of assistance and would take a nice young postulant with £200, but she must be educated, in modern style, not as a teacher—it would serve them greatly just now. You are such a good look out—perhaps you would cast your eye on one—provided she had not means enough for you—as you may now take time and look high.[40]

Write to me when you have time.

Pray for your ever affectionate
M. C. McAuley

Love to Dear Sr. Vincent—and all my grandchildren.

Tuesday—could not finish for yesterday's post.

Autograph: Silver Spring

192. To Sister Teresa Carton   [Galway]
   Baggot Street   [c. October 5, 1840][41]

My Dearest Sister Teresa

I can scarcely believe that so many days have passed since I left dear Baggot St.—such constant business of one kind or other going on here. We had high Mass & Benediction here yesterday.

(1845), Glasgow (1849), Roscommon (1853), Ennis (1854), and Edinburgh (1858)—all before Mary Elizabeth Moore's death in 1868.   **38** The Mercy convent on Baggot Street, Dublin was the "mother house" not in any governmental sense, but simply spiritually: as a source of spiritual guidance, the site of the original inspiration and vocation of the Sisters of Mercy, the place where the leaders of the first foundations outside of Dublin received their initial training as Sisters of Mercy. The heart of the maternal role played by this house was of course the character and spirit of Catherine McAuley herself, its founder and leader.   **39** Mary Vincent Harnett (Limerick), Mary Teresa Purcell (Tullamore), Mary Josephine Warde (Cork), and Mary Josephine Trennor (Carlow) were each the "second" sister from Baggot Street at the time of the founding of their respective convents. Whenever the potential for leadership seemed to decline at Baggot Street, Catherine McAuley often wished to have these "heads" back in Dublin again. The irony is that new leaders at Baggot Street always seemed to emerge when needed, as the following decades demonstrated.   **40** Catherine often encouraged the various foundations to help one another grow by directing postulants to the ones in need of additional members.   **41** Catherine must have left Dublin shortly after the profession ceremony on Thursday, September 24, arriving in Galway no later than Wednesday, September 30, for the reception ceremony there on October 1. The "high Mass and Benediction here yesterday"

The House of Mercy is very nicely appointed—I will bring you a suit of the uniform dress. They are going to commence a Laundry. Two go to situations today & 2 more come in—all are much interested & greatly pleased. The inhabitants say it is the best Institution that ever was in Galway.[42] I am interrupted and will be obliged to continue so.

I was ill on Wednesday night and from six o'c Thursday morning—my stomach & just as when I was here before.[43] Thank God I have been pretty well since, but very anxious to get away. I find it is the spa-kind of water which affects me.

I hope to find all as well as I left. Give my affectionate love to each. God bless you, my Dear Sister Teresa.

Your ever affectionate
M. C. M.

Autograph: Dublin, Mercy

193. To Sister M. Frances Warde　　　　　　　　　　　**Baggot St.**
Carlow　　　　　　　　　　　　　　　　　　　　**October 12, 1840**

My ever Dear Child and Sister

We were obliged to hasten back here—as the Revd. Mr. Butler arrived to conduct Sisters M. de Sales and M. Xavier to London. His health is so bad, he is quite impatient to return lest the weather should change—but I am now writing as if you were always with me and knew as formerly all the affairs.[44]

(noted in paragraph one of this letter) must have occurred on Sunday, October 4, which suggests that this undated letter was written on or near October 5. Since Catherine did, in fact, go to Limerick on her return journey to Dublin, as evidenced by Letters 193 and 195, and since she also had to be back in Dublin by October 11 (in order to put Mary de Sales White, one of her travelling companions, on the boat to England on October 12, as noted in Letter 193), she probably visited Limerick around October 6–10. Neumann (235) and Bolster (150) both date this letter October 9, but that date is too late for a letter written from Galway, where Catherine was affected by the "spa-kind of water." This letter, addressed on the cover simply to "My Dear Sister Teresa" was evidently enclosed in another letter to Baggot Street, now no longer extant. 42 Galway records indicate that "During the early years at St. Vincent's [the convent in Galway] there was a House of Mercy where poor girls of good character were trained in domestic work. This had to be given up when the Industrial School was acquired [some time after 1851]" (*Convent* 17, 22). 43 Catherine's illness probably occurred on Wednesday night, September 30, and on the morning of October 1, the day Mary Joseph (Christina) Joyce and Mary de Sales (Ismena) McDonnell received the habit. Clarke recounts Mary de Sales's future life (10–14). 44 Catherine McAuley had planned to visit Carlow on the way from Limerick to Dublin, but Peter Butler of Bermondsey, acting on the request of Dr. Thomas Griffiths of London (see paragraph two) had already arrived in Dublin to escort the two sisters to be lent to Bermondsey: Mary de Sales White, who had been one of Catherine's travelling companions on the trip to Galway, and Mary Xavier O'Connell. Consequently, Catherine and Mary de Sales had to hurry back to Dublin, foregoing a visit to Carlow. They left Mary Teresa (Catherine) White in Limerick, in an effort to strengthen her health. She had been Catherine's second travelling companion on the circular trip to Galway and Limerick.

Just as our journey to Galway drew near, I received a most interesting letter from the Bishop of London—asking for two professed Sisters, to forward some views—which he does not fully explain, but asks the favor so much in the name of God, that it would be impossible to refuse. Though very distressing & inconvenient—they sail this evening. We are, I trust, to bring them back—when leaving Birmingham. I suspect they are thinking of another House more central in London, though I have not heard it unequivocally expressed.[45]

Tuesday, 13th—I began this yesterday and could not finish—saw my poor Sisters on board, the same packet we sailed in first—and though the cabin was full of hightoned persons, the good little stewardess recognized us and said most triumphantly, "This is the *Queen*—that you went in to found a Convent in London." The Revd. Mr. Butler & Revd. Mr. Maddack accompanied them.[46] The former who came for them has been waiting at the Shelbourne since two days before I returned, in great terror lest the Irish air would disagree with him. Poor man, he is in a very precarious state, affected like Father Rafter.[47]

We left Galway with a determination to go to you—but a letter was sent after us to Limerick—pressing a speedy return, lest the weather would change, which

---

45 The Bermondsey Annals for this period—in Clare Moore's handwriting—alludes to several reasons, not including a new house in London, why the presence of two sisters from Baggot Street was needed in Bermondsey. In July Dr. Griffiths had appointed Mary Clare Agnew as mistress of novices (with a view to Clare Moore's imminent departure from London). "This change, however, was not productive of good effects, either because this Sister was not sufficiently acquainted with the obligations of that most important office, or that our Lord permitted trials and contradictions for the sanctification of those whom He had chosen." When Dr. Murphy arrived to take Clare Moore back to Cork, Dr. Griffiths represented to him "the still unsettled state of the Convent," and Dr. Murphy consented to Clare's remaining in London "some time longer." After requesting that Catherine McAuley "send two professed Sisters," Dr. Griffiths then "made enquiries relative to Sister Mary Xaveria Latham, and Sister Mary Vincent Weller, two of the Novices [received in Bermondsey on December 12, 1839] who had expressed much discontent, and finding that they were the persons chiefly in fault, his Lordship ordered them to be dismissed." Mary Vincent left in September, but "it was with difficulty" that Mary Xaveria "was at length prevailed on" to leave in October (Bermondsey Annals 1:16–17).

The Annals cites the "great danger in admitting persons into a Convent, who have been for any length of time in other religious Communities, as they are liable to find fault with regulations differing from those to which they had been accustomed" (1:17–18), but other factors were evidently operative as well. In June 1841, Catherine McAuley will note Mary Clare Agnew's "self-importance as to opinion" and her fondness for "extremes in piety" (Letters 282 and 284); in August 1841 she will be aware of "the Irish malediction" that fell on Clare Moore in her first years in Bermondsey (Letter 290). Dr. Thomas Griffiths's firmness in late 1840, as well as Clare Moore's own wisdom, which had presumably inspired his, undoubtedly saved the Bermondsey community from irreversible decline. However, Catherine McAuley is at this point, so far as the extant correspondence reveals, ignorant of the true difficulties in Bermondsey.

46 The Reverend Maddack [or Maddock?] has not been identified—at least not as a priest in the London District. John Maddocks was a priest of Lancashire, assigned to St. Nicholas Church in Liverpool, and Walter Maddocks, also of Lancashire, was a priest assigned to the chapel in Wigan (*Irish Catholic Directory* [1840] 322–23). 47 Michael Rafter, parish priest in Killeshin (Carlow-Graigue), had died on January 16, 1840.

Mr. Butler dreaded so much. I think it now providential I did not go to Carlow, lest I should be tempted to take Sr. Aloysius away. This month will be more useful to her than any she has passed. Mother de Pazzi is most anxious for her return—Mr. O'Hanlon desires me most positively not to think of it.

We are scattering our nice little professed—Sister Teresa Mary we left in Limerick, almost native air.[48] On the journey to Galway she had evident signs of deep engagement of the liver. The Bishop of Limerick knows her Mamma—and was quite pleased at her being left. They have a sweet community.

I feel quite deserted this morning—dear Sister de Sales has been my mother for some time, plaiting my coifs, etc., etc. May God bless them and receive the offering to His greater glory.

We had a most splendid ceremony in Galway. Mr. Mathew[49] arrived at the church in Mrs. Reddington's carriage—and three more of her carriages following close with different members of her family, all to compliment him. We came next—the two beautiful postulants[50] and my poor self in Mr. Joyce's carriage. Sister Mary Teresa, M. Catherine and Teresa Mary in Mr. McDonnald's [McDonnell's] carriage.[51] Sister de Sales, Sr. M. de Chantal[52] and a lay Sister in the Bishop's carriage. Miss McD had a white satin dress from Dublin—so made up as to turn into a cope. We saw it all in pieces before we left. Her good family would do anything for religion. Miss Joyce had white satin & lace dress over. Both wore white wreaths on their hair The sermon was delightful. Mr. Mathew has become quite eloquent since I heard him before. The Convent was crowded after the ceremony—all anxious to see him. The families of both Sisters supplied a grand *déjeuner*.

Thank God I am at rest again and now I think the name of another foundation would make me sick—but they say I would get up again. Indeed the thought of it at present would greatly distress me. On this late occasion I travelled one hundred miles a day, which is very fatiguing except on Railways.

Praying God to grant you every blessing—and trusting I shall soon see you,

I am your own old affectionate

M. C. McAuley

Poor Dr. Fitzgerald is much altered but looks better than I expected. His mind seems as sound as ever. He says our english Sisters are not to be compared to his "Mercy Girls" in Carlow.

Autograph: Silver Spring

---

48 Mary Teresa (Catherine) White. 49 Theobald Mathew, the "apostle of temperance." 50 Christina Joyce and Ismena McDonnell. 51 Mary Teresa (Amelia) White, the superior, Mary Catherine Leahy, and Teresa Mary (Catherine) White rode in Mr. McDonnell's carriage. 52 Mary de Sales White, Mary de Chantal O'Beirne, a Galway novice, and an unidentified Galway lay sister rode in the carriage of Dr. George Joseph Plunket Browne, the bishop of Galway.

194. To Cardinal Giacomo Filippo Fransoni　　　October 14, 1840
Prefect, Congregation for the Propagation
of the Faith[53]

May it please your Eminence

A petition was laid before the Sacred Council—humbly praying for confirmation of the Rule of our Blessed Lady of Mercy. This was accompanied by letters of approval from the Bishops in whose Diocese branches of the Institute have been founded. The answer conveyed to the petitioners was most consoling. It gave promise that the Rule would be confirmed at the next meeting of the Sacred Congregation. This was joyfully communicated to Ecclesiastical authorities, who are anxious to establish more Houses in England and Ireland, which they think would be greatly facilitated by the full approbation of the Holy See, as all orders of the Clergy would then cooperate in promoting an order which they deem very conducive to the Interests of Religion.

It is most respectfully represented to your Eminence that when the petition was presented—in December, there were twelve Houses in full operation. Two have since been added.

One hundred and forty two Sisters are now devoted to God and His poor in this order. They have been advised to solicit the valuable aid which your Eminence can afford, and which they most humbly and most respectfully beg for the greater glory of God.

Mary Catherine McAuley
Convent of our Lady of Mercy, Baggot Street, Dublin
October the 14th 1840

Autograph: Propaganda Fide, SRC, Irlanda, vol. 27, f. 340 rv

195. To Sister M. Elizabeth Moore　　　Convent, Baggot St.
Limerick　　　October 18, 1840

My Dearest Sister Mary Elizabeth

I have been speaking so romantically of Limerick that the English Sisters asked would it be possible for them to see it after their Profession, should they succeed, etc., etc. This is a long look-out—till next August. I at first answered

---

53 This autograph letter to Cardinal Fransoni, now preserved in the Archives of Propaganda Fide, Rome, is written on very thin blue-gray paper. No envelope or cover has been filed with the letter. However, an Italian translation of Catherine McAuley's letter is filed in the same volume, as folio 341, and a summary of the letter is filed as folio 343v and signed by Cardinal Paola Polidori, with the dates "21 Nov. 1840" and "11 November 1840." I have not been able to ascertain what action, if any, the letter prompted in Rome. Papal confirmation of the Rule did not take place until June 6, 1841.

that it would not be possible. Sister Mary Cecilia begged to say it would—and
that Limerick was the only convent so many could visit—as the travelling to each
by the Boat would be only 30 shillings there and back—and no coach could carry
them elsewhere. Stopping at Shannon Harbour, etc., would make it about £2 to
each.[54] This they seemed to think no difficulty. If 9 went it would be £18.[55]
Ought I to sanction such application of money if it were found on a hill? The
Rational and the Irrational powers have been contending ever since the thought
was suggested. They discoursed as follows:

R –   would not so much money accomplish some good & useful object?

IrR –   perhaps that money might not be forthcoming for any other purpose, but
        lie dead & doing nothing.

R –   would not a mere visit of such distance tend to dissipate the fruit of their
        meditations for & after profession?

IrR –   seeing a branch of the Institute, so short a time formed, now fully and
        regularly established, might rather serve to strengthen their pious resolu-
        tions and to animate their hopes for what they were about to undertake.

R –   could they not be told of it—surely they would not entertain any doubt.

IrR –   what we are told by unquestionable authority inspires confidence—but
        what we see confirms it.

R –   where would they lie down at night?

IrR –   anywhere.

R –   they could not get into the Refectory.

IrR –   they could get in, but it would be difficult to get out, I admit—there
        would be more fun than feeding.

Well now, after all this nonsense, I was seriously thinking of a great improvement might be made in the refectory if the wall was removed and the passage
added up to the Kitchen—the door of Kitchen opening into refectory.[56] It would
make a great addition tho' it appears little now—or if the kitchen wall was also
moved—and a little from the Kitchen also added—the K[itchen] would be large

---

54 Catherine imagines their taking inland passage boats on the Grand Canal from Dublin to Shannon
Harbour, near Banagher, where they could take a steam boat on the River Shannon to Limerick. If
they stopped at Shannon Harbour, and were picked up there by carriage or Bianconi car, the trip
would cost £2 per person; it would cost less per person if they went by boat all the way to Limerick,
though the journey by water would take more time. Passage boats departed for Shannon Harbour
from Ringsend, Dublin, at 7:00 a.m., and at 2:00 p.m. for connection with the steamer to Limerick
(*Dublin Directory* [1839] 183–84).   55 The nine travellers would be the seven English sisters: Mary
Juliana Hardman, Mary Xavier (Ann) Wood, Mary Vincent (Lucy) Bond, Mary Cecilia (Eliza)
Edwards, Marianne Beckett (who was apparently still in the Baggot Street community), Margaret
Polding, and Caroline Borini, as well as Mary Cecilia Marmion, mistress of novices, and Catherine
McAuley.   56 Having just returned from Limerick the week before, Catherine envisioned how the
refectory and kitchen there could be improved. As one who had partially designed or at least cri-
tiqued the construction of several new convents, and lived in many, she had developed a practical
architectural sense about what worked in terms of convenience.

enough. If any difficulty arises from obstructing/breaking the passage through the Hall, a small slip could be taken for that purpose—the Pantry taken down—a good press would do very well. Look at it with all your brains and you will soon make a great improvement. We find the Kitchen opening into Refectory most convenient.

If you wrote such a letter as this is, I would be seriously alarmed for your poor head.

I hope Sister Mary Teresa[57] will write soon to say she is getting quite strong. Three letters to announce the safe arrival of Dear Sisters Mary de Sales and Mary Xavier—a most affectionate one from Mother Mary Clare—returning thanks. We are to have profession and reception in about three weeks.[58]

Mother de P. and I have kept up a regular concert of sighing & moaning since the Sisters went—but this day I was resolved not to be outdone, or even equaled, so commenced groaning for every sigh she gave, and our sorrows have ended in laughing at each other.

Good-bye for about a month. God bless you and all with you. My affectionate love to dear Sister Mary Teresa—and each one of the sweet family.

Your ever attached
M. C. McAuley

My Dearest Sister Mary Vincent, give me a real true opinion on the disputed question you will hear of, but oh for pity's sake, speak in a whisper—or it will fly—that we are all—english and Irish—going to move.

Pray for your ever affectionate

M. C. M.

Get all the prayers you can for our valuable Sister Teresa who is looking very bad this day—and for my poor James McAuley who is in the last stage of consumption. Thanks be to God, he has complied with all religious obligations & is quite resigned to die.[59]

Autograph: Limerick

---

57 Mary Teresa (Catherine) White, who had stayed in Limerick when Catherine returned to Dublin. 58 The next ceremony at Baggot Street took place on November 26, 1840: Mary Elizabeth (Clare) Butler professed her vows, and Margaret Polding and Caroline Borini received the habit, taking the names Mary Magdalen and Mary Angela, respectively. On December 15, 1840, Mary Rose (Catherine) Lynch professed her vows. In this letter, written on October 18, Catherine McAuley is anticipating the ceremony on November 26, which was originally scheduled for November 19. (The Dublin Register incorrectly dates Mary Elizabeth Butler's profession, October 26, which cannot be accurate, given the information in Catherine's extant letters.) 59 This last paragraph is a postscript to the whole letter. It is written on side four of the stationery. The note to Mary Vincent Harnett is written below the closing, at about mid-page on side three. Catherine's nephew James Macauley, the eldest of her sister Mary's three sons, was now living in Blackrock and afflicted with consumption, like his two sisters, Mary and Catherine, and his brother Robert. James was twenty-five years old. His death came on April 29, 1841 (Burke Savage 351).

196. To Sister M. de Sales White Convent, Baggot Street
Bermondsey   October 18, 1840

My Dear Sister Mary de Sales

 We were all delighted to hear of your safe and happy arrival. I am sorry my dear Sister Mary X[avier] was sick, but it soon passed away. After we parted, I was greatly tempted to return and go with you to Liverpool—but I soon discovered this was a vain temptation, as if I could preserve you from any danger—and I felt you did not want any more care than God provided for you.

 Mother Mary de Pa[zzi] and I have kept up the most musical sighing or groaning in the Bishop's parlour. I thought she was far surpassing me—and yesterday I determined not to be outdone and commenced such a moaning as brought all to an end.

 We are as usual. Poor Sister Teresa[60] coughing very much. Sister Mary Aloysius greatly disappointed at not being brought to her old home, which Father O'Hanlon will not hear of. He says the winter in Carlow will strengthen her lungs—as it is native air. He is confined to his Room for some days—do not forget to mention him when you write.[61]

 I wrote to Galway to mention you got safe. You must write soon to Sister Mary Teresa.[62] Tell Sister Mary X[avier][63] she must give us a few lines occasionally—10 lines from each of you will be quite sufficient, about once a month.

 Give my best love to dear Mother Mary Clare—and to every dear Sister.

Believe me always your affectionate
Mary C. McAuley

 Be sure give my most affectionate love to your namesake in religion[64]—tell dear Sister Mary Clare Agnew I never forget her—love to Sister Mary Augustin.[65] Tell Revd. Mr. Butler I beg to return thanks for his kind letter. Do not forget these little matters.

May God bless you.

Autograph: Liverpool

197. To Sister M. Frances Warde   Baggot St.
Carlow   October 26, 1840

My Dearest Sister Mary Frances

 I feel quite anxious to do anything in my power to forward the pious wishes of little Sr. Maher. I rejoice in seeing a good Sister added to our order anywhere,

---

60 Teresa Carton. 61 Evidently Redmond O'Hanlon was ill, but well enough to insist on Mary Aloysius Scott's remaining in Carlow (since August 15) where her health could be restored. 62 Mary de Sales's sister, Mary Teresa White, the superior in Galway. 63 Mary Xavier O'Connell had also been loaned to the Bermondsey community. 64 Mary de Sales (Barbara) Eyre, in Bermondsey. 65 Mary Augustin (or Austin) Taylor, a member of the Bermondsey founding community.

but I would think it imprudent to press what Mr. Croke is opposed to.[66] He never took such interest as he does now, and it is most fortunate and a great blessing indeed, that he has taken the part of a guardian, in full authority. All will go on well now, please God.

I forget the little Sister[67]—if her manners are not too plain—if she is rather nice than otherwise, and able to visit the poor, etc., etc.—I think they would take her in Galway, provided what is promised would be secured. Mr. Daly requires that. If she is very plain or speaks badly, she would not be acceptable to him. He is to the Sisters a second Father Maher,[68] and most particular—he would not take a Co. Galway person on such terms, but from a quarter where it will not be known, I think I can induce him to take her. You would not bring me into discredit with him, and if the dear little Sr. is not such as I describe, you will tell me. The few they have are remarkably nice. Mr. D.[69] is with them some time of every day. He objected to a very nice young person to whom an uncle had left £300—because previous to that—she was for a few months only at [a] most respectable dress & milenary [sic] warehouse in Clare St.[70] He said the Co. Galway people would find out anything, and that it would be a certain injury. Miss Maher—if as I have said—rather nice—will be much more likely to remain happily in Galway, than Charleville.

I have had a letter from England—they have three Sisters in bad Typhus fever—names are not mentioned, I suppose we do not know them. God preserve them. A bad case also in Tullamore—the 6th since they went there. No deaths, thank God.

My poor James is in the last stage of decline in Kingstown. I am as much there as possible.[71] Pray & get prayers for him. I hope I may be here when Mrs. Warde comes.[72]

God bless you and all with you.

Ever your affectionate
M. C. McAuley

Autograph: Silver Spring

66 Catherine McAuley is still working to find a convent for Anna Maria Maher, but advises against pressing Charleville where Thomas Croke is parish priest. See also Letter 173, note 13, and Letter 182. 67 That is, Anna Maria Maher. 68 In light of her first impression, Catherine McAuley favorably compares Peter Daly in Galway with the community's dear friend James Maher in Carlow-Graigue—a comparison that will not hold up over time. 69 Father Peter Daly. 70 Catherine probably refers to a warehouse on Clare Street, Dublin. 71 Remembering the grief she felt at being absent when her nephew Robert died in early January 1840, Catherine McAuley visits James as much as possible. 72 This Mrs. Warde is Frances Warde's sister-in-law. A fragment of an autograph letter in the Windham archives may be addressed to her, but the fragment is cut along the left side and too incomplete to be reproduced.

198. To Miss Caroline White **Baggot Street**
Dundalk **October 26, 1840**

My Dear Caroline

I am indeed truly afflicted to hear of your darling sister's dangerous state.[73] May God comfort and support her afflicted family, but chiefly her Father and Mother. What is this poor miserable world but a place of sorrow and continued disappointment. God be praised, it is not our fixed abode, only the weary Road that leads to it. Oh what would we do, if in place of 70 or 80 years, God had appointed three or four hundred for our journey.

We also are in most painful anxiety. I have had a letter from London, saying they have three in bad typhus fever. The names are not mentioned, I suppose they are strangers to us. May God preserve the two dear Sisters we have lent them.[74] I was not able to go with them, but hope to go for them. They have also bad fever in Tullamore, one in great danger—I should rather say, in great hope of being united to her God.[75] For although to us who remain, these events are deeply afflicting, surely to those who are taken in innocence and purity of life, it must be a most joyful circumstance, when we compare what they leave, with what they are going to possess—not for a few fleeting years—but for all Eternity.

We will pray most fervently for you all. May I hope for a line, soon as you can. I will write when I hear from London.

God bless and preserve you, my Dear Child.

Your affectionate
M. C. McAuley

My Dear Sister M. T. in Galway & all with her are well, thank God.

Autograph: Liverpool

199. To Sister M. Teresa White **Baggot St.**
Galway **October 28, 1840**

My Dearest Sister Mary Teresa

I had a letter from Caroline yesterday saying how very dangerously ill dear Christina was. I had one from Mamma this morning to say there was a little change for the better. We are praying fervently for her, and three poor Sisters

---

73 Christina White, the sister of Mary Teresa White in Galway and Mary de Sales White in London, was evidently severely ill. 74 Mary Ursula O'Connor, Mary Scholastica Burroughs, and Anna Maria Ross, a postulant, had typhus in London (see Letters 200, 201, 205, and 206). Caroline White's sister, Mary de Sales White, was one of the sisters lent to the Bermondsey community. 75 The Tullamore Annals records that in late 1840 Mary Aloysius Deverell, a novice preparing for profession of vows, "was seized with a violent fever, which however did not last long, thank God. The Ceremony was postponed until she should become quite strong" (37).

in London. I had a letter from Sister M. de Sales this day. She says 2 are in great danger—one, Sister Ursula[76]—the others are strangers to us.

Sister Mary Frances writes again about little Sister Maher[77] and recommends her so strongly, I would advise you to take her—if Father Daly has not objection. Her brother says he will give £15 per year for 10 years and defray every expense up to profession. In your letter on the subject say that the first year should be paid in advance—and some security given for the remainder. I suppose her brother's note would be enough. Make out a full list of all she should bring—remember 4 cloaks, desk & work box—it may not be so easy to get a supply after—Bed, etc., etc. Mother Frances wishes you to write what she can shew to her friends. She adds—"Sister Maher is nice in mind and manner." While she was in Carlow, Dr. Fitzgerald was continually complaining of so many members from one family.[78] He said they would make a sysme [schism]—& not having money—and that it never was approved in the church. You know he has strange notions and must be humoured. I am quite certain she was parted with deep regret. All these circumstances will be preserved in silence. You never will let the temporal wants of a Sister be known beyond its proper limits.

My fingers are so stiff I cannot write more. With most affectionate regards to all, including your good Father,[79] I am your ever attached etc.

M. C. McAuley

I will write very soon to my dear Sister M. Catherine.[80]

I wrote to Caroline yesterday and I have written to your poor Mamma this day quite affectionately, just what you would like.

Autograph: Galway

200. **To Sister M. de Sales White**   Convent, Baggot Street
    Bermondsey   October 31, 1840

My Dearest Sister Mary de Sales

I need not say your letter afforded my great consolation, for although it conveyed the distressing account of the poor Sisters, yet under such circumstances it gives great comfort to hear of those who continue in health. May God preserve my poor Sister Mary Clare.[81] I know she will not give herself any rest—

---

76 Mary Ursula (Mary) O'Connor had received the habit on December 12, 1839, while Catherine McAuley and Mary Teresa White were in Bermondsey.   77 Anna Maria Maher: see Letters 173, 182, and 197.   78 According to the Carlow Register and Carlow Annals, in October 1840 there were five Mahers in the Carlow community: Mary de Sales (Mary) Maher from Killeany, Queen's County; Mary Clare (Eliza) Maher and Mary Cecilia (Ellen) Maher, half-sisters from Freshford, Co. Kilkenny; Mary Catherine (Kate) Maher and Mary Teresa (Teresa) Maher, sisters from Kilrush, Co. Kildare.   79 Peter Daly.   80 Mary Catherine Leahy, a founding member of the Galway community.   81 Mary Clare Moore, the superior in Bermondsey.

while able to stand. The happy state of the dear Sisters gives to the trial all that sweetens and makes it lighter.

I often reflect on the words of poor Miss Bourke[82] in Galway, when she discovered that I found some difficulty in telling her the Sacraments were to be administered—"ah darling Revd. Mother, what were we created for, or what is our existence prolonged for, but to attain a happy death." The affectionate manner proved how perfectly her mind was prepared and how sweetly resigned she was. Your constitution, on that occasion, and Mother Mary Clare's on many others, proved not to have any predisposition for fever.

Whatever God pleases, a fever and His love—what better. But it is most pleasing to Him that we use all prudent precaution. To act otherwise would bespeak confidence in our prepared state which we have but weak foundation for. Duty only should bring us in the way of contagion.

No change here since we parted, save that I do not see my dear Sister Mary de S[83]—dusting and polishing all about the altar on Friday. I am pleased to hear you are refectorian. I believe you never had that office before. Sister Juliana[84] will take great care of all your little brushes etc. You know when she leaves you will be returning, if almighty God is pleased to favor our arrangements. Any alteration He wishes will be our joy and delight.

Sister Mary Aloysius says she perfectly is recovered. Mr. O'Hanlon will not approve of her coming to Dublin for some time, tho' we want her very much. Little Sister Mary Teresa , eating heartily, and what is more wonderful, drinking our full quantity of Tea, which she could only taste. Munster air and the kindred spirit of her country has done wonders for her in so short a time.[85]

Father Mathew has been to visit Carlow—administered the pledge to 25 thousand, celebrated Mass for our Sisters, "and to my great mortification," says Sr. Aloysius, "told before several Priests, that Revd. Mother had taken the pledge and one of her daughters in Galway."[86] What an affliction for those who still love their freedom far as it may be enjoyed. I did not know till now that Sr. M. A. was an anti Mathewite. One hundred and twenty pounds collected after his sermon, to which he added sixty—it is to erect a Boys school.

Letter yesterday from Galway—all well—likely to get two Postulants. The dear little Widow White[87] calls—Mother de Pazzi says she will soon be a very holy Nun. They have had some profound conversation—I am not in the Cabinet. Sister Agnes gone to Kingstown, like a Lamb, without—pleasure or reluctance.[88]

---

82 Mary Bourke had died of typhus in Galway on June 11, 1840. Catherine McAuley spells her name "Burke."   83 That is, the recipient of this letter herself, Mary de Sales White.   84 Mary Juliana Hardman, now a novice.   85 Mary Teresa (Catherine) White, a native of Carrick-on-Suir, was still in Limerick and wonderfully restored in health.   86 Catherine McAuley did indeed take the pledge of total abstinence on some occasion, though exactly where and when is not known with certainty.   87 The widow of William White, Mary de Sales's brother who died in early 1839. See Letter 118.   88 Mary Agnes (Mary) O'Connor had professed her vows on September 24, 1840. In 1846, she became the founder of the Sisters of Mercy in New York City.

Now my own dear child, as I know you are anxious to be good—take the advice I here give you. Keep away from your mind all impatience to hear of or from any of us—and above all things, do not let it appear that you feel any. You shall have letters, please God, twice a month, between you and my Dear Sister Mary Xavier, to whom I will write in a few days. Her letter was very nicely written. I would not give it for five shillings, it comforts me to look at it. Neither of you have said—where you parted the Priest & his sister.

Mother de P unites in fondest love to each of her poor children. May God bless you both.

Your ever affectionate Mother in Christ,
Mary C. McAuley

Sister Magdeline asked did you remember her—Father O'Hanlon desired his best blessing to you & Sr. X[avier].

Autograph: Liverpool

November–December 1840

The year 1840, the last full year of Catherine McAuley's life, ended with new foundations of Sisters of Mercy in Wexford on December 8 and Birr, Co. Offaly, on December 27, with plans underway for foundations in Birmingham and Newfoundland, and with invitations for Nottingham and probably Westport. The final months of 1840 also brought familiar sorrows and joys: the shocking deaths of two novices in London from typhus; a gradual worsening of her nephew James's consumptive condition; the pleasure of a short visit to Carlow; relief at Mary Aloysius Scott's recovery of health; and amusement at Daniel O'Connell's complimentary speech about the Sisters of Mercy, at Carrick-on-Suir.

Although Catherine fussed a bit during this period—about the durability and appearance of the fabric used for veils and cloaks in Carlow and Wexford, and about the recruiting methods of the convent in Naas, the extant letters of these months reveal that she had larger worries on her mind: the pension school now opened in Kingstown was severely under-enrolled; and at least six sisters had to be professed, received, or admitted prior to her departure for Birr on December 26. The residue of fatigue from her earlier travels this year led her to admit, just twice, that she was "worn out."

But the most striking feature of this period is Catherine McAuley's fidelity to her duty, as she perceived it, of letter-writing to the "foreign powers", her playful term for the superiors and other sisters in the foundations outside of Dublin. The twenty-two extant letters from her in these months represent only a fraction of the letters she actually wrote. Yet of these, thirteen were written to sisters in Carlow, Galway, Limerick, London, Naas and Wexford. Although she was in no sense the superior of these sisters or their communities (except the two sisters lent to London), Catherine evidently felt a deep obligation to support and encourage them, by her affection, her good humor, and her sharing of news, when visits were not possible. Their "ever affectionate M. C. McAuley" was a disciplined correspondent, doing what she could to sustain the grace of God within them, writing not just to the superiors of these convents, but to the novices and young professed sisters—she who was almost universally twice their age.

One paragraph in the letter to Mary de Sales White in London on December 20 summarizes the purity of heart that gave Catherine McAuley strength, in her travels and labors, and that would, she prayed, give strength to her sisters:

> We have one solid comfort amidst this little tripping about: our hearts can always be in the same place, centered in God—for whom alone we go forward—or stay back. Oh may He look on us with love and pity, and

then we shall be able to do anything He wishes us to do—no matter how difficult to accomplish—or painful to our feelings. If he looks on us with approbation for one instant each day—it will be sufficient to bring us joyfully on to the end of our journey. Let us implore Him to do so at this season of love and Mercy. (Letter 220)

201. To Sister Mary Clare Moore   November 6, 1840
     Bermondsey

Dear Rev. Mother

I seize the first opportunity to congratulate with you & all the Dear Sisters of the House of Mercy on this first martyr of charity offered to Almighty God. Greater love than this no man hath, that a man lay down his life for his friends. Sister Ursula has exercised this greatest act of charity, & is I trust now enjoying its infinite reward from her benevolent Saviour, who has promised to recompense even a cup of cold water given in his name.[1] I have offered the adorable Sacrifice in thanksgiving for this especial blessing bestowed upon her, & likewise in expiation of any imperfection which may have accompanied the sacrifice of herself.

Though the temporary separation [is] painful to her Dear Sisters, they will not fail to thank the Almighty for this greatest of blessings vouchsafed to their House of Mercy; it is I hope a pledge of future graces.

Mention my kindest regards & fervent prayers for every blessing to all the Sisters, especially to the two invalids,[2] and if your duties allow you the time, I shall be happy to receive a letter from you by Monday evening's post, addressed to New Hall in Chelmsford, which will I hope & pray contain a favourable account of the sick Sisters, & of your own health.

1 Mary Ursula (Mary) O'Connor, a novice, died of typhus in Bermondsey on November 1, 1840. The Bermondsey Annals records her illness and death: "Among the sick persons visited by the Sisters there was a poor woman in great misery, with a family of seven children living in Brewer's Turning, Vine Yard. While the Sisters were attending her, the Typhus Fever seized on her poor children, and from them, three of our Sisters caught the infection. Sister Mary Ursula O'Connor was the first who manifested symptoms of the disease. On the 21st of October . . . the Physician was called in, but notwithstanding all remedies, the Fever increased rapidly ... In her last sickness, the extraordinary resignation and joy she evinced under the most dreadful pains and agonies surprised and edified even the Physician who attended her." She "expired tranquilly on Sunday, the feast of All Saints . . . being about forty years of age. She was interred on the following Wednesday, in the Vaults of the Church immediately beneath the Altar Steps" (1:19–20).   2 "Sister Mary Scholastica [Frances] Burroughs [also a novice] became ill [of typhus] a few days after Sister Mary Ursula's fever had commenced; her sufferings too were intense, and every remedy unavailing . . . she died on Thursday the fifth of November about nine o'clock a.m. and was buried in the same grave with Sister Mary Ursula on the Saturday" (Bermondsey Annals 1:20). Dr. Griffiths was unaware of her death when he wrote this letter. Anna Maria Ross, a postulant, "was the third who caught the fever, but she recovered from it." She received the habit on December 8, 1840, taking the name Mary Teresa, but subsequently left the community (Bermondsey Annals 1:21).

Believe me, with sincere gratitude & respect, Dear Rev. Mother
>   Yours very faithfully in Christ
>   + Thomas Griffiths

Autograph: Bermondsey

202. To Dr. Thomas Walsh   **Convent of Our Lady of Mercy**
>   **Baggot Street**
>   **November 6, 1840**

My Lord
     It affords me very great pleasure to inform you that your spiritual daughters
continue to advance in the love and practise of religious discipline. God seems
to have given them a right understanding of their state and its obligations, and
there is every reason to hope that your Lordship will have the consolation to see
them performing their duties in such manner as will merit your approbation, and
give much edification to your poor people.
     Dear Sister Juliana[3] is remarkably well, passing from one charge to another,
determined to be acquainted with all. Sister Caroline Borina [Borini], who came
to try change of air, is quite strong and healthy—likely to be a very desirable
addition indeed. She and Sister Polding are preparing most ardently for their
religious clothing. We hope to have the ceremony on the nineteenth.[4]
     My Lord, I enclose accounts for the half year in the first outfit.[5] Each Sister
is provided with four cloaks. The annual expense in future will not exceed one
pound. I give you a copy of our distribution of time, my Lord, which has been
found well adapted to the duties of our order.[6] It is contained in our observances,
not in our Rule, and therefore subject to any alteration that place or circumstances might require. I have the honor to remain
>   My Lord, most respectfully our obedient servant
>   Mary C. McAuley

Autograph: Birmingham

---

3 Mary Juliana Hardman.   4 Caroline Borini and Margaret Polding actually received the habit at
Baggot Street on November 26, 1840, taking the names Mary Angela and Mary Magdalen respec-
tively.   5 The autograph of the hand-printed account for Juliana Hardman, signed by Catherine
McAuley, is preserved in the Mercy archives in Handsworth, Birmingham. It lists the following
expenses totalling £20.10.11½: "Pension—half year £12.10.0, Clothing—£7.9.4, Books—6.4½,
Medicine—5.3." On the back of the autograph, in a different hand, are listed the total half-year
expenses for Miss Edwards (£12.10.0), Miss Wood (£18.18.3½) and Miss Bond (£19.4.8½).   6
The horarium enclosed for Dr. Walsh is Letter 203.

203. Dr. Thomas Walsh [November 6, 1840]

Daily distribution of Time

5½	To Rise
6	Assemble in choir, Angelus, small hours,[7] meditation
7	Make up cells etc.
7½	Mass
8¼	Breakfast
9	Lecture
9½	Prepare for School—Visitation of Sick—Instruction of adults
10	These duties entered upon
11¾	Particular examen—visit to The Blessed Sacrament
12	Angelus, & Acts of Faith, Hope, and Charity, Litany of Jesus
4	Dinner
5	Vespers, Litany of The Blessed Virgin
5½	Lecture
6	Angelus & Mattins and Lauds, Litany for happy death
6¾	Supper
7	Recreation
9	Examen—Litany of Saints, morning meditation prepared
10	All in Bed

Sisters engaged in the visitation of the sick are exempt from any choir duty from 10 till 4, but all in choir at Office and all attend Lectures. The Rosary is said by obligation, but no time marked. It is often said going on the visitation.

[Mary C. McAuley]

Autograph: Birmingham

204. Draft of Horarium[8] [Undated]

We are called at half past five—assemble in Choir at six—Angelus Domini—Office, Meditation & Mass—all over at eight. Quarter past 8 Breakfast. After

---

7 Prime, Terce, Sext, and None.   8 This autograph is clearly a draft as it contains many crossings-out and revisions. Catherine McAuley is known to have occasionally adjusted the times in the horarium at Baggot Street, to accommodate the demands of the works of mercy in which the sisters were engaged. She would also have helped each new foundation to draft its own horarium. As she noted in Letter 202 to Dr. Thomas Walsh, the horarium was "subject to any alteration that place or circumstances might require." This draft horarium differs from the previous horarium only in its elaboration of responsibilities in the House of Mercy, its insertion of a brief recreation period after dinner, and its commentary on the merriment at recreation and the happiness of religious life. Catherine's comments suggest that she drafted this horarium with a view to sharing it with a priest or bishop seeking a new foundation or with a prospective postulant. A notation appended to the

Breakfast the Sisters attend to their different employments till 9—when we have public lecture for all. At half past 9 the Sisters appointed to visit the sick prepare to go out and those who have charge of the school prepare for it. The Sister who superintends the distressed persons takes her place in the work room. Revd. Mother and a Senior Sister sit in an adjoining room to receive and answer applications.

At a quarter to 12 we again assemble in Choir for particular examen, Angelus, Acts of F[aith], H[ope], C[harity], Litany of Jesus—then resume our employments. Those who went out first are now returned—when others go, who return about 3. Dinner for the House of Mercy at 3, our Dinner at 4—after D[inner] recreation in the Community Room for half an hour, but as the Sisters who read & attend Table and the lay Sisters have yet to dine, it is not called general recreation.

At five Vespers in Choir—half past 5, Public lecture for all till 6—then Angelus & Mattins & Lauds. Quarter to 7 Tea. From 7 to 9 general recreation, and you never saw such a happy & merry party, nor never will except in a religious Community.

At 9 examen, night prayers, morning meditation read, & then to rest.

This one day—is our whole life. You might suppose the daily and uninterrupted repetition of the duties were tiresome. It is not so. Religious life affords more lively solid lasting happiness than all the variety this world could give.

[M. C. McAuley]

Autograph: West Hartford

205. To Sister Mary Vincent Harnett   Convent, Baggot St.
Limerick   November 8, 1840[9]

My dear Sister M. Vincent

I received your welcome letter and was quite amused with all your projected arrangements for the proposed visitors.[10] "Man proposeth," etc.[11] We have a con-

autograph by a later hand says, "Horarium: First Sisters of Mercy Baggot Street," but that notation may not be precisely accurate. Mary Clare Moore says that when Catherine McAuley first came home to Baggot Street from George's Hill "Supper was at 8, no silence; that only lasted a few weeks. Supper went to 7 and silence" (Sullivan, *Catherine McAuley* 97).   9 No autograph of this letter has been found. However, there are four early handcopies: one that Mary Vincent Harnett herself had prepared for Josephine Warde in Cork, which is dated "Nov. 8th 1840"; and three dated "November 1840"—in the Baggot Street volume of manuscripts called "Annals" (51–52), in the Brisbane Book of Transcriptions (91–93), and in the small book of Baggot Street Manuscript Copies (96–98). The letter in abbreviated form also appears in Harnett's *Life*, 173–74. The text given here is that in the handcopy prepared by the recipient.   10 The "proposed visitors" may be sisters from Tullamore who, Catherine suggested, might go to Limerick to learn the system of education (see Letter 190). However, the Tullamore Annals for 1840 does not speak of any sisters going to Limerick for such instruction, although it does speak of the great success of the poor school and pension school in Tullamore (34–36).

tinuation of melancholy news from London—a second Sister dead, and a third in a very doubtful state.[12] The fever of most malignant character—the poor remains obliged to be enclosed in the coffin soon after the soul departed. Mother M. Clare says "My heart is gone". She has great fatigue and anxiety—pray God to preserve her and all the Sisters. We fancied that Sisters M. de Sales and M. Xavier were going for some additional good work, but you see God designed otherwise and has arrested the progress, no doubt to give more contempt to all earthly plans, and more animation to work with increased fervor, seeing life and death so closely, so intimately united. Surely we have not an hour to spare—it has forced me to conclude for another foundation which we had quite declined.[13] Pray for the intention.

The Sisters in all other quarters well, thank God. We hope to have the Reception of the two English Sisters that came last and Profession of Sister Butler on the 19th. Sr. M. Aloysius is most anxious to return from Carlow, says she is quite well. Probably she will go on the next foundation.[14] We expect St. John's[15] will come about in May or June. We announced that whoever could take tea without milk should go there as Superior, it being very difficult to procure it. Mother de Pazzi commenced this morning and has declared herself so far an efficient candidate.

We shall soon have a very thin house, if God is not pleased to send us a new batch, and if 4 go to Newfoundland, and 9 to Birmingham[16] and two to the last named[17]—15 vacated cells would be a curiosity here. This will be great relief to my poor little house steward—Sr. M. Teresa[18]—who was often perplexed to make out a bed—so much that I used to try to avoid her when an addition was on the way—and when we met [we] were sure to have the following little dialogue. Sr. M. T.: "Revd. Mother, I hear there is another Sister coming." "Yes, have you

---

11 "Man proposes, but God disposes" (Prov. 16.9 and 19.21). This statement is also in Thomas à Kempis, *Imitation of Christ*, Book 1, ch. 19—the place where Catherine McAuley likely encountered it. Clare Moore claims that Catherine's "Favourite Book" was "'The Following of Christ,' especially the Chapters 30th of Book 3rd, and 8th of Book 4th" (*Practical Sayings* 35). These chapters are "Of Craving the Divine Aid, and Confidence of Recovering Grace" and "Of the Oblation of Christ on the Cross and of Resignation of Ourselves" (Thomas à Kempis 126–28 and 206–207). 12 See Letter 201.   13 Probably Catherine refers to the foundation in Birr, which Theobald Mathew had requested on behalf of the parish priest, and for which she will depart from Dublin on December 26.   14 That is, on the foundation to Birr.   15 The foundation of the first community of Sisters of Mercy in St. John's, Newfoundland, occurred on June 3, 1842, under the leadership of Mary Ursula Frayne and Mary Francis (Mary Ann) Creedon. This was a year later than Catherine McAuley expected when she wrote this letter.   16 The nine will be the seven women now preparing for Birmingham, Catherine McAuley, and her travelling companion.   17 The Birr foundation. 18 Before her September–October trip with Catherine McAuley to Galway and Limerick, where she now remained, Mary Teresa (Catherine) White had served, as Catherine said, as "house steward"—assigning beds in the religious community at Baggot Street and generally looking after the house. At this time there were at least thirty-six women in the Dublin community, some of them living in Kingstown or Booterstown, but most of them at Baggot Street. In early November 1840, at least seventeen of these were novices or postulants.

any objection." "Where is she to sleep?" "In my lap." "Oh, I declare, Revd. Mother, it is impossible to make any more room. The Sisters are dreadfully crowded. Come look at the dormitory." Read this for her, and she will rejoice at the prospect of 15 spare beds. She must come home soon—we cannot have our poor reduced forces scattered. Give my affectionate love to her, and my dear Mother M. E. and every dear Sister. Be sure to pray for your sincerely attached

M. C. McAuley

Harnett handcopy: Cork; handcopies: Brisbane and Dublin, Mercy

206. To Sister M. Frances Warde   Convent, Baggot Street
Carlow   November 9, 1840

My Dearest Sister Mary Frances

We continue to receive melancholy accounts from London—a second Sister dead, and the third in a most afflicting state, tendency to mortify. My poor Sister Mary Clare almost exhausted. You would not know her writing. She says, "My heart is gone." The first that died was received when I was there, the others are strangers to me. Sisters M. de Sales & M. Xavier[19] continue well. The former has afforded the greatest assistance. What a scene of trial we sent them to. This is the way of God['s] providence. I suppose all will go on well to shew us that what we think a draw back will be followed by greater progress. If they should have a new foundation—it will not be without the cross.

I had a letter from Sister Mary Teresa, and I believe she has written under the direction of Mr. Daly. He has had the charge of the Presentation Convent for 20 years, and is quite attentive to every trifle. He is a most generous Priest— but has not means proportioned to his undertakings, and is always engaged for [far?] too much.[20]

I believe Sister M. Aloysius must soon try what she is able to do, so tell her to prepare, as she says she is quite well. Nothing more likely to keep her so than reasonable occupation of mind and body. She has got petting enough for one season.[21]

I believe we are retiring from business—no postulants on the way. When the english party leave we shall have plenty of vacant Beds. Perhaps some may be thinking of us now. Whatever God pleases.

My poor James[22] continues in the same state, apparently, but I suppose he is getting nearer to the grave each day. He is really pious, wishes the Priest to

---

19 Mary de Sales White and Mary Xavier O'Connell in Bermondsey.   **20** Catherine had probably received a reply from Mary Teresa White, superior in Galway, expressing Peter Daly's view that Anna Maria Maher could not be admitted as a postulant in Galway because of her relatively small dowry.   **21** At this point Catherine plans to name Mary Aloysius Scott as superior of the foundation in Birr to be established at the end of December 1840.   **22** Catherine McAuley's nephew James Macauley was seriously ill with "consumption" (tuberculosis).

visit him frequently, and receives the Holy Communion as often as persons in his state can. He has a good young man attending him at night—and the Sisters are with him every day. He is quite cheerful—and speaks of his death most happily. This is great consolation. Continue to pray for him. Robert's last wish was that the Sisters would pray for the repose of his poor soul.[23]

My earthly joys are cut down, thank God, but the joys of my state are many, and I feel the most lively gratitude. I would not write so soon—but to tell you of London. God Almighty bless and preserve you. A thousand loves to Sr. Aloysius—and each, etc.

Your ever affectionate
Mary C. McAuley

I did not see Sister M. Aloysius's note till this moment. I have the full value of 1/6 in the nice socks she sends me. Tho' some fine days have passed without bringing me to St. Leo's, not many more will do so.[24]

The music books are just delivered with a charge of 1/6. Dr. Tuomy came to town a few days since. He would have brought it.[25]

Autograph: Silver Spring

207. To Charles Cavanagh, Esq.   [Baggot Street]
Thursday, November 10 [1840]

Dear Sir

Mr. Thomas Butler who hands you this wishes to give such security as you shall approve for £25 per an[num]—during the life of his sister—previous to her profession with us.[26]

---

23 Catherine recalls her nephew Robert Macauley who died of tuberculosis in early January 1840 while she was in Bermondsey.   24 St. Leo's was the name of the Mercy convent in Carlow. When Catherine returned from Galway in early October, she hoped to visit Carlow soon, but still had not done so. In fact, she had not been to Carlow in well over a year—since she stopped there on her way to Dublin from Cork in late August or early September 1839.   25 Dr. John Tuomy, A.M., M.B., Carlow, was a Licentiate of the Royal College of Surgeons in Ireland (*Dublin Directory* [1839] 152). He was one of the two Carlow doctors who attended Julia Redmond when she had typhus in late February 1840 (Carlow Annals). The music books were delivered by post or courier, with a charge of one shilling and sixpence. Catherine had to pay the same charge for the socks Mary Aloysius Scott sent her, but felt they were worth it.   26 Thomas Butler's sister was Mary Elizabeth (Clare) Butler who was preparing for her profession of vows on November 26, 1840. As dowry, he wished to promise £25 a year during her life. In 1843 Mary Elizabeth became a member of the Liverpool foundation; she served as a nurse during the Crimean War and died in Balaclava of typhus on February 23, 1856. The Dublin and Liverpool Registers say she professed her vows on October 26, 1840, but that date is incorrect, in view of Catherine McAuley's comments in this dated letter and in Letter 205, which was clearly written in November. Catherine had initially planned the ceremony for November 19, as certain letters indicate, but for some reason—perhaps Dr. Murray's schedule—it was changed to November 26 (see Letter 212).

Mr. Butler is a most excellent man, one of the Poor Law guardians.[27] I believe his sister has no other claim on him than what his kind affection gives her. He has a large family.

Dear Sir, very gratefully, etc.,

M. C. McAuley

Autograph: Dublin, Mercy

208. To the Reverend John Hamilton

Convent, Baggot St.
November 12, 1840

Very Reverend Sir

The Revd. Mr. Mathew made a request of me, some time since, which it is now in my power to comply with. I shall feel most grateful if you will give him the enclosed note.[28]

Very Reverend Dear Sir, most respectfully, etc.

Mary C. McAuley

Autograph: Dublin Diocese, Murray Papers AB3/34/15, no. 18

209. To Sister M. Frances Warde
Carlow

Friday, November 13, 1840

My Dearest Sister Mary Frances

I was writing to Father O'Hanlon yesterday, to tell him that I was going to Carlow on Saturday, when I received a note from Jane O'Dwyer, asking permission for herself and Sister Marcella[29]—to come to Father Mathew's Mass here, as she heard we were "to enjoy that favor." I did not till then recollect that he was to be in Dublin on Sunday, of course did not hear he would celebrate Mass for us—that I suppose to be mere conjecture. I believe he leaves Dublin on Wednesday, perhaps sooner—but untill then I must remain.[30]

---

27 Evidently Thomas Butler served as a Poor Law guardian in a Union outside of the city of Dublin, but the exact location has not been identified.   28 The note Catherine McAuley sent to Theobald Mathew, through John Hamilton, presumably contained her agreement to found a Mercy community in Birr at the end of 1840, in response to his longstanding request that she send sisters there. A severe schism wracked the Catholic community in Birr, and Father Mathew hoped the presence of Sisters of Mercy might bring healing. For a discussion of the schism, occasioned by two priests, Michael Crotty and William Crotty, but also initially by some measure of episcopal mishandling, see Murphy, *Diocese of Killaloe*, 2:100–133. See also Letter 173.   29 Jane and Marcella O'Dwyer have not been identified. They were presumably lay friends of the Baggot Street community. "Sister Marcella [Flynn]," as transcribed in Bolster's *Correspondence* (166), cannot be correct, as there was no Sister Marcella in the Baggot Street community at this time. Catherine McAuley often capitalized "Sister" and "Brother" when referring to siblings.   30 The "Catholic Annals" in the *Irish Catholic Directory* for 1842 notes

I am sorry we miss the ceremony.[31] I intended to bring one of the English novices—who has got that kind of cough which a little change of air often removes. She has it rather too long, but is otherwise in good health. Kingstown or Booterstown is rather sharp.

If Mr. M[athew] should come here on Monday, I could go on Tuesday. If not, I must wait while we could have any hope—which must end on Wednesday. Then I could go on Thursday. I think it likely he will leave Dublin Tuesday evening or early on Wednesday, as he is published for some distant part of the Co. Leitrim on Thursday, so I suppose I could go on Wednesday.[32] Sister M. Cecilia sent immediately, to bespeak the second Beads.[33]

We have not heard from London since, which surprises me.

As usual, Sisters drop in here out the sky. When I wrote last, I said we were done—since that, two have nearly concluded to enter on the 8th of December.[34] Three are to be received on Monday in Limerick, and two to enter—Miss Griffin, cousin to dear little Sr. Potter—and Miss O'Connor of Mallow.[35] Mr. O'Connell['s] speech in Carrick has brought Sisters of Mercy quite into fashion.[36]

It is said that the Publicans of Dublin are in terror at Father Mathew's approach—another visit, they say, will break them up. You can scarcely form an

---

that on Sunday, November 15, 1840, "V. Rev. T. Mathew preached in the Metropolitan church [St. Mary's], Dublin, towards the expense of completing that cathedral. The attendance was most respectable and numerous, and the proceeds most liberal" (395). 31 In Carlow, on Monday, November 16, 1840, Ellen Lanigan and Ellen O'Brien were scheduled to receive the Mercy habit, taking the names Mary Clare and Mary Magdalen respectively. Catherine McAuley had hoped to go to this ceremony, but was prevented by Father Mathew's possible visit. 32 Catherine had earlier hoped to arrange a profession and reception ceremony at Baggot Street on Thursday, November 19 (Letter 205). That event was already re-scheduled to November 26 because here she is speaking of going to Carlow on Wednesday, November 18. The Carlow Annals for 1840 records that "Towards the end of November, Rev. Mother McAuley came to take home her amiable child [Mary Aloysius Scott], having for travelling companion Sr. M. Julianna Hardman, wearing the white veil. We observed with deep regret that the health of our venerated Foundress was declining, and that she did not take the necessary care of herself." The Annals notes that Catherine remained a few days in Carlow and "presented the four professed Sisters with black veils of the same material as that now generally worn; the gossamer, she considered, was 'too like a bit of millinery.'" 33 Evidently the Carlow community was short one set of the large rosary beads worn on the outside of the habit—and needed for its clothing ceremony on November 16. 34 The sisters dropping "out the sky" were unexpected postulants entering the Baggot Street community. On December 8, 1840, Frances Vigne and Teresa MacDonnell entered the community (see Letter 215). 35 Ellen Griffin—cousin of Mary Teresa Vincent Potter and sister of the well-known poet Gerald Griffin—entered the Limerick community on Saturday, November 14, 1840; Elizabeth Mulqueen, on Monday, November 16, 1840. Miss O'Connor has not been identified. On Thursday, November 19, 1840 three women received the habit in Limerick: Mary McNamara, taking the name Mary Clare; Anne McNamara, taking the name Mary Catherine; and Mary Purcell, taking the name Mary Baptist. Catherine McAuley's dates for these events are incorrect. 36 Daniel O'Connell, MP, had recently given a speech at Carrick-on-Suir on repeal of the 1801 Union of Ireland with Britain. See an excerpt from the speech in Letter 210. Catherine McAuley remained deeply amused by the newspaper report of his dramatic celebration of the "educated" foot of the Sister of Mercy, peeping from under her black cloak as she hastened on her errand of mercy.

idea of the moral improvement throughout the country. We passed through populous towns on fair and market days without hearing one angry voice. Men, women & children dressed—and all so peaceable and happy. This proves to us what the special grace of God can produce—tho' bestowed but on one man—yet so as to go forth amongst millions, through the agency of his touch. Creatures who never could keep a promise made to God or man—and who frequently violated the most solemn oath, when intemperance was in question—persons, of strong mind and good education, never have given evidence of such resolution as these millions of weak, ignorant, obstinate creatures are now manifesting.[37]

Sister M. C. just came to bid me say she will have the beads to send by Purcell's coach tomorrow. Love to dear Sister M. A. and all.[38]

Your ever affectionate
M. C. McAuley

Autograph: Burlingame

210. To Sister M. Catherine Leahy[39]   **Convent, Baggot Street**
      Galway   **November 13, 1840**

My Dearest Sister Mary Catherine

I should have written sooner—to thank you for your kind letter and the copy of regulations, etc. I am delighted to find you are so happy—you never will be otherwise, while the spirit of your religious vocation animates your actions, the daily review and interior interrogation: what had God in view when calling me to this state, etc. etc.? do I endeavour in every thought, word & action to correspond with His intention in my regard? As I am certain this is the course you follow, happiness must await you—even when you have much to deplore and many charges to make against yourself.

We have not heard from London since the account of the second death. God, I trust, will spare the rest.

Did you hear what a handsome tribute of regard Mr. O'Connell paid to the Sisters of Mercy in his speech at Carrick—it is bringing them quite into fash-

---

37 Theobald Mathew will visit Dublin on November 15 and 16, administering the pledge of total abstinence to thousands. On her various travels through Ireland Catherine McAuley had seen the widespread results of his ministry. As here, she was especially moved by the vast amount of good that could be accomplished through the agency of a single person who is pure of heart.   38 Mary Cecilia Marmion will have the second set of rosary beads to send on November 14. Catherine sends love to Mary Aloysius Scott.   39 Mary Catherine Leahy had gone to Galway from Baggot Street, as one of the founding community. Catherine McAuley initially intended that after the first six months Catherine Leahy would succeed Mary Teresa White as superior in Galway, and Teresa would return to Baggot Street. Perhaps the character of Peter Daly prevented this, or Catherine McAuley thought better of the idea. Teresa White remained in Galway until 1855, and then founded a Mercy community in Clifden on the coast of Connemara.

ion. As a test of my humility, I have it in my desk—to look at occasionally, and will copy it for you—

"No country on the face of the earth is like Ireland. Look at the fairest portion of creation, possessing all the virtues that adorn and endear life, forsaking their homes, their families and friends, etc., etc. Look at the Sisters of Mercy, wrapped in coarse black cloaks—hear, hear—they are seen gliding along, persons apparently poor—while a slight glance at the foot shews the educated Lady. They are hastening to the lone couch of some sick fellow creature fast sinking into the grave with none to console, none to sooth [*sic*]. They come with consolation and hope, and bring down with their prayers the Blessing of God on the dying sinner, on themselves, and on their country—cheers—oh such is too good to be oppressed. Great cheering."[40]

The foot has afforded great amusement at recreation, each claiming for her own foot the compliment paid to all. They have lately made some very nice cloth Boots, and got them soled & caped [capped] with leather. When finished they do not cost quite 4 shillings. Dear Sister M. de Sales[41] commenced the work—and it now goes on rapidly. They are exceedingly neat & warm—any kind of stocking will do. I have been long recommending these home made Boots, both for neatness and economy.

I have just got a letter from my poor Mother Mary Clare—the third Sister recovering. Their trial has been great indeed. She says—"picture us to yourself going to the vault with one dear Sister on Wednesday, and with another on Saturday following."[42] They caught this malignant fever attending a poor family—all of whom recovered. Such is the mysterious Providence of God. I look forward now to their greater progress—to shew that "His ways are not like our ways—nor His thoughts like our thoughts."[43]

Tell dear Mother Teresa[44]—I think she did well in every little matter she stated to me. Give my most affectionate love to each. Tell my dear Sister M. Chantel,[45] I will soon have the pleasure of writing to her and to my other dear grandchildren. All unite in love to you, etc. etc.

Believe me ever your attached
M. C. McAuley

Give my respectful regards to Father Daly.

---

40 Daniel O'Connell had been a supporter of the Sisters of Mercy ever since the House of Mercy opened on Baggot Street in 1827. His daughter Kate initially helped out in the poor school there, according to Mary Ann Doyle and Mary Clare Moore, and O'Connell himself used to carve at the Christmas dinner given for poor children in the neighborhood. He lived for a time at 30 Merrion Square, a few streets from the house on Baggot Street. See Sullivan, *Catherine McAuley* 50, 54, 86, 89 and 94.   41 Mary de Sales White, now in London.   42 In Bermondsey, Mary Ursula O'Connor died of typhus on November 1 and was buried on November 4; Mary Scholastica Burroughs died, also of typhus, on November 5 and was buried in the same grave on November 7.   43 Isaiah 55.8.   44 Mary Teresa White, the superior in Galway.   45 Mary de Chantal O'Beirne, a novice in Galway.

Sr. M. Teresa[46] comes home from Limerick—to be the travelling companion.

3 to be received on Monday in Limerick—2 to enter—2 expected here on the 8th of December.[47] You have all the news now.

I have had such urgent letters from the zealous good PP of Birr,[48] that we can no longer resist and propose going there about the 26 of next month. Sister Scott—I hope will be able to commence—with Sr. Blake—who will succeed Sr. A—when they are joined by 3—the former to return.[49]

Autograph: Galway

211. **To Sister M. Catherine Meagher**   Convent, Baggot St.
     Naas   [c. November 18, 1840][50]

My Dear Sister M. Catherine

I am very happy to receive a note from you and regret exceedingly that it is impossible to admit the young person. We are always crowded to excess at this season—so many leaving Dublin, dismissing servants and few engaging any, we have every day most sorrowful applications from interesting young creatures, confectioners & dress makers, who at this season cannot get employment and are quite unprotected. I am sure I spoke with two yesterday who were hungry, tho' of nice appearance.

Their dejected faces have been before me ever since. I was afraid of hurting their feelings by offering them food & had no money. The poor law Tax has deprived us of much help. We find it very difficult to keep up the poor Institution.

My best love to all—believe me

your ever affectionate
M. C. McAuley

Photostat of autograph: Mercy, Dublin

46 Mary Teresa (Catherine) White, now temporarily in Limerick, will be Catherine McAuley's travelling companion to Birr in late December.   47 See Letter 209, notes 34 and 35.   48 John Spain, parish priest in Birr and vicar general of the diocese of Killaloe.   49 At this point Catherine anticipates that when three women from Birr or the surrounding country have joined the Birr community, Mary Gertrude Blake may succeed Mary Aloysius Scott as superior of the Birr community, and Mary Aloysius may return to Baggot Street. In the end this early plan did not come to pass. Mary Gertrude Blake did not go to Birr in late December 1840. Mary Aloysius Scott remained the superior in Birr until a few months before her death there on May 31, 1844. Mary Gertrude then went to Birr as interim superior for one year, before responding to a request of Frances Warde to go to Pittsburgh in November 1845.   50 The autograph of this undated letter was once in Naas, but currently cannot be located. The photostat of the letter in Mercy Congregational Archives, Dublin, is dated "July 1841" in the index to the bound volume of photostats titled *Letters of Mother McAuley 1841*, but that date cannot be correct. Neumann dates this letter "[November 18, 1840]"

212. To Sister M. Frances Warde
Carlow

Convent, Baggot St.
November 24, 1840[51]

My own Dear Sister Mary Frances

The very first prayer or praise I offered on my arrival was to return most grateful thanks to God for the sweet and heavenly consolation I received in my visit to Carlow, and to implore His blessing and gracious protection for those who have been so instrumental in bringing this branch of the Institution to its present flourishing and happy state.[52] My anxiety about your opening in Wexford encreases every hour—and you must not think me tiresome, if I repeat again what experience has imprinted on my mind.[53]

Commence the visitation soon as possible—let four go out some days at the same time if only for one hour. Do not let the least difference appear in dress—shape of Bonnet, etc., etc. They are so long expected, every eye will be turned on them, and while we place all our confidence in God—we must act as if all depended on our exertion, etc. I must stop now—but I can scarcely do so—though I could only repeat what you know as well as I do. I have sent for the veiling and cloth to make a cloak for you—you must go out a little—and all in the same cloaks.[54] Entreat Father Maher to remain until you get an addition—and of all things, get him to preach at the profession—this will give life to the whole. Never cease begging Father Maher to assist in forming the new branch. A good beginning is of great importance. [55]

3 o'c—I have not got the veiling yet, though we sent before 9 o'c.

God bless you—and each of the dear Sisters. All well here, etc.

Your ever affectionate
Mary C. McAuley

Mr. Strange has just called for the copy of the will.[56]

(255–56), and Bolster dates it "[18–23 November 1840]" (168–69). I tend to agree with the November 1840 dating, given the letter's content. Those who came to Dublin or elsewhere in Ireland for the summer months and then hired servants—for example, middle and upper class landowners from England who kept houses in Ireland—left when the weather turned colder. Commercial hiring in Dublin was also to some extent dependent on this summer population. **51** As Catherine McAuley indicates in the last postscript paragraph, this letter was written over a two-day period, November 24–26, after she returned from Carlow. **52** Catherine McAuley visited the Carlow community for a few days sometime between November 18 or 19 and November 23. **53** Frances Warde and the Carlow community will establish a new foundation of Sisters of Mercy in Wexford on December 8, 1840. **54** These sentences are Catherine McAuley's only extensive recorded discussion of religious clothing. In her biography of Catherine McAuley in the Bermondsey Annals, Mary Clare Moore claims: "Although very careful to have her own exterior appearance and that of her Religious suitable to the holy dignity of their calling, her under clothing was always of the meanest description" (Sullivan, *Catherine McAuley* 114). **55** James Maher of Carlow-Graigue will accompany the foundation to Wexford. **56** Lawrence Strange had two daughters in the Carlow community, both novices: Mary Rose (Rosina) entered on October 15, 1838; Mary Elizabeth (Hester), on December 21, 1839. A third daughter, Fanny, will enter on June 5, 1841, later taking the name Mary Aloysius. The Stranges were cousins of Dr. Nicholas Wiseman.

Do not wear the cashmere in Wexford, my darling child—the cape is not nice.

You must waste some time with visitors—and introduce the Sisters. Make Sister M. T.[57] come forward on all occasions while you are with her—that she may learn the manner of acting when you are not.

I promised my little Fanny a broach [brooch] to fasten her collar & six kisses on the back. It was my dear Mary Teresa's.[58]

Sister Aloysius remarkably well—Mr. O'H says he never saw her so healthy looking. God, I trust, will preserve her so until we go.

I send you the beautiful veils, and I wish I could have the comfort of seeing you with it on. It is a present—and the cloak—which I got lighter than we generally wear—get it made immediately—before the cold comes.

This has been written these two days. I got your welcome letter just as we were coming out from the ceremony—& by the same post a conclusive one for Birr.

Autograph: West Hartford

213. To "Little Fanny Warde"[59]   [November 24–26, 1840]
Carlow

> Though this is very dear to me
> For reasons strong and many
> I give it with fond love to Thee
> My doat'y—"little Fanny"[60]
>
> Six kisses too from out my heart
> So sweet tho' from a Granny
> With one of them you must not part
> My doat'y—"little Fanny"
>
> What shall I wish now let me see
> Which I wish most of any
> That you—a nice good child shall be
> My doat'y—"little Fanny"

[Mary C. McAuley]

Autograph: Silver Spring

---

57 Mary Teresa (Maria) Kelly professed her vows in Carlow on June 11, 1839. On December 8, 1840, she will become the founding superior of the Wexford community.   58 Little Fanny Warde was the niece of Frances Warde. The brooch Catherine McAuley sent her, with a poem-letter (Letter 213), had belonged to Catherine's beloved niece Mary Teresa Macauley.   59 Catherine McAuley folded into thirds the paper (4 inches x 6 inches) on which she wrote this poem, and then addressed it to "Little Fanny Warde," with quotation marks.

60 In 1936, Mary Paul Xavier Warde, Frances Warde's grandniece and a member of the Sisters of Mercy in Manchester, New Hampshire, annotated a typed copy of this poem, saying that it was

214. To Sister M. Frances Warde   Convent
    Carlow   November 30, 1840

My Dear Sister Mary Frances

There cannot be any objection to your wearing the Cashmere cloaks if you prefer them. I believe the Sisters every where think they have a more religious appearance. It must be difficult to preserve them nice looking in winter. The frequent cleaning in Dublin would soon make them look very badly.

I hope most sincerely Mr. Lacy will not furnish the convent in a worldly style, but a few days since, I heard "the fashion of Naas" spoken of.[61]

Father Dan Nolan said Mass for us this day & yesterday. He only heard of his brother's death on Saturday, tho' the account was in Dublin when we came from Carlow. He feels it very much. He returns this day.

Sister Aloysius goes on very well—tho' we have had great fog. She does not look so well, I think, but says she is free from any uneasiness. It will seem long to me till she is again in clear fresh air.[62]

While providing for the head and shoulders, do not neglect the poor feet, to which the[63] Repealer has directed particular attention—O'Connell's speech at a public dinner—Carrick-on-Suir:

"No country on the face of the earth is like Ireland. Look at the fairest portion of creation, educated and possessing all the virtues that adorn and endear life, forsaking their homes, their families and friends, entering a Convent in the morning of their days to devote long lives to piety and the promotion of virtue. Look at the Sisters of Mercy—hear, hear—wrapped in their long black cloaks, they are seen gliding along the streets, in this humble attire, while a slight glance at the foot shews the educated Lady. Thus they go forth, not for the purpose of amusement or delight. No, they are hastening to the lone couch of some sick fellow creature fast sinking into the grave, with none to console, none to sooth [*sic*]. They come with hope and consolation, and bring down with their prayers the blessings of God on the dying sinner, on themselves, and on their Country—cheers— oh such a Country is too good to continue in slavery—great cheering."

written "not to Mother Warde, but to a younger Fanny Warde, my father's sister." Mary Paul Xavier's father was Frances Warde's nephew John Warde, the son of Frances's brother John. Carroll says that young Fanny lost her father in 1839, when he died in England leaving his widow and four children; she also claims that young Fanny eventually died of consumption (*Leaves* 1:255). Catherine McAuley speaks of this young fatherless family in her letter to Frances Warde on June 6, 1840 (Letter 173).

The typescript has "doat'g" which is annotated "darling." However, the word in the autograph is clearly "doat'y," with exactly the same meaning: darling, fond, silly in the sense of lovable.

61 The Mercy convent in Naas, founded from Carlow, opened on September 24, 1839.   62 The fresh air in Birr, Co. Offaly.   63 Catherine McAuley wrote "to which to Repealer," clearly a slip of the pen.

This afforded great amusement here—each claiming for her foot the tribute of praise.

Sister Mary Teresa the Less[64]—is on her way home from Limerick. I am quite distressed to find the P.P. is taking the trouble to accompany her, tho' an inconvenient time to leave home.[65] She is to be the travelling companion—the only one I had. We must have another ceremony of Profession before I go. I fear poor Dr. M[urray] will get a surfeit.[66]

I am trying to fill this up—and cannot. God Almighty bless you—your old favorite prayer. Give my love to all—and respectful remembrance to Father Maher.

Your ever affectionate
M. C. McAuley

Sister M. Aloysius sends a thousand loves, etc.

Autograph: West Hartford

215. To Sister M. de Sales White   Convent, Baggot Street
Bermondsey   December 7, 1840

My very Dear Sister Mary de Sales

I know a few lines will be acceptable to you—a long letter is a formidable concern for me. All well here. Sister M. Aloysius in good health and spirits, making diligent preparation for her mission to Birr—Sister M. Rose to be professed on the 15th, as her assistant—a postulant, Sister Anna Maria, to make the third—little Sister M. Teresa my companion. Perhaps I have told this already. I must keep a memorandum book to mark where I wrote and what I said. My memory is beginning to puzzle me.

The founders leave Carlow for Wexford this day, and Sister Susan goes from this to join them tomorrow, as she was designed for Wexford.[67] Two enter on tomorrow, Miss MacDonnell and Miss Vigne, a convert—both well educated and young—18 & 23.[68]

I shall now feel very anxious to hear of the Holy Profession of your dear religious namesake.[69] Give her my most affectionate regards, and tell her the best prayers I can say shall be offered for her.

---

64 That is, Mary Teresa (Catherine) White.   65 John Brahan was parish priest of St. Mary's, Limerick, where the Mercy convent was located.   66 In addition to the ceremony on November 26 (previously planned for November 19), at which Mary Elizabeth Butler professed her vows and Mary Magdalen (Margaret) Polding and Mary Angela (Caroline) Borini received the habit, Catherine was planning a ceremony for December 15, when Mary Rose (Catherine) Lynch, destined for the Birr foundation, would profess her vows. Apparently Daniel Murray presided on both of these occasions.   67 Susan Wall, a postulant, had entered the Baggot Street community for the upcoming Wexford foundation. She joined the founding party in Wexford on December 8.   68 Teresa MacDonnell and Frances Vigne.   69 Mary de Sales (Barbara) Eyre professed her vows at the convent in Bermondsey on April 22, 1841.

When I went for Sister M. A. to Carlow I saw the Doctor. He is very well—and all his family—so near an increase that Mrs. W could not venture to the Convent.[70] Their little Margaret is quite a smart pupil at the pension school—in deep affliction on the day I was there—for getting a bad judgment.

All well in Galway. They are beginning to press us now for Westport.[71] We must refer that matter to Father Daly. It gives me great consolation & relief to find Carlow so prepared to divide. I think they will now keep it up. Liverpool is expected to be the next. In about another year Limerick will be starting. Cork could step out, but Doctor Murphy will be slow and sure.

Sister M. Aloysius looks remarkably well. She will be a nice little Mother Superior. Sister Teresa is much better since she took the pledge.[72] I suppose the wine that I thought so necessary was not good for her. Twenty one Sisters now belong to the total temperance society for whom Masses are offered occasionally—and a daily memento made by the Apostle of Temperance. The convent in Birr is dedicated to him. He is now generally called an Apostle, by Bishops, Priests, etc.—and is said to have received a special Commission. His cooperation has been faithful indeed—no labor—or endless importunity ever wearies him. For days together he is speaking & standing amidst multitudes, an object of wonder—which is so truly distressing to a mind like his. He sent us all silver medals—& others to our poor people. Sr. M. Cecilia was first in the last Batch though she had determined not to be one. Mary Duffy, a most ardent aspirant—Ann Quin—who attends the door—would not take it—she thought it quite awful—and we did not urge her.[73]

[December] 8th—our two postulants arrived—Teresa MacDonnell and Frances Vigne. The former you have heard of—she was a deliberator, and has yet something doubtful in her manner—the other, prompt and promising. Time will tell more.

The Sisters went yesterday to Wexford—Sr. Wall joins them this day.

[December] the 9th—and my poor letter not finished. I have a round of letters to write before I move for the foundation and must make them all shorter than this.

Give my very fond love to my dear Sister M. Xavier. Mother de P., M. Cecilia, M. Aloysius, Sr. Magdeline,[74] and many more unite in affectionate remembrance to you both.

Pray for me and believe me ever your attached Mother in Christ
Mary C. McAuley

---

70 Mary de Sales White's brother Matthew Esmonde White, MD and his family lived in Carlow where he served as a physician at the Carlow Lunatic Asylum. The Asylum served the counties of Carlow, Kildare, Kilkenny, and Wexford (Lewis 263). Their son was born before December 20 (see Letter 220).   71 The first convent of Mercy in Westport was founded from Carlow in 1842.   72 Teresa Carton.   73 Mary Duffy and Ann Quin were residents of the House of Mercy on Baggot Street.   74 Mary Magdalen Flynn, one of the earliest members of the Baggot Street community.

This paper is so thin, the writing can be seen through. I must give you a grand cover. God almighty bless you—both.

I wrote to Mr. Daly, and said I was marking out a nice little plan—"go to Birmingham in August, to Bermondsey in September, to Galway in October for the Profession—and to see the new Convent in great progress."

I forgot to tell you little Sister Mary Teresa is come home—to accompany me to Birr. She is very well. I find I have written this already.

Autograph: Liverpool

216. To Catherine McAuley   Violet Hill, Newry
                                                      December 10, 1840

Dear Rev. Mother

I most cordially participate in the joy you feel on seeing your holy order spreading its branches so rapidly and so prosperously through Ireland and England, and with you and all the holy members of that order I return my most fervent thanks to God for its happy increase and diffusion, and I beseech him that what is going on so well may succeed every day still better. [At the same time while I dwell with delight on that heart cheering view, I am only the more anxious that as your cares and responsibility increase, so may also your vigilance and strength. An empire extended, the more is it liable to fall by decay in some of the parts, so in the sacred societies by which the virtues of the Gospel are propagated, unless with their growth. I cannot say, however, that I feel painfully anxious.][75]

It has indeed exceeded all my expectations and has exemplified in a very striking manner the reasonableness of that conviction which Religion establishes.

[Michael Blake]

Author's transcript: Dromore

217. To John Hardman, Jr.   Convent, Baggot Street
        Birmingham   December 14, 1840

Dear Sir

I beg to thank you for the Bank order just received. I am sorry to find your excellent Father is not as well as usual.[76] This is always a very trying season. We

---

[75] The sentences in brackets are in the draft letter in Dr. Blake's Journal of Letters, but it is unclear whether he meant to include them in the letter or struck them out.   [76] The bank order was payment of the half-year expenses of his sister Juliana at Baggot Street. See Letter 202, note 5. John Hardman, Sr. was in failing health, but lived well beyond the foundation in Birmingham in August 1841.

feel great anxiety here about him, so much that I should almost fear it would weaken the ardent spirit which now animates the Birmingham party, if we were not to have a hope of seeing him, but we shall, please God—and also the happiness of uniting with him in prayer as he is to be one of our Community in the Convent chapel.

Your dear gentle Sister and companions are remarkably well, and although very happy and always cheerful—yet they occasionally feel a holy impatience for the completion of their term, which is so much in accordance with their destination, that we could not wish to see them divested of it.

Requesting my very best regards to your respected family, and most earnestly wishing them and you—all the graces and blessings of this happy season—I remain
Dear Sir, with much esteem, very faithfully, etc., etc.
Mary C. McAuley

Autograph: Birmingham

218. To Sister M. Frances Warde   Convent— Tuesday
       Wexford   December 15, 1840

My Dearest Sr. M. Frances
The ceremony just over and I as usual—tired doing nothing.[77]

Your accounts from Wexford are very gratifying, and from what you say of the Orphan House, I should think it quite suitable. I recollect one of the objections started here—was that the engraved stone—with "Orphan House"—could not be removed, and that the Sisters would be regarded as Matrons of the Establishment. This, I think, could never be. I am certain the title would be changed immediately, no matter what stone was up. Sr. M. Teresa[78] said she would prefer it to any House in the Town, except the Parochial House. You might propose having "Institution of Mercy" substituted, as some public tribute seemed necessary to the memory of the Benefactors.

Sr. Teresa takes the paper to look for arrivals at Hotels every day for one halfpenny. She pointed out to me this morning a paragraph from the Wexford paper—announcing the arrival of "Sisters of Charity." I immediately sent the following, which will appear tomorrow: "Sisters of Mercy"—"The beloved and venerated Doctor Keating, Catholic Bishop of Ferns, has brought a branch of this order into the Town of Wexford, from the flourishing Establishment in Carlow."

We got another little Sr. this morning—nice little creature—light purse.

I would advise you to sanction the Orphan House being changed into a Convent. The Bishop seemed quite anxious it should be so, and it is a pity to have such a good concern so partially employed.

---

77 On December 15, 1840, Mary Rose Lynch professed her vows.   78 Mary Teresa (Amelia) White, now in Galway, lived in Co. Wexford in her early life.

I have not a moment more.

I am fonder of Sister Aloysius since she came from Carlow than ever I was. She feels such affectionate gratitude, that a letter from Wexford—makes her grow quite red and she is all impatience to hear it. She will write soon—never ceased working since she came for the foundation.

May God Almighty bless you and all with you—and in Carlow.

Your ever affectionate
M. C. McAuley

Autograph: Silver Spring

219. To Sister M. Frances Warde   December 17, 1840
     Wexford

My Dearest Sister Mary Frances

I this day received the enclose[d]—to which I returned the following answer:

> My Dear Sr. M. J.[79]
>
> I have seldom heard anything more extraordinary than your expectation of a Sister who never was spoken to on the subject—until she heard Revd. Mr. Doyle came for her. I did not know that she or her friends ever heard there was a Convent in Naas. If the least intimation had been made to me— she would not have been admitted here—of this you may rest assured. But how could such arrangement take place without any communication with you—she laughs at it and says she thought the Superioress was the person to act on such occasions. She was educated in two Convents and seems to know the usual regulations.
>
> Worldly persons never can tran[s]act religious affairs. I am distressed very much, Dear Sr. M. J.—to hear you say—"I wrote two letters to you, etc., etc., but just at that time I got the painful intelligence of my Dear Sister which engaged All my thoughts since." I hope not, Dear Sr. M. J. This would be a bad way to make religious houses flourish.
>
> Your enclosure came safe. The veiling will be ready on Saturday. Earnestly wishing you all the graces and blessings of this Holy Season, I remain, etc., etc., your affectionate—

I thought this a short mode of explaining the whole matter to you.[80] I wish the young Sr. had gone to Naas—but now she would not think of it. God forbid—

---

79 Mary Josephine Trennor, the superior of the convent in Naas, founded from Carlow on September 24, 1839. 80 The issue seems to have been the following: A young woman entered the Baggot Street convent who those in Naas had hoped would enter the Naas convent. With Mary Josephine Trennor's apparent acquiescence, Gerald Doyle, the parish priest, and the Barretts came to Baggot Street to solicit the young woman's departure for Naas. Catherine McAuley and apparently the postulant herself were ignorant of the desires in Naas until the conversations at Baggot Street.

I should ever get a Sr.—by disappointing the hopes of another House. I need not give you any caution—not to speak of her letter. She would reasonably think it was not sent in as a mark of approbation, but I think it well you should know that Mr. & Mrs. Barrett are her agents—in procuring Sisters, or endeavouring to do so. You might say that I felt greatly mortified on hearing that Mrs. Barrett had promised to bring the Sr. in question, and that she acceded to it without taking any part. Mrs. Barrett told me she & Mr. B. conducted the whole matter, and never spoke with the intended postulant. This is very disedifying and will create much idle talking. Mr. Hume[81] was here this day. He says nothing could equal the disappointment. I had the Sr. called to him and she repeated exactly what I have written. Did you ever hear such a strange proceeding? I pressed her to go—but she would not consent. Sr. M. J. will never advance the good work in this way,

I have two letters to write for this post—they shall be 5 lines & half. God almighty bless you.

Your ever affectionate
M. C. McAuley

Dr. Warde's prescription shall be carefully followed—what alarm you must have felt at the floods—3 letters from London yesterday—all well.

We go to Birr by Tullamore. I did not know it was so near till we got an invitation. Sleep there on Saturday 26th—and go into Birr St. John's day, after our devotions—only 20 miles. Sister M. Aloysius seemed quite happy to hear of the stop—or rest—which shews there is something yet to fear. This foundation ought to be made from Tullamore—it is quite a shame to be such creep-mouses— in such a cause. I will give bitter scolding, and 3 cheers for Carlow.

I hope you have had the happiness of seeing the truly charitable Mr. R. Devereux[82]—he was so kind to call on me—and as usual—it was not a mere visit of compliment. He always brings us what Sr. Teresa calls "good luck." Mr. O'Connell came next day with £5 and an unknown with £10. We remark something of this kind always after Mr. D's visit.

I had a strong remonstrance from the Revd. Mr. Butler, London—about the new branches getting any other name—than "Lady of Mercy." He alludes to "Apostle of Temperance"—and says—"It (the order) will soon degenerate if this is let to pass—we shall seek in vain for a Convent of The 'Sisters of Mercy.'" If he hears of an "Orphan House" I will certainly get another letter—his pious pride is quite wounded.

Autograph: Silver Spring

---

81 George Hume, curate in Naas.   82 Mr. Richard Devereux was a major benefactor of the new convent in Wexford, founded from Carlow on December 8, 1840. The founding community were Mary Teresa Kelly, superior, Mary Gertrude (Joanna) Kinsella, Mary Aloysius (Julia) Redmond, Mary Bridget (Margaret) Hackett, and Susan Wall, the postulant from Baggot Street.

220. To Sister M. de Sales White   [December 20, 1840]
Bermondsey

My Dearest Sister M. de Sales

I think sometimes our passage through this dear sweet world is something like the Dance called "right and left." You and I have crossed over, changed places, etc., etc.—your set is finished—for a little time you'll dance no more—but I have now to go through the figure—called Sir Roger de Coverly—too old for your memory. I'll have to curtsie and bow, in Birr—presently, to change corners—going from the one I am in at present to another, take hands of every one who does me the honor—and end the figure by coming back to my own place. I'll then have a Sea Saw dance to Liverpool—and a Merry Jig that has no stop to Birmingham— and, I hope, a second—to Bermondsey—when you, Sister M. Xavier and I will join hands—and dance the "Duval" Trio, back on the same ground.[83]

We have one solid comfort amidst this little tripping about: our hearts can always be in the same place, centered in God—for whom alone we go forward— or stay back. Oh may He look on us with love and pity, and then we shall be able to do anything He wishes us to do—no matter how difficult to accomplish— or painful to our feelings. If He looks on us with approbation for one instant each day—it will be sufficient to bring us joyfully on to the end of our journey. Let us implore Him to do so at this season of love and Mercy.

I am greatly comforted by the good account I hear of you. My poor old child[84] says you are a comfort to her—for which God will bless you, as her place is very arduous & trying.

Pray much for your affectionate

M. C. McAuley

I am rejoiced to hear of the Baptism of your nephew. I wish the Princess Royal was such a fortunate child.[85]

I have so exhausted my words and thoughts writing a round of foundation circulars to each of the foreign powers that I never could have written this had not a lively spirit inspired me to dance through it—Air by Roderige—"Where ever duty calls me" ♫ ♫ ♫[86]—*no crotchet.*[87]

Autograph: Liverpool

83 Mary de Sales White and Mary Xavier O'Connell had been lent to the Bermondsey community in mid October 1840. Catherine intended to bring them back to Dublin when she went to England to found the Birmingham community in August–September 1841. In this paragraph Catherine uses as metaphors five English country dances that she had learned years before, perhaps in the Callaghan household. She never lost her love for dancing, and once closed a letter to the Baggot Street community with the injunction: "Dance every evening" (Letter 228).   84 Mary Clare Moore, superior of the Bermondsey community, was one of the first twelve sisters in the Baggot Street community; in the years prior to her departure for Cork in July 1837, she had been a very talented help to Catherine McAuley, which Catherine never forgot.   85 Victoria, the daughter of Queen Victoria and Prince Albert, was born in 1840. She was the first of their nine children.   86 More research needs to be done on this passage, but I suspect that Catherine is turning into a song a line on

221. **To Sister Mary Joseph Joyce** [Baggot Street]
     Galway [c. December 20, 1840]

My Dearest Sister M. J.[88]

I am delighted to find you continue so happy, indeed I had no fears that you would not—from the first visit I felt that you were to be a happy addition to our number. How gratifying it is to hear that your dear Papa is so fully satisfied.

A very nice interesting young person—who is most anxious to unite with us here—has exactly the same difficulties to contend with that you had at first.[89] On our last ceremony day, I thought we had succeeded in prevailing on her to remain, as you did—but a Priest was soon sent for her, and she like a poor faint-hearted soul was afraid to stay—if she had, all would have been settled now. I told her your story, but could not impart any share of your pious determination. A man not half the size of Dr. Browne[90] alarmed her—and though all in tears at going, the little coward would not stay. She is promised at Easter, but I fear much it will be Christmas again before that promise is redeemed.

Nothing like Christian courage—the Church would not have one martyr to rejoice in without it. Your little branch is beginning to be spoken of. You will soon increase, and once you begin, you will go on. That is our way. I shall be looking forward with delight to the time of holy Profession. I frequently cheer my spirits with the view of it—to me, an old traveller, it does not appear distant.

I think we are done with foundations for a long time. Birr will entirely exhaust us.

Will you present my respects to Papa and Mamma. My affectionate remembrance to the little dove with the Roman cloak.[91]

Praying God to grant you an increase of spiritual blessings, I remain

My dear Sister M. J., your much attached
M. C. McAuley

Autograph: Galway (severely damaged); handcopies: Brisbane and Dublin, Mercy

---

obedience from Alonso Rodriguez's *The Practice of Christian and Religious Perfection*, a work she is known to have read often to the Baggot Street community. 87 Catherine is evidently using the word "crotchet" in two senses: to say that her dance metaphors are no mere whim or caprice, and to assert that the musical notes she has penned before the expression "no crotchet" are not quarter notes (crotchets), but symbols of an even more lively tempo. The "lively spirit" that has animated her letter writing is, she believes, no fanciful whim, but a gift of God, kindly accompanying her persevering attempt to fulfill her relatively heavy duties of correspondence. 88 Mary Joseph (Christina) Joyce was now a novice. She had received the habit on October 1, 1840, while Catherine McAuley was in Galway. 89 Christina Joyce's parents, very religious and wealthy citizens of Galway, were initially reluctant to allow their daughter to enter the Sisters of Mercy, given the promising future they assumed she would have as a married woman. No one could foresee that she would die of cholera in 1849, contracted while caring for disease- and famine-stricken patients in Galway (*Convent* 14). 90 Dr. George J. P. Browne, bishop of Galway. 91 The "little dove" (one of Catherine's favorite terms of endearment for young girls) was Mary Joseph Joyce's little sister

222. **To Sister M. Elizabeth Moore**   Convent
     Limerick   December 20, 1840

> Don't miss one word of this very nice letter
> I often write more—but seldom write better.

My Dear Sister Mary Elizabeth

You must have the well known—Mrs. Moore—once more before we part. I must tell you what others say & what I have already said, for my poor stock in trade is quite exhausted. I wrote to Mother Mary Ann[92] asking—could she let five go to sleep—on Saturday 26th—and could our devotions on Sunday, breakfast & visit to the new Convent by over by 12 o'c—2 post carriages ready to start for Birr. I prayed her to answer quickly—plainly & briefly. She writes as follows:

> "Céad Míle Fáilte"[93]—good dry lodging, entertainment for man and beast—Coffee for teetotalers—Mass at 8 o'c, Breakfast 9½—visit the new Convent at 10—2 first rate chaises from head Inn—at the door at 12—refreshments with the P. P. of Eglish (Father Murtagh) half way—arrive in Birr—4 o'c P.M. No fog till 5. Dear Revd. Mother, affectionately."

Sister Aloysius heard this read with great surprise. She did not suppose there was so much life in that quarter—if she had not read it she would be certain it fell out of my poor head.

As I must go through the rounds of writing—called "the foundation circulars," after having finished—to Mother M. Clare, England—and Sister Xavier—I really did not know what to say to my poor Sister M. de Sales, from whom I have two or three unanswered letters, when some lively spirit suggested the thought of dancing through it. I wrote as follows—it has made them laugh here—and if it has the same effect on you, I will think the time well spent in running it over again.

> My Dear Sr. M. de S.
>
> I have just thought that our passage through this sweet world is something like the dance—Right & Left—you and I have crossed over, changed places, etc. Your sett is finished for a little time, but I have now to go through the long figure— called "Sir Roger De Coverley"[94]—too old per-

---

who had received a beautiful new cloak during her family's trip to Rome, just prior to Christina's entrance into the Galway convent.   92 Mary Ann Doyle, the superior in Tullamore.   93 "A hundred thousand welcomes"—in Irish. Unfortunately this letter from Mary Ann Doyle is no longer extant.   94 The "Sir Roger de Coverley" is a very old English song and country dance brought to Ireland in the eighteenth century and distinctively naturalized by Irish dancers. It is a slip jig and corresponds with the native Irish Hey dance; it is called the Virginia Reel in the United States (Scholes 534 and Jewitt 31–32). The "Sir Roger" is a long dance involving several figures danced by a large group of facing couples, the top gentleman and bottom lady leading off the first figure, the top couple then dancing the "strip the willow" figure, and the same couple finally inviting the two lines of dancers

haps for your memory. I'll have to curtsie & bow in Birr—to change cornors—leaving the one I am now in for another—take hands of all—who will present theirs, and end the figure by coming back to my own place. Next—a Sea Saw dance to Liverpool—and a merry Jig that has no stop— to Birmingham—another to Bermondsey—when Sister M. Xavier, you and I will join hands and dance the "Duval Trio"—back on the same ground.

We have one solid source of happiness amidst—all this tripping: we can keep our hearts fixed on God. Neither change of motion or place can deprive us of this—and if he will vouchsafe to look towards us for one moment each day with complacency, we shall get on joyfully to the end of our journey. Oh let us implore Him to do so at this season of Mercy and Love.

Now what shall I say to yourself—worn out as I am. You don't require much. Your path is now "strewed with" flowers—for the Bazaar—and all the pretty dolls & toys—will bring you back to the gaiety and innocence of childhood, and when you see them changed into Bread & Broth and Blankets,[95] your heart will rejoice, and your offering will—I trust—be rendered fully acceptable by the pure love which produces it.

May God grant you every blessing. I will write to you from Birr.

Pray often for your ever affectionate

M. C. McAuley

My best love to my Dear Sister Vincent and each dear Sister. Will you offer my respectful remembrance to Revd. Mr. Brahan.

Autograph: Limerick

223. To Dr. Daniel Murray

Baggot Street
December 22, 1840

My Lord

I am exceedingly sorry to inform your Grace, that our little plan of a pension school in Kingstown has not yet succeeded.[96] At anytime during the summer

---

through an arch to begin the dance again, themselves now at the bottom of the group. Catherine McAuley's description of the travels she anticipates shows a thorough firsthand knowledge of the "Sir Roger de Coverley." **95** The proceeds of the bazaar in Limerick will be used in their House of Mercy and on visitations to the sick poor. **96** The sisters had left the branch house in Kingstown in November 1838 because the Baggot Street community could not afford to pay the £450 bill—wrongfully assigned to them by the parish priest and builder—for converting the coach house and stable on the Kingstown property into a school for poor girls. A lawsuit had been brought against Catherine McAuley by James Nugent, the builder of the poor school. The suit was settled in 1838 in his favor, and the Baggot Street community eventually had to pay the remaining £375. In April 1840 they returned to Kingstown at the archbishop's request, with the hope of defraying their expenses by operating a pension school for tuition-paying middle class children, while still conducting the poor school.

we had not more than six—now only three. Before we were proceeded against for building the poor school—my Lord—the extra expenses incurred by every distinct establishment were defrayed by a Miss McGuinness [Magenis] from Newry—who not being found eligible for a Sister remained as a Benefactress, but was so great an oddity we were obliged to part.

We would not have returned to Kingstown—my Lord—had not Mr. Hamilton[97] expressed very strong desire on the part of your Grace, that we should do so—saying that a portion of some means left at your disposal was allotted to this purpose. I have made every exertion in my power, my Lord, to keep it up for eight months, but cannot go on without some assistance. It would not add more than fifty pounds a year to have the Sisters with us here. It will be more than one hundred to keep them there. If we had even what would sustain it during the winter months, we might make another trial of the school—in spring.[98]

I have the honor to remain, My Lord,

most respectfully etc.

Mary C. McAuley

Autograph: Dublin Diocese, Murray Papers AB3/34/15, no. 19

---

97 John Hamilton, secretary to Dr. Murray.   98 Some temporary financial help was evidently provided. The Sisters of Mercy remained in Kingstown until after Catherine McAuley's death, then departed once again in the early 1840s, only to return soon after, and this time permanently.

January–February 1841

"With all around me covered with snow, and my poor fingers petrified, I will endeavour to write a few lines to you"—thus Catherine McAuley wrote on January 20, 1841 from Birr, the new foundation of Sisters of Mercy in the central table land of Ireland where she spent the first six weeks of 1841 (Letter 230). In Birr, her "poor Bethlehem," she trudged through the snow and cold, visiting families bitterly wounded by the longstanding schism in the local church. Yet despite the seriousness of their mission of reconciliation, she was amazingly refreshed in Birr: by the newborn enthusiasm of Mary Aloysius Scott, the superior, by the "pure sparkling spring water," and by the humorous comments their presence in the town elicited. As she wrote to Baggot Street in early January: "Hurra for foundations, makes the old young and the young merry" (Letter 226).

True, Dr. Patrick Kennedy, bishop of Killaloe, was "no great patron of nuns" (Letter 230), the parish priest was too busy to help them, and Father Theobald Mathew disappointed—by not responding to mail and not coming to the reception ceremony on February 2. But still there were causes for laughter: Catherine's own makeshift petticoat, her whole wardrobe soaked with mud and melted snow; the tiny tea cups—"baby toys" compared to "a real Baggot Street drink of tea" (Letter 233); and "the sweet little Mice" (Letter 238).

When Catherine returned alone to Dublin on February 10, after a coach journey of ten hours, new concerns commanded her attention. Mary de Pazzi Delany had been very ill; Cecilia Marmion was worn out, training at least fifteen novices and postulants and entertaining numerous bishops who were in Dublin for the solemn consecration of St. Andrew's Church and for their annual synod in early February; typhus struck the Wexford and Limerick communities, and the London influenza hit six at Baggot Street; Anna Maria Maher was still searching for a convent to enter; Marianne Beckett had gone to England, trying to discern her faith and her vocation; and a great change had overcome Catherine's nephew James, now dying in Blackrock.

The nineteen extant letters of these two months—all of them written to Sisters of Mercy—conclude in the first week of Lent, the last Lenten season of Catherine McAuley's life. In a profoundly reflective letter to Mary de Sales White and Mary Xavier O'Connell in London, Catherine cautions against excessive fasting: "You will be far more mortified in taking that which you do not like to take, than in abstaining from it," and then remarks, with her proverbial common sense: "Let us take one day only in hands at a time, merely making a resolve for tomorrow. Thus we may hope to get on—taking short careful steps, not great strides" (Letter 241).

224. To Sister M. Angela Dunne   **[Birr]**
     Charleville   **[Early January, 1841][1]**

[Dear Sister Mary Angela]

We left Dublin on Saturday, the 26th of December 1840, arrived in Tullamore at three o'clock, found all well and happy. I am sure I do not know how they contrived to get us five beds. We had Mass in the choir on Sunday morning from Dr. O'Rafferty, who is now quite versed in our foundation affairs. We left Tullamore at twelve o'clock, and reached our present abode at six. We were very busy persons all Monday; bespoke our tables, entrance-bell, tin teapot, chairs, etc.; received visitors, and commenced our retreat at the usual time; left the reception room, and lived in our cells.[2] How sweet, how blessed is our life, which affords much consolation and enjoyment when all that the world values is shut out from us. Everywhere I thought the sun was shining even too much. I do not think any one in the midst of all the Christmas festivities was so happy as we were.

This is a fine old house; one room is as large as our old school-room in Baggot Street. It is beautifully situated; open country all about, and view of gardens and fields. Our garden is small. I have never seen, to any convent, such a one as in Charleville. We are quite close to the parish church—a fine building. Father Spain[3] is very kind. We have some hope of being joined by postulants. One candidate has started already.

I suppose you heard that Sister Mary Frances, and six sisters, are gone to Wexford.[4] She remains for two months. Sister M. Aloysius Scott is Superior here; she is delicate. I trust God will restore her. She has been a most edifying, humble sister.

Praying God to grant to you, and to each of us, the full benefit of our renovation,[5] and Divine grace to perform all our holy resolutions, and begging you to pray for me ...

                                   [M. C. McAuley]

Published transcription: Harnett, Life 177–78

1 No autograph or early handcopy of this letter has been found. However, Mary Vincent Harnett, a careful early biographer who knew Catherine McAuley personally at Baggot Street and in Limerick, includes the letter, as presented here, in her *Life* (177–78). 2 The foundation of the Sisters of Mercy in Birr, in the diocese of Killaloe, occurred on December 27, 1840. In the founding party were Mary Aloysius Scott, the new superior, Mary Rose (Catherine) Lynch, who had just professed her vows on December 15, and Anna Maria McEvoy, a postulant from Baggot Street, as well as Catherine McAuley and Mary Teresa (Catherine) White, her travelling companion. In Birr and in all the existing Mercy convents a spiritual retreat was observed on the last three days of the calendar year, beginning on the night of December 28, after celebration of the feast of the Holy Innocents. 3 John Spain, vicar general of the diocese of Killaloe and parish priest in Birr. 4 Mary Teresa Kelly, the superior; Mary Bridget Hackett, Mary Gertrude Kinsella, Mary Aloysius Redmond, novices; and Susan Wall, a postulant, were the community in Wexford founded from Carlow. Kate Farrell joined them as a postulant on December 27, 1840. 5 Here Catherine uses "renovation" to refer to the individual renewal of vows that took place in all Mercy convents on January 1 each

225. **To Sister M. Frances Warde**
    Wexford

Convent of Our Lady of Mercy
St. John's, Birr
[January 2–3, 1841]

My Dearest Sister M. Frances

I am anxious to write to you from my strange habitation—how many new beds have I rested in. When I awake in the morning, I ask myself where I am—and on the last two or three foundations, I could not recollect for some minutes.

This is a good old house—delightfully situated—fields or garden all round it. Just now it appears like a fine summer day, as close to the main street of the town as Baggot St. is to little James St.—yet quite remote from all other buildings—walls or hedges in every direction. It must be particularly healthy. Ten or twelve Sisters could be very well accommodated. There is one fine room nearly as large as our first school room, now Community Room.[6]

Sister Aloysius remarkably well. I firmly believe—Father Mathew has been the agent of her final recovery—he has prayed so much for the Birr foundress. The first good was done by sending her to you—taking her out of the Doctor's hands.[7]

Our journey here was quite free from fatigue. We travelled to Tullamore on Saturday—got good sleep—Sunday morning devotions & breakfast over by 10—went to the new Convent, to which a passage has been made through the garden of the old. It is a beautiful edifice, a grand tribute to religion, an ornament to the Town. I had no idea of its extent. The stairs, which are the finest I ever saw—were not even planed [planned] when I was there last. The Community room—a little longer than our old community room—with rich stucco work. Dr. O'Rafferty[8] complained of the center piece for a hanging lamp—and desired the superintending man to order a vine wreath round it with the leaves much raised. The choir or chapel is in preparation and will be nice indeed. There are 2 reception rooms about the size of Baggot St. parlour—noviciate 24 feet—Infirmary same—Community R[oom] & 30 cells—store rooms—closets—and water brought through the entire House by conductors, so that a pipe may be put anywhere. The school rooms are very fine and connected to the Convent. The entire concern is a great sight from the Canal boat. One of the little foundresses, Sr. M. Rose, said she thought it was a Palace. I am sure God is preparing a distinguished place in Heaven for the generous excellent man who has erected it.[9] If I said much more it would not be too much—it will last for centuries.

---

year: "The Sisters shall on the first day of every year make a renewal of their vows to excite in their hearts an encrease of fervour in the service of their Heavenly Spouse by so solemn a recollection of the obligations they have contracted" (Rule 14.2, in Sullivan, *Catherine McAuley* 308).   6 Throughout this letter Catherine compares the Birr house to the Baggot Street house, with which Frances Warde is familiar.   7 Dr. Dominic Corrigan had been attending Mary Aloysius Scott in Dublin and Booterstown before Catherine sent her to Carlow in mid August 1840.   8 Dr. James O'Rafferty, parish priest in Tullamore and vicar general of the diocese of Meath.   9 Michael Molloy, a distiller in Tullamore and a major benefactor of the Mercy community there.

We got 2 post carriages at 12 o'c—and stopt for dinner with our dear friend, Father Murtagh, P.P. of Eglish, within 4 miles of Birr. Our own P.P., Doctor Spain—Dean & V[icar] G[eneral]—with one of his curates was invited to meet us— 4 Priests & 5 Sisters[10]—a teetotaler entertainment. Coffee served immediately after dinner—arrived at home before 6—said our 2 Thirty Days Prayer, and went to rest.

On Monday, saw 5 or 6 ladies—one candidate, Miss Egan, 24 years old, a fine young person, educated in Thurles Convent.[11] Got 2 turkeys, a leg of mutton, bowl of butter—provision for retreat—which is now happily over. Made our renovation[12] in the Public church—in the midst of a crowded congregation. Your patient was up before five and did not breakfast till after ten. She has risen every morning since we arrived at 5½—looks remarkably well. After Mass the Vicar said: "My dear people, I have a present to make you—I have a new year's gift for you, the most gratifying that a Pastor could have. I present you the Sisters of Mercy, who by their example and pious instruction will draw upon our town the blessings of Heaven—I recommend them to your respectful attention, and I beseech God to bless them and you." We had great laughing at breakfast—saying he might have tried us a little longer—not to make a present of us so soon.

We get a choir made up next week—and an appointed place in the church— which is so near we will not require cloaks or bonnets. You have now nearly all the news.

The unfortunate Crotty is indefatigable in his evil works—he is joined by Mr. Carlile, who was one of the Commissioners of education.[13] They have the

---

10 See Letter 224, note 2.   11 Susan Egan entered the Birr community on February 2, 1841.   12 Renewal of vows.

13 To do justice to the Crottyite schism in Birr requires the chapter of his book that Ignatius Murphy has devoted to it (100–133). By early 1841 Michael Crotty was away from Birr, having left in 1840 and, prior to that, having married in the Church of England (Murphy 128–29). However, his cousin William Crotty was still in Birr, as was James Carlile, a prominent clergyman in the Presbyterian Church, who was now engaged in missionary work in Birr, having resigned as one of the commissioners of national education sometime in 1839. At first William Crotty and James Carlile seem to have collaborated, Crotty having become affiliated with the Presbytery of Dublin in 1839 (Murphy 129). However, "tension between William Crotty and Carlile ... eventually ... led to Crotty's transfer [by the Presbytery] to Roundstone in Connemara in 1841" (Murphy 130).

The difficulties surrounding the Crottys' behavior, including insubordination to successive bishops, dated back to the early 1820s, such that by 1833 Catholic bishops expressed reservations about the validity of the marriages these priests had witnessed, and the confessional absolutions they had offered were thought to be null and void (Murphy 123). Meanwhile, the Catholic people who had been drawn to the ministry of these energetic priests were left vulnerable and divided—by the priests' behavior and by the "essentially hardline" response of Church authorities. Murphy quotes a letter, about an entirely different case, in which John Ennis, parish priest of Booterstown, says that "rigid & prompt severity produced in the case of Crotty of Birr, wounds & woes, marriages & profanations still to be deplored" (qtd. in Murphy 133). It was some of these wounds that Theobald Mathew thought the ministry of the Sisters of Mercy might assuage, if not altogether heal.

James Carlile's missionary intentions in Birr appear to have been straightforwardly proselytizing, convinced as he and many others were at this time that "popery," by which they meant Roman Catholic faith and practice, was harmful to the people.

same church—and preach the same doctrine, "that nothing is to be feared but popery." This speaks well for National education—had Mr. Carlile found it likely to injure the Catholic Church he would not have abandoned it. We have not met any poor Crottyite yet—but expect to see them soon, for they are most unhappy tho' still obstinate—the common punishment of rebellion in religion.

I am delighted to hear Sr. Susan is so useful. We had a very respectable Lady enquiring for Sr. Susan Wallplate. I just thought of the coincidence: our only Susans are Wall and Wallplate. God grant the second may be as faithful and edifying as the first—Sister Martha is a real treasure.[14] Our Postulant here[15] is quite a different person from what she was in Baggot St.—useful in every way. Nothing like foundations for rousing us all.

God almighty bless you, my Dear Sister M. F., and grant us all grace to keep the holy resolutions we made in our retreat.

Your ever affectionate
M. C. McAuley

I will expect a long letter for this.

Autograph: Silver Spring

226. To Sister M. Cecilia Marmion	Convent, Saint John's, Birr
Baggot Street	January 4, 1841

My Dear Sister Mary Cecilia

Here we are surrounded by Newfoundland ice—obliged to keep hot turf under the butter to enable us to cut it. Tell Sister M. Frances[16] I am obliged to take hold of some person to keep me up. Sister Mary Rose & I walked one mile and half yesterday in all the snow to visit an unfortunate family who were followers of Crotty. Our excuse for going uninvited was that they had a son, 26 years old, killed by a fall from a House since we came. The Priest told us to say we came to offer them consolation. We were pretty well received— until a Crottyite Lady arrived—who probably saw us going and came, though in all her little speeches, which she did in profusion, and looking deeply at me, said—"We are all sinners." I bowed as low as Sister Vigne does dancing Sir R[oger de Coverley]. It was snowing greatly and she seemed resolved to wait till it would cease, but finding us disposed to wait her out—which I made known by settling our seats close to the fire—and talking about Father Mathew and the pledge. The old couple—who are now childless—acknowledged it was wonderful—tho' not for some time. They

---

14 Susan Wall was the postulant from Baggot Street who entered the Wexford community. Mary Martha (Susan) Wallplate (or Walplate) was then a professed lay sister in the Dublin community; on August 28, 1843, she became a founding member of the Liverpool community. 15 Anna Maria McEvoy. 16 Mary Frances Boylan, in the Baggot Street community, whose profession of vows had been delayed until September 24, 1840, because of illness.

kept—quite at her side—merely saying it was a good thing. Our Lady retired, and I did all I could to awaken the poor people to a sense of their state. They both promised to come to us, but I fear they have been too long perverse to hope that one visit would produce effect—sysmaticks [schismatics] for eight years.

I wish to tell you what seemed first to draw them a little. They have been deluded by the false charity of the unfortunate fallen Priest—who used to distribute amongst them all that was collected at the church—tho' not his to bestow. It belonged equally to the other clergymen—he was only curate—and in opposition to his Pastor would carry out the money in this way.

They are all replenished with the perverted Texts of Scripture. I asked them, would it not seem that Saint Paul feared we might mistake such conduct for charity—when he said, If you give your goods to feed the poor, etc., etc. I asked—did they not think our Blessed Saviour had tender charity for the poor—and yet when he dwelt amongst them in our mortal state, He did not take any money to give them or remove them from their poverty, which made them dear to him—and which He made choice of for Himself—that when they were constantly about Him, He did not think of relieving their wants until He feared lest they should feint, but was ever attending to their spiritual necessities, and only mindful to prepare them to share in His own Glory, teaching them to bear their short trials and afflictions in submission to the Divine Will, and promising them all the treasures of Heaven for ever & ever. [I] asked them was He not master of all the wealth of this world—did He not love the Poor in a particular manner, [and] which—He or Mr. Crotty—was the best judge of what was good for them, and did He not desire to do all that would make them happy—here by the gifts of His Grace, and hereafter by a share in His Kingdom. They were moved a little. What an awful thing is the loss of Grace. A perverse spirit seems to hold the heart—and force it on to ruin.

Mr. Spain just called to say he had a letter from a lady—asking the terms of admissing [admission] & saying her attention was attracted by an article in the N[ews] Paper. Some visitors were here—and we heard no more.

We had our retreat very happily—shut up reception rooms—retired upstairs—and went through all our exercises most regularly, made the renovation of vows in the Public church—& witnessed by thousands to the great delight of Mr. Spain. Sister Aloysius was up that morning by mistake at half past 4— and fasting till 10—up every morning since we came at our usual hour—and out on the mission almost every day. She has been with a desperate Crottyite who struck the Priest. She was very successful—made him cry heartily. Her appetite and spirits are remarkably good.

On New Year's day, after Mass, Dr. Spain said—"My dear people, I have a new year's gift for you—I have a present to make you, such as is most gratifying to a Pastor's feelings. I present you the 'Sisters of Mercy.'" etc., etc. When we came home, Sister Anna Maria was most humorous. She said, quite in a whining melancholy voice—"He might have kept us a little longer, he need not have given us away so soon." She did it so well that I really thought she was distressed. She is all life and spirits—nothing like foundations for bringing forth. I expect Birmingham will rouse all your dormant faculties—and that you will return, a New Light—not a Crottyite.

Did my sing-song visitor call since?[17]

I have a little secret to tell you—don't proclaim it. I have my morning cloak on for a petticoat—the end of the sleeves sewed up to make Pockets. All my wardrobe is washing. I came home yesterday—with at least half yard deep of mud—melted snow—and I have not a cold in my head. I was out 5 hours. Hurra for foundations, makes the old young and the young merry. When next I write I hope [I] will announce two concluded for.

I got my dear Mother de Pazzi's letter on Saturday. Tell her to keep Sr. M. Clare close to the Register.[18] Tell me the extent of the injury done in Fr[ancis] St. church, and by what accident.[19]

Give me a true and faithful account of your charge—to each of whom give my most affectionate love. I often wish I had dear Sister Lucy Vincent to dress the evening fire, which is sometimes forgotten.[20]

Butter, milk, and bread, Dublin price—Tea higher—meat much cheaper, good for 4d—all Turf—manners very like Dublin—no Irish.[21]

3 minutes to 4. God bless you all.

Your very affectionate
M. C. McAuley

Let my poor Sr. Teresa read this—I trust she is pretty well.

Autograph: Mercy, Dublin

227. To Sister M. Frances Warde[22]   **[Birr]**
    Wexford   **[January 12, 1841]**

[Dear Sister Mary Frances]

We are getting quite at home here. Sister M. Aloysia strong and lively, Sister Martha a real treasure, and our postulant useful in every way, quite a different

---

17 The autograph is damaged here—only "si" appears visible; "since" is provided from a handcopy in Mercy Congregational Archives, Dublin. The "visitor" has not been identified.   18 Catherine wants Mary Clare Augustine Moore to work on illuminating a Register—for Baggot Street or another convent.   19 On Christmas 1840, an "awful calamity [occurred] in the new Catholic church of St. Nicholas Without, Francis-street, Dublin, at High Mass, at 6 o'clock in the morning, owing to a most unfounded report that the gallery was falling; four or five persons, on rushing out, lost their lives" (*Irish Catholic Directory* [1842] 398).   20 Mary Cecilia Marmion, the recipient of this letter, was mistress of novices. Sister Lucy Vincent is Mary Vincent (Lucy) Bond, whom Catherine called "Lucy Vincent" to distinguish her from Mary Vincent (Ellen) Whitty, also in the Baggot Street community at this time. Since Mary Vincent Bond will go to Birmingham in August 1841, the problem of two sisters with the same name will then be solved.   21 According to Catherine McAuley, good meat could be had for four pence, and no Irish language was spoken in Birr.   22 No autograph, early hand-

person from what she was in Baggot-street. Nothing like Foundations for rousing us all. Our expected Sister is really in affliction at not joining us. Her father does not refuse consent, but says he must have time to prepare his mind. He cried here on Sunday. I fear she must make a *runaway*.[23] We hear of other postulants, but nothing near a close. You will see by the writing that I can scarcely hold the pen. I feel so grateful to God for the prosperity of Wexford, that, if we should not get a postulant for a month, it would not cast me down. I never saw such frost; the cold is intense—every place covered with snow.

Sister M. Clare says they have a more severe winter in London than has been for a century. What sailors call the 'white swan' (a cloud of snow floating in the air) has been seen off Winchester. She expects two Sisters immediately, daughters of the principal merchants in Portugal.[24] Dear Sisters Xavier and de Sales well—all well in Baggot-street.

My poor James has rallied a little. My good, affectionate Sister M. Genevieve is his constant nurse, gives all her day to him, and, when she finds it necessary, goes again in the evening.[25] She has become quite fond of him, and, provided he does nothing without her leave, grants whatever he wishes. He won't even open a book that is lent him till she approves of it. How good God is to him!

A long poetic epistle from Sister M. Ursula, who says:

> Sister Genevieve's garden is locked up in snow,
> So she cannot exert herself there,
> But a certain sick child whom you tenderly know,
> Has all her affectionate care.

---

copy, or photocopy for this letter has been found. It appears only in Austin Carroll's *Life* (384–86), where the date is given, but no recipient is identified. Since it is a long letter, containing material that does not appear in other letters, it is included in this edition. From the more intimate nature of the last paragraph, it is assumed to have been written to Frances Warde, in Wexford at the time. However, the first three sentences of the letter suggest that the version Austin Carroll received may have been a pastiche of two or more letters, or that she herself may have combined letters. Moreover, "Aloysia" is incorrect; Mary Aloysius Scott did not use that form, nor did Catherine of her. And Martha Wallplate was not in Birr at this time, as seems implied here. Carroll may have used part of Letter 225.   23 Susan Egan entered the convent in Birr on February 2, 1841.   24 One of these sisters was Margaret Anne Duff who entered the Bermondsey convent on June 22, 1841; the other woman has not been identified.   25 Mary Genevieve (Catherine) Jarmy, now living in Booterstown, had volunteered to care for Catherine McAuley's nephew James Macauley who was dying slowly of consumption near Booterstown. She was the widow of Captain William Jarmy. She had entered the Baggot Street convent on September 24, 1833 and professed her vows on July 1, 1835. In the early records she is said to be "old" although her exact age is not given. Degnan says she was "in her seventy-second year" when Catherine McAuley died in 1841 (343). When Mary Genevieve died on July 19, 1858, she would then have been about eighty-eight or eighty-nine years old, which is possible, but does not seem likely. However, in her *Life* of Catherine McAuley, Carroll claims that when Catherine Jarmy entered in 1833 she was "three times as old as" Mary McCann, also a widow who entered in 1833 (231). Tradition affirms that Mary Genevieve Jarmy was the oldest member of the early Baggot Street community, possibly older than Catherine McAuley herself.

No sign of our Pastor's return here as yet,
Some think that next month he'll be home;
Others think that a bishopric surely he'll get,
Or be kept for the College at Rome.

Slow workmen here—no choir yet. Sister M. Aloysia is out every day. She has a sick priest and an old lady in her own charge. Sister M. Teresa has two unfortunate Crottyite families, obstinate, though most miserable in mind. I never saw anything so like the description the French Priest, Monsieur De Luers [Luynes], gave at George's Hill,[26] of some possessed persons he saw in a remote part of France, who could not bear the Sign of the Cross. These unhappy people will not raise the hand to make it or even suffer you to help them; and while they pour out dreadful curses on the miserable man that deluded them, they will not move one step to obtain reconciliation. It seems as if they could not. I never saw schismatics before. They are worse in appearance than heretics. The latter think they are right; the others *know* they are wrong, and yet are obstinate. If any of them make the Sign of the Cross when we are with them, it is in the style of a stubborn child, who is forced to say what is against his will.

They are not persecuting me with letters to return. God bless Father O'Hanlon, he put an end to that in Baggot-street. When I returned from Galway, I looked so ill, that he particularly asked what had distressed me. I told him the uneasy state my mind was kept in with accounts from St. Mary's, saying, "I would not be home before Sister Aloysia's death," etc., etc., and this when I had a death-bed to attend at Sr. Teresa's.[27]

[M. C. McAuley]

Published transcription: Carroll, Life 384–86.

228. To Sister M. Cecilia Marmion   Convent, Birr, upper Baggot St.
Baggot Street   January 15, 1841

My Dear Sister M. Cecilia

I had a letter from Mr. O'Hanlon. Should poor Miss B[eckett] return, you will act exactly as he directs.[28] I had also Mother de Pazzi's letter. She does not

---

26 In the Derry Manuscript, Mary Ann Doyle says that Henry de Luynes, a French priest, celebrated Mass at Baggot Street in 1831: "Having been introduced to our dear foundress at George's Hill, he at her request visited this house and held some general as well as many private conferences with the Sisters" (Sullivan, *Catherine McAuley* 58). In the Bermondsey Annals, Clare Moore also speaks of Monsieur de Luynes's visit at length (Sullivan, *Catherine McAuley* 94–95).   27 Carroll writes "St. Teresa's," but she must mean "Sr. Teresa's"—i.e. the Mercy convent in Galway, where Teresa White was superior and where Mary Bourke had died of typhus on June 11, 1840, while Catherine was there. The alarming accounts from Baggot Street (i.e. St. Mary's) about Mary Aloysius Scott's health had been sent by Mary de Pazzi Delany.   28 Marianne Beckett, one of the first English postulants to come to Baggot Street (on April 29, 1840), had left the convent and returned to England,

say what description of chimney piece. I think Mr. O'Rafferty got black marble, at a stone yard in Baggot Street for £2/10. Sister Teresa knows where, could say Mr. O'R had purchased there.[29] Mr. Bush is what poor Father Burke used to call a queet saint.[30]

Our mission goes on very well. Some of the old obstinate party are preparing for confession. Sister M. Aloysius—perfectly at home—the most vigilant clever manager I have met [in] some time. I never knew till now the loss she must have been to her Father's large family.[31] We put our candles under a Bushel. She is in excellent health—has departed from her Carlow rules—was up at 5 o'c—and out visiting in the snow, when she would have been in Bed in Baggot Street—as was usual. Sister M. Teresa cheerful and active, always employed. Sr. Rose as usual. Sister A[nna] M[aria] most zealous. All have met Priests here who knew them.[32] A P[arish] P[riest] within 5 miles was curate to Sr. M. R[ose's] uncle, and a Revd. Mr. Tynan, living in the Town, was intimate with Sr. Aloysius's Father & Mother before she was born. We hear of McAuleys frequently amongst the poor—but not of the Crotty party yet.

We are now here 19 days and have been to the P[arish] Church every morning but one, not attended with any inconvenience. On the first Sunday of the month,[33] we had our usual morning exercises—30 days prayer, Lecture, Office for the dead—all before Mass—Breakfast 10½—no distress or injury to old or young. Our expected postulant still lingering—her father crying here on Sunday. I think we shall have two before the 30 days prayer is out—and the same in Wexford.

Had a letter from London. Two postulants concluded for there—one from Liverpool—2nd, the daughter of a rich Portugal merchant.[34] My dear Sister Mary

presumably sometime in late 1840. It is not known for certain whether she received the habit on August 10, 1840, or remained a postulant at that time. She was a convert and evidently experienced some difficulties of faith (see Letters 232 and 260); Catherine McAuley often expressed solicitude for her. On February 9, 1842, Marianne entered the convent of the Sisters of Mercy in Birr; she received the habit, taking the name Mary Anastasia, on August 16, 1842, and professed her vows on October 6, 1844. Her friend and spiritual director was the Honorable and Reverend George Spencer, "a convert himself and great-great-grand uncle of the present Earl Spencer" (O'Brien 26). Starting in August 1846, Mary Anastasia served as assistant to the superior of the Birr community, Mary Vincent (Susan) Egan; after Mary Vincent Egan's death on December 17, 1860, she was elected superior and "for the remainder of the century, except for three years, she was Rev. Mother of the Birr community" (O'Brien 28, 39–40).   29 Evidently black marble, like that obtained by James O'Rafferty, parish priest in Tullamore, was needed for some purpose at Baggot Street (or possibly in Birr), and Catherine is confident that Teresa Carton will find it at the nearby stone yard.   30 Mr. Bush, possibly a priest, has not been identified, beyond his being "a queer saint," as defined by the now deceased Daniel Burke, OSF, the former chaplain of the House of Mercy on Baggot Street.   31 Apparently her mother Elizabeth had died some time before Mary Aloysius Scott entered the convent in 1835.   32 Catherine McAuley mentions Mary Teresa (Catherine) White, her travelling companion to Birr, and Mary Rose Lynch and Anna Maria McEvoy, founding members of the Birr community.   33 According to the Rule of the Sisters of Mercy which Catherine McAuley composed, the sisters "shall ... devote the first Sunday of every month to a preparation for a happy Death" (Rule 14.1, in Sullivan, *Catherine McAuley* 308).   34 See Letter 227, note 24.

Clare wishes most anxiously to return to her old home when she leaves Bermondsey, and begs me to petition Doctor Murphy which I suppose would be quite unavailing. She says they are doing so well in Cork that she is not required, and it would be great comfort to her and to us—if he would let her return to her favorite home.[35] Sisters de Sales and Xavier very well.

Most amusing accounts from Limerick of their Bazaar—two long letters —at the end: "To be continued." Letter from Galway—all well, an increase expected. Wexford taking the lead—a Wexford news paper sent here says—"The most visible change has taken place in our Town since the arrival of the Sisters of Mercy."

My clothes are not dry yet—the morning cloak still as a substitute & the sleeves as pockets keep me in mind of John Gilpin's belt—with the 2 jars meeting behind. No fire drying here—the turf ashes spoils [sic] every thing. Flannel never dries in frost.[36]

No answer from Father Mathew. Ceremony waiting on him. The place where our Convent stands has no particular denomination. We have proposed calling it Baggot Street. This little nonsensical proposition produced such immoderate laughing that I really was alarmed for Sr. Aloysius. I never saw her laugh in such a manner, and I was choaking. However, Baggot St. it is.

Returning from Mass this morning, a sweet looking old country woman stopt me, putting 6 pennys into my hand. I said—"for the sick poor." "No, honey, for the Sisters, for yourselves." We have two great comforts here—excellent Bread in the Dublin household form and pure sparkling spring water. I have not had one moment's indisposition and Sr. A. M. laughs at the stirabout that broke her tooth. I am beginning to cherish the Primate's opinion, "that too many women living together engenders troublesome humours of mind and Body."[37]

Sister Aloysius has just called me with a great iron sledge in her hand. She saw, through a small aperture, a long room, instantly broke through a slight partition, and discovered a spacious apartment with cornice, skirting, grate & chimney piece—3 windows—full as large as our present community room. The Bishop when residing here[38]—not requiring so much room—gave it up for oats and hay—

35 Mary Clare Moore will visit Baggot Street, her "favorite home," briefly in June 1841, before proceeding to Cork; she will be recalled to London in December 1841.   36 See Letter 226 for Catherine's account of the mud and melted snow on her clothes, and the need for a substitute petticoat. Once again she draws pleasure from the legendary tale of John Gilpin (see Letter 172, note 8). In William Cowper's poem, John Gilpin dashes along on his horse, with two stone bottles of homemade wine, to please his wife, attached to his leather belt on either side. But then his runaway horse breaks into a tremendous gallop, the two bottles "swinging at each side," and before long "The bottles twain behind his back / Were shatter'd at a blow" and "all might see the bottle necks / Still dangling at his waist" (Cowper 356–57). Catherine McAuley's keen memory of this poem and her obvious amusement in it, and in her own predicament, are testimony not only to her sense of humor, but also to her lack of pretension. She enjoyed whatever brought laughter, even at her own expense.   37 Catherine is probably contrasting, favorably, the small size of the community in Birr to the much larger community on Baggot Street.   38 Dr. Patrick Kennedy, the bishop of Killaloe at the time, had been administrator or parish priest in Birr from 1826 until his

getting up by a ladder to one of the windows. It will make 6 fine cells. She is now making out a House of Mercy—of stable and coach house. I never cease thanking God for giving me courage to bring her into action, and she is delighted.

We hope our little choir will be nicely finished. We have got a table, like the novaship—as well made—chairs the same colour—no cane or Rush to be got. They are stuffed and covered with black Saxony cloth.

I hope my dear Sr. Teresa is keeping warm—and that I will have the happiness to see her pretty well. She may expect to see me as smart as a young girl. If you are not smart and strong—hold down your head, when my animated countenance appears.

Direct—Convent, Sr. of Mercy, Baggot St., Birr.

Your affectionate
M. C. McAuley

Dance every evening.

No cross—but good appetites and little money.

Tell Sr. Teresa to send me a copy of the best words she has in a collection Book—soon as she can.

Sr. M. T. takes 2 cups of Tea overflowing—3 pieces of Bread.[39]

What does Sr. T[40] pay for the children's bonnets?

If the Birmingham foundation is as merry as this, we may look forward to it without dismay.

Birr fashion. Mr. Egan, Father to the Sr. we expect, goes to Dublin on Monday. If he visits the Convent, I hope he will meet every attention, and see the House, etc. etc. Speak of his daughter as a Sister—be very gracious.

Autograph: Dublin, Mercy

229. To Sister Teresa Carton   Convent, Birr
    Baggot Street   January 19, 1841

My Dearest Sister Teresa

Your affectionate letter was truly acceptable to me, and the delightful speech of Mr. O'Connell was quite a treat to me, and the Bishop's nice note to Mr. Flanagan. We teetotalers may rejoice now indeed. I never liked anything better

---

appointment as coadjutor to Dr. Patrick MacMahon in November 1835 and his episcopal consecration in January 1836. In June 1836 he became bishop of Killaloe on the death of Dr. MacMahon (Murphy 126). By 1839, and perhaps earlier, he had moved his residence to Castleconnell (*Irish Catholic Directory* [1839] 241) and thence to Six-Mile-Bridge, near Quin and Ennis, by 1840 (*Irish Catholic Directory* [1840] 293).   39 Catherine is marveling at the renewed health and appetite of Mary Teresa (Catherine) White since her sojourn in Limerick prior to their coming to Birr.   40 In Catherine's letters, "Sr. T." or "my poor Teresa" is nearly always Teresa Carton, but the initial in this postscript written vertically across the letter may be "Fr."— for Frances Boylan.

than I now like a good drink of water. My health is remarkably good, thank God. Our long fasts have agreed well with all. Sister Aloysius feels strong, and takes the most active part—she was out for hours when the weather was severe, came in very wet—but got no cold.

Sister Mary Rose afforded me great recreation yesterday evening. She and Sister M. Teresa had been visiting an old man who has deserted his religion. He is becoming quite penitent. He said to Sr. M. Teresa, "Well, since the first day I saw you I never had you from my thoughts, you are the most heavenly young woman I ever met." In another place they were standing together, when an old sinner said, "Well, if God did no[t] send his ministers to convert me, sure he sent his little ones."[41] They could scarcely keep from laughing, when they looked at each other. In another place—a woman who came from a neighbouring cabin to look at them said, "Such purty little jewels—as fair as an Egg." Sister M. Rose cannot avoid laughing, but says she hold[s] her head down and keeps her handkerchief to her face.[42]

I have just got a letter from Sister Angela. Mrs. Dan Clanchy died on the 13th day of Typhus fever. You may remember seeing her in good health—the day the english Sisters were received. Sr. Angela remained with her to the last.[43]

We have great accounts from Wexford, our old dear Sister Frances dashing away. We have been every week expecting an addition here—but not yet come. We cannot fix Sister A[nna] Maria's reception, till we hear from Father Mathew. We like her very much. She is quite animated.

Tell my Dear Sister Martha a Mrs. Stokes, a widow, called here to enquire for her. I am rejoiced to hear our Laundry is improving. I am sure my dear Sisters will leave nothing in their power undone. God bless them all. I am so happy to hear our children are good. Give my blessing and love to them.

It grieves me to hear of the cough and chest. This is a very fine day—we had good light this morning at 6 o'clock.

I am likely to be interrupted as we expect the Vicar, Dr. Spain, and I would not like to miss one post—thanking you, *my own* good child, for your nice note. All unite in love to you and heartily wish you were here. May God bless and preserve you. Pray for

your ever affectionate
M. C. McAuley

Do you remember Letitia Keating, the eldest child of poor Mrs. Keating who was School Mistress at Bray. She is a most destitute creature—12 years old, her unfortunate Father idleing about—it distressed me to see her.

---

41 Inserting the "t" may ruin Catherine McAuley's attempt to replicate the old man's speech.   42 Evidently Mary Teresa White and Mary Rose Lynch had little experience in the country; Mary Rose was a Dublin woman; Mary Teresa, though born in Carrick-on-Suir, had lived in Dublin for at least seven years.   43 Mrs. Dan Clanchy of Charleville was the wife of Daniel Clanchy, Esq., "one of the most respected Catholic magistrates in the country" (Carroll, *Leaves* 1:133). Mary Clanchy, of the same family, was an important benefactor of the Charleville community. Mary Angela Dunne, the superior in Charleville, was devoted to this family.

Remember me particularly to the good Mrs. Manning, who I hope calls to see you. Do not be uneasy about me. I have got all my wardrobe—I made the most of it for amusement. God bless you, dear.

Sister Aloysius will be extremely obliged to Sr. M. Clare, if she will send her a sketch of the Tabernacle soon as possible.

I got a great parcel from Limerick—to help me in making out a page for the collection Book[44]—and when I had it compleated it went astray or was burnt—for we could never find it. I made out another and put it on the top of door, till some person coming in threw it down. Sr. Aloysius thought it was the lost one coming from the ceiling. We have got 2 children—sisters, 7 & 10 years old—they did not commence yet.

Autograph: Dublin, Mercy

230. To Sister M. de Sales White
Bermondsey

Convent, Birr
January 20, 1841

My Dearest Sister Mary de Sales

With all around me covered with snow, and my poor fingers petrified, I will endeavour to write a few lines to you & my dear Sister M. Xavier. I feel satisfied that you are both affording all the assistance in your power—and I humbly pray God to bless your exertions and render your service useful to the valuable Establishment in Bermondsey—from this till August—when I hope to have the happiness of going for you—should God be pleased to spare me till then.

We have not added to our few—yet we expect two about the end of the month. You never saw Sister M. Aloysius so strong. She has been up every morning at our early hour, most active, out every day. She has succeeded in bringing several of the unfortunate scismatics [schismatics] to seek reconciliation. You have heard of the great injury done by the apostate Crotty. We meet many who have not been present at Mass for ten or twelve years—and in almost every poor family, there is still a deluded member to be met—who through some evil infatuation follows the unhappy man—though about three years since, when he yielded to remorse, he told them publickly "he was leading them astray," but soon returned to the destructive work again.

All the poor souls receive the Sisters with affection and confidence. An obstinate sinner said yesterday, "Well, when I would not hear God's ministers, he sent his little ones to convert me." This was quite a source of recreation, as Sisters M. Teresa & M. Rose were the little ones. It is likely the poor man did not speak in reference to their littleness of stature.

---

44 The "collection book" was the notebook in which the door-to-door collection of clothing, blankets, and money for the poor was recorded.

We are obliged to go to the Public church every morning. It is as near as the church at Bermondsey, if the corridore was an uncovered passage, a very splendid edifice—the Bell cost one hundred and twenty pounds – in England to be sure. The Bishop resides forty miles distant—Doctor Kennedy —I fear, no great patron of Nuns. It was from his Diocess the Ursulines came to Galway. The Presentation branch that succeeded them in Lifford are not likely to remain. You remember Dr. Brown[45] told us they complained of having no Bishop. I have made an humble petition to his Lordship, but cannot say what its fate may be. Indeed at this season, 40 miles is a long drive. Poor old Dr Crotty came to Charleville from Cove—and when I regretted his taking so much trouble, he said when we did not decline travelling from Dublin to his charge, he could not avoid coming to meet us.[46]

Mrs. Dan Clanchy of Charleville died this month of violent Typhus fever— the Sisters were constantly with her. May God have mercy on her—she was a most charitable kind person. She was in Baggot St. the day the english Sisters were received and enquired most particularly for Mother M. Clare.

Most dashing accounts from your old Town—Sr. Frances attracting all round her—the orphan House preparing, & the wings to be raised equal to [the] front— and 20 cells with corridore all around—House of Mercy in one wing—orphan H. in the other. One hundred a year secured for the purpose—Mr. R. Devereux most generous.[47] I expect the next letter will announce a third Sister. No addi-

---

45 Dr. George J. P. Browne, bishop of Galway.

46 In expressing admiration for the graciousness of Dr. Bartholomew Crotty, bishop of Cloyne and Ross, Catherine McAuley is, by contrast, alluding to Dr. Patrick Kennedy's aloof manner. Over the next decade her assessment proved true. After John Spain, the kindly and accommodating parish priest in Birr, died on May 10, 1848:

> Bishop Kennedy then decided to return from Sixmilebridge and live in Birr. For a year and a half he deprived the Sisters of the privileges they had hitherto enjoyed and forbade Rev. Mother M. Vincent [Egan] to receive any more postulants ... Through the influence of Mother M. Cecilia Marmion, Baggot St., Archbishop Murray of Dublin mediated and convinced Bishop Kennedy to revoke his decree and restore to the community all privileges.
>
> What these privileges were we do not know. Years later when Mother M. Anastasia [Beckett] was asked to explain she refused to comment ... However, a study of the register reveals that no Sisters were professed in the years 1848–50 though five had completed their novitiate, three of them having been received in 1846. They were all professed in 1851.
>
> Towards the end of 1849 Bishop Kennedy became seriously ill and lingered on till November 1850, nursed and tended by the Sisters. His last intelligible words implored God to shower "abundant benedictions, in time and eternity on the Sisters of Mercy" who did much to "ease and comfort him in his last illness." (O'Brien 35, 37)

47 Frances Warde was still in Wexford with the founding party who had arrived on December 8, 1840, having spent the night of December 7 in Enniscorthy at the residence of Dr. James Keating, bishop of Ferns. They lived in temporary housing in Wexford until the conversion of the former, but little used, "orphan house" into a convent, with adjoining space for works of mercy, was completed in 1842. Neumann gives long excerpts from the Wexford Annals to illustrate the early poverty of this

tion to poor Galway yet. I feel great tenderness for that branch—as the youngest until I leave this. Limerick goes on fast. We are invited to Ennis—but indeed we are come to our resting place, no more from poor Baggot Street. We are come to the centre—this is called the Table Land of Ireland—very fine light air. All well in Dublin, Booterstown and Kingstown. Poor Miss Beckett—most anxious to return. I think we shall have seven new Sisters before you return, to fill up the places of those who will go to Birmingham.

The Railway seems to be much dreaded now—do you hear of many accidents?

Sister Mary Teresa's House of Mercy[48] is doing great good, thank God. Mr. Daly says there are no nuns like his own. I had a letter from him in which he says—"Now remember, I tell you in time, you must bring Mary de Sales to the Profession."

Sister Teresa sent me a great parcel yesterday, temperance speeches etc. She has her cough, says the Laundry improves daily, and that the dormitory is crowded. This is very consoling.

My fingers are very cold & stiff.

Let me have a long letter when you have time. Tell me particularly how my old dear Revd. Mother's health is—all about dear Sr. C. Agnew, Sr. M. Augustin, Sr. M. de Sales[49]—and the little ones. How is Mr. Butler, is not the choir a great addition to the happiness of all,[50] are you getting a nice english accent—is my dear Sister Xavier always well?

I suppose I shall not return for about 3 weeks—and I never parted a Sister who entered more fully and cordially on her new obligations than Sister M. Aloysius has already done. God bless her—and everyone of my very dear Sisters in England and Ireland. Be sure to pray for your ever affectionate

M. C. McAuley

All desire love etc.

Autograph: Liverpool

231. To Sister M. Angela Dunne   Convent, Birr
     Charleville   January 20, 1841

My Dear Sister M. Angela

I received your letter conveying the account of poor Mrs. Clanchy's death. I am exceedingly sorry, and feel very much for her afflicted family.

---

community, and the generosity of its principal lay benefactor, Richard Devereux (262–67). Corish notes that in Wexford "we see the Redmond and Devereux families in particular transforming the whole appearance of the town, with Richard Devereux (1795–1883) providing his church with much of its physical structures ... he was a great support in the provision of the Catholic schools of the nuns and brothers" (*Irish Catholic Experience* 173–74).   48 In Galway.   49 Mary de Sales Eyre.   50 The convent chapel in Bermondsey was solemnly blessed on December 17, 1840, "the Sisters all walking in procession with white cloaks and lighted tapers" (Bermondsey Annals 1:22).

As to your enquiry about the Rule, etc., Doctor Murray obtained the full approbation of his Holiness for our Order—in the year 1835. When His Grace compiled the Rule,[51] and when it was compleated, affixed his seal & signature, but we did not ask a confirmation of it from the Holy See until we reduced it to practice. When I was in London last January, a petition to that effect was presented, accompanied by letters of strong recommendation from Dr. Murray, Dublin—Dr. Murphy, Cork—Dr. Ryan, Limerick—Dr. Haley [*sic*], Carlow—Dr. Crolly, Primate—Dr. Kinsella, Kilkenny—Dr. Cantwell, Tullamore[52]—Dr. Griffiths, London. Revd. Mr. Colgan of the Carmelite order, Dublin, was the bearer of a most gracious answer—he wrote to me to say that if he could remain some time longer he would carry home the documents. I spoke with Dr. Cullen, President of the Irish College at Rome—when in Dublin last summer—he said it was certainly granted, but that they were slow in issuing final documents.[53]

I do not understand what you mean by the other question—the vow is that of all religious orders—"poverty, chastity and obedience—to the end of life"—the fourth of enclosure has been added to suit other communities.[54]

Present my best respects to Revd. Mr. Constant, and tell him I shall be most happy to communicate any information he wishes, and beg him to accept my thanks for the kind interest he has manifested.[55]

Doctor Spain sent me a paper with an account of your ceremony.[56] Please God your establishment will now go on very well. Two more good Sisters will soon come. We hope for two here, about the end of the month.

You did not say anything of Mrs. L. and her daughter.

All unite in love to you. Remember me to each of the Sisters, and believe me always

your affectionate
M. C. McAuley

My hand is quite stiff.

Autograph: Charleville

---

51 "When" is used here in the sense of "then." Actually, Catherine McAuley herself "compiled" the Rule; it was then reviewed and slightly revised by Dr. Murray.   52 The letter Catherine says was written by Dr. John Cantwell, bishop of Meath, has not been located in the archives of Propaganda Fide, or elsewhere.   53 The Rule was approved by the Congregation for the Propagation of the Faith on July 20, 1840, and forwarded to Pope Gregory XVI sometime during the following year; papal confirmation was granted June 6, 1841. The confirmation was announced by the Congregation in a decree dated July 5, 1841. However, this Latin decree and the approved Rule, printed in Italian, were not mailed from Rome until July 31, 1841. The post reached Dublin after August 20, 1841.   54 Sisters of Mercy have never taken a vow of enclosure. For a discussion of the "fourth vow" of service, see Letter 155, note 79. It seems clear from this paragraph that Catherine McAuley did not think of the words "service of the poor, sick, and ignorant" in the vow formula as precisely a fourth vow.   55 John Constant was a curate in the Charleville parish (*Irish Catholic Directory* [1841] 313). Perhaps he had been asked to preach at some event on behalf of the Sisters of Mercy.   56 Elizabeth Walsh entered the Charleville community on September 12, 1840; Eleanor Teresa Hogan, on October 3, 1840. Their recent reception of the Mercy habit is the ceremony to which Catherine refers.

232. To Sister M. Cecilia Marmion   **Convent, Baggot Street, Birr**
Baggot Street   **January 21, 1841**

My Dear Sister Mary Cecilia

Sister M. Aloysius is exceedingly obliged to her Sisters for their contributions to her poor Bethlehem.

I have no objection to Sister Veronica changing her name to any you mention.[57] We did not fix on Sister Anna Maria's until yesterday. Finding she had Teresa in Confirmation,[58] I prayed her to add Louisa and make up my favorite name "Anna Maria Louisa Teresa"—and as she is a very careless walker—and many wet ways to pass—we agreed that it would keep her in mind, to add "Keep out of the gutter, you dirty s - - t"[59]—which would serve as an act of humiliation—three or four times a day. She was quite satisfied.

You say Birr appears to be my Pet foundation—not that I have been over-indulged. All is cool and quiet. We cannot say "tis too much to last long"—but we may most reasonably hope for a little more—love—and when it comes, it will be lasting, since it is perfectly free from all symptoms of rapture.[60]

Mr. Egan is said to be the chief earthly author of the convent—and indeed it would appear so—but not a word on that subject.[61]

We hope to have the reception on Tuesday week—if the Vicar approves. He is so much engaged with Country Stations, he cannot spare much time to us—and what he promises to do he forgets. I think when I am gone, he will call more frequently. He thinks perhaps that I am sufficient. Sister M. Aloysius likes him, and would rather have all to begin as it is most likely to continue.

Dr. Spain has been just here—says we have no chance of Father Mathew. So much for his own branch. I proposed Tuesday week—said he would let us know tomorrow.

I feel very much for poor Miss B[eckett]—and wish I knew what to do.

If the balm of a good conscience will not keep you in health and spirits—

---

57 Mary Veronica (Elinor) Cowley at Baggot Street changed her name to Mary Aloysius before her profession of vows on May 4, 1841.   **58** The photostat of the autograph is a little confusing here. Catherine McAuley writes "Finding she I had Teresa ..." but then clearly crosses out "I". "Finding she had Teresa ..." fits the sense of the sentence because Catherine asks Anna Maria McEvoy to "add" only "Louisa."   **59** Catherine McAuley clearly writes "s - - t," knowing that "slut" is the word in the expression. Presumably she has in mind not the secondary, but the primary meaning of the noun: a slattern, a woman who is careless of her appearance, and hence dirty or slovenly. Poor Anna Maria will mind the puddles henceforth! Previous published editions of this letter have altered the sentence, expurgating the word (Neumann 300–301; Bolster 194–95). The autograph of this letter, once said to be in Oak Lea, Sunderland, England, cannot now be found; it may have been destroyed among papers held by a sister who died of tuberculosis. The extant handcopies of this letter have "slut" or "s - - t."   **60** In a veiled way, Catherine McAuley is commenting on the absence in Birr of the sort of enthusiastic support on the part of the bishop and parish priest that she experienced in other foundations.   **61** John Egan was the father of Susan Egan, a young woman planning to enter the Birr community on Tuesday, February 2.

send to the Medical Hall for The Balm of Mecca. You must be young and handsome when I see you.[62]

Your ever affectionate
M. C. McAuley

Photostat of autograph: Dublin, Mercy

233. **To Sister M. Cecilia Marmion**   [Convent, Birr]
     Baggot Street   [c. January 30–31, 1841][63]

My dear Sr. Mary Cecilia

When my letter to Sr. de Pazzi was gone—I found the patterns which should have been enclosed. The lamp arrived safe. Sr. M. Aloysius likes it very much—the chains are long enough for Baggot Street, but they are easily shortened.

Give my best love to my dear Sr. Teresa, and a thousand thanks for the account of the consecration—it came when we were at breakfast and supplied the want of a real Baggot Street drink of tea—which I begin to long for. The cups were provided when we came—they are baby toys compared to ours. I am ashamed to ask for five, and six would not supply the deficiency.[64]

Dr. Spain received a most kind letter from Mr. Mathew, saying that the unavoidable disappointment to us has given him "great uneasiness"—he promises every assistance in a few months. I think it is probable there will be three candidates. A very nice young person, Miss Usher, who would not meet any opposition, has spoken a little seriously.

I am delighted you have so many bishops—it always brings blessings from Heaven. I hope you are not withholding all aid you can give, and that your flock are always nice.

We had our new seats in the church this morning and our new child in full costume, the piano tuned and Miss Usher to play. She is considered a first rate, but I would fear the breaking of the instrument—she dashes away so.

I am greatly improved in every way, more mild and patient—lecture better, have thought of many new explanations. I hope you will think so.

It looks like summer just now, so mild and all so green about us. Tell my dear Sr. Aloysius alias Veronica that I have promised Sr. M. Rose, that she shall

---

62 Catherine is trying to tease Mary Cecilia into good spirits and health, aware of the difficulties at Baggot Street whenever she is absent and Mary de Pazzi Delany longs for her return.   63 No autograph, photostat, or photocopy of this letter has been located. However, at least three early undated handcopies are extant: in the Baggot Street Book of Manuscripts called "Annals" (56), in the small Baggot Street Book of Manuscript Copies (103), and in the Brisbane Book of Transcriptions (132–33). The text given here is that in the "Annals" except where noted. The content of the letter suggests that it was written from Birr before Letter 234. The Brisbane handcopy attaches four postscript paragraphs, included here, one of which is written on January 31.   64 Catherine liked large tea cups—not small ones that needed to be filled several times to equal a "real" cup of tea. See also note 72.

come to the public ceremony in June—this has given her new life.[65] Whisper it very secretly to her. Either you or Mother de Pazzi must also come. It will only be a 4 days absence.

Give my affectionate love [*missing words*].

Your attached etc., etc.

M. C. McAuley

No account from Wexford yet—I hope the ceremony took place on the 29th [27th]—tomorrow perhaps will bring a letter.

Sunday—31 January—pray that we may get through the runaway on Tuesday—I dread it—My Mamma could give a scolding etc., etc.[66]

I wish you knew the price of these cheques, the one with the cross is exactly what we have—yard wide, 9d per yard.[67]

I had a note from Sr. Gertrude—Kingstown—this day—it would surprise you.

Handcopies: Dublin, Mercy and Brisbane

234. To Sister M. Frances Warde
Carlow

Convent [Birr]
February 3, 1841

My Dearest Sister M. Frances

I received your kind letter, and am delighted to hear your ceremony went on.[68] I did not expect a full account of it—that would be unreasonable—but was uneasy lest any interruption should have occurred.

The postulant here was admitted to the holy habit yesterday in the convent choir. Miss Egan entered, a very fine nice person about 24. The grand public ceremony is to be in June. It is expected there will be a third in time to join the two who are in their first attire.[69]

Poor Miss Maher—no chance here.[70] Money, money is the theme. I entreated in favor of a candidate, with £16 per year & £100 in hand—it was regarded quite insufficient. A convent never yet succeeded in this Diocese, it is supposed from imprudent arrangements. The Bishop has given strict charges to the Vicar who is Superior.[71]

---

65 Catherine has promised Mary Rose Lynch in Birr that her friend Mary Aloysius Cowley will come from Baggot Street to the reception ceremony later that year in Birr. 66 Catherine feared that in order to enter the Birr convent Susan Egan might have to run away from home. She did, but the next day her family apologized for resisting her decision (Birr Annals). 67 Catherine is speaking of fabric—for some articles of clothing or furnishing. 68 At a ceremony in Wexford on January 27, 1841, Mary Bridget (Margaret) Hackett and Mary Gertrude (Joanna) Kinsella, who had come from Carlow, professed their vows. 69 Anna Maria McEvoy received the habit on February 2, 1841, taking the name Mary Magdalen (which she evidently later changed to Mary Clare). On the same day Susan Egan entered the Birr community, joining Mary Anne Heenan, a postulant who had entered on January 22. 70 Catherine McAuley is still searching for a convent for Anna Maria Maher. For a full account of her eventual entrance into the Kinsale community and her subsequent founding of the community in Cincinnati, Ohio, see Molitor, "Mary Teresa Maher of Cincinnati." 71 According to the Rule, the bishop or his delegate was the ecclesiastical superior of the

I leave this on Monday. Doctor Wiseman is in Dublin, is to say Mass and exhort in Baggot St. Sr. M. C[ecilia] wrote to me pressingly. Some remarks have been made on my being absent twice during the short noviciate of the english Sisters. The english Bishops think superiors should be with their charge.[72]

Sister M. Aloysius—about in all the bitter cold, a very busy little woman—entering on her new state very quietly and efficiently.

Mrs. Stain, who was Miss Kate Byrn, resides in this Town—knew Sr. Aloysius in the St[reet] and came to see her—Mrs. Dignans, also a very nice person—and an old Priest who has always known her Papa. A first cousin of Miss Fitzpatrick of Nenagh—who is married to Mr. Byrn of Bays Well—is likely to join. We saw little to expect at first—now a bright light is dawning.

I will write soon from Baggot Street. Poor Sr. de Pazzi has been very ill. Sr. M. Cecilia had three Bishops to entertain on Sunday & 2 yesterday. She is delighted with Dr. Crolly & Dr. Wiseman—Dr. Meyler accompanied the latter.[73]

Sr. Aloysius unites in affectionate love—to you. Give mine to all, and believe me ever your fondly attached

Mary C. McAuley

I had a letter from Sister Traynor [Trennor] begging I would make Naas my way home, which I promised to gratify her in, but now must not make a moment's delay.[74] I would have left immediately on receipt of Sr. Cecilia's letter, but had promised the new Postulant to read & explain part of the Rule for her, at which I will work diligently to help poor Sr. Aloysius, who cannot speak much. She has got a Lay Sister, as nice looking as Sister Lucy—strong & good-humoured. God bless you.

I am most happy at the advice you gave relative to Sr. M. J.'s niece.

I had a very nice letter from Sr. M. J. in Cork—all well.

Since I wrote this & mentioned it to Sr. M. Aloysius, I have found her crying, and must try to remain a little longer.

Autograph: Silver Spring

---

community. Dr. Patrick Kennedy had designated John Spain, vicar general, to serve in this capacity. 72 Dr. Nicholas Wiseman, coadjutor to Dr. Thomas Walsh, vicar apostolic of the Central District, England, was in Dublin to preach at the solemn consecration of St. Andrew's Church, Westland Row, on Friday, January 29, 1841, and to give a Charity Sermon on February 7. The "remarks" about Catherine McAuley's absence from Baggot Street were presumably made by Dr. Wiseman, who recalled her long trip to Galway shortly after the English sisters arrived in Dublin on April 29, 1840. Coming from Birmingham, Dr. Wiseman took a protective interest in the young women who would found the Birmingham community later in 1841. 73 According to the *Irish Catholic Directory* for 1842, among the bishops in Dublin to attend the consecration of St. Andrew's on January 29, 1841, were, in addition to Dr. Murray and Dr. Wiseman, Drs. John Murphy (Cork), John Ryan (Limerick), and William Crolly (Armagh)—all friends of the Sisters of Mercy (399). The Irish bishops were also in town for the synod of bishops on February 2–5, 1841 (400). 74 Catherine had evidently promised Mary Josephine Trennor that she would spend at least a night in Naas on her way back to Dublin, but now she cannot do so.

235. To Sister M. Teresa White   Convent [Birr]
Galway   February 3, 1841

My ever Dear Sr. M. Teresa

I am so frozen, so petrified with cold, I can scarcely hold the pen. What comfort it gives me to hear of your continued happiness. I could not express the gratitude I feel for Mr. Daly's affectionate kindness to you, and next to the Glory given to almighty God I rejoice that his expectations have not been disappointed. Your little Institute is much spoken of. One year more will forward it greatly, please God.

Our postulant was received here yesterday in a quiet little choir like your own. Miss Egan entered, a very nice person—also a lay Sister, making three in 6 weeks. Sr. M. Aloysius continues well. She has met some Kilkenny friends— a Priest who has known her Papa 20 years—and Mrs. Stain who knew her in the street. Sister M. Rose has met a Priest who was curate to her Uncle, and Sister Anna Maria—another Priest—so they are getting quite at home.

We have been applied to about little Miss Maher. I did hope Sr. Frances [Warde] would get her into Wexford Convent.

A letter just now from Sister M. Cecilia. Poor Sr. de Pazzi has been very ill. Sr. Cecilia had 3 Bishops to entertain on Sunday and 2 yesterday—Doctors Crolly, Murphy, Ryan, Kinsella, and Wiseman from Oscott. He is to give them an exhortation some morning this week.

I had written to say I would return on Monday—which has been over ruled. I must stay a week or 10 days more. Some remarks have been made on my being twice absent during the noviciate of the Birmingham Sisters. English Bishops think superiors ought to be with their charge.

I had a letter from my dear Sr. de Sales—she speaks with delight of our cherished hope—of going to Galway in October. I trust you will have 2 or 3 postulants before that.

I feel very much for my poor Sr. Tighe. She was most fondly attached to her sister—send the enclosed.[75]

I will not expect a letter from you till I return to our old dear habitation, where I shall never again see all my dearly beloved Sisters—all strange faces. They all say that the first separation from kindred, etc., was a joyful sorrow, but that the separations in religion are bitter sorrows. What must it be to me who never met one unkind Sister yet.

This is a gloomy subject—will we all meet in Heaven—oh what joy—even to think of it.

God bless you, my very dear Sister Mary Teresa—give my affectionate love to dear Sr. M. Catherine and each of the happy flock.

---

75 The sister of Catherine's old friend Mary Louis or Lewis (Fanny) Tighe had recently died. Catherine wishes Teresa White to forward a letter to Fanny, at the Presentation Convent in Galway.

Believe me your fondly attached

M. C. McAuley

Autograph: Galway

236. To Sister M. Cecilia Marmion

Baggot Street

Convent [Birr]

February 5, 1841

My Dear Sister M. Cecilia

On receiving your last letter, I commenced writing to say I would be home on Monday next, but Sr. Aloysius was greatly agitated, and although I have these feelings always to encounter, yet in her case I was afraid of excitement and gave up. We have spoken quietly and rationally on the subject—and she is satisfied I should return Monday week.[76]

We have had a great battle to make about Miss Egan. Thank God it is all over. She is worth a little trouble, now in her Postulant's dress. Sister M. Magdeline looks very well in her white veil, another is likely to come.[77] Miss Egan is the most important person to catch in this Town. Her father keeps 7 clerks, some of them brothers to the curates, but not one dines at their Table. As we hope to meet so soon I will tell you no more.

I feel the frost most acutely in my right side from my hip to my ankle. I have put on a great flannel bandage with camphorated spirit—and trust in God it will, like a dear good old acquaintance, carry me safe back.

Don't say a word of Miss Egan—where it could be mentioned outside (I mean of any difficulty). Mr. E[gan] has a sister in Dublin who knows every Priest—and half the world.

Trusting I shall find you all well in one week, I remain, with great affection,

M. C. McAuley

I will not write again—except any disappointment occurs. The Coach leaves this at 8 o'c—arrives at the Hibernian Hotel, Dawson St.—half past 6.

Autograph: Dublin, Mercy

---

76 Catherine McAuley wrote this letter on Friday, February 5. She had planned to return to Baggot Street on Monday, February 8, but Mary Aloysius Scott's reluctance to have her leave Birr so soon caused her to propose departing on Monday, February 15. However, she actually left Birr on Wednesday, February 10, as Letter 237 indicates. 77 Mary Magdalen (Anna Maria) McEvoy received the habit on February 2, 1841. While Catherine McAuley was in Birr, two more women entered the community who would later become professed sisters: Mary Anne Heenan, on January 22, 1841, and Susan Egan, on February 2, 1841. Mary Anne was from Borrisokane, Co. Tipperary; Susan became superior of the community in 1845 and served in that capacity until her death in 1860.

237. To Sister M. Frances Warde   Convent, Baggot St.
                                                        February 11, 1841

My Dearest Sr. M Frances

   Doubtful where you are I just forward a few hasty lines to tell you I arrived at 6 o'clock yesterday, very much fatigued. I left Sr. M. T[eresa] till the ceremony is over—in May or June.[78] They will do well, please God, in a little time. Sr. Aloysius continued in good health. The air is remarkably fine. Dr. Kinsella's Diocess comes within 2 or 4 miles of her—she has great hope of seeing him. She is twenty five miles nearer to Kilkenny that she was in Dublin. Perhaps one of her sisters may unite with her.[79] God bless you. I am called.

                                                        Your ever affectionate
                                                        M. C. McAuley

   I am surprised to find the Presentation order in such a tottering state that their own name is not sufficient to support them—they have been obliged to add ours. But—as I hear Mr. Maher intends to have the affair of *honor* settled at the 15 Acres—I must refrain from all further remark.[80]

Autograph: Silver Spring

238. To Sister Mary Aloysius Scott   Convent, Lower Baggot Street
   Birr   February 13, 1841

My Dearest Sister M. Aloysius

   How I rejoice in this mild weather for sake of my poor Sisters in Birr. I found all here, etc., etc., just as we left them. Dr. Wiseman was gone—he celebrated Mass twice and gave an ex[h]ortation.[81]

   I have a letter from Limerick—now—to say Sister O'Farrell is in fever—the sacraments administered. No opinion to rest on—till Monday. May God restore her. Sr. Elizabeth has every hope.[82]

---

78 Mary Teresa (Catherine) White, Catherine McAuley's travelling companion, remained in Birr until the reception ceremony of Mary Anne Heenan and Susan Egan in May 1841. Perhaps her staying to assist in Birr was what enabled Catherine to return to Dublin earlier than February 15 (see Letter 236). Catherine travelled home alone, in two successive coaches; the trip took ten hours. 79 Dr. William Kinsella, the bishop of Ossory, lived in Kilkenny, Mary Aloysius Scott's home town. Her sister Mary Ann Scott entered the Birr community in January 1842 (Birr Annals). 80 Evidently some publication misnamed the Presentation Sisters the Sisters of Mercy. Here Catherine McAuley humorously claims that Father James Maher is going to avenge the misrepresentation at the Fifteen Acres, a famous duelling field in Phoenix Park, Dublin (Kelly 234). 81 After the consecration of St. Andrew's Church on January 29, Dr. Nicholas Wiseman remained in Dublin to give the Annual Charity Sermon in support of the "Parochial Female Free Schools ... under the care of the Religious Sisters of Charity." The sermon was set for Sunday, February 7, at the Church of the Conception (St. Mary's), Marlborough Street, according to a printed flier in the Dublin Diocesan Archives (Hamilton Papers PI/36/4, no. 143). 82 Sister O'Farrell apparently recovered; at least, no extant letter announces her death. Having entered the Limerick community in September or October 1838,

A letter from London—all there well. Miss Beckett gone to her friend in England, quite reconverted to the Catholic faith.[83]

Four candidates for admission—two of whom will probably close.

The Bishops had a most cordial meeting, all past differences at an end, thank God. Dr. Kinsella very well, enquired most particularly for you.

I could scarcely do justice—in description—to the kindness of the 2 Coach men. The first, from the time we left Birr, at every stage was quite compassionate to me, offering to carry me into the Inns, to get to a fire, really uneasy about me. When changing he recommended me to the second, who was equally kind & neither sought any payment. I mention this as I never met anything of the sort before.

When we arrived in Dublin my 'weak side' was stiff, and I was quite bent or sunk[84] in size. A car was waiting for me, with a very small man as driver. The good coach man said, "is this little man come for this little woman?" Yes. "Oh then I'm glad—she's lost with cold and hunger." Mother de P & Sr. M. Clare were in the car. I was not able to laugh then, but we all have laughed plenty since at my good hearted coach man. I would really like to see them again. I had Mr. Carlile far as Mount Mellick. If I can judge of a countenance, his spiritual influence will not be extensive.[85]

Sister Teresa is as usual.

I must have a letter from you—and Sister Mary Teresa in turn. Write every second to Mother de Pazzi—between you both, 3 letters in a month, till we meet again—one to me—one to Sr. de P.—and one to Sr. M. Cecilia—is not this reasonable. It is quite useless to write to more than one of us at any time—by addressing them to each, all will be gratified.

A promise to bring Sister M. Aloysius—late Veronica—to the reception has perfectly reconciled her to wait for her own ceremony till after Easter, when we

---

and received the habit on December 4, 1838, she is still in the community in February 1841, yet she does not appear in the Limerick Register. However, a sister by the name of Mary Joseph (Anne) Farrell *is* listed in the Limerick Register: she entered on December 1, 1843; received the habit on July 11, 1844; "was admitted by dispensation to make her religious profession on 2 October 1845"; and went to Mallow on October 13, 1845. In Mallow she served as superior from 1847 until her death in 1875. One suspects that "Sister O'Farrell" may be "Anne Farrell", and that after her severe attack of fever in 1841, she left the Limerick community only to return two and a half years later. The fact that Anne Farrell was allowed "by dispensation" to profess her vows after only fifteen months of novitiate suggests that some circumstance—such as her having earlier served at least a year's novitiate—was taken into account. I am very grateful to Scholastica Stokes, RSM, Limerick, for her help in researching this question.   83 Marianne Beckett's English friend was the Honorable and Reverend George Spencer, an Anglican priest who had converted to the Roman Catholic Church. In 1841 he was at St. Mary's College, Oscott, near Birmingham (*Irish Catholic Directory* [1841] 329). See also Letter 228, note 28.   84 Catherine wrote "sunk," not "shrunk" as one might have expected.   85 See Letter 225, note 13, regarding James Carlile, a Presbyterian minister teaching in Birr. See also Finlay Holmes, *The Presbyterian Church in Ireland*, especially chapter 4 on Presbyterian outreach in nineteenth-century Ireland (84–122).

hope to have a good number. The postulant, Sr. Teresa, still stands on doubtful ground. I must give you a little dialogue between her and Sister Mary—who is greatly improved, or else I did not see her fully before.[86] On hearing the Profession was not to be, she said—"Sr. Teresa, let us be very good now and we will surely get in."

"What a hurry you're in—perhaps you might soon—get out again. I have no doubt you'd have taken the habit the very day you came to the Convent—but that's not the way I like to do things."

"Oh, well, you can wait as long as you please, but I cannot wait for you."

"Can you not indeed? And do you think I'd come after you?"

"It's too bad, but I must get ready."

"You shall not get before me."

She read at Dinner yesterday, first time & Mother Cecilia had to help her up—on the seat—reading good—great efforts—to go on.

Sr. Fanny[87] all that is most desirable.

I have seen the Srs. in Booterstown—quite well, their poor patient much changed. Kingstown is too far till the noise of the wheels are [*sic*] out of my head.[88] Be sure give me a particular account of Father Birmingham.[89]

All unite in most affectionate love to you, Sr. M Teresa, Sr. Rose & Sr. Magdeline. Give mine to my dear Sisters Susan & Mary Ann—also to Ann Blake. Remember me most kindly to Mrs. Egan & Mr. Agness—Miss Williamson, if you see her. Give my best respects to Dr. Spain, Mr. Tuhy [Tuohy] and Mr. Kennedy.[90] You will be weary of this before you can read it. Pen as usual bad.

Dr. Murphy said he would soon send a branch of Srs. to Kinsale with Sr. M. J. at the helm—and have Mother Clare in her old station at Cork.[91]

Pray for me, your old comrade. How are the sweet little Mice?

Your ever most affectionate

M. C. McAuley

Autograph: Dublin, Mercy

86 Catherine McAuley reports the following dialogue between Teresa MacDonnell, a postulant who had entered on December 8, 1840, and a "Sister Mary," probably Mary Lawless, a postulant who entered on December 15, 1840, though possibly the sister is Mary Liston, a novice whose profession was delayed—because of Catherine's absence and the Lenten season—until May 4, 1841. The dialogue begins with Mary speaking.   87 Frances Vigne entered the Baggot Street community on December 8, 1840.   88 In Blackrock, near Booterstown, Catherine's nephew James Macauley was severely ill with consumption. Since Kingstown is a greater distance from Dublin, she had not yet been there since her return from Birr late on February 10.   89 A Reverend "J. Birmingham" was parish priest in Borrisokane, near Birr (*Irish Catholic Directory* [1841] 304).   90 Edmund Tuohy and Philip Kennedy were curates in Birr at this time (*Irish Catholic Directory* [1841] 304).   91 The plans of Dr. John Murphy, bishop of Cork, did not come to pass. A community in Kinsale was founded from Limerick in 1844, with Mary Frances Bridgeman as superior; Josephine Warde remained in Cork; and Clare Moore returned to London in December 1841.

239. To Sister M. Teresa White **Baggot Street**
  Galway February 16, 1841[92]

My ever Dear Child and Sister

Here am I again since Thursday, as usual weary of foundation work—and ready for more. I find two invitations here—indeed they must wait.

It is needless for me to say that each of your letters affords me very great consolation. May Almighty God continue His graces and blessing. How I long to hear you have a postulant. Miss Egan who has joined in Birr is the young person Sister O'Beirne mentioned. She seems very desirable indeed.

Sister M. Aloysius is the most active little woman you can imagine—no symptoms of weakness. Dear little Sr. M. Rose looks like an angel instructing the poor unfortunate people who have been led astray by the scismatical [schismatical] party. She has them constantly around her.

The Wexford foundresses have met an early cross. The assistant Sister in typhus fever—Sister Kinsella—a fine young woman.[93] Fever in Limerick also, I fear a bad case—Sr. O'Farrell, one of the first.

I must conclude with most affectionate love to my dear Sr. Mary Catherine and each of our very dear Sisters. All pretty well here—a few slight colds. Called away—

May God bless you, my ever Dear Child

Your affectionate
M. C. McAuley

Sr. de Sales very anxious to return to dear Ireland—a few months more will bring that about, please God. Dr. Murphy says Sr. M. Clare must return to Cork—at easter.

Doctor Wiseman said Mass here twice & gave the community a delightful ex[h]ortation. I was not at home. Dr. Browne did not call.

Autograph (severely damaged): Silver Spring; handcopies: Dublin, Mercy and Brisbane

240. To Sister M. Frances Warde **Convent, Baggot St.**
  Carlow February 18, 1841[94]

My Dear Sister M. Frances

I am most anxious to hear of the dear Sister in Wexford. It is too much to

---

92 The autograph of this letter, which is said to have been once in Belize, is very severely damaged, with pieces missing. Fortunately there are two early handcopies: one in the Mercy Congregational Archives, Dublin, that may have been made by Teresa White herself, and one in the Brisbane Book of Transcriptions. The text given here follows the autograph, supplemented by the Dublin handcopy.   93 Mary Gertrude (Joanna) Kinsella went on the foundation to Wexford as a novice. She professed her vows there on January 27, 1841. She recovered from this attack of typhus, but lived only six more years, dying in Wexford on October 27, 1847.   94 Neumann reads the date of this letter as February 13 (306–307), but it is definitely February 18.

ask you—who have so much to write. A line from any of the Sisters would be very acceptable. They have fever in Limerick. The last account rather favorable, one of the first that joined—before I left.

It is an early cross for the poor Sisters in Wexford—please God it will not end in death. I feel very anxious to hear, and Mr. O'Hanlon will expect me to let him know. His care and anxiety for us all increases every day. He said yesterday—"this is my fourteenth year amongst you."[95]

God bless you & all, my dear child & Sister.

Your ever affectionate
M. C. McAuley

Autograph: Silver Spring

241. To Sister M. de Sales White   **Baggot Street**
    Bermondsey   **February 28, 1841**

My Dearest Child

I have felt quite anxious to write to you and my dear Sister M. Xavier—but my old cough has made me so nervous that I could not—nor cannot now write distinctly. You must read with patience.

We have imported the London Influenza—six on the Infirmarian's list— Sister Lucy Vincent[96] has been very ill indeed, the only english patient amongst them. Poor Mother M. Cecilia, Sr. M. Austin, Sr. M. Ann, Sr. Fanny Vigne— a postulant— Sr. Vincent Whitty & Sr. Lucy—all going on well.[97] I often think of my old Galway Nurse that would not allow me a little stirabout.

Now, my dearly beloved child, I hope you are exceedingly cautious as to the fast of Lent—remember, obedience is above every other sacrifice, and you will be far more mortified in taking that which you do not like to take, than in abstaining from it. You have not sufficient strength to fast. Take a good collation in the morning, the usual allowance here— and some light supper. Take in the day a crust— or something if you have a long walk. Sister M. Xavier will I know take care—in this particular—I lay this obligation on you.[98]

---

95 Redmond J. O'Hanlon, ODC, prior of the Discalced Carmelite community on Clarendon Street, Dublin, was appointed confessor of the Baggot Street community on June 4, 1829, and later Dr. Murray's deputy as ecclesiastical superior, but he had become a solicitous friend of the community as early as the opening of the House of Mercy on September 24, 1827.   **96** Mary Vincent (Lucy) Bond, whom Catherine McAuley sometimes called Lucy Vincent, to distinguish her from Mary Vincent Whitty.   **97** The sisters mentioned are Cecilia Marmion, Mary Austin Horan, Mary Ann Teresa O'Brien, Frances Vigne, Mary Vincent (Ellen) Whitty, and Mary Teresa (Maria) Breen, whom Catherine McAuley often called Lucy Teresa, or simply Lucy, perhaps to distinguish her from Mary Teresa (Amelia) White and Mary Teresa (Catherine) White when they were in Baggot Street.   **98** Ash Wednesday was February 24 in 1841. Catherine is writing on the first Sunday of Lent.

How rapidly the days, weeks & months are passing. Another month ended, that seemed but a few days begun. If we have not forfeited the friendship of almighty God—but have been trying to love Him more and more and to serve Him faithfully, they were Blessed days for us. Oh let us endeavour to make these days such as we should wish the past to have been. Let us enter into the spirit of the Church—making this to us a truly penitential season, mortifying the pride of self opinion, performing all with an humble heart—keeping the first Lenten admonition engraved on our heart—"You are but dust, and unto dust will soon return." Our poor Bodys [*sic*] only, but our precious immortal souls—after passing through these few years of pilgrimage, pain and sorrow—will, if we are faithful, soon enter on the joys of a blissful Eternity.

The simplest and most practical lesson I know—my Dear Sister de Sales— is to resolve to be good today—but better tomorrow. Let us take one day only in hands—at a time, merely making a resolve for tomorrow. Thus we may hope to get on—taking short careful steps, not great strides.

God bless you, my Dear children. Pray fervently for your ever affectionate Mother in Christ—

M. C. McAuley

Do all you can to comfort my Dear Mother M. Clare. I will not expect to hear from you during Lent—except something should make it necessary—but you shall hear from us.

Autograph: Liverpool

242. To Sister M. Teresa Purcell   [Baggot Street]
Tullamore   [Early 1841][99]

My Dearest Sister Mary Teresa

I congratulate you on your happy increase, which you and I love so much that we will never frighten a candidate away for not having a bag of money. We

[99] The dating of this undated autograph letter is a problem. Both Neumann (290) and Bolster (183) date it "Early 1841." It was probably written from Dublin and enclosed in a letter to Mary Ann Doyle, the superior in Tullamore. One reason for placing it in early 1841, although it may have been written even earlier, is that Mary Cecilia Marmion went to Birr sometime between March 1 and March 10, 1841, to restore her health (see Letter 244), stopping in Tullamore en route. Catherine's reference to Cecilia's looking forward to seeing Teresa may be to this upcoming reunion, or to Cecilia's return trip through Tullamore, with Catherine McAuley, in May 1841 (see Letter 268). However, the Tullamore Annals does not help to date the letter, in terms of explaining any recent "happy increase" in the Tullamore community. Four sisters, including two lay sisters, received the habit in Tullamore on September 8, 1840, but after that apparently no postulant entered and no ceremony occurred until October 1841. However, a postulant may have entered who did not persevere, and hence is not listed in the Tullamore Register. If this letter was written earlier than 1841, it has not been possible so far to find a date that would satisfy the contents of the letter.

will sooner give half our share—than not multiply. The Lord and Master of our House and Home is a faithful provider. Let us never desire more than enough. He will give that and a blessing.

Sister Mary Cecilia looks forward with delight to the time of seeing you. Remember me affectionately to Mr. Murtagh[100] and believe me

your attached Mother in Christ
M. C. McAuley

Autograph: Tullamore

---

[100] Walter Murtagh, curate in Tullamore when the sisters arrived there in April 1836, became parish priest in Eglish in 1837, but remained extraordinary confessor of the community and thus visited Tullamore several times a year.

One notices several important themes in Catherine McAuley's letters in March and April 1841: the persistence of her cough; the impending heartache of her nephew James's death; the ever increasing obligations of corresponding with sisters in the foundations outside of Dublin, especially in "poor Birr," the most recent of the foundations; concern about the future of Mary Clare Moore, who will be leaving London, and about Redmond O'Hanlon, recovering from influenza; and great care to see the health of Cecilia Marmion improved. Of the twenty extant letters of this period all but two are written to Sisters of Mercy, nine of them to Mary Aloysius Scott or Cecilia Marmion in Birr.

Here one also sees characteristic details that flesh out the human portrait of Catherine McAuley, and endear her to observers: her unavailing efforts to doctor herself, her barely suppressed annoyance at the pokiness of Clare Augustine's art work, her occasional weariness, her efforts to be a serious-minded mistress of novices, her playfulness with the postulants and novices, her delight in the St. Patrick's day parade of teetotallers, her need to work around the moods and preferences of the nonetheless beloved Mary de Pazzi Delany, and, always, her gratitude that, despite all, "The blessing of unity still dwells amongst us—and oh what a blessing—it should make all things else pass into nothing" (Letter 257).

243. Sister M. Frances Warde   [Baggot Street, Dublin]
Carlow   [March 5, 1841]

My Dearest Sister Mary Frances

I am sorry to find by your letter this morning that they are saying too much about my loss of health. My rather new visitant, a cough—has been with me very constantly since the first Sunday after my return. To please my kind tormentors, I took one large bottle of medicine and put on a small blister[1] from which I (for want of faith perhaps) did not receive any benefit. I am now doctoring myself as I have Sister Teresa—very warm flannel entire dress—mellow barley water, old fashioned sugar candy—a little Hippo[2] at night—and I think—*Mr. Time* taken into account—I am doing very well. I do think that a cough has made

---

[1] A poultice. [2] "Hippo," in this case, derives from the name of Hippocrates, the Greek physician, and was probably a generic name for spiced wine, or a honey-based liquid, used for medicinal purposes—especially in respiratory ailments.

a resting place with me—and will be no unusual visitor in future. I am now going to hide from the Doctor who is gone up to four influenza patients.

Sister Mary Clare Moore[3] is a character—not suited to my taste or my ability to govern—though possessing many very estimable points. She teased and perplexed me so much about the difficulty of copying the two pages, that I was really obliged to give up—unwilling to command lest it should produce disedifying consequences. She said it would take the entire Lent—indeed you can have no idea how little she does in a week—as to a day's work, it is laughable to look at it. She will shew me 3 leaves, saying, I finished these to day—3 rose or lilly [sic] leaves.

The little girl I wrote to Wexford about has annoyed me greatly. She is a still silent little creature and let her married sister speak for her until Wednesday, when they both called and said she did not like to go to Wexford, and that the very reason her sister had for desiring it was the chief cause of her objection— a long connection of her Brother-in-law's. She is not half alive and wishes to hide her little head. I was quite angry with her and really scolded. I told her it was no matter that myself and the superioress in Wexford had the trouble of writing, but that it was quite too much that the Bishop should be spoken to, etc. etc. She has been in a Carmelite Convent six months and has indeed got the holy art of keeping custody of eyes, for she seldom opens them.

She next applied to come here by Mr. Smith's direction—but her means not being sufficient I declined and asked them to select one of the young Houses. Now her sister says she will most gladly forego some portion of her share of property to get her settled here—if Mr. S. will consent. She says her Husband would be most willing to do so. If it is arranged—I shall have a nice task opening the eyes of the little Carmelite. However, I will have all the talk, for she is as meek as a Dove. I did hope she would have fancied poor Birr, which I represented as it deserves, but carefully avoided recommending any in particular. I think a little girl won't [would?] give me so much to do & undo in future.[4]

The Mamma of the first Sr. who joined in Wexford—I forget the name— was here yesterday getting the direction to cross and Bead maker—cincture, etc.[5] It was most consoling to hear her describe the feelings of all parties regarding the Sisters of Mercy. She said the Bishop is now most anxious to get a branch in Enniscorthy. She particularly spoke of "Mrs. Kelly" as a general favorite[6] and said all were looking forward to see Mrs. Warde again at the reception of three— thinks she has another daughter will join them, & speaks of it with delight.

---

3 Mary Clare Augustine Moore, the artist.   4 Unfortunately, it has proved impossible to determine whether Catherine McAuley wrote "won't" (the *t* is not crossed) or "would" (there is no *d*)— and the two words convey opposite senses. The young woman in question has not been identified, except as a person directed by John Smyth, a curate at Sts. Michael and John's, or possibly by Patrick Smyth, a curate at St. Nicholas Without on Francis Street.   5 Kate Farrell was the first postulant to join the Wexford community, exclusive of Susan Wall who joined from Baggot Street. 6 Mary Teresa Kelly, the superior in Wexford.

You may think I have a pretty sound lungs yet—since I read every word of Mr. Maher's delightful sermon to the Sisters in Community Room, taking a little water occasionally. It is greatly spoken of as an admirable explanation of the two states—and equally instructive to both.[7]

I must wait for change of air, till May or June—when I have in view another toilsome journey to Birr, but it would not stand without aid. I had a most kind letter from Father Mathew yesterday. God bless him. He cannot appoint the time yet—but says he soon will. Four are preparing here to play & sing. All possible excitement is required.

God preserve and bless you, my dearest old Child.

M. C. McAuley

A letter from London. Sr. M. Clare does not yet know what Dr. Murphy will do with her. He said here she must return to Cork at Easter—and adds what I have no recollection of, that I promised the 2nd M. Clare[8] to do some wonderful things. I dare not venture to contend with him.

Autograph: Silver Spring

244. **To Sister M. Cecilia Marmion**	**Convent, Baggot St.**
Birr	**March 11, 1841**

My Dear Sister M. Cecilia

I am sorry you wrote until you were fully rested. In about ten days I expect to hear of great improvement, please God.[9]

Father O'Hanlon came yesterday & he advised me [to] take off the cloak— and drive out to Booterstown to day. I have done both, tho' half an hour before I would not have cut 2 inches off for a pattern, I felt so afraid of making a patient of myself again. I think I am much better, not coughing much. He was delighted I sent you away and says you will get strong and fat. He was very angry, exceedingly angry, when told of Sister Aloysius keeping damp clothes on—and charged me to tell her it would not be pleasing to God. This has spared me the pain of scolding, as I intended. Such a mild admonition would never proceed from me on such an aggravated occasion.

I brought Sr. Justina in today, and of course talk followed.[10] I have been a most attentive person ever since, read lecture, heard & corrected reading at one o'c, received sinners to repentance at 9 o'c—got into many of the secrets of your holy office, and acquitted myself like anything but a new beginner. I will have

---

7 James Maher of Carlow-Graigue preached at the profession ceremony in Wexford on January 27, 1841. 8 That is, Mary Clare Augustine Moore, the artist. 9 Catherine McAuley had sent Cecilia Marmion to Birr in an effort to strengthen her health. 10 Catherine brought Mary Justina Fleming, a novice, back to Baggot Street from Booterstown where she had been staying. It is not clear what community dynamics were behind the "talk" that followed.

all in great order for you. Sister Julianna cried—her mother, for one day, got a good lecture, etc.[11] Sr. Genevieve has slight influenza.

An excellent school at Booterstown, quite an unusual number. Mr. McCormick recovered—Mr. Ennis expected on Patrick's Day.[12]

Did you tell Sister M. Aloysius my 2 reasons for wishing you or she would say something to the Vicar as to your visit—first, that he would not regard me Mistress General, and 2nd—her as a Proprietor who could invite Sisters, etc—but as she knows his feelings now much better than I do, she will act accordingly.[13]

You were so disappointed at no poetry coming from Birr, in all the fine air—perhaps you would like a little now you are there.

> No Dr. now is to be seen—
> No Bottles either blue or green—
> no sopha [sofa]—pillow, stool or screen
> The Dr. called the day you went,
> To help to get you through the Lent
> A Box of Pills and Bottle Big—
> Enough to carry in the gig
> he'd like they should be sent by post—
> the carriage 16d [pence] at most
> but as no customer was found
> he took them back quite safe & sound
> I'd wish to shield you next from Love—
> except what takes its flight above.
> A Sister whose last tye [tie] is broken—
> on this subject thus has spoken
> Oh never never shall my heart—
> with any creature share a part
> Tho' it was said by ancient bard
> That not to love was very hard
> and in truth he must confess—
> not to be loved was nothing less.

---

11 During Cecilia Marmion's absence, Catherine McAuley took on the responsibilities of mistress of novices at Baggot Street, directing the training of well over a dozen novices and postulants, as she had done years before when the congregation was just beginning. This included helping novices like Juliana Hardman get over their tears.   12 John McCormick, curate in Blackrock and an old friend of Catherine McAuley and the Sisters of Mercy, recovered only temporarily. He died six months later, on September 17, 1841, at age sixty-eight (*Irish Catholic Directory* [1842] 437). John Ennis, parish priest in Booterstown, was finally expected home, after his long assignment in Rome as a spokesman for the Irish bishops on the merits of the national education system, under review by the Vatican.   13 Catherine McAuley was always eager to affirm the governmental autonomy of the individual foundations, and to correct any misperception that she retained authority over them. She also did not want to convey the impression to John Spain, the parish priest in Birr, that a superior could add to her community simply by inviting members from other convents.

But—it was worse than all, he'd prove—
to be deprived of what we love.
[*Illegible word*]—yet do you not know full well, my Dear—
such love should never enter here
by many pangs—you've learnt to know—
It ever ends in pain & woe.
These things, my Dear, do not forget—
Let none again e'er see your pet.
And lest—an angry dart X should strike—
in future, love them all alike.

I am rejoiced to hear of Mr. Birmingham's recovery. I could not make up my mind to his dying this time.

Sr. Lucy V[incent] asked leave to write to you immediately—No.

All send fond love. Give mine to each, share & share alike.

God bless you and make you a good child of your affectionate Mother

M. C. McAuley

X Dart—alluding to love Dart

Δ—the 3 oldest black veils will scarcely be able to read.[14]

Autograph (severely damaged): Dublin, Mercy

245. To Sister Mary Aloysius Scott [Baggot Street]
    Birr [c. March 19, 1841]

My Dearest Sister M. Aloysius

I am greatly comforted to find all in Birr going on so well—may God continue His blessing to you all. We are as usual on the encrease, a prospect of two soon after easter. One of them did not appear till this morning. She is about 20—Daughter of a stipendary magistrate, a nice person. All pretty well.

An historian who is writing the remarkable events of the 19th century called last week for some particulars, number of Sisters, etc., etc.—including all.[15] I said a week would alter that part—I have just heard from Carlow that three are about to enter.

Will you make my poor Sr. M. Cecilia strong? Do not confine her too much. Milk, coffee—and crisp thin toast might help her appetite—I cannot eat my toast

---

14 These two footnotes to her poem are Catherine McAuley's own, but the meaning of each is obscure. Moreover, the Δ symbol she used for the second footnote cannot be found in the poem because the autograph has been severely damaged by folding and tape.   15 M. J. Brenan, OSF, published his *Ecclesiastical History of Ireland* in 1840. Catherine McAuley is listed as a subscriber (v), and on pages 411–12 of volume 2, Brenan discusses Catherine McAuley and the Sisters of Mercy, noting that 190 members "have embraced this institute since its foundation in 1831" (412).

except it's very thin and well toasted. Want of appetite is troublesome to ourselves and to others.

I have the old man's cough yet, tho' as cautious as possible—never go to the choir at 9 o'c. I am generally in a little perspiration at that time. I have been down in the morning at our usual hour—since Saint Patrick's Day, thank God. This is a great relief to me. I am doing Mother Cecilia's business—well as I can. I think some would wish her safe at home when they come on private concerns—in future I will have the Poker in my hand.[16]

Father Mathew says—"I cannot now appoint the day, but confide in me. I will not disappoint—you shall hear soon again."[17]

Dear Sr. Aloysius, send me a memorandum of the little account we made up. If I brought a copy—I have lost it. Tell me what I yet owe—and what I am to purchase in time.

Mother de Pazzi is determined she will not be envied for her quiet sitting in the B[ishop's] parlour. She has never been one quarter of an hour here since, except to read the morning Lecture when I am in the novaship. She has now got another sorrow—Sr. M. Clare going to Cork at easter. I did not know till now—there was so strong a cord there. She feels most acutely on these love occasions—I suppose it is to be attributed to her constitution. I wish most heartily this trial was over.[18]

God bless and preserve you, my very dear child. I pray this every day.

Remember your affectionate
M. C. McAuley

Autograph: Dublin, Mercy

246. To Sister M. Cecilia Marmion   [Baggot Street]
    Birr   Saturday, March 20, 1841

My Dear Sr. M. Cecilia

Your letter this morning gave me great comfort—thanks be to God you are improving in health. Continue to be obedient—and I will expect to meet you again in this world, looking as if your Lent did not last all the year round. I am better, tho' coughing. I really think 3 drinks of the "Waters of Birr" would cure me. My poor Sister Teresa was very bad last week—weak, complaints of different character. What served one encreased another. She is better today. Fever

---

16 Catherine McAuley is evidently enjoying her temporary reputation for severity as acting mistress of novices.   17 Theobald Mathew still cannot set a date for the reception ceremony in Birr in May.   18 At the request of Dr. John Murphy, Mary Clare Augustine Moore was scheduled to go to Cork with her sister Mary Clare when she returned from Bermondsey. Mary de Pazzi was close to the Moore sisters, and apparently already anticipated the loss. Catherine McAuley wishes this new provocation of de Pazzi's uneasiness were over, rather than pending.

again in Limerick, a fine creature—Sr. M. Clare.[19] The Dr. has said—of dangerous kind. He is mistaken, I hope.

All your charge well—and very good. Sister Angela[20] taking most active part in getting the children ready for Confirmation on Tuesday next—they have made 80 new Bonnets. I believe they will make up 100—they are as nice as the first we ever had—100 Hymns of the Holy Ghost printed on cards to take in their hand. The Sisters are quite animated and long for Tuesday to see them dressed.[21] Mr. Farrelly attending to the confessional most kindly, and daily instructions in school. I am to finish the course on Monday. The grand oratorio in W[estland] R[ow] given up—the 3d—a matter of ridicule. Poor Mr. Gormley singing alone.[22]

The delightful exhibition on Patrick's day will never be forgotten. 70,000 Teetotallers marched in the most orderly edifying manner—all wearing scarfs of Irish manufacture, the Priests of each division attending in splendid Carriages. Mr. O'Connell—4 beautiful milk white horses dressed in blue and silver—four out riders, in blue velvet jackets, caps, white overalls. Mr. Yore—4 jet black— in crimson & gold. Mr. Flanagan—4 bays—with amber & blue. Dr. Meyler—4 dressed in scarlet and gold. His Excellency looking at them and Dr. Murray in his carriage at a cornor [corner] of Mer[rion] Square, standing till all passed— the servant saluting them. It is said there never was such a sight in the world— think of 70,000—without a single accident—or window broken.[23]

I should have commenced telling you that the two sweet little Doves entered yesterday, your child at 6 in the morning.[24] She got her dress on for St. Joseph. They are exactly the same size. When we wanted to distinguish them by name, I asked little M[argaret] Dwyer—"Have you a second name?" Yes, Margaret Teresa. Not intending to have that which would sound like a religious name, I waited the arrival of the other[25]—"Have you a second name?" Yes, Margaret Teresa. Both heartily weary of the world—in their youth—the same coloured hair—heads the same size. We have determined on calling them—The Twins— the first we had. Sr. Mary[26] is the Mother of the Twins—the second born will

19 Mary Clare McNamara in Limerick had typhus.   20 Mary Angela (Caroline) Borini, a novice, or Mary Angela Maher, a professed sister.   21 On Tuesday, March 23, 1841, Dr. Murray "administered the Sacrament of Confirmation to nearly 1,300 children and others" in the Church of St. Paul, Arran Quay, Dublin (*Irish Catholic Directory* [1842] 404). Presumably it was for this ceremony that the children at Baggot Street were prepared. It was not unusual at this time in Ireland for the sacrament to be conferred on a very large number of people at one time. The *Directory* notes that "upwards of two hundred children from the poor house" received the sacrament on this occasion (404).   22 This reference has not been identified, as intriguing as it is.   23 Catherine describes the St. Patrick's Day parade with the detail of an eye-witness, suggesting that she too must have been standing on Merrion Square or had carefully read a newspaper account.   24 Margaret Teresa Dwyer entered the Baggot Street community on March 19, 1841.   25 Margaret Teresa Geraghty also entered on March 19, 1841.   26 "Sr. Mary" is probably Mary Lawless, the postulant who entered immediately before Margaret Dwyer and Margaret Geraghty (i.e., on December 15, 1840); she was therefore, by custom, the "mother" of the newcomers.

have her dress on tomorrow. You never saw two sweeter little Duckeys—one[27] greatly disappointed at your absence.

God bless you and grant you to increase in strength.

Your ever affectionate

M. C. M.

Autograph: Bermondsey

247. **To Sister M. Cecilia Marmion**   **[Baggot Street]**
      Birr   **[c. March 22, 1841]**

My Dear Sister M. Cecilia

I felt great indignation at the pretended difficulty in understanding my lively expressive Ballad.[28] Oh how could you forget— the lide de di—impossible. But you have become a dignatory—and cannot give ear or time to—folly.

I am almost infatuated with the darling heavenly little Sr. Margaret D[wyer]. I never met in this great world a sweeter little Dove, all animation, candor and real good sense. I declared she should be Queen of the order in general. This was taken up quite seriously, and a strong opposition party formed, headed by M. de P.—who has been reserved to my poor Queen—from the first. This roused all my energy—and I prepared an Address, giving notice that it would be presented next evening.

At the appointed time, a cradle, dressed in artificial flowers, ribbons, etc. etc., was brought in—to put Queen Mab to sleep—before the young fairies would come to take her.[29] She was most unmercifully teased by Sr. Magdelin, Sr. M. Ann—Sr. M. Clare [Augustine], ditto, ditto. She really looked terrified, and called on me for help. The loyal party assembled round her—all the English—Srs. Veronica, Vincent, Elizabeth, Justina, Frances—etc., etc. and rescued her. I acted as Prime Minister, ordered the cradle to be demolished & the wreath placed on her Majesty's head. Sr. Angela executed this order—and got a most severe and serious lecture from M. de P. You would be surprised to hear the little Sr. Mary—she was really sharp—I was afraid too much so. "The people will walk over your Majesty in the St[reet]. On the ceremony day—the Bishop or Dr. Meyler will have to put their hand over the rail of the sanctuary to feel for you. Will you be pleased to give your dress to make a frock for a nice little [girl] of 7 years old?"

All taken sweetly. The only thing she said that appeared like being hurt— was "Oh Mother de Pazzi—I see you are against me."

---

27 Margaret Teresa Dwyer had visited Cecilia Marmion at Baggot Street many times before entering. "Duckey" is here a term of endearment.   28 See Letter 244.   29 Queen Mab, the diminutive queen of the fairies in English folklore.

This was a most useful little war—it let me see what I did not penetrate with all my skill. The other little Margaret is coming on—a dear little thing but not a Queen—that is, quite a distinguished person.

Mrs. Dwyer comes often, declaring she would not submit to any such regulations. We are obliged to submit. All the preparations going on well, thanks be to God. All the children good and happy.

This is a little private note for your own amusement.

Revd. Mr. Ennis desired to be particularly remembered to you—he got a relic of St. Cecilia— and forgot it at the Irish College in Rome—he says he has written a desperate letter for it.

Take good care of yourself. Do not write for 10 or 12 days—and then you will be able to give me good news.

God bless you.

Your affectionate
M. C. McAuley

Autograph: Dublin, Mercy

248. To Catherine McAuley

Eaton House, Liverpool
March 26, 1841

Dear and respected Mother

I take the liberty of addressing you as a child to beg the favour which I have long wished for of being really admitted as one among your Community. I deferred writing again to Sister Juliana[30] or acknowledging the very kind lines you were so good as to add to her last letter,[31] until I could take this decisive step, and now the consent of my parents enables me to do so. I think you know the difficulty I have had to obtain this, being the only daughter with them, and how much I feel in leaving my present happy home; but I have also long had a strong desire to dedicate myself to the service of God, and my neighbour in the admirable Order of Our Lady of Mercy, & I think I have met with trials sufficient in the world to prove that this desire comes from the Almighty, and from a conviction it is in that state I shall meet with the most abundant means for working out my eternal salvation; it is with the advice of my director I now humbly beg to be admitted a Postulant in your House.

I know I have many many faults; I have so long followed my own will and inclinations, that no doubt I shall feel difficulty in submitting them entirely to obedience, and my idle habits will repine at a life of continual activity, but I trust

---

30 Mary Juliana Hardman from Birmingham was a friend of Jane Frances Gibson from Liverpool before either of them entered the Sisters of Mercy; they corresponded after Juliana entered the Baggot Street community on April 29, 1840.   31 As Catherine McAuley explains in Letter 249, the "kind lines" were added by Cecilia Marmion, the mistress of novices, not by Catherine.

our good God will give me grace proportioned to my necessities. I feel determined to make every effort in my power to become a virtuous Spouse of Christ, and prove my gratitude for the inestimable grace of a Religious vocation.

I cannot tell exactly the time when I shall be able to leave home, but I think the second or third week after Easter. Should I be allowed to spend 2 years in the Noviceship, with the intention of returning to England at the end of that time? I feel very desirous of doing what little good I can in my own country, where I see instruction and good example are so much needed but above all, I wish to be guided by what *you* think most advisable for me & for the advancement of God's honour and glory.

Believe me, ever, with sincerest respect

Your most obedient Child
Jane Frances Gibson[32]

Handcopy: Liverpool

249. To Jane Frances Gibson   Convent, Baggot Street
     Eaton House, Liverpool   March 28, 1841

My Dear Miss Gibson[33]

I have been favored with your very pleasing communication, and am delighted at the near prospect of receiving you as a member of our Community.

Your note to Sister Juliana excited great pity—what pain indeed it must give you to wound the affection of your very estimable Parents, who make this generous sacrifice for God's glory and your happiness. It is a great triumph over nature. The grace must flow from our Divine Redeemer who came on earth, not to bring the delusive enjoyment which we call peace—but a Heavenly Sword sharpened on the cross to cut those dearest ties that have such strong hold on the heart, and thus to draw all to Himself, you who—in obedience to His call—will enter into His immediate service, and your respected Parents, who cooperate with His designs by not placing an obstacle in your way.

The appointed term of our probation is two years and half—six months consideration, and two years noviciate. The annual pension—twenty five pounds, at Profession six hundred pounds. For new establishments the time previous to making vows is reduced to one year and quarter. We have every reason to hope much for the Birmingham foundation. The Sisters in preparation continue to give the most unquestionable evidence of an ardent desire to under-

---

32 The simplicity of this letter requesting admission to the Sisters of Mercy underlies the long and fruitful religious life of Mary Liguori (Jane Frances) Gibson (1819–1881) who entered the Baggot Street community on May 16, 1841, became one of the founding members of the Liverpool community in August 1843, and from 1849 to 1881, except for three years, served as superior of the Sisters of Mercy in Liverpool (Smith 19–21).   33 See Letter 248, note 32.

stand perfectly the obligations of religious life, and to enter into the real spirit of their state.

I shall feel most happy to see you amongst them. They have made impressions here—so favorable to english Sisters, that we shall ever rejoice to add to their number.

The few lines you mention were written by our Mistress of Novices. This is the first time I have had the happiness to address you.

Earnestly begging God to grant you every grace and blessing, I remain with sincere affection

My Dear Miss Gibson, your ever faithful, etc., etc.

Mary C. McAuley

Autograph: Liverpool

250. To Sister M. Frances Warde Baggot St.
Carlow March 29, 1841

My Dearest Sister Mary Frances

I really forget if I wrote to you since Sr. M. Cecilia went to Birr, but think I did not. She was very weak—and had some complaints similar to the last which poor Sr. M. Francis had, and being at the same period of the year, we became a little supersticiously affected.[34] An unexpected favorable opportunity offered, and I sent her to Birr, and as we had designed that she should go to assist at their ceremony in May, I had not so much difficulty to surmount—all having a strong objection to move merely for health. She is nearly three weeks there, better but still very weak, getting exactly the same management you gave Sr. Aloysius— says she can eat, drink, sleep or pray only as directed, "and seeing that each of us cannot have our own way, I seek refuge in submission."

I am a very busy woman now, minding my Novaship, etc., etc. All go on well. Our english Sisters edify us very much—they give the most unquestionable evidence of sincere desire to understand perfectly the obligations of religious life and to enter into the real spirit of their state. We have now a darling indeed, a most angelic little soul, Margaret Dwyer, Dr. Tumy's [Tuomy's] granddaughter. Tho' she has been a constant visitor for two years, I did not think she was what I find her—Sr. M. Cecilia often told me I would be agreeably surprised. I have called her The Queen of [the] Order—she is just her Majesty's size. I am certain if ever a human body was formed without gall—it is she. The other little one is coming to life and we get a third little one from england in easter week.[35] They would not do for foundations tho' we have a

---

34 Mary Francis Marmion, Mary Cecilia's sister, died of consumption on March 10, 1840.   35
Frances Gibson will enter on May 16, 1841, about five weeks after Easter (April 11).

little flock in Birr doing very well. Sr. Dwyer plays & sings most sweetly, a well cultivated voice and finger. You could not avoid making a pet of her—she is such a dove like creature.

I have been told two or three times that you are going to Liverpool—and Sisters of Charity also. Matters with you are not closed—or you would tell me.[36]

We expect Sister M. Clare from London on the 26 April—she returns to Cork with Dr. Murphy—& the other Mary Clare which he made imperative. Four will be professed in London in easter week[37]—so she will leave eight black veils. Lady Barbara Eyre, thank God, will be one of them. She found it difficult to relinquish *all*, and no other terms would be acceded to.

Sister M. Clare is working indeed at the Register. She is quite ashamed to leave it unfinished. I hope to get a safe way of sending it to you—for Sr. M. Cecilia to copy what she likes.[38]

I have heard three or four times of the Wexford Sisters—Mr. Whitty[39] told us they are to get the Parochial House—& that Mr. D[evereux] gave £80 to prepare it for them. God will ever bless him.

All well in Tullamore, Charleville—and Galway. They have had fever again in Limerick—now recovering. Ground taken for a convent in Galway in a most desirable situation next to the College House.

I had a very kind letter from Mr. Mathew. He promises to preach in Birr at their ceremony—what an agent he has been in the hands of God.

Let me soon hear from you.

What a round of business poor Sr. M. Clare[40] has gone through—now only entering her 31 year—first 2 years in Cork—then to London—now back—and I believe soon to another foundation, but I am not told where. Sisters de Sales White and O'Connell are to return in September, please God.

Give my best love to each. Be sure present my respectful regards to Mr. Maher and Dr. Fitzgerald.

Believe me your ever most affectionate

M. C. McAuley

---

36 Over the next five months a three-way conversation evolved, about a foundation in Liverpool, Catherine McAuley urging authorities in Liverpool to let the foundation be made from Carlow, but Dr. George Hilary Brown in the end insisting that the foundation come from Baggot Street.   37 Four novices at the convent in Bermondsey will profess their vows on April 22, 1841: Mary de Sales Eyre, Mary Agnes Birch, Mary Teresa Boyce, and Mary Joseph Hawkins (Bermondsey Annals 1:25).   38 Evidently Clare Augustine Moore was illuminating the Baggot Street Register at this time. It would then be sent to Carlow so that Mary Cecilia Maher, an artist in the Carlow community, could copy whatever art work she wished into the Carlow Register.   39 Possibly William Whitty, the father of Mary Vincent (Ellen) Whitty, a novice, or her priest-brother Robert Whitty, or George Whitty, parish priest in Castlebridge (*Irish Catholic Directory* [1840] 290).   40 Mary Clare (Georgiana) Moore, now in London, was born on March 20, 1814, so she was actually now entering her twenty-eighth year—even younger than Catherine McAuley calculated.

Mary Brooks—when preparing for Confirmation last week—said, "ah, let me be called after Mrs. Warde." Sister Teresa was delighted and told it all over the [place].

Autograph: Silver Spring

251. To Sister M. Teresa Purcell   [Baggot Street]
    Tullamore   [c. March 30, 1841]

My Dear Sister M. Teresa

Your very interesting young friend called yesterday. I should indeed feel most happy to forward her views, but must have more certainty of the Establishment she mentioned, which is only in prospect at present. One year's noviciate here would, I know, be a useful preparation, as the more experience we acquire, the more capable [we are] of discerning deficiency and making some improvement. Our Noviciate goes on very well now, thank God.

My poor Sister M. Cecilia would have been delighted to go to Tullamore, but Mr. O'Hanlon said what I knew, of course, that there was not room, and to me it would be great relief, for Sister de Pazzi would never make the least objection—for what reason I know not, but she objects to a move anywhere else. When Carlow was mentioned for Sr. Aloysius Scott as near her native air, Sister de Pazzi cried and grieved—begging she would be sent to Tullamore. I believe she thinks there is more of our first fervor there than any where else. It will amuse you to hear that when she & I have a little fret—it is followed by—a wish—"that she was in Tullamore."[41]

We have a little trial just now—a dear Sr. in fever—the symptoms all good, thanks be to God. This is the 6th day.[42]

I expect a summons to Birr, when Mr. Mathew appoints his day to preach. I have this moment received the enclosed from Sr. M. Cecilia. If we return by Tullamore, how could we get 4 beds—it seems a most unreasonable thing—2 go from this, and 2 there are to return.[43]

Give my affectionate love to all, and believe me your ever faithfully attached

M. C. McAuley

My cough remains as constant as your sweet little Mother's did.

Autograph: Tullamore

41 The Tullamore convent was very crowded; the new convent, under construction, would not be ready for occupancy until August 15, 1841 (Tullamore Annals 41). Mary de Pazzi Delany was fond of Mary Ann Doyle and Teresa Purcell, the leaders of the Tullamore community.   42 The sister in fever is Mary Vincent (Ellen) Whitty, a novice, originally from Wexford.   43 The ceremony in Birr, at which Theobald Mathew will preach, will eventually be set for May 20. Catherine McAuley will go from Dublin with a travelling companion, and the two will return to Dublin bringing Cecilia Marmion and—according to Catherine's present plan—Teresa (Catherine) White who had been temporarily in Birr to assist the new community.

252. To Sister M. Teresa White   [Baggot Street]
Galway   March 31, 1841

My Dearest Sister M. Teresa

I beg to offer to you and each of our dear Sisters most grateful thanks for your nice collection for the lottery. All Dublin seems compleatly tired of these little works. Not one will engage in them as formerly. The spirit has fled to Limerick, Galway, Cork, etc., etc. For seven years we were wonderfully successful.[44] You have enriched our little store very much. My poor Sr. Teresa is as usual indefatigable trying to sell tickets at one shilling to her customers for servants—indeed she is all we have acting in the matter, and fifty pounds is the extent of our hope, which added to the profit of Laundry work will get us through this year. The Work Houses have not lessened our number—we have at this moment 52, and to speak of the poor House to any of them is a kind of condemnation. There is such a mixture of immoral persons—unavoidably admitted, that the reduced, moral, orderly person cannot bear to go.[45]

I believe I have already told you that we expect Sr. M. Clare here on the 26th April. She is to return with Dr. Murphy to Cork—4 are to be professed in easter week—Lady B[arbara] at last, thank God, surrenders all—which was rather difficult to her.[46] 6 professed of their own will remain and our two, who return at the appointed time, but I suppose you hear all from Sr. de Sales.

My poor Sr. M. Cecilia is not much improved, but I have every hope when the weather changes she will receive great benefit—the air is so good. I had a few lines from her yesterday. She says it is reported that Crotty is getting several preachers to Birr, to recover some of his congregation stolen by the Sisters of Mercy. Thank God, the poor deluded souls are returning fast—and preparing to approach the Holy Sacraments. Little Sr. M. Teresa is following them every where and begs we will unite in the 30 days prayer during April for the conversion of the apostate leader—I must write to moderate her zeal—I am really afraid she would speak to him if they met in any poor place which would be exceedingly wrong.

My Dearest child, pray most fervently next month and get all the prayers you can—that God may direct me in making arrangements for Birmingham—I

---

44 The annual bazaars in support of the House of Mercy, that had been such a successful source of income for several years, were now falling off in Dublin. Apparently, the novelty of these fashionable occasions had dulled, but the financial need had only increased.   **45** John O'Connor presents a chart that shows the "No. of inmates for which [each] Workhouse was originally designed." The South Dublin Union, the workhouse nearest Baggot Street, first admitted people on April 24, 1840, and was said to accommodate 2000 people in the adapted building of the old Foundling Hospital (J. O'Connor 235, 261). O'Connor notes that in the "punishment book" kept in each workhouse, the Master of the workhouse was empowered to "punish any pauper" for "Using obscene or profane language … insulting any person … Threatening to strike or assault any person … Not duly cleansing his person" and other behaviors. The very list suggests that these behaviors occurred in an atmosphere where people were treated as "paupers, serving a life sentence for the crime of poverty" (108).   **46** See Letter 250, note 37.

am a little perplexed. Another english Sr. coming at easter. All are truly good religious, but I am at a great loss about a superior—I do not know what to do.

My God bless and protect you and all. Give my best love to each of our dear Sisters, and believe me always you fondly attached Mother in Christ.

M. C. McAuley

All well here—Kingstown merely existing—Sr. Blake presiding[47]—Booterstown as usual.

I am delighted to hear you have a prospect of encrease. Three are expected to enter in Carlow—at easter. In all we counted that there will be eleven added to the order at Easter.

Autograph (damaged): Galway

253. **To Sister Mary Aloysius Scott**   [Baggot Street]
     Birr   [April 1841]

My Dear Sister M. Aloysius

How very grateful I feel to God for continuing His favors to you—and amidst all your little difficulties, preserving you in health and spirits. Your improvements, according to report, are very great. Sr. M. Cecilia must have been surprised to see your Community Room. I do not think they have so large in any of the Convents.

I am delighted to find Mr. Birmingham able to return to his Parish. Revd. Mr. Egan called here yesterday, he saw you about 10 days since. He told me Father Frank was a very frequent visitor.[48]

Father Mathew's letter was quite consoling. He says—"I had a long conversation with the Bishop, he is proud of the foundation." He promises that nothing he can at present foresee shall interrupt his preaching at your ceremony.[49]

I hope you are getting in love with your charge—it was a great mistake to think that my wish for St. John's was to relase [release] myself from my responsibility. No indeed—I think it a sweet occupation. The spirit of penance alone would take me from it. When I see my poor efforts for their improvement blessed with success, I think—none so happy as I am. Never talk of your fears again—

47 Mary Gertrude (Elizabeth) Blake had been appointed local superior in Kingstown in March 1841, to relieve Clare Augustine Moore who came back to Baggot Street to work on the Register before going to Cork.   48 In the *Irish Catholic Directory* for 1841, a "Rev. J. Birmingham" is listed as the parish priest of Borrisokane, near Birr (304). "Rev. Mr. Egan" and "Father Frank" have not been identified. Catherine may have meant to write "Mr. Egan"—the father of Susan Egan in Birr.   49 As of April 12, Theobald Mathew still had not set a date for the reception ceremony in Birr. However, Letter 261, written on April 19, indicates that by then he had chosen May 20 for the ceremony. This paragraph may suggest that this letter was written in mid April after the May date was set.

they are wild—as Robin run a the hedge.⁵⁰ Take care of yourself—and be a good Mother Superior—you could not be a better thing at this side the grave.

Very good news from Galway—a New Convent commenced with large garden in the centre of the Town—a Sister about to enter. I suppose your garden & little lawn will be lovely in April and May.

I often smile when I think on your enjoying Mother de P. sitting in the B[ishop's] parlour. I do not think she sat here one quarter since Sr. M. C[ecilia] went. I do not know if she ever sits down till dinner. She certainly has a great deal of worldly matters to attend to every day.⁵¹

God bless you, my Dear Sr. M. Aloysius. A thousand loves to your Children in Christ. Glorious title, Mother of Children in Christ. Again, may God bless you.

Your ever affectionate
M. C. McAuley

Mother de P—love 10,000 times.

Autograph: Dublin, Mercy

254. To Sister M. Cecilia Marmion   [Baggot Street]
    Birr   [April 6, 1841]

My Dear Sister M. Cecilia

I have all that is satisfactory to communicate to you. The Sisters of the Novaship are truly edifying, and admirably formed—so far as they are advanced. You have great reason to rejoice and return many thanks to God for blessing your humble efforts. It is my greatest happiness to be with them. Their tempers are regulated so that they seem always prepared for humiliating remarks—which you know I am not sparing of. It comforts me more than I can express to find them so initiated in the real spirit of their state—may God continue to bless them.

I am doing my share—regularly, thank God, novices and postulants in turn, the Rule every evening with scolding, coaxing etc., etc. The lay novice very promising. The little Mary Lawless dancing in and out of the habit—which is made—and the once doubtful Sr. Teresa—most rationally happy—the Revd. Mr. O'Connell told her brother. He was delighted. I was very much pleased with

---

50 Catherine McAuley is probably referring to St. John's, Newfoundland, not St. John's parish, Birr, where the Mercy convent was located. As early as 1838 she had expressed a willingness to go herself to Nova Scotia (see Letter 124, note 18). Perhaps as she prepared Mary Francis Creedon, now a novice, for the eventual foundation in Newfoundland, she also expressed a willingness or a desire to go there—even as she increasingly knew that she would be unable to go. Here she is assuring Mary Aloysius that she need not fear such a separation, calling her fears as wild as "robin run in the hedge," which was the popular name for several wild plants including ground-ivy, goosegrass, and bindweed (OED). The red-flowered campion was popularly called "robin in the hedge" (OED).   51 Apparently when an attack of melancholy or depression was upon her, Mary de Pazzi Delany would sit at length during the day in the Bishop's Parlour, the guest parlour at Baggot Street. However, when her spirits were raised, she abandoned this practice.

your note to her—it was exactly what I like—is not this miraculous. An old torment, even tearing notes and letters to pieces—I read it out for all and took great pains to do it justice—no more was required.[52]

How I long for the note that will tell me you are getting stronger. We commenced the 30 Days Prayer on Thursday in place of the Psalter[53]—the substance of petition, That God will graciously direct all the arrangements to be made for the establishment of the Convent in Birmingham. As I gave previous notice & entreated the pious co-operation of all, I am sure we have it. I do not wish you to say the long prayer but—think of the intention at Mass when you can.

I do not expect to hear of your health oftener than every 10 days—till we meet.

If Dr. Spain would write now to Father Mathew—he probably would appoint the day—he is somewhere near Tullamore.

A cruel April fool trick was played on Thursday—great placards all over the city to announce that the "Apostle of Temperance" was to administer the pledge at the Custom house. The poor people—men, women & children—were running in hundreds under all the heavy rain to get his blessing—he was then in the North.

A most desirable young person called this week—with some serious thoughts—I will wait a little before I say more—like Sr. Teresa—she means to look about. She is quite nice—and no impediment seems to be in the way.

Sr. Teresa's brother wrote a note full of joy & affection on hearing she was to be received. I have taken a great fancy to this man.

God bless you. Pray for your affectionate

M. C. M.

The very nice young person alluded to has just been here—said the Angelus with me in the B[ishop's] parlour. Pray God to direct her and if He has no objection, ask Him to send here. It would be very useful.

Autograph: Dublin, Mercy

255. To Sister M. Frances Warde   [Baggot Street]
     Carlow   Easter Saturday [April 10, 1841][54]

My Dearest Sister Mary Frances

I have just received your welcome letter. I am rejoiced to hear you are going

---

52 Catherine McAuley distrusted particular attachments and "favorite" friendships in religious communities—what she called "pets" in relationships—because such favoritism could lead not only to emotional preoccupation, but to divisiveness and partisanship, and could thus diminish the union and universal charity that should, in her view, characterize religious communities. She felt that novices should learn the discipline of large-heartedness early in their training.   53 Catherine refers here to the long prayer called the "Psalter of Jesus." See Letter 98, note 31.   54 One is loathe to correct Catherine McAuley, yet that may be necessary. She dated this letter "Easter Saturday" which in present-day parlance would have been April 17; however, I believe, that she meant "Holy

to Wexford. I often meditated writing a petition to Doctor Healy[55] to that effect—but was afraid of being a busybody.

I have found the second visit to a new branch exceedingly useful, not for what we can say or do—for our experience in religious life has been so short—that a good faithful Sister to whom God has imparted grace—may be said to know as much of spiritual life as we do—yet it is certainly most useful to give assistance for some time. It animates the new beginners and gives confidence to others. I have been told that it made parents & guardians give countenance and say that they did not fear a failure when there was such attention—not only from their own Bishop—but also the Bishop from whose Diocess they came. It bespeaks a warm interest in the success of the new branch and will be found conducive thereto. It was not thought we would succeed in Galway, where there was [sic] five old established nunneries. Dr. Browne on our second visit said from the altar: "It is impossible the order of Srs. of Mercy should fail—where there is such unity and such affectionate interest is maintained, as brings them one hundred miles to encourage and aid one another, and this is their established practice, to look after what has been newly commenced." Several persons told me it was more useful to say these few words than I could suppose. They have purchased ground and a new Convent is to be erected immediately—3 are preparing to join.

I am gratified to hear you are so soon to return to Carlow. It is too young to be left long.

All here as usual—a Profession & reception—immediately. I wish it was over.[56]

We were thinking of each other just at the same moment. I got your former letter on the day you got mine. I also got your answer to mine.

The usual interruptions about marketing, etc. I will conclude—begging God to grant you and all with you His very best Blessings—to guide you in what you are about to engage in, and bring you safe back to your charge.

Pray for your ever affectionate
M. C. McAuley

The change of air will cure your cough, please God.

Autograph: Silver Spring

Saturday" which was April 10 in 1841. She has received word that Frances Warde is "going" to Wexford. In Letter 256, written on April 10, 1841, she says "Sr. Frances goes on Monday [April 12] to Wexford for the ceremony." According to the Wexford Register, a reception was held in Wexford on Friday, April 16, at which Kate Farrell, Mary Walsh, and Susan Wall received the habit, taking the names Mary Francis, Mary Josephine, and Mary Clare, respectively. If this letter is written, on April 17, as Catherine's "Easter Saturday" might imply, then Frances Warde is already in Wexford, and the ceremony is over.   55 Dr. Francis Haly, bishop of Kildare and Leighlin.   56 Catherine is anticipating the profession and reception ceremonies to be held at Baggot Street on May 4, 1841.

256. To Sister Mary Aloysius Scott
Birr

My Dearest Sr. M. Aloysius

I rejoice with you all on the arrival of Easter Sunday, and hope soon to hear a good account of my poor Sr. M. Cecilia. I had a few lines from Carlow this day. Sr. M. F. says she had a letter from her—in which she said you were taking the same care of her (Sr. M. C.)—as Sr. Frances did of you. God grant it may be equally successful.

Mother de P. very ill this week—recovering. All the rest as usual.

Sr. Frances goes on Monday to Wexford for the ceremony.[57]

My Dear Sr. M. A., will you prevail on Dr. Spain to write to Father Mathew. He is promising in all directions—I fear he will forget us.

My cough is constant. A move now would be useful indeed, but I cannot go till he names the time.

The blessing of meats, etc., and many other interruptions, making preparations for 32 etc., etc.[58]—compels me to conclude, praying God to grant you and all with you—His very best blessings at this truly joyful season.

Pray for your ever affectionate
M. C. McAuley

Write soon to poor Mother de Pazzi.

Autograph: Dublin, Mercy

257. To Sister M. Elizabeth Moore
Limerick

My Dearest Sr. M. Elizabeth

I am impatient to send you a few hurried lines, rejoicing that our sorrowful meditations are at an end—and humbly beseeching God [to] impart to us all some portion of those precious gifts and graces which our Dear Redeemer has purchased by His bitter sufferings—that we may endeavour to prove our love and gratitude, by bearing some resemblance to Him—copying some of the lessons He has given us during His mortal life, particularly those of His passion.

---

57 See note 54 above. However, the "Annals" of the *Irish Catholic Directory* for 1842 incorrectly lists this event on May 7, 1841, and also says incorrectly that "the Misses Walsh, Farrell, and Doyle—took the initiatory vows and were received into the above religious and highly useful order" (407). The order is not mentioned "above," and no vows are taken when a novice receives the habit.
58 Those having Easter Sunday dinner at Baggot Street will include not only the members of the religious community living there, but also the residents of the House of Mercy who are not employed outside the House on Easter. Since there were about fifty-two women and girls residing in the House at this time, according to Letter 252, Catherine may not be including any of them in the thirty-two, but calculating their number separately.

Poor Sr. de Pazzi has been very ill and is not yet well. Preparations for Reception & Profession—not one old helpmate. Sisters Cowley, Byrn and dear Sister Mary—Lay—to be professed; Sisters Teresa McDonnell, M[ary] Lawless & F[rances] Vigne—to be received, & a Lay Sr. for the english Mission.[59] Not one prepared voice for the choir—add to this my blunders—and Mother de Pazzi's over zeal & excitement, and you will have a picture of a charming ceremony. God will help us through it.

All are good and happy. The blessing of unity still dwells amongst us—and oh what a blessing—it should make all things else pass into nothing. All laugh and play together, not one cold stiff soul appears. From the day they enter, all reserve of an ungracious kind leaves them. This is the Spirit of the order indeed— the true Spirit of Mercy—flowing on us—that notwithstanding our unworthiness, God never seems to visit us with angry punishment. He may punish a little in Mercy—but never in wrath. Take what He will from us—He still leaves His holy peace—and this He has graciously extended to all our Convents. Thousands of thanks and praises to His Holy Name.

God preserve and bless you, My Dear Sister M. Elizabeth. With affectionate love to all, believe me your ever sincerely attached

M. C. McAuley

Autograph: Limerick

258. To Sister Mary Vincent Harnett   [Baggot Street]
Limerick   [April 12, 1841?][60]

My dearest Sister Mary Vincent

I cannot close the cover without saying a few words to you. I rejoice exceedingly at the account I have heard of your school and your poor women—it is greatly spoken of by persons who have connections in Limerick. The improvement in the school has been represented to the Board.[61] I earnestly pray God to

---

59 Catherine lists those who will profess their vows and those who will receive the habit at the ceremony on May 4, 1841: Mary Aloysius (Elinor) Cowley, Mary Camillus (Teresa) Byrn (Catherine's cousin and godchild), and Mary (Eliza) Liston; and the postulants Teresa MacDonnell, Mary Lawless, and Frances Vigne. The lay sister preparing for the English mission is possibly a Sister Margaret.   60 No autograph of this letter has been found. However, there are three early handcopies—all undated: the handcopy in Cork, which the recipient had prepared and numbered "2nd"; a copy in the Baggot Street Manuscript Book called "Annals" (49); and one in the Brisbane Book of Transcriptions (88–89). This letter was, according to its first sentence, enclosed in the cover of a letter to Elizabeth Moore. It may have been enclosed in an earlier letter than Letter 257 (April 12, 1841), perhaps in 1839 or 1840, but no other logical date for the letter has been identified.   61 That is, the Board of Commissioners of the national education system. Daniel Murray, archbishop of Dublin, was a commissioner. Catherine may have heard this positive report from him.

preserve you in health and to bless you with His Divine grace, granting you renewed vigor every day to carry you happily to the journey's end.

I have not seen your Father or Brother since we heard of them through Sister Blake.[62]

Again I pray God to bless you. Your letter was most acceptable to me. Give my particular love to Sisters Mary & Anne. I will write to all soon. Remember me most kindly to Miss Reddin [Reddan].

Pray for your ever affectionate

M. C. McAuley

Tell Sister M. E. to write to me the name of the wine Mr. O'B. gave me.[63] Beg of Sister Bridgman to try to get me a copy of Mr. Marrain's [Murrane's] delightful Sermon—her Aunt perhaps could get it.[64]

Harnett handcopy: Cork; handcopies: Brisbane, and Dublin, Mercy

259. Poem on "Mercy"[65]								[Undated]

> Sweet Mercy! soothing, patient,[66] kind
> Softens the high and rears[67] the fallen mind

---

62 Mary Vincent Harnett was born in Milltown, Co. Dublin, south of the city. Her mother died when she was eight or nine years old. Her father, Maurice Harnett, one-time proprietor of a mercantile establishment in Dublin, lived in the suburbs of Dublin, with his only son. Perhaps Mary Gertrude Blake in Kingstown (Dún Laoghaire) had seen the father and son there. See Sullivan, *Catherine McAuley* (130, 366 n. 1).   63 Catherine may be referring to a priest in Limerick by the name of O'Brien, possibly to Dr. Richard Baptist O'Brien, who in 1839 went to Halifax, Nova Scotia, for five years as president of St. Mary's College there (Mac Suibhne 147). He is known to have met with Catherine on at least one occasion (see Letter 124, note 18), but perhaps more. Possibly he was in Limerick when she visited in early October 1840. Although Catherine had taken the pledge of total abstinence—probably in Galway, in May or June 1840—the correspondence of early 1841 indicates that her cough was growing much worse, and that some means of suppressing it was needed. Presumably she is inquiring about the wine for herself.   64 Two more sentences, in much smaller handwriting, are added to this postscript in the handcopy prepared for Mary Vincent Harnett, the recipient—possibly by her or her scribe or by a later hand. The sentences do not appear in the other two handcopies and are not included in the text presented here because they do not seem, in view of their content, to belong to this letter. The sentences are these: "Sr. M. Aloysius getting quite [well?]—little Sr. M. Ann out of hope of going to Heaven this time. She has been 25 days in bed—very ill indeed—my poor child"—which might suggest an 1840 date. 65 Some present-day writers and editors have given this poem on Mercy the date September 24, 1828 or December 9, 1830, and these dates—symbolic as they are, but for which there is no verification in the primary source material—have now become quasi-authoritatively (but, I believe, incorrectly) attached to the poem.   The fact is that the poem cannot be accurately dated. Indeed, what is known about the poem is very limited: Harnett claims that Catherine McAuley "on one occasion, quite impromptu, wrote the following lines" (*Life* 112); Carroll says, "One evening the Sisters asked her to write them a verse on Mercy. She immediately composed, quite impromptu, the following lines" (*Life* 261); Clare Moore presents the poem as one of the "Favourite Verses of our Foundress" (*Practical Sayings*, 37–38); and the Limerick Annals inserts the poem after its transcription of Letter

Knows with just rein, and even hand to guide
Between false fear, and arbitrary pride
Not easily provoked, and soon forgives[68]
Feels for all,[69] and by a look relieves
Soft peace she brings where e'er[70] she arrives
Removes our anguish and reforms our lives
Lays the rough paths[71] of peevish nature even
And opens in each heart a little heaven.[72]

Handcopies: Limerick and Dublin, Mercy

---

257 saying, "From the allusion to the 'Spirit of Mercy' in the above [i.e. in Letter 257] this may be the appropriate place to insert some lines which she wrote extempore on the word, a little time before in Baggot Street" (1:86–87).

No autograph of this poem has been located, and no photostat or photocopy of it has been discovered. However, there are at least three early and nearly identical handcopies: in the Limerick Annals, in the Dundalk Manuscript, and in the small "Baggot St. Ms. Copies of poems and letters" as well as the text published in 1868 in Moore's *Practical Sayings*. The text given here is that in the Baggot Street handcopy. The footnotes indicate where the Limerick or other texts differ from the Baggot Street text.

I have chosen to place the poem in the 1841 sequence, rather than among "Undated" texts at the end of this edition, simply on the strength of its placement in the Limerick Annals after Letter 257, even though I regard the poem as presently undatable. And while the poem is said to be Catherine McAuley's own composition, one cannot absolutely rule out the possibility that she transcribed some or all of it from another, published source.

66 The Limerick text inserts "gentle" here.   **67** The Limerick text has "raises" for "rears."   **68** The Limerick text reads: "Not soon provoked, and easily forgives."   **69** The Dundalk Manuscript has "Feels love for all … "   **70** The Limerick text has "wherever" for "where e'er." The Baggot Street text actually has "wher'eer" which seems too confusing to repeat.   **71** The Limerick text has "path" for "paths."

72 In the published texts in Harnett (1865), Carroll (1866), and Moore (1868), the last two lines of the poem are not included. Moreover, their identical versions have many variations in wording from the Baggot Street text: "mild, and" for "gentle" (l. 1); "lifts" for "rears" (l. 2); "soft" for "just" (l. 3); "Nor yields to fear nor knows exacting pride" (l. 4); "it" for "and" (l. 5); "Is all to" for "Feels for" and "with" for "by" (l. 6); "it" for "she" twice (l. 7); and "pains" for "anguish" and "crowns with peace" for "reforms," although Carroll has "crowns with joy" (l. 8). Thus their version reads as follows, which may be the original wording, though this is not certain:

Sweet Mercy, soothing, patient, mild, and kind
Softens the high and lifts the fallen mind,
Knows with soft rein and even hand to guide
Nor yields to fear, nor knows exacting pride.
Not soon provoked, it easily forgives,
Is all to all, and with a look relieves
Soft peace it brings wherever it arrives
Removes our pains, and crowns with peace [joy] our lives.

260. To Sister M. Cecilia Marmion [Baggot Street]
     Birr [April 1841][73]

My Dear Sister M. Cecilia

I look forward with great hope that we shall soon have a very [good] account of the state of your health. All going on very well here—preparations for ceremony, etc., etc.

Tell my dear Sr. M. A[loysius] she will hear of a miracle amongst us—soon as we can execute a commission. From Saturday till Monday morning when I left—she had an alarm. We would send many messages—& distinct written orders before a proper clock would be sent. A note from Dr. Spain would be respectfully attended to and he has opportunities every day—and now that he shews such kind interest he would not refuse.[74] Let me know has the Convent bell been put up.

Francis[75] was just here transacting some affairs for me—he is very well.

I know the note from Miss Beckett will be consoling to you. I wrote to express the great pleasure it gave me. Thanks be to God she seems now out of danger.[76]

My old cough is tormenting me, some stings in my chest. I believe I must go to Birr.

All well in Limerick, etc. The little M[argaret] Dwyer—full of delight as her hour draws nigh—a little disappointed at Mother Cecilia's absence.[77]

God bless you. Most affectionate love to all.

Pray for your faithful
M. C. McAuley

Mother de Pazzi is the most active busy person you could see—general providore for both Houses—laundry superintender. I have not seen her for half an hour in the Bishop's Parlour since you went—indeed she has much to attend to as I am quite a Lady.[78]

Autograph: Dublin, Mercy

---

73 Neumann (329–30) and Bolster (221–22) both date this undated autograph letter April 12, 1841. The only problem with that estimate is the sharp contrast between the comment on Mary de Pazzi's ill health in Letter 257 (written on April 12) and her vigorous activity as reported in this letter. 74 The meaning of these somewhat playful sentences is obviously clear to Catherine McAuley, but not to the present-day reader. 75 Francis Marmion, an attorney, was the brother of Mary Cecilia. 76 Evidently Marianne Beckett, now in England, had resolved her religious doubts and difficulties. Her note to Catherine McAuley has not been located. 77 Margaret Teresa Dwyer was preparing for reception of the habit. However, her reception did not occur until August 19, 1841. That fact might raise questions about the dating of this letter except that only from March to early May 1841 was Catherine McAuley in Baggot Street and Cecilia Marmion in Birr. 78 Catherine was not above putting a bright face on Mary de Pazzi's condition so as not to worry Cecilia when she was recuperating. See also Letter 261 regarding Catherine's own health.

261. To Sister M. de Sales White
Bermondsey

Convent
April 19, 1841

My Dear Sister M. de Sales

I fully intended writing to you on Easter Monday, but was prevented by an accident. Rising to light the taper candle for sealing letters, I found my right foot fastened in the train of my habit—in disengaging it, the ancle [ankle] turned and I was a criple [cripple] for some hours only, though obliged to be assisted by two. In a little time we found the sinews were strained but no more injury. However, you know my Mistresses would make a Nurse child of me. The old Galway cough continues. I do not know what it intends to do with me.

Sister Vincent Whitty in slight fever, with very favorable symptoms. All the rest well, thank God. We have a very sweet little Postulant called the Queen— most promising in every respect. We are expecting two. I have just had a note from Sr. M. Cecilia. She is improving very much.

Father Mathew has appointed Ascension day for the ceremony in Birr. We shall all be back before June, please God. The English Sisters will then be near remote retreat for profession.[79] What a thin House they will leave here—ten are to go, 8 their own stock—& two of us. We shall be obliged indeed to gather in our scattered troops, or the duties of this Convent—with its two poor dependants, Kingstown & Booterstown—should be at an end. Be quite ready to come at a short notice. If able I will go for you, but 'tis very probable the journey to Birmingham will be more than I can well go through—if I cannot go—one of the good Priests will.

Disengage your heart if it is entangled in dear Bermondsey Convent—for we cannot leave you one week beyond the time appointed. I hope to have Sr. M. Teresa from Galway sooner than I expected,[80] and with all, we shall be poorly provided with hands. We will endeavour to make up in fervor and good will. The impression made on our minds, by forty days meditation on Christ's humiliations, meekness and unwearied perseverance, will help us on every difficult occasion, and we will endeavour to make Him the only return He demands of us—by giving Him our whole heart—fashioned on His own model—pure, meek, merciful and humble. All will then be easy and sweet—no agitation, no particular desire—except to please and glorify God.

Pray for your portion of Easter Grace, before the extra Treasury is closed. Pray fervently & constantly—do not give up until All is given you.

May God preserve and bless you.

Your affectionate
M. C. M.

Autograph: Liverpool

79 Those preparing for profession of vows made a remote retreat of two months, using special daily meditations for this purpose. Catherine McAuley envisions that the sisters going to Birmingham will profess their vows in mid August. 80 Catherine still plans that Mary Teresa White will return from Galway to Baggot Street, and that Mary Catherine Leahy will take over as superior in Galway. This change did not occur.

262. To Sister M. Frances Warde [Baggot Street]
    Carlow [April 24, 1841][81]

My Dear Sister M. Frances

We have had much trial here since you went to Wexford. A Sister in fever—slight, thank God—now up.[82] Another has thrown up blood—three times in one day—she is better.[83] A third—one of the english—Erysipelas in the head and face—good symptoms.[84] In the midst of all this alarm, a note from Sr. Genevieve—"Come as fast as possible. James is dying and wants to see you." My cough was very severe—and so much encreased by going as the door & window were obliged to be open. I got on a blister on that night. The weakness passed away—I fear my poor child will have many such—he is in a most heavenly state of mind—imploring God's forgiveness and quite happy.[85]

Dr. Furlong called. He gave me a delightful account of everything, but the sermon. He was greatly pleased & surprised. It is his young friend that has fever—she is a great favorite—most deservedly.[86]

Sr. M. Cecilia improving. Mr. Mathew has fixed Ascension day for the ceremony in Birr[87]—so that we shall be without her for another month, too much—making preparation for Profession & reception here when God sent us sickness—He knows what is good for us.

Just got a letter from england—their ceremony over, four professed and one received. Lady Barbara fixed at last—an humble Sr. of Mercy, the first titled Lady who became a Nun in England—or Ireland—for a long time.[88] There have been Honorables—but not an Earl's daughter for centuries.

Our poor Teresa seems almost gone—this variable weather has such an effect on her. She takes so little nourishment & is coughing exceedingly.

God bless you, my ever dear Sr. Frances.

Your truly affectionate
M. C. McAuley

81 The postmarks on this letter are Dublin "AP 24/41" and "Carlow AP 25/1841." Frances Warde had apparently already returned to Carlow from Wexford. 82 Mary Vincent Whitty, a novice. 83 This may be Mary Justina Fleming, a novice, whose health deteriorated during 1841. She died in Tullamore on December 10, 1841 (Tullamore Annals 45). 84 Erysipelas is an acute febrile disease caused by a streptococcal organism and involving inflammation of the skin, usually of the face (Carmichael 720). The English novice has not been identified. 85 Mary Genevieve Jarmy, who lived in the Booterstown branch house, was caring for Catherine McAuley's eldest nephew James Macauley who was dying of consumption. 86 Dr. Thomas Furlong was parish priest of Killegay in the diocese of Ferns and professor of rhetoric and belles lettres at St. Patrick's College, Maynooth (*Irish Catholic Directory* [1841], 297, 389). He knew Mary Vincent (Ellen) Whitty whose family was in Wexford. Dr. Furlong evidently preached at the reception ceremony in Wexford on April 16, 1841. However, a physician by the name of Furlong also lived in Wexford, and it may have been he who visited Baggot Street on this occasion. 87 May 20, 1841. 88 In the Bermondsey convent on April 22, 1841, the following professed their vows: Mary de Sales (Barbara) Eyre, Mary Agnes (Louisa) Birch, Mary Teresa (Elizabeth) Boyce, and Mary Joseph (Sarah) Hawkins. The sister who received the habit was Mary Francis, a lay sister who "was afterwards dismissed, having been tried for more than two years, and found unequal to the duties of the Institute" (Bermondsey Annals 1:25).

All over for the present about Sr. M. Clare returning. Dr. Murphy read a letter he received from the Bishop of London—which induced him to consent to her remaining till June—I suppose they will then petition for more. It would have been easier—and more safe—for her to have left the charge in three months than now. Had the arrangement rested with me—I would never have consented to her remaining longer than I remained—since she was destined to return. They will find a change now rather dangerous—but God will direct all.

Autograph: Silver Spring

263. To Sister Mary Aloysius Scott   [Baggot Street]
    Birr   Wednesday, April 28, 1841

My Dear Sister M. Aloysius

We have a letter from Miss Gibson saying she leaves home for Baggot Street on the 14th of May.[89] I had every hope of getting to Birr soon after our ceremony which takes place on the 4th—and if you desire it very much—I might leave the admission of Miss G[ibson] to Mother de Pazzi who is remarkably well, thank God, but great pressing will be necessary, tho' I feel the want of some change very much.

I really think a few drinks of the waters of Birr—hot and cold—will cure me. Do you not think it absolutely necessary, that I should conduct the retreat. Sister M. Cecilia is out of office—and you are not capable.[90]

I would wish to go on the 8th to Tullamore, rest on Sunday there—& go to you on Monday morning.

I wish you had a Postulant. Miss Furlong who Sr. M. Cecilia speaks of will not even be permitted to call here since her Mamma found she was so disposed. I spoke to her Father, who rejected the thought of it most conclusively. Sr. M. C. seems to think she could go anywhere, if much means were not required.

God bless you, my Dear Sister Aloysius. What chattering we will have soon, please God.

                     Pray for your ever affectionate[91]
                           M. C. McAuley

I am rejoiced to hear you are to have the Bishop. We must try to make a conquest—and gain his affections.[92]

---

89 Jane Frances Gibson from Liverpool entered the Baggot Street community on Sunday, May 16. 90 Catherine McAuley obviously wants—and needs—to go to Birr as soon as possible. She is trying to formulate reasons, other than her own health, why this is a necessity—for example, that she is needed to conduct the eight-day retreat for the sisters who will receive the habit in Birr on May 20. 91 As Catherine closes this letter, she does not realize that her nephew James Macauley will die the next day, April 29, in his twenty-sixth year. 92 Catherine hopes to win greater support from Dr. Patrick Kennedy, bishop of Killaloe. However, see Letter 230, note 46.

I expect to be astonished at Sr. M. Cecilia's appearance. If she looks better than I do as to health—she must be greatly changed indeed, for I am not altered in looks, tho' weary of this old cough.

Mr. O'Hanlon has just been here—after recovering from Influenza, & proposed going to Birr with us if I would go after the ceremony—please God, we will go on Thursday in the coach—4 of us.[93]

Autograph: Dublin, Mercy

---

93 The departure for Birr is now scheduled for Thursday, May 6.

May–June 1841

Ever since her trip to Galway in May–June 1840, Catherine McAuley had suffered from what she called an "old man's cough," a harbinger, as she may have realized, of the consumption that would claim her life on November 11, 1841. Yet May and June 1841 were extremely busy and encouraging months for her: first, of course, there was the sad burial on May 1 of her eldest nephew James, the last (as she thought) of her sister's children, so that she had "nothing now to draw me for one hour from my religious Sisters" (Letter 265); then on May 4, she saw three novices profess their vows and four postulants receive the habit at Baggot Street; she was in Birr from May 7 to May 23, helping to prepare the two Birr postulants for their reception of the habit on May 20; at Baggot Street seven novices were preparing for foundations in Birmingham, England and Newfoundland; plans were emerging for a future foundation in Liverpool; and indeed, by late June the convent on Baggot Street was filled with the fervor and humor of well over a dozen novices and postulants in whom she delighted, she who was typically forty years their senior.

Only later, in the last six weeks of Catherine's life, when she was sixty-three and dying, would there be any evident diminution of her activity. For now, there was Frances Gibson, a postulant from Liverpool, to be welcomed; new veiling to be sent to Carlow; the journey to and from Birr, with "a cross driver, slow horses, and broken harness" to be accepted; "our old beloved companion," the returning Mary Clare Moore, now "very thin," to be embraced; the "obstinate cough" of Justina Fleming, a novice, to be worried over; and Bishop John England to be teased when he came looking for sisters for Charleston. The sensitive, generous, playful fire of her affection was undiminished. These were months of poetry, grateful remembrances, sympathy for Frances Warde, concern over "creepy crawly" Naas, encouragement of her "last born child, poor Birr," and the kind of deep prayer that Catherine McAuley never discussed in her letters.

264. To the Reverend John Hamilton

Baggot Street
[May 1, 1841][1]

Very Reverend Dear Sir

Will you be so kind to favor us with your presence at the ceremony of reception on Tuesday the 4th Inst.—at one o'clock.

1 This undated request that John Hamilton attend a reception ceremony at Baggot Street could

Very respectfully etc., etc.
Mary C. McAuley

I hope you will be so kind to grant this earnest request.

Autograph: Dublin Diocese, Murray Papers AB3/34/15, no. 21

265. To Sister M. Frances Warde   Baggot Street
   Carlow   May 1, 1841[2]

My Dear Sister M. Frances

We are very busy people here, preparing for 7 on Tuesday—4 received & 3 professed.[3] I had written this much yesterday & was interrupted. This morning I got your welcome letter. I am delighted to hear you are going to Naas.

To create some pious excitement, my cough was worse last night—than any cold night in winter. Mr. O'Hanlon has had this Influenza very severely. I thought we were going to part him, he looked so badly. Thank God he is recovering. He, I and two Sisters go to Birr on Thursday the 6th—I will have 12 or 13 days before the ceremony there, and perhaps the cough will get better. A wonderful change in Sr. M. Cecilia. All think the air quite similar to Carlow.

---

have been written only on September 1, 1838 or May 1, 1841—prior to the reception ceremony on Tuesday, September 4, 1838 or Tuesday, May 4, 1841, respectively. Since there was also a profession ceremony for three sisters on the morning of May 4, 1841 (hence the one o'clock time of the reception ceremony), but no profession of vows on September 4, 1838, the probable date of this letter is Saturday, May 1, 1841—the earliest possible date in the same month ("inst.") as the ceremony. Profession ceremonies took place during the celebration of the Eucharist, and were therefore scheduled in the morning, given the required fast before receiving Holy Communion; reception ceremonies were not conducted within the celebration of the Eucharist, though they could occur immediately before Mass, or afterwards as in the case of the reception ceremony in Bermondsey on December 12, 1839. At least two early copies of the *Form of Ceremony for the Reception and Profession of the Sisters of Our Lady of Mercy* are extant: Frances Warde's copy of the one printed in Dublin in 1834 (Mercy Congregational Archives, Dublin) and one printed in London in 1840 (Bermondsey Archives). 2 Catherine McAuley dates this letter May 1, 1841. However, as she indicates in the second sentence, she wrote most of the letter on Sunday, May 2. 3 On May 4, 1841, Mary Aloysius Cowley, Mary Camillus (Teresa) Byrn (Catherine McAuley's cousin and godchild), and Mary Liston will profess their vows; and Frances Vigne, Mary Lawless, Teresa MacDonnell, and, apparently, a woman named Margaret, destined "for the English mission" will receive the habit. Frances Vigne will take the name Mary de Sales; the religious names of Mary Lawless and Teresa MacDonnell are not known as they did not remain in the Sisters of Mercy. At a Chapter of the Baggot Street community held on May 12, 1843 "Miss Teresa McDonnell was dismissed from the Novitiate" (Acts [4]). The available information about "Margaret," compiled by John MacErlean, SJ, is very incomplete. Margaret Teresa Dwyer and Margaret Teresa Geraghty did not receive the habit at this ceremony, though some of Catherine McAuley's letters seem to suggest that they will; they were approved for reception of the habit by a Chapter held on July 18, 1841, and received the habit on August 19, 1841.

My poor dear James is in Eternity.[4] He died like a saint. Though parched
with thirst, he would not take a drop of water without making the sign of the
cross, or let his pillow be moved till he said some little prayer. He never was
impatient for five minutes, tho' six months without being up one entire day. He
received the Holy Viaticum every eighth day, and lived to the last 8th—so as to
receive two hours before he expired. He would never let the crucifix be removed
from a table at his bed side, even when his Uncle[5] came. Tell this to Doctor
Fitzgerald, it will give him pleasure to find that the religious impressions did not
pass away. You will pray fervently for him, I know.

I have nothing now to draw me for one hour from my religious Sisters where
all my joy on earth is centered.[6] Every year's experience of their worth attaches
me more strongly, and I am as ardent for new ones as if I was beginning. I suppose it is the spirit of my state, and my first children—Sr. de P[azzi] excepted—
seem to have it also.

Thank you for the nice Saint Catherine. We had no folly here on her day[7]—
so many in retreat. Indeed I was very glad.

God bless you and all with you.

Pray for your ever most affectionate
M. C. McAuley

Autograph: Silver Spring

266. To Sister M. Juliana Hardman[8]   **Convent [Birr]**
Baggot Street   **May 13, 1841**

My Dear Sister Juliana[9]

My not answering your letter yesterday was unavoidable, particular circumstances prevented me. As your good Mother must be anxious to know the result

---

4 Catherine's nephew James Macauley died on April 29, 1841, in his twenty-sixth year. From her
description of his death, it appears that Catherine was with him. He was buried on Saturday, May
1, the day this letter was started.   5 Catherine's brother, Dr. James McAuley, was a Protestant.   6
Apparently Catherine assumes that her nephew William Macauley is lost at sea or dead from some
other cause.   7 April 30, the day after James's death, was the liturgical feast of St. Catherine of
Siena, and Catherine McAuley's feast day. Frances Warde had sent her a small commemorative
card containing a drawing of St. Catherine, on the back of which was written: "From Sister Mary
Francis [*sic*] Warde to her beloved Spiritual Mother, Mary Catherine McAuley," and in a later, different handwriting, "Brought by Revd. Mother Mary Elizabeth [Moore] from Dublin 1841
November 11th." The card is now in the Limerick Archives.   8 The cover of this letter, posted
from Birr, is addressed to "Miss Hardman, Sisters of Mercy, Baggot Street, Dublin."   9 Mary
Juliana Hardman, then a novice in the Baggot Street community, was preparing for the upcoming
foundation in her native Birmingham, England, to which she and others would journey after her
profession of vows on August 19. She became the first superior of the Birmingham community in
September, and served in that role until 1876. She died on March 24, 1884.

of her enquiry, will you, my dear, write immediately and say that the person she refers to may be admitted to Mass "on account of her infirmity"—and whoever is really necessary to afford her assistance, but this permission cannot extend to any member of her family, except there is a part of the Chapel, distinct from what the Sisters are to occupy. We always have discretionary power to admit an individual occasionally to Mass, but not to give them an established liberty to attend. Mark, particularly, that it is in consideration of her 'Infirmity' that we give the general permission.[10]

The Sisters in the second day of their retreat, very fervent and most happy.[11]

I look forward with anxiety to our return, which I hope to accomplish the day after the ceremony, tho' I dare not say so yet. If Mr. Mathew should celebrate Mass in the Convent—on Friday, I suppose we could not go.[12]

I hope you will have 'Sister Fanny' on Saturday.[13] Give her my most affectionate welcome. Don't tell her I give severe lectures or sharp reproofs—speak of me, as a quiet easy simple goodnatured person, such as you know I am. Tell her how I simpathise with poor Sisters addicted to crying, how tenderly I compassionate their weakness, in fine, tell her all that will make a favorable impression at first. If I should—unfortunately—fail to realize it in [*missing word*], she will perceive the kindness of your intention, and admire the charity with which you speak of your superior.

Mother M. Aloysius, M. Cecilia, M. Teresa—and the travellers, with dear Sister M. Rose[14]—unite in fond regards to all. Pray for me and believe me

---

10 Mary Juliana's father and his third wife were the principal benefactors of the Birmingham convent, then under construction. Evidently Barbara Hardman, Juliana's stepmother, had requested that an infirm friend or relative be allowed to attend Mass regularly in the Birmingham convent chapel. 11 Catherine McAuley had gone to Birr to help prepare the two postulants, Mary Anne Heenan and Susan Egan, for their reception of the habit on Ascension Thursday, May 20. During their eight-day retreat before the ceremony, Catherine instructed them each day about the nature of religious life as a Sister of Mercy. The names they chose at reception were Mary Joseph and Mary Vincent, respectively. 12 Theobald Mathew took a great interest in the Birr foundation, because of the role he thought the sisters could play in reaching out to those affected by the schism. He was scheduled to preach at the reception ceremony on Thursday, May 20, and Catherine thinks he may stay and celebrate Mass on Friday, May 21. 13 Jane Frances Gibson from Eaton House, Liverpool, entered the Sisters of Mercy, Baggot Street, on Sunday, May 16, 1841. She became part of the founding community in Liverpool in late August 1843. In this letter Catherine McAuley playfully tells the novice Mary Juliana to give Fanny a favorable, if not wholly accurate, impression of the superior, that is, herself. Mary Juliana would have seen the humor in her words. When Catherine assumed the responsibilities of mistress of novices during Mary Cecilia Marmion's absence earlier in the year, Mary Juliana herself had felt the difficulties, and the tears, of learning to be a good Sister of Mercy. In fact, Catherine often expressed admiration for her fervor and generosity and that of the other Birmingham novices. 14 Mary Aloysius Scott and Mary Rose Lynch were founding members of the Birr community, Teresa (Catherine) White had been lent to Birr in the early months, Cecilia Marmion was in Birr to regain her health, and the "travellers" were Catherine herself and her travelling companions, Mary Aloysius Cowley and another unidentified sister. Catherine had brought two to enhance the singing at the ceremony.

your ever affectionate
Mary C. McAuley

I need not say much about the cough—if I bring it back—it will speak for itself—if not, we have no objection to part this one Companion.

Autograph: Birmingham

**267. To Sister Mary Aloysius Scott   Tuesday, May 25, 1841
        Birr**

My Dear Sister Mary Aloysius

We are all safe arrived, got excellent Horses at Birr and most attentive driver—reached Tullamore quarter to one.[15] The fine little boy who brought the great Trunk would not take any payment—"ah sure ma'am, I'll be ped [paid] at home." It distressed me to hear him say—ped—he is such a fine creature. Offered him 6d [pence] for himself—"ah no ma'am—haven't I a shillen— to get my supper and my bed and breakfast."

Most cordial welcome in Tullamore.[16] Sister M. Cecilia continued to evince so much alarm or dislike to the canal—that we arranged to go on posting, got an excellent roomy chaise, drove 28 miles in 4 hours—had then only 19. At 12 o'c started, but met a cross driver, slow horses—and broken harness—kept us five hours & quarter on that short stage—a confined carriage. Sister Cowley who sat at our feet has not stood up—quite well yet.

All well here. Father O'Hanlon celebrated Mass for us this morning—looks very well. He regretted writing such an imperative letter to me, about going to Limerick—but said it was impossible to get—aft[er?]—Sr. Elizabeth called all the Community and engaged each of them to say a considerable number of paters etc., for him—offer so many communions and visits to the sick for him, second Masses—it said he could not refuse anything asked on such terms.[17]

15 Mary Cecilia Marmion, Mary Aloysius Cowley, Catherine McAuley, and another sister from Dublin left Birr by stage coach on the morning of Sunday, May 23.   16 They stayed the night in Tullamore. The Tullamore Annals reports: "In May [1841] Rev. Mother McAuley visited Tullamore again for the sixth and last time. She was on her way from Birr, where she had assisted at the first public ceremony. Her health was evidently breaking down, and the sisters saw with grief that she could not long withstand the labors and fatigues of her numerous foundations. She was accompanied by Mother M. Cecilia Marmion, the Mistress of Novices in Baggot St., and two other Srs." (40).   17 The meaning of these sentences is not clear. Evidently Father Redmond O'Hanlon had written to Catherine in Birr, asking her to return to Baggot Street as soon as possible, because he was going to Limerick, at Elizabeth Moore's request. An alternative interpretation is that Catherine herself was contemplating visiting Limerick from Birr, but there is no other evidence that Catherine had such a trip in mind. The Limerick Annals, written some years later, does not report a specific visit of Redmond O'Hanlon at this time, but notes: "Rev. Raymond [*sic*] O'Hanlon, our Foundress's sincere and long tried friend, continued ever to be regarded with most sincere esteem and gratitude by Mother Mary Elizabeth.

The new Sister—Fanny—looks very delicate, a nice person.[18] Another proposal—quite serious—since we left.

Now for my old cough—very frequent since 9 o'c last night. I will use the Crotty oil again—and the Iceland Moss.[19]

Mother de Pazzi is remarkably well and most active—Sister Teresa as usual.

Give a thousand loves to my dear Sister M. Teresa—Mary Rose, Mary Magdeline, Mary Joseph & Mary Vincent.[20] May God bless them. I hope you thanked Mrs. Egan for all her kindness to me. I shall never forget her great good nature & continued attention.

God bless and guide you, my Dear Sister M. Aloysius. Pray for your ever affectionate

[M. C. McAuley]

Autograph (with the signature cut off): Dublin, Mercy

268. To a Sister of Mercy[21]   [1841?]

My Daughter Grand
From Typpe's Land
how very kind you've been
In sending me
Such poetry
As I have seldom seen

Every year on the Feast of St. Raymond [January 23] she regularly reminded the Community to offer prayers for his client—who from time to time came down to visit her [here?]. He evinced great interest in this Convent and its Inmates to his death. He wrote here too occasionally, and was much pleased when he heard that all was progressing happily, and the glory of God still further promoted by new Foundations" (1:96). The word I have read as "aft" may be "off," and the words I read as "it said" [i.e., a letter from O'Hanlon or from Limerick said] may be "he said."   18 Frances Gibson, from Liverpool.   19 "Crotty oil" was either an oil remedy peculiar to Birr, or a medicinal invention of Catherine McAuley. "Iceland moss" is "a species of edible lichen, *Cetraria islandica*, having certain medicinal properties; hence Iceland moss jelly, starch" (OED).   20 Mary Teresa (Catherine) White, Mary Rose Lynch, and the novices Mary Magdalen McEvoy (who apparently later changed her name to Mary Clare), Mary Joseph (Mary Anne) Heenan, and Mary Vincent (Susan) Egan—the latter two having just received the habit and new names on May 20.   21 This poem, the autograph of which is preserved in the Brisbane archives, was written to a sister who entered one of the foundations in Ireland outside of Dublin. Catherine McAuley often called these sisters her "grand daughters," as distinct from those who went to the foundations from Dublin, her "daughters" in a sense. The only clue to the identity of the recipient is the second line of the poem, "From Typpe's [or Tippe's] Land"—which is possibly a reference to Tipperary. (I am grateful for extended conversations with Ken MacGowan, Hon. Secretary, and Peter Costello, Hon. Librarian, Central Catholic Library, Dublin, for suggestions that eventually led me to this tentative conclusion.)

If the recipient of this short poem was a sister coming from Tipperary, among the prime candidates, if not the only one, is Mary Joseph (Mary Anne) Heenan, a sister who entered the Birr

Description strong
and not too long
of each dear Sister given
creates desire
To see them nigher—
e'er [ere] they go to Heaven

A fond Adieu
I'll bid to you
grandaughter [*sic*] dear & sweet
and hope—I will
that we may still
In this poor world—meet

[Mary C. McAuley]

Autograph: Brisbane

269. To Sister M. Frances Warde   Baggot Street
Carlow   May 28, 1841

My Dearest Sister M. Frances

It distressed me very much to hear from Mr. O'Hanlon that your good director was changed. I know it is an affliction to you—but rest assured, God will

---

community on January 22, 1841, and received the habit on May 20; Catherine McAuley was in Birr
on both occasions, spending a total of five weeks in Mary Anne's company. Mary Anne's native
town was Borrisokane, Co. Tipperary, about twelve miles southwest of Birr, Co. Offaly. Borrisokane
is in the riding (an administrative unit of the county) called North Tipperary, sometimes colloqui-
ally called "North Tip."

The recipient of the poem had sent Catherine McAuley some poetry, in response to which
Catherine sends her this brief poem, with the hope that she will see her again in "this poor world."
As it turned out, Catherine made only one more trip before her death, to and from Birmingham,
England, through Kingstown and Liverpool, August 20 to September 21, 1841—if indeed this poem
was sent to Birr after May 24, 1841.

Mary Joseph Heenan was a lay sister, and Catherine McAuley was particularly devoted to and
affectionate towards lay sisters, seeing in their work a close resemblance to the ministry of Jesus: "constantly engaged serving others, but never requiring any care or attendance for Himself" (see Sullivan,
Catherine McAuley 269, 271). One thinks, in particular, of Catherine's affection for Teresa Carton (who
in 1844 became a choir sister), Martha Wallplate and Mary Liston at Baggot Street, Mary Shanahan
and Anne Hewitt in Limerick, and Mary Teresa Boyce and Mary Joseph Hawkins in Bermondsey.

The presence of the autograph in Brisbane is no help to identifying the recipient. The autographs of five other poems in Brisbane were sent to Ursula Frayne in Booterstown, Mary Teresa
Vincent Potter in Limerick, and Anna Maria Harnett, then at Baggot Street—none of whom seems
to fit a "Typpe's Land" connection. Ursula and Anna Maria were from Dublin, and Ellen Potter
was from Adare, Co. Limerick. Finally, Tippeenan Lower and Tippeenan Upper were townlands
in County Kildare, but I have not been able to identify any Sister of Mercy in Catherine McAuley's
acquaintance who came from either townland. Thus, one is left with a tender-hearted autograph
poem to an unknown recipient—though Mary Joseph Heenan seems the likely recipient.

send some distinguished consolation.[22] This is your life, joys and sorrows mingled, one succeeding the other. Let us not think of the means [God] has employed to convey to us a portion of the Holy Cross, being ever mindful that it came from Himself. You remember what Father Gaffney[23] said to us when in retreat—"If the entire cross upon which Christ died was sent to this House, how impatient would each Sister be to carry it, and she who was permitted to keep it the longest—would be the most favored. Far better and more profitable for you to receive with all your heart the cross which God will send you in any form or shape He pleases." I earnestly hope that you will receive this trial so as to render it valuable to you.

The Ceremony in Birr went on very well. Father Mathew received thousands into the temperance society—he has got a most sorrowful or plaintive manner of saying, "ah, don't pull me." The Bishop went through the ceremony as if he performed it every week—he is a nice celebrant—and very kind & pleasing.[24]

Bernard Cavanagh paid a visit here when I was away—asked to see the Nuns. Sr. de Pazzi appeared—he said—"Did you ever hear of Bernard Cavanagh?" Yes. "What did you hear of him, what does the Public say of him?"—We know very little of public opinion. "Would you like to see him?"—I am not very anxious. "I am he." He asked to see the school, said many spiritual things—thin but not wasted or remarkable—features good, but expression of countenance weak and simple or foolish. Mr. Mathew says he is not an impostor—but certainly a lunatic.[25]

All are well here. The usual encrease. We have again 3 postulants, expecting 2 more. Sister M. Cecilia is not as much better as I hoped—she has no appetite. I fear she never will have strength. Sr. Teresa a shadow.

The Sisters in Tullamore well—remove to their New Convent next month. I expected to hear you were in Naas—poor Naas is like the little chicken that belongs to the clutch called—creepy crawly. I wish it would take a start.

My love to all.

Pray fervently for your ever affectionate
M. C. McAuley

Autograph: West Hartford

22 Daniel Nolan had been a curate in Killeshin (Carlow-Graigue), but was now assigned as curate in Sandcroft, near Kildare (*Irish Catholic Directory* [1841] 294). The Carlow Annals for 1841 notes: "Early in July, our extraordinary Confessor, Rev. Daniel Nolan received an appointment to a curacy about fifteen miles hence, and Rev. John Magee was named to fill his place." Father Dan Nolan, whom Catherine McAuley called "my son," was the brother of the deceased and much-loved Dr. Edward Nolan, on whom Frances Warde had earlier relied. Presumably Father Dan was her "good director." 23 Myles Gaffney, dean of St. Patrick's College, Maynooth, and frequent retreat director for the Sisters of Mercy. Catherine may be recalling their first retreat together in 1832. 24 Dr. Patrick Kennedy, bishop of the diocese of Killaloe. 25 Bernard Cavanagh has not been identified.

270. To Sister M. Frances Warde [Baggot Street]
 Carlow [June 3, 1841][26]

My Dearest Sister Mary Frances

Father O'Hanlon has been telling me that your Community have not adopted the thick veil—and for very good reason indeed, because your spiritual authorities do not approve of it. Mr. O'Hanlon admired the veil you wore and says he advised you to keep it. Would you then send me the veiling I got for your use. We seldom get any so nice. It would be quite a treasure to me now.

Sr. M. Cecilia has been expecting to hear from you. I trust you have not been ill.

It was only this morning Fr. O'H told me or I would have asked you for it sooner—like our old veiling—it is very difficult to get it of the degree of thickness resembling Nuns Crape—we could get it thicker which they would pass for the real kind—& the colour is generally bad.

I heard yesterday Father Maher was in Dublin lately, which grieved me—as he did not call.

I look forward with fear and trembling to my Birmingham journey—I have really got a surfeit. The Sisters for that foundation continue to be all that we could desire—not a troublesome one amongst them. I hope you have gratifying accounts from Wexford. All I hear from chance visitors is delightful.

Give my love to each. I do not despair of visiting Saint Leo's again, please God. I suppose all is beautiful around you now. Father O'H says there is nothing like it.[27]

Remember me respectfully to Doctor Fitzgerald, Father Maher, and believe me ever your affectionate

M. C. McAuley

My Dear Sr. F.

I have just read your letter and am comforted to hear that the seeming great cross is not so heavy as was apprehended, thanks be to God.[28]

Miss Gibson, our postulant, is not the person you speak of—her father is of Eaton House, 5 miles from Liverpool, of large property. She has left all the vanities of this life. She mentioned the other Miss Gibson, a relative still in Liverpool. They are both Fannys. Sister Juliana's sister is married to a cousin of this Miss G.[29] I enclose a very nice letter she wrote me. Since her arrival, we have heard there are three more coming—but no more of them, not even their names.

---

26 This letter, with its long postscript to "Sr. F," was treated by previous editors as two separate letters (Neumann 342–44 and Bolster 231–32), but the autograph (a single folded sheet with text on sides 1, 2, and 3 and the address and postmarks on side 4) shows that it is a single letter, posted from Dublin on June 3, 1841.   27 The comments on Redmond O'Hanlon suggest that he had visited Carlow recently, and possibly also Limerick (see Letter 267, note 17).   28 Presumably Catherine is referring to the reassignment of Daniel Nolan (see Letter 269, note 22).   29 The postulant at Baggot

We expect Sr. M. Clare on the 14th[30]—I suspect it will be again deferred. She has been left too long—it is a good instruction for other foundations. I fear it will be difficult to get Srs. de Sales and Xavier.[31] They must come when 9 leave this for Birmingham. We could not do without them.

Pray for your attached
M. C. M.

Autograph: Silver Spring

271. To Dr. Thomas Walsh[32]   [Baggot Street]
[c. June 17, 1841][33]

My Dear L[ord] and Very Revd. F[ather]

The votes of the Community having passed for the Profession of your spiritual daughters, we feel most anxious to make our solemn vows [34] to you & earnestly & respectfully pray your Lordship to grant us this great indulgence.

The season is so favorable for crossing,[35] and we would all pray so fervently to God to protect you, that we humbly hope your Lordship would find no inconvenience in your short visit to the Capital of Ireland.

The words contained in the vows seem to require the presence of our Ecclesiastical Superior. Rule—"under the authority—& in presence of you, my Very Revd. Father in God, Dr. Walsh, etc., etc."[36]

Street is Frances Gibson. Juliana Hardman had three sisters or half-sisters who survived to adulthood—Lucy Hardman Powell, Mary, and Elizabeth. Mary Hardman became a Sister of Mercy in 1843, and Elizabeth became an Augustinian Sister; perhaps William Powell, the husband of Lucy, was Frances Gibson's cousin. I am very grateful to Barbara Jeffery, RSM, archivist of the Birmingham collection, for sharing her extensive knowledge of the Hardman family.   30 According to the Bermondsey Annals, after the profession ceremony there on April 22, 1841, "Bishop Murphy wrote to require the immediate return of the Mother Superior, Sister Mary Clare Moore, to her Convent in Cork, and she left London, accompanied by Revd. Father Butler on the 14th of June, in order to meet Bishop Murphy in Dublin as he had directed" (1:25). Coming by overnight boat to Kingstown, she would have arrived in Dublin on June 15. On Saturday, June 12, Dr. Thomas Griffiths had appointed Mary Clare Agnew superior of the Bermondsey community.   31 Mary de Sales White and Mary Xavier O'Connell, lent to the Bermondsey community in October 1840, will return to Dublin in September 1841, as planned. 32 This autograph draft letter, composed by Catherine McAuley and in her handwriting, was presumably then prepared in fair copy and signed by the four novices from Birmingham. The autograph letter they actually sent to Dr. Walsh has not been located.   33 The book of Acts of the Chapter of professed sisters at Baggot Street records the following decision: "June 17th 1841: By the majority of the votes of the Chapter Sisters Mary Vincent Whitty, M. Justina Fleming, M. Frances [*sic*] Creedon, M. Xavier Wood, M. Juliana Hardman, M. Vincent Bond and M. Cecilia Edwards were admitted to the holy Profession" ([3]). The vote to admit to profession needed to occur two months before the intended date for the profession of vows. The present letter could not have been written before this decision, i.e. before June 17. Earlier editors have dated the draft June 14. The autograph draft is undated.   34 Catherine McAuley is not using the words "solemn vows" in a technical, canonical sense.   35 That is, crossing the Irish Sea, from Liverpool to Kingstown.   36 Rule 20.5 (Sullivan, *Catherine McAuley* 316).

Confiding in your charity & kindness for a favorable answer—and begging your intercession for us with God, now more than ever, we have the honor and happiness to remain

Dear respected V. Revd. Father
your devoted children in C. J.,
[Sister M. Juliana Hardman]
[Sister M. Xavier Wood]
[Sister M. Vincent Bond]
[Sister M. Cecilia Edwards]

Autograph: Dublin, Mercy

272. To Sister M. Frances Warde   Baggot Street
Carlow   June 19, 1841

My Dearest Sister Mary Frances

Our old beloved companion, Sister Mary Clare, leaves this on Monday, accompanied by the Pastor of Bermondsey for Carlow. Mr. Butler goes on Mr. Taylor's invitation, and dear Sr. M. Clare avails herself of the opportunity of going to see you.[37] The House in London, thanks be to God, is well established, and three more likely to be formed.

Dr. Murphy met his child here and is quite proud of her return. His Lordship expressed a wish that Mr. Butler would go to see the Convent, etc., etc.

All pretty well here. My cough better. God bless you, my Dear Sr. M. F.

Pray for your affectionate
M. C. McAuley

Autograph: Silver Spring

273. To Sister M. de Sales White   [Baggot Street]
Bermondsey   [c. June 19, 1841][38]

My Dearest Sister M. de Sales

I have only ten minutes now at my disposal, and only time to say that altho' we have another Sr. de Sales,[39] the old place in our hearts is yet vacant for you.

---

37 Mary Clare Moore and Peter Butler left for Carlow, en route to Cork, on Monday, June 21 or Tuesday, June 22 (see Letter 274). The reunion of Clare Moore and Frances Warde brought together two of the first and most talented members of the Baggot Street community. They had become residents there in 1830 and 1828, respectively; Clare was now twenty-seven, and Frances about thirty-one. James Ignatius Taylor was vice-president of Carlow College. In 1843, on the death of Dr. Andrew Fitzgerald, Dr. Taylor became president. 38 The autograph of this letter is undated, but since it was hand-delivered, Catherine McAuley may have given it to Peter Butler before he left for Carlow, Limerick, Cork, and then London. He may have returned to London by boat from southern Ireland. 39 Mary de Sales (Frances) Vigne had received the habit on May 4, 1841.

What a number of new faces you will see—all learners and no teachers—all to [be] guided—and none to guide them—all children of a few months old.

Take care that you both return fit to be Mothers, or I will not have any patience. Mr. Daly said you looked better than he ever saw you.[40] I trust the beauty of my Daughter emanated from within. I look up to you both with great expectations. Do not disappoint me.

You must forgive this short note.

A new child entered Galway on Monday, another to join on the 2nd of July.[41] They are slow in progress.

God bless you, my Dearest Sister de Sales.

Pray for your ever affectionate
M. C. McAuley

Autograph: Liverpool

274. To Sister M. de Sales White   [Baggot Street]
Bermondsey   [June 24, 1841][42]

[Dear Sister Mary de Sales]

Our beloved Mother Mary Clare left us on Tuesday morning for Carlow, accompanied by Rev. Mr. B[utler], who had a most pressing invitation from the Vice-President of the college. They proposed going to Limerick this day, and thence to Cork, where they are in joyful expectation of their old Mother Superior. She is very thin, and while here had not any appetite. I trust, when the excitement of parting and meeting is at an end, she will get a little stronger. The report she gives of the dear Bermondsey convent is consoling indeed. She says it is going on so happily, and Rev. Mr. B[utler] thinks it most permanently established. It will increase rapidly, please God. I hope dear Reverend Mother Clare will not be too indulgent, but keep you all in good order.[43]

We shall leave this house so badly provided when going to Birmingham, that we thought it would be necessary to get you and Sister Xavier home before we left, but I am now satisfied to wait till I return, though indeed I see the necessity as clearly as those who do not deem it prudent to wait so long.[44] But we will

40 Peter Daly of Galway was apparently in London on business.   41 Agnes Smith, a lay sister, entered the convent in Galway in 1841. She will die in Galway on May 10, 1849, during the epidemic of cholera that followed the worst years of the Famine.   42 No autograph, photostat, or photocopy of this letter has been discovered. However, it is published, apparently in its entirety, in Harnett's *Life* (185–86). Harnett says that on "the 24th of June [1841]" Catherine McAuley "wrote the following letter to Mother Mary de Sales" (185).   43 Mary Clare (Elizabeth) Agnew was now the superior of the Bermondsey community, as of June 12, 1841.   44 Evidently there was a difference of opinion at Baggot Street about whether Mary de Sales White and Mary Xavier O'Connell should return from Bermondsey sooner than late September.

get you both so much improved by the good example you have had, and the active practice of our duties, that you will soon help us to get all in order—that is, to teach all the new children.

We expect to hear of a great addition to the community in Cork—we hear four or five are waiting the arrival of Mother M. Clare.[45]

I had a letter this day from Galway—a new Sister entered since last I heard. There are two postulants now, and a third is expected on the 2nd of July. Sister de Chantal is in retreat for profession.[46]

Rev. Mr. Daly proposes laying the first stone of the new convent on the 24th of September. I must be home from Birmingham by that time. Mother M. Clare and Rev. Mr. B[utler] admire the convent there very much.[47] They say it is too nicely gilt for contemplation—you are tempted to be wholly employed in admiration. Mother de Pazzi begs her best love, and give mine most fondly to Reverend Mother, Sister M. Augustin, Sister Xavier, and all my dear sisters. Do not forget Sisters Teresa and Joseph.[48] Pray for me very fervently, and believe me always your affectionate

[Mary C. McAuley]

Published transcription: Harnett, Life 185–86

275. To Sister Mary Aloysius Scott   [Baggot Street]
Birr   June 30 [1841]

My very Dear Sister M. Aloysius

I seem to be almost forgetting my last born child, poor Birr. You have heard, my constant attention has been engaged by a passing visit from our beloved old companion, Sister Mary Clare, who is now safe at home in Cork. Revd. Mr. Butler returned to England yesterday. Dr. Murphy and Sr. M. A. Clare[49] left this for Cork. Mother M. C. went some days since with Mr. Butler.

I cannot say how delighted I feel—at the account of your numerous children. This will really and effectually undermine all the old Crotty roots and branches.[50]

---

45 Of those who entered the Cork community in 1841, after Mary Clare Moore's return, apparently only Mary Teresa (Mary) Wildridge remained (Cork Register). She professed her vows on June 14, 1844, and some time before her death in September 1848 compiled the biographical manuscript about Catherine McAuley known as Cork MS 1.   46 Mary de Chantal (Anne) O'Beirne professed her vows in Galway on June 26, 1841, after an eight-day retreat.   47 Clare Moore and Peter Butler may have seen the newly built convent in Birmingham, now almost completed, on their journey from London to Liverpool, and thence to Dublin.   48 Catherine McAuley sends love to Mary Clare Agnew, the superior, Mary Augustin Taylor, Mary Xavier O'Connell, the lay sisters Mary Teresa Boyce and Mary Joseph Hawkins, and the other "dear sisters" in the Bermondsey community at this time of whom she would have met only Mary de Sales Eyre.   49 Mary Clare Augustine Moore (Catherine McAuley puts the A. before Clare).   50 The poor school sponsored by the Sisters of Mercy in Birr grew rapidly: "Even before Catherine McAuley's departure in

Have you heard of the great rage for missions, the Bishops of foreign districts going about to get all the religious Sisters they can. Doctor England from Charleston celebrated Mass here this morning and gave a most animating ex[h]ortation— in a loud voice—he said, "Fear nothing. Follow Paul in peril, pestilence & famine, that you may be his glorious associate for time & Eternity. The moment you get into his path, you will feel as if in Heaven."[51]

After Breakfast we assembled all the troops in the community room, from all quarters—Laundry, Dining Hall, etc., etc.—by chance 2 were in from Kingstown. We made a great muster. The question was put by his Lordship from the chair— who will come to Charleston with me to act as Superior, etc. The only one who came forward offering to fill the office was Sr. Margaret Teresa Dwyer—which afforded great laughing.[52] I had arranged it with her before, but did not think she would have courage. His Lordship was obliged to acknowledge that we are poor dependants on the white veil & caps—we certainly look like a community that wanted time to come to maturity, reduced to Infancy again as we are.[53]

I was quite disappointed at Sister Mary Teresa's not writing to me.[54] I wrote her a long letter, and having just got a suitable cover I return the only line she wrote me—saying you had not time tho' it was to her I wrote. Tell Sr. M. Rose[55] her little note was most acceptable. I will write to her soon.

I am glad you have got a Lay Sister.[56] Have you any chance of Miss R. How is poor Ann Blake. I hope Sr. M. Magdelin supported the character of Mother

February the sisters had put a school for poor children on a firm footing with more than 400 pupils, some of whom had transferred from a school run by Crotty" (Murphy 166).   51 Dr. John England (1786–1842), a native of Cork City and a graduate of Carlow College, was named the first bishop of Charleston (a diocese embracing Georgia and the Carolinas) in 1820. In the decade before his death in 1842, he visited Ireland several times and "is credited with stirring a zeal for the missions among the Catholic people of Ireland at a time when they themselves were only rebuilding a church recovering from centuries of penal laws" (McEvoy 28–29). The Carlow Annals records that Dr. England visited the Mercy convent in Carlow in 1840, "but altho' all admired the fervour of the good Bishop, none volunteered to join his standard." Three years later Frances Warde and other Carlow sisters will go to Pittsburgh to found the first Mercy convent in the United States on December 21, 1843.   52 Margaret Teresa Dwyer, then a postulant, was small in size. She was preparing to receive the Mercy habit on August 19, 1841.   53 The impish Catherine McAuley was nonetheless acting on a sound assessment. Of those in the Baggot Street community at this time, at least seventeen were novices or postulants, of whom at least eight were planned for England and one for Newfoundland. The twenty-five professed members of the community, as of this date, including Catherine herself, were engaged in works of mercy at six locations: operating the poor school (300 girls), House of Mercy (60 or more residents), public laundry, visitation of the sick, and large novitiate at Baggot Street; serving the schools and visitation of the sick at the branch convents in Booterstown and Kingstown; and temporarily serving in Bermondsey, Birr, and Cork. Moreover, of these twenty-five, three (Agatha Brennan, Monica Murphy, and Catherine herself) will die within a year, and within five years eleven will go to new foundations in Newfoundland, Liverpool, London, Pittsburgh, New York City, and Perth, Australia.   54 Mary Teresa (Catherine) White, still in Birr.   55 Mary Rose Lynch.   56 According to the Birr Annals, Mary Weir (or Wier) entered the Birr community on June 1, 1841; the Register of the Killaloe communities says the date was June 21, 1841. She received the habit in January 1842, taking the name Mary Aloysius.

Superior well, as she had the task only for one day.[57] How is "our Cow."[58] Poor Sister M. Cecilia is still, what I fear she will continue, very delicate—just as usual—not worse. Sr. Justina, a troublesome obstinate cough. Sr. Elizabeth just recovering from Influenza.[59] All the rest well. Mother de Pazzi wonderfully well after taking leave of the two Mary Clares.[60] I believe she is getting disengaged.

Give my respectful regards to Doctor Spain, Mr. Tuhy [Tuohy] and Kennedy—& my best love to each. Mother M. de Pazzi & Sr. M. C[ecilia] unite in most affectionate love with

your ever attached
M. C. McAuley

Autograph: Dublin, Mercy

---

57 On December 28, 1840, the feast of the Holy Innocents, Anna Maria McEvoy—later named Mary Magdalen (and still later, Mary Clare)—would have been the youngest (and only) postulant in the Birr convent and, according to custom, would have been invited to play the role of "Mother Superior" on that day.   58 "Our Cow" is probably a real cow, belonging to the Birr community or the parish or at least grazing nearby. Both Ignatia Neumann (347) and Angela Bolster (235) have identified "our Cow" as a humorous reference to Mary Aloysius Cowley, a young professed member of the Baggot Street community. She had visited Birr in May with Catherine McAuley, but had returned with her on May 24 (see Letter 267), so she was not in Birr on this date.   59 Mary Justina Fleming, a novice, had consumption, and Mary Elizabeth Butler was one of several at Baggot Street who had influenza in mid 1841.   60 Mary Clare (Georgiana) Moore and her sister Mary Clare Augustine (Clare) Moore were now in Cork. Mary de Pazzi Delany was especially fond of both of them.

July–August 1841

In the summer months of 1841 there was much work to be done, and Catherine McAuley's correspondence was heavy. Dr. Thomas Youens and Dr. George Hilary Brown, vicar apostolic of the Lancashire District, England, were encouraged to seek the new foundation for Liverpool from Carlow; Dr. Thomas Walsh—and in his absence, Dr. Daniel Murray—was pressed to set a date for the August ceremony; Mary Aloysius Scott was assured that affiliation with the national system of education was beneficial; Mary Ann Doyle was supported in her interpretation of the vow of poverty; Frances Warde was consoled when Carlow was not chosen for the foundation in Liverpool; and Teresa White was congratulated on the wonderful progress in Galway. Closer to home, Catherine herself—"Father McAuley," as she quipped—conducted the annual retreat at "poor Baggot Street"; ten novices and postulants received daily instructions from her prior to their profession and reception ceremony on August 19; and plans were made for the journey to Birmingham on August 20–21.

The one way the summer of 1841 differed from the past was Catherine's cough—now more persistent, especially at night; now aggravated somewhat by speaking and always by fresh air; now on the minds of her companions, near and far. Only at the end of August, when she declined an invitation from Dr. George J. P. Browne in Galway, did Catherine herself, now in Birmingham, plainly describe the situation: "if I remain any time in a room with a window open, I am coughing all night and disturbing the poor Sisters who are near me ... to travel in October would be very imprudent indeed" (Letter 299). But during these months her emotional energy was characteristically directed elsewhere: hoping, finally, to receive official word that Gregory XVI had confirmed the Rule and Constitutions; feeling relief that, as she thought, all in Bermondsey was "going on remarkably well"; grieving the serious illness of Justina Fleming, a novice, and dreading—ironically, as it turned out—the "severe trial" Justina's death would be to those at Baggot Street; sending kisses to little Fanny Warde in Carlow; comforting Frances Gibson in the death of her sister, and taking her to England to console her parents.

When Frances Warde invited Catherine to come to Carlow for the annual retreat in August, she was deeply grateful, even tempted, but she declined: "it would be delightful to me to accept ... but think of all that must be left behind ... It is quite impossible for any one in my situation to think of pleasing themselves. My pleasure must be in endeavouring to please all" (Letter 291). Catherine spent July and August 1841 trying to do just that. She did not admire Pugin's "gilded figures of saints" in the Birmingham chapel—"by no means calculated to inspire devotion" (Letter 298)—but her whole heart, if not her full voice, was in the *Te Deum laudamus* prayed there in the late afternoon on August 21, 1841, at the inauguration of what was to be her last new foundation of Sisters of Mercy: "*Fiat misericordia tua, Domine, super nos; quemadmodum speravimus in te. In te, Domine, speravi; non confundar in aeternum.*" ¹

276. To John Hardman, Jr.²   [July 1841]
Birmingham

Furniture wanted for the Convent³

A straw and hair mattress for the Beds.

Small press, not too high, that will answer for a wash hand stand with a small drawer and cupboard underneath for Linen. [*Catherine McAuley's drawing provided to the left.*]

The Chairs in the Noviceship & Community rooms not heavy (what we have are cane seats).

The refectory tables to be of plain deal, not painted, of this form. [*Catherine McAuley's drawing provided to the left.*]

The side tables to be 2 ft. 5 in. high and two feet in width, the length in proportion to the Room.

The top table seven feet two inches in length and 2 ft. 6 inches in width.⁴

The Community room and Noviceship Tables 4 feet in width, and 2 ft. 5 in. in height.

1 "Let thy mercy, O Lord, be upon us; as we have put our trust in thee. In thee, O Lord, have I put my trust; let me not be confounded for ever."   2 On the reverse side of the single sheet of this autograph, in handwriting that may be that of John Hardman, Jr., is written: "Particulars of Furniture, etc., for the Convent as sent by Mrs. McAuley, July 1841."   3 This list of furniture is not in Catherine McAuley's handwriting, but was probably dictated by her.   4 Traditionally, as here, the refectory table in Mercy convents was horseshoe-shaped, with the superior, the assistant, the bursar, and sometimes the mistress of novices seated at the top table. The members of the community sat at the outside of the side tables.

The length of the Tables must be according to the size of the rooms, but there should be a good space left for passing at each end of the room.

[Catherine McAuley]

Autograph: Birmingham

277. Decree of Confirmation of the Rule and Constitutions of the Sisters of Mercy

July 5, 1841

Whereas a Society of very pious Ladies, called Sisters of Mercy, established with the approbation of the Most Reverend Father Daniel Murray, Archbishop, and founded especially by the zeal of the religious lady, Catherine McAuley, has been erected in Dublin; and whereas very many bishops have begged the Apostolic See to confirm this Society, the Sacred Congregation for the Propagation of the Faith, at a General Meeting held on the 20th day of July in the year 1840, having before it the *relatio* of the Most Eminent and Reverend Lord, Paul Polidori, Cardinal of the Holy Roman Church; and having pondered attentively the great benefits that have already accrued and those that may justly be expected in the future from the establishment of this Society which devotes itself sedulously to the special end of helping the poor and relieving the sick in every way, and safeguarding by the exercise of charity and religion women who find themselves in circumstances dangerous to virtue, decided and decreed to supplicate our Most Holy Lord that he might deign to confirm the Rules and Constitutions of this Society in the form in which they have been described above, prescribing at the same time that the Vows taken by the Sisters admitted to this Society should be simple, until such time as the Holy See may judge otherwise.

When this judgment of the Sacred Congregation had been related to our Most Holy Lord, Pope Gregory XVI, by the Most Reverend Father Ignatius Cadolini, Archbishop of Edessa, Secretary to the Sacred Congregation, His Holiness, in an audience on the 6th day of June in the year 1841, fully approved it and kindly confirmed the Rules and Constitutions under consideration, as indicated above.

Given at Rome, from the offices of the Sacred Congregation for the Propagation of the Faith, on this 5th day of July, in the year 1841.

J. Ph. Card[inal] Fransoni, Prefect
I[gnatius], Archbishop of Edessa, Secretary

Autograph (Latin): Propaganda Fide, SC Irlanda, vol. 27, f. 498r; official publication:
La regola e le costituzioni delle religiose nominate Sorelle della Misericordia *(26)*[5]

---

5 This decree was officially published, beyond the records of the Congregation for the Propagation of the Faith, by inserting it as the final page (page 26) in the official hardbound publication of the confirmed Rule and Constitutions of the Sisters of Mercy, namely *La regola e le costituzioni delle religiose nominate Sorelle della Misericordia*. Copies of this publication were sent to the bishops of the dioceses in which the Sisters of Mercy were then located. See Letter 288, written on July 31, 1841,

278. To Jane Frances Gibson   [Lancaster]
Baggot Street   [July 15, 1841]

My dear and esteemed Friend

Your most welcome letter gives me inexpressible delight. I thank God you are so happy and doing so well. I trust in His good and holy providence that you will persevere to the end and gain your immortal crown of supereminent brilliancy. You have, for the love of God and your neighbor, chosen the better part; therefore fear nothing, for the hand of God will support and guide you.

Now for an answer to your question. Undoubtedly I am as firmly fixed as ever in my purpose of having a convent of Sisters of Mercy in Liverpool. A house and ground are purchased, and Dr. Youens is indefatigable in his exertions to prepare for your reception. It is not in my power to fix the time when it will be ready, but I have written to Dr. Youens to give you information on this head immediately.[6] Do not hesitate to write to me on any subject on which I can give you satisfaction at any time. I shall always be delighted to hear from you. I have been very unwell since I had the pleasure of seeing you at Eaton House ...

I recommend myself and flock to your pious prayers and those of the community, and remain, my dear child, with great esteem,

Very sincerely yours in Christ
+ G[eorge Hilary] Brown
[Vicar Apostolic, Lancashire District]

Published transcription: Carroll, Leaves 2:363–64

279. To Sister M. Frances Warde   [Baggot Street]
Carlow   [Mid July 1841][7]

My Dearest Sister M. Frances

When Father O'Hanlon called here on his return from Carlow—he said to me, "Oh my dear, I am delighted to see you so much recovered, you are looking quite yourself"—by this you will judge, he does not urge me to change the air.

---

with which Cardinal Fransoni forwards ten copies to Dr. Daniel Murray with the request that he distribute to "the Superior of the House ... in your diocese ... one copy of the Rule and Constitutions." In the same letter, Cardinal Fransoni reports that the Rule and Constitutions "were with the approval of His Holiness [Gregory XVI] confirmed." This decree was translated by John MacErlean, SJ, in the middle of the twentieth century; the translation was recently reviewed and slightly modified by Mary Eymard Hyland, RSM.   6 The newly created ecclesiastical district of Lancashire, England, in which Dr. George Hilary Brown was vicar apostolic, included the city of Liverpool where efforts were underway to establish a convent of Sisters of Mercy. Several letters in July and August 1841, to and from Catherine McAuley, discuss whether the foundation should be made from Carlow or Baggot Street. As a native of Liverpool, Frances Gibson, a postulant at Baggot Street, was willing and eager to be a member of the future foundation. Dr. Thomas Youens was pastor of St. Nicholas parish, Copperas Hill, Liverpool. Early records in the archives of the Sisters of Mercy, Liverpool, speak of Dr. Youens as vicar general of the Lancashire District, a role he filled soon after 1841.   7 Mary Ignatia Neumann

What a time it would be to desert my post—7 Sisters in preparation for pro-fession—& 3 for reception. I am quite renovated by a delightful addition to the flock—on Wednesday last—the first Scotch Sister that has joined an Irish com-munity. Sister Cecilia became acquainted with Mrs. Capt. Osbourne, a Scotch lady—who goes every year to see her friends in Edenburgh [*sic*]—and through her this sweet Sister came[8]—22 years old, most interesting. The variety of accent is now quite amusing at recreation. She never was out of Scotland before. We get on Wednesday a very nice niece of Doctor Murray's—Miss Elizabeth Murray of Sheep Walk, Co. Wicklow, the daughter of his youngest & favorite Brother, 24 years old.[9] She is like the Bishop. So that we will have 2 to succeed to the caps.[10]

Father O'H told us you had a grand breakfast for the Liberator etc., etc. We are praying all day long for the preservation of good Father Maher. As we are constantly hearing something of the Carlow election—we cannot forget to add, God preserve Father Maher.[11]

dates this undated letter "[July 19, 1841]" which may be correct (348). 8 Eliza Munro entered on Wednesday, July 14, 1841—which suggests that this letter was written before July 21. No further information about her is available. 9 Elizabeth Murray evidently entered the Baggot Street com-munity on Wednesday, July 28 or Tuesday, July 27 (see Letter 280). No further information on her is available. 10 That is, two women to succeed the three postulants ("caps") who will receive the habit in mid August. The book of Acts of the Chapter of professed sisters at Baggot Street records that on "July 18, 1841: By the majority of the votes of the Chapter, Sisters Margaret Teresa Dwyer, Margaret Teresa Geraty [Geraghty] and Jane Frances Gibson were permitted to receive the holy habit of Religion" (3). This may have been the last Chapter over which Catherine McAuley presided.

11 The Carlow Annals for 1841 records the visit and election campaigning in Carlow of Daniel O'Connell, MP:

> A county election caused great excitement in the town just at this time, the great "Liberator" Dan O'Connell having come to solicit the votes of the freeholders for his younger son John. He remained a month in town, and every evening from a raised platform in front of his hotel, he addressed his crowded audience, and having done speaking he would retire as if to take a short rest, but really to beg God's blessing on his labours; Father [James] Maher told us that these moments were always employed by the grand old patriot, in saying his beads. On Sundays he went to Confession in our Sacristy or rather in the screened off por-tion of our chapel, whence his fervent act of contrition could be distinctly heard by all out-side, then heard Mass and received Communion most devoutly. He also breakfasted here on these occasions together with His Lordship and some of the priests.

James Maher was also a "grand old patriot," as well as confessor, at this time, to Daniel O'Connell. Like the deceased Bishop Doyle ("J. K. L.") whom he admired and served, James Maher was an indefatigable proponent of the rights of the poor Irish, issuing long public letters and speeches against the tithes, the poor law, "exorbitant rents," evictions, "boroughmongers," unsympathetic gentry, misinformed magistrates, and "aristocratic incapables" (Moran xliii–lxv). The *Letters ... Memoir*, published by his nephew (Patrick Moran), contains the texts of many of Father Maher's impassioned letters. However, in the election of the summer of 1841, O'Connell's party lost. Writing to a friend in October, Maher said:

> You have heard of our defeat at the last elections ... The loss of the election was perhaps the means employed by Heaven to save the lives of the people. The Tories were so

Mr. Lacy of Wexford called here yesterday. He says all goes on well in the convent. The ardent zeal of Sister Kelly he says delights everyone.[12] I am rejoiced that poor sickly Naas is recovering fast. It has been a little Martyrdom to Sister M. Joseph[ine Trennor]—so much to be done & so few to help her.

We have some expectation that Dr. Walsh will come over to receive the vows of his spiritual children—and Doctor Wiseman to preach. It is impossible more interest could be manifested, than is at the other side. I sent Dr. Walsh's letter to the Bishop—who says in reply—"This is a high honor to all concerned."[13]

God bring us through it—His Divine help only can.

God bless and preserve you—and all with you.

Pray for your ever affectionate

M. C. M.

Do not speak of the english Bishop, etc., as it is not decided—until we get another letter.

Autograph: Silver Spring

280. To Sister Mary Aloysius Scott Baggot St.
Birr July 20, 1841

My Dear Sister M. Aloysius

I am very sorry to find any displeasure existing towards the education Board. Ever since the decision of the Cardinals it is regarded with additional confidence, and Dr. Murray, its chief patron.[14] This is the peace to be prayed for—and the

---

enraged that they would have had recourse to violence if they were losing. Twenty at least voted who had no more right to vote than you had in the county. A petition has been lodged against the return ... The Repeal question is making great progress ...; half of the Bishops, I believe, have declared in favor of it (qtd. in Moran lxvi).

12 James Lacey was a curate in Wexford (*Irish Catholic Directory* [1840] 291). Mary Teresa Kelly was the superior of the Mercy community there. 13 Dr. Thomas Walsh's letter to Catherine McAuley appears to be no longer extant. She sent it to Dr. Murray who returned it (see Letter 280). Carroll quotes a portion of Dr. Walsh's letter: "I shall have great pleasure indeed in receiving the vows of my dear daughters in Jesus Christ, and the more so as I have a beautiful convent, the admiration of all who see it, furnished with every requisite, ready for them to commence their works of mercy" (*Life* 399; *Leaves* 2:310–11). Carroll may be quoting from Catherine's letter of August 3, 1841 (Letter 290) where the same excerpt from Dr. Walsh's letter is shared with Teresa White. 14 At their annual synod in early February 1841, the Irish bishops unanimously responded to the positive word from the Vatican that Pope Gregory XVI would leave the question of cooperating with the national education system in Ireland to their own individual judgments, in their respective dioceses—thus bringing to naught the considerable effort of Dr. John MacHale, the archbishop of Tuam, to get Rome to condemn the system completely as a danger to the faith of Catholic children. Dr. Daniel Murray was one of the commissioners of education, and Catherine McAuley— aware of the opinions of bishops and priests whose wisdom she respected—supported collaboration with the system as then operative. Presumably, Dr. Patrick Kennedy of Killaloe and his vicar gen-

plenty—is Miss Ryan, I suppose.[15] Prayer will do more towards both than all the money in the Bank of Ireland. Let us pray well and never grow weary.

We admitted on Wednesday last a most interesting Scotch Sister, the first in Ireland—22 years old, very very nice in manner & appearance. She has been three years wishing to be an—Irish Nun—never was out of Scotland before, name—Eliza Munro! She understood house linen would be required—and has brought 12 large pair of sheets—12 Table cloths & 24 napkins, Scotch manufacture. Sister M. Cecilia's acquaintance with Mrs. Osbourne of Booterstown, who is from Edenburgh [*sic*], opened the way to this addition, which seems truly desirable.[16] So that we cannot fall out with the worldlings alltogether, but must try to have a select few.

We expect on Tuesday Miss Murray of Sheep Walk, Co. Wicklow, niece to the Bishop—and another not yet ready. So we shall have heads for the considering caps—before the present owners—or occupiers—get the "cap of Wisdom".[17]

We had a long visit from Mr. Pusie [Pusey], professor of Oxford College, whose new opinions have created so much interest. His appearance is that of a negligent author—such as some of the poets are described. His manner most pleasing—his countenance is not expressive of a strong mind—but in conversation he does not betray any imbecility except the wanderings of all protestants. He says they must get back their title—Catholic—expressed his firm belief in the real presence—says we are a safe sound branch from the old Root, with many incumbrances & superfluous practices—not of importance in any way. The orthodox Greek, another sound branch—and his own, the reformed Catholic branch, the third. He was extremely guarded not to say anything which might offend—and apoligied [*sic*] for once calling the Pope—Bishop of Rome—or Romish Bishop.[18]

What shall I say of the sweet delightful fruit and Butter—which is certainly some of the best I ever saw—it is fresh and nice yet. I have some delightful Ras[p]berry Vinegar Sr. Lucy Vincent made me—and they had all grand pies as you directed.

I sent a Habit to Sr. M. Teresa—I hope it will not be too small.

We have just had some proposals from Liverpool—and believe we shall have some postulants over.

Write soon. Give my affectionate love to all. Did you hear we have reason to expect Dr. Walsh will come over to receive the vows of his spiritual children—& Dr. Wiseman to preach. I sent Dr. Walsh's letter to our Bishop. Returning it, he says—"This is indeed a high honor to all concerned"—8 to be

---

eral, Dr. John Spain, parish priest in Birr, were hesitant—no doubt affected by their unfortunate experience with the schismatics and proselytizers in Birr.   15 Apparently Miss Ryan was considered a possible candidate for the Sisters of Mercy in Birr. No further information on her has been discovered.   16 See note 8 above.   17 See notes 9 and 10 in Letter 279.   18 Catherine McAuley's discussion of Dr. Edward B. Pusey (1800–1882), the well-known Anglican clergyman and theologian, is obviously unaffected by his considerable reputation as a leader of developments in the Church of England.

Professed and 3 received—one for Liverpool. Doctor Pusie [Pusey] invited himself if quite agreeable.

Pray well for your ever affectionate

M. C. McAuley

Take care of my last born—Birr.

Present my respects to Doctor Spain and remember me to Mrs. Egan.

Autograph: Dublin, Mercy

281. To Dr. Thomas Youens[19]   [Baggot Street]
Liverpool   [c. July 24, 1841]

Respected Revd. Father

I this day received a letter from my dear Sister Warde of Carlow, speaking of your intended Institute. She tells me all the arrangements she intended to make—if she should be called upon—and they seem to me exceedingly good.

She makes me perfectly understand what Sisters she designed to give—who are truly desirable. Some of them would, I think, bring the usual portion. Indeed all she proposes, Revd. Father, far exceeds what we could do—and I am now as ardent as my youthful Sister, praying & trusting that nothing may retard the good work.

Very little preparation would be necessary on your part, Revd. Father, and we might sail together for Birmingham & Liverpool. I have been speaking with Sister Fanny G[ibson]—& find she would go at once with the Liverpool foundation.[20]

Recommending myself, etc., etc., to your charitable remembrance.

I remain, etc., etc.

[M. C. McAuley]

Autograph: Silver Spring

19 This unsigned autograph is the draft of the letter Catherine McAuley sent to Thomas Youens, pastor of St. Nicholas Church, Copperas Hill, Liverpool, in the Lancashire District, where Dr. George Hilary Brown was vicar apostolic. The actual autograph letter sent to Dr. Youens has not been located.   20 Catherine McAuley is now fully aware that she does not have the personnel at Baggot Street to send a foundation to Liverpool, except the postulant Jane Frances Gibson. She is doing her best to encourage Dr. Youens to seek a founding community from Carlow, with the hope that the two parties might travel together to Liverpool and Birmingham in August. Apparently Father James Maher and Dr. Youens were friends and had already had a conversation along these lines, which has occasioned Frances Warde's intended "arrangements." In Letter 250, written to Frances on March 29, 1841, Catherine had said: "I have been told two or three times that you are going to Liverpool ... Matters with you are not closed—or you would tell me." Catherine may have initially intended to send a foundation to Liverpool from Dublin, and she certainly wished to be informed of plans made in the various convents outside of Dublin, but it is probably exaggerated to say that she is simply "showing tolerance" of the arrangements Frances Warde is making (see Bolster, ed. 240).

282. To Sister M. Frances Warde
Carlow

[Baggot Street]
Saturday, July 24, 1841

My Dear Sr. M. Frances

A few days before Dr. Youens came to Dublin, our Sister Gibson had a letter from Doctor Brown, her Bishop, who seemed to wish to make arrangements here for Liverpool.[21] If he has had any consultation with Dr. Griffiths of London, or Dr. Walshe [*sic*] of Birmingham they would endeavour to impress him with the feeling that establishments in England ought to be made from the chief or Mother House, as they term it, in Ireland, as they attribute whatever little difficulty has been found in Bermondsey to that want. And certainly in that instance more experience was required, to take down some of Sr. Agnew's self importance as to opinion and bring her well through a noviciate, but the case in question is a very different one.[22] The Sister you offer as superior—is to remain—and her dispositions are well suited. Dr. Youens is so anxious, it is a pity to have any impediment, and if our little plans could be formed, perhaps we might sail together— after our ceremony. I think you would do well to send the enclosed note to Dr. Youens—(with Mr. Maher's approbation).[23] He would shew it to the Bishop who, I am told, is endeavouring to got more persons to come here for preparation— do it without delay.

Pray for your affectionate
M. C. McAuley

Autograph: Silver Spring

283. To Sister Mary Ann Doyle
Tullamore

Baggot Street
July 24, 1841

My Dear Sister Mary Ann

You are on the secure high road of the Cross—have the most strong and lively confidence that your Convent will be firmly established, for it certainly

---

21 Dr. Brown's letter (Letter 278) must have reached Dublin by July 17 or 18; evidently Dr. Thomas Youens visited Dublin, and presumably Carlow, around July 20. The present letter may imply that, while in Dublin, he came to see Catherine McAuley at Baggot Street. 22 At this point Catherine was well aware of some "difficulty" in Bermondsey, though not, I believe, of its severity. What she knew would have come from Clare Moore or Peter Butler during their visit in June. Clare Moore was twenty-four years old when Elizabeth Agnew, about forty, entered the Cork community in April 1838. 23 The "enclosed note" was either a note from Catherine McAuley herself to Dr. Youens which she thought Frances Warde could forward, or a note from Catherine to Frances which, again, could be forwarded to Dr. Youens in support of Frances's proposal. If it was the former, it may actually be the fair copy of Letter 281 in which Catherine encourages Dr. Youens and Dr. Brown to seek the foundation from Carlow; if it was the latter, it was a note from Catherine to Frances in which she commends Frances's plans—in this case, perhaps it was the enclosed "note written by you to Mrs. Warde" to which Dr. Youens refers in Letter 286.

will. "Be just & fear not." Acquit yourself with justice towards God—let no temporal consideration influence your words or actions, when the duty of your state is in question. I could not think any person with very cautious worldly views—worthy to be admitted to holy Profession. It is not a disposition to bestow gifts, like benevolent persons in the world, that bespeaks generosity of mind for the religious state. It is bestowing ourselves most freely and relying with unhesitating confidence on the Providence of God.[24]

When our innocent—yet very sensible, Sister Chantell [de Chantal] (McCann) was about to hand over all she possessed, making it impossible to ever command one shilling, her Mother told her she ought to have some security, as many persons were of the opinion this House would not be established—and said to her, What would you do then? She answered—"Won't I have my sweet Lord?"—and sweet He was to her indeed to the very last moment.[25] Tho' we may not often have the consolation to meet such noble universal disengagement as hers—yet a spirit directly opposite, I humbly hope will never make its abode amongst us.

Do not fear offending any one. Speak as your mind directs and always act with more courage when the "mammon of unrighteousness" is in question. Let me know when you are closely pressed, and I will divide with you, be it ever so little.[26]

I wish I could hear of your getting up a lottery or raffle occasionally. Sr. M. Teresa has made £80 in Galway at different times. If you had two good prizes—and all the rest trifles, you would sell £25 worth of tickets between this and Christmas at 1 s[hilling] per ticket—by giving 10 to every [one] you know to sell them. The drawing could be in the school room—3 blanks to a prize. We have just had one—and did not expend more than £1-10.

Write soon. Most earnestly praying God to direct and strengthen you—

I remain with great affection etc., etc.

M. C. McAuley

Give my best love to all.

Autograph: Bermondsey

---

24 Evidently a novice preparing for profession of vows in Tullamore wished to set aside some of her own money for her future personal use, before she professed the vow of poverty by which she would forever renounce all right to administer any assets legally held in her name. Mary Ann Doyle, realizing that the Tullamore community was in need of professed members, may have been tempted to accede to the novice's wish, which Catherine McAuley calls a "very cautious worldly" view. Catherine then gives an important definition of the generosity of mind distinctive of vowed religious life. The next profession ceremony in Tullamore was held on October 18, 1841. 25 Mary de Chantal McCann, the widow of Dr. John McCann, a Dublin physician, had entered the Baggot Street community in October 1832 and professed her vows on July 1, 1835. She died of typhus fever on October 27, 1837. See Letters 27 and 56. 26 Catherine may be thinking of Matt. 6.24 and 1 Tim. 6.9–10. When the Tullamore community is in financial straits, she will divide with it whatever money the Baggot Street community has.

284. To Sister M. Frances Warde [Baggot Street]
     Carlow [c. July 26–27, 1841][27]

My Dearest Sister M. Frances

Your letter this morning gratified me very much. The arrangement you propose seems very desirable, and if we could all start together,[28] I have no doubt that Sister Gibson would join at once. I have been speaking with her—she is a treasure to religion, a sweet docile animated creature, all alive—and delighted with her duties.

Sister M. Cecilia you know is a general favorite. Perhaps there never was a more beloved Mistress of Novices. They call the novaship—Paradise—tho' the best discipline is kept up. Her going away will make it easier for any novice or postulant to be moved.[29] Indeed it will be another great blow to poor Baggot Street—which has passed through many sorrows. The sweet little Scotch Sr. said to me—"What shall I do when Mother Cecilia is gone." I am so much confined to one room that they seldom see me before evening.[30]

Do all you can to forward the Liverpool foundation. Sr. Fanny[31] thinks she knows 2 who would join immediately—if Dr. Youens gets Beds, etc. Other matters could be got when you arrive. He says the House is very large. There is no time to spare.

Your ever affectionate
M. C. McAuley

Having heard from a Priest some unfavorable reports of Bermondsey, I wrote to Mr. Butler, begging him to tell me the real state. I this moment rec'd the enclosed—read it and send it again to me when you are writing. 2 left under angry circumstances, I believe they are enemies—Sr. Agnew is fond of *extremes* in piety, that is her greatest error. She wrote to me in the greatest alarm—about a most trifling matter—if you and I were to write on such subjects—we would never be done.[32]

Autograph: Silver Spring

27 Neumann dates this letter "[July 26, 1841]" (354); Bolster dates it "28 January 1841" (195), which cannot be correct, given the content of the letter (a response to Frances's response to Letter 282).   28 For Liverpool and Birmingham, sailing from Kingstown in mid August.   29 Catherine McAuley had already decided that Mary Cecilia Marmion would remain with the new Birmingham community for the first two or three months, until they got settled—taking over Catherine's own role of helper after she departed from Birmingham.   30 Catherine's acknowledging that she is currently confined to one room, with its windows closed, during the day—probably the parlor on the street floor of the house—is her first extant indication that she is now forced to make some accommodation to ease her persistent cough.   31 Frances ("Fanny") Gibson.

32 Peter Butler's letter about the Bermondsey community is, unfortunately, not extant. In March 1841, according to the Bermondsey Annals, two novices in the community—Mary Bernard Murray and Mary Angela Browne—were dismissed for reasons of health and deficiency "in the requisite qualities and dispositions" (1:24), but Catherine McAuley would have heard about this at least by June when Clare Moore returned to Ireland. Of Clare Agnew's conduct as superior, the Bermondsey

285. To Sister M. Frances Warde   Convent, Baggot St.
     Carlow   July 28, 1841

My Dear Sister M. Frances

As we shall want all our little exhibitions for the Ceremony, I hope you can send the Register. I felt a great want in not having it to shew Dr. Pusie [Pusey], the Oxford professor who spoke of illuminated works. Those little affairs are a good fill up and spare the trouble of talking much. I hope there is no fear of not having it.[33]

The progress in Galway exceeds all expectation, as there were five Convents before us. They are now 9 in number—2 to be professed and 3 received in October.[34]

Poor "Father Crotty"—is greatly afflicted—the Sisters in Birr have four hundred & fifty children in their school—his school is quite deserted. He calls them "poor deluded Dupes."

God almighty bless you and all.

                                                  Your affectionate
                                                  M. C. McAuley

Autograph: Silver Spring

Annals says only the following, in Mary Clare Moore's handwriting (which signifies that this portion of the Annals was written after December 10, 1841):

> When Sister Mary Clare Agnew became Mother Superior, she was very anxious to introduce certain customs which she desired to see established in the Community, and changed many of the regulations, which had always been observed, without consulting the feelings of the Sisters, or even apprising them that such alterations would be made—which caused much dissatisfaction among them. In other ways too she gave umbrage, and estranged the minds of the Sisters from her, so that she found her office very insupportable; and being naturally of an enthusiastic temper, and fond of novelty, she turned her attention to other Orders, where she hoped to find greater satisfaction. She fixed her thoughts principally on the Order of La Trappe, and went so far as to enter into a correspondence with the Superiors of it, without acquainting those appointed to guide her or seeking their advice. (1:26)

At the end of July 1841 Catherine McAuley might have known some, but certainly not all, of this story. Mary de Sales White and Mary Xavier O'Connell were, of course, still in Bermondsey, but Catherine would not undermine the authority of the superior by soliciting information from them. On August 3, she tells Teresa White in Galway: "Most satisfactory letters from London, all going on remarkably well" (Letter 290).

33 In late March or April 1841, Catherine McAuley sent the illuminated Baggot Street Register to Carlow so that Mary Cecilia Maher could copy some of its artwork into the Carlow Register. Because talking makes her cough, Catherine hopes to have the Register back in time to show it to guests at the ceremony in August.   34 Mary Joseph Joyce and Mary de Sales (Ismena) McDonnell will profess their vows in October 1841, not in 1842 as in Clarke (12). Because the Galway Register is incomplete, it is not possible to identify the nine members of the Galway community at this time, or the three who will receive the habit in October.

286. To Catherine McAuley

[Liverpool]
[July 30, 1841][35]

By yesterday's post I received your letter and also a letter from Mr. Maher enclosing a note written by you to Mrs. Warde. At the moment these letters arrived I was preparing to write to you as I had just returned from a journey to Lancaster and Weld Bank, where I had been to confer with the Bishop and his Grand Vicar on the subject of the Convent.[36] After describing how much I was delighted and edified with all I saw and heard in Carlow, his Lordship's conclusion was that he intended to treat with the Mother House, and desired me write to Ireland to that effect. It was just when I was about to execute this order that the letters from Ireland arrived.

[Thomas Youens]
[Pastor, St. Nicholas, Copperas Hill]

Catherine McAuley's handcopy: Letter 289

287. To Sister Mary Aloysius Scott
Birr

Convent
July 31, 1841

My Dear Sister M. Aloysius

I long to hear how you have got through the Dog days. Not one animal has suffered from excessive heat in Dublin.

How does your school go on. Mr. Egan says it is a grand sight—has Dr. Spain applied to the Board.[37] Tell me all the news before retreat. No time appointed for our ceremony yet—perplexed with disappointment. I ought to say—delighted, the bad spirit spoke first.

Our poor Sister Justina is very ill. Her Father sent Dr. Corrigan to attend her in Booterstown. She has been blistered, leeched and kept on low diet—the strength is greatly exhausted—yet still she hopes to be Professed at the next ceremony, which is extremely doubtful.[38] All the rest well. My cough as usual.

Good accounts from Tullamore, Carlow, Cork, Limerick, Galway, London—a most satisfactory letter yesterday from Revd. Mr. Butler.

35 No autograph of this letter has been located. The only source for it is Catherine McAuley's own transcription of this one paragraph in Letter 289, where she says that Dr. Youens dated the letter July 30. Since the letter appears to settle the question of the Liverpool foundation, it seems wise to include it in its proper chronological sequence, as well as in Letter 289, where more of the letter is paraphrased.   36 Dr. George Hilary Brown, vicar apostolic of the Lancashire District in which Liverpool was located, resided at this time in Lancaster, a town on the northwest coast of England north of Liverpool. The Revd. R. Thompson, vicar general of the district, resided in Weld Bank (*Irish Catholic Directory* [1841] 333, 335).   37 The Board of National Education.   38 Mary Justina Fleming did profess her vows on August 19, 1841. She died of consumption less than four months later, on December 10.

We had a visit from Dr. England of Charleston and Mrs. Borgia (Nun)—
who accompanied him to look out for Postulants. She came here in a Private
Carriage with 2 fashionables without cloak, Bonnet or hood—an Ursuline dress—
veil, thin black gause [*sic*]—frightful.[39]

Won't you pray fervently that we may all have a profitable holy retreat—
may almighty God help us to make it well. We are to have no other conductor.[40]

Sister M. Frances wrote to me to say—Dr. Cullen had communicated to Mr.
Maher that the Rule was confirmed.[41]

Pray fervently for me—your poor old Mother. Give my fond love to all.

Your ever affectionate
M. C. McAuley

Autograph: Dublin, Mercy

288. To Dr. Daniel Murray[42]

Rome
July 31, 1841

Most Illustrious and Reverend Lord

Along with this letter Your Grace will receive ten copies of the Rule and
Constitutions of the Congregation of the *Sisters of Mercy*, which, after they had
been accurately examined by the Sacred Congregation, were with the approval
of His Holiness confirmed. Your Grace will, I am sure, be pleased to hear from
me of the happy outcome of this matter which, as is evident from your letters,
you have very much at heart.

Your Grace will take care that the Superior of the House of the above mentioned Congregation which has been erected in your diocese receives one copy
of the Rule and Constitutions.

In the meantime I pray God may long preserve Your Grace in health and
happiness.

---

39 Mrs. Borgia is probably Revd. Mother Mary Borgia MacCarthy, an Irish Ursuline born in Cork
who was superior of the Ursuline community in Charleston, South Carolina, founded in late 1834
at Dr. John England's request (T. J. Walsh 246–49). Always conscious of the immense educational
needs of the people in his diocese, John England was now back in Ireland with Mother Borgia,
trying to secure more sisters to teach in his schools. Catherine McAuley deeply admired the great
educator Saint Angela Merici, the founder of the Ursuline order and one of the patron saints of
the Sisters of Mercy. Her blunt one-word comment on Mother Borgia's habit—"frightful"—was
no doubt an exaggeration, but a humorous one. Catherine seems to have strongly disliked thin veils!
40 In Letter 289, Catherine says that in the absence of a retreat director she will herself conduct
the annual retreat at Baggot Street, though her deeper belief is expressed here: they will "have no
other conductor" than God.   41 Dr. Paul Cullen, then rector of the Irish College in Rome, had
communicated to his uncle, James Maher, the news that Catherine McAuley will hear officially only
after she returns from England on September 21. See Letter 288.   42 This letter, written in Latin,

Rome, from the Office of the S[acred] C[ongregation for the] Prop[agation of the] Faith

31st day of July 1841
Ever at Your Grace's service
Giacomo Filippo Card[inal] Fransoni, Prefect

I[gnatius], Archbishop of Edessa, Secretary

Autograph (Latin): Dublin Diocese, Murray Papers AB3/31/9, no. 162

289. To Sister M. Frances Warde   **[Baggot Street]**
    Carlow   **[Early August 1841]**

My Dear Sister M. Frances

Before I received your last letter, I had written the enclosed to Dr. Youens. I have this morning a letter from him. He says—"By yesterday's post"—his letter is dated 30th & did not reach [here] till this morning. [He writes]:

> I rec'd your letter & also a letter from Mr. Maher, enclosing a note written by you to Mrs. Warde. At the moment these letters arrived, I was preparing to write to you as I had just returned from a journey to Lancaster and Weld Bank where I had been to confer with the Bishop and his Grand Vicar on the subject of the Convent. After describing how much I was delighted and edified with all I saw & heard in Carlow—his Lordship's conclusion was that he intended to treat with the Mother House & desired me write to Ireland to that effect. It was just when I was about to execute this order that the letters from Ireland arrived.

Dr. Youens adds that he must again confer with the Bishop—before he can give a conclusive answer to my last note. He says as to the time of going it could not be before November or December—as his holding is not fully secure until then. Let us fervently pray that almighty God may direct & govern in this as well as all that concerns us. Dr. Youens requests I will write to him before he again sees the Bishop—I have only to say that we have no colony to give.

I need not wish you a holy & happy retreat. Father Whitty told me Dr. Furlong had 23 lectures or explanatory discourses prepared for you.[43] Father McAuley conducts the retreat in poor Baggot St.[44]

---

and the accompanying packet did not reach Daniel Murray until sometime after the ceremony at Baggot Street on August 19. Catherine McAuley left Dublin for Birmingham on the evening of August 20, not yet having seen a copy of the confirmed Rule and Constitutions. The letter was translated by John MacErlean, SJ, in the middle of the twentieth century; the translation was recently reviewed and slightly modified by Mary Eymard Hyland, RSM.   **43** Dr. Thomas Furlong was professor of rhetoric and belles letters at St. Patrick's College, Maynooth.   **44** Catherine McAuley was being softly playful here, about herself, but she did not use the title "Father"

God bless & preserve you and send you every blessing.

Pray for your affectionate

M. C. McAuley

We are perplexed about the english Profession. Dr. Walsh who had promised to come over was called to London on some law affairs. We hear he is now gone to travel & Dr. Murray could not make any engagement until we hear from him.

Autograph: Silver Spring

290. To Sister M. Teresa White   **Convent**
Galway   **Tuesday, August 3, 1841**

My Dearest Sister M. Teresa

It seems very long to me since I wrote to you, but if you knew all the weary writing I have had you would fully excuse me. We are exceedingly perplexed about the english profession. When I was in Birr, Doctor Wiseman came over to preach at the consecration of Westland Row. When visiting here, he recommended that Dr. Walsh should be invited to perform the ceremony for his spiritual children.[45] With our Bishop's full approbation, the request was made, which was most kindly acceded to. He concludes thus, "I shall have great pleasure indeed, in receiving the vows of my Dear Daughters in J. C.—and the more so— as I have a beautiful Convent, the admiration of all who see it—furnished with every requisite—ready for them to commence their works of Mercy."

By Doctor Murray's direction, we left the day to Dr. Walsh's appointment. We next hear that he is summoned to London on law affairs—and since—that he and Dr. Wiseman are on the continent, but cannot find them by letter or letters. Doctor Griffiths of London says he has some matters of importance to communicate to Dr. Walsh—and he cannot find him. In this perplexity, Dr. Murray would not make any appointment, so perhaps we may go on to the end of the month, as I said in my letter of thanks to Dr. Walsh that any time after the 15th would answer.

---

lightly. According to the Bermondsey Annals, she "entertained a profound respect for the sacred Ministers of Religion, and taught the Sisters to observe the same in word and manner. The Chaplain of the Convent, the Reverend D[aniel] Burke, had been there for eight years, and was consequently a very intimate friend, yet she always used the word 'Sir' in addressing him, and told the Sisters they ought to say it also to all Priests; with other persons she did not like it, as she thought it quaint or old-fashioned, but she said they ought to venerate Priests" (Sullivan, *Catherine McAuley* 118). Catherine's reverence for the ordained priesthood did not, of course, prevent her from teasing priests and bishops or showing them affection.   45 On January 29, 1841, the new St. Andrew's Church on Westland Row was solemnly consecrated. Dr. Nicholas Wiseman was coadjutor to Dr. Thomas Walsh, vicar apostolic of the newly configured Central District in which the city of Birmingham was located. The sisters destined to found a Mercy community there were in that sense his "spiritual children."

I need not say that my heart rejoices at your very great progress. It has been very great indeed—7 added to your community in so short a time, and 4 of them so very desirable. Mr. O'Hanlon says he would have thought it good progress in 3 years—where there are so many Institutions long established. It affords great comfort to my mind, and gives great promise of lasting good.[46]

We have five postulants, a 6th comes on the 15th—Mother de Pazzi's sister, 18 years younger. The last who came from Winchester Convent—a 7th from Liverpool in September. We have a niece of the Archbishop's—Miss Murray of Sheep Walk.[47]

I have also had a writing business about the Liverpool foundation. Doctor Youens, a most pious respectable english Clergyman, has been making some arrangements for it in Carlow—as he knows Mr. Maher. Doctor Brown—the Bishop—wishes to treat with the Mother House—and I fear my poor Sister M. Frances will be disappointed as she has such genuine ardour & a kind of real innocent pious anxiety, to be engaged in such works. I am sorry—and still hope she may be chosen—hence I have manifested all the indifference that Mr. Daly[48] *admired so much* & given 7 lines of writing in reply to a sheet full—ever praying that God may produce the effect He most desires.

Most satisfactory letters from London, all going on remarkably well. All well in Cork. Sr. M. C[lare] recovering her looks and simple Irish manners—she was too much infected with the—precise—when she came home. I hope my dear Srs. de Sales & Xavier will come back in their own native style—as the Irish malediction did not fall on them & wherever it not fall—we could not wish for any change.[49] As my last poetic production has been on this subject, I send a copy of it to dear Sister M. Catherine as a tribute of affectionate remembrance, not insinuating that the curse has fallen on her.[50]

---

46 The earliest Galway records are incomplete. This prevents any detailed understanding of the membership of the community in the first years and the "progress" that so pleased Catherine McAuley.   47 The five postulants who had already entered were Margaret (a lay sister whose surname has not been discovered), Margaret Teresa Dwyer, Margaret Teresa Geraghty, Elizabeth Murray (Daniel Murray's niece), and Frances Gibson, who had attended the Benedictine convent school in Winchester, England (Carroll, *Leaves* 2:358). Ellen Delany, the much younger sister of Mary de Pazzi Delany, will enter on August 15, and Mary Anne Consitt, born in Durham and destined for the Liverpool foundation, on August 31, while Catherine McAuley is in Birmingham. 48 Peter Daly, parish priest in Galway.   49 Every member of the Bermondsey community—except Mary Clare Moore, the initial superior, and the two sisters lent for a year from Dublin—was English born and bred. Two or three—certainly Clare Agnew and Mary de Sales Eyre—were upper class English women. Although the Bermondsey Annals is silent about this source of tension (no doubt because Clare Moore herself was the object of the snobbery), Catherine McAuley's letters allude to ethnic prejudice and to a desire on the part of some in Bermondsey to be rid of the Irish presence and influence. The irony of the situation—which Catherine McAuley could not know—is that in December 1841, Clare Moore, Dublin born and bred and then twenty-seven, returned to Bermondsey as superior—an office she held, except for fifteen months, until her death in 1874— and led that community in remarkably widespread and welcomed missionary service to the people of England.   50 Catherine's "last poetic production" cannot be found, nor can it be identified—

You have heard that Sr. M. C. Augustine Moore is gone to Cork with her Sister. Sr. M. Joseph Delaney here—and poor Father Walsh in great woe for his two stars, the most valuable, he says, we ever had in our order.[51]

You now know as much as if you were in the Bishop's Parlour.[52]

Sr. Margaret, Lay Sister, is the most improved young person I ever saw— no complaints now of any kind.

The school in Kingstown never was so numerously attended, Booterstown much encreased & a great number here. We calculate that 600 poor children in the Archdiocess receive daily tuition from our Sisters, thanks be to God. Birr going on well—four hundred & fifty children at their school—all have left Mr. Crotty's—and he is worse than ever, railing against Priests & Nuns. Sr. Aloysius in strong health.

I fear much we are about to have a severe trial, dear Sr. Justina very ill— and will not leave us—all the appearance of decline. Dr. Corrigan attending at her father's request—he would not have been our choice.[53]

Let not a word contained in this letter reach an ear that would carry it to the world.

Give my most affectionate love to each—and believe me, with the fondest attachment

your own old Mother

M. C. McAuley

Be sure remember me to Father Daly.

Let us pray fervently during the retreat & all will go on well.

Autograph: Galway

---

unless she is referring to her acrostic poem for Peter Butler in which she tackled the "wild Irish" aspersion (Letter 153). However, that poem is assumed to have been written a year and a half earlier than the present letter, while she was still in Bermondsey.   51 Mary Joseph (Alicia) Delaney, also from Durrow, Co. Kilkenny, but apparently no close relation to M. de Pazzi Delany, had gone to Charleville as part of the founding community in October 1836 and professed her vows there in June 1837; she returned to the Baggot Street community in 1839, and departed from the Sisters of Mercy in 1848. Mary Clare Augustine Moore, like Teresa White before her, had been superior of the branch house in Kingstown in early 1841. She returned to Baggot Street, before departing for Cork in late June. William Walsh was a curate in Kingstown. Probably it is he who is in "great woe"—at Kingstown's loss of "two stars": Teresa (or M. Joseph Delaney?) and Clare Augustine. 52 Every Convent of Mercy tried to maintain, if it had the space, one tidy living room for greeting guests—which it often called the "bishop's parlour"; the best furniture went there. At Baggot Street, this parlour was on the street floor and was, I believe, the room that is today called the Callaghan Room (containing furniture from Coolock bequeathed to Catherine McAuley by William Callaghan). In 1841, when the community at Baggot Street was so large and when Catherine's cough prevented her from climbing the stairs too many times in a day, the professed sisters, or at least some of them, occasionally had evening recreation with her in the bishop's parlour, the rest of the community using the large community room on the floor above.   53 Not since March 10, 1840 (the day Mary Francis Marmion died), had a sister died at Baggot Street, and Catherine dreads the severe trial she anticipates in the death of Mary Justina Fleming—especially in view of her

291. **To Sister M. Frances Warde**
Carlow

Wednesday Morning
[August 4, 1841]

My Dearest Sister M. Frances

I am sure I need not say that it would be delightful to me to accept the invitation to St. Leo's—but think of all that must be left behind. They would feel it very much indeed. It is quite impossible for any one in my situation to think of pleasing themselves. My pleasure must be in endeavouring to please all.

We hope the english Sisters will be then in retreat for profession, tho' no arrangement is yet made—expecting Dr. Walsh's answer. At least we hope they will not have much more delay, as Sister Juliana's Father is thought to be in a dying state & her family are pressing her return.[54]

Speaking does not injure me. I am giving them instructions every day for more than a month—thanks be to God, they love instruction—and are most anxious to profit by it.[55]

I will write to you immediately after retreat—if I hear what we are to do. Dr. Murray could not receive any application until Dr. Walsh's [letters] gives his final answer.

I believe we are going to have a great trial—Sister Justina—Mr. Hume's relative, a fine creature, with every symptom of decline. If possible, I will get her to return to her home—she would have more chance of recovery & we would be spared the sorrowful scene.

May God bless and protect you, etc., etc. Give 5 kisses to my little Fanny.[56]

Your ever affectionate
M. C. McAuley

I just mentioned at recreation having some thought of going to Carlow for the retreat, etc.—& had at least 15 up in a minute: "Ah will you bring me etc., etc."

It is probable Father Gaffney would have come to us had we pressed him, but his stomach etc., got ill last time, & indeed he was greatly distressed. You

---

misgivings about Dr. Dominic Corrigan's medical treatment. He was not particularly recognized as an expert in diseases of the chest. The dramatic irony here is now obvious; the first "severe trial" coming upon the community will be Catherine's own death in November.   54 The inconvenience of not knowing when in August the profession and reception ceremony would occur was considerable. On that date hinged the timing of an eight-day retreat; the profession of seven sisters, including one who was dying and four destined for Birmingham; the reception of three; the subsequent journey of nine sisters and two priests by boat and train to Birmingham; and the visit, as soon as possible, to Mary Juliana Hardman's father, thought then to be dying. Dr. Murray would not set a date until Dr. Walsh had clearly rescinded his decision to come, and the latter could not be reached. Catherine's fretting about the date was well justified.   55 For one month before reception of the habit and two months before profession of vows, the sisters anticipating these ceremonies engaged in preparatory instructions and meditations. Catherine herself instructed the ten sisters preparing for the ceremonies in August.   56 Little Fanny is Frances Warde's young niece, the child of her deceased brother, to whom Catherine McAuley had sent, months before, a poem and Mary Teresa Macauley's brooch (see Letters 212 and 213).

may suppose Sister de Pazzi is not sighing for a repetition, as I positively refused [*illegible words: four and a half short lines have been heavily crossed out*].[57]

Autograph: Silver Spring

292. To the Reverend Michael Gibson[58]   Convent, Baggot St.
Liverpool   Dublin
                                            August 6, 1841

Reverend Father

    We have received with very great regret the account of your valued Sister's death,[59] but, as we this day commence our annual Retreat, in which Sister Fanny joins, preparatory to her Religious clothing, I think it better not to communicate the afflicting event to her before the morning of the Assumption, lest entering upon a Retreat of eight days with her mind greatly depressed might be too much for a constitution rather delicate; when the Retreat is over, and all are free to sympathize with her, I have every reason to hope that she will meet this great trial with renewed fortitude, and humble resignation to the holy Will of God.[60] All the aid in our power shall be afforded to the dear departed soul.

> I remain, Reverend Father
> Respectfully yours in Xt
> Mary C. McAuley

Handcopy: Liverpool

293. To John Hardman, Jr.   **Dublin**
Birmingham   **August 13, 1841**

Dear Mr. Hardman,

    I have just time, before the post starts, to write that all things are settled, to our satisfaction. Dr. Walsh has written from London, requesting Dr. Murray to

---

57 Among the defaced words one clause may be very faintly discerned: "this is not a house to bring a Priest into who ..." Presumably Catherine feels that they already have enough sickness at Baggot Street. However, as later letters will reveal, Myles Gaffney was well enough to travel to Birmingham with the founding party on August 20.   **58** Michael Gibson was the priest-brother of Jane Frances (Fanny) Gibson, then twenty-two. He may have been a faculty member at Ushaw College, Durham, at this time. He was president of the College in 1844 (Smith 13).   **59** Further information on Mrs. Leigh, Fanny Gibson's eldest sister, has not been discovered (Smith 6). In Letter 295 Catherine McAuley spells her surname "Lee."   **60** Catherine's decision to withhold news of her eldest sister's death from Fanny Gibson for eight days is striking. Fanny could not have gone to the burial in any event. Although the sisters at Baggot Street would have undoubtedly found ways to reach out and console her—even though they were all on retreat—perhaps Catherine most feared the harmful effects of Fanny's dealing with the death when she was alone, in silence, unoccupied with other work. It was apparently at this point that Catherine made the further decision to take Fanny, who would then be a novice, as her travelling companion to Birmingham later in August so that she could visit her family in Liverpool.

receive the vows of the good Sisters, and His Grace of Dublin has fixed Thursday next, the 19th, for the Ceremony. On the 20th in the evening, please God, we will all start for Birmingham, & will leave Liverpool on the 21st by the 10½ o'clock train.

Mrs. McAuley & I have thus arranged matters. If there should be any change, I will write to you again. I need not say to you, to tell this good news, as soon as possible, to your good Father.

I am, Dear Mr. Hardman

Yours very sincerely
M[yles] Gaffney

Mrs. McAuley will accompany us. [61]

Autograph: Birmingham

294. To Catherine McAuley

Mount Brown, [Dublin]
August 13, 1841

Mr. C[ornelius] P. Shannon's compliments to the Sisters of Mercy—begs to inform them that no prohibition exists against their visiting the South Dublin Union Workhouse—and on the part of the Catholic guardians of the board, he respectfully solicits a renewal of their attendance on the sick and infirm of their persuasion.[62]

[C. P. Shannon]

Autograph: Dublin, Mercy

61 This letter is the earliest extant document indicating that the issue of the August ceremony was resolved, and a day chosen for the event (August 19). Myles Gaffney, dean of the college at Maynooth and longtime friend of Catherine McAuley and the Sisters of Mercy, had earlier visited Mr. John Hardman, Sr. in Birmingham (see Letter 295). He is presumably writing this letter on Catherine McAuley's behalf. He will, with Redmond O'Hanlon, accompany the founding party to Birmingham.   62 Cornelius P. Shannon was an elected Poor Law Guardian from St. James's Ward, living on Mount Brown. This letter, addressed to "Mrs. McAuley, Convent, Baggot St.," contains a notation in the upper right corner that may be in the same hand as the letter: "Permission for visiting the Poor House."

When the Board of Guardians met on July 29, 1841—having been elected on March 25, 1841— Mr. Shannon gave notice that he would introduce a motion permitting the Sisters of Charity and the Sisters of Mercy to visit the Catholic sick and infirm in the workhouse. On August 5 he withdrew his notice, acknowledging that nothing in the minutes of the Board prohibited their visiting. He then wrote the present letter. However, at a subsequent meeting of the Board (August 26), a Guardian claimed that in the absence of a resolution the Sisters of Charity had no permission to visit (the claim may also have included the Sisters of Mercy, the two religious congregations being often confused in the mind of the public). Mr. Shannon thereupon moved a resolution, but two of the Guardians then argued by proposed amendment that "The Chaplain being the responsible Officer of this Board for imparting Religious consolation to the members of their several flocks ...

295. To Sister M. Frances Warde
Carlow

[Baggot Street]
[August 16, 1841]

My Dearest Sister M. Frances

I was aware the confirmation of the Rule was granted, but I have not received it yet—probably his Grace may bring it on Thursday to the ceremony. All the dear english Bishops disappointed.[63]

As Sister Juliana's Father is in his last illness, we sail on Friday. Mr. Gaffney saw him in his bed. He said if he only lived half an hour after our arrival he would be happy. The whole family have been such generous friends to [*missing word*] that Dr. Walsh writes to Dr. Murray begging there may not be any delay. Young Mr. Hardman gave 15 hundred £ towards the Cathedral—and now has given five hundred & fifty for an organ and purchased a nice little one for the Convent. Mr. Gaffney promised the good old Father he would bring his child to him, and he kindly returns with us on Friday.

Poor Sister Fanny G[ibson] had a sorrowful letter coming out of retreat—the death of her sister, Mrs. Lee. She is a delicate creature, and looks so like a ghost since she rec'd the sad communication ...[64]

... he thinks Carlow the best of all air, but advised we should wait a little. What relief for me if God is pleased to spare me from witnessing another fine young creature going to the Tomb. I will write to you from Birmingham immediately.

Ellen Delaney entered yesterday.[65] She is a very gentle nice young person, slight and very thin, such a contrast to her Sister de Pazzi.

What a heavenly retreat you had. I am heartily sorry you are not going on the mission[66] to impart some of its fruits while they are new, but you will treasure them up—for a future day. These good Bishops take their own full time, to consider any little affair, and those that are, like myself, rather impatient for an answer, may just as well make up the mind to wait for one.

---

the Board do not deem it expedient to admit other persons for that purpose" (Typed notes, Mercy Congregational Archives, Dublin). The amendment failed, but the motion carried, allowing the "ingress and egress" of the Sisters.

The South Dublin Union Workhouse, opened for admissions on April 24, 1840, was located on the grounds of the old Foundling Hospital in Kilmainham, Dublin, south of the Liffey (J. O'Connor 261). Considerable research remains to be done, for which primary source materials exist, on the ministries of the Sisters of Mercy in the workhouses of Ireland over the next decades. Although Catherine McAuley abhorred these warehouses, with their indiscriminate treatment of the varieties of poor people, she would not abandon to the government those confined in them.

63 That is, the English bishops, Dr. Walsh and Dr. Wiseman, are now not coming to the profession ceremony of the English novices on August 19. 64 Between this sentence and the next, a portion of this autograph letter is missing, probably a whole sheet or half sheet with writing on both sides. The portion was missing in 1969 when Neumann published her edition, and in the 1940s and 1950s when Mary Dominick Foster assembled the volumes of photostat copies in Dublin. No available fragments seem to fit in this gap. The "he" of the next sentence is undoubtedly Redmond O'Hanlon; the dying sister is Justina Fleming. 65 August 15, 1841. 66 To Liverpool.

God Almighty bless you and all with you. Pray much for your ever affectionate

M. C. M.

Autograph: Silver Spring

296. To Sister M. Frances Warde [Baggot Street]
     Carlow [August 19, 1841]

My Dearest Sister M. F.

The ceremony just over—the poor Bishop very much fatigued, had 10 Sisters to officiate for.[67] Dr. Furlong favored us with his presence. We had the celebrated Dr. Pusey & his daughter, who engrossed all Dr. Murray's attention.

We sail tomorrow.[68] I received the enclosed at 9 last night—and am not much wiser. I do not know what the arrangements in Lancaster were—time will tell us all about it.[69]

I am very uneasy.

Dr. Murphy of Cork received an account of the confirmation of our Rule. Dr. Murray has not yet & is much surprised.

Pray for me. God bless you.

Your affectionate
M. C. M.

Autograph: Burlingame

67 On August 19 at Baggot Street, seven sisters professed their vows: Mary Vincent Whitty, who in 1860 will found a community in Brisbane, Australia, after many years of creative leadership in the Dublin community; Mary Francis Creedon, who in 1842 will found the Sisters of Mercy in Newfoundland; Mary Justina Fleming, who will die on December 10, 1841, in Tullamore, where she went in hope of improving her health; and Mary Juliana Hardman, Mary Xavier Wood, Mary Vincent Bond, and Mary Cecilia Edwards, who on August 21 will found the community in Birmingham, England, with Juliana Hardman later appointed their superior. In addition, three women received the habit that day: Margaret Teresa Dwyer, whose name in religion is not known; Margaret Teresa Geraghty, who took the name Mary Baptist, and went on the foundation to Liverpool in August 1843; and Frances Gibson, who took the name Mary Liguori, and went on the foundation to Liverpool in August 1843. In 1849 Mary Liguori succeeded Mary de Sales White as superior of the Liverpool community and served in that capacity for twenty-nine years. 68 The group sailing at night on August 20 from Kingstown to Liverpool and then going by train to Birmingham included the founding community—Juliana Hardman, Mary Xavier Wood, Mary Vincent Bond, Cecilia Edwards, Mary Magdalen Polding (a novice), and Mary Angela Borini (a novice); Mary Cecilia Marmion, who would assist the new community until late December; Redmond O'Hanlon, Myles Gaffney, Catherine McAuley, and her travelling companion, Mary Liguori Gibson. This was Catherine McAuley's last journey to establish a new foundation of the Sisters of Mercy—her ninth in less than five and a half years. 69 Whatever communication Catherine McAuley received about the Liverpool foundation, the document seems to be no longer extant.

297. To Sister M. Frances Warde   Convent, Birmingham
     Carlow   [c. August 25, 1841]

My Dearest Sister M. F.

I could not get half an hour till this moment to write to you—so many persons calling etc., etc. We had our ceremony on Thursday and sailed on Friday—got here about 4 o'c on Saturday, had scarcely time to put on guimps etc., when we were summoned to the choir, where the Right Revd. Dr. Wiseman in full Pontificals recited the *Te Deum*—said a few animating words & concluded with fervent prayer for the aid of almighty God.[70]

The Convent is beautiful—and fully furnished for 20 Sisters. Mr. Pugin would not permit cloth of any kind on the rooms—rush chairs and oak Tables—but all is so admirable, so religious, that no want can be felt. The whole building cost but three thousand pounds. I would say 6—without hesitation. We expect a Sister in a few days—many are spoken of—but one concluded for.[71]

Very bad accounts of Dr. Brown—'tis said his recovery is very doubtful.[72] Father O'H[anlon] came with us. We were most happily circumstanced travelling—9 of us—Father Gaffney, who was our Guardian Angel, & Mr. O'H., & Dr. Brown, Bishop of Kilmore—who was going to Leamington—joined us, which made up 6 for each Train Carriage, & we had not one stranger amongst us. Mr. O'Hanlon most kindly went to London to bring Sisters de Sales & Xavier to me. I expect them this day.

Old Mr. Hardman whose death was expected has rallied wonderfully. They are a most holy family.

I am afraid of being interrupted again—and in half an hour I will be too late for the Post. We cannot miss the time here—as the clock chymes the quarters. The Convent bell weighs 140 pounds—it is hard work to ring it.

God almighty bless you, my Dear Sister M. Frances. Love to all.

                                        Pray for your affectionate
                                                    M. C. M.

Sister M. Cecilia desires her love. My respects to Dr. Fitzgerald & Father Maher.

The ceiling of the choir is blue & gold with the word—Mercy—in every type and character all over it.

Autograph: Pittsburgh

---

70 This ceremony in the chapel of the new convent in Birmingham took place in the late afternoon on August 21, 1841.   71 Lucy Powell, a niece of Mary Juliana Hardman, entered the Birmingham convent on August 28, 1841 (Birmingham Register).   72 Dr. George Hilary Brown, vicar apostolic of the Lancashire District, had evidently become very ill during August. He recovered.

298. To a Sister of Mercy[73]

[Birmingham]
[Late August 1841]

The convent is very nice indeed. They tell me it cost three thousand pounds, though there is not one rib of stucco, or one panelled door, except in the chapel. I have never seen so plain a building. I have seldom seen such a general favourite as Mr. Pugin is in this part of England. Nothing is perfect that he does not plan and execute. He has manifested much taste, yet I do think some of his plans would admit of improvement; for example, he has brought the cells close to the chapel-door, which will, I fear, be attended with some inconvenience. I do not admire his gilded figures of saints; they are very coarse representations, and by no means calculated to inspire devotion. The stained glass and the ceiling of the chapel, with the word 'Mercy' at least one hundred times, in varied characters, are very beautiful. It may be said the sisters are surrounded with mercy.

[M. C. McAuley]

Published transcription: Harnett, Life *189–90*

299. To Dr. George Joseph Plunket Browne
Galway

Convent of our Lady
of Mercy
Birmingham
August 30, 1841

Dear and much respected Lord

I have just had the honor to receive your esteemed letter, and deeply regret that I am not to have the happiness of uniting with my beloved Sisters on the joyful occasion of their holy Profession.[74] Even in this very warm weather, my Lord, if I remain any time in a room with a window open, I am coughing all night and disturbing the poor Sisters who are near me. I propose returning to Baggot Street on the 20th of September, and expect to be confined to a close room, as the least blast—makes me very troublesome for several days together, but to travel in October would be very imprudent indeed, my Lord.

How I wish your Lordship could see this beautiful convent—executed by Mr. Pugin in the ancient monastic style. I almost think you would try to get such in Galway, for your Daughters of Mercy.[75]

73 No autograph, photostat, photocopy, or handcopy of this letter has been discovered. It appears only in Harnett's *Life* (189–90), and there only partially. One suspects that Harnett, without citing the recipient, is quoting a paragraph from a letter to Elizabeth Moore or to herself—one of the last letters Elizabeth or she might have received from Catherine McAuley. Harnett explains that Catherine is here describing the Birmingham convent.   74 In Galway, Mary Joseph Joyce and Mary de Sales McDonnell were preparing for profession of vows in October. Catherine McAuley had long spoken of attending this ceremony. Mary de Sales later went to Westport, and founded the convent in Sligo in 1846. She died in 1854 (Clarke 12).   75 Catherine's view of the architectural

The good Bishop here celebrated Mass for us yesterday, and this day Doctor Wiseman is giving a course of Lectures in the grand Cathedral, commencing with the novel opinions of the 16th century, placing before the congregation the arguments and reasoning of both parties. Doctor Walsh said there were at least twelve hundred persons yesterday at the preparatory discourse, some hundreds of whom were Protestants. It is expected they will produce many converts.

My Lord, I should now apologise for encroaching on your valuable time. Begging to thank your Lordship for all your kindness to me and Sisters, and entreating your charitable remembrance, I have the honor to remain,

My Lord, most respectfully
your obedient servant
M. C. McAuley

My Lord, Sister M. de Sales desires her most respectful remembrance.[76]

Autograph: Galway

---

work of Augustus Welby Pugin softened somewhat, after she saw his design of the Birmingham convent.   **76** This postscript indicates that Mary de Sales White and Mary Xavier O'Connell had already come to Birmingham from London and were ready to return to Dublin with Catherine McAuley and Mary Liguori (Frances) Gibson. Mary de Sales, the sister of Teresa White, superior in Galway, had met Dr. George J. P. Browne, bishop of Galway, when she accompanied Catherine and Teresa on the founding journey to Galway in May 1840, and again in October 1840.

September–November 1841

The final months of Catherine McAuley's life were, until two or three weeks before the end, not unlike the previous ten years. She travelled home from Birmingham on September 20–21; she grieved the death of a priest devoted to the poor; she wrote affectionate letters to several sisters; she reviewed her copy of the confirmed Rule and Constitutions of the Sisters of Mercy and met with an official from Rome about some "evident mistakes"; she admitted she had had a "surfeit of travelling"; she arranged for the dying Justina Fleming to receive care in Tullamore where the air was better for her; she responded to the claim of a building supplier that she owed £130 for "timber and slates"; she secured a £20 legacy bequeathed to the community; and, in one extant letter, she acknowledged that she had twice seen a physician specializing in ailments of the chest who said her right lung was "diseased."

Catherine's letters of this period are written in the same strong hand as her earlier letters though one notices an occasional missing or repeated word in some of the autographs. The correspondence presented here ends with the official announcements of her final illness, and of her death on November 11, 1841. These letters are followed by three undated documents: two poem-transcriptions and her most detailed statement about the "spirit" of the religious order she had founded.

Only in the last two weeks of her life, when Catherine McAuley was bedridden, was there any alteration of her ministry. Then the humility that had long characterized her self-perception took the form of relinquishing to others, with encouraging confidence in their abilities, some of her personal responsibilities as superior, and doing what she could, in the days that remained, to shore up the fragile financial condition of the Baggot Street community. She had seen in the new postulants and novices at Baggot Street and in the foundations beyond Dublin some of "the fire Christ cast—kindling." In the end her own inner fire burned with exquisite compassion, even to her requesting the sisters gathered about her in her last hours "to get a good cup of tea ... when I am gone and to comfort one another" (Mary Vincent Whitty to Mary Cecilia Marmion, November 12, 1841, in Sullivan, *Catherine McAuley* 243).

300. **To Sister Teresa Carton**[1]   Convent [Birmingham]
     Baggot Street   Monday, September 6, 1841

My Dear Sister Teresa

I am going to give you some cautions and commissions. Mother de Pazzi tells me the parlours are colouring. I hope you will be very careful not to get fresh cold—do not go to sit in the room until it is perfectly dry—I hope the chimneys of both were well swept before the ceilings were whitened.[2]

Bespeak an Iron Bedsted wherever you can get it made in one week—the direction as follows [*a portion of the autograph is here cut out*].[3]

You will try to get this done exactly, make the person read it well—he will think the Bed too near the ground—but it is to be so. The pattern of the cheque is in my Desk or flat Box—get it also.[4] Have the Infirmary very well cleaned. Move your Bed to where Sister M. Clare's is,[5] and clear out your corner for mine, where I will not hear the noise of the street. I will want a fire.

When I think of the day you will get this—I suppose the 8th, it seems impossible to have it done, in time. You may try—& it would be ready in a day or two after. You are not to leave the room—a little coughing will never disturb me. I am much better there. Some days—very bad appetite, I do not like the bread or butter, it is quite different.

Do not have any hurry about getting the Bed done. It will be time enough— the 3rd Bed to be taken away.

It is strange to me, my Dear Sr. Teresa, to write so much about myself— and give such trouble. My [*illegible word*] love to all.

Your ever affectionate
M. C. McAuley

Autograph (severely damaged) and photocopy: Dublin, Mercy

1 This autograph letter written from Birmingham is severely damaged. It was preserved for a long time by strips of tape. It was also recently conserved by a process that all but removed the handwriting as well as the damaging effects of the tape. However, a photocopy made before the autograph was sent to the conservator contains the handwriting, though faintly. The photocopy as well as the autograph have been used in presenting the text of this important letter in which Catherine McAuley asks to have an infirmary bed prepared for her use after she returns from Birmingham. 2 By "colouring" Catherine means "being painted." She is concerned that Teresa Carton's lung condition may be worsened by the dampness of rooms in which the paint has not yet dried. 3 The "direction"—i.e., the address and other instructions—for the workman who will make the iron bedstead has been cut off the bottom of sides 1 and 2 of the autograph, evidently so that Teresa Carton could take that piece of the letter with her to the workman's shop. 4 The "cheque" was apparently the checkered (or "chequered") fabric that was used for the curtains around each sister's bed and perhaps for the bed covering. Catherine is not referring to a means of paying for the bedstead. 5 Mary Clare Augustine Moore had gone temporarily to Cork in June 1841. The room Catherine McAuley is asking to have arranged, the room in which she eventually died, is now preserved as "Catherine's Room," on the first floor of Mercy International Centre, Baggot Street, Dublin.

301. **Statement** [September 1841]

Institution of Mercy established in[6]

The Sisters of this Religious order are particularly devoted to the education of poor girls—visitation of the sick and the protection of young women of good character.

In the visitation of the sick, the Sisters are obliged by their regulations to employ every practicable means to promote cleanliness, and to be exceedingly cautious in the distribution of relief, making every enquiry that may lead to a true knowledge of each case. The Sisters carry nourishment and clothing to the Sick, and very seldom give money except for fire and light. It would be impossible to give a just description of these scenes of sorrow, where in addition to the anguish of death, all around are in want and misery, and even when a poor family are not deprived of their usual support—the weak and sick are often found pining away unable to partake of it.

When the funds of a new Establishment are not sufficient to provide a House of Mercy, for the protection of destitute young women, the Sisters procure Lodgings, and afford assistance to as many as their means will admit until suitable employment is obtained. If after being placed in situations, they are found diligent and strictly correct, yet are obliged to leave from ill health, incapacity or their services being no longer required, they may return to the care of the Sisters until again provided for, but if dismissed with any charge of dishonesty ...

[M. C. McAuley]

Autograph (severely damaged) and photocopy: Dublin, Mercy

6 The heading is incomplete in the autograph. Apparently Catherine McAuley wrote a notice like this one, for the newspapers or other public display, each time a new foundation of the Sisters of Mercy was established in a city or town. John MacErlean wrote the following note about this autograph: "The blue ink is similar [presumably to that used in Letter 300]; if written 6 Sept. '41 it must have been written in Birmingham ... I am inclined to think this is the original (6 Sept. '41) for the benefit of English enquirers" (Typescript inserted in bound volume of photostats, *Letters of Mother McAuley: 1841*, Mercy Congregational Archives, Dublin). The autograph is one sheet of paper, and like Letter 300 it is damaged by faulty conservation. The last words, "charge of dishonesty," are written in Catherine McAuley's hand on the back of the sheet. Evidently she did not complete the statement. Reading the autograph is helped by reference to an early photocopy.

Similar notices appeared almost annually in the *Irish Catholic Directory*. For example, in the *Directory* for 1837, under the heading "Institution of Mercy, Baggot-Street," appears a paragraph descriptive of the "free school," the visitation of the sick, and the House of Mercy (157). An almost identical paragraph (to the 1837 version) appears in the *Irish Catholic Directory* for 1839 (181–82). The version Catherine wrote in 1841, as presented here, is much more detailed about the visitation of the sick and the House of Mercy.

302. To Sister Mary Aloysius Scott
Birr

[Birmingham]
[September 17, 1841]

My Dearest Sister M. Aloysius

I have been very weak and sick for the last 12 or 14 days. We return on Monday. I did not intend to write till we changed quarters, but your account of poor Father Toohey [Tuohy] has so distressed me.[7] You may be sure we will pray most fervently for him. I hope you will let us know how he goes on—I shall be most anxious to hear—I am delighted you visit him—& have every hope of his recovery. Endless visitors coming in here & I cannot leave the one aired room without coughing violently. God bless & preserve you.

Your ever affectionate
M. C. McAuley

As your note is not dated, I do not know when it was written. It was delivered here—12 o'c this day, Friday 17th.

Autograph: Dublin, Mercy

303. To Sister Mary Aloysius Scott
Birr

[Baggot Street]
[September 21, 1841]

My Dearest Sr. M. Aloysius

After writing a few lines to Mother Cecilia to tell her we got safe—I wish to tell you how sincerely I regret the death of dear Father Toohey [Tuohy].[8] May God receive him into everlasting happiness. He was a kind creature to the Poor & I suppose it is a disguised blessing, that God has called him in all his youthful fervor before coldness or indifference towards the poor would render him less acceptable to Almighty God.

Just half an hour before we left Birmingham yesterday, I received your letter, and one from Carlow—Galway & Bermondsey—I could not go there[9]—nor ever go out, even to the Garden.

May God preserve & bless you all.

Your ever affectionate
M. C. M.

Autograph: Dublin, Mercy

7 "Edmund Toohey" is listed as a curate in Birr in the *Irish Catholic Directory* for 1841 (304), as well as in the *Directory* for 1840 (293) and for 1839 (244). However, in the "Clerical Obituary" for 1841, he is listed on September 17 as "Edward Tuohy, C. C. Birr" (*Irish Catholic Directory* [1842] 437). 8 The curate's death occurred on September 17, 1841, the same day as the death, at age sixty-eight, of Catherine McAuley's old friend John McCormick, curate in Blackrock. Father McCormick had welcomed Catherine's sister Mary back into the Catholic church in 1827 (Sullivan, *Catherine McAuley* 41, 47). As Catherine wrote this letter she may have been unaware of John McCormick's death, having just arrived home from Birmingham that morning. 9 That is, to Bermondsey.

304. To Sister Mary Ann Doyle
Tullamore

Baggot St.
September 24, 1841[10]

My Dear Sister M. A.

I am now going to give you a little trouble, or rather to beg you to accept it. A dear much valued Sister in a most delicate state thinks she would receive benefit from change of air which has been prescribed for her. Mr. O'Hanlon, our ever dear good Father, would go with her on Monday next, if you can admit her. I need not recommend her to your tenderness, I know she will experience every mark of affection tho' a stranger. All expenses of course will be defrayed. Write me a line immediately, that we may have her ready. She is one of the last professed—Sister M. Justina.[11]

I received your letter in Birmingham and will reply to it soon. I am going to propose myself—as Deputy to Doctor O'Rafferty in the guardenship [*sic*] of your Convent.[12] Your good Bishop was *much* mistaken as to property here—we have ever confided largely in Divine Providence—and shall continue to do so.[13] God bless you.

Your ever affectionate
M. C. McAuley

Autograph: Tullamore

305. To Sister M. Frances Warde
Carlow

Convent [Baggot Street]
September 25, 1841

My Dearest Sister M. Frances

I received your note about half an hour before we left Birmingham. We had a weary passage from Liverpool—kept 3 hours waiting for water & did not arrive in Kingstown till 9 o'c.[14] The poor Sisters had comfortable Tea etc. for us. We rested there till 12 o'c. Sister Xavier is much improved—Sister de Sales just the same poor "skin & bone."[15]

10 On the cover of this posted letter addressed to "Mrs. Doyle, Convent, Tullamore" Catherine McAuley wrote "Speed." 11 Mary Justina Fleming, who had just professed her vows on August 19, was now in Booterstown. Catherine hopes to send her—with Redmond O'Hanlon and Mary Vincent Whitty accompanying her—to Tullamore on Monday, September 27. 12 This is a remarkable offer, given what is now known about Catherine McAuley's health at this time. It supports the view that Catherine was not yet aware that she was dying, although two days later (see Letter 306), she will report that she has seen the physician twice. In general, the correspondence of the next seven weeks suggests that very few, possibly excluding Catherine herself, thought that she was in her last illness, until very near her death. 13 Evidently Dr. John Cantwell, bishop of Meath, who resided in Mullingar, was under the false impression that there was considerable money at Baggot Street that could assist the Tullamore convent. 14 On Tuesday morning, September 21, 1841. 15 Mary Xavier O'Connell and Mary de Sales White, who had been helping out in Bermondsey

I had with me the young novice, Sr. Gibson—she has had great family afflictions.[16] Her poor Papa now in London after some severe operation—& her
Mamma's letters such as tis wonderful she could bear. Never did I see a vocation
so proved. Doctor Youens who is an intimate friend had her Mamma to meet us
at his house[17]—we dined with him as the Packet did not sail till near eight. He
brought us to look at the place where he intends to build a Convent. It is very
well suited, quite close to the Town with 3 good approaches to it. The present
House, he says, shall remain for a "House of Mercy." We "dressed for dinner"
so he and some of his Priests have now seen the full costume which they like very
much.[18] He seems quite ardent in the matter. He sent a Sister in my absence—
for that foundation, a Miss Concitt[19]—a very nice person indeed. Dr. Brown is
gone to travel for health. He arranged with Dr. Youens to proceed as Dr. Walsh
did—to have english subjects prepared in the Mother House.[20]

Sister Juliana Hardman was appointed Superior before I left. Sister M.
C[ecilia] will be home at Christmas—which will be great relief here.[21]

I think Birmingham will be a most flourishing House—and Bermondsey is
all alive since "Paddy" left—such has been the promise given by some unknown
letter writer. Amongst the most amiable, we could clearly discover—a desire that
John Bull should be the head on all occasions. Lady Barbara, Sister de Sales, has
gone out to visit the sick though she never did so while our Sisters were there.
Miss Kellet has or is about to join them. She takes her "dear Jane's cell"—two
more are concluding. I am sure they will go on now with great ardor.[22]

---

for almost a year, went from London to Birmingham in late August, and then returned to Dublin
with Catherine McAuley on September 20–21.   16 Catherine is speaking of Mary Liguori (Frances)
Gibson, who had received the habit at Baggot Street on August 19 and then accompanied Catherine
to Birmingham, with a stop in Liverpool on their return trip.   17 Dr. Thomas Youens, pastor of
the parish in Liverpool where an eventual foundation of the Sisters of Mercy will be situated (in
1843).   18 When the sisters were travelling, they wore travelling attire that was different from their
habits and veils.   19 Mary Anne Consitt, who was born in Durham, England in 1817, entered the
Baggot Street community for the future foundation in Liverpool on August 31, 1841, while Catherine
McAuley was in Birmingham.   20 Dr. George Hilary Brown, vicar apostolic of the Lancashire
District, has now settled that he wants the Liverpool foundation to come from Baggot Street, not
from Carlow as Catherine McAuley and Frances Warde had once hoped.   21 When Catherine left
Birmingham, Mary Cecilia Marmion was asked to remain there until after the profession ceremony
of Mary Magdalen Polding and Mary Angela Borini. That ceremony, as well as the reception of
Lucy Powell who had entered the Birmingham community on August 28, took place in St. Chad's
Cathedral, Birmingham, on December 6, 1841. A manuscript account of the early days in
Birmingham, written in November 1909, says that Cecilia returned to Dublin in January 1842
("Account of Foundation of St. Mary's Hunter's Road ... 1841–1856," [5]–[6]). However, the book
of Acts of the Chapter at Baggot Street records that on January 2, 1842, Mary Cecilia Marmion
"was elected to the offices of Mother Assistant and Mistress of Novices" ([4]), the election to these
two offices having been delayed until her "return ... from Birmingham" ([3]). Hence, she must have
returned to Baggot Street before January 2, 1842, probably in mid or late December. In a letter to
Cecilia written on November 16, 1841, Mary Vincent Whitty reminds her that Catherine McAuley
"got Mother Elizabeth [Moore] to write to you to hurry home" (Sullivan, *Catherine McAuley* 245).
22 Here Catherine reflects on the early Irish-English tension in the Bermondsey community. She

I am afraid of being interrupted. May God bless you and all.

Your ever affectionate
M. C. McAuley

Autograph: Silver Spring

306. To Sister Mary Aloysius Scott   Sunday [or Friday] Morning
Birr   Baggot Street
                                                                                    [September 26 or 24, 1841][23]

My Dear Sister M. Aloysius

I write in haste as you have done, to prevent your sending any fruit. My Dear, those who are not accustomed to pack fruit—could never send it such a journey without [its] being greatly injured. I hope you have the charity to eat some fresh fruit off the trees, walking in the garden—as that is the way fruit is most beneficial to delicate constitutions. How happy it would make me if I knew you were doing all in your power to keep up your strength amidst such a variety of occupations, and so constant. God send you help soon.

Sister Justina has been in the Doctor's hands and is gone to Booterstown.[24] The poor cook, Sr. Elizabeth, also gone, after influenza.

---

also notes that Henrietta Kellet from Wexford will enter the Bermondsey convent on September 27, 1841. "Jane" may be Mary Xaveria (Jane) Latham, who had been dismissed from the community in October 1840, or more likely Mary de Sales (Jane) White who was also from Wexford. The "two more … concluding" in September 1841 were Georgina Booker who entered on October 7, 1841, and Elizabeth Baxter, on November 20, 1841 (Bermondsey Annals 1:17, 27). These two women became devoted members of the Bermondsey community, Mary Aloysius Booker eventually serving as mother assistant of the community before the death of Mary Clare Moore in 1874.

While Catherine McAuley was aware of some problems in Bermondsey, in its early years and in the months before her death, she was not in the end alarmed by them, and died believing, so far as one can tell from her extant correspondence, that the community would go on "with great ardor." She was conscious of Mary Clare Agnew's flaws as a superior (June—December 1841), but apparently did not know of their severity nor did she anticipate the imminent outcome: Clare Agnew's removal from office and Clare Moore's return as superior on December 10, 1841. The problems in Bermondsey came to a head as Catherine was dying, and those knowledgeable of the crisis evidently spared her this worry, so far as one can tell from extant records.

23 In the editions of Neumann (374–76) and Bolster (259–60) this letter is dated September 20, 1841, but that date is not correct. Catherine McAuley was still in Birmingham and then in Liverpool on Monday, September 20. On Monday night she took the overnight steam packet from Liverpool, arriving in Kingstown (Dún Laoghaire) on Tuesday morning, September 21. Previous editors also read Catherine's "Sunday" (or "Friday"?) as "Tuesday." Catherine wrote briefly to Mary Aloysius Scott on September 21 (see Letter 303), but the present letter was written on Sunday, September 26, or on Friday, September 24, 1841. Admittedly, Catherine's handwriting here is very difficult to decipher.   24 See Letter 304. Although Justina Fleming is ill in Booterstown, a more restful place for her than Baggot Street, Catherine awaits word from Mary Ann Doyle that Justina will be welcomed in Tullamore.

My cough very variable—one night bad, another good. Five minutes in a room with a window ever so little open brings on an hour's coughing, great expectoration, yet I am not weak—tho' I cannot say I have any appetite.

Mr. O'Hanlon particularly requested I would consult Dr. Stokes.[25] I have seen him twice. On his first visit he looked like a person who had made a great discovery. On his second—Mother de Pazzi conducted him out and returned with such sorrow in her countenance that I entreated her to tell me his opinion.

My Right Lung was "diseased"—I have now less confidence than ever in the faculty,[26] and you know my stock was small enough. I do not think my lung is affected. I am now dead to the poor children—not to read, speak—give out office, etc. I tell you all these particulars—to give you the benefit of experience.[27] If my lung is actually engaged—the progress will not be checked, and the fact of no debility—not half so much as I have had when my gums were enflamed—shews that it cannot be.

Ordering a linament to be applied to my chest—he desired my servant to do it. Mother de P—has got that appointment. I call every night for my servant. Sister M. Catherine[28] administers medicine & Sr. L[ucy] Vincent[29] is head cook—making nice rennet whey, light puddings, etc., etc. I am very sure her Majesty[30] is not attended with half so much care, often most ungraciously received by a poor unfortunate peevish old sinner, who never required any particular care or attention before, and who is more weary of it than of the delicacy that occasions it. To the affectionate often repeated question—Revd. Mother, what could you take—the best answer is—My heart, you teise [tease] me very much.

As we should carefully examine the motive of our actions—I here humbly confess that my chief motive—just now—is to shew that one of the most distinguished amongst our medical professors may be mistaken[31]—and that we should not immediately take up their opinions.

God bless you and all with you, my ever dear Sister M. Aloysius.

Pray for your affectionate
M. C. McAuley

25 Dr. William Stokes, MD (1804–1878), was one of the most distinguished physicians in Ireland. In 1825, "he published ... 'An Introduction to the Use of the Stethoscope,' one of the earliest treatises on the subject in English." His treatise on "Diseases of the Chest," published in 1837, was a landmark in its day and "will always be useful as a model of medical exposition" (*DNB* 54:401–403). 26 That is, the faculty of medicine. 27 Catherine is mindful of the possibility that Mary Aloysius Scott's lung disease will recur. In this letter she gives for Mary Aloysius's benefit more detail about her own illness than in any other extant letter. 28 Mary Catherine Gogarty, a novice. 29 Mary Vincent Whitty, whom Catherine mistakenly calls "Lucy Vincent," the name she had once used for Mary Vincent (Lucy) Bond (now in Birmingham) when there were two Mary Vincents in the Baggot Street convent. 30 Queen Victoria. 31 Catherine probably knew that Dr. William Stokes was rarely if ever mistaken about diseases of the chest, but she did not wish to alarm Mary Aloysius or any Sister of Mercy.

I should add that it was not the Dr. desired me not read, etc.—it was Fr. O'Hanlon. The Dr. in a melancholy tone—left me to my own wishes—I might take any thing I liked. He seemed evidently to regard the case as hopeless.

Autograph: Dublin, Mercy

307. Dr. Nicholas Foran[32]   [Late September–October 1841]
Waterford

Much respected Lord

When I was just about to leave Ireland—with some english Sisters who had made preparation here to form an Establishment in Birmingham—the Revd. Dr. Kirby[33] called to convey a message from your Lordship signifying your desire to have a branch of our Institute formed in Waterford. I would feel greatly delighted indeed, my Lord, to do all in my power to promote the desired object, and as experience has afforded me some useful information on the subject, I will take the liberty of suggesting the best mode of proceeding. If your Lordship, through the agency of your respected Clergy, could meet three, four, or five educated persons with mar[k]ed vocations—good constitutions, young if possible, who would come to the Mother House[34] to prepare for their own—this Establishment is so extensive, my Lord, it affords constant instruction by practice & example—and if your Lordship could send such Ladies as I have [described] I would have every hope of returning them to you—acquainted with their state as Religious—and well practiced in the corporal and spiritual works of Mercy. I have the honor to remain, my Lord,

Yours with great respect,
your humble servant in J.C.
M. C. M.

Autograph: Merion

308. To Sister M. Juliana Hardman   Saint Mary's, Baggot Street
Birmingham   October 2, 1841

My Very Dear Sister Mary Juliana

I am most happy to hear that the little affairs at Saint Ethelreda's go on so

---

32 Dr. Nicholas Foran was bishop of the diocese of Waterford and Lismore. This autograph is the draft of the letter Catherine McAuley actually sent to him. That letter has not been found. 33 Dr. Tobias Kirby, an Irish priest, was vice-rector of the Irish College, Rome, at this time, serving under the then rector, Dr. Paul Cullen. 34 Catherine McAuley here refers to the Baggot Street convent as the "mother house" though she does not mean the term in any governmental sense. She is simply acknowledging the fact that the convent on Baggot Street was the first convent of the Sisters of Mercy and bore the special responsibilities of the "first born."

well.[35] I am not yet quite comfortable, in the Community room or refectory. What would I not give to see my dear nurse coming with her whey.[36] I believe that would not satisfy, I should want to see them all. May God protect and bless them.

I have great consolation, in reflecting on the arrangements we have made. Every day I feel a strong conviction that it was the best mode of proceeding. The only thing that embitters it a little is the recollection that it gave pain to you.[37]

We like our new English Sr. very much indeed.[38] She is getting quite impatient for another, as her month is out. I think we should feel strange now without a little mixture of England amongst us.

They had a grand ceremony in Naas a few days since, and some wild reporter has published—that we have spread into eighty branches. I suppose the answer to his enquiry was—eighteen, which includes those not yet established, though arranged for.[39] Should you hear of this great flourish, be sure, contradict it.

Sister Vincent returned yesterday from Tullamore. Poor Sr. Justina wonderfully relieved by the change, yet there is no reason to hope that it will be more than temporary.[40]

I shall be looking most anxiously for a long letter, tho' not deserving as I am so often heard exclaiming against them. I am quite certain of hearing that all goes on happily, and that each of my most dear Sisters will give their whole heart to the good work in which God has engaged them, with a pure intention of pleas-

---

35 The convent in Birmingham was initially named St. Etheldreda's. Its name was later changed to St. Mary's (Dickinson et al. 13–15).   36 While Catherine McAuley was in Birmingham, Juliana Hardman or another of the founding community had nursed her with the watery part of milk that is separated from the curd in the process of making cheese. Whey is rich in nutrients.   37 Mary Juliana Hardman (1813–1884) was named superior of the Birmingham community on September 6, 1841, two weeks before Catherine left Birmingham. She was then twenty-eight years old. She served as superior for thirty-five years.   38 Mary Anne Consitt entered the Dublin community on August 31, 1841.   39 The "eighteen branches" Catherine counts are Dublin, Tullamore, Charleville, Carlow, Cork, Limerick, Naas, Bermondsey, Galway, Wexford, Birr, Birmingham, the branch houses in Kingstown and Booterstown, and four foundations already "arranged for": Newfoundland (1842), Westport (1842), Liverpool (1843), and one other. Carroll notes that the Westport convent was founded on September 9, 1842 from Carlow, "at the request of Very Rev. Dean Burke, who, applying to the holy foundress herself for a foundation, was recommended by her to Carlow, Baggot Street being at the moment unable to supply him" (*Leaves* 2:531–32). The eighteenth foundation Catherine has in mind cannot be identified with certainty. It may be Waterford (see Letter 307), but no foundation occurred in that city in the 1840s; a convent in Cappoquin, also in the diocese of Waterford and Lismore, was founded from Wexford in 1850 (Carroll, *Leaves* 1:407). She may be aware of arrangements underway for a convent in Sunderland, England, founded from Cork on October 15, 1843, or she may be thinking of the convent requested for Ennis, or for Nottingham, which was founded on February 6, 1844 from Birmingham (see Letter 188).   40 Mary Vincent Whitty and Redmond O'Hanlon accompanied Mary Justina Fleming to Tullamore. The Tullamore Annals says of her: "Poor child! She gradually sank, but yet survived her beloved Mother [Catherine McAuley] whose death had a great effect on her. She died on the 10th December and was waked in the Convent Chapel ... the first death of a religious in Tullamore ... Her remains were conveyed to Dublin, by her father who came in tears to perform this last sad office to his beloved daughter, and buried with the Community in Baggot St. as there was no Cemetery prepared here as yet" (45).

ing Him. And my own dear Sister Juliana will do all in her power to fill the place allotted to her, and will pray fervently for those animating graces which will lead us on in uniform peace, making the yoke of our Dear Redeemer easy, etc., etc.

My fondest love to each dear Sister. My respectful and best regards to your good Father and Mother—you will tell me particularly how dear Father is. Remember me to Brother—and give my affectionate love to Mrs. John and my Sister Mary if returned.[41] I hope you do not encroach on her privileges.

The school persons not arrived yet.[42]

I kept for the last what I know you will like to hear—that every person who has seen me since my return, thinks I look much better.

Pray for me and believe me, my own ever Dear Sr. Juliana, your affectionate

Mary C. McAuley

Autograph: Birmingham

309. **To Sister M. Frances Warde**[43]   St. Mary's
    Carlow   Feast of St. Francis
                                        [October 4, 1841]

My Dear Sr. M. Frances

The poor Sr. whose case we consider hopeless—as to this poor life—is now 10 days in Tullamore. She revived very much—but no lasting strength has returned. Blessed is the sweet spotless soul—getting rapidly out of this miserable world. We have our own cemetary at length prepared but I am sure she will

---

41 Catherine sends greetings to all the Hardman family, including Juliana's elder sister Mary and her sister-in-law, Mrs. John Hardman, Jr. Mary Hardman entered the Birmingham community in 1843, became superior of the Maryvale Convent of Mercy in 1854, and died in 1855 (Carroll, *Leaves* 2:314).   42 The meaning of "The school persons not arrived yet" is obscure. The words are preceded and followed by dashes, the first a bit longer. It is unclear whether the words go with the comment about Mary Hardman's privileges and so pertain to Birmingham, or whether they begin a new paragraph and a new thought pertaining to Baggot Street. The latter is probably the case, but even then the reference is not clear.   43 This autograph letter to Frances Warde is the most severely damaged of all the autographs: it is in pieces that are damaged at the edges, with some parts missing, so it cannot be re-assembled into a whole letter. When the autograph in its present state was sent from Our Lady of Mercy Convent in St. Louis, Missouri, where it was found, to the archives of the Sisters of Mercy in Bethesda, Maryland in 1967 (and thence in the early 1990s to Silver Spring) it was already without a closing or signature (Mary Kevin Trower to Mary Stella Maris Bergin, March 29, 1967, Archives, Silver Spring). It is possible that a whole page is missing. I have included here, in brackets, the end of the letter as given in M. Angela Bolster, *Correspondence*, 264. However, where Bolster has "Sr. M. Ursula Frayne is my nurse," in Letter 311 for which the autograph is extant Catherine writes "Sr. de Sales [White] … is my constant affectionate Nurse." Possibly both women served in that capacity at different times. Ursula Frayne was the superior in the branch house in Booterstown, but evidently came frequently to Baggot Street during Catherine's illness. Mary Ignatia Neumann does not include the letter in her edition.

find the first place in the nice vault at Tullamore as cheerful as any part of the
Convent. May God support & comfort her to the end.

I would indeed like much to go to you—if I could do so without a journey
of 80 miles. If ever any poor creature got—what is called a surfeit[44]—Irish &
English—I have.

Singing just beside me or all the noise they make in the Community [*damaged, illegible words*] at my hour of retiring would not [disturb] me, tho' close to
them, but the sound of a carriage wheel rouses me at once. I have but little
appetite.

[My affectionate Sr. M. Ursula Frayne [[Mary de Sales White?]] is my nurse,
and never ceases thinking of something for me.

God bless you and all your charge. You will not forget

your ever affectionate
M. C. McAuley]

Autograph (severely damaged): Silver Spring

310. To Sister Mary Aloysius Scott   **[Baggot Street]**
    Birr   **Monday, Feast of St. Francis Assisi**
                                            [October 4, 1841]

My Dearest Sister M. Aloysius

I was thinking of my poor children in Birr during the night at different times
tho' I had quite enough of sleep. I made a kind of resolution to write this day, and
altho' the duty is now Mother de Pazzi's, yet I must keep my nocturnal resolution.

I am comforted by the recollection that poor Father Edmond[45] was not a frequent visitor. You would feel the loss so much more. I suppose you will often
see Father Frank Healy—not too often—you will all be better engaged.[46] I hope
Father F. will be as great a favorite with the poor as his Predecessor. I am sure
he will.

What is my dear Sister Vincent[47] doing? She ought to have great grand children before this. We met in Birmingham a most pious Nobleman, Lord Clifford.
He told us that he was asked for advice in a case of some difficulty. His Lordship
replyed—"Let the offended or afflicted person—repeat 3 Hail Marys 3 times a
day for eleven days. I never knew this remedy to fail." The desired effect was

---

44 That is, a surfeit of travelling.   45 Edmund Toohey or Tuohy, curate in Birr, died on September
17, 1841.   46 Frank Healy has not been identified. A Reverend James Healy was curate in
Ballingarry and Kilcoman, in the diocese of Killaloe, at the time (*Irish Catholic Directory* [1841]
304). Ballingarry is about thirteen miles southwest of Birr.   47 Mary Vincent (Susan) Egan, a
novice, had received the habit on May 20, 1841. Catherine was in Birr for the ceremony, and she
is here chiding Mary Vincent for not inspiring more young women—who would be Catherine's
"great grandchildren"—to enter the Birr community, by praying them in, as it were.

produced. Now, my Sister M. Vincent must not be offended—but she ought to be afflicted. Let her reflect on her loss until she becomes somewhat afflicted. She will then be a proper cliant [client] in this case and will obtain the benefit so often experienced and even very lately.

Why do they never write a line to their grandmother—Sister Vincent, Sr. M. Ann, my own conquest Sr. Magdeline, or my old own child, Sr. M. Rose—it is but just punishment for their neglect that their generations do not spring up.[48]

Birmingham is very promising—Sr. Juliana appointed superior—the second week we were there. Sr. Cecilia to be home before Christmas. This is the best arrangement we ever had—pleasing to Bishops, Priests, etc., etc.—to all but the dear amiable poor soul who is now Revd. Mother.

Pray who gave you such a false account of me, I am just as you saw me. Pray fervently that God may grant me the grace of a holy penitential preparation and the grace of a happy death. God bless you all.

Your ever affectionate
M. C. M.

We hear of many parcels going to Sr. M. Teresa[49]—what are they?
This is now called St. Mary's. Your child is Saint John's.[50]

Autograph: Dublin, Mercy

311. To Sister M. Teresa White[51]   Convent [Baggot Street]
Galway   October 7, 1841

My very Dear Sister M. Teresa
How heartily I rejoice that all difficulties have been surmounted, and our dear, dear Srs. Professed, thanks be to God. How I felt for them, kept in public till three o'clock fasting, but the holy delightful view that God inspired them to take of their mortified Redeemer at that hour—was well calculated to support and animate them.[52]

---

48 Again, Catherine is teasing Mary Vincent Egan, Mary Joseph (Mary Anne) Heenan, Mary Magdalen McEvoy, and Mary Rose Lynch for not writing to her, telling them it's only just that they have no new postulants in Birr—beyond Mary Wier (Weir) who entered on June 1, 1841— because they don't write to their "grandmother" (herself).   49 Mary Teresa (Catherine) White, of the Baggot Street community, remained in Birr from the time of the founding in late December 1840 until January 1843. In 1848, she "retired from religious life" (Dublin Register).   50 That is, the Baggot Street convent was now called St. Mary's, and the Birr convent, St. John's. After Catherine McAuley's death, the Baggot Street convent began to be called St. Catherine's.   51 The autograph of this letter has been damaged by what appear to be ink blotches. However, the writing is legible with the help of an early handcopy at Mercy Congregational Archives, Dublin. 52 On October 1, 1841, in Galway, Mary Joseph (Christina) Joyce and Mary de Sales (Ismena) McDonnell professed their vows. Clarke provides important information about Mary de Sales beyond that in the Galway records (11–15); Mary Joseph Joyce died of cholera in 1849.

My poor Sr. de Sales⁵³ was disappointed at not going to you, but as she is my constant affectionate Nurse, it was well for me, and indeed I am a troublesome child. I have felt the last heavy days very much—great increase of cough. Thank God this mild day has revived me.

You never mention Miss Lynch, your neighbour, or Miss Curran.⁵⁴ How do they go on. Your Mamma was here since we returned. She looks as well as I ever saw her, tho' she has been seriously ill.

Sister Mary Cecilia is to be home before Christmas, Sr. Juliana Hardman appointed Superior before I left.

We are now preparing a foundation for Liverpool.

I must try to write a few lines to my grandchildren.⁵⁵ God bless & protect you.

Pray for your affectionate
M. C. McAuley

Autograph: Galway

312. To Sister Mary Joseph Joyce   [Baggot Street]
Galway   [October 7, 1841]⁵⁶

My Very Dear Sister Mary Joseph

How sincerely, how joyfully, I congratulate you on the completion of your ardent hopes and wishes.⁵⁷ What a sweet and blessed union you have formed. Now it is that you must prove your love and gratitude by going hand in hand with your Divine Redeemer, nothing to interest you but what relates to His greater Glory. May He grant you every grace and blessing, and make you one of His dearest and best beloved.

Pray for your ever affectionate
Mary C. McAuley

Autograph: Galway

313. To Dean Bernard Burke⁵⁸   October 8, 1841
Westport

Many thanks, dear Reverend Father, for the kind concern you express about my health. I am really quite a fine lady, doing nothing but looking on, keeping

---

53 Mary de Sales White, Teresa's sister, would have been Catherine McAuley's travelling companion to Galway, had Catherine been able to make the journey. 54 See Letter 176, note 46. Miss Lynch did not enter the Sisters of Mercy, but at her death in 1845 willed the Magdalen Asylum she had founded on Lombard Street in Galway to the Sisters of Mercy. I am grateful to Teresa Delaney, Galway archivist, for this information. 55 That is, the young sisters in Galway. 56 This letter was not posted; it was probably enclosed in Letter 311. 57 The profession of her vows in early October 1841. 58 Bernard Burke was parish priest in Westport, Co. Mayo, and dean of the

up the little remnant for the foundations, and, above all, for Westport. Earnestly begging your charitable remembrance, I remain, dear respected Reverend Father, your very grateful Sister and servant in Christ

Mary C. McAuley

Published transcriptions: Harnett, Life *192, and Carroll,* Life *425*

314. **To Sister M. Frances Warde**   **[Baggot Street]**
      Carlow   **Tuesday, October 12, 1841**

My Dear Sister M. Frances

The Very Revd. Dr. Kirby, V[ice] P[resident] of the Irish College, Rome, called here the day before he sailed. I mentioned to him some evident mistakes in the Copy of our Rule. He told me to select them and forward the document to him, with Dr. Murray's signature, & said we would without any more trouble obtain permission to rectify the evident mistakes.[59]

I have felt the last bad change in the weather very much.

Father O'H brought your affectionate note. I humbly hope I am done with travelling for some time. If ever any poor sinner got a surfeit of it I have.

I forgot to add—what will occur to yourself—that I was cautioned not to speak of any mistake in the R[ule].[60]

God almighty bless you.

Your ever affectionate
M. C. McAuley

I have just received your welcome letter. How grateful I ought to be for all your anxiety. We shall meet again, please God, *but not at present.* I am sorry to hear poor Dr. Fitzgerald is suffering so much. Tell him I pray with all the fervor I can for his comfort, etc.[61]

Autograph: Silver Spring; published transcription: Carroll, Life *427*

---

archdiocese of Tuam. As noted earlier, he had asked Catherine McAuley for a foundation of Sisters of Mercy in Westport, and she referred him to Frances Warde. The foundation was made from Carlow on September 9, 1842. Dean Burke gave the Westport community "his own house and two hundred pounds towards the erection of a convent, for which the Marquis of Sligo gave a beautiful site of three acres." Dr. John MacHale, archbishop of Tuam, "gave seven hundred and seventy pounds for the same object" (Carroll, *Leaves* 2:532). No autograph or early handcopy of this letter has been discovered. However, the letter is published in Harnett's *Life* (192) and in Carroll's *Life* (425). The text presented here is Harnett's, with Carroll's closing. **59** Dr. Tobias Kirby (1804–1893) was a native of Tallow, Co. Waterford. He became rector of the Irish College, Rome, in 1850 when Dr. Paul Cullen became archbishop of Armagh (MacSuibhne 2:116). His relations with the Congregation for the Propagation of the Faith were strong, and he evidently was willing to negotiate the correction of the mistakes in the text of the Rule. However, corrections do not appear to have been ever requested (see Sullivan, *Catherine McAuley* 271–85). **60** Catherine writes "until" after "R[ule]," and then crosses it out. **61** The autograph of this letter presently consists

315. **To Catherine McAuley**   **Poolbeg St., Dublin**
                                                        October 13, 1841

Mrs. McAuley
    Madam,
    We beg leave to inform you that the Booterstown Convent is indebted to us
for the last 4 years about £130 for Timber & Slates supplied for its erection.[62]
We have waited expecting some arrangements would have been made to pay off
the debt & have on several occasions called on Revd. Mr. Ennis but as yet nothing has been done.
    As members of the Committee we assisted by contributions & otherwise to
forward the Building, and it is really too bad that after such a lapse of time it
should still remain our Creditor.
    Had that good Lady Mrs. Verschoyle lived, we are persuaded we would be
long since paid off—we find she left twenty guineas[63] a year to the Convent, and
we offered Revd. Mr. Ennis to accept of that sum as security until our debt
would be discharged. He refers us to you and in the event of your refusing to
accede to our terms, we will be obliged (very much against our inclination) to
issue an execution and attach the Convent where our property is.
    We are convinced that from your well known benevolent disposition you will
at once enter into an arrangement for the liquidation of our just claim and spare

---

of only sides 1 and 2, ending with the signature "M. C. McAuley"; this was apparently also the
case when the photostat in Mercy Congregational Archives was made in the mid twentieth century.
However, the transcription of the letter in Carroll's *Life* (427) contains the important postscript
which is included here. I believe there was, indeed, a side 3 and a cover (side 4) in the original
autograph, and that the postscript was on side 3 and is authentic.
    Since this is Catherine McAuley's last extant letter to Frances Warde—and possibly her last
actual letter to her—Frances may have especially cherished the portion with the postscript, with its
assurance, "We shall meet again, please God, *but not at present.*" She may have separated this portion of the autograph in order to keep it for herself, and it was thus disconnected early on from the
rest of the autograph.
62 Less than a month before her death, Catherine McAuley received this letter from the suppliers
of timber and slates for the construction of the Booterstown convent, asking her to pay the £130
debt or suffer the loss of the convent—presumably until the debt was paid. Catherine evidently
gave the letter to Charles Cavanagh, because a notation on the back, I believe in his handwriting,
reads: "Booterstown. Application for bill of timber & slates for B.Town"; Catherine responded to
the Dowlings in Letter 316, written two days later. How the debt was discharged is not known.
Booterstown convent remained, and is to this day, a convent of the Sisters of Mercy. Earlier letters of Catherine McAuley make clear that the convent was under construction before the Sisters
of Mercy were invited to live in it. Patrick Doyle, predecessor to John Ennis, parish priest of
Booterstown, negotiated with the committee responsible for building the convent and seeking a religious community to live in it and minister to the poor people about whom Mrs. Barbara Verschoyle,
the donor, was deeply concerned. She died in 1837, leaving Mr. James C. Bacon the agent of her
estate. Perhaps Mr. Bacon or Father Ennis stepped in to resolve the issue of the debt, or an agreement was reached to forfeit to the Dowlings the twenty guineas a year which the convent received
from Mrs. Verschoyle's bequest.   63 Twenty guineas (21 shillings each) was equivalent to £21.

us the trouble of proceeding, which must more or less annoy you and the other Ladies of your community stopping there.

Respectfully, Madam,
we are your obedient servants
M. & M. Dowling[64]

Autograph: Dublin, Mercy

316. To M. and M. Dowling   Baggot Street
      Poolbeg Street, Dublin[65]   October 15, 1841

Gentlemen

I would have replyed immediately to your communication, but have not been well for some days. When the Convent in Booterstown was nearly compleated, Mr. Bacon[66] called on me, most kindly requesting I would point out any little alteration that would render it more suitable. I then asked for the cross doors[67] which were immediately put up. Twenty guineas a year left by Mrs. Verschoyle[68] is the only fund to meet extra expenses which every distinct establishment must incur. It is small—but not so to us who would not get more for six hundred pounds.[69]

As to any legal proceedings, there is no occasion to have recourse to them. The Sisters can return here, and whoever has a just claim may take possession of the House until their demand is satisfied, if there is no other means of providing for it.

I am quite sure Mr. Bacon never expected any circumstance of this nature,

---

64 The *Dublin Directory* for 1842 lists at 24 Poolbeg Street "M. and M. Dowling, timber and slate merchants," and notes their other locations at 20 Luke Street, and Crofton Place, Kingstown. 65 The exact recipients of this letter cannot be unquestionably identified. Previous editors have said that the letter was addressed to "Board of Trustees, Booterstown Convent" (Bolster 266) or "Board of Trustees, Booterstown" (Neumann 383). Letter 315, previously unpublished and which Catherine McAuley would have received on October 13 or 14, seems to suggest the immediate reason for the present letter: an unpaid bill of £130 for timber and slates, with the threat of law proceedings and an "execution" to "attach the Convent where our property is"; that letter is signed by M. and M. Dowling. As the Dowlings indicate in their letter, they were members of the "Committee" in Booterstown who assisted in the development of the convent in 1837–1838. 66 James C. Bacon was the agent for the estate of Barbara Verschoyle, the donor of funds to establish the Booterstown convent, and the widow of Richard Verschoyle of Mount Merrion, Blackrock, who had been an agent of Richard Lord Viscount Fitzwilliam. Mrs. Verschoyle died on January 25, 1837, in her eighty-fifth year (Neumann 120). 67 Doors reinforced by cross beams of wood or iron for greater security. 68 See note 66 above. 69 The meaning of this sentence is somewhat obscure. Presumably it is the annual "twenty guineas," and not the convent itself, that Catherine regards as "small," but what she means by the "more" that the community "would not get ... for six hundred pounds" is unclear. I think she means that, given their vow of poverty, the community lives frugally and would not spend £600 in a year for "extra expenses" even if they had that sum.

as he called on me several times, to say all was ready for us. Mrs. Verschoyle was then dead for some time.

> I remain, Gentlemen, your obedient servant, etc.,
> Mary C. McAuley

Photostat: Dublin, Mercy[70]

317. To Charles Cavanagh, Esq.

Baggot Street
October 18, 1841

Dear Sir

Mrs. Ryan, a widow lady who lived very much at the Shelbourne Hotel, bequeathed me twenty pounds. Mr. Boylan, a solicitor (I believe), was appointed to make the payments. He came here—accompanied by Mr. O'Hagan with a document for me to sign—but I have not received the money tho' I hear all the legacies are paid.

When you have a moment to spare, will you be so kind—to ask Mr. O'Hagan about it.[71]

> I remain, Dear Sir, with much respect and gratitude, etc., etc.
> M. C. McAuley

Autograph: Dublin, Mercy

318. To Charles Cavanagh, Esq.

[Baggot Street]
[October 1841]

Dear Sir

Will you be so kind to call on Mr. Felix Boylan—for twenty pounds bequeathed to me by the late Widow Ryan.[72]

> I am, with much respect, etc.
> M. C. McAuley

Autograph: Dublin, Mercy

---

70 The autograph cannot now be found. It was once said to be in "Oak Lea Convent, England," according to a notation filed with the photostat.   71 Charles Cavanagh's notation on the letter: "Got the £20 afterwards from Mr. Boylan and handed same to Mrs. Delany for her." Arthur O'Hagan was a law partner of Charles Cavanagh.   72 Charles Cavanagh's notation on this undated letter: "Mr. Boylan paid the money to the convent 26 October 1841."

319. **To Sister Mary Ann Doyle**   **Convent of our Lady of Mercy**
     Tullamore   **[Baggot Street]**
                                                     November 10, 1841

Dear Revd. Mother

　　With feelings of the deepest and most bitter regret it devolves on me to announce to you that our very dear and much beloved Revd. Mother is considered to be past hope of recovery.

　　May Almighty God in His Infinite Mercy prepare us all for the heavy affliction that awaits us.[73]

Ever[74] your affectionately attached
In J. C.
Sister M. Ursula Frayne

Autograph: Bessbrook

320. **Last Will and Testament**   **August 20, 1841**
     and Codicil   **and November 11, 1841**

　　This is the last **Will and Testament** of Catherine McAuley of the Convent of our Blessed Lady of Mercy, Baggot Street, Dublin.[75] I devise and bequeath all my real and personal Estate and appoint all the real and personal Estate over which I have any power of appointment unto the Most Reverend Daniel Murray of the City of Dublin, Doctor of Divinity, The Very Reverend William Yore, V.G., The Very Reverend R. J. O'Hanlon & Mary Delaney, Amelia White,[76] Ann Markey, Marcella Flinn, Teresa Byrn, Mary Carton, Mary Cecelia Marmion, members of the Institute known by the name of the Sisters of Mercy, and the Survivor and Survivors of them, In trust for the use of the Members of the said Convent of our Blessed Lady of Mercy, Baggot Street, Dublin, this 20th day of August 1841.

　　Signed, sealed and published by the said Testator

Catherine McAuley
[Seal]

73 Identical or similar letters to this one were presumably sent to the superiors of all the foundations of Sisters of Mercy in Ireland and England. This letter reached Tullamore on November 11, 1841, the day Catherine McAuley died in the evening, about ten minutes to eight. Mary Ursula Frayne, the superior of the branch house in Booterstown, had evidently come in to Baggot Street to assist Mary de Pazzi Delany, Catherine McAuley's assistant.   74 Mary Ursula Frayne wrote "Every," not "Ever"—a slip of the pen.   75 Catherine McAuley signed her last Will and Testament on August 20, 1841, the day she sailed for Birmingham. The text presented here, which follows the autograph exactly, preserves all the spelling of names in the original. It should be noted that the document was written by the solicitor's office, and only Catherine McAuley's signature is in her handwriting.   76 Although Mary Teresa (Amelia) White was the superior of the Galway community at this time, it was Catherine McAuley's early understanding that Teresa remained a member of the Dublin community, on loan to Galway, and that she would return to Baggot Street when the Galway community was firmly established, and Mary Catherine Leahy could assume the role of superior. Catherine died without confirming this understanding; thus the move did not occur.

as and for her last Will and Testament in presence of us who have at her request, in her presence, and in presence of each other, subscribed our names as Witnesses hereto:

Mary Coleman, Anna Maria Coleman, Anna Matilda Kieron, Witnesses[77]

I hereby by way of **Codicil** to my Will bearing date the twentieth of August one thousand eight hundred and forty one ratify and confirm same and declare that I mean by the Members of the Convent therein mentioned Mary Delany, Amelia White, Anne Markey, Marcella Flinn, Teresa Byrne, Mary Carton and Mary Marmion therein mentioned, and Catherine Jarmey, Clara Frayne, Anne Murphy, Alicia Delany, Jane White, Mary Maher, Jane O'Connell, Anne O'Brien, Eliza Blake, Frances Boylan, Mary O'Connor, Clare Butler, Susan Walpole, Marianne Brennan, M. A. Duggan, Ellen Cowley, Eliza Liston, Ellen Whitty, Mary Anne Creedon, professed Sisters of the Institute of the Sisters of Mercy at present residing in or belonging to the House in Baggot Street[78] wherein I now reside called and known by the name of the Convent of Mercy, Baggot Street, in the City of Dublin, and declare that all my real freehold and personal property of every kind and description whatsoever after paying all my just debts and funeral expense shall be vested in [them], and I do accordingly devise and bequeath the same unto the Trustees named in my Will and the Survivor of them and the Heirs, Executors and Administrators of such Survivor, In trust for the said professed Sisters of said Institute, and the Survivors and Survivor of them, and thereby appoint the Most Reverend Doctor Murray, the Very Reverend William Yore[79] and the Very Reverend R. J. O'Hanlon, Executors of my said Will and of this Codicil. In Witness whereof I have hereunto set my hand and seal this eleventh day of November, one thousand eight hundred and forty one.[80]

Catherine McAuley

77 The women who witnessed the Will have not been identified.   78 The sole purpose of the Codicil to Catherine McAuley's last Will and Testament, beyond reaffirming the Will, was to add to it the names of all the professed members of the Baggot Street community, some of whom had not been listed in the Will. If one examines the Dublin Register, one discovers that only the following professed sisters are not listed in the Codicil, probably for the reasons noted: Mary Clare Augustine (Clare) Moore and Mary Justina (Annie) Fleming, who were now residing in Cork and Tullamore, respectively; Mary Teresa (Catherine) White and Mary Rose (Catherine) Lynch, who were now residing in Birr; and Teresa (Maria) Breen, who appears to have been inadvertently omitted by the solicitor or in the list given to the solicitor. Martha (Susan) Wallplate's name is incorrectly given as "Walpole." The names of the postulants and novices in the community are intentionally not listed.
79 William Yore was vicar general and precentor of the archdiocese of Dublin at this time, and parish priest of St. Paul's.   80 On a copy of Catherine McAuley's last Will and Codicil, Charles Cavanagh wrote the following on November 16, 1841: "I have received from the Most Revd. Doctor Murray assignment of premises in Baggot Street from Catherine McAuley to Michael Sullivan, Gentleman, dated 8 April 1829—also assignment of same premises from Michael Sullivan to The Most Revd. Dr. Murray, Catherine McAuley, Anna Maria Doyle & Catherine Josephine Byrn." Cavanagh is noting that he has received from Daniel Murray the legal documents establishing the Baggot Street Trust

Signed, Sealed and Published by the said Catherine McAuley in the presence of Us, who at her request, in her presence, and in the presence of each other, have subscribed our names as Witnesses hereto.

Charles Cavanagh
Arthur O'Hagan.

Autograph: Dublin, Mercy

321. To Sister Mary Ann Doyle   **Convent of Sisters of Mercy**
Tullamore   **Baggot St.**

Friday Morning [November 12, 1841]

Dear Revd. Mother

Our dear and much beloved Revd. Mother is gone to receive the rewards of her good works. She departed this life after receiving the last Sacraments, between the hours of 7 and 8 yesterday evening. May Almighty God strengthen us all, and enable [us] to submit with calm resignation to this heavy affliction. The Office and High Mass for the repose of her soul will take place on Monday at 11 o'clock.

Your affectionately attached
In J. C.
Sister M. Ursula Frayne

Autograph: Bessbrook

322. Transcribed Poem[81]   [1840–1841]

> Lifeless ah no, both faith and art have given
> That passing hour a life of endless zest

---

on April 8, 1829, whereby Catherine McAuley assigned the property to Dr. Murray, should she or her associates be unable or fail to fulfill the stated purposes of the House on Baggot Street.

Catherine McAuley's Will was probated on April 5, 1842. The document of probate (now in Mercy Congregational Archives, Dublin) declares that the appointed Executors—Daniel Murray, William Yore, and Redmond J. O'Hanlon—"have by an instrument in writing under their respective hands and seals freely and absolutely renounced all their right title and interest of, in and to the burden of the execution of said will and codicil." Thus Mary de Pazzi Delany and Mary Cecilia Marmion, then the superior and assistant of the Baggot Street community, became the sole executors of Catherine McAuley's will, most of the properties and assets of the community having been formerly held in her name.

81 Mary Vincent Whitty penned the following note at the end of this autograph transcription in Catherine McAuley's handwriting: "Our venerated Foundress M. C. McAuley's writing—found amongst her papers after her death. Nov. 1841. S. M. V. W."

And every soul who loves the food of Heaven
May to that Table come a welcome guest

Lifeless ah no, while in my heart are stored
Sad memories of my Brethren changed or gone
Familiar faces—now not round our board
And still that silent supper lasting on

While I review my youth, what I was then
What I am now—and you beloved ones all
It seems as if these were the living men
And we the coloured shadows on the wall

Their good effect remains unchanged by time
In every view they teach, excite—inspire
while our weak efforts always in decline
extinguish more than kindle holy fire

It was a holy usage to record
Upon each refectory's side or end
The last mysterious Supper of our Lord
That meanest appetites might upward tend

Within the Convent Palace of old Spain
Rich with the gifts and monuments of Kings
Hung such a picture, said by some to reign
The sovereign glory of these wondrous things

A painter of far fame in deep delight
Dwelt on each beauty he so well discerned
While in low times, a grey Geronomite
This answer to his extacy returned

"Stranger—I have received my daily meal
"In this good company now three score years
"And thou whoever thou art canst hardly feel
"How time these lifeless Images endears"[82]

[M. C. McAuley]

Autograph: Brisbane

---

82 The style and vocabulary of this poem suggest that although the autograph is in Catherine McAuley's handwriting, the poem may not be wholly her own composition, but rather a transcription of or inspired by an unknown, probably published, source. The poem focuses on the faces of the disciples in a painting of the Last Supper as an evocative symbol of the faces of friends and co-workers who have moved on to other places or have died. The themes of loving memory and the deathless character of good example that pervade the poem capture the attitudes Catherine McAuley always had toward her companions in the Sisters of Mercy. That she retained this autograph, when

323. Transcribed Poem[83]   [Undated]

Since Trifles make the sum of human things
and half our misery from mere trifles springs
since life's best joys consist—in peace and ease

---

she destroyed so many other personal papers before her death, is testimony to her affection for her "beloved ones" and her undying gratitude for "their good effect": remembering them "endears" and brings to life the "lifeless Images" of the painting.

Considerable effort has been expended, so far to no avail, to try to find the original source of this poem if it is not Catherine McAuley's own composition. Research on this intriguing problem will continue. The "grey Geronomite" in stanza seven seems to suggest that Catherine is transcribing or transforming another poet's work. The themes and images of William Wordsworth's "Lines suggested by a Portrait from the Pencil of F. Stone" (in the 1840 edition of his *Poetical Works*, 5:131–36) are very similar to those in Catherine's transcription. While Wordsworth's poem initially describes a portrait of a young woman, it moves to a discussion of the "God-like" power of art to confer on those portrayed a kind of immortality: "here do they abide, / Enshrined for ages" (ll. 89–90). His poem then focuses on the words of a "mild Jeronymite" as he contemplates Titian's painting of the Last Supper on the refectory wall of the Monastery of the Escorial in Spain, a work commissioned by King Philip II. In Catherine's poem the speaker also likens her memories of absent faces to those of a "grey Geronomite" as he gazes on the faces of Titian's painting in "the Convent Palace of old Spain." Although no lines of Catherine's poem correspond exactly with any of Wordsworth's lines, it is possible that the overall meaning of his poem inspired hers. It is also possible that another poem, by a different and so far unknown poet, but on the same theme and painting, was her original source. The concept of the reproduction of living witness—the continual "inspiration" passing from one to another—is of course an important motif in the poem, as in Catherine McAuley's own life and work.

83 Catherine McAuley copied, with some revision, most of the lines of this autograph poem from a much longer poem by the English religious writer Hannah More (1745–1833). More's poem, entitled "Sensibility: An Epistle to the Honourable Mrs. Boscawen," is contained in *The Works of Hannah More, in Four Volumes* published in Dublin in 1803 (1:85–96). "Sensibility" is 386 lines long. Catherine transcribed only eighteen lines of More's poem: ll. 295–305, 309, 311–314, and 337–38. After l. 314 and before the couplet, she inserted four lines of her own composition, replacing More's illustrations of "petty strife" and "sacred joys" with her own examples of compassion. In twelve of the eighteen lines she transcribed from More's poem, Catherine altered the wording, sometimes extensively. The eighteen lines as the appear in More's poem are as follows:

> Since trifles make the sum of human things,
> And half our misery from our foibles springs;
> Since life's best joys consist in peace and ease,
> And tho' but few can serve, yet all can please;
> O let th' ungentle spirit learn from hence,
> A small unkindness is a great offence.
> To spread large bounties, tho' we wish in vain,
> Yet all may shun the guilt of giving pain:
> To bless mankind with tides of flowing wealth,
> With rank to grace them, or to crown with health,
> Our little lot denies; yet lib'ral still,
> ...
> The gift of ministring to other's ease,
> ...

and few can save or serve, but all can please
oh, let the ungentle spirit—learn from hence
a small unkindness is a great offence
large bounties to bestow, we wish in vain
but all can shun the guilt of giving pain
to bless mankind with tides of flowing wealth
with power endue them, or to crown with health
our little lot denies, but Heaven decrees
to all the gift of ministering to ease
the gentle offices of patient love
beyond all purchase, and all price above
the mild forbearance of another's fault
the taunting word suppressed as soon as thought
the pitying look—proceeding from the heart
the tear of sympathy, about to start
on these Heaven bade the sweets of life depend
commencing here, a love which ne'er shall end
But cold reserve, and slights—unmixed with hate
make up in measure, what they want in weight.[84]

[M. C. McAuley]

Autograph: Dublin, Mercy

324. "The Spirit of the Institute"[85]   [Undated]

To devote our lives to the accomplishment of our own salvation and to promote the salvation of others is the end and object of our order of Mercy. These two works are so linked together by our rule and observances that they recipro-

---

> The gentle offices of patient love,
> Beyond all flattery, and all price above;
> The mild forbearance at a brother's fault,
> The angry word suppress'd, the taunting thought;
> ...
> Small slights, neglect, unmix'd perhaps with hate,
> Make up in number what they want in weight.

84 See Letter 166, note 56, for a possible reference to this poem. The original autograph of the poem as Catherine McAuley shaped it is in a manuscript notebook of her early writings in Mercy Congregational Archives, Dublin. However, she may have later made a copy of the poem, in 1840, for Joanna Reddan—or the reference in letter 166 may have nothing to do with this poem.   85 Catherine McAuley's original manuscript of this statement on the spirit of the Institute of the Sisters of Mercy (or "The Mercy Ideal" as it is sometimes called) is contained in a manuscript notebook of her writings which is preserved in the Bermondsey archives. The autograph is undated, but its location in the manuscript notebook with other early transcriptions suggests that it may have been written as early as Catherine McAuley's novitiate days at the Presentation Convent, George's Hill,

cally help each other. We should often reflect that our progress in spiritual life consists in the faithful discharge of the duties belonging to our state, as regards both ourselves and our neighbour, and we must consider the time and exertion which we employ for the relief and instruction of the poor and ignorant—as most conducive to our own advancement in perfection, and the time given to prayer and all other pious exercises—we must consider as employed to obtain the grace, strength and animation—which alone could enable us to persevere in the meritorious obligations of our state, and if we were to neglect these means of obtaining Divine support we would deserve that God should stop the course of His graces, to make us sensible that all our efforts would be fruitless, except we were continually renewed and replenished with His Divine Spirit. God speaking to us by His inspired Apostle says—Attend to thyself.

The employments which regard our neighbour require that we should be very well grounded in humility and patience—in order to be truly serviceable to them without any prejudice to ourselves.

Saint Augustin says—everything has its particular worm—no matter how sweet and good it is in its nature. All kinds of fruit, of wood, of grain has a worm that eats it if not separated from it. There is the worm of a plum, the worm of an apple, the worm of a pear. Let us take care of the worm of good works which is vanity arising from self-approbation and esteem. Hence the Holy Scripture cautions us saying, "Recover thy neighbour according to thy power and take heed to thyself that thou fall not ..." (Sir. 29.20), and again, "What would it profit to gain the whole world and lose our own souls" (Matt. 16.26).

Therefore reason and well ordered charity require that we should not neglect ourselves for the advantage of others, or for any consideration whatever. We

---

Dublin. There is no documentary evidence to support (or deny) the view that it was written in 1841, specifically to address the existing tension, between contemplation and the works of mercy, in the Bermondsey community. The fact that the manuscript is now located *in* Bermondsey is not a conclusive argument that it was written *for* Bermondsey.

The essay is not wholly an original composition of Catherine McAuley, but rather an abbreviated, and slightly altered transcription of a treatise by Alonso Rodriguez: "Of the end for which the Society of Jesus was instituted—the means which are conducive to this end; and which regard all Religious ...," in Volume 3 of his masterwork, *The Practice of Christian and Religious Perfection*, first published in Spain in 1609. An English translation, published in Kilkenny, Ireland, in 1806, was evidently Catherine's source; in the passages she uses, her wording is in many instances identical to that in the Kilkenny edition of Rodriguez's work. For a sentence-by-sentence comparison of the two essays and an analysis of the portions of Rodriguez's work which Catherine uses, see Sullivan "Catherine McAuley's Theological and Literary Debt to Alonso Rodriguez" in *Recusant History* (May 1990).

The statement is presented here, not as a personal letter, but as a communal communication from Catherine McAuley who undoubtedly read, or spoke, its contents to many groups of Sisters of Mercy. The essay was published in the editions of Neumann (385–91) and Bolster (242–46), but before its dependence on the treatise of Alonso Rodriguez was known. The text presented here follows the autograph exactly, and readers will notice some differences from previous renderings. The autograph of the statement is untitled; I have given it the title used by both Neumann and Bolster, which I find preferable to "The Mercy Ideal."

should not relent or grow negligent in our own improvement. We might often repeat the words of the Psalmist saying, "Teach me goodness, discipline and knowledge." Goodness first, as particularly necessary to incline our hearts to pity for our suffering brethren. Discipline next—that we may so regulate our time and actions, as to serve them with zeal and prudence—and knowledge, that we may impart such instruction as will lead them to God, and keep ourselves faithful in our duty. There is no charity, says the wise man—like to this: "Take pity on thy own soul, by rendering it pleasing to God." We must always keep in memory the words of Saint Paul, "that we go into the middle of a perverse world" (Phil. 2.15), and this must teach us to be extremely on our guard. We must try to be like those rivers which enter into the sea without losing any of the sweetness of the water. We must, in the midst of the rudeness, impiety and impatience which we shall witness, preserve meekness, piety and unwearied patience, but in order to do this we must prepare—by application to spiritual exercises—prayer, examen, lecture, penance, self denial. From each of these we draw new aid and the grace of Jesus Christ which will accompany us in all we undertake with a pure intention of pleasing Him alone.

Albertus the Great was wont to say that in Divine knowledge a greater advancement was made by piety and prayer than by study, and in proof of this assertion, he alleged the words of Holy Scripture: "I desired to have a right knowledge and God gave it to me, I invoked the Lord and He filled me with the spirit of wisdom" (Wis. 7.7).

It was thus that Saint Thomas became so learned and enlightened which made him say, that he was indebted to prayer for all he knew, and not to his labour or studies. We read of Saint Bonaventure that when he taught Divinity in Paris, with a great deal of reputation, and when he attracted the esteem and admiration of all the world, Saint Thomas of Aquin going one day to see him, begged of him to shew him the Books he had made use of for his studies, upon which Saint Bonaventure led him to his cell and shewed him some very common books that lay upon his table. And when Saint Thomas told him he had a desire to see those other books from which he had acquired so many wonderful things, the Saint then shewing him his oratory upon which he had his crucifix, "Behold," Father says, "all my Books, and behold here, pointing to the crucifix, the chief book from which I derive all I teach and write. It is by casting myself at the feet of Christ crucified, and supplicating light, that I have made greater progress, and gained more true knowledge than by reading any Books whatsoever."

The great Apostle Saint Paul says: "I desired to be separated from Jesus Christ for the sake of my brethren" (Rom. 9.3). Saint Chrysostom interprets these words thus, "The Apostle says he wished to be separated from the contemplation of Jesus Christ and the peace and happiness which this constant union would afford him in order to apply himself to the instruction and consolation of those who required his assistance," and all the Doctors of the church agree that in this, Saint Paul made an act of charity sovereignly perfect and they give it as an example to prove that the corporal and spiritual works of mercy, which draw religious from a life of contemplation, so far from separating them from the love of God, unite them much more closely to him, and render them more valuable in His holy service.

Clement of Alexandria makes use of some comparisons to set forth this truth. "The more water, says he, that we draw from fountains the clearer and the more wholesome it is to drink, but when the pump is not in frequent use, the water gets foul and muddy. The more we use a knife the brighter it grows, but without sufficient use it will grow rusty." Do we not also perceive, adds this eminent Doctor, that those who instruct others—improve themselves, by the very act. That which we say to and for others cannot but regard ourselves. If we pray for their conversion, let us always mentally join ourselves to them, praying that we may be truly converted from whatever is in us contrary to the sanctity and purity of our state. If we pray for their happy death, let us always offer the prayer for our own happy death, and thus if we have occasion to repeat the same petition frequently during the day, we are most happily preparing for our own last hour and in all probability saying many more prayers—to that effect—than those who are entirely devoted to contemplative life.

We learn by visiting prisons and hospitals, and by reconciling quarrels, what misery there is in the world, and come thereby to have a greater esteem for our vocation by which we have the unspeakable happiness of being separated from it, and all the occupations which our holy state enjoins, so far from being any occasion of remissness, that on the contrary they help to keep us more carefully on our guard, and to excite us more and more to virtue and perfection.

Add to what has been said the graces which God pours down on those who are engaged in the more active works of charity, and if a great reward has been promised to such as administer to the corporal wants and miseries of their fellow beings, what may we not justly hope for those, who being constantly engaged in the spiritual instruction of the ignorant—which is far more important—add to it also whatever temporal relief and comfort they can procure by all the exertion in their power. Saint Peter Chrysologus compares those who administer spiritual and corporal aid to the nurses of Princes—as says he, great care is taken that the nurses of Kings' Children be supplied with whatever will strengthen and cherish them, so the King of Kings takes care that those who attend to the care of His most dear poor, to whom He is Father, shall be nourished and animated with the choicest food from His heavenly Table, that they may the better fulfill an office so dear to His Paternal heart. We may then truly say to these poor objects of our care what Saint Paul said to the Philippians and Thessalonians: "You are my joy and my crown," because through you we draw down on ourselves the mercy and grace of our Lord.

We ought therefore to make account, that our perfection and merit consists in acquitting ourselves well of these duties, so that though the spirit of prayer and retreat should be most dear to us, yet such a spirit as would never withdraw us from these works of mercy, otherwise it should be regarded as a temptation rather than the effect of sincere piety. It would be an artifice of the enemy, who transforming himself into an angel of light, would endeavour to withdraw us from our vocation under the pretence of labouring for our advancement. We ought to give ourselves to prayer in the true spirit of our vocation, to obtain new vigor, zeal and fervor in the exercise of our state, going on with increasing efforts, so that we may say with holy Job—"If I go to Bed to sleep, I will say when shall I rise again, and in the morning I will be impatient until the evening approaches" (Job 7.4).

"The works of God are all perfect" (Deut. 32.4)—in the order of Grace as well as nature. He never calls any person to any state or for any end without giving the means and necessary helps to carry them through all the difficulties of it, and this being sufficiently established, it is not to be doubted, but that when God institutes a religious order, He gives at the same time the Grace that is necessary for such an order, and for all those who are called to that order, that all may attain to the perfection for which it was designed, hence none can attribute to themselves the success that may attend their exertions, because it is the fruit which God intended to produce when he instituted the order and granted the means to propagate it. It follows from what has been said that each society of Religious receives a grace particularly adapted to the duties which they are called to perform. We ought then have great confidence in God in the discharge of all these offices of mercy, spiritual and corporal—which constitute the business of our lives, and assure ourselves that God will particularly concur with us to render them efficacious as by His infinite mercy we daily experience, and this proceeds, as we have said before, from the grace belonging to the vocation or grace of the order.

We read in the first chapter of Maccabees what is much to this purpose. Some of the chief men among the Jews, speaking of the great victories the Maccabees had obtained against the Gentiles, wished to do the same—saying, "Let us also make for ourselves a name." For this purpose they gathered all their troops together, and went forth against the enemy, but the success did not answer their expectations, for though numerous and powerful, they were defeated, and here the Holy Scripture takes notice, that they were not called or designed by God to accomplish this end. And in order to excite and animate us in our daily occupations, let us imagine that God says to us, as we read in holy Scripture, "Fear nothing, it is I who have called you—take courage, and be of resolution", for in the execution of the duties to which I have called you—you are safe, and may confidently say with holy David—"Though I should have to walk in the midst of the shades of night, I will fear nothing because thou art with me." By this we see how much some religious deceive themselves, who hearkening only to their own sentiments, imagine that they would serve God better in some other House or other engagements. This is generally (indeed I may say always) delusion and artifice of the enemy, as experience has sufficiently proved. Once we are, by the grace of Almighty God, brought to religion, all we have then to do—

is to surrender entirely our own will, and give ourselves up generously to be directed & governed as children brought forth in Jesus Christ.

I shall now speak of the most effectual means of rendering ourselves useful to our neighbour, and also the advancement of our own salvation, for these two things, as I have already said in the beginning of this treatise, are so linked together that whatever contributes to the one must necessarily promote the other.

The first means which the saints have recommended to render us most useful to others, is to give good example and to live in sanctity. Saint Ignatius says as follows, "In the first place," says he, "the good example which we give by leading a most holy and Christian life has the greatest power over the minds of others, wherefore we ought to take great care to edify as much as possible by our actions and words." It was for this reason that our Blessed Saviour marked the way to Heaven by His example. "Jesus Christ", says Saint Luke, "began to do and to teach" (Acts 1.1), thus signifying to us that we should do first what we would induce others to do. It is an established opinion that the way to virtue and to piety is shorter by example than by precept. Saint Bernard speaking on this matter says—"Example is very efficacious and a very proper lesson to persuade because it proves that what it teaches is practicable and this is what has most influence on all."

"Our weakness is so great," says Saint Augustin, "that we can hardly be moved to do what is right except we see others do it." The apostle well understood the truth and force of this when he said—"Be ye imitators of me, as I am of Jesus Christ" (1 Cor. 11.1). Saint Basil and St. Chrysostom, speaking of those who teach by their words only, say they are not true religious, but merely comedians, that is players, who act a part upon the stage, but possess nothing of what they represent. We may represent humility very well in our words, also the vanity of this world and the contempt that ought to be felt for it, but if we are not striving to be really humble and to contemn heartily whatever would separate us from the love of God, our efforts, however diligent they may be, cannot be acceptable or meritorious in the sight of Heaven.

[M. C. McAuley]

Autograph: Bermondsey

A Chronology of Catherine McAuley's Life[1]

September 29, 1778   Catherine Elizabeth McAuley is born of Catholic parents in Dublin. Though the exact year of her birth cannot be verified, it is general practice to use 1778. Her sister Mary may have been born in 1781, or earlier.

April 26, 1783   Birth of CMcA's brother, James William.

July 18, 1783   Her father, James McGauley, makes his will and dies shortly afterwards.

1798   Death of CMcA's mother, Elinor Conway McAuley.

1801   CMcA moves in with Protestant relatives, the Armstrongs.

1803   She moves into the home of a Protestant couple, William and Catherine Callaghan on Mary Street, Dublin, as household manager and companion to Catherine Callaghan. Later in the year she moves with the Callaghans to Coolock House, a twenty-two acre estate northeast of Dublin.

August 18, 1804   CMcA's sister, Mary McAuley, marries Dr. William Montgomery Macauley, a Protestant apothecary.

October 3, 1819   Death of Catherine Callaghan.

1821   CMcA's brother, Dr. James McAuley, a surgeon and now a Protestant, marries Frances Ridgeway.

January 27, 1822   William Callaghan signs his last will and a codicil designating CMcA as his sole residuary legatee.

August 9, 1822   Death of Anne Conway Byrn, CMcA's cousin. CMcA adopts ten-year-old Catherine Byrn, having adopted the baby, Teresa Byrn, in 1821.

November 10, 1822   Death of William Callaghan.

May 11, 1823   Dr. Daniel Murray becomes archbishop of Dublin.

c. 1823–1824   William Callaghan's will is finally settled.

June 22, 1824   CMcA leases property on Baggot Street in southeast Dublin to build a house to serve poor women and children.

July 1824   Dr. Michael Blake, parish priest of Saints Michael and John's and CMcA's friend, lays the first stone for the house.

August 11, 1827   Burial of Mary McAuley Macauley, CMcA's sister. She leaves five children: Mary, James, Robert, Catherine, and William, ages sixteen to five.

September 24, 1827   Feast of our Lady of Mercy: the House on Baggot Street opens as a school for poor young girls and a residence for

1 This chronology is a shortened and slightly modified version of the chronology in Sullivan, *Catherine McAuley and the Tradition of Mercy*, 9–25.

	homeless girls and women. Anna Maria Doyle and Catherine Byrn move in and begin these works of mercy.
May 15, 1828	Death of Edward Armstrong, a priest of Dublin and CMcA's close friend and spiritual director in relation to the project.
May or June 1828	CMcA moves into Baggot Street with Teresa Byrn, age seven.
June 22, 1828	Frances Warde becomes a resident member.
September 10, 1828	CMcA explains that Baggot Street is a place devoted to "the daily education of hundreds of poor female children and the instruction of young women who sleep in the house" (Letter 6).
September 15, 1828	CMcA sells Coolock House.
September 24, 1828	Daniel Murray gives permission for the House on Baggot Street to be called "of our Lady of Mercy."
November 22, 1828	Daniel Murray receives Mary Macauley, CMcA's niece, into the Catholic Church, and permits the community to visit the sick in their homes and hospitals.
January 25, 1829	Death of CMcA's brother-in-law, Dr. William Macauley. Each of his five children chooses her as legal guardian. She is now the adoptive mother of nine, including Catherine and Teresa Byrn, Ellen Corrigan, an orphan, and Ann Rice, a homeless child.
March 2, 1829	CMcA registers her nephews—James, Robert, and William Macauley—as boarders at Carlow College.
April 8, 1829	She establishes the Baggot Street Trust, which assigns the House of Mercy to Daniel Murray should she and her associates cease to fulfill the purposes for the House.
June 4, 1829	Dr. Murray dedicates the chapel in the House and opens it to the public, the funds generated from Sunday collections to be used to support the women and girls sheltered there. He assigns Daniel Burke, OSF, as chaplain to the House of Mercy, and Redmond O'Hanlon, ODC, as confessor to the community.
September 8, 1829	Margaret Dunne joins the community.
November 22, 1829	CMcA's niece, Mary Macauley, joins the community.
November 30, 1829	Elizabeth Harley joins the community.
Early 1830	In the midst of clerical and lay criticism, CMcA and her associates decide, against her earlier judgment, to found an unenclosed religious congregation of women dedicated to the service of the poor, sick, and ignorant.
June 10, 1830	Georgiana Moore joins the community.
July 12, 1830	Mary Anne Delany joins the community.
September 8, 1830	As preparation for founding the Sisters of Mercy, CMcA,

Anna Maria Doyle, and Elizabeth Harley enter the Presentation Sisters at George's Hill, Dublin, and begin their novitiate on December 9, 1830.

June 28, 1831   Death of Caroline Murphy at Baggot Street. She is buried in the Carmelite vault at Saint Teresa's Church, Clarendon Street, the first of thirteen Sisters of Mercy who will be buried there.

December 12, 1831   At George's Hill, CMcA and her two associates—now called in religion, Mary Ann Doyle and Mary Elizabeth Harley—each "vow perpetual poverty, chastity and obedience, and to preserve until the end of my life in the Congregation called the Sisters of Mercy, established for the Visitation of the Sick Poor, and charitable instruction of poor females." Thus they found the Sisters of Mercy.

December 13, 1831   Daniel Murray appoints CMcA the first superior.

January 23, 1832   Seven women at Baggot Street receive the habit of the Sisters of Mercy at the first reception ceremony: Mary Josephine (Catherine) Byrn, Mary Frances (Frances) Warde, Mary Angela (Margaret) Dunne, Mary Teresa (Mary) Macauley, Mary Clare (Georgiana) Moore, Mary Magdalen de Pazzi (Mary Anne) Delany, and Mary Agnes (Anna) Carroll. Mary Aloysius (Anne) O'Grady is also received on her deathbed.

February 7, 1832   Mary Aloysius O'Grady dies at Baggot Street.

April 25, 1832   Mary Elizabeth Harley dies at Baggot Street

March–December 1832   Cholera epidemic in Dublin. At the Board of Health's request, CMcA and other sisters work for months, in shifts from 8:00 a.m. to 8:00 p.m., in a cholera hospital set up on Townsend Street.

June 10, 1832   Anne Moore enters the community. She will receive the habit and the name Mary Elizabeth on October 8, 1832, and profess her vows on October 8, 1834.

December 1, 1832   Mary Josephine (Catherine) Byrn transfers to the Dominican Convent in Cabra.

January 24, 1833   Four women profess their vows at the first profession ceremony on Baggot Street: Mary Frances Warde, Mary Angela Dunne, Mary Clare Moore, and Mary de Pazzi Delany.

March 17, 1833   Dr. Michael Blake is consecrated bishop of Dromore. Walter Meyler succeeds him as parish priest of St. Andrew's.

November 3, 1833   CMcA's niece, Mary Teresa Macauley, professes her vows in a private ceremony.

November 12, 1833	Mary Teresa Macauley dies just after midnight.
December 8, 1833	CMcA sends to Rome two original chapters of the future Rule and Constitutions of the Sisters of Mercy, and a petition for approbation of the Sisters of Mercy. These chapters—on the Visitation of the Sick and the Protection of Distressed Women—will be additions to the Rule and Constitutions of the Presentation Sisters, which CMcA will revise for the Sisters of Mercy.
January 28, 1834	CMcA's niece, Catherine Macauley, who had lived at Baggot Street since 1828–1829, enters the community. She will receive the habit and the name Mary Anne Agnes on July 3, 1834, and profess her vows on October 22, 1836.
September 4, 1834	Mary Carton enters the community at Baggot Street, as a lay sister. She will receive the habit and the name Teresa on July 1, 1835, and profess her vows on July 1, 1837.
October 1834	Dr. Walter Meyler decides to close the convent chapel to the public, thereby cutting off needed funds for the House of Mercy.
March 24, 1835	CMcA opens a branch house in Kingstown (Dún Laoghaire), as a place of convalescence for sick sisters at Baggot Street. She gives buildings on the property to create a school for the poor girls she sees "loitering about the roads." She will be subsequently charged with the entire cost of the renovation.
March 24, 1835	The Holy See sends Dr. Murray a letter commending the Sisters of Mercy and granting them its apostolic benediction. The community receives this welcome communication on May 3, 1835.
April 21, 1836	CMcA founds a Convent of Mercy in Tullamore, Ireland. Mary Ann Doyle is appointed superior.
October 29, 1836	CMcA founds a Convent of Mercy in Charleville, Ireland. Mary Angela Dunne is named superior.
February 5, 1837	Anna Maria Harnett enters the community. She will receive the habit, taking the name Mary Vincent, on July 1, 1837, and profess her vows on October 24, 1838.
April 11, 1837	CMcA founds St. Leo's Convent of Mercy in Carlow, Ireland. Mary Frances Warde is appointed superior.
July 6, 1837	CMcA founds a Convent of Mercy in Cork. Mary Clare Moore is appointed superior.
August 7, 1837	CMcA's niece, Mary Anne Agnes (Catherine) Macauley, dies at Baggot Street.
August 15, 1837	CMcA's godchild, Teresa Byrn, who had been living at Baggot Street, enters the community. She will receive the

	habit and the name Mary Camillus on February 21, 1838, and profess her vows on May 4, 1841.
Autumn 1837	Daniel Burke, OSF, chaplain since 1829, resigns to accompany the new vicar apostolic of the Cape of Good Hope, Dr. Patrick Griffith. A disagreement begins between CMcA and Walter Meyler over appointment of a chaplain for the House of Mercy.
November 1837	In Kingstown CMcA falls and breaks her wrist.
June 1838	CMcA opens a branch house in Booterstown, as a possible replacement for the Kingstown convent.
July 1838	Receiving a legacy of £1000, CMcA decides to build a commercial laundry at Baggot Street, as income for the House of Mercy.
September 24, 1838	CMcA founds a Convent of Mercy in Limerick. Mary Elizabeth Moore is appointed superior.
November 1838	The community withdraws from Kingstown.
December 1838	CMcA's nephew, William (Willie) Macauley, goes to sea. She loses contact with him, and later presumes that he has died at sea.
September 24, 1839	The Carlow community founds a Convent of Mercy in Naas. Mary Josephine Trennor is appointed Superior.
November 18, 1839	CMcA, Mary Clare Moore, the two English sisters who made their novitiate in Cork, and others depart for Bermondsey, London, arriving on the night of November 19.
November 21, 1839	A Convent of Mercy is established in Bermondsey. Mary Clare Moore is appointed temporary superior.
Late 1839–early 1840	CMcA sends to Rome for final approval and papal confirmation the text of the Rule and Constitutions of the Sisters of Mercy.
January 4, 1840	CMcA's nephew, Robert Macauley, dies of consumption.
Mid-January 1840	CMcA returns to Dublin and is "confined to bed" for two weeks.
March 3, 1840	Paul Gavino Secchi Murro, consultor of the Congregation for the Propagation of the Faith, submits a positive report on the proposed Rule and Constitutions of the Sisters of Mercy.
March 6, 1840	With Dr. Murray's permission, CMcA appoints Mary de Pazzi Delany, to be her assistant; Mary Aloysius Scott, bursar; and Mary Cecilia Marmion, mistress of novices.
April 1840	CMcA re-opens the house in Kingstown at Dr. Murray's request.
Early May 1840	CMcA founds a Convent of Mercy in Galway. Mary Teresa White is appointed superior.

July 20, 1840   In Rome, the Congregation for the Propagation of the Faith approves the Rule and Constitutions of the Sisters of Mercy and later forwards its recommendation to Pope Gregory XVI.

December 8, 1840   The Carlow community founds a Convent of Mercy in Wexford. Mary Teresa Kelly is appointed superior.

December 27, 1840   CMcA founds a Convent of Mercy in Birr. Mary Aloysius Scott is appointed superior.

March 31, 1841   Fifty-two women and girls are crowded in the House of Mercy on Baggot Street at this time.

April 12, 1841   CMcA writes: "My old cough is tormenting me."

April 29, 1841   James Macauley, Catherine's eldest nephew, dies.

May 16, 1841   Frances Gibson enters the Baggot Street community for an eventual foundation in Liverpool (1843).

June 6, 1841   Gregory XVI confirms the Rule and Constitutions of the Sisters of Mercy.

June 14, 1841   Mary Clare Moore returns to Baggot Street from Bermondsey, and a week later goes to Cork to resume the role of superior.

July 5, 1841   The decree of papal confirmation of the Rule is promulgated in Rome. Cardinal Fransoni sends this information to Dr. Murray on July 31, with copies of the approved text in Italian.

August 19, 1841   Four young women destined for the foundation in Birmingham profess their vows at Baggot Street. Mary Vincent Whitty, future founder of the Sisters of Mercy in Brisbane, also professes her vows on this day, as does Mary Justina Fleming, who will die on December 10.

August 20, 1841   CMcA draws up her will. In the evening she and the founding party for Birmingham sail to Liverpool and proceed by rail to Birmingham.

August 21, 1841   CMcA founds a Convent of Mercy in Birmingham.

September 6, 1841   Mary Juliana Hardman, who professed her vows on August 19, is appointed superior of the Birmingham community.

September 6, 1841   CMcA sends instructions to Teresa Carton at Baggot Street about preparing space for her in the infirmary.

September 20, 1841   She leaves Birmingham, arrives in Kingstown on the morning of September 21, and proceeds to Baggot Street.

September 26, 1841   She writes to Mary Aloysius Scott in Birr, saying she has seen Dr. William Stokes twice. He says her right lung is "diseased."

October 12, 1841   Writing to Frances Warde about "some evident mistakes in the copy of our Rule," CMcA adds: "I have felt the last bad change in the weather very much."

October 18, 1841   She asks Charles Cavanagh to secure £20 bequeathed to her by Mrs. Ryan.

Late October 1841   Unaware it has been received, CMcA again asks Mr. Cavanagh to secure the £20. This is apparently her last extant letter.

c. October 29, 1841   CMcA becomes bedridden. She is suffering from pulmonary tuberculosis complicated by an abscess.

November 8, 1841   Redmond O'Hanlon anoints her on Monday night.

November 11, 1841   CMcA signs the codicil to her will. She is visited by her brother James, his wife Frances, Dr. William Stokes, and several priests, including Redmond O'Hanlon, Myles Gaffney, and Walter Meyler.

She asks Teresa Carton to "tell the Sisters to get a good cup of tea—I think the Community Room would be a good place—when I am gone, and to comfort one another, but God will comfort them" (Mary Vincent Whitty to Mary Cecilia Marmion, November 12, 1841).

Catherine McAuley dies, about ten minutes to eight in the evening.

November 15, 1841   After the Solemn Office and Requiem Mass, she is buried in the earth, like the poor, as she had wished.

Works Cited

A[gnew], E. C. *Geraldine; a Tale of Conscience.* 3 vols. London: Dolman, 1837–1839.

Backscheider, Paula R. *Reflections on Biography.* New York: Oxford University Press, 1999, 2001.

Blake, Donal S. *Mary Aikenhead (1787–1858): Servant of the Poor.* Dublin: Caritas, 2001.

Bolster, M. Angela. *Mercy in Cork, 1837–1987.* Cork: Tower Books, 1987.

——, ed. *The Correspondence of Catherine McAuley, 1827–1841.* Cork: The Congregation of the Sisters of Mercy, Diocese of Cork and Ross, 1989.

Brenan, M. J. *An Ecclesiastical History of Ireland from the Introduction of Christianity into that Country to … [1839].* 2 vols. Dublin: John Coyne, 1840.

Burke Savage, Roland. *Catherine McAuley: The First Sister of Mercy.* Dublin: M. H. Gill, 1949.

Byrne, Michael. *Tullamore Catholic Parish: A Historical Survey.* Tullamore: Leinster Leader, 1987.

Carmichael, Ann G. "Erysipelas." *The Cambridge World History of Human Disease.* Ed. Kenneth F. Kiple. Cambridge: Cambridge University Press, 1993. 720–21.

Carrigan, William. *The History and Antiquities of the Diocese of Ossory.* Dublin: Sealy, Bryers & Walker, 1905.

[Carroll, Mary Austin]. "Joanna Reddan: A Sketch." *The Irish Monthly* 20, no. 227 (May 1892): 225–236.

——. *Leaves from the Annals of the Sisters of Mercy.* 4 vols. vol. 1. Ireland. New York: Catholic Publication Society, 1881; vol. 2. England, Crimea, Scotland, Australia and New Zealand. New York: Catholic Publication Society, 1883; vol. 3. Newfoundland and the United States. New York: Catholic Publication Society, 1889; vol. 4. South America and the United States. New York: P. O'Shea, 1895.

——. *Life of Catherine McAuley.* New York: Sadlier, 1866.

Cartwright, Frederick F. *Disease and History.* New York: Thomas Y. Crowell Co., 1972.

Catholic Directory, Almanack, and Registry … , A Complete. Dublin: Printed for the Proprietor, 1836–1842. Called the *Irish Catholic Directory.*

Clarke, Frances, *A Brief History of the Sisters of Mercy, Diocese of Elphin, 1846–1994.* Athlone: Temple Printing Co., n.d.

Coakley, Davis. *Irish Masters of Medicine.* Dublin: Town House, 1992.

——. *Robert Graves: Evangelist of Clinical Medicine.* Dublin: Irish Endocrine Society, 1996.

Comerford, M[ichael]. *Collections Relating to the Dioceses of Kildare and Leighlin.* vol. 1. Dublin: James Duffy and Sons, 1883.

Convent of Our Lady of Mercy, St. Vincent's, Galway: 1840–1940. Galway: n.p., n.d.

Corish, Patrick J. "The Catholic Community in the Nineteenth Century." *Archivium Hibernicum* 38 (1983): 26–33.

——. *The Irish Catholic Experience: A Historical Survey.* Dublin: Gill and Macmillan, 1985.

Courtney, Marie Therese. "'The Careful Instruction of Women.'" *Sisters of Mercy in Limerick.* n.p.: Limerick Leader, 1988. 14–22.

——. "Fearless Mother Elizabeth Moore." *Sisters of Mercy in Limerick.* n.p.: Limerick Leader, 1988. 31–37.

——. "The 'Nuns' of St. Mary's." *Sisters of Mercy in Limerick.* n.p.: Limerick Leader, 1988. 5–8.

Cowper, William. *The Poetical Works of William Cowper. A New Edition.* London: Thomas Tegg, 1845. "The Diverting History of John Gilpin." 353–61.

Crawford, E. Margaret. "Typhus in Nineteenth-Century Ireland." *Medicine, Disease and the State in Ireland, 1650–1940.* Eds. Greta Jones and Elizabeth Malcolm. Cork: Cork University Press, 1999.

Degnan, Mary Bertrand. *Mercy unto Thousands: Life of Mother Mary Catherine McAuley.* Westminister, Maryland: Newman Press, 1957.

[Dickinson, Dominic, Anna Moloney, Imelda Keena, and Joan McNamara]. *Trees of Mercy: Sisters of Mercy of Great Britain from 1839.* Wickford, Essex: Sisters of Mercy, 1993.

Dictionary of National Biography: From the Earliest Times to 1900. Eds. Leslie Stephen and Sidney Lee. London: Smith, Elder & Co., 1893. "Henry Marsh," 36:211; "William Stokes," 54:401–403; "Helen Maria Williams," 61:404–405.

Documentary Study for the Canonization Process of the Servant of God Catherine McAuley, Founder of the Congregation of Sisters of Mercy, 1778–1841: Positio Super Virtutibus. Ed. Mary Angela Bolster. 2 vols. Rome: Congregation for the Causes of Saints (Prot. N. 1296), 1985.

Donnelly, N[icholas]. *A Short History of some Dublin Parishes.* Parts 1–26. Dublin: Catholic Truth Society, [1906–1913]. Reprinted as *Short Histories of Dublin_Parishes.* Blackrock, Dublin: Carraig Chapbooks, n.d.

Donoghue, Mary Xaverius [Frances]. *Mother Vincent Whitty: Woman and Educator in a Masculine Society.* Melbourne: Melbourne University Press, 1972.

Dublin Almanac and General Register of Ireland. Dublin: Pettigrew and Oulton, 1839–1842. Called the *Dublin Directory.*

Enright, Séamus. "Women and Catholic life in Dublin, 1766–1852." *History of the Catholic Diocese of Dublin.* Eds. James Kelly and Dáire Keogh. Dublin: Four Courts, 2000. 268–93.

Fitzgerald, Thomas W. H. *Ireland and Her People: A Library of Irish Biography.* 3 vols. Second edition. Chicago: Fitzgerald Book Co., 1909–1911.

Form of Ceremony for the Reception and Profession of the Sisters of Our Lady of Mercy. Dublin: J. Byrn, 1834.

Form of Ceremony for the Reception and Profession of the Sisters of Our Lady of Mercy. London: C. Richards, 1840.

Foster, Kenelm. "Introduction." *I, Catherine: Selected Writings of Catherine of Siena.* Ed. and trans. Kenelm Foster and Mary John Ronayne. London: Collins, 1980.

French, Roger K. "Scurvy." *The Cambridge World History of Human Disease.* Ed. Kenneth F. Kiple. Cambridge: Cambridge University Press, 1993. 1000–1005.

[Gaffney, Myles]. "*La Regola e le Costituzioni delle Religiose nominate Sorelle della Misericordia.*" *Dublin Review* 22 (March and June 1847): 1–25.

Gahan, William A. *The Christian's Guide to Heaven: or, A Complete Manual of Catholic Piety.* Fourteenth edition. Dublin: Reynolds, 1804.

[Harnett, Mary Vincent]. *A Catechism of Scripture History Compiled by the Sisters of Mercy for the Use of the Children Attending Their Schools.* Revised by [Edmund] O'Reilly. London: Charles Dolman, 1852.

——. *The Life of Rev. Mother Catherine McAuley.* Ed. Richard Baptist O'Brien. Dublin: John F. Fowler, 1864.

Healy, Kathleen. *Frances Warde: American Founder of the Sisters of Mercy.* New York: Seabury Press, 1973.

Heaney, Seamus. "Mossbawn: Two Poems in Dedication for Mary Heaney 1. Sunlight." *Opened Ground: Selected Poems 1966–1996.* New York: Farrar, Straus and Giroux, 1998.

Hemmeon, J. C. *The History of the British Post Office.* Harvard Economic Studies. vol. 8. Cambridge: Harvard University Press, 1912.

Holmes, Finlay. *The Presbyterian Church in Ireland*. Blackrock, Co. Dublin: The Columba Press, 2000.

Jewitt, Diana. *Traditional British and Other Dances for National Curriculum*. London: English Folk Dance and Song Society, 1997.

Jones, Greta and Elizabeth Malcolm, eds. *Medicine, Disease and the State in Ireland, 1650–1940*. Cork: Cork University Press, 1999.

Keena, M. Imelda, ed. *The Letters of William Montgomery McAuley*. London: Institute of Our Lady of Mercy, n.d.

Kelly, James. *'That Damn'd Thing Called Honour': Duelling in Ireland, 1570–1860*. Cork: Cork University Press, 1995.

Kerr, Donal. "Dublin's forgotten archbishop: Daniel Murray, 1768–1852." *History of the Catholic Diocese of Dublin*. Eds. James Kelly and Dáire Keogh. Dublin: Four Courts Press, 2000. 247–67.

Killerby, Catherine Kovesi. *Ursula Frayne*. South Fremantle, Western Australia: The University of Notre Dame Australia, 1996.

Kiple, Kenneth F., ed. *The Cambridge World History of Human Disease*. Cambridge: Cambridge University Press, 1993.

Lappetito, M. Michael [Joanne]. "Our Life Together in Mercy: Toward an Apostolic Spirituality." Burlington, Vermont: The Federation of the Sisters of Mercy of the Americas, 1980.

Levin, Jeffrey. "Periodontal Disease (Pyorrhea)." *The Cambridge World History of Human Disease*. Ed. Kenneth F. Kiple. Cambridge: Cambridge University Press, 1993. 924–926.

Lewis, Samuel. *A Topographical Dictionary of Ireland … with Historical and Statistical Descriptions*. London: S. Lewis & Co., 1837.

MacSuibhne, Peadar. *Paul Cullen and his Contemporaries*. 5 vols. Naas: Leinster Leader, 1961–1965.

[McAuley, Catherine?]. *Cottage Controversy*. New York: P. O'Shea, 1883, 1964.

McEvoy, John. *Carlow College, 1793–1993*. Carlow: St. Patrick's College, 1993.

McGrew, Roderick E. *Encyclopedia of Medical History*. New York: McGraw-Hill, 1985.

Meagher, William. *Notices of the Life and Character of His Grace Most Rev. Daniel Murray, Late Archbishop of Dublin, as Contained in The Commemorative Oration*. Dublin: Gerald Bellew, 1853.

Mitchell, James. "Father Peter Daly (c. 1788–1868.)" *Journal of the Galway Archeological and Historical Society* 39 (1983–1984): 27–114.

Molitor, Margaret. "Mary Teresa Maher of Cincinnati." *The MAST* [Mercy Association in Scripture and Theology] *Journal* 5.1 (Fall 1994): 26–34.

Monaghan, Phelim, ODC. "Discalced Carmelites in Ireland." Unpublished manuscript. Discalced Carmelites, Marlborough Road, Dublin.

Monsell, J. S. *Cottage Controversy; or, Dialogues between Thomas and Andrew, on the Errors of the Church of Rome*. 1838. Second edition. Limerick: Goggin, 1839.

[Moore, Mary Clare, ed.]. *A Little Book of Practical Sayings, Advices and Prayers of our Revered Foundress, Mother Mary Catharine [sic] McAuley*. London: Burns, Oates and Co., 1868.

Moran, Patrick Francis, ed. *The Letters of Rev. James Maher, D. D. … With a Memoir*. Dublin: Browne & Nolan, 1877.

More, Hannah. "Sensibility: An Epistle to the Honourable Mrs. Boscawen." *The Works of Hannah More in Four Volumes*. 4 vols. Dublin: D. Graisberry, 1803. 1:85–96.

Muldrey, Mary Hermenia. *Abounding in Mercy: Mother Austin Carroll*. New Orleans: Habersham, 1988.

Murphy, Ignatius. *The Diocese of Killaloe*. vol. 2: 1800–1850. Dublin: Four Courts Press, 1992.

Neumann, Mary Ignatia, ed. *The Letters of Catherine McAuley, 1827–1841*. Baltimore: Helicon, 1969.

Normoyle, M. C. *A Tree Is Planted: The Life and Times of Edmund Rice*. Second Edition. Private Circulation. Rome: Congregation of the Christian Brothers, 1976.

O'Brien, Pius. *The Sisters of Mercy of Birr and Nenagh*. Ennis: Congregation of the Sisters of Mercy, Killaloe, 1994.

O'Connor, John. *The Workhouses of Ireland: The fate of Ireland's poor*. Dublin: Anvil Books, 1995.

O'Connor, M. Loreto. "Helena Heffernan, a True Limerick Woman." *Sisters of Mercy in Limerick*. n.p.: Limerick Leader, 1988. 23–26.

O'Donnell, E. E. *The Annals of Dublin, Fair City*. Dublin: Wolfhound Press, 1987.

[O'Flanagan, Mary Padua]. *The Life and Work of Mary Aikenhead, Foundress of the Congregation of Irish Sisters of Charity, 1787–1858*. London: Longmans, Green and Co., 1924.

Oxford English Dictionary, The Compact Edition. Glasgow and New York: Oxford University Press, 1971.

Petrie, George, ed. *The Petrie Collection of the Ancient Music of Ireland*. vol. 1. Dublin: M. H. Gill, 1855.

Poor Man's Manual of Devotions; or Devout Christian's Daily Companion. Dublin: D. Wogan, 1819.

Praying in the Spirit of Catherine McAuley: A Collection of Prayers Written or Compiled by the Sisters of Mercy of the Americas. Ed. [Doris Gottemoeller, et al.]. Chicago: Institute of the Sisters of Mercy of the Americas, 1999.

"Pugin, Augustus Welby." *New Catholic Encyclopedia*. New York: McGraw-Hill, 1967.

Purcell, Mary. "Dublin Diocesan Archives: Hamilton Papers (6)." *Archivium Hibernicum* 49 (1995): 48–81.

——. "Sidelights on the Dublin Diocesan Archives." *Archivium Hibernicum* 36 (1981): 44–50.

[Purcell, Mary Teresa]. *Retreat Instructions of Mother Mary Catherine McAuley*. Ed. [Mary Bertrand Degnan]. Westminster, Maryland: Newman Press, 1952.

Rodriguez, Alonsus. *The Practice of Christian and Religious Perfection*. Kilkenny: John Reynolds, 1806.

Rushe, Desmond. *Edmund Rice: The Man and His Times*. Dublin: Gill & Macmillan, 1981.

Scholes, Percy A. *The Concise Oxford Dictionary of Music*. Second edition. Ed. John Owen Ward. London: Oxford University Press, 1964.

Sheehy, David. "Dublin Diocesan Archives: Murray Papers (7)." *Archivium Hibernicum* 42 (1987): 49–74.

Smith, M. Aquinas. *A Liverpool Pioneer in Mercy's Path: Life and Letters of Mother M. Liguori Gibson*. Liverpool: n.p., n.d.

Sullivan, Mary C. *Catherine McAuley and the Tradition of Mercy*. Notre Dame, Indiana: University of Notre Dame Press, 1995; Dublin: Four Courts Press, 1995.

——. "Catherine McAuley's Spiritual Reading and Prayers." *Irish Theological Quarterly* 57 (1991): 124–46.

——. "Catherine McAuley's Theological and Literary Debt to Alonso Rodriguez: The 'Spirit of the Institute' Parallels." *Recusant History* 20 (May 1990): 81–105.

——. "The Prayers of Catherine McAuley." *Praying in the Spirit of Catherine McAuley*. Ed. [Doris Gottemoeller, et al.]. Chicago: Institute of the Sisters of Mercy of the Americas, 1999. 47–75.

——, ed. *The Friendship of Florence Nightingale and Mary Clare Moore*. Philadelphia: University of Pennsylvania Press, 1999.

Talbott, John H. *A Biographical History of Medicine*. New York and London: Greene and Stratton, 1970. "Sir Dominic John Corrigan (1802–1880)," 1058–1060; "William Stokes (1804–1878)," 1060–1063.

Thomas à Kempis. *Of the Imitation of Christ*. London: Oxford University Press, 1903, 1935.

Walsh, Dolores. *Grow Where You Are Planted: A History of the Tullamore Mercy Sisters, 1836–1996*. Ferbane, Ireland: Brosna Press, 1996.

Walsh, T. J. *Nano Nagle and the Presentation Sisters*. Dublin: M. H. Gill, 1959.

[Whitty, Mary Vincent]. *Mercy Women Making History From the Pen of Mother Vincent Whitty*. Brisbane, Queensland: Sisters of Mercy Brisbane Congregation, 2001.

Williams, Helen Maria. *Poems*. Second edition. 2 vols. London: T. Cadell, 1791.

——. *Poems on Various Subjects*. London: G. and W. B. Whittaker, 1823.

Wordsworth, William. "Lines suggested by a Portrait from the Pencil of F. Stone." *The Poetical Works of William Wordsworth*. 6 vols. London: Edward Moxon, 1840. 5:131–36.

List of Letters

44	April 29, 1837	John Murphy to Catherine McAuley
45	June 7 [1837]	Catherine McAuley to John Hamilton
46	June 20, 1837	Catherine McAuley to Charles Cavanagh, Esq.
47	[1837]	Catherine McAuley to M. Frances Warde
48	July 1, 1837	Catherine McAuley to Andrew Fitzgerald, OP
49	July 27, 1837	Catherine McAuley to M. Elizabeth Moore
50	August 8, 1837	Catherine McAuley to Andrew Fitzgerald, OP
51	[August 15-30, 1837]	Catherine McAuley to M. Frances Warde
52	August 31, 1837	Catherine McAuley to M. Elizabeth Moore
53	October 3, 1837	Catherine McAuley to Mary de Pazzi Delany
54	October 12, 1837	Catherine McAuley to M. Frances Warde
55	October 17, 1837	Catherine McAuley to M. Teresa White
56	[October 23, 1837]	Catherine McAuley to M. Frances Warde
57	[late October– early November 1837]	Catherine McAuley to M. Josephine Warde
58	November 6, 1837	Andrew Fitzgerald, OP, to Catherine McAuley
59	November 22, 1837	Catherine McAuley to John Hamilton
60	November 22, 1837	Catherine McAuley to M. Frances Warde
61	[late November– early December 1837]	Catherine McAuley to M. Frances Warde
62	[December 8, 1837, or later in December]	Catherine McAuley to M. Frances Warde
63	December 12, 1837	Michael Blake to Catherine McAuley
64	[November–December 1837]	Catherine McAuley to M. Frances Warde
65	[December 1837]	Catherine McAuley to M. Frances Warde
66	December 19, 1837	Catherine McAuley to John Hamilton
67	December 20, 1837	Catherine McAuley to M. Angela Dunne
68	December 23, 1837	Catherine McAuley to M. Frances Warde
69	January 10, 1838	Catherine McAuley to James Maher
70	[January 1838]	Walter Meyler to Catherine McAuley
71	January 17, 1838	Catherine McAuley to M. Frances Warde
72	January 23, 1838	Catherine McAuley to James Maher
73	[January 25, 1838]	Poetic Exchange: Catherine McAuley and Mary Francis Marmion
74	January 27, 1838	Catherine McAuley to M. Josephine Warde
75	[February 1838]	Catherine McAuley to Mary Vincent Deasy
76	February 6, 1838	Catherine McAuley to John Hamilton
77	February 15, 1838	Catherine McAuley to James Maher
78	February 17, 1838	Catherine McAuley to M. Frances Warde
79	[late February-March 1838]	Catherine McAuley to M. Frances Warde
80	[March 13, 1838]	Catherine McAuley to M. Frances Warde
81	March 24, 1838	Catherine McAuley to M. Frances Warde
82	April 9, 1838	Catherine McAuley to M. Frances Warde
83	April 11, 1838	Catherine McAuley to John Hamilton
84	April 6, 1838	Catherine Divine to John Hamilton
85	[c.April 25, 1838]	Catherine McAuley to M. Frances Warde
86	[April 1838]	Catherine McAuley to M. Frances Warde
87	May 9, 1838	John Martin to Charles Cavanagh, Esq.

88	May 15, 1838	Catherine McAuley to M. Frances Warde
89	[late May 1838]	Catherine McAuley to M. Frances Warde
90	June 16, 1838	Catherine McAuley to M. Frances Warde
91	[early July 1838]	Mary Ann Doyle to Catherine McAuley
92	July 3, 1838	Catherine McAuley to Andrew Fitzgerald, OP
93	[Mid 1838]	Catherine McAuley to M. Ursula Frayne
94	August 23, 1838	Catherine McAuley to M. Frances Warde
95	August 31, 1838	Catherine McAuley to James McAuley, Esq.
96	October 1, 1838	Catherine McAuley to M. Teresa White
97	[October 1838]	Catherine McAuley to M. Magdalen Flynn
98	October 25 [1838]	Catherine McAuley to M. Frances Warde
99	October 25, 1838	Michael Blake to M. Elizabeth Moore
100	November 1, 1838	Catherine McAuley to M. Teresa White
101	November 15, 1838	Catherine McAuley to Mary de Pazzi Delany
102	November 17, 1838	Catherine McAuley to M. Frances Warde
103	[December 9, 1838]	Catherine McAuley to M. Elizabeth Moore
104	[December 1838]	Catherine McAuley to Joanna Reddan
105	December 19, 1838	William Walsh to Catherine McAuley
106	[c.January 2, 1839]	Michael Blake to Catherine McAuley
107	[early 1839]	Catherine McAuley to M. Teresa Vincent Potter
108	[January 6, 1839]	Catherine McAuley to M. Frances Warde
109	January 7, 1839	Catherine McAuley to M. Frances Warde
110	January 13, 1839	Catherine McAuley to M. Elizabeth Moore
111	[January 25, 27, 1839]	Catherine McAuley to M. Frances Warde
112	[January 26, 1839]	Catherine McAuley to Charles Cavanagh, Esq.
113	[February 1839]	Catherine McAuley to M. Frances Warde
114	February 7, 1839	Catherine McAuley to John Hamilton
115	February 14, 1839	Catherine McAuley to Charles Cavanagh, Esq.
116	February 19, 1839	William Walsh to John Hamilton
117	[April 17, 1839]	Catherine McAuley to Charles Cavanagh, Esq.
118	[late April 1839]	Catherine McAuley to M. Frances Warde
119	[April 30, 1839]	M. Ursula Frayne to Catherine McAuley
120	[April 30, 1839]	Catherine McAuley to M. Ursula Frayne
121	May 2, 1839	Catherine McAuley, Notation
122	May 11, 1839	Catherine McAuley to M. Frances Warde
123	[May-July 1839]	Catherine McAuley to Mary Vincent Harnett
124	[May-August 1839]	Catherine McAuley to M. Frances Warde
125	[June-July 1839]	Catherine McAuley to Mary de Sales
126	July 24, 1839	Catherine McAuley to M. Elizabeth Moore
127	September 23, 1839	Catherine McAuley to M. Frances Warde
128	September 27, 1839	Catherine McAuley to M. Frances Warde
129	September 30, 1839	Catherine McAuley to John Hamilton
129a	October 1 [1839]	Catherine McAuley to Mrs. Dunn
130	[October 1839]	Catherine McAuley to M. Ursula Frayne
131	October 18, 1839	Catherine McAuley to M. Josephine Warde
132	October 25, 1839	Catherine McAuley to Mrs. Turnbull
133	October 30, 1839	Michael Blake to Catherine McAuley
134	October 30, 1839	John Ryan to Catherine McAuley
135	November 5, 1839	William Kinsella to Gregory XVI

136	November 6, 1839	Catherine McAuley to Emily Molloy
137	November 8, 1839	William Crolly to Catherine McAuley
138	November 12, 1839	Daniel Murray to Gregory XVI
139	November 13, 1839	Catherine McAuley to Francis Haly
140	November 13, 1839	Catherine McAuley to John Murphy
141	[November 15, 1839]	Catherine McAuley to Charles Cavanagh, Esq.
142	[November 17, 1839]	Catherine McAuley to M. Frances Warde
143	November 18, 1839	John Murphy to Gregory XVI
144	November 22, 1839	Francis Haly to Giacomo Filippo Fransoni
145	[November or December 1839]	Catherine McAuley to Gregory XVI
146	December 3, 1839	Thomas Griffiths to Giacomo Filippo Fransoni
147	December 3, 1839	Thomas Griffiths to Gregory XVI
148	December 17, 1839	Catherine McAuley to M. Elizabeth Moore
149	December 24 [1839]	Catherine McAuley to M. Josephine Warde
150	December 26, 1839	Catherine McAuley to M. Angela Dunne
151	[November 1839-January 1840?]	Catherine McAuley to M. Teresa Vincent Potter
152	[November 1839-January 1840?]	Catherine McAuley, Poem-transcription
153	[December 1839-January 1840]	Catherine McAuley to Peter Butler
154	[December 1839-January 1840]	Catherine McAuley to Peter Butler
155	[December 1839]	M. Teresa Vincent Potter to Catherine McAuley
156	[January 1840]	Catherine McAuley to M. Teresa Vincent Potter
157	January 18, 1840	Catherine McAuley to M. Elizabeth Moore
158	January 30, 1840	Catherine McAuley to M. Frances Warde
159	February 1, 1840	Thomas Walsh to Catherine McAuley
160	February 4, 1840	Catherine McAuley to Thomas Walsh
161	February 26, 1840	Catherine McAuley to Charles Cavanagh, Esq.
162	February 29, 1840	Catherine McAuley to M. Elizabeth Moore
163	March 2, 1840	Catherine McAuley to M. Frances Warde
164	March 10, 1840	Catherine McAuley to M. Frances Warde
165	March 12, 1840	Catherine McAuley to M. Frances Warde
166	March 14, 1840	Catherine McAuley to M. Elizabeth Moore
167	[March 19, 1840]	Catherine McAuley to M. Elizabeth Moore
168	[March 21, 1840]	Catherine McAuley to M. Elizabeth Moore
169	March 24, 1840	Catherine McAuley to M. Elizabeth Moore
170	April 9, 1840	Catherine McAuley to Thomas Walsh
171	April 20, 1840	Catherine McAuley to Mary Vincent Harnett
172	[c.May 12, 1840]	Catherine McAuley to the Sisters at Baggot Street
173	June [6, 1840]	Catherine McAuley to M. Frances Warde
174	[c.June 7, 1840]	Catherine McAuley to Marianne Beckett
175	June 10, 1840	Catherine McAuley to M. Elizabeth Moore
176	June 30, 1840	Catherine McAuley to M. Frances Warde
177	July 1, 1840	Catherine McAuley to M. Elizabeth Moore
178	July 20, 1840	Paolo Polidori to the Cardinals of the Congregation for the Propagation of the Faith
179	July 27, 1840	Catherine McAuley to M. Teresa White
180	July 28, 1840	Catherine McAuley to M. Elizabeth Moore
181	July 30, 1840	Catherine McAuley to John Hamilton
182	July 30, 1840	Catherine McAuley to M. Frances Warde
183	August 1, 1840	Daniel Murray to John Hamilton

184	August 1, 1840	Catherine McAuley to M. Frances Warde
185	August 4, 1840	Andrew Fitzgerald, OP, to Catherine McAuley
186	August 5, 1840	Catherine McAuley to M. Frances Warde
187	[Mid 1840]	Augustus Welby Pugin to John Hardman, Esq.
188	August 5, 1840	Catherine McAuley to Thomas Walsh
189	[August 17, 1840]	Catherine McAuley to M. Frances Warde
190	August 20, 1840	Catherine McAuley to Mary Ann Doyle
191	September 7, 1840	Catherine McAuley to M. Elizabeth Moore
192	[c.October 5, 1840]	Catherine McAuley to Teresa Carton
193	October 12, 1840	Catherine McAuley to M. Frances Warde
194	October 14, 1840	Catherine McAuley to Giacomo Filippo Fransoni
195	October 18, 1840	Catherine McAuley to M. Elizabeth Moore
196	October 18, 1840	Catherine McAuley to M. de Sales White
197	October 26, 1840	Catherine McAuley to M. Frances Warde
198	October 26, 1840	Catherine McAuley to Caroline White
199	October 28, 1840	Catherine McAuley to M. Teresa White
200	October 31, 1840	Catherine McAuley to M. de Sales White
201	November 6, 1840	Thomas Griffiths to Mary Clare Moore
202	November 6, 1840	Catherine McAuley to Thomas Walsh
203	[November 6, 1840]	Catherine McAuley to Thomas Walsh
204	[Undated]	Catherine McAuley, Draft of Horarium
205	November 8, 1840	Catherine McAuley to Mary Vincent Harnett
206	November 9, 1840	Catherine McAuley to M. Frances Warde
207	November 10 [1840]	Catherine McAuley to Charles Cavanagh, Esq.
208	November 12, 1840	Catherine McAuley to John Hamilton
209	November 13, 1840	Catherine McAuley to M. Frances Warde
210	November 13, 1840	Catherine McAuley to M. Catherine Leahy
211	[c.November 18, 1840]	Catherine McAuley to M. Catherine Meagher
212	November 24, 1840	Catherine McAuley to M. Frances Warde
213	[November 24-26, 1840]	Catherine McAuley to "Little Fanny Warde"
214	November 30, 1840	Catherine McAuley to M. Frances Warde
215	December 7, 1840	Catherine McAuley to M. de Sales White
216	December 10, 1840	Michael Blake to Catherine McAuley
217	December 14, 1840	Catherine McAuley to John Hardman, Jr.
218	December 15, 1840	Catherine McAuley to M. Frances Warde
219	December 17, 1840	Catherine McAuley to M. Frances Warde
220	[December 20, 1840]	Catherine McAuley to M. de Sales White
221	[c.December 20, 1840]	Catherine McAuley to Mary Joseph Joyce
222	December 20, 1840	Catherine McAuley to M. Elizabeth Moore
223	December 22, 1840	Catherine McAuley to Daniel Murray
224	[early January, 1841]	Catherine McAuley to M. Angela Dunne
225	[January 2-3, 1841]	Catherine McAuley to M. Frances Warde
226	January 4, 1841	Catherine McAuley to M. Cecilia Marmion
227	[January 12, 1841]	Catherine McAuley to M. Frances Warde
228	January 15, 1841	Catherine McAuley to M. Cecilia Marmion
229	January 19, 1841	Catherine McAuley to Teresa Carton
230	January 20, 1841	Catherine McAuley to M. de Sales White
231	January 20, 1841	Catherine McAuley to M. Angela Dunne
232	January 21, 1841	Catherine McAuley to M. Cecilia Marmion

281 [c.July 24, 1841]   Catherine McAuley to Thomas Youens
282 July 24, 1841   Catherine McAuley to M. Frances Warde
283 July 24, 1841   Catherine McAuley to Mary Ann Doyle
284 [c.July 26-27, 1841]   Catherine McAuley to M. Frances Warde
285 July 28, 1841   Catherine McAuley to M. Frances Warde
286 [July 30, 1841]   Thomas Youens to Catherine McAuley
287 July 31, 1841   Catherine McAuley to Mary Aloysius Scott
288 July 31, 1841   Giacomo Filippo Fransoni to Daniel Murray
289 [early August 1841]   Catherine McAuley to M. Frances Warde
290 August 3, 1841   Catherine McAuley to M. Teresa White
291 [August 4, 1841]   Catherine McAuley to M. Frances Warde
292 August 6, 1841   Catherine McAuley to Michael Gibson
293 August 13, 1841   Myles Gaffney to John Hardman, Jr.
294 August 13, 1841   Cornelius P. Shannon to Catherine McAuley
295 [August 16, 1841]   Catherine McAuley to M. Frances Warde
296 [August 19, 1841]   Catherine McAuley to M. Frances Warde
297 [c.August 25, 1841]   Catherine McAuley to M. Frances Warde
298 [Late August 1841]   Catherine McAuley to a Sister of Mercy
299 August 30, 1841   Catherine McAuley to George Joseph Plunket Browne
300 September 6, 1841   Catherine McAuley to Teresa Carton
301 [September 1841]   Catherine McAuley, Statement
302 [September 17, 1841]   Catherine McAuley to Mary Aloysius Scott
303 [September 21, 1841]   Catherine McAuley to Mary Aloysius Scott
304 September 24, 1841   Catherine McAuley to Mary Ann Doyle
305 September 25, 1841   Catherine McAuley to M. Frances Warde
306 [September 26 or 24, 1841]   Catherine McAuley to Mary Aloysius Scott
307 [late September-October 1841]   Catherine McAuley to Nicholas Foran
308 October 2, 1841   Catherine McAuley to M. Juliana Hardman
309 [October 4, 1841]   Catherine McAuley to M. Frances Warde
310 [October 4, 1841]   Catherine McAuley to Mary Aloysius Scott
311 October 7, 1841   Catherine McAuley to M. Teresa White
312 [October 7, 1841]   Catherine McAuley to Mary Joseph Joyce
313 October 8, 1841   Catherine McAuley to Bernard Burke
314 October 12, 1841   Catherine McAuley to M. Frances Warde
315 October 13, 1841   M. and M. Dowling to Catherine McAuley
316 October 15, 1841   Catherine McAuley to M. and M. Dowling
317 October 18, 1841   Catherine McAuley to Charles Cavanagh, Esq.
318 [October 1841]   Catherine McAuley to Charles Cavanagh, Esq.
319 November 10, 1841   M. Ursula Frayne to Mary Ann Doyle
320 August 20, 1841   Catherine McAuley, Last Will and Testament and
     and November 11, 1841   and Codicil
321 [November 12, 1841]   M. Ursula Frayne to Mary Ann Doyle
322 [1840-1841]   Catherine McAuley, Transcribed Poem
323 [Undated]   Catherine McAuley, Transcribed Poem
324 [Undated]   Catherine McAuley, "The Spirit of the Institute"

Index

The following index is an alphabetical subject index, giving page references for persons, events, and other important topics. When a footnote is indexed, the page number and the note number are given: for example, 124 n. 21, 127 nn. 33, 35. An abbreviation is used for references to Catherine McAuley (C McA). Letters written *to* and/or *from* a person are generally listed by the *number* of each letter—at the end of the entry, before any cross-references. However, since the letters written to and from Catherine McAuley and those written to Mary Frances Warde are so numerous, in their entries the reader is referred to the List of Letters published at the end of this volume.

CPSIA information can be obtained
at www.ICGtesting.com
Printed in the USA
LVOW08*0740260517

535914LV00020B/526/P